Managerial Accounting
Concepts for Planning, Control, Decision Making

RAY H. GARRISON, D.B.A., C.P.A.
Brigham Young University

1976

BUSINESS PUBLICATIONS, INC. Dallas, Texas 75243
IRWIN-DORSEY INTERNATIONAL Arundel, Sussex BN18 9AB
IRWIN-DORSEY LIMITED Georgetown, Ontario L7G 4B3

First Printing, January 1976
Second Printing, July 1976

ISBN 0-256-01780-8
Library of Congress Catalog Card No. 75–22674
Printed in the United States of America

Managerial Accounting
Concepts for Planning, Control, Decision Making

To
Mary Jean

Preface

THIS TEXT is designed for a one term course in managerial accounting, to be used by students who have already completed one or two terms of basic financial accounting. Its emphasis is on uses of accounting data internally by managers in setting plans and objectives, in controlling operations, and in making the myriad of decisions involved with the management of an enterprise. The book looks at managerial accounting through the eyes of those who must depend on accounting data in much of their work. This approach provides a solidly managerial framework within which to introduce concepts. It also makes it easier to portray the internal accountant in his true roll—that of a key participant in the basic functions of management. Although the emphasis of the book is on uses of accounting data, care has been taken to not sacrifice the student's need for basic technical understanding. To this end, topics are covered in enough depth to insure full comprehension of basic concepts. Thereby the student is able to proceed with intelligence and confidence in applications of concepts to organizational problems.

Organizations today are faced with *many* problems that demand the best that the accountant and the manager have to give. The last two or three decades have been characterized by dramatic changes in technology, in societal values, in consumer markets, in energy availability, and in points of concentration of wealth and capital. As a result of these changes, the role of the accountant has also changed substantially. Internally, he has come to be known as a *management accountant*—one who sits with top management and who is a key supplier of information needed for a variety of management purposes. The work of the management accountant is pervasive in its impact—so pervasive that any student of business needs a clear understanding of what it involves if he expects to be adequately prepared to assume responsibility in an organization. This is why managerial accounting classes have become so widely required as a basic element in the training of all business students.

A paramount objective in writing this book has been to make a clear and balanced presentation of relevant subject material. Effort has been made to draw examples and homework problems, where appropriate, from service-oriented as well as from profit-oriented situations, and from non-manufacturing as well as from manufacturing situations.

ORGANIZATION

The book is divided into three parts. Part I is a five chapter sequence covering the fundamentals of managerial accounting. It is designed to provide a groundwork for the managerial applications which follow in Part II. Cost terms and concepts, product costing, cost behavior analysis, and cost-volume-profit relationships are all covered as part of this essential groundwork.

Part II is a nine chapter sequence devoted exclusively to uses of managerial accounting data. It includes chapters on segmented reporting, budgeting and standard costs, flexible budgets, contribution analysis, and control of decentralized operations. In order to emphasize uses of cost data in decision making, chapters are also included on relevant cost analysis, pricing, and capital budgeting.

Part III is a four chapter sequence designed to provide the student with expertise in some specialized areas. Because of the growing importance of mathematical techniques in directing the affairs of organizations, several mathematcal applications of cost data are covered here, including inventory models, linear programming, and probability analysis. In recognition of the preference of some schools to cover statement analysis and funds analysis as part of the managerial stem, chapters on these topics are also provided in Part III.

The text contains over 600 questions, exercises, and problems for in-class use or for student assignment. Having a broad range of carefully prepared and well-coordinated assignment material available is essential to any successful accounting course. The assignment material has been painstakingly developed (and classroom tested) to focus on concepts, and to assist the student in integrating his knowledge. The questions can be used to stimulate in-class discussion, or they can be used by the student as a study guide. Questions are designed to cover the essential points in a chapter, and are arranged in the order in which these points appear in the chapter material. The exercises are short problem situations, designed to give emphasis to essential concepts and relationships in the chapter. The problems are longer and more rigorous than the exercises, and are generally arranged in order of increasingly difficulty and/or time required for solution.

USING THE TEXT

Flexibility in meeting the needs of courses varying in length, content, and student composition has been a prime concern in writing the book. Sufficient text material is provided to permit the instructor to choose topics and depth of coverage as desired. The text materials have been extensively classroom tested in both regular daytime and evening program courses. The instructors using the materials have ranged from professors with many years' teaching experience to graduate students teaching their first course.

The instructor's manual accompanying the text contains a number of suggested course outlines for use in courses of various lengths.

USE OF THE GENERIC SINGULAR PRONOUN

The English language lacks a generic singular pronoun signifying he *or* she. For this reason the masculine pronouns he and his are used to some extent in this book for purposes of succinctness and to avoid repetition in wording. As used, these pronouns are intended to refer to both females and males.

ACKNOWLEDGMENTS

I am indebted to many people for help and encouragement in the writing of this book. Literally scores of changes were made in the final product as a result of comments and suggestions received from colleagues and students who first used the materials in mimeograph form. For this help I am grateful. Thanks must also go to those who provided insightful reviews of the manuscript at various stages. Included among these are Stephen L. Busby, Indiana University; Robert W. Koehler, The Pennsylvania State University; E. Dee Hubbard, Brigham Young University; Lester E. Heitger, Indiana University; and Lloyd Seaton, Jr., The University of Arkansas. I particularly appreciate the capable assistance of Gary A. Yamashita, California State University, Hayward, who assisted in preparing homework materials for Chapters 6, 7, and 12. Carol Myer, Mary Ann Matheson, and Roland Li provided capable and efficient service in typing the manuscript.

My appreciation is also extended to the National Association of Accountants and to the American Institute of Certified Public Accountants for permission to quote from their publications. Selected materials from the Uniform CPA Examinations, copyright 1950 through 1972 by the American Institute of Certified Public Accountants, Inc., are used and adapted by permission.

Provo, Utah
December 1975   RAY H. GARRISON

Contents

Outline: *Measuring Direct Materials Cost. The Job Cost Sheet. Measuring Direct Labor Cost. Application of Manufacturing Overhead. Computation of Unit Costs. A Summary of Document Flows.* Job Order Costing—The Flow of Costs: *The Purchase and Issue of Materials. Labor Costs. Actual Overhead Costs. Application of Manufacturing Overhead. Nonmanufacturing Costs. Cost of Goods Finished. Cost of Goods Sold. A Summary of Cost Flows. A General Model of Product Cost Flows.* Problems of Overhead Application: *The Concept of Underapplied and Overapplied Overhead. Disposition of Underapplied and Overapplied Overhead Balances.* Appendix: Process Costing and the Concept of Equivalent Units.

part two
Uses of Managerial Accounting Data

Flexible Budgets: *Characteristics of a Flexible Budget. Deficiencies of the Static Budget. How the Flexible Budget Works. The Measure of Activity—A Critical Choice.* The Overhead Performance Report—A Closer Look: *The Problem of Budget Allowances. Spending Variance Alone. Both Spending and Efficiency Variances.* Fixed Costs and the Flexible Budget. Fixed Overhead Analysis: *Denominator Activity. The Fixed Overhead Variances. Cautions in Fixed Overhead Analysis.* Summary Problem on Overhead Analysis.

Responsibility Accounting: *The Functioning of the System. The Flow of Information. Expanding the Responsibility Accounting Idea. Investment, Profit, and Cost Centers. Measuring Management Performance.* Rate of Return for Measuring Managerial Performance: *The Rate of Return Formula. Factors Underlying Rate of Return. Operating Income and the Asset Base.* Controlling the Rate of Return: *Increase Sales. Reduce Expenses. Reduce Operating Assets. The Problem of Allocated Expenses and Assets.* The Concept of Residual Income. Transfer Pricing: *The Need for Transfer Prices. Transfer Prices at Cost. Transfer Prices at Variable Cost. Transfer Prices at Market Price. Illustrating the Market Price Approach. The Problem of a Change in Market Price. Transfers at Negotiated Market Prices. The Matter of Opportunity Cost. Divisional Autonomy and Suboptimization.*

Cost Concepts for Decision Making: *Identifying Relevant Costs. Cost Relevance versus Cost Precision.* Sunk Costs Are Not Relevant Costs: *Book Value of Old Equipment. Partially Completed Inventory.* Future Costs That Do Not Differ Are Not Relevant Costs: *An Illustration. Why Isolate Relevant Costs?* Adding and Dropping Product Lines: *An Illustration of Cost Analysis. Beware of Allocated Fixed Costs.* The Make or Buy Decision: *The Advantages of Integration. An Example of Make or Buy. The Matter of Opportunity Cost.* Utilization of Scarce Resources: *Contribution in Relation to Scarce Resources. The Problem of Multiple Constraints.* Joint Product Costs and the Contribution Approach: *The Pitfalls of Allocation. The Contribution Approach to the Problem.*

The Economic Framework for Pricing: *Total Revenue and Total Cost Curves. Marginal Revenue and Marginal Cost Curves. Elasticity of Demand. Limitations to the General Models.* Pricing Standard Products: *Cost-Plus Pricing Formulas. The Absorption Approach. The Contribution Approach. Using Cost-Plus Data. Why Use Cost Data in Pricing?* Pricing

New Products: *Test Marketing of Products. Pricing Strategies. Target Costs and Product Pricing.* Special Pricing Decisions: *Pricing a Special Order. The Variable Pricing Model.* Criticisms of the Contribution Approach to Pricing. The Robinson-Patman Act.

chapter 1

Managerial Accounting—A Perspective

MANAGERIAL ACCOUNTING is concerned with providing information to *managers,* that is, to those who are *inside* of an organization and who are charged with directing and controlling its operations. Managerial accounting can be contrasted with financial accounting, which is concerned with providing information to stockholders, creditors, and others who are *outside* of an organization.

Because it is manager oriented, any study of managerial accounting must be preceded by some understanding of the management process, and by some understanding of the organizations in which managers work. Accordingly, the purpose of this chapter is to examine briefly the work of the manager, and to look at the characteristics, structure, and operation of the organizations in which this work is carried out. The chapter concludes by examining the major differences and similarities between financial and managerial accounting.

ORGANIZATIONS AND THEIR OBJECTIVES

An organization can be defined as a group of people united together for some common purpose. A bank providing financial services is an organization, as is a university providing educational services, and the General Electric Company producing appliances and other products. An organization consists of *people,* not physical assets. Thus, a bank building is not an organization; rather, the organization consists of the people who work in the bank and who are bound together for the common purpose of providing financial services to a community.

The common purpose toward which an organization works is called

1

its *objective.* Not all organizations have the same objective or objectives. For some organizations the objective is to produce a product and earn a profit. For other organizations the objective may be to render humanitarian service (the Red Cross), to provide aesthetic enrichment (a symphony orchestra), or to provide government services (a water department). To assist in our discussion, we will focus on a single organization, the Discount Furniture Marts, Inc., and look closely at this organization's objectives, structure, and management and at how these factors influence its need for managerial accounting data.

Setting Objectives

The Discount Furniture Marts, Inc., is a corporation, and its owners have placed their money in the organization with the thought in mind of earning a return, or profit, on their investment. Thus, one objective of the company is to earn a profit on the funds committed to it. The profit objective is tempered by other objectives, however. The company is anxious to acquire and maintain a reputation for integrity, fairness, and dependability. It also wants to be a positive force in the social and ecological environment in which it carries out its activities.

The owners of the Discount Furniture Marts, Inc., prefer not to be involved in day-to-day operation of the company. Instead, they have outlined the broad objectives of the organization, and have selected a president to oversee the implementation of these objectives. Although the president is charged with the central objective of earning a profit on the owners' investment, he[1] must do so with a sensitivity for the other objectives which the organization desires to achieve.

Strategic Planning

The implementation of an organization's objectives is known as strategic planning. In any organization strategic planning occurs in two phases:

1. Deciding on the products to produce and/or the services to render.
2. Deciding on the marketing and/or manufacturing methods to employ. That is, deciding on the best way to get the intended product and/or service to the proper audience.

---

[1] As stated in the preface, the English language lacks a generic singular pronoun signifying he *or* she. For this reason the masculine pronouns he and his are used to some extent in this book for purposes of succinctness and to avoid repetition in wording. As used, these pronouns are intended to refer to both females and males.

The set of strategies emerging from strategic planning is often referred to as an organization's *policies,* and strategic planning itself is often referred to as *setting policy.*[2]

Phase One Strategy. There are several strategies that the president of the Discount Furniture Marts, Inc., could employ in achieving the stated central objective of earning a profit. The company could specialize in office furniture. It could specialize in appliances, it could be a broad "supermarket" type of furniture outlet, or it could employ any one of a number of other product and/or service strategies.

A decision has been made that the company's strategy will be to sell only home furnishings, including appliances. The president, for one reason or another, has rejected several other possible strategies. He has decided, for example, not to service appliances. He has also decided not to sell office furniture, or to deal in institutional-type furnishings.

Phase Two Strategy. Having decided to concentrate on home furnishings, the president of the Discount Furniture Marts, Inc., is now faced with a second strategy decision. Some furniture companies handle only the highest quality home furnishings, thereby striving to maintain the image of a "quality" dealer. Markups are usually quite high, volume is quite low, and promotional efforts are directed toward a relatively small segment of the public. Other furniture dealers operate "volume" outlets. They try to keep markups relatively low, with the thought that overall profits will be augmented by a larger number of units sold. Still other dealers may follow different strategies. The selection of a particular strategy is simply a matter of managerial judgment. The Discount Furniture Marts, Inc., has decided to operate "volume" outlets, and to focus on maintaining a "discount" image.

Every organization must make similar strategy decisions. The set of strategies resulting from these decisions may not be written down, but they exist nonetheless and are a central guiding force in the organization's activities and in its need for accounting information.

The Work of Management

The work of management centers around what is to be managed—the organization itself. Essentially, the manager carries out four broad functions in an organization:

1. Planning.
2. Organizing and directing.
3. Controlling.
4. Decision making.

---

[2] For an expanded discussion of strategic planning, see Robert N. Anthony, *Planning and Control Systems: A Framework for Analysis* (Boston: Division of Research, Harvard Business School, 1965).

These activities are carried on more or less simultaneously and often under considerable stress, urgency, and pressure. Rarely (if ever) will a manager stop to examine which function he is engaged in at that particular moment. Perhaps he couldn't tell even if he tried, since a specific action might touch on all four.

Planning. In planning, the manager outlines the steps to be taken in moving the organization toward its objectives. We saw the planning function in operation in the Discount Furniture Marts, Inc., as the president decided on a set of strategies to be followed. The president's next step will be to develop further, more specific plans (of both a short-and long-term nature), that can be communicated throughout the organization. These plans will serve to coordinate, or to meld together, the efforts of all parts of the organization toward the company's objectives.

Organizing and Directing. In organizing, the manager decides how best to put together the organization's human and other resources in order to carry out established plans. As a customer enters one of the Discount Furniture Marts, Inc.'s stores, the results of the manager's organizational efforts should be obvious in several ways. Certain persons will be performing specific functions, some directly with the customer, and some not. Some persons will be overseeing the efforts of other persons. The store's physical assets will be arranged in particular ways, and certain procedures will be followed if a sale is made. These and a host of other things, seen and unseen, will all exist to assure that the customer is assisted in the best way possible.

In sum, the organization that is apparent in most companies doesn't simply happen; it is a result of the efforts of the manager who conceives the structure that is needed to get the job done, whatever the job may be.

In directing, the manager oversees day-to-day activities, and keeps the organization functioning smoothly. Employees are assigned to tasks, disputes between departments or between employees are arbitrated, questions are answered, on-the-spot problems are solved, numerous small routine and non-routine decisions are made involving customers and/or procedures, etc. In effect, directing is that part of the manager's work which deals largely with the routine and with the here and now.

Controlling. In controlling, the manager takes those steps that are necessary to insure that every part of the organization is functioning at maximum effectiveness. To do this he studies the accounting and other reports coming to him, and compares these reports against the plans set earlier. These comparisons may show where operations are not proceeding effectively, or where certain persons need help in carrying out their assigned duties. Control, in large part, is a function of obtaining useful *feedback* on how well the organization is moving toward its stated objectives. This feedback may suggest the need to replan, to set new strategies, or to reshape the organizational structure. It is a key ingredient to the effective management of any organization. As we shall see shortly, the generation of feedback to the manager is one of the central purposes of internal accounting.

Decision Making. In decision making, the manager attempts to make rational choices between alternatives. Decision making isn't a separate management function, per se; rather, it is an inseparable part of the *other* functions already discussed. Planning, organizing and directing, and controlling all require that decisions be made. For example, when first establishing its organizational strategies, the Discount Furniture Marts, Inc., had to make a decision as to which of several available strategies would be followed. Such a decision is often called a *strategic decision*, because of its long-term impact on the organization. In organizing and in directing day-to-day operations, as well as in controlling, the manager must make scores of lesser decisions, all of which are important to the organization's overall well-being. All decisions are based on *information*. In large part, the quality of management's decisions will be a reflection of the quality of the accounting and other information which it receives.

As the reader may have noted, the work of management follows a quite well-defined cycle. This cycle, sometimes referred to as the planning and control cycle, is illustrated in Exhibit 1–1.

EXHIBIT 1–1
The Planning and Control Cycle

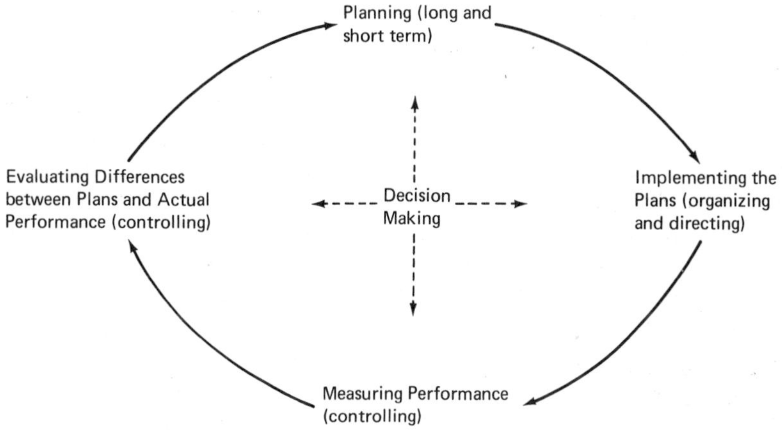

Organizational Structure

Just as organizations are made up of people, management accomplishes its objectives by working *through* people. The president of the

Discount Furniture Marts, Inc., could not possibly execute all of the company's strategies by himself. He must rely on other people to carry a large share of the management load. This is done by the creation of an organizational structure that will permit a *decentralization* of management responsibilities. For example, the Discount Furniture Marts, Inc., has three stores, with each store having a furnishings department and an appliances department. Each store has a store manager, as well as a separate manager over each department. In addition, the company has a purchasing department and an accounting department. These organizational relationships are shown in Exhibit 1–2.

EXHIBIT 1–2
Organization Chart, Discount Furniture Marts, Inc.

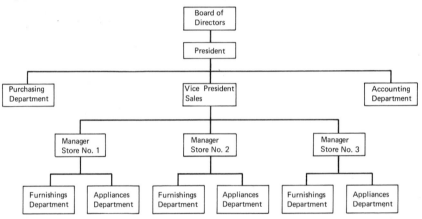

The arrangement of boxes shown in Exhibit 1–2 is commonly called an *organization chart.* Each box depicts an organizational unit, as discussed above, and the lines between the boxes show the relationship of one organizational unit to another. The chart tells us, for example, that the managers of the stores are responsible to the vice president in charge of sales. In turn, the latter is responsible to the company president (as is the manager of the purchasing department, and the controller), who in turn is responsible to the board of directors. In essence, an organization chart shows the *responsibility relationships* between managers of an organization.[3]

An organization chart also depicts *line* and *staff* authority in an organization. Any organizational unit whose activities are *directly* related to the basic objectives of the organization is a line unit. Refer to Exhibit

---

[3] For further discussion, see W. Jack Duncan, *Essentials of Management* (Hinsdale, Ill.: The Dryden Press, 1975), chapter 13.

1–2. One of the objectives of the Discount Furniture Marts, Inc., is to earn a profit through sales of furnishings and appliances to customers. Therefore, the furnishings and appliances departments in each store are line units. Moving upward on the chart, the stores themselves are line units, as is the position of the vice president in charge of sales. The units represented by these boxes are all *directly* involved in meeting the company's stated objectives.

A staff unit is one which provides services and assistance to other units in the organization. The purchasing department in the Discount Furniture Marts, Inc., is in a staff position, since its only function is to support and serve the line departments by doing their purchasing for them. The company has found that better buys can be obtained by having one central purchasing unit for the entire organization. Therefore, the purchasing department has been organized as a staff department to perform this service function. It cannot be called a line department, since it is involved only *indirectly* with the basic objectives of the organization, and since its role is *supportive* in nature. By this line of reasoning, the accounting department is also a staff department, since its purpose is to provide specialized accounting services to other departments.

The Discount Furniture Marts, Inc.'s organization chart shows only two staff departments. In a larger organization there would be many more staff departments, including perhaps finance, engineering, medical services, cafeteria, personnel, advertising, and research and development.

The Controller

The manager in charge of the accounting department is known as the *controller*. He is a member of the top management team, and is an active participant in the planning, control, and decision-making processes. Although the controller does not "control" in terms of line authority (remember, accounting is a staff function), as chief information officer he is in a position to exercise control in a very special way. This is through the reporting and interpreting of data needed in decision making. By the supplying and interpreting of relevant and timely data, the controller exerts an influence on decisions and plays a key part in directing an organization toward its objectives.

Because of his position as a member of the top management team, the controller's time generally is kept free of technical and detailed activities. He oversees the work of others, directs the preparation of special reports and studies, and advises top management in special problem situations. The organization of a modern controller's office is shown in Exhibit 1–3.

Since the focus of this book is on managerial accounting, we are

EXHIBIT 1–3
Organization of the Controller's Office

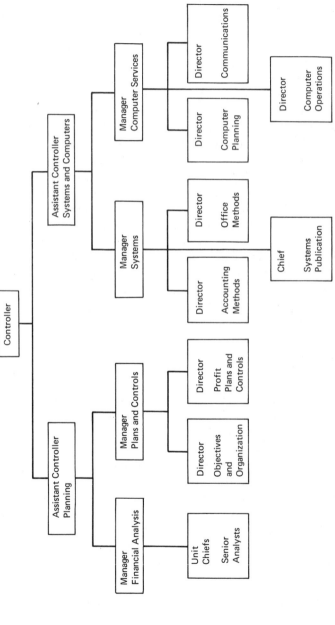

Source: W. Joseph Littlefield, "Developments in Financial Organizations: 1915–1965." *Financial Executive*, vol. 33, no. 9 (September 1965), page 14, supplement. Reproduced by permission from the Financial Executives Institute, Inc.

particularly interested in the work of the controller and the department he manages. The information which the accounting department generates is used throughout an organization in many different ways, as we shall see in chapters following.

Organizations Have Basic Similarities

Organizations can be classified into three basic groups:

1. Profit-oriented business enterprises that are privately owned and operated as corporations, partnerships, and proprietorships.
2. Service-oriented agencies and associations that are either publicly or privately controlled, such as the Red Cross, the YMCA, and the Salvation Army, and that are usually operated as nonprofit corporations.
3. Service-oriented agencies such as the Department of Defense, a state university, and a city water department that are created and controlled by government bodies.

Each of these groups contains thousands of organizations. Each organization may be unique in its own right, but nearly all will share the following basic similarities:

1. Each will have an objective or group of objectives toward which it is working.
2. Each will have a set of strategies designed to assist in achieving the basic objective or objectives.
3. Each will have a manager or managers who plan, organize, direct, and control the organization's activities, and who make numerous decisions of both a long- and short-term nature.
4. Each will have an organizational structure that shows responsibility relationships between various managers, and that shows line and staff relationships.
5. Each will have an insatiable need for information to assist in the execution of its strategies.

Because of these basic similarities, much of what we say in this book about managerial accounting and its uses will have almost universal application among organizations. To the extent that organizations differ, some of our topics will of necessity be more narrow in their focus. It is our intent, however, to be concerned with the nature and uses of managerial accounting data in all types of organizations; for this reason, the reader will find chapter examples and problems relating to organizations that are service-oriented as well as to those that are profit-oriented.

THE MANAGER'S NEED FOR INFORMATION

Information is the "motor" that makes management go. In the absence of a steady flow of information management would be powerless to do anything. Fortunately, a large part of management's information needs are satisfied within the structure of the organization itself. As suggested by the organization chart in Exhibit 1–2, there are channels of communication extending throughout an organization through which the various levels of management can communicate. Through these channels, policies and instructions are submitted to subordinates, problems are discussed, formal and informal contacts are made, reports and memos are transmitted, and so on. Without these channels of communication, it would be impossible for management to function effectively.

The management of an organization also depends on specialists to provide a large part of its information needs. Economists, marketing specialists, organizational behavior specialists, accountants, and others all provide information to management and advise on various phases of the organization's activities. The economist, for example, provides information on contemplated economic conditions. The marketing specialist provides information essential to effective promotion and distribution of goods and services, and the organizational behavior specialist assists in the structure and functioning of the organization itself.

Accounting Information

The information provided by accounting is essentially financial in nature, helping the manager to do three things:

1. Plan effectively and focus attention on deviations from plans.
2. Direct day-to-day operations.
3. Arrive at the best solution to the operating problems faced by the organization.

Plan Effectively. The plans of management are expressed formally as *budgets*, and the term *budgeting* is often applied to management planning generally. Budgets are usually prepared on an annual basis, and express the desires and goals of management in specific, quantitative terms. For example, the Discount Furniture Marts, Inc., plans sales by month a full year in advance. These plans are expressed as departmental budgets, which are communicated throughout the organization.

But planning is not enough. Once the budgets have been set, the president and other managers of the Discount Furniture Marts, Inc., will need information inflows that will indicate how well the plans are working out. Accounting assists in this information need, by supplying *performance reports* that help the manager focus in on problems and/or opportunities that otherwise might go unnoticed. If the performance report on a particular department indicates that problems exist, then the manager will need to find the cause of the problems and take corrective action. If the performance reports indicate that things are going well, then the manager's time is free to do other work. In sum, performance reports are a form of feedback to the manager, directing his attention toward those parts of the organization where managerial time can be used most effectively.

Direct Operations. The manager has a constant need for accounting information in the routine conduct of day-to-day operations. As a departmental manager in the Discount Furniture Marts, Inc., prices new items going onto the display floor he will rely on cost information provided by accounting to insure that prices are properly computed. The company's store managers will rely on other accounting information such as sales volumes and inventory levels as they attempt to prepare advertising programs. And the purchasing department manager will rely on still other accounting information in evaluating costs of storage, handling, etc. In these and a score of other ways the work of the accountant and the manager are inextricably connected in the conduct of day-to-day operations.

Solve Problems. Accounting information is often a key factor in analyzing alternative methods of solving a problem. The reason is that various alternatives usually have specific costs and benefits that can be measured and used as an input in deciding which alternative is best. Accounting is generally responsible for gathering available cost and benefit data, and for communicating it in a usable form to the appropriate manager. For example, the Discount Furniture Marts, Inc., may discover that competitors are making inroads on the company's business. In deciding between the alternatives of reducing prices, increasing advertising, or doing both in an attempt to maintain its market share, the company will rely heavily on cost/benefit data provided by accounting. It is important to note here that the needed information may not be in readily available form; in fact, accounting may find it necessary to do a large amount of special analytical work, including some forecasting, in order to prepare the needed data.

Information Must Be in Summary Form

An essential element of managerial accounting information is that it be in summary form. In your study of financial accounting you learned that an accounting system handles an enormous amount of detail in recording the results of day-to-day transactions. The bulk of this detail is of no interest to the manager, however. The manager's interest is in the *summaries* that are drawn from the accounting records, and it is on these that he relies in his work. For this reason, we spend only a minimum of time in this book on the underlying detail in a managerial accounting system. The bulk of our time is spent on learning the *kinds* of summarized data needed by the manager, and learning how these data are *used* in directing the affairs of organizations.

COMPARISON OF FINANCIAL AND MANAGERIAL ACCOUNTING

In our discussion of managerial accounting we have noted that it differs in several ways from financial accounting. To assist the reader in a transition from the study of financial accounting to the study of managerial accounting, it is desirable at this point to summarize these differences, as well as to point out certain similarities between the two fields of study.

Differences between Financial and Managerial Accounting

In all, we can identify eight major differences between financial and managerial accounting:

1. Managerial accounting focuses on providing data for internal uses by the manager.
2. Managerial accounting places much more emphasis on the future.
3. Managerial accounting is not governed by generally accepted accounting principles.
4. Managerial accounting emphasizes relevance and flexibility of data.
5. Managerial accounting places less emphasis on precision, and more emphasis on nonmonetary data.
6. Managerial accounting emphasizes the segments of an organization, rather than just looking at the organization as a whole.
7. Managerial accounting draws heavily from other disciplines.
8. Managerial accounting is not mandatory.

Internal Uses by the Manager. For internal purposes, the manager does not need the same kinds of information as needed externally by stockholders and others. The manager must direct day-to-day operations, plan for the future, solve problems, and make numerous routine and non-routine decisions, all of which require their own special information inputs. Much of the information needed by the manager for these purposes would be either confusing or valueless to stockholders and others, because of the form in which the information is prepared and used.

Emphasis on the Future. Since a large part of the overall responsibilities of a manager have to do with *planning*, a manager's information needs have a strong future orientation. Summaries of past costs and other historical data are useful in planning, but only to a point. The difficulty with summaries of the past is that the manager can't assume that the future will simply be a reflection of what has happened in the past. Economic conditions, customer needs and desires, competitive conditions, etc., are constantly changing, all of which demand that the manager's planning framework be built in large part on estimated data that may or may not be reflective of past experience.

By contrast, financial accounting records the *financial history* of an organization. Financial accounting has little to do with estimates and projections of the future. Rather, entries are made in the accounting records only after transactions have already occurred.

Generally Accepted Accounting Principles. Financial accounting statements must be prepared in accordance with generally accepted accounting principles. The reason is that these statements are relied on by persons outside the organization. These outside persons must have some assurance that the information they are receiving has been prepared in accordance with some common set of ground rules; otherwise, great opportunity could exist for fraud or misrepresentation, and confidence in financial statements would be destroyed. The managers of a company, by contrast, are not governed by generally accepted accounting principles in the information which they receive. Managers can set their own ground rules on the form and content of information which is to be used internally. Whether these ground rules conform to generally accepted accounting principles is immaterial. For example, management might direct that for internal uses fixed assets be stated at appraised value, depreciation be ignored, revenue be recorded before it is realized, and that certain costs be omitted from inventory, even though all of these procedures would be in violation of generally accepted accounting principles. In sum, the manager is free to reshape data as he desires internally in order to obtain information in its most useful form.

Relevance and Flexibility of Data. Financial accounting data are expected to be objectively determined, and to be verifiable. For internal uses, the manager is often more concerned about receiving information that is relevant and flexible than he is about receiving information that is completely objective or even verifiable. By relevant, we mean *pertinent to the problem at hand.* So long as information inflows are relevant to problems which must be solved, the manager may view objectivity and verification as matters of secondary importance. The manager must also have information that is flexible enough to be used in a variety of decision-making situations. For example, the cost information needed for pricing transfers of goods between sister divisions may be far different from the cost information needed for pricing sales to outside customers.

Less Emphasis on Precision.   When information is needed, speed
is often more important than precision. The more rapidly information
comes to a manager, the more rapidly he is able to move on problems.
For this reason, the manager is often willing to trade off some accuracy
for information that is immediately available. If a decision must be
made, waiting a week for information that will be slightly more accurate
may be considered less desirable than simply acting on the information
that is presently available. Thus, in managerial accounting, estimates
and approximations may be more useful than numbers that are accurate
to the last penny. In addition, managerial accounting places considerable
weight on nonmonetary data. Salesmen's impressions concerning a new
product, information on weather conditions, and even rumors could be
helpful to the manager, even though this information is nonmonetary
in nature.

Segments of an Organization.   Financial accounting is primarily concerned with reporting of business activities for a company as a whole.
By contrast, managerial accounting focuses less on the whole, and more
on the parts, or segments, of a company. These segments may be the
product lines, the sales territories, the divisions, the departments, or
any other way that a company can be broken down. In financial accounting, it is true that some companies do report some breakdown of revenues and costs, but this tends to be a secondary emphasis. In managerial
accounting, segmented reporting is the primary emphasis.

Draws on Other Disciplines.   Managerial accounting extends beyond
the boundaries of the traditional accounting system, and draws heavily
from other disciplines including economics, finance, statistics, operations
research, and organizational behavior. These "outside" sources give managerial accounting a strong interdisciplinary flavor as well as a decidedly
pragmatic orientation.

Not Mandatory.   Financial accounting is mandatory; that is, it must
be done. Financial records must be kept so that sufficient information
will be available to satisfy the requirements of various outside parties.
Often the financial records that are to be kept are specified by regulatory
bodies, such as the Securities and Exchange Commission (SEC). Even
if a company is not covered by SEC or other regulations, it must meet
certain financial accounting requirements if it is to have its statements
examined by professional outside accountants. In addition, *all* companies
must keep adequate records to meet the requirements of taxing authori-
ties. By contrast, managerial accounting is not mandatory. A company
is completely free to do as much or as little as it wishes. There are
no regulatory bodies or other outside agencies that specify what is to
be done, or for that matter, whether anything is to be done at all.
Since managerial accounting is completely optional, the important ques-

tion is always "Is the information useful?" rather than "Is the information required?"

Similarities between Financial and Managerial Accounting

Although differences do exist between financial and managerial accounting, they are similar in at least two ways. First, both rely on the accounting information system. It would be a total waste of money to have two *different* data-collecting systems existing side by side. For this reason, managerial accounting makes extensive use of routinely generated financial accounting data, although it both expands on and adds to these data, as discussed earlier. Second, both financial and managerial accounting rely heavily on the concept of *responsibility*, or *stewardship*. Financial accounting is concerned with stewardship over the company *as a whole;* managerial accounting is concerned with stewardship over its *parts*, and this concern extends to the last person in the organization who has any responsibility over cost. In effect, financial accounting may be viewed as being the apex, and managerial accounting as filling in the bulk of the pyramid underneath, from a responsibility accounting point of view.

THE EXPANDING ROLE OF MANAGERIAL ACCOUNTING

Managerial accounting is in its infancy. Historically, it has played a secondary role to financial accounting, and in many organizations it still is little more than a by-product of the financial reporting process. Events of the last two decades have spurred the development of managerial accounting, however, and it is becoming widely recognized as a field of expertise separate from financial accounting.

Increased Needs for Information

Among the events which have spurred the development of managerial accounting we can note increased business competition, a severe cost-price squeeze, and rapidly developing technology. The changes brought about by these events have intensified the manager's need for information, and particularly for financial information beyond that contained in the traditional income statement and balance sheet. Consider the following:

> Over the last two decades products have become obsolete at accelerating rates. Various sceintific breakthroughs have resulted in the development of many new basic components, such as the transistor and the electronic "chip," which have literally revolutionized many industries

and their products. Scientific researchers report that this "revolution" is only in its beginnings.

Dramatic changes have taken place in production methods over the last two decades. The term "automation" was coined in the early 1950s to describe a process that was new at the time. Today, many products are produced virtually untouched by human hands. Oil refinery operations are controlled by massive computers, machine tools are electronically controlled, and there are even some entire manufacturing plants where workmen do little more than monitor instrument panels.

Modes of management and methods of decision making have been affected by the development of powerful new quantitative tools such as linear programming, probability analysis, and decision theory. These new tools, which have come from the mathematical and statistical sciences, are becoming indispensable in day-to-day decision making.

Whole new industries have emerged as a result of various technological breakthroughs. A few short years ago petrochemicals and laser beams were little more than laboratory novelties, and space exploration was little more than a dream. Today the petrochemical industry stands as a powerful competitive force in the business environment, laser beams are used in everything from cutting steel to delicate eye surgery, and students work amazingly complex mathematical computations on tiny electronic calculators that are a direct outgrowth of aerospace exploration.

In some industries, costs have more than doubled over the last ten years. These cost increases have forced the companies involved to make many adjustments, including modification of products, changes in methods of marketing, and the discovery of new sources and means of financing.

The economic impact of these and other factors has been far-reaching. As managers have grappled with the effects of increased competition, escalating costs, and evolving technology, the role of managerial accounting has expanded many-fold from what was common in earlier years. Looking to the future, we can expect this role to expand even further as new concepts and applications are explored and perfected.

The Certificate in Management Accounting (CMA)

Specific recognition is given to the management accountant as a trained professional in the National Association of Accountants' (NAA) *Certificate in Management Accounting* program. The purpose and operation of the program are described in the following excerpts from a brochure issued by the NAA:

> More and more people—inside the business world and out—realize the significant changes which have been taking place for years in accounting and in the role of the accountant in business. No longer is

he simply a recorder of business history. He now plays a dynamic role in making business decisions, in future planning and in almost every aspect of business operations. This new accountant is called a Management Accountant and he sits with top management because his key responsibility is developing, producing and analyzing information to help management make sound decisions. Many management accountants make their way to top management positions.

In response to the needs of business and at the request of many in the academic community, the National Association of Accountants has established a program to recognize professional competence in this field—a program leading to the Certificate in Management Accounting.

The CMA program requires candidates to pass a series of uniform examinations and meet specific educational and professional standards to qualify for and maintain the Certificate in Management Accounting. NAA has established the Institute of Management Accounting to administer the program, conduct the examinations and grant certificates to those who qualify.

The objectives of the program are threefold: (1) to establish management accounting as a recognized profession by identifying the role of the management accountant and the underlying body of knowledge, and by outlining a course of study by which such knowledge can be acquired; (2) to foster higher educational standards in the field of management accounting; (3) to assist employers, educators and students by establishing objective measurement of an individual's knowledge and competence in the field of management accounting.

SUMMARY

Understanding organizations and the work of those who manage organizations helps us to understand managerial accounting and its functions. All organizations have basic objectives, and a set of strategies for achieving those objectives. The setting of strategy, sometimes called strategic planning, is one of the basic functions of the manager, as well as planning of a more short-term nature. In addition to planning, the work of the manager centers on organizing and directing day-to-day operations, controlling, and decision making.

The managers of an organization choose an organizational structure that will permit a decentralization of responsibility, by placing managers over specific departments and other units. The responsibility relationships between managers are shown by the organization chart. The organization chart also shows which organizational units are performing line functions and which are performing staff functions. Line functions relate to the specific objectives of the organization, whereas staff functions are supportive in nature, their purpose being to provide specialized services of some type.

A large part of the information needs of management are provided within the structure of the organization itself. Channels of communication exist between various levels of management, through which information flows. Management also calls on various specialists to provide information, including the economist, the engineer, the operations research specialist, the accountant, and others. The information provided internally by the accountant is used by management in three ways: (1) to plan, and to monitor how well plans are working out; (2) to direct day-to-day operations, including setting prices, advertising policy, etc.; and (3) to solve problems confronting the organization.

Since managerial accounting is geared toward the needs of the manager, rather than toward the needs of stockholders and others, it differs substantially from financial accounting. Among other things, it is oriented more toward the future, it is not governed by generally accepted accounting principles, it has less emphasis on precision, it emphasizes segments of an organization (rather than the organization as a whole), it draws heavily on other disciplines, and it is not mandatory. The role of managerial accounting is expanding rapidly, and has become recognized as a field of professional study through which professional certification can be obtained.

QUESTIONS

1–1. Contrast financial and managerial accounting.

1–2. What objectives might be important to the managers of a profit-oriented organization, other than earning a profit?

1–3. A Little League baseball team is an organization. Describe such a team in terms of its objectives, its strategies, its organizational structure, the work of its manager(s), and its need for information.

1–4. Some persons consider strategic planning to be the most important work a manager does. In what ways might this be true? In what ways might it be false?

1–5. Assume that the central objective of a college basketball team is to win games. What strategies might the team follow to achieve this objective?

1–6. Managerial accounting isn't as important in the government as it is in private industry, since the government doesn't have to worry about earning a profit. Discuss this allegation.

1–7. What function does *feedback* play in the work of the manager?

1–8. "Essentially, the job of a manager is to make decisions." Discuss this statement.

1–9. What is the relationship, if any, between information and decision making?

1–10. Choose an organization with which you are familiar. Prepare an organization chart depicting the structure of the organization you have chosen. (The organization you choose should be sufficiently complex so as to have at least one staff function.) Be prepared to place your organization chart on the board, if your instructor so directs.

1–11. A student planning a career in management commented, "Look, I'm going to be a manager, so why don't we just leave the accounting to the accountants?" Discuss this comment.

1–12. Accountants are sometimes compared to journalists, in that the accountant doesn't just "report" information to the manager, he "editorializes" the information. What implications does this hold for the accountant "managing the news" so to speak?

1–13. "The term controller is a misnomer, because the controller doesn't 'control' anything." Discuss this statement.

1–14. A production superintendent once complained, "Accounting is a staff function. Those people have no right to come down here and tell us what to do." Do you agree? Why or why not?

1–15. What are the major differences between financial and managerial accounting? In what ways are the two fields of study similar?

part one
Managerial Accounting Fundamentals

chapter 2

Cost Terms, Concepts, and Classifications

As EXPLAINED in Chapter 1, the work of management centers on (1) planning, which includes setting objectives and outlining the means of attaining those objectives, and (2) control, which includes the steps taken or means used to insure that objectives are realized. In order to discharge his planning and control responsibilities, the manager needs *information* about his organization. In large part, the information needs are for data on the *costs* of the organization.

In financial accounting, the term cost is defined as the sacrifice made in order to obtain some good or service. The sacrifice may be measured in cash expended, property transferred, service performed, and so on. This definition is easily stated, and widely accepted in financial accounting.

In managerial accounting, the term cost is used in many different ways. The reason is that there are many different types of costs, and these costs are classified differently according to the immediate needs of management. In this chapter we look at some of these different types of costs, and at some of the ways in which the manager classifies them for his own use internally.

GENERAL COST CLASSIFICATIONS

Costs are associated with all types of organizations—business, non-business, service, retail, manufacturing, etc. Generally, the kinds of costs that are incurred, and the way in which these costs are classified, will depend on the type of organization involved. Cost accounting is as much applicable to one type of organization as to another, and for this reason we focus on both manufacturing and nonmanufacturing companies in this book.

What costs are incurred in a manufacturing firm? In a nonmanufacturing firm? How are these costs classified and used by the manager? In this section we seek answers to these and other questions. Our discussion is necessarily general in nature, but the concepts which we develop can be applied to nearly any manufacturing or nonmanufacturing organization.

Manufacturing Costs

A manufacturing firm is more complex than a merchandising firm or other type of organization. The reason is that the manufacturing firm is broader in its activities, embracing all functions of production, marketing, and administration. An understanding of the cost structure of a manufacturing firm provides a broad, general understanding of costing that can be very helpful in understanding the cost structures of other types of organizations.

Manufacturing involves the transformation of raw materials into finished products, through use of labor and factory facilities. By contrast, merchandising is the marketing of products without changing their basic form or content. The cost of a manufactured product is made up of three basic elements:

1. Direct materials.
2. Direct labor.
3. Manufacturing overhead.

Direct Materials. A wide variety of materials can go into the manufacture of a product. These are generally termed raw materials. The term is somewhat misleading in that "raw materials" seems to imply basic, natural resources. Actually, raw materials is inclusive of any materials input into a product, and the finished product of one firm can become the raw materials of another firm. For example, the finished lumber products of a sawmill become the raw material of a construction company.

Direct materials are those materials that become an integral part of a company's finished product, and which can be conveniently traced to it. This would include, for example, the sheet steel in a file cabinet, or the wood in a table. Some items of materials may become an integral part of the finished product, but may be traceable into the product only at great cost and inconvenience. Such items might include the glue used to put a table together, or the welding materials used to bond the sheet metal in a file cabinet. Glue and welding materials would be called *indirect materials,* and would be included as part of manufacturing overhead.

Direct Labor. The term direct labor is reserved for those labor costs which are directly traceable to the creation of products. The labor costs of assembly line workers, for example, would be direct labor costs, as would the labor costs of carpenters, bricklayers, and machine operators. Labor costs which cannot be traced directly to the creation of products are termed *indirect labor,* and are treated as part of manufacturing overhead. Indirect labor would include the labor costs of janitors, foremen, materials handlers, engineers, and night watchmen. Although the efforts of these workers are essential to production, it would be either impractical or impossible to accurately relate the costs to specific units of product. Hence, such labor costs are treated as indirect labor.

Manufacturing Overhead. Manufacturing overhead can be defined very simply as including all costs of manufacturing except direct materials and direct labor. Included within this classification one would expect to find costs such as indirect materials, indirect labor, heat and light, property taxes, insurance, depreciation on factory facilities, repairs, maintenance, and all other costs of operating the manufacturing division of a company.

Manufacturing overhead is known by various names. Sometimes it is called manufacturing expense, factory expense, overhead, factory overhead, or factory burden. All of these terms are synomyous with "manufacturing overhead."

Manufacturing overhead combined with direct labor is known as *conversion cost.* This term stems from the fact that direct labor costs and overhead costs are incurred in the *conversion* of materials into finished products. Direct labor combined with direct materials is known as *prime cost.*

Nonmanufacturing Costs

Traditionally, most of the focus of managerial accounting has been on manufacturing costs and activities. The reason is probably traceable to the complexity of manufacturing operations, and to the need for carefully developed costs for pricing and other decisions. However, costing techniques are now coming into use in many nonmanufacturing areas. Firms are going beyond the traditional selling and administrative expense classifications, and are developing data to show costs of servicing customers by age classification, by geographical location, etc. Cost breakdowns of these types provide data for control over selling and administrative functions in the same way that manufacturing cost data provide for control over manufacturing functions.

The subclassifications of nonmanufacturing costs usually consist of the following:

1. Marketing or selling costs.
2. Administrative costs.

Marketing or selling costs would include advertising, selling, shipping, salesmen's travel, sales salaries, etc. Administrative costs would include both executive and clerical costs which cannot logically be included under either production or marketing. Examples of such costs would include executive compensation, general accounting, secretarial, public relations, etc.

Period Costs

In addition to manufacturing and nonmanufacturing cost classifications, costs can be classified as being either *period* costs or *product* costs. Period costs are discussed in this section, and product costs are discussed in the following section.

Period costs are those costs which can be identified with measured time intervals, rather than with goods delivered or services provided. Office rent is a good example of a period cost. Assume that office rent is $500 per month. This amount will have to be paid each month without regard to the amount of business activity which occurs during the month. Thus, the office rent is matched against revenues on a *period* basis, and for this reason it is said to be a period cost.

Virtually all costs in the nonmanufacturing category are treated as period costs and deducted from revenues in the period that they are incurred. The reason is that nonmanufacturing costs are generally more easily identified with a time period than they are with services provided or with goods delivered. Thus, advertising, executive compensation, secretarial costs, etc., would all be considered period costs.

Product Costs

Some costs are better matched against products produced than they are against periods of time. Such costs should not be treated as expenses in the period they are incurred; rather, they should be treated as expenses in the period in which the related products *are sold*. This means that if costs are incurred during one period, and the related products are not sold until a following period, then the costs should not be treated as expenses until the following period when sale takes place. The deferral of costs is necessary in order that the costs be properly matched against the benefits which they have brought about. The benefits in this case would be the sales revenues obtained in the later period.

To illustrate the idea of a product cost, assume that a company pays factory rent of $5,000 per year. If the goods which are produced in the factory during the current year are not sold until next year, then the factory rent should not be charged as an expense of the current period. The factory rent should follow the products into the next period, and be charged to expense in that year, as the products are sold.

Any cost incurred in the manufacture of a product should be treated as a product cost, rather than as a period cost. This would include direct materials, direct labor, and manufacturing overhead. As suggested by the discussion above, these costs should be viewed as attaching to units of product as the units are produced. Manufacturing costs are treated as product costs even if they accrue on a time basis. For example, the factory rent discussed above would accrue on a time basis, but it still would be a product cost rather than a period cost, since it is involved with the *manufacture* of products.

COST CLASSIFICATIONS ON FINANCIAL STATEMENTS

In your prior accounting training you learned that firms prepare periodic reports for creditors, stockholders, and others to show the financial condition of the company and the company's earnings performance over some specified interval. The reports you studied were probably those of merchandising firms, such as retail stores, which simply purchase goods from suppliers for resale to customers.

The financial statements prepared by a *manufacturing* firm are more complex than the statements prepared by a merchandising firm. As stated earlier, manufacturing firms are more complex organizations than merchandising firms, since the manufacturing firm must produce its goods as well as market them. The production process gives rise to many costs that do not exist in a merchandising firm, and somehow these costs must be accounted for on the manufacturing firm's financial statements. In this section we focus our attention on how this accounting is carried out, from a cost classification point of view.

The Income Statement

Exhibit 2–1 compares the income statement of a merchandising firm to the income statement of a manufacturing firm.

Notice in the case of a merchandising firm that the cost of goods sold simply consists of the purchase cost of the goods from a supplier. By contrast, the cost of goods sold in a manufacturing firm consists of many different costs which have been incurred in the process of manufacturing the goods which have been sold.

The income statement of a manufacturing firm is supported by a schedule of *cost of goods manufactured* (see Exhibit 2–1). This schedule shows the specific costs which have gone into the goods which a company has manufactured during a period. Notice that it contains the

EXHIBIT 2–1

Income Statement Data
Merchandising Firms versus Manufacturing Firms

Merchandising Firms

The cost of goods sold to customers comes from the purchased cost of these goods from an outside supplier.

Sales			$50,000
Cost of goods sold:			
Opening inventory		$ 8,000	
Add purchases		31,000	
Goods available for sale		39,000	
Ending inventory		9,000	30,000
Gross margin			20,000
Less operating expenses:			
Administrative expense		8,000	
Selling expense		9,000	17,000
Net income			$ 3,000

Manufacturing Firms

The cost of goods sold to customers comes from the manufacturing costs which have been incurred in the manufacture of the goods. These costs consist of Direct Materials, Direct Labor, and Manufacturing Overhead (see below).

Sales			$80,000
Cost of goods sold:			
Opening finished goods inventory		$10,000	
Add cost of goods manufactured		55,000	
Goods available for sale		65,000	
Ending finished goods inventory		15,000	50,000
Gross margin			30,000
Less operating expenses:			
Administrative expense		10,000	
Selling expense		11,000	21,000
Net income			$ 9,000

Manufacturing Firms—Schedule of Cost of Goods Manufactured

Direct materials			$16,000
Direct labor			20,000
Manufacturing overhead:			
Indirect materials		$ 3,000	
Indirect labor		6,000	
Lubricants		500	
Utilities		1,700	
Insurance		1,300	
Depreciation—Factory		4,000	
Property taxes		2,000	18,500
Total manufacturing costs			54,500
Add: Beginning work in process			10,000
			64,500
Deduct: Ending work in process			9,500
Cost of goods manufactured			$55,000

three elements of cost—direct materials, direct labor, and manufacturing overhead—which we discussed earlier as being the costs which go into any produced item. Also notice at the bottom of the schedule that one must add the beginning work in process to the production costs of a period, and deduct the ending work in process, in order to determine the cost of goods completed during a period. Work in process means goods partially completed at the beginning or end of a period.

The Balance Sheet

The preparation of the balance sheet, or statement of financial condition, is also more complex in a manufacturing firm than in a merchandising firm. A merchandising firm has only one class of inventory—goods purchased from suppliers which are awaiting resale to customers. By contrast, manufacturing firms have three classes of inventory—goods purchased as raw materials to go into manufactured products (known as "raw materials"), goods only partially complete as to manufacturing at the end of a period (known as "work in process"), and goods completed as to manufacturing but not yet sold to customers (known as "finished goods").

The current asset section of a balance sheet of a manufacturing firm is compared to the current asset section of a balance sheet of a merchandising firm in Exhibit 2–2. The inventory accounts shown in these current

EXHIBIT 2–2

Current Asset Data
Merchandising Firms versus Manufacturing Firms

Merchandising Firms

	Current assets:		
	Cash		$ 10,000
	Accounts receivable.		60,000
A single inventory account,	Merchandise inventory		150,000
consisting of goods purchased	Prepaid expenses		3,000
from suppliers.	Total.		$223,000

Manufacturing Firms

	Current assets:		
Three inventory accounts,	Cash		$ 15,000
consisting of materials to be	Accounts receivable		90,000
used in production, goods	Inventories:		
partially manufactured, and	Raw materials.	$ 12,000	
goods completely	Work in process.	60,000	
manufactured.	Finished goods	140,000	212,000
	Prepaid expenses		4,000
	Total.		$321,000

asset sections constitute the *only difference* between the balance sheets of the two types of firms.

Product Costs—A Closer Look

Earlier in the chapter we defined product costs as being the costs which go into the manufacture of goods. We need to take a closer look at product costs to see more clearly how the costing process affects the income statement and balance sheet of a manufacturing firm.

Product costs are often called *inventoriable* costs. The reason is that partially completed units or unsold units go into inventory, and the costs involved in their manufacture follow them into the inventory accounts. Thus the term inventoriable costs. The concept of an inventoriable or product cost is a key concept in managerial accounting, since these costs can end up on the balance sheet *as assets* (either as work in process or as finished goods) if manufactured products are only partially completed or are unsold at the end of a period.

Exhibit 2–3 illustrates the cost flows in a manufacturing firm. Notice

EXHIBIT 2–3
Cost Flows and Classifications

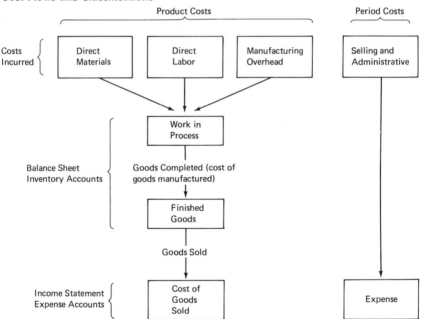

that direct materials, direct labor, and manufacturing overhead are added into work in process. As goods are completed, their cost is transferred from work in process into finished goods. As goods are sold, their cost is then transferred from finished goods into cost of goods sold.

Those costs which are placed in work in process initially are inventoriable or product costs. We indicated earlier that these costs would include *all costs* associated with *operating the factory*. By contrast, selling and

administrative costs and other costs associated with marketing and administration are not inventoriable costs, since they have nothing to do
with the *manufacture* of a product. Rather, they are treated as period
costs, and go directly to expense accounts as they are incurred.

An Example of Cost Flows. Assume that a firm prepays insurance
for two years at a total cost outlay of $4,000, with one half of the
amount applying to each year. How much of each year's $2,000 insurance
cost would be an expense of the period, and how much would be added
to the products of the period as part of their manufactured cost? To
answer this question we need to know how much of the insurance coverage applies to factory operations, and how much applies to merchandising operations (selling and administrative activities). Let us assume
that $1,500 applies to the factory, and that the remaining $500 applies
to the selling and administrative end of the company. In this case, $1,500
of the insurance would be an inventoriable cost, and would be added
to the cost of the goods produced during the period. This portion of
the period's insurance cost would not become an expense until the goods
produced during the period were sold (which might not be until the
following period). Until the goods were sold, this element of insurance
cost would remain as part of the asset, inventory (either as part of
work in process or as part of finished goods), along with the other
costs of producing the goods.

By contrast, the $500 of the insurance cost associated with the selling
and administrative end of the company's activities would go to expense
immediately, as a charge against the period. The cost flows are dia-
grammed in Exhibit 2–4.

A Summary of Product and Period Costs. The chart in Exhibit 2–5
contains a summary of product and period costs in both manufacturing
and merchandising firms.

EXHIBIT 2–4

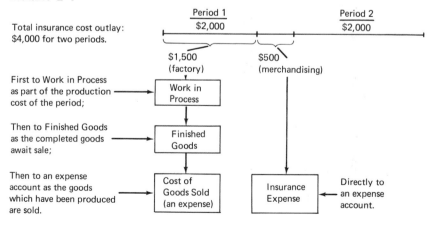

EXHIBIT 2–5
A Summary of Product and Period Costs

Type of Firm	Product Costs	Period Costs	Treatment
Merchandising firm	Cost of purchased inventory from suppliers		Treated as an asset (inventory) until the goods are sold. Then the cost is taken to expense as cost of goods sold.
Manufacturing firm	Direct materials Direct labor Manufacturing overhead (consists of all costs of production other than direct materials and direct labor)		Treated as product costs. These costs go into inventory accounts until the associated goods are completed and sold. Then they are taken (released) to expense as cost of goods sold.

Both merchandising and manufacturing firms		Selling expenses:
		   Salesmen's salaries
		   Depreciation on sales equipment
		   Insurance on sales equipment
		 Administration expenses:
		   Secretarial salaries
		   Depreciation on office
		     equipment
		   Insurance on office
		     equipment
			Treated as expenses immediately. Classified as *operating* expenses and deducted *from* gross margin.

The reader should study this exhibit with care, noting particularly the treatment of each type of cost as shown in the extreme right column.

FURTHER CLASSIFICATION OF LABOR COSTS

Of all of the costs of production, labor costs often present the most difficult problems of segregation and classification. Although firms vary considerably in their breakdown of labor costs, the following subdivisions represent the most common approach:

Direct labor (discussed earlier)
Indirect labor (part of manufacturing overhead)
   Janitors
   Foremen
   Materials handlers
   Engineers
   Night watchmen
   Maintenance
   Idle time
   Overtime premium
Payroll fringe benefits

The costs under indirect labor should not be viewed as being inclusive, but rather as being representative of the kinds of costs that one might expect to find there. Certain of these costs require further comment.

Idle Time

Idle time represents the costs of direct labor workers who are unable to perform their assignments due to machine breakdowns, materials shortages, power failures, etc. For example, if a press operator earning $4 per hour works 40 hours during a given week but is idle for 3 hours due to breakdowns, his labor cost would be allocated as follows:

Direct labor ($4 × 37 hours) $148
Manufacturing overhead (indirect labor, as idle time) ($4 × 3 hours).   12
Total $160

Overtime Premium

The overtime premium paid to *all* factory workers (direct labor as well as indirect labor) is considered to be part of manufacturing overhead. It is *not* assignable to any particular order or batch of production.

At first glance this may seem a strange practice. After all, overtime is always spent working on some particular batch of goods. The reason for the practice is that production is scheduled on a *random basis*. It would be unfair to charge an overtime premium against a particular batch of goods simply because the batch *happened* to fall on the tail end of the daily scheduling sheet.

To illustrate, assume that two batches of goods, order A and order B, each take three hours to complete. The production run on order A is scheduled early in the day, but the production run on order B isn't scheduled until late in the afternoon. By the time the run on order B is completed, two hours of overtime have been logged in. The necessity to work overtime was a result of the fact that *total* production exceeded the regular time available. Order B was no more responsible for the overtime than was order A. Therefore, all production should share in the premium charge that resulted. This method of handling overtime premium is much more equitable as between production runs, and doesn't penalize one run simply because it happens to fall late in the day.

Let us again assume that a press operator in a plant earns $4 per hour. He is paid time-and-a-half for overtime (time in excess of 40 hours a week). During a given week he works 44 hours, and has no idle time. His labor cost for the week would be allocated as follows:

Direct labor ($4 × 44 hours)	$176
Manufacturing overhead (overtime premium) ($2 × 4 hours)	8
Total	$184

Payroll Fringe Benefits

An item that is not so clearly defined as to its proper classification is payroll fringe benefits. Payroll fringe benefits would include employment-related costs paid by the employer, such as employee insurance programs, hospitalization plans, and annuity and retirement plans. Many firms treat all such costs as indirect labor, by adding them in total to manufacturing overhead. Other firms draw a distinction between the payroll fringe benefits relating to direct labor costs, and those relating to indirect labor costs. These firms treat payroll fringe benefits relating to direct labor as *additional* direct labor costs. Only the payroll fringe benefits relating to indirect labor are added to manufacturing overhead.

COSTS AND CONTROL

The cost classifications which are used to prepare financial statements may not be the same cost classifications which a manager uses to control operations and to plan for the future. For control purposes costs are often classified as variable and fixed, direct and indirect, and controllable and noncontrollable.

Variable and Fixed Costs

One of the most widely used cost classifications is by cost behavior. Cost behavior means how a cost will change with respect to changes in business activity. As the volume of business activity increases or decreases, a cost may increase or decrease as well, or it may remain constant. Obviously, if a cost is to be controlled properly, one must know whether the cost can be expected to change under various operating conditions. If it can be expected to change, one must know by how much.

Variable Costs. Variable costs are costs which vary in direct proportion to changes in the volume or level of activity. Direct materials is a good example of a variable cost. The amount of direct materials needed in production will vary in direct proportion to the number of units produced. If a company produces automobiles, then each auto produced will require one battery. As the volume of autos produced increases or decreases, the number of batteries used will increase or decrease proportionately. Thus, the batteries will be a variable cost of producing automobiles. If the batteries cost $10 each, then the total cost of batteries in relationship to production can be charted as follows:

Number of Autos Produced	Total Cost of Batteries at $10 Each
1	$ 10
10	100
100	1,000
1,000	10,000

There are many examples of variable costs, including direct materials, direct labor, and some items of manufacturing overhead in a manufacturing firm. In a merchandising firm, cost of goods sold would be a variable cost, as would commissions to salesmen.

Fixed Costs. Fixed costs are costs which remain constant in total regardless of changes in the volume or level of activity. Unlike variable costs, fixed costs are unaffected by changes in volume. To illustrate, assume that a firm pays $5,000 per month to rent a piece of equipment. The equipment might be used to its full capacity, or it might not be used at all, but this would not affect the fixed rental fee.

Since a fixed cost does not change in total amount, a problem sometimes arises in trying to cost units of product. The problem arises from the fact that as more units are produced, the amount of fixed cost per unit *decreases*. This is because the same total fixed cost is spread over more units as output is increased. The opposite happens when production falls off—the amount of fixed cost per unit *increases* as the unchanged total fixed cost is spread over fewer units.

To illustrate, assume again that a company rents a piece of equipment for a fixed monthly rental cost of $5,000. Assume that the equipment is capable of producing up to 1,000 units of product each month. The per unit cost for the equipment rental is shown below for output levels of 10 units, 100 units, and 1,000 units each month:

Monthly Rental Cost	*Number of Units Produced*	*Average Cost per Unit*
$5,000.	10	$500
5,000.	100	50
5,000.	1,000	5

Examples of fixed costs include depreciation, insurance, property taxes, rent, supervisory salaries, and advertising.

Direct and Indirect Costs

Costs are often classified as being either direct or indirect. However, the terms have no meaning unless one first identifies a unit or object to which the costs are to be related. For example, if the unit or object under consideration is a unit of product, then direct labor and direct materials would be direct costs. The reason is that they can be obviously and *physically* traced to the unit under consideration. Manufacturing overhead, by contrast, would be an indirect cost of a unit of product. The reason is that manufacturing overhead is not directly identifiable with any particular product, but rather is incurred as a consequence of general, overall operating activities.

In short, the distinction between direct and indirect costs hinges on the unit or object under consideration. The sales manager's salary would be a direct cost of the sales division, but it would be an indirect cost of the products sold *within* the division. Similarly, a production superintendent's salary would be an indirect cost of departments within a company, but it would be a direct cost of the company itself. The following guidelines prevail in distinguishing between direct and indirect costs:

1. If a cost can be conveniently and physically traced to a unit under consideration, then it is a direct cost with respect to that unit.
2. If a cost must be allocated in order to be assigned to a unit under consideration, then it is an indirect cost with respect of that unit.

Controllable and Noncontrollable Costs

Like direct and indirect costs, whether a cost is controllable or non-controllable depends on the point of reference. *All* costs are controllable at some level or another in a company. Only at the lower levels of management can some costs be considered to be noncontrollable. Top management has the power to expand or contract facilities, hire, fire, set expenditure policies, and generally exercise control over any cost as it desires. At lower levels of management, however, authority may not exist to control the incurrence of some costs, and these costs will therefore be considered noncontrollable *so far as that level of management is concerned.*

A cost is considered to be controllable at a particular level of management if that level has power to *authorize* the cost. For example, entertainment expense would be controllable by a sales manager if he had power to authorize the amount and type of entertainment for customers. On the other hand, depreciation of warehouse facilities would not be controllable by the sales manager, since he would have no power to authorize warehouse construction.

Direct Costs and Controllability. Students are sometimes inclined to assume that direct costs and controllable costs are the same thing. However, a cost can be direct to a department, but yet not be controllable by that department. For example, depreciation on equipment used exclusively by one department would be a direct cost of that department. But this cost would not be controllable by the department if it had no authority to authorize equipment purchases.

Cost Behavior and Controllability. There is also a tendency to assume that all fixed costs are noncontrollable, and that all variable costs are controllable. Cost behavior should not be confused with controllability. Just because a cost is fixed is no reason to assume that it is not controllable. For example, advertising is a fixed cost, but the amount is entirely controllable by top management policies. Similarly, many salaries are fixed, but their amount is controllable at some level within an organization.

Time and Controllability. In some situations there is a time dimension to controllability. Costs which are controllable over the long run may not be controllable over the short run. A good example is advertising. Once an advertising program has been set and a contract signed, management has no power to change the amount of spending. But when the contract expires, advertising costs can be renegotiated, and thus management can exercise control over the long run. Another example is plant acquisition. Management is free to build any size plant it desires, but once a plant is built management is largely powerless to change the attendant costs over the short run.

OTHER COST CONCEPTS

There are three other cost concepts with which we should be familiar as we start our study of managerial accounting. These concepts are differential costs, opportunity costs, and sunk costs.

Differential Costs

In making decisions, managers compare the alternatives before them. Each alternative will have certain costs associated with it that must be compared to the costs associated with the other alternatives available. A difference in cost between one alternative and another is known as a *differential* cost. Differential costs are also known as *incremental* costs, although technically an incremental cost should refer only to an increase in cost from one alternative to another. Differential cost is a broader term, including both increases and decreases in costs between alternatives.

The accountant's differential cost concept can be compared to the economists's marginal cost concept. In speaking of changes in cost and revenue, the economist employs the terms marginal cost and marginal revenue. The revenue that can be obtained from selling one more unit of product is called marginal revenue, and the cost involved in producing one more unit of product is called marginal cost. The economist's marginal concept is basically the same as the accountant's differential concept.

Opportunity Costs

An opportunity cost can be defined as the potential benefit that is foregone in rejecting some course of action. To illustrate, assume that a firm is considering investing a large sum of money in land to be held for future expansion. Rather than being invested in land, the funds could be invested in high-grade securities. If the land is acquired, there will be an opportunity cost associated with the purchase. The opportunity cost will be the investment income that could have been realized if the securities had been purchased instead.

Opportunity cost is not usually entered on the books of an organization, but it is a cost that must be explicitly considered in every decision that a manager makes. Virtually every alternative has some opportunity cost attached to it. In the example above, if the firm decided to purchase the securities rather than the land, opportunity costs would still be present: the costs associated with trying to obtain suitable land at an acceptable price at some later date.

In short, every alternative course of action facing a manager has a mixture of good and bad features. In rejecting a course of action, the good features must be given up along with the bad. The net good features of a rejected alternative become the opportunity costs of the alternative that is selected.

Sunk Costs

A sunk cost is a cost that has already been incurred, and which cannot be changed by any decision made now or in the future. Since sunk costs cannot be changed by any present or future decision, they should not be used in analyzing future courses of action.

To illustrate the notion of sunk cost, assume that a firm has just acquired a special-purpose packaging machine for $50,000. Since the outlay has already been made, the $50,000 investment in the machine is a sunk cost. What has happened in the past is done; that is, the investment in this case *has been made*. The investment may have been unwise, but the associated costs are "out of the window" so far as decision making is concerned. For this reason, such costs are said to be *sunk*.

SUMMARY

Although the term "cost" has a fairly distinctive meaning in financial accounting, it can be used in many different ways in managerial accounting. In this chapter we have looked at some of the ways in which it is used by the manager in order to organize and classify data.

We have learned that costs can be classified as being either period costs or product costs. Period costs are incurred as a function of time, rather than as a function of goods produced. Product costs relate to goods produced, and basically consist of the costs associated with operating the factory. We have found that product costs fall into one of three categories—direct materials, direct labor, and manufacturing overhead. These costs go first into work in process. As goods are completed, the costs come out of work in process and go into finished goods. As goods are sold, the costs come out of finished goods and go into cost of goods sold. The costs of partially completed or unsold goods appear as assets on the balance sheet of a manufacturing company, as work in process inventory or as finished goods inventory.

We have found that costs can also be classified as being either variable or fixed, direct or indirect, and controllable or noncontrollable. In addition, we defined differential costs, opportunity costs, and sunk costs. A differential cost is the difference in cost between two alternatives. An opportunity cost is the benefit that is foregone in rejecting some course of action, and a sunk cost is a cost that has already been incurred.

All of these cost terms and classifications are basic to managerial accounting. We shall use them repeatedly, as well as refine them further, in chapters ahead.

QUESTIONS

2–1. What are the three major elements in the cost of a manufactured product?

2–2. Distinguish between merchandising and manufacturing.

2–3. Distinguish between the following: (*a*) direct materials, (*b*) indirect materials, (*c*) direct labor, (*d*) indirect labor, and (*e*) manufacturing overhead.

2–4. Explain the difference between a product cost and a period cost.

2–5. Describe how the income statement of a manufacturing firm differs from the income statement of a merchandising firm.

2–6. Describe how the balance sheet of a manufacturing firm differs from the balance sheet of a merchandising firm, so far as current assets are concerned.

2–7. Why are product costs sometimes called inventoriable costs? Describe the flow of such costs in a manufacturing firm from point of incurrence until they finally become expenses on the income statement.

2–8. Is it possible for costs such as salaries or depreciation to end up as assets on the balance sheet? Explain.

2–9. Of what value is the schedule of cost of goods manufactured? How does it tie into the income statement?

2–10. Give at least three terms that may be substituted for the term "manufacturing overhead."

2–11. Ronald Jones operates a stamping machine on the assembly line of the Dustin Manufacturing Company. Last week Mr. Jones worked 45 hours. His basic wage rate is $5 per hour, with time-and-a-half for overtime. How should last week's wage cost be allocated as between direct labor and manufacturing overhead?

2–12. "A variable cost is a cost that varies per unit of product, whereas a fixed cost is constant per unit of product." Do you agree? Explain.

2–13. Under what conditions is a cost controllable at a particular level of management?

2–14. Define the following terms: differential cost, opportunity cost, sunk cost.

EXERCISES

2–1. Carey Products, Inc. produces automobiles. During March, 19X1, the company purchased 5,000 batteries at a cost of $10 per battery. It withdrew 4,800 batteries from the storeroom during March. Of these, 200 were used to replace batteries in cars being used by the company's traveling sales staff. The remaining 4,600 batteries were placed in cars being produced by the company; 90 percent of these cars were completed in all respects by the end of March. Of the cars completed during the month, 20 percent were unsold at March 31.

There were no inventories of any type on March 1, 19X1.

Required:

As of March 31, 19X1, determine the cost of batteries that should appear in the following accounts:

    a. Raw Materials.
    b. Work in Process.
    c. Finished Goods.
    d. Cost of Goods sold.
    e. Selling Expense.

2–2. Robert Peterson works on the assembly line of Carter Manufacturing Company. Mr. Peterson is paid $5 per hour. On Friday of last week Mr. Peterson worked 10 hours, including two hours of overtime. The first six hours of the day were spent on product X and the last four hours were spent on product Y. The company authorized the overtime in order to be able to start the next week on a fresh batch of orders. Mr. Peterson receives time-and-a-half for overtime.

Required:

    1. What portion of Mr. Peterson's labor cost should be allocated to product X? To product Y?
    2. Should any portion of Mr. Peterson's labor cost be allocated to manufacturing overhead? Explain.

2–3. Ornate Glass Products, Inc. manufactures glass products to special order. The company is considering two orders for the forthcoming year, only one of which can be accepted due to capacity constraints. Order #1 would bring in revenues of $120,000 and increase overall costs in the company by $70,000. Order #2 would bring in revenues of $105,000 and increase overall costs by $50,000.

    The company operates in a building purchased three years ago at a cost of $150,000. The equipment used to produce the glass products cost $65,000 three years ago. It costs $20,000 each year (not considering depreciation) to operate the equipment, regardless of the type of order being worked on, and in addition to the costs mentioned above. Fire is always a danger around glass production, so the company has just taken out a one-year fire insurance policy at a cost of $5,000.

Required:

    1. Identify the sunk costs.
    2. Identify the differential costs and revenues. (Notice that the company has two alternatives. It can choose, first, whether to produce or not produce. If it chooses to produce, it can choose between order #1 and order #2.)
    3. Identify the opportunity costs of each order.

2–4. The accounting records of Pressboard Binders, Inc. show the following information for 19X7:

Beginning finished goods inventory	$16,000
Ending finished goods inventory	14,000
Beginning work in process inventory	8,000
Ending work in process inventory	9,000
Direct labor	12,000
Indirect labor	7,000
Maintenance of factory equipment	2,000
Insurance on factory equipment	500
Insurance on office equipment	300
Rent on factory facilities	5,000
Depreciation of office equipment	500
Direct materials	10,000
Indirect materials	1,000
Depreciation on factory equipment	1,500

Required:

1. Prepare a schedule of cost of goods manufactured for 19X7.
2. Prepare a schedule of cost of goods sold for 19X7.

2–5. Classify the following costs as being inventoriable (I) or noninventoriable (N) in a manufacturing company:

1. Depreciation on salesmen's cars.
2. Rent on equipment used in the factory.
3. Lubricants used for maintenance of machines.
4. Salaries of finished goods warehouse personnel.
5. Soap and paper towels used by workmen at the end of a shift.
6. Foremen's salaries.
7. Heat, water, and power consumed in the factory.
8. Materials used in boxing units of finished product for shipment overseas.
9. Advertising outlays.
10. Workman's Compensation Insurance.
11. Depreciation on chairs and tables in the factory lunchroom.
12. The salary of the switchboard operator for the company.
13. Depreciation on a Lear Jet used by the company's executives.
14. Rent on rooms at a Florida resort for holding of the annual sales conference.
15. Replacement of small cutting tools broken on the assembly line.

2–6. Selected cost information from the records of Call Company is given below for the month of March, 19X5:

Factory utilities	$12,000
Finished goods inventory, March 1	18,000
Finished goods inventory, March 31	22,000
Direct labor cost	20,000
Administrative salaries	6,000
Indirect materials	14,000
Factory insurance	4,000
Sales commissions	5,000
Other factory costs	10,000
Work in process, March 1	17,000
Work in process, March 31	11,000
Direct materials used in production	32,000

Required:

1. Prepare a schedule of cost of goods manufactured for March 19X5.
2. Prepare a schedule of cost of goods sold for March 19X5.

2–7. The Meriwell Company was organized on May 1, 19X1. On that date the company purchased 5,000 plastic emblems, each with a peel-off adhesive backing. The front of the emblems contained the company's name, accompanied by an attractive logo. Each emblem cost the Meriwell Company $2.

During May, 4,500 emblems were drawn from the raw materials inventory account. Of these, 500 were taken by the sales manager to an important sales meeting with prospective customers, and handed out as a promotional gimmick. The remaining emblems drawn from inventory were affixed to units of the company's product. Of the units of product having emblems affixed during May, 80 percent were fully completed as to production during the month, and were transferred from work in process to finished goods. Of the goods fully completed as to production, 60 percent were sold during the month.

Required:

1. Determine the cost of emblems that would be in each of the following accounts at May 31, 19X1:
   a. Raw Materials.
   b. Work in Process.
   c. Finished Goods.
   d. Promotional Expense.
   e. Cost of Goods Sold.
2. Specify whether each of the above accounts would appear on the balance sheet or on the income statement at May 31.

PROBLEMS

2–1. *Cost Identification.* Jerry Genius has invented a new type of mousetrap. After giving the matter much thought, Jerry has decided to quit his $1,200 per month job with a computer firm and produce and sell the mousetraps full-time. Jerry has rented a garage which will be used as a production plant, and the rent has been paid for three months in advance at $150 per month. He has a number of tools and some equipment purchased several years ago at a cost of $4,000 which will be used in production.

Jerry has rented a room in the house next door for his sales office. The rent is $75 per month. One month's rent has been paid. He has arranged for the telephone company to attach a recording device to his home phone to get off-hours messages from customers. The device will increase his monthly phone bill by $20. In addition, he is charged $.50 for each message recorded on the device.

The cost of materials for each mousetrap will be $2.50. Jerry will supervise production, but the actual work will be done by employees who will be paid $.50 for each completed mousetrap. Jerry has $5,000 in savings at 6 percent interest. The savings will be withdrawn and used to get the business going. Advertising will cost $300 per month.

Required:

From the foregoing information, identify one or more examples of each of the following types of costs. (Note: A single item may be identified as more than one type of cost.)

a. Variable cost.
b. Fixed cost.
c. Product cost.
d. Period cost.
e. Opportunity cost.
f. Differential cost (between the alternatives of producing the mousetraps and not producing the mousetraps).
g. Overhead cost.
h. Sunk cost.

2–2. *Allocation of Payroll Costs.* Ben Newberry is employed by the Kopper Corporation, and works in the company's assembly plant. He assembles component parts that go into various of the company's products. During a recent week, Mr. Newberry worked a total of 50 hours. His time was spent as follows:

Assembly of gearboxes (part of a finished product)	46 hours
Idle time	4 "
Total time reported.	50 hours

Mr. Newberry is paid $5 per hour. The Kopper Corporation has determined that the cost to the company for payroll fringe benefits is $1 per hour. The company treats those payroll fringe benefits relating to direct labor hours as being added direct labor cost. Payroll fringe benefits relating to indirect labor are added to manufacturing overhead. Mr. Newberry is paid time-and-a-half for time worked in excess of 40 hours per week.

Required:

1. Allocate Mr. Newberry's wages for the week reported as between direct labor cost and manufacturing overhead.
2. Allocate the payroll fringe benefits for the week reported as between direct labor cost and manufacturing overhead.

2–3. *Cost Identification.* Hal Goodwin began dabbling in pottery several years ago as a hobby. He has enjoyed the pottery work so much that he has decided to quit his job with an areospace firm and manufacture pottery products full time. He is hopeful that he can make enough from pottery sales to equal at least the $1,500 per month he is now getting from his aerospace job.

Mr. Goodwin has decided to manufacture the pottery in the basement of his home. The basement is now being used as a rental apartment, and is bringing in rental revenues of $200 per month. Mr. Goodwin has some pottery wheels and other equipment which cost

$2,000 several years ago. These items will be used in the pottery manufacturing operation. Mr. Goodwin has agreed to rent additional equipment from a rental company at a monthly fee of $200. The equipment will be used to manufacture the pottery. Two months advance rent has been paid, which is not refundable.

Mr. Goodwin figures that the cost of clay and glaze will be about $1.00 for each finished piece of pottery. He will hire several workers to produce the pottery at a labor rate of $2.00 per pot. Having the manufacturing operation in his home will cause Mr. Goodwin's insurance to go up $25 per month. In addition, an answering device attached to his home phone for recording after-hours calls for orders will increase his monthly phone bill by $30. He is also charged $.50 per call recorded on the device.

In order to sell his products, Mr. Goodwin feels he must advertise heavily. He has entered into an advertising contract with a local advertising firm. He has made an initial payment of $500 for advertising, and will pay an additional $100 per month for one year under the contract.

Required:

Prepare an answer sheet with the following column headings:

Name of the Cost	Sunk Cost	Variable Cost	Fixed Cost	Product Cost	Period Cost	Opportunity Cost

Differential Cost	Overhead Cost

List the different costs associated with Mr. Goodwin's pottery operation down the extreme left column (under "Name of the Cost"). Then place an "X" under each heading which helps to describe the type of cost involved. There may be X's under several column headings for a single cost (i.e., a cost may be a sunk cost, a fixed cost, and a period cost; you would place an X under each of these column headings opposite the cost).

2–4. *Schedule of Cost of Goods Manufactured, and Cost Behavior.* Various sales and cost data for Black Enterprises for 19X6 are given below:

Direct labor	$ 15,000
Indirect labor	5,000
Factory supplies	500
Work in process, beginning	12,000
Work in process, ending	13,500
Sales	100,000
Selling expenses	11,000
Finished goods, beginning	10,000
Finished goods, ending	9,000
Depreciation—factory	27,000
Administrative expenses	14,000
Utilities, factory	2,000
Direct materials	12,000
Maintenance, factory	1,000
Indirect materials	4,000
Insurance, factory	1,000

Required:

1. Prepare a schedule of cost of goods manufactured for 19X6.
2. Prepare an income statement for 19X6.
3. Assume that the company produced 10,000 units of product during 19X6. What would be the per unit cost of direct materials? What would be the per unit cost of factory depreciation? Assume that factory depreciation is a fixed cost, computed on a straight-line basis.
4. Assume that the company expects to produce 15,000 units of product during the coming year. What total cost and what per unit cost would you expect the company to incur for direct materials at this level of activity? For factory depreciation? Assume no change in cost behavior patterns.
5. Explain any difference in unit costs between parts 3 and 4.

2–5. *Supply Missing Production and Sales Data.* Supply the missing data in the cases below. Each case is independent of the others.

	Case #1	Case #2	Case #3	Case #4	Case #5
Sales	$10,000	$15,000	$12,500	$18,000	$20,000
Opening finished goods.	2,000	4,000	3,000	?	6,000
Cost of goods manufactured. .	8,000	?	11,000	?	11,000
Ending finished goods	?	3,000	?	4,000	7,000
Cost of goods sold	7,000	?	10,000	13,000	?
Gross margin	3,000	5,000	?	5,000	?
Operating expenses	1,000	1,500	1,500	2,000	5,000
Net income	2,000	3,500	1,000	3,000	5,000
Direct materials	3,000	4,000	3,000	2,000	5,000
Direct labor	?	2,000	4,000	4,000	3,000
Manufacturing overhead	4,000	2,000	?	3,000	5,000
Total manufacturing costs . . .	9,000	?	?	?	?
Beginning work in process . . .	2,000	?	2,500	5,000	?
Ending work in process	?	4,000	2,500	2,000	4,000
Cost of goods manufactured. .	8,000	9,000	11,000	?	?

2–6. *Fixed and Variable Cost Behavior.* By analyzing costs of prior periods, Harper Company has determined that variable manufacturing overhead costs amount to $.38 for each machine hour worked in the plant. The company has also determined that fixed manufacturing overhead costs (such as for insurance, depreciation, etc.) amount to $5,200 per month.

Two machine hours are required to produce one unit of finished product.

Required:

1. Assume that during July Harper Company produced 8,000 units of product. What amount of manufacturing overhead should have been incurred?

2. Assume again that 8,000 units were produced during July. What was the manufacturing overhead cost per unit? How much of this cost was variable? How much was fixed?
3. Assume that 10,000 units were produced during August. What was the manufacturing overhead cost per unit? How much of this cost was variable? How much was fixed?
4. Compare the July variable and fixed per unit costs to the August variable and fixed per unit costs. Which per unit costs differ? Why do they differ?

2–7. *Cost Classification.* Various costs associated with the operation of a factory are given below.

1. Electricity for operation of machines.
2. A foreman's salary.
3. Sand in a cement factory.
4. Lubricants for machines.
5. Direct labor payroll fringe benefits.
6. Property taxes.
7. Janitorial salaries.
8. Factory cafeteria food costs.
9. Laborers assembling a product.
10. Glue in furniture production.
11. Rent on a factory building.
12. Lease cost of equipment to produce units of product.

Classify each cost as being either variable or fixed with respect to volume or level of activity. Also classify each cost as being either direct or indirect with respect to units of product. Prepare your answer sheet as shown below:

	Cost Behavior		To Units of Product	
Cost Item	Variable	Fixed	Direct	Indirect
Example: Factory insurance		X		X

2–8. *Statements from Incomplete Data.* Cedrick Hardluck, the chief accountant of Foremost Enterprises, accidentally tossed the company's cost records into a wastebasket. Realizing his error, he raced to the incinerator but was successful in retrieving only a few scraps from the roaring blaze. From these scraps he has been able to determine the following facts about the current year, 19X4:

1. Sales totaled $100,000 during 19X4.
2. The beginning inventories for the year were:

    Work in process $12,000
    Finished goods   6,000

3. Direct labor is equal to 25 percent of conversion cost.
4. The work in process inventory decreased by $2,000 during 19X4.

5. Gross margin during 19X4 was equal to 55 percent of sales.
6. Manufacturing overhead totaled $24,000 for 19X4.
7. Direct labor is equal to 40 percent of prime cost.
8. Administrative expenses for 19X4 were twice as great as net income, but only 25 percent of selling expenses.

Mr. Hardluck must have an income statement and a schedule of cost of goods manufactured ready for the board of directors in an hour.

Required:

Prepare the income statement and schedule of cost of goods manufactured needed by Mr. Hardluck. The board wants these items in the format shown in Exhibit 2–1 in the text for a manufacturing firm.

2–9. *Cost of Goods Manufactured, and Cost of Goods Sold.* The information given below was taken from the books of Shaw Manufacturing Company:

Inventories at January 1, 19X2:

Work in process	$30,000
Finished goods	60,000

Inventories at December 31, 19X2:

	Work in Process	Finished Goods
Direct materials	$12,000	$18,000
Direct labor	20,000	40,000
Factory overhead	18,000	?
Total.	$50,000	?

Other information for the year ended December 31, 19X2:

Cost of goods manufactured.	$630,000
Factory overhead (equal to 90% of direct labor cost)	225,000

No raw material inventories are maintained. Raw materials are purchased as used in production.

Required:

1. Prepare a statement of cost of goods manufactured for the year 19X2, in as much detail as the data permit.
2. Assume the following additional information for the year 19X2:

Sales	$750,000
Selling expenses.	70,000
Administrative expenses	30,000

Prepare an income statement for the year 19X2.

2–10. *Preparing Manufacturing Statements.* The Marcos Company has just completed operations for the year 19X3. The company's assistant accountant (who is very inexperienced) prepared the following income statement for the year's activities:

MARCOS COMPANY
Income Statement
For the Year Ended December 31, 19X3

Sales		$320,000
Operating expenses:		
Insurance expired during the year	$ 4,000	
Utilities paid during the year	10,000	
Direct labor cost	60,000	
Indirect labor cost	12,000	
Depreciation on factory equipment	16,000	
Raw materials purchased during the year	120,000	
Rent paid	40,000	
Selling and administrative salaries.	32,000	294,000
Net income		$ 26,000

You have been asked to assist the Marcos Company in preparing a corrected income statement for the year 19X3. The following additional information is available:

1. The Marcos Company is a manufacturing firm that produces a product for sale to outside customers.
2. 80 percent of the rent paid applies to factory operations; the remainder applies to selling and administrative activities.
3. No raw materials were on hand on January 1. Some $15,000 of the raw materials purchased during 19X3 were still on hand at December 31. The remainder was used in production during the year.
4. 70 percent of the insurance expired, and 90 percent of the utilities paid apply to factory operations; the remainder apply to selling and administrative activities.
5. Work in process and finished goods inventories were:

	January 1	December 31
Work in process	$42,000	$48,000
Finished goods	54,000	40,000

Required:

1. Prepare a statement of cost of goods manufactured for 19X3.
2. Prepare a corrected income statement for 19X3.

chapter 3

Cost Accumulation for Product Costing

As DISCUSSED in Chapter 2, product costing is the process of assigning manufacturing costs to manufactured goods. An understanding of this process is vital to any manager, since the way in which a product is costed can have a substantial impact on reported net income, as well as on the current asset section of the balance sheet.

In this chapter we look at product costing from the *absorption* approach. The approach is so named because it provides for the absorption of all manufacturing costs, fixed and variable, into units of product. In Chapter 7 we look at product costing from another point of view, and then discuss the strengths and weaknesses of the two approaches.

THE NEED FOR FACTORY UNIT COST DATA

In studying product costing, we will focus initially on *unit cost of production,* an item of cost data generally regarded as being highly useful to managers.

Managers need unit cost data for a variety of reasons. First, unit costs are needed in order to cost inventories on financial statements. The units of product remaining on hand at the end of an operating period must have costs attached to them as the units are carried forward on the balance sheet to the next period.

Second, unit costs are needed for determination of a period's net income. The cost of each unit sold during a period must be placed on the income statement as a deduction from total sales revenue. If unit costs are incorrectly computed, then net income will be equally incorrect.

Finally, managers need unit cost data to assist them in a broad range of decision-making situations. Without unit cost data, managers would find it very difficult to set selling prices for factory output. A knowledge of unit costs is also vital in a number of special decision areas, such as whether to add or drop product lines, whether to make or buy production components, whether to expand or contract operations, and whether to accept special orders at special prices. The particular unit costs that are relevant in this variety of decision-making situations will differ, so we need to learn not only how to derive unit costs, but also how to differentiate between those costs that are relevant in a particular situation and those that are not. The matter of relevant costs is reserved until Chapter 12. For the moment we are concerned with gaining an understanding of the concept of unit cost in its broadest sense.

TYPES OF COSTING SYSTEMS

The type of costing system used to measure unit costs will depend heavily on the nature of the manufacturing process involved. Basically, two costing systems have emerged in response to variations in how the manufacturing process can be carried out. These two systems are commonly known as *process costing* and *job order costing*.

Process Costing

Process costing is employed in those situations where manufacturing involves a single product that is produced for long periods at a time. Examples of industries that would use process costing include cement, flour, brick, and gasoline manufacturing. All of these industries are characterized by a basically homogeneous product that flows evenly through the production process on a more or less continuous basis.

The basic approach to process costing is to accumulate costs in a particular operation or department for an entire period (month, quarter, year), and then to divide this total by the number of units produced during the period. The basic formula for process costing would be:

$$\frac{\text{Total Costs of Manufacturing}}{\text{Total Units Produced (gallons, pounds, etc.)}} = \text{Unit Cost per Gallon, Pound, etc.}$$

Since one unit of product (gallon, pound, etc.) is completely indistinguishable from any other unit of product, each unit bears the same average cost as any other unit produced during the period. This costing technique results in a broad, average unit cost that applies to many thousands of like units flowing in an almost endless stream off of the assembly or processing line.

Job Order Costing

Job order costing is used in those manufacturing situations where many *different* products, jobs, or batches of production are being produced each period. Examples of industries that would typically use job order costing include special order printing, furniture manufacturing, and machine tool manufacturing.

These types of industries require a costing system in which costs can be assigned separately to each independent order (such as a special printing job) or batch of goods (such as a production run of ten special-purpose machines), and distinct unit costs determined for each separate item produced. Obviously, a job order costing system will entail problems of record keeping and cost allocation that are not present under the process costing system. Rather than dividing total costs of production by many thousands of like units, under job order costing one must somehow divide total costs of production by a few, basically unlike units.

Regardless of whether one is dealing with process costing or job order costing, the problem of determining unit costs involves a need for *averaging* of some type. The essential difference between the process and job order approaches lies in the way this averaging is carried out. Since the job order approach is the most versatile of the two costing methods, we will focus on it for our initial discussion of product costing.[1]

JOB ORDER COSTING—THE GENERAL OUTLINE

In the preceding chapter the point was made that there are three broad categories of costs involved in the manufacture of any product:

1. Direct materials.
2. Direct labor.
3. Manufacturing overhead.

As we study the operation of a job order costing system, we will look at each of these costs, and at the way in which each is involved in the costing of a unit of product. In studying job order costing, it is our purpose to gain a broad conceptual perspective of the system and the way in which it operates.

Measuring Direct Materials Cost

The production process begins with the transfer of raw materials from the storeroom to the production line. The bulk of these raw mate-

---

[1] See the Appendix for a discussion of process costing.

rials will be traceable directly to the goods being produced, and will therefore be termed direct materials. Other materials, generally termed indirect materials, will not be charged to a specific job, but rather will be included within the general category of manufacturing overhead. As discussed in Chapter 2, indirect materials would include costs of glue, nails, and miscellaneous supplies.

Raw materials are drawn from the storeroom on presentation of a materials requisition form. A materials requisition form is shown in Exhibit 3–1.

EXHIBIT 3–1
Materials Requisition Form

Materials Requistion Number __14873__		Date __March 2, 19X2__	

Job Number to be Charged __2B47__
Department __Milling__

Description	Quantity	Unit Cost	Total Cost
M46 Housing	2	$123	$246
G7 Connector	8	52	416
			$662

The materials requisition form is a basic, detailed source document that forms the basis for entries in the accounting records.

The Job Cost Sheet

The cost of direct materials is entered on a job cost sheet, similar to the one presented in Exhibit 3–2. A job cost sheet is prepared for each separate job initiated into production. Normally, the job cost sheet is prepared by the accounting department upon notification by the production department that a production order has been issued for a particular job. The production order is issued only on authority of a sales order from the sales department indicating that a firm agreement in terms of quantities, prices, and shipment dates has been reached with the customer.

As materials are issued, the accounting department makes entries

EXHIBIT 3–2
The Job Cost Sheet

JOB COST SHEET

Job Number____2B47_____   Date Initiated____March 2, 19X2_____
                                    Date Completed_____

Department____Milling_____
Item____Special order coupling_____   Units Completed_____
For Stock_____

Materials		Direct Labor			Manufacturing Overhead		
Req. No.	Amount	Card	Hours	Amount	Hours	Rate	Amount
14873	$662						

Cost Summary		Units Shipped		
Materials	$	Date	Number	Balance
Direct Labor	$			
Overhead	$			
Total Cost	$			
Unit Cost	$			

directly on the job cost sheet, thereby charging the specific job noted on the sheet with the cost of direct materials used in production. When the job is completed, the total cost of materials used can be summarized in the "cost summary" as one element involved in determining the unit cost characteristics of the order.

Measuring Direct Labor Cost

Direct labor cost is accumulated and measured in much the same way as direct materials cost. Direct labor would include those labor charges that are directly traceable to the particular job in process. By contrast, those labor charges that cannot be traced directly to a particular job, or that can be traced only with the expenditure of great effort, are treated as part of manufacturing overhead. As discussed in Chapter 2, this latter category of labor costs is termed indirect labor, and would include such tasks as maintenance work, lubrication, and clean-up.

Labor costs are generally accumulated by means of some type of work record prepared each day by each employee. These work records, often termed *time tickets* or *time sheets*, constitute an hour-by-hour summary of the activities and assignments completed during the day by the employee. When working on a specific job, the employee enters the job number on his time sheet and notes the number of hours spent on the particular task involved. When he is not assigned to a particular job, the employee enters the type of indirect labor tasks to which he was assigned (such as clean-up, maintenance, etc.), and the number of hours spent on each separate task.

At the end of a day, the time sheets are gathered and the accounting department carefully analyzes each in terms of the number of hours assignable as direct labor to specific jobs, and the number of hours assignable to manufacturing overhead as indirect labor. Those hours assignable as direct labor are entered on individual job cost sheets (such as in Exhibit 3–2), along with the appropriate charges involved. When all direct labor charges associated with a particular job have been accumulated on the job cost sheet, the total can be summarized in the "cost summary" section. The daily time sheets, in essence, constitute basic source documents used as a basis for labor cost entries into the accounting records.

Application of Manufacturing Overhead

Manufacturing overhead must be considered along with direct materials and direct labor in determining unit costs of production. However, the assignment of manufacturing overhead to units of product is often a difficult task. There are several reasons why this is so.

First, as explained in Chapter 2, manufacturing overhead is an *indirect* cost to units of product, and for this reason can't be traced directly to a particular product or job. Second, manufacturing overhead includes a conglomeration of unlike items, involving both variable and fixed costs. It ranges from the grease used in machines to the annual salary of the production superintendent. Finally, firms with strong seasonal variations in production often find that even though output is fluctuating, manufacturing overhead costs tend to remain relatively constant. The reason is that fixed costs generally constitute a large part of manufacturing overhead.

Given these problems, about the only acceptable way to assign over-head costs to units of product is to do so in an *indirect* manner, through an allocation technique. The approach is to choose some base, common to all jobs worked on during a particular period, which measures so far as possible each job's utilization of, or benefits from, the manufacturing overhead incurred. The trick, of course, is to choose the right base so that the overhead application will be equitable as between jobs. Probably the most widely used bases are direct labor hours and machine hours, although direct labor cost is also used to some extent. Once a base is chosen, it is divided into the *estimated* total manufacturing overhead costs of the period in order to obtain a rate that will be used to apply to jobs as they are processed.

The Need for Estimated Data. Notice our emphasis on the use of *estimated* data in computing an overhead application rate. *Actual* overhead costs are rarely, if ever, used in overhead costing. The reason is that actual overhead costs are not available until after a period is over. This is too late for costing purposes, since prices must be set on customer orders, and other decisions involving costs must be made on a day-by-day basis as the year progresses.

For this reason, rather than using actual overhead costs, most firms *estimate* total manufacturing overhead costs at the beginning of a year, and *estimate* the direct labor hours (or whatever base is being used) that will be worked during the year, and develop an overhead rate *in advance* based on these estimates. An overhead rate based on estimated data is known as a *predetermined overhead rate.*

The Predetermined Overhead Rate. The formula for computing a predetermined overhead rate is:

$$\frac{\text{Estimated Total Manufacturing Overhead Costs}}{\text{Estimated Total Units in the Base (direct labor hours, etc.)}} = \text{Predetermined Overhead Rate}$$

In assigning overhead costs to the job cost sheet (and thereby to units of product), the predetermined overhead rate is multiplied by the number of direct labor hours (or whatever the base is) worked on the job, and the total amount entered on the job cost sheet. To illustrate, assume that a firm has estimated its total manufacturing overhead costs for the year to be $300,000, and has estimated 100,000 total direct labor hours for the year. Its predetermined overhead rate for the year would be $3 per direct labor hour, as shown below:

$$\frac{\$300,000}{100,000 \text{ Direct Labor Hours}} = \$3/\text{Direct Labor Hour}$$

If a particular job required 54 direct labor hours to complete, then that job would be allocated $162 (54 × $3) of manufacturing overhead cost. This allocation is shown on the job cost sheet in Exhibit 3–3.

Whether the application of overhead is made slowly as the job is worked on during the period, or in a single application at the time of completion, is a matter of choice and convenience to the company involved. If a job is not completed at year end, however, overhead

EXHIBIT 3–3
A Completed Job Cost Sheet

JOB COST SHEET

Job Number___2B47_____   Date Initiated___March 2, 19X2_____
                                      Date Completed___March 8, 19X2_____

Department___Milling_____
Item___Special order coupling_____   Units Completed___150_____
For Stock_____

Materials		Direct Labor			Manufacturing Overhead		
Req. No.	Amount	Card	Hours	Amount	Hours	Rate	Amount
14873	$ 662	47	12	$ 36	54	$3/DLH	$162
14875	538	23	30	120			
14912	238	76	8	24			
	$1,438	18	4	20			
			54	$200			

Cost Summary		Units Shipped		
Materials	$ 1,438	Date	Number	Balance
Direct Labor	$ 200	3/8/X2	—	150
Overhead	$ 162			
Total Cost	$ 1,800			
Unit Cost	$ 12*			

* $1,800 ÷ 150 units = $12 per unit.

should be applied to the extent needed to properly value the work-in-process inventory.

Computation of Unit Costs

With the application of manufacturing overhead to the job cost sheet, total costs of the job can be summarized in the "cost summary" section (see Exhibit 3–3 for an example of a completed job cost sheet). The cost of the individual units in the job can then be obtained by dividing the total costs by the number of units produced. The completed job cost sheet is then ready to be transferred to the finished goods inventory file, where it will serve as a basis for either costing unsold units in the ending inventory, or charging expense for units sold.

A Summary of Document Flows

The sequence of events just discussed is summarized in Exhibit 3–4. A careful study of the flow of documents in this exhibit will provide

EXHIBIT 3–4
The Flow of Documents in a Job Order Cost System

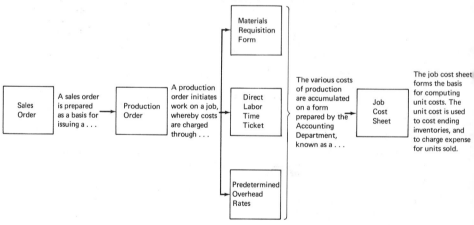

an excellent visual review of the overall operation of a job order costing system.

JOB ORDER COSTING—THE FLOW OF COSTS

Having obtained a broad, conceptual perspective of the operation of a job order costing system, we are now prepared to take a look at the flow of actual costs through the system itself. We shall consider a single month's activity for a hypothetical company, presenting all data in summary form.

The Purchase and Issue of Materials

During the month of April, the Rand Company purchased $60,000 in raw materials for use in production. Fifty thousand dollars of this amount was direct materials and $10,000 was indirect materials. The purchase is recorded in entry (1) below:

Raw Materials. 60,000
    Accounts Payable. 60,000 (1)

"Raw materials" is an inventory account. Whatever raw materials remain in it at the end of a period will appear on the balance sheet under the inventory classification.

During April the Rand Company drew $50,000 in raw materials from the storeroom for use in production. Entry (2) records the issue of the materials to the production departments.

Work in Process. 40,000
Manufacturing Overhead. 10,000
    Raw Materials. 50,000 (2)

The materials charged to *Work in Process* represent direct materials assignable to specific jobs on the production line. *The Work in Process account is a summarized total of the costs appearing on individual job cost sheets for jobs in process at any point in time.* This concept is illustrated in Exhibit 3–5.

Notice from Exhibit 3–5 that a portion of the materials drawn were not assignable directly to any specific job, and were therefore charged

EXHIBIT 3–5
Raw Materials Cost Flows

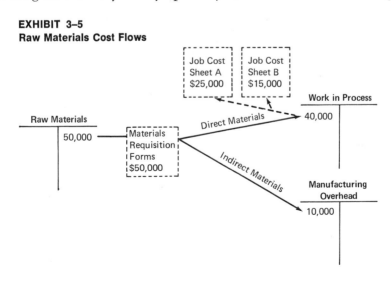

to Manufacturing Overhead. These costs will remain in the Manufacturing Overhead account until the time comes to allocate them to Work in Process (and to the individual job cost sheets) by use of the predetermined overhead rate. The cost of these indirect materials would have been one of the costs included in the estimated total Manufacturing Overhead at the beginning of the period when the predetermined overhead rate was computed.

Labor Costs

As work is performed in various departments of the Rand Company from day to day, employee time tickets are generated, collected, and forwarded to the Accounting Department. There the tickets are costed according to the various rates paid to the employees, and the resulting costs classified in terms of being either direct or indirect labor. This costing and classification for the month of April resulted in the following entry:

```
Work in Process. . . . . . . . . . . . . . . . . . . . . . . . .   55,000
Manufacturing Overhead . . . . . . . . . . . . . . . . . . .   15,000
    Wages Payable  . . . . . . . . . . . . . . . . . . . . . . .            $70,000   (3)
```

As with raw materials, the amount charged to Work in Process represents the labor costs chargeable directly to specific jobs. It will equal the total of the direct labor charges on the individual job cost sheets. This concept is illustrated in Exhibit 3–6.

The labor costs charged to Manufacturing Overhead represent the indirect labor costs of the period, such as maintenance, janitorial work, and clean-up. As in the case with raw materials, the labor costs going

Labor Cost Flows
EXHIBIT 3–6

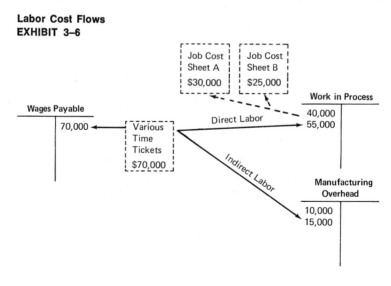

into Manufacturing Overhead will remain there until allocated to Work in Process through use of the predetermined overhead rate.

Actual Overhead Costs

As actual manufacturing overhead costs are incurred, they are not charged to Work in Process. Rather, they are recorded in a *Manufacturing Overhead account.* To illustrate, assume that the Rand Company incurred the following general factory costs during the month of April:

Utilities (heat, light, and power)	$15,000
Supervisory salaries	5,000
Rent on equipment	10,000
	$30,000

The entry to record the payment of these factory costs would be:

Manufacturing Overhead	30,000	
Cash		30,000 (4)

In addition, let us assume that the Rand Company recognized $25,000 in accrued property taxes during April, and recognized $5,000 in insurance expired on factory buildings and equipment. The entry to record these items would be:

Manufacturing Overhead	30,000	
Property Taxes Payable		25,000
Prepaid Insurance		5,000 (5)

Let us further assume that the company recognized $10,000 in depreciation on factory assets during April. The entry to record the accrual of depreciation would be:

Manufacturing Overhead	10,000	
Accumulated Depreciation		10,000 (6)

In short, *all* manufacturing overhead costs are recorded directly into the Manufacturing Overhead account as they are incurred day-by-day throughout the period. Notice from the entries above that the recording of *actual* manufacturing overhead costs has had no effect on the Work in Process account.

Application of Manufacturing Overhead

How do manufacturing overhead costs find their way into the Work in Process account? The answer is that they enter into the Work in Process account by means of the predetermined overhead rate. The process of charging Work in Process with manufacturing overhead is called the *application* or *absorption* of overhead. The amount of manufacturing overhead to be absorbed by a particular job is obtained by multiplying the predetermined overhead rate by whatever base is being used to measure overhead utilization, as discussed earlier in the chapter.

We shall assume that the base being used by the Rand Company is direct labor hours. We shall also assume that the Rand Company has developed a predetermined overhead rate of $6 per direct labor hour. During the month, 15,000 direct labor hours were worked on various jobs. The entry to record the application of manufacturing overhead would be:

```
Work in Process.........................  90,000
    Manufacturing Overhead.................         90,000  (7)
```

The process of applying manufacturing overhead to jobs in Work in Process is shown in T-account form in Exhibit 3–7.

EXHIBIT 3–7
The Flow of Costs in Overhead Application

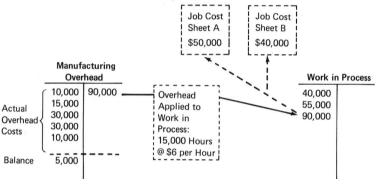

The Concept of a Clearing Account. The Manufacturing Overhead account operates as a *clearing* account. Actual factory costs are charged to it as they are incurred day by day throughout the period. At certain intervals during the period, usually when a job is completed, these costs are relieved from the account and applied into Work in Process. By this time the individual costs have *lost their separate identity*, and are simply treated as unidentified parts of an average overhead application figure called the predetermined rate.

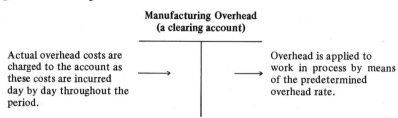

Since the predetermined overhead rate is based on estimates, the overhead *applied* may be more or less than the *actual* overhead costs incurred during a period. For example, notice from Exhibit 3–7 that the Rand Company's actual overhead costs are $5,000 *greater* than the overhead applied to Work in Process. We will reserve discussion of what to do with this $5,000 balance until a later section in the chapter titled, "Problems of Overhead Application."

Nonmanufacturing Costs

In addition to incurring taxes, salaries, utilities, etc., as part of the operation of the factory, manufacturing firms will also be incurring these same kinds of costs in relation to other parts of their operations. For example, there will be salaries, utilities, etc., arising from activities in the "front office" where secretaries, top management, and others work. There will be identical kinds of costs arising from the operation of the sales staff. The costs of these nonfactory operations should *not* go into manufacturing overhead since the incurrence of these costs is not related to the manufacture of products. Rather, these costs should be treated as expenses of the period, as explained in Chapter 2, and charged directly to the income statement. To illustrate, assume that the Rand Company incurred the following costs during the month of April:

Top management salaries	$30,000
Secretaries' salaries	10,000
Salesmen's commissions	25,000
	$65,000

The entry to record payment of these salaries and commissions would be:

Salaries Expense	40,000	
Commissions Expense	25,000	
Cash		65,000 (8)

Since these items go directly into expense accounts, they will have no effect on the costing of the Rand Company's production for the month of April. The same will be true with all other selling and administrative expenses incurred during the month, including advertising, depreciation of salesmen's automobiles, utilities for the administrative offices, depreciation of office equipment, etc.

Cost of Goods Finished

When a job has been completed, the finished output is transferred from the production departments to the finished goods warehouse. By this time the Accounting Department will have charged the job with direct materials and direct labor cost, and the job will have absorbed a portion of manufacturing overhead through the application process discussed earlier. A transfer of these costs must be made within the costing system that *parallels* the physical transfer of the goods to the finished goods warehouse. The transfer within the costing system will be to move the costs of the completed job out of Work in Process, and into the Finished Goods inventory account.

In the case of the Rand Company, we have placed $185,000 into Work in Process during the month:

Direct materials	$ 40,000
Direct labor	55,000
Manufacturing overhead	90,000
Total costs in work in process	$185,000

Of this total, let us assume that goods costing $170,000 were completed during the period. The entry to record the transfer of the completed units into Finished Goods would be:

Finished Goods	170,000	
Work in Process		170,000 (9)

The $15,000 balance remaining in Work in Process ($185,000 — $170,000) represents the cost of goods started during the month, but not completed at month-end. As explained in Chapter 2, this balance will appear under the caption "Work In Process Inventory" in the inventory section of the balance sheet.

Cost of Goods Sold

As units of product in Finished Goods are shipped to fill customer orders, the unit cost appearing on the job cost sheets is used as a basis for transfering the cost of the sold items from the Finished Goods inventory account into the Cost of Goods Sold account. If a complete job is shipped, as in the case where a job has been done to a customer's specifications, then it is a simple matter to transfer the entire cost appearing on the job cost sheet into Cost of Goods Sold. In most cases, however, only a portion of the units involved in a particular job will be sold. In these situations, the unit cost is particularly important in knowing how much product cost should be removed from Finished Goods and charged into Cost of Goods Sold.

For the Rand Company, we will assume that during the month of April goods were sold that had a production cost of $105,000. These goods were sold at a selling price of $150,000. The entries to record the sale would be:

Cash	150,000	
Sales		150,000 (10)
Cost of Goods Sold	105,000	
Finished Goods		105,000 (11)

With entry (11) the flow of costs through our job order costing system is completed.

EXHIBIT 3–8
A Summary of Cost Flows—The Rand Company

Cash			
XX	(4)	30,000	
(10) 150,000	(8)	65,000	

Accounts Payable		
	XX	
(1)	60,000	

Capital Stock	
	XX

Prepaid Insurance		
XX	(5)	5,000

Wages Payable		
	XX	
(3)	70,000	

Retained Earnings	
	XX

Raw Materials			
Bal.	5,000	(2)	50,000
(1)	60,000		
Bal.	15,000		

Property Taxes Payable		
	XX	
(5)	25,000	

Sales	
	(10) 150,000

Work in Process			
Bal.	30,000	(9)	170,000
(2)	40,000		
(3)	55,000		
(7)	90,000		
Bal.	45,000		

Cost of Goods Sold	
(11) 105,000	

Finished Goods			
Bal.	10,000	(11)	105,000
(9)	170,000		
Bal.	75,000		

Salaries and Commissions Expense		
(8)	40,000	
(8)	25,000	

Accumulated Depreciation		
	XX	
(6)	10,000	

Manufacturing Overhead			
(2)	10,000	(7)	90,000
(3)	15,000		
(4)	30,000		
(5)	30,000		
(6)	10,000		
Bal.	5,000		

Note: XX = Normal balance in the account (e.g., Cash normally carries a debit balance).

Explanation of entries:
(1) The purchase of raw materials.
(2) The issue of raw materials into production.
(3) The recording of labor costs.
(4) The recording of overhead costs.
(5) The recording of overhead costs.
(6) The recording of overhead costs.
(7) The application of overhead costs into work in process.
(8) The recording of salaries and commissions expense.
(9) The transfer of cost of goods manufactured into finished goods.
(10) The sale of goods.
(11) The recording of cost of goods sold.

A Summary of Cost Flows

To pull the entire Rand Company example together, a summary of cost flows is presented in T-account form in Exhibit 3–8. The flows of costs through the exhibit are keyed to the numbers (1) through (11). These numbers relate to the numbers of the transactions (1) through (11) appearing on the preceding pages.

Exhibit 3–9 presents a schedule of cost of goods manufactured and a schedule of cost of goods sold for the Rand Company.

EXHIBIT 3–9
Schedules of Cost of Goods Manufactured and Cost of Goods Sold

Cost of Goods Manufactured

Direct materials:		
Raw materials inventory, April 1	$ 5,000	
Add purchases of raw materials	50,000*	
Total raw materials available	55,000	
Deduct raw materials inventory, April 30	15,000	
Direct materials used in production		$ 40,000
Direct labor		55,000
Manufacturing overhead:		
Indirect materials	10,000	
Indirect labor	15,000	
Utilities	15,000	
Supervisory salaries	5,000	
Rent	10,000	
Property taxes	25,000	
Insurance	5,000	
Depreciation	10,000	
Actual overhead costs	95,000	
Less underapplied overhead	5,000	90,000
Total manufacturing costs		185,000
Add: Beginning work in process		30,000
		215,000
Deduct: Ending work in process		45,000
Cost of goods manufactured		$170,000

Cost of Goods Sold

Opening finished goods inventory	$ 10,000
Add cost of goods manufactured	170,000
Goods available for sale	180,000
Ending finished goods inventory	75,000
Cost of goods sold	$105,000

Notes: Notice on the schedule of cost of goods manufactured that underapplied overhead must be *deducted* from actual overhead costs, and only the *difference* ($90,000 above) added to direct materials and direct labor. The reason is that this $90,000 difference represents the amount of overhead *applied* to work in process, and therefore to units of product.

If overhead had been overapplied during the period, then the overapplied overhead would have been *added* to actual overhead costs on the schedule of cost of goods manufactured in order to obtain the amount of overhead applied to work in process.

* Raw materials, direct. Indirect materials are in manufacturing overhead.

A General Model of Product Cost Flows

The flow of costs in a product costing system can be presented in general model form, as shown in Exhibit 3–10. This model applies as much to a process costing system as it does to a job order costing system. Visual inspection of the model can be very helpful in gaining a perspective as to how costs enter a system, flow through it, and finally end up as cost of goods sold on the income statement.

EXHIBIT 3–10
A General Model of Cost Flows

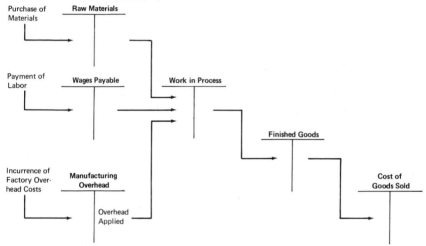

PROBLEMS OF OVERHEAD APPLICATION

The Concept of Underapplied and Overapplied Overhead

Since companies use a predetermined overhead rate to apply overhead to Work in Process, there generally will be a difference between the amount of overhead applied and the actual overhead costs incurred during a period. The reason is that a predetermined overhead rate is based on *estimates,* and the estimates rarely if ever will be the same as what actually happens in the way of costs and activity. In the case of the Rand Company, for example, $90,000 of overhead was applied to Work in Process, whereas *actual* overhead costs totaled $95,000 for the month (see Exhibit 3–7). The difference of $5,000 is termed *under-applied* overhead, for the obvious reason that the Rand Company applied $5,000 less to Work in Process than it actually incurred in overhead cost. Had the tables been reversed, and the company applied $95,000 of overhead to Work in Process, while incurring actual overhead costs of only $90,000, then a situation of *overapplied* overhead would have existed.

As suggested above, under- or overapplied overhead is a result of differences between the estimates used in computing the predetermined overhead rate and the actual activity of a period. To illustrate, let us refer again to the formula used in computing the predetermined overhead rate:

$$\frac{\text{Estimated Total Manufacturing Overhead Costs}}{\text{Estimated Total Units in the Base (direct labor hours, etc.)}}$$
$$= \text{Predetermined Overhead Rate}$$

If the estimated cost or estimated level of activity used in this formula differs from the actual cost or actual level of activity for a period, then either under- or overapplied overhead will result. Assume, for example, that two firms have prepared the following estimated data for the year 19X1:

	Company A	Company B
Predetermined overhead rate based on	machine hours	direct labor cost
Estimated manufacturing overhead for 19X1	$100,000	$120,000 (*a*)
Estimated machine hours for 19X1.	50,000	− (*b*)
Estimated direct labor cost for 19X1.	−	$ 80,000 (*b*)
Predetermined overhead rate (*a*) ÷ (*b*)	$2 per machine hour	150% of direct labor cost

Now assume that the *actual* overhead costs and the *actual* level of activity for 19X1 for each firm are as shown below:

	Company A	Company B
Actual manufacturing overhead costs.	$99,000	$128,000
Actual machine hours	48,000	−
Actual direct labor cost	−	$ 88,000

Since in Company A the actual level of activity is less than the estimated level of activity, the company ends the year with underapplied overhead. The opposite is true in Company B. The actual level of activity exceeds the estimated level of activity, so the company ends the year with overapplied overhead. The computations are shown below:

	Company A	Company B
Actual manufacturing overhead costs.	$99,000	$128,000
Manufacturing overhead applied to work in process during 19X1:		
48,000 *actual* machine hours × $2	96,000	
$88,000 *actual* direct labor cost × 150%		132,000
Underapplied (overapplied) overhead.	$ 3,000	($ 4,000)

Disposition of Underapplied and Overapplied Overhead Balances

What disposition should be made of any underapplied or overapplied balance remaining in the manufacturing overhead account at the end of a period? Generally any balance in the account is treated in one of two ways:

1. Closed out to Cost of Goods Sold.
2. Allocated between Work in Process, Finished Goods, and Cost of Goods Sold, in proportion to the ending balances in these accounts.

Most firms follow the first approach, and simply close any remaining balance out to Cost of Goods Sold. This approach has the advantage of simplicity. It has the disadvantage of some loss of accuracy in costing.

The second approach (allocation) is more accurate than the first approach, since it assigns overhead costs to where they would have gone in the first place had it not been for the errors in the estimates going into the predetermined overhead rate. Although the second approach is more accurate, it is used less often in actual practice than the first approach, because of the time and difficulty involved in the allocation process. Most firms feel that the greater accuracy simply isn't worth the extra effort that allocation requires, particularly when the dollar amounts are very small.

SUMMARY

Unit cost of production is one of the most useful items of cost data to a manager. There are two methods in widespread use for determining unit costs. These are job order costing and process costing. Job order costing is used in those manufacturing situations where units of product are not alike, as in production of special-order machine tools. Process costing is used in those manufacturing situations where units of product are homogeneous, as in the manufacture of cement.

Materials requisition forms and labor time tickets control the assignment of direct materials and direct labor cost to production. Indirect manufacturing costs are assigned to production through use of a predetermined overhead rate. Since the predetermined overhead rate is based on estimates, the actual overhead cost incurred during a period may be somwhat more or somewhat less than the amount of overhead applied to production. Such a difference is referred to as underapplied or overapplied overhead. The underapplied or overapplied overhead of a period can be either (1) closed out to Cost of Goods Sold, or (2) allocated between Work in Process, Finished Goods, and Cost of Goods Sold.

The detailed discussion in the chapter has focused on job order costing. A discussion of process costing is contained in the Appendix following, for those who wish to study this costing method in more depth.

Appendix: Process Costing and the Concept of Equivalent Units

In the main body of the chapter we stated that firms which produce basically homogeneous products such as bricks, flour, and cement employ a costing approach known as *process* costing. Process costing is generally used in place of job order costing whenever a firm has units of product that are indistinguishable from each other, and which flow in a constant stream off of an assembly line or out of a processing plant. Our purpose in this section is to look at some of the more important features of process costing systems.

COMPUTING UNIT COSTS

Several basic steps are involved in the structure and operation of a process costing system. These steps can be outlined as follows:

1. Identify individual processing centers.
2. Accumulate the material and processing costs for each separate processing center over some specified period.
3. Measure the output of each separate processing center.
4. Divide the material and processing costs by the period's output to get the unit cost of production for each separate processing center.
5. Add the unit costs of each separate processing center to get the total cost for a fully processed unit of product.

We will now examine each of these steps in some detail.

Identify Processing Centers

Processing centers are locations in the factory where work is done directly on the goods being produced. For example, a brick factory might have two processing centers—one for mixing and molding clay into brick form, and one for firing the molded brick. There are two critical features to any processing center. First, the activity performed in the processing center must be performed uniformly on all units going through it. And second, the output of the processing center must be homogeneous.

The processing centers for producing a product such as bricks would probably be organized in a *sequential* pattern. Sequential processing centers are illustrated in Exhibit 3–11. The flow of units goes from left to right, with all units undergoing processing in all processing centers.

EXHIBIT 3–11
Sequential Processing Centers

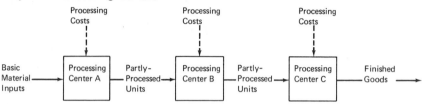

A different type of processing pattern, known as *parallel* processing, is required in some firms. Parallel processing is used in those situations where all units do not go through all processing centers. For example, the petroleum industry may input crude oil into one processing center and then use the refined output for further processing into several different end products. Each end product may undergo several steps of further processing after the initial refining, some of which may be shared with other end products and some of which may not. The concept of parallel processing is illustrated in Exhibit 3–12.

EXHIBIT 3–12
Parallel Processing Centers

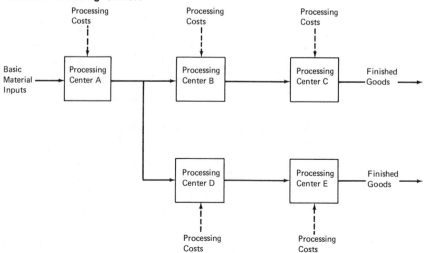

Accumulate Material and Processing Costs

Cost accumulation is simpler in a process costing situation than in a job order costing situation. The reason is that costs only need to be identified by processing center—not by separate jobs. This means that costs can be accumulated for longer periods of time, and that just one allocation is needed at the end of a period to assign the accumulated costs to the period's output.

Generally, materials costs and processing costs will be accumulated separately during a period. Materials costs, of course, would be the materials going into the product. These may be raw materials from the warehouse, or they may be the output from the prior process. Processing costs are the labor and overhead costs incurred in the processing center.

Measure the Output of the Period

After materials and processing costs have been accumulated for a period, the period's *output* must be computed so that appropriate unit costs can be determined. If a processing center has no work in process at the beginning or at the end of a period, this is a simple task. The period's output will simply equal the *completed* units turned out during the period.

If a processing center has work in process at the beginning or at the end of a period, however, *completed* units alone will not accurately measure total output. The reason is that part of the costs of the period will relate to the partially completed units in the ending inventory. These partially completed units will have to be considered along with the fully completed units in measuring the period's output. However, the partially completed units will be measured on an *equivalent units* basis. For example, 100 units 60 percent complete would be equivalent to 60 fully completed units. Therefore, the ending inventory in this case would be said to contain 60 *equivalent units of production.* These equivalent units of production would have to be added to the fully completed units as a step toward computing the total output of the period.

By the same line of reasoning, the *beginning* inventory could also contain equivalent units of production. In this case, however, the equivalent units would relate to work done in the prior period, and the equivalent units would have to be *deducted* from the completed units of the current period. For example, if the beginning inventory contains 200 units 40 percent complete at the start of the period, then the equivalent of 80 units will have already been completed before processing in the current period begins. These 80 equivalent units of production will have to be deducted from the current period's final completed output as a step toward computing the period's *actual* output.

To further illustrate the concept of equivalent units of production, assume the following data:

The Regal Company produces a product that goes through three processing centers—Mixing, Molding, and Firing. During 19X1, the following activity took place in the Mixing Processing Center:

	Materials		Processing	
	Pounds	Percent Completed	Pounds	Percent Completed
Beginning inventory	500	90%	500	50%
Pounds of raw material entered into the processing center	9,000	—	9,000	—
Ending inventory	200	40	200	10
Completed during the period and transferred to Molding	9,300	—	9,300	—

Required:

Compute the output for 19X1 in the Mixing Center.

Since the work in process inventories are at different stages of completion for materials and for processing, two output figures will have to be computed—one for output in terms of materials and one for output in terms of processing. Actually, this is a common practice since material costs and processing costs are normally accumulated and accounted for separately in a processing center, as mentioned earlier. The output computations are shown below:

	Material	Processing
Completed and transferred to Molding	9,300 lbs.	9,300 lbs.
Add: Equivalent units in ending inventory:		
200 lbs. × 40 percent	80 lbs.	
200 lbs. × 10 percent		20 lbs.
	9,380 lbs.	9,320 lbs.
Deduct: Equivalent units in the beginning inventory:		
500 lbs. × 90 percent	450 lbs.	
500 lbs. × 50 percent		250 lbs.
Output for 19X1 (equivalent units of production)	8,930 lbs.	9,070 lbs.

In our example, the actual output for the period is less than the number of units completed and transferred to the next processing center. The reason is that the work in process inventory was reduced during the year. In those cases where the work in process inventory is increased (in terms of equivalent units) the actual output of the period will be greater than the units completed and transferred out.

Compute Unit Costs

Once costs have been accumulated by the processing centers, and the period's output has been determined, unit costs can be computed. Generally, this is a fairly simple task involving no more than dividing the accumulated costs by the period's output. To illustrate, assume that the Regal Company in the preceding section has accumulated the following costs for 19X1 in the Mixing processing center:

Materials.......................	$ 44,650
Processing	81,630
	$126,280

Using the output figures computed in the preceding section, the unit costs for the Mixing processing center for 19X1 would be:

Materials: $\dfrac{\$44,650}{8,930 \text{ lbs.}} = \$ 5/\text{lb.}$

Processing: $\dfrac{\$81,630}{9,070 \text{ lbs.}} = 9/\text{lb.}$

Total cost .... $14/lb.

Since the output of the Mixing center is transferred to the Molding center, the $14/lb. unit cost of the Mixing center becomes the *materials input cost* of the Molding center. In effect, as materials are transferred from processing center to processing center, the *processing* costs of the prior center lose their identity as processing costs, and simply become part of the material input cost of the new processing center.

Add All Unit Costs to Obtain Fully Processed Cost

By the time a unit of product has passed through all processing centers it will have accumulated its total costs of production. That is, the Molding center in the preceding section will add its own processing costs onto the $14-per-unit materials cost received from the Mixing center (and perhaps add some more materials costs of its own as well), and then pass the processed units on to the next processing center. By the time a unit of product has passed through all processing centers its costing will be complete.

As an alternative, some firms account for the costs of each processing center separately and don't pass costs on from one center to the other. In these cases, when a unit of product has gone through all processing centers, the costs incurred in the separate centers are totaled individually, and the final unit cost computed.

THE FLOW OF UNITS BETWEEN PROCESSING CENTERS

As mentioned earlier, the units completed in one processing center flow directly into the next processing center. Processing centers are usually required to account for the units on which they work during a period. To illustrate how such an accounting is made, assume the following data:

	Mixing		Engraving		Firing	
	Units	% Completed	Units	% Completed	Units	% Completed
Opening inventory	2,000	40	3,000	60	1,500	70
Units initiated into production.	10,000					
Ending inventory	1,000	80	2,000	30	3,000	60

A processing center accounts for the units worked on during a period by means of a *production report.* Although a production report can take various forms, the one illustrated in Exhibit 3–13 is typical in format.

EXHIBIT 3–13
Production Report—Units Processed

	Mixing	Engraving	Firing
Units to be accounted for:			
Opening inventory in units	2,000	3,000	1,500
Units initiated into production, or transferred in from the prior center	10,000	→ 11,000	→ 12,000
Total units available	12,000	14,000	13,500
Units accounted for as follows:			
Transferred out during the period (total units available, minus ending inventory)	11,000 ———	12,000 ———	10,500
Ending inventory	1,000	2,000	3,000
Total units accounted for	12,000	14,000	13,500
Equivalent units of production:			
Units transferred out during the period (above)	11,000	12,000	10,500
Add: Equivalent units in the ending inventory:			
1,000 units × 80%	800		
2,000 units × 30%		600	
3,000 units × 60%			1,800
	11,800	12,600	12,300
Deduct: Equivalent units in the opening inventory:			
2,000 units × 40%	800		
3,000 units × 60%		1,800	
1,500 units × 70%			1,050
Output for the period (equivalent units of production)	11,000	10,800	11,250

TRANSFER COSTING PROBLEMS

In those cases where the units in the opening inventory carry the same per unit costs as incurred during the period, no problems exist in transferring costs from one processing center to another. But in those cases where the per unit costs in the opening inventory differ from the per unit costs incurred during the period, a problem arises over the per unit rate to use in transferring the units in the opening inventory to the next processing center when these units are finally completed. Should they be transferred at the per unit rate in the opening inventory, or should they be transferred at the per unit rate incurred during the current period to bring them to a full state of completion? Or should they be transferred at still some other rate? Generally speaking, when the per unit costs in the opening inventory differ from the per unit costs of the current period, firms will either assume a Fifo cost flow or a moving average cost flow.

Fifo Cost Flow

Under a Fifo cost flow, the units in the opening inventory are transferred at a figure that includes *both* the prior period and the current period costs. All other units completed during the period are simply transferred at the current period cost. To illustrate, assume the following data:

	Amount	Percent Completed	Processing Cost
Opening inventory	400 lbs.	60%	$ 1,440
Ending inventory	600 lbs.	80	
Entered into production	2,000 lbs.	–	13,260
Completed and transferred out	1,800 lbs.	–	

The output for the current period would be:

Completed and transferred out	1,800 lbs.
Add: Equivalent units in the ending inventory: ·	
600 lbs. × 80 percent	480 lbs.
	2,280 lbs.
Deduct: Equivalent units in the opening inventory:	
400 lbs. × 60 percent	240 lbs.
Total output (equivalent units of production)	2,040 lbs.

The cost per unit for the current period's output would be:

$$\frac{\$13,260}{2,040 \text{ lbs.}} = \$6.50/\text{lb.}$$

By contrast, the cost per unit for the equivalent units in the opening inventory would be:

$$\frac{\$1,440}{400 \text{ lbs.} \times 60\% = 240 \text{ lbs.}} = \$6.00/\text{lb.}$$

If a Fifo cost flow is assumed, the 1,800 lbs. completed and transferred would be broken into two segments—one segment consisting of the 400 lbs. in the opening inventory, and one segment consisting of the remaining 1,400 lbs. completed and transferred. The two segments would be costed as follows:

	First 400 lbs.	Remaining 1,400 lbs.	Total Cost Transferred
Cost in opening inventory	$1,440		$ 1,440
Cost required to complete the units in the opening inventory:			
400 lbs. × 40% × $6.50	1,040		1,040
Cost required to complete all remaining units transferred:			
1,400 lbs. × $6.50		$9,100	9,100
	$2,480	$9,100	$11,580

The units in the ending inventory would be costed at the current period's unit cost of $6.50 per equivalent unit.

All of the costs associated with a period's operations are usually summarized on a production report, such as follows:

PRODUCTION REPORT–COSTS
Processing Costs

Processing costs to be accounted for:
Costs in the opening inventory . . . . $ 1,440
Costs added during the period 13,260
    Total costs to be accounted for. $14,700

Processing costs accounted for as follows:
Costs transferred to the next department $11,580
Costs in the ending inventory (600 lbs. × 80 percent × $6.50) 3,120
    Total costs accounted for $14,700

Moving Average Cost Flow

A much simpler method of costing transfers can be found in the moving average approach. The moving average approach simply strikes an average between the unit costs in the opening inventory and the unit costs incurred during the current period. This is accomplished by adding together the costs in the opening inventory and the costs incurred during the period, and dividing the sum by the total output of the period, plus the equivalent units in the opening inventory. The formula can be expressed as follows:

$$\frac{\text{Cost in the Opening Inventory, plus Cost Incurred during the Period}}{\text{Equivalent Units in the Opening Inventory, plus Output for the Period}} = \text{Average Cost}$$

Computation of the average cost for the data in the preceding section would be as follows:

$$\frac{\$1,440 + \$13,260 = \$14,700}{240 \text{ lbs.} + 2,040 \text{ lbs.} = 2,280 \text{ lbs.}} = \$6.447/\text{lb.}$$

All 1,800 lbs. transferred out during the period would be costed at $6.447 per pound. The 480 equivalent units in the ending inventory (600 lbs. × 80 percent) would also be costed at $6.447 per pound and carried forward to the next period at this rate. These ending inventory costs would then be averaged in with the next period's costs to get an average cost for use in that period—thus, the term *moving average* cost.

Comparison of Moving Average and Fifo

Any major difference in unit costs as between the moving average and Fifo methods is likely to be traceable to erratic movements in raw materials prices. Processing costs usually will not fluctuate widely from month to month, due to the continuous nature of the flow of goods in process costing situations. In addition, inventory levels in most companies tend to remain quite stable, thereby adding to the general stability of unit costs.

From a standpoint of *cost control,* the Fifo method is superior to the moving average method. This is because current performance should be measured in relation to the costs of the *current* period only, and the moving average method inherently mixes these costs with the costs of *prior* periods.

On the other hand, the moving average method is simpler to apply than is the Fifo method. Because of its greater ease of use, some contend that it is more widely used in actual practice. However, specific evidence to support this point is not available.

Other Transfer Problems

Many other problems can exist in attempting to cost transfers between processing centers. For one thing, it is common to have materials shrink

As a further step, some firms deduct from the total contribution margin generated by a salesperson the amount of the traveling, entertainment, and other expenses which he incurs. This encourages the salesperson to be sensitive to his own costs in the process of making sales.

The Concept of Sales Mix

Sales mix can be defined as the relative proportion of total units sold (or total sales dollars) which is represented by each of a company's several product lines. To illustrate the concept, assume that a company has three product lines—Line A, Line B, and Line C. During 19X1, sales were as follows:

	Line A		Line B		Line C		Total	
	Amount	%	Amount	%	Amount	%	Amount	%
Sales	$20,000	100%	$50,000	100%	$30,000	100%	$100,000	100
Less variable expenses	15,000	75	30,000	60	24,000	80	69,000	69
Contribution margin	$ 5,000	25%	$20,000	40%	$ 6,000	20%	$ 31,000	31
Sales mix.	20%		50%		30%		100%	

The company's sales mix would be 20 percent Line A, 50 percent Line B, and 30 percent Line C, since Line A accounts for $20,000 of the total $100,000 in sales, etc.

Sales mix is an important concept. Most firms have more than one product line and for planning purposes need to know the relative weight of each in total sales. These weights are obtained by analyzing the sales mix. In addition, sales mix has an impact on break-even analysis, as well as on other aspects of cost-volume-profit computations.

Sales Mix and Break-even Analysis. One of the assumptions underlying break-even analysis is that the sales mix will not change. To illustrate, assume that the company represented by the sales data above has fixed costs totaling $15,500. The break-even point for 19X1 would be $50,000 in sales—the total fixed costs of $15,500 divided by the *average* P/V ratio of 31 percent.

$$\frac{\text{Total fixed costs } \$15,500}{\text{P/V ratio } 31\%} = \$50,000 \text{ sales to break even}$$

But $50,000 in sales represents the break-even point for the company only so long as the sales mix does not change. *If the sales mix changes, then the break-even point will also change.* To illustrate, assume that the sales mix shifts away from Line B (a 50 percent P/V ratio), toward Line C (only a 30 percent P/V ratio). Assume that the sales mix in 19X2 is:

in quantity as processing takes place. For example, processing may cause evaporation resulting in less units (gallons) transferred out than transferred in from the prior process. In other cases, spoilage is common, again resulting in less units transferred out than transferred in. Problems such as these are easily handled in a process costing system, but they are more applicable to advanced managerial accounting courses and will not be considered here.

QUESTIONS

3–1. Distinguish between job order costing and process costing.

3–2. What is the essential purpose of any costing system?

3–3. What is the purpose of the job cost sheet in a job order costing system?

3–4. What is a predetermined overhead rate, and how is it computed?

3–5. Why do firms use predetermined overhead rates rather than using actual manufacturing overhead costs in applying overhead to units of product?

3–6. Explain why some production costs must be assigned to products through an allocation process. Name several such costs. Would such costs be classified as *direct* or as *indirect* costs? Why?

3–7. A company assigns overhead to completed jobs on a basis of 75 percent of direct labor cost. The job cost sheet for Job 313 shows that $4,000 in direct material has been used on the job, and that $8,000 in direct labor time has been incurred. If 1,000 units were produced in Job 313, what is the cost per unit?

3–8. Explain how a sales order, a production order, a materials requisition form, and a labor time ticket are involved in the production and costing of products.

3–9. What is underapplied overhead? Overapplied overhead? What disposition is made of these amounts at period end?

3–10. Barnaby Company applies overhead to completed jobs on a basis of 80% of direct labor cost. If Job 467 shows $10,000 of manufacturing overhead applied, how much was the direct labor cost on the job?

3–11. What is the purpose of a production report in a process cost accounting system?

3–12. Why is cost accumulation easier under a process cost system than under a job order cost system?

3–13. Distinguish between sequential processing centers and parallel processing centers.

3–14. What are equivalent units of production? Give an example, showing equivalent units in both the beginning and the ending inventory.

3–15. In process costing, how is it possible for direct labor and manufacturing overhead (processing costs) to become part of materials cost?

EXERCISES

3–1. Estimated cost and operating data for the forthcoming period for three companies are given below:

	Company A	Company B	Company C
Direct labor hours	12,000	15,000	20,000
Manufacturing overhead	$90,000	$120,000	$150,000
Machine hours.	20,000	20,000	25,000
Direct labor cost	$60,000	$ 75,000	$100,000
Predetermined overhead rates are based on	Direct labor hours	Direct labor cost	Machine hours

Required:

1. Compute the predetermined overhead rate to be used in the forthcoming period for each company.
2. Assume for Company B that $80,000 of direct labor cost actually is incurred. How much overhead will be applied to work in process?
3. Assume for Company C that 30,000 machine hours are actually worked during the forthcoming period. How much overhead will be applied to work in process? If actual overhead costs total $175,000 will overhead be over- or underapplied? By how much?

3–2. The Slater Manufacturing Company produces a product that is subject to wide seasonal variations in demand. Unit costs are computed on a quarterly basis, by dividing each quarter's manufacturing costs (material, labor, and overhead) by the quarter's production in units. The company's quarterly unit costs for the most recent year are given below:

	First Quarter	Second Quarter	Third Quarter	Fourth Quarter
Direct materials.	$16,000	$ 8,000	$ 4,000	$12,000
Direct labor	30,000	15,000	7,500	22,500
Variable manufacturing overhead.	12,000	6,000	3,000	9,000
Fixed manufacturing overhead	30,000	30,000	30,000	30,000
Total manufacturing costs.	$88,000	$59,000	$44,500	$73,500
Number of units produced.	20,000	10,000	5,000	15,000
Cost per unit	$4.40	$5.90	$8.90	$4.90

The company is concerned about the variation in unit costs, and wonders if its costing system needs revision.

Required:

1. How would you suggest that the Slater Manufacturing Company's costing system be changed?
2. Recompute the company's unit costs in accordance with your suggestion in Part 1.

3–3. The Carter Company began operations on January 2, 19X5. The following activity took place in the work in process account for the month of January:

Work in Process

Direct materials	10,000	To finished goods	79,000
Direct labor	30,000		
Manufacturing overhead	45,000		

The Carter Company uses a job order costing system, and applies manufacturing overhead to work in process on a basis of direct labor cost. At the end of January, only one job was still in process. This job (Job 15) has been charged with $2,000 in direct materials cost.

Required:

Complete the following job cost sheet for partially completed Job 15:

Job Cost Sheet—Job 15 (as of January 31, 19X5)

Direct materials. . . . . $_____
Direct labor . . . . _____
Manufacturing overhead . . . . _____
　　　　Total cost to January 31. . . . . _____

3–4. Selected *actual* cost data for four companies for the year just ended (19X5) are given below:

	Company			
	W	X	Y	Z
Direct labor hours worked.	5,000	8,000	15,000	12,000
Machine hours worked	15,000	25,000	20,000	30,000
Direct labor cost	$25,000	$40,000	$75,000	$60,000
Direct materials cost	12,000	18,000	15,000	20,000
Manufacturing overhead cost	20,000	50,000	72,000	95,000
Predetermined overhead rate	150% of direct material cost	$7 per direct labor hour	100% of direct labor cost	$3 per machine hour

Required:

1. For each company, compute the amount of overhead applied to work in process during 19X5.
2. Based on your computations in part 1 above, for each company compute the amount of over or under application of overhead for 19X5.
3. Assume that Company X produced 10,000 units of product during 19X5. What is the cost per unit (assume no work-in-process inventories)?

3–5. Listed below are a number of routine transactions in a manufacturing company. Give the journal entry or entries that would be made to record each transaction, using account titles only (use Xs in the place of dollar amounts).

a. Purchase of raw materials on account.
b. Requisition of raw materials for use in production (both direct and indirect materials).
c. The accrual of wages payable to factory employees (both direct and indirect labor).
d. The accrual of wages payable to administrative personnel.
e. The accrual of property taxes on the factory building.
f. The expiration of prepaid insurance on both factory and administrative facilities.
g. Recording of depreciation on factory equipment.
h. The application of manufacturing overhead to production.
i. The completion of production on a number of jobs.
j. The sale and shipment of completed goods to customers (all sales on account).
k. Recognition of cost of goods sold to customers.

3–6. Estimated cost and operating data for three companies for 19X5 are given below:

	Company X	Company Y	Company Z
Units to be produced.	10,000	8,000	12,000
Machine hours.	50,000	10,000	6,000
Direct labor hours	12,000	16,000	36,000
Direct labor cost	$ 48,000	$64,000	$144,000
Manufacturing overhead	150,000	40,000	60,000

Predetermined overhead rates are computed on the following bases in the three companies:

Company	Overhead Rate Based On
X	Machine hours
Y	Direct labor hours
Z	Units produced

Required:

1. Compute the predetermined overhead rate to be used in each company during 19X5.
2. Assume that during 19X5, 18,000 actual direct labor hours are worked in Company Y. How much overhead will be applied to work in process?
3. Assume that during 19X5, 48,000 actual machine hours are worked in Company X. How much overhead will be applied to work in process? If actual overhead costs total $149,000 for 19X5, will overhead be over- or underapplied? By how much?

3–7. The following data relate to the manufacturing activities of Pearl Company for 19X7:

Raw materials inventory, January 1 . . . . $ 5,000
Raw materials inventory, December 31 4,000
Purchases of raw materials during 19X7 30,000
Work in process inventory, January 1 7,000
Work in process inventory, December 31 7,500
Actual manufacturing overhead incurred 48,000
Direct labor cost (10,000 hours) 40,000
Predetermined overhead rate . . . . $5 per DLH

Required:

1. Compute the amount of under- or overapplied overhead for 19X7.
2. Prepare a schedule of cost of goods manufactured for 19X7.

3–8. (Appendix) The cost records associated with Pressboard, Inc.'s process costing system show the following selected data for July 19X5:

	Units	% Complete
Process A:		
Opening inventory	4,000	80
Closing inventory	3,000	40
Units started into production	?	—
Process B:		
Opening inventory	5,000	60
Closing inventory	4,000	70
Units received from Process A	31,000	—

Units of product are introduced into production at the start of Process A, and flow through both processes.

Required:

Prepare a production report for July 19X5.

3–9. (Appendix) Mauer Company uses a process costing system. At the end of 19X3, the company's cost records revealed the following information:

	Process A		Process B	
	Units	% Completed	Units	% Completed
Opening inventory	4,000	40	6,000	70
Ending inventory	3,000	60	4,000	25
Units entered into production.	9,000		10,000	
Units completed and transferred out	10,000		12,000	

Required:

Compute the 19X3 output (equivalent units of production) for both Process A and Process B.

3–10. (Appendix) Faber Company began business on July 1, 19X8. The company uses a process costing system. Data for the month of July are given below:

	Units	% Completed	Material Cost
Entered into production	20,000		$60,000
Completed and transferred to finished goods.	15,000		
Ending inventory	5,000	40	

Processing costs for July totaled $85,000. All materials are added at the beginning of the production process.

Required:

1. Compute the Faber Company's output for July for both materials and processing.
2. Compute the total cost per unit transferred to finished goods.

3–11. (Appendix) The Superior Pulp Company processes wood pulp for various manufacturers of paper products. The company prepares a monthly production report on its two processes. Cost and other data on these two processes for June 19X8 are presented below:

	Tons of Pulp	% Completed
Process #1:		
Opening inventory, June 1.	16,000	60
Ending inventory, June 30.	20,000	35
Started into processing during the month	125,000	–
Process #2:		
Opening inventory, June 1.	8,000	90
Ending inventory, June 30.	15,000	25
Received during the month from Process #1	?	–

The wood which forms the basis for the finished pulp is introduced at the beginning of Process #1, and flows evenly through both processes.

Required:

Prepare the company's production report for June 19X8.

3–12. (Appendix) The following data are available for one month's activity in a company having a process costing system:

	Amount	Percent Completed	Processing Cost
Opening inventory	500 lbs.	40%	$ 1,650
Entered into production	3,800 lbs.	–	29,541
Completed and transferred out	3,350 lbs.	–	
Ending inventory	950 lbs.	30%	

Required:

1. Compute the equivalent units of production.
2. The company uses a Fifo cost flow. Prepare a schedule showing the cost of units transferred out during the month. Be sure to distinguish between the units in the opening inventory and the units started and completed during the month.

3–13. (Appendix) The Sincere Refining Company opened a new refinery on May 1, 19X6. The company uses a process costing system. Data for the first month's operations are given below:

	Gal-lons	Processing % Com-pleted	Raw Materials Cost
Entered into production during the month	85,000	–	$510,000
Completed and transferred to finished goods.	76,000	100	?
Ending inventory, May 31	9,000	70	?

All materials are added at the beginning of the refining process. The cost records for May indicate that processing costs totaled $205,750 for the month.

Required:

1. Compute the output (equivalent units of production) for May for both materials and processing.
2. Compute the total cost per gallon of finished product transferred to finished goods.

PROBLEMS

3–1. *Straightforward Job Order Costing Journal Entries.* Prepare journal entries to record the following transactions completed during 19X5 in the Atlantic Manufacturing Company:

1. Raw materials were purchased on account for use in production, $97,000.
2. Raw materials were requisitioned for use in production, $90,000 (80 percent direct, 20 percent indirect).
3. Salaries and wages of factory and other employees were incurred and paid:

Direct labor (20,000 hours)	$90,000
Indirect labor	16,000
Selling expense	25,000
Administrative expense	30,000

4. Heat, light, and power costs were paid on the factory, $16,000.
5. Other miscellaneous factory costs were incurred and paid, $34,000.

6. Miscellaneous administrative expenses were incurred and paid, $12,000.
7. Depreciation was recorded on factory buildings and equipment, $10,000.
8. Manufacturing overhead was applied to production at a rate of $4.75 per direct labor hour.
9. The cost of goods completed during 19X5 was $260,000.
10. Goods were sold to customers during 19X5 at a total selling price of $400,000. The manufactured cost of these goods was $250,000.

3–2. *Journal Entries for a Job Order Cost System, with T-Accounts.* At the beginning of the current year, Maple Products had the following inventory amounts on its balance sheet:

Raw materials.	$12,000
Work in process	20,000
Finished goods	35,000

Maple Products estimated that it would incur $60,000 in manufacturing overhead during the year, and that it would operate at a level of 15,000 direct labor hours. During the current year, the following transactions were completed:

a. Purchased raw material on account, $8,000.
b. Raw materials were issued to production, $16,000. 90% of these materials were direct, and 10% were indirect.
c. Factory payrolls were paid, $49,000. 80% of the factory payroll was direct labor, and 20% was indirect labor. 14,000 direct labor hours were worked.
d. Administrative payrolls were paid, $12,000. Sales payrolls were paid, $10,000.
e. Depreciation on factory equipment, $8,000.
f. Factory utilities paid, $7,000.
g. Various administrative expenses incurred and paid, $20,000.
h. Various selling expenses incurred and paid, $15,000.
i. Various manufacturing overhead costs incurred and paid (other than those indicated above), $30,000.
j. Manufacturing overhead was applied to production.
k. Completed production for the current year, $106,600.
l. Sales to customers for the current year were:

Selling price	$160,000	
Cost.	?	(Ending finished goods inventory, $21,600)

Required:

1. Prepare journal entries to record the above transactions.
2. Prepare T-accounts for Raw Materials, Manufacturing Overhead, Work in Process, Finished Goods, and Cost of Goods Sold. Post the appropriate parts of your journal entries to these T-accounts to determine the ending balance in each account. (Don't forget to enter the opening balances in the inventory accounts.)

3. Prepare the necessary journal entry to close the balance in the manufacturing overhead account to Cost of Goods Sold.

3-3. *Computation of Overhead Rates, and Costing Units of Product.* Dorsey Company uses a job order costing system. The company uses predetermined overhead rates in applying manufacturing overhead to individual jobs. The predetermined overhead rate in Department A is based on machine hours, and the predetermined overhead rate in Department B is based on direct labor cost. At the beginning of 19X5, the company's management made the following estimates for the year:

	Dept. A	Dept. B
Direct labor hours.	20,000	45,000
Machine hours.	60,000	90,000
Direct labor cost	$ 80,000	$180,000
Manufacturing overhead	150,000	216,000

Job #237 was initiated into production on August 1, and completed on September 15. The company's cost records show the following information on the job:

	Dept. A	Dept. B
Direct labor hours	30	40
Machine hours.	74	85
Materials placed into production	$450	$250
Direct labor cost	120	160

Required:

1. Compute the predetermined overhead rate that should be used during 19X5 in Department A. Compute the rate that should be used in Department B.
2. Compute the total overhead cost applied to Job #237.
3. What would be the total cost of Job #237? If the job contained 100 units, what would be the cost per unit?
4. At the end of 19X5, the records of Dorsey Company reveal the following *actual* cost and operating data for all jobs worked on during the year.

	Dept. A	Dept. B
Direct labor hours	22,000	48,000
Machine hours.	61,000	95,000
Direct labor cost	$ 89,000	$195,000
Manufacturing overhead	153,000	232,000

What was the amount of underapplied or overapplied overhead in each department at the end of 19X5?

3-4. *Schedule of Cost of Goods Manufactured.* The following data have been taken from the cost records of the Supreme Manufacturing Company for the month of March:

Work in process inventory, beginning.	$ 40,000
Work in process inventory, ending	50,000
Raw materials inventory, beginning.	12,000
Raw materials inventory, ending	15,000
Finished goods inventory, beginning	30,000
Finished goods inventory, ending.	28,000
Depreciation, factory equipment	30,000
Factory supplies	5,000
Supervisory salaries.	20,000
Lubricants.	12,000
Indirect labor	10,000
Direct labor	150,000
Purchases of raw materials.	120,000
Predetermined overhead rate.	50% of direct labor cost

Required:

1. Compute the underapplied or overapplied factory overhead for March.
2. Compute the cost of direct materials used in production for March.
3. Using the data developed in parts 1 and 2, prepare a schedule of cost of goods manufactured.

3–5. *Job Order Costing; Computation of Work in Process Inventory.* Aspen Corporation employs a job order cost system. For 19X5 the company has computed a predetermined overhead rate of $2 per direct labor hour. On March 1 the company's inventory balances were:

Raw materials.	$30,000
Work in process	40,000
Finished goods	70,000

During March, the following data were recorded:

Purchases of raw materials on account	$ 50,000
Issue of direct materials to production.	60,000
Direct labor cost incurred (15,000 hours)	75,000
Manufacturing overhead cost incurred and paid.	32,000
Cost of goods manufactured.	180,000

Required:

1. Prepare journal entries to record the transactions indicated by the March data.
2. Assume that on March 31 the Finished Goods Inventory balance is $60,000. Compute the cost of goods sold for March. Prepare the journal entry to record the cost of goods sold on the company's books.
3. What was the overapplied or underapplied overhead for the month?
4. What was the March 31 balance in Work in Process?

3–6. *Job Order Cost Flows, and Computation of Work in Process.* The Dolby Manufacturing Company's inventory accounts contained the following balances at the beginning and at the end of 19X6:

	Beginning of Year	End of Year
Raw materials	$20,000	$22,000
Work in process	35,000	32,000
Finished goods	60,000	68,000

During 19X6, the following costs were added into production:

Direct materials	$ 50,000
Direct labor	80,000
Manufacturing overhead (based on direct labor cost)	120,000

Required:

1. What was the cost of goods completed (manufactured) during 19X6?
2. What was the cost of goods sold for 19X6?
3. Direct labor made up $10,000 of the $32,000 ending Work in Process Inventory balance. Supply the information missing below:

Direct materials	$?
Direct labor	10,000
Manufacturing overhead	?
Work in process inventory	$32,000

3–7. *T-Account Analysis of Cost Flows.* Selected ledger accounts of the Barnaby Company are given below for the year 19X8:

Raw Materials Inventory

Jan. 1 Bal.	15,000	19X8 credits	?
19X8 debits	50,000		
Dec. 31 Bal.	12,000		

Manufacturing Overhead

19X8 debits	74,000	19X8 credits	?

Work in Process

Jan. 1 Bal.	35,000	19X8 credits	188,000
Direct materials	48,000		
Direct labor	60,000		
Overhead	75,000		
Dec. 31 Bal.	?		

Factory Wages Payable

19X8 debits	67,000	Jan. 1 Bal.	4,000
		19X8 credits	66,000

Finished Goods

Jan. 1 Bal.	60,000	19X8 credits	?
19X8 debits	?		
Dec. 31 Bal.	48,000		

Cost of Goods Sold

19X8 debits	?		

Required:

1. What was the *actual* manufacturing overhead cost incurred during 19X8?
2. How much of the actual manufacturing overhead in part (1) consisted of indirect materials?
3. How much of the actual manufacturing overhead in part (1) consisted of indirect labor?
4. What was the cost of goods manufactured for 19X8?
5. What was the cost of goods sold for 19X8?
6. If overhead is applied to production on a basis of direct labor cost, what rate was in effect for 19X8?
7. Was manufacturing overhead over- or underapplied for 19X8? By how much?

3–8. *Alternative Methods of Disposing of Under- or Overapplied Overhead.* Alex Company uses a job order cost system. The company uses predetermined overhead rates, based on direct labor hours, in applying manufacturing overhead to jobs. Estimated cost and operating data for 19X6 are given below:

Estimated direct labor hours.	30,000
Estimated direct labor cost	$ 90,000
Estimated factory overhead	120,000

At the end of 19X6, Alex Company's cost records revealed the following actual cost and operating data:

Direct labor hours.	32,000
Direct labor cost	$ 68,000
Factory overhead	130,000
Raw materials inventory	8,000
Work in process inventory	25,000
Finished goods inventory	50,000
Cost of goods sold	175,000

Required:

1. Compute Alex Company's predetermined overhead rate for 19X6.
2. Compute the underapplied or overapplied overhead for 19X6.
3. Assume that Alex Company closes any underapplied or overapplied overhead directly to cost of goods sold. Prepare the appropriate journal entry.
4. Assume that Alex Company allocates any underapplied or overapplied overhead to the appropriate accounts. Prepare the journal entry to show this allocation.
5. How much higher or lower will net income be for 19X6 if the underapplied or overapplied balance is allocated rather than closed directly to cost of goods sold?

3–9. *T-Account Analysis of Job Order Costs.* Wire Products, Inc. operates under a job order cost system. At the beginning of the current year the company showed inventory balances as follows:

Raw material . . . . $ 8,000
Work in process 17,900
Finished goods 20,000

During the current year, the following transactions were completed:

a. Raw materials were acquired from suppliers on account, $20,000.
b. Raw materials were requisitioned for use in production, $22,000 (80 percent direct, 20 percent indirect).
c. Factory payrolls were accrued, $40,000 (75 percent direct, 25 percent indirect).
d. Cash payments were made:
   To suppliers, $19,000.
   To employees for payrolls, $40,000.
   For factory utilities, $6,000.
   For factory rent, $12,000.
   For miscellaneous factory costs, $3,660.
e. Overhead was applied to jobs on a basis of 115 percent of direct labor cost.
f. The ending Work in Process Inventory was determined to be $16,000.
g. The ending Finished Goods Inventory was determined to be $14,000.

Required:

1. Enter the above transactions directly into T-accounts.
2. As stated in item (f) above, the ending balance in Work in Process was $16,000. Factory overhead constituted $5,750 of this balance. The management of Wire Products, Inc. would like to know how much of the balance consisted of direct material and direct labor. Complete the following schedule:

Direct materials . . . . $?
Direct labor . . . .   ?
Factory overhead   5,750
Total work in process. $16,000

3. What was the underapplied or overapplied factory overhead for the year?
4. Wire Products, Inc. follows the practice of allocating any under-applied or overapplied overhead balance to the pertinent accounts. Prepare a *general journal entry* to show this allocation.

3–10. *Analysis of Job Order Cost Sheets.* The Speedy Print Shop does a wide variety of printing work on a custom basis. For this reason, the company uses a job order cost system. During the month of May, six jobs were worked on. A summary of the job cost sheets on these jobs is given below.

Job No.	Direct Materials	Direct Labor	Factory Overhead	Total Cost of Job
216	$ 410	$ 360	$288	$1,058
217	850	790	632	2,272
218	110	85	68	263
219	1,500	1,140	912	3,552
220	950	850	680	2,480
221	270	115	92	477*

* Ending work in process.

The Speedy Print Shop has used the same overhead rate on all jobs. Job No. 216 was the only job in process at the beginning of the month. At that time it had incurred direct labor costs of $150, and total costs of $570.

Required:

1. What is the apparent predetermined overhead rate used by the Speedy Print Shop?
2. Assume that during May factory overhead was overapplied by $600. What was the *actual* factory overhead cost incurred during the month?
3. What is the total amount of direct materials placed into production during May?
4. How much direct labor cost was incurred during May?
5. What is the cost of goods manufactured for May?
6. If the finished goods inventory increased by $1,000 during May, what would be the cost of goods sold for the month?

3–11. *Comprehensive Problem in Job Order Costing.* Archer Products, Inc. uses a job order cost system. The company applies overhead to jobs on a basis of 125 percent of direct labor cost. The following transactions took place during 19X5:

1. Raw materials purchased for use in production, $15,000.
2. Raw materials requisitioned for use in production (all direct materials), $17,000.
3. Utility bills received and paid on the factory, $4,000.
4. Wages and salaries paid during the year, $30,000 (70 percent direct labor, 10 percent indirect labor, 5 percent sales salaries, and 15 percent administrative salaries).
5. Depreciation recorded on machinery and equipment used in the factory, $8,000.
6. Depreciation recorded on office equipment, $2,000.
7. Miscellaneous overhead costs incurred (credit Accounts Payable), $12,000.

✓ 8. Miscellaneous selling and administrative expenses incurred (credit Accounts Payable):

Selling	$ 7,000
Administrative.	10,000

9. Manufacturing overhead was applied to jobs, ___?___.

10. Cost of jobs completed during the year, ___?___ (the ending balance in the Work in Process inventory account for 19X5 was $7,000; the beginning balance is given below.)

11. Sales for the year totaled $100,000.

12. Cost of goods sold for the year totaled $60,000.

The balances in the inventory accounts at the beginning of 19X5 were:

Raw materials	$4,000
Work in process	5,000
Finished goods.	3,000

Required:

1. Prepare journal entries to record the above transactions.

✓ 2. Post your entries to T-accounts. (Don't forget to enter the opening inventory balances above.) Determine the ending balances in the inventory accounts and in the Manufacturing Overhead account.

3. Prepare a schedule of cost of goods manufactured and a schedule of cost of goods sold.

4. Assume that Archer Products, Inc. closes any balance in the Manufacturing Overhead account out to Cost of Goods Sold. Prepare the necessary journal entry.

5. Prepare an income statement for 19X5. Ignore income taxes.

✓3-12. *Straightforward Process Costing Problem.* (Appendix)   Oaks Processing Company produces a detergent compound in two separate processes—blending and boxing. In the blending process (three pounds of material are introduced at the start of the process for each unit (consisting of three pounds of blended materials) transferred to boxing. Processing costs are incurred uniformly throughout the blending process. Cost records for the blending process for June show:

In process on June 1, 300 units one third processed.
In process on June 30, 200 units one half processed.
Put into process during June, 2,700 pounds of material.
Transferred to boxing during June, 1,000 units.
Cost of June 1 work in process, $3,700.
Cost of materials added during June, $8,100.
Cost of processing during June, $11,000.

Oaks Processing Company costs units on a first-in, first-out cost flow basis.

Required:

1. Compute the output (equivalent units of production) of the blending process for June for both materials and processing.
2. Compute the per unit materials and processing cost incurred during June.
3. Compute the cost of the units transferred to the boxing process during June.
4. Compute the cost of the ending Work in Process Inventory in the blending process at June 30.

3–13. *Cost Flows through Work in Process: Average Cost Method.* (Appendix) Lubricants, Inc., produces a special kind of grease that is widely used by race drivers. The grease is produced in three processes: refining, blending, and packaging. Raw oil products are introduced at the beginning of the refining process, with processing costs being incurred evenly throughout the operation. The refined output is then transferred to the blending operation. The following incomplete Work in Process account is available for the month of March for the refining operation:

Work in Process—Refining

March 1 inventory (5,000 gal., 1/5 complete)	4,850	Completed and transferred to Blending (? gal.)	?
March costs added: Raw oil materials (30,000 gal.)	15,000	March 31 inventory (7,000 gal., 3/5 complete)	?
Labor	30,000		
Overhead	32,400		

The materials cost in the opening inventory is $.55 a gallon. The company costs units of product by the average cost method.

Required:

1. How many gallons of refined materials were transferred to the Blending Process during March?
2. Compute the units of output (equivalent units of production) in the Refining Process during March for both materials and processing.
3. What average cost of processing should be used for March? What average cost of materials? (Carry answers to three decimal places.)
4. Determine the cost of the units transferred to Blending during March.
5. Determine the cost of the ending Work in Process Inventory at March 31.

3–14. *Unit and Cost Flows under Sequential Processing.* (Appendix) Product Specialties, Inc., produces a unique seasoning which is in strong demand by restaurants for seasoning chicken and certain other meats. The seasoning is produced in three consecutive processes: Compounding, Cooking, and Packaging. The following information has been taken from production reports for the month of July:

	Beginning Inventory		Units Introduced for Processing	Ending Inventory	
	Units	% Complete		Units	% Complete
Compounding Process	8,000	20	30,000	6,000	40
Cooking Process.	4,000	60	?	5,000	70
Packaging Process.	?	80	?	3,000	60

During July, 34,000 units were transferred from the Packaging Process to the finished goods warehouse. All units flow through all three processes. Raw materials are added only at the beginning of the Compounding Process. Processing costs are incurred evenly throughout each production process.

Required:

1. Determine the number of units introduced for processing in the Cooking and Packaging processes during July.
2. Determine the number of units in the July beginning work in process inventory for the Packaging Process.
3. Compute the total output (equivalent units of production) relating to (*a*) materials and (*b*) processing in the Compounding Process, and relating to processing in the other two processes.
4. Assume the following cost data relating to the Compounding Process:

	Opening Inventory	Costs Added	Ending Inventory
Materials	$ 7,200	$28,500	?
Processing	8,800	33,600	?
	$16,000	$62,100	?

Compute the cost of the units transferred from Compounding to Cooking during July. Product Specialties, Inc., determines production costs on an average cost basis.

3–15. *Computation of Unit Costs of Production.* (Appendix) Kimber Manufacturing Company was organized on January 2 of the current year. The company operates a process costing system. The main product, Throgles, goes through three processes before production is complete. These processes are: Molding, Sanding, and Firing. Selected data from cost and production reports for the current year are given below:

	Molding	*Sanding*	*Firing*
Costs added to production:			
Raw Materials.	$33,000	none	none
Processing	6,000	27,000	15,000
Units started into production or			
transferred *in* during the			
current year.	44,000	?	?
Ending inventory:			
Number of units	6,000	4,000	5,000
Stage of completion	1/3	1/2	1/5

The raw materials are added at the beginning of the Moulding Process. Processing costs are incurred evenly throughout each process.

Required:

1. Determine the number of units transferred *out* of each process during the current year.
2. Calculate the total output (equivalent units of production) in terms of (*a*) materials and (*b*) processing for Molding, and in terms of processing for Sanding and Firing.
3. Compute the unit cost added in each process.
4. Compute the final cost of a complete Throgle.

3–16. *Production Report; Fifo Cost Flow.* (Appendix) Production and cost data for one department of a company using a process costing system are presented in the following tabulation:

Production:
Units in process, May 1; 30% complete as to processing   12,000
Units received from the prior department   90,000
Units completed and transferred out. . . . .   ?
Units in process, May 31; 70% complete as to processing   8,000
Costs:
Work in process inventory, May 1 . . . . $ 5,040
Materials used during the month   244,800
Processing costs incurred during the month   139,200

Materials are added in this department when processing is one half completed. Costing is handled on a Fifo basis.

Required:

1. Prepare a production report for the month for units processed. Show equivalent units on your report for both materials and processing.
2. Compute unit costs for the month's production for both materials and processing.
3. For both materials and processing costs, compute:
    a. The amount of cost transferred out during the month.
    b. The amount of cost assigned to the ending Work in Process Inventory.

3–17. *Production Report; Average Cost Flow.* (Appendix) Following are production and cost data for one month in a department of a company that computes unit costs by the average cost method:

Production data:

Units in process, March 1; 60% complete as to process.	15,000
Units received from the prior department	105,000
Units completed and transferred to finished goods	?
Units in process, March 31; 20% complete as to processing	9,000

Cost data:

Work in process inventory, March 1:

Materials costs	$ 58,920
Processing costs.	27,900
Materials used in production during the month	398,400
Processing costs incurred during the month	321,780

All raw materials are added in this department when processing is one third completed.

Required:

1. Prepare a production report for the month for units processed. Show equivalent units on your report for both materials and processing.
2. Compute unit costs for the month's production for both materials and processing.
3. For both materials and processing costs, compute:
   a. The amount of cost transferred out during the month.
   b. The amount of cost assigned to the ending Work in Process Inventory.

3–18. *Unit Costs; Fifo Cost Flow.* (Appendix) The Leaky Valve Company produces valves in three separate processes. The company's accountant (who is very inexperienced) has prepared a summary of production and costs for the finishing department for April:

Finishing department costs:

Beginning work in process inventory, 450 units. All materials included, but only 60% complete as to processing costs	$ 1,860
Raw materials placed in production during the month, sufficient to produce 1,950 units (includes cost transferred in from the preceding department)	6,240
Processing costs incurred during the month	3,420
Total departmental costs	$11,520

Finishing department costs assigned to:

Units completed and transferred to finished goods, 1,800 @$6.40	$11,520
Ending work in process inventory, 600 units. All materials included, but only 30% complete as to processing costs.	–0–
Total departmental costs assigned	$11,520

The company's inexperienced accountant assigned no cost to the ending Work in Process, since these units were only partially completed. The company computes unit costs on a Fifo cost flow basis. The president of the Leaky Valve Company is confused by the information presented, and would like some new computations made.

Required:

1. Compute the equivalent units of production for the month for both materials and processing, and determine the cost per unit for each.
2. Compute the cost per unit and the total amount of cost that should have been assigned to the 1,800 units transferred to Finished Goods during the month.
3. Compute the cost per unit and the total amount of cost that should have been assigned to the ending Work in Process.

3–19. *Cost Flows through Work in Process; Fifo Cost Method.* (Appendix) ZAB, Inc., produces a very popular low-calorie soft drink. Two processes, blending and bottling, are used to produce the drink. All materials are added at the beginning of the blending process, with processing costs being incurred evenly throughout the operation. The blended liquid is then transferred to the bottling operation where it is put into bottles ready for distribution.

The following incomplete Work in Process account for the blending process is available for the month of June 19X8:

Work in Process–Blending

June 1 inventory (3,500 gal., 40% complete)	1,582	Completed and transferred to Bottling (72,000 gal.)	?
June costs added:			
Materials (? gal.)	22,200	June 30 inventory (5,500 gal.,	
Processing	32,758	70% complete)	?

The company costs units of product by the Fifo cost method.

Required:

1. How many gallons of material were put into production during the month?
2. Compute the units of output (equivalent units of production) in the Blending process during June for both materials and processing.
3. What are the per unit (gallon) costs for materials and processing for the work done during June?
4. Compute the cost of the units (gallons) transferred to Bottling during June.
5. Compute the cost of the ending Work in Process Inventory.

chapter 4

Cost Allocation for Planning and Control

BEFORE we conclude our discussion of product costing, we need to give some further consideration to the matter of cost allocation. The concept of cost allocation was introduced in the preceding chapter in connection with the allocation of manufacturing overhead to units of product through the use of a predetermined overhead rate. We need now to discuss the matter of cost allocation further by introducing the concept of a *normalized* overhead rate, and by considering the problem of allocation of service department costs.

NORMALIZED OVERHEAD RATES

Many firms hesitate to set predetermined overhead rates on the basis of the anticipated production of a single period if that production is subject to wide variations. The reason is that rates based on a single period's activity may result in high per unit production costs in periods when production is low, and in low per unit production costs in periods when production is high. The problem arises from the fact that fixed costs often make up a large part of manufacturing overhead, and that these costs go on unchanged regardless of the level of production activity. When production is low, then the fixed overhead costs are spread over a small number of units, resulting in a high cost per unit. When production is high, then the fixed overhead costs are spread over a large number of units, resulting in a lower cost per unit.

The Impact of Fluctuating Overhead Rates

To illustrate the problems that can result from permitting overhead rates to fluctuate as production fluctuates, assume the following data:

Manufacturing overhead (assume all fixed) $6,000
Time required to produce one unit of product . . . . . 1 machine hour

Anticipated production and sales:

	Production		Sales in Units
Year	Number of Units	Total Machine Hours, at One Hour per Unit	Sales in Units
19X1	2,000	2,000 MH	2,000
19X2	3,000	3,000 MH	2,000

19X1 predetermined overhead rate:

$$\frac{\$6,000}{2,000 \text{ Machine Hours}} = \$3 \text{ per Machine Hour}$$

19X2 predetermined overhead rate:

$$\frac{\$6,000}{3,000 \text{ Machine Hours}} = \$2 \text{ per Machine Hour}$$

If we further assume that each unit of product requires $4 in direct materials cost, and $2 in direct labor cost, then the cost of a single unit of product produced in 19X1 and in 19X2 would be:

	19X1	19X2
Direct materials	$4	$4
Direct labor	2	2
Manufacturing overhead	3	2
Total cost per unit	$9	$8

Notice that the per unit cost is lower in 19X2 than in 19X1 as a result of 19X2's overhead rate being lower than 19X1's. This is the only difference in cost data between the two years.

Many managers feel that this type of difference in unit cost, which arises from using fluctuating overhead rates, can result in distorted financial statements. Such statements can be confusing to statement users, both within and without the firm. To illustrate, if 2,000 units of product are sold in both 19X1 and 19X2, 19X2 will show a greater total gross margin even though the same number of units is sold in each year (assume a selling price of $12 per unit):

	19X1	19X2
Sales (2,000 units @ $12 ea.)	$24,000	$24,000
Cost of goods sold:		
2,000 units @ $9 ea	18,000	
2,000 units @ $8 ea		16,000
Gross margin	$ 6,000	$ 8,000

The only reason why 19X2 shows a higher gross margin than 19X1 is that more units were *produced* in 19X2 than in 19X1. As stated above, the higher level of production resulted in a lower overhead cost per unit, and therefore in a larger margin per unit sold. Yet a stockholder using these data might be misled into thinking that the increased gross margin reported in 19X2 was a result of efficiencies that will continue into the future, rather than simply being the result of a temporary imbalance between production and sales.

The Concept of a Normalized Overhead Rate

The company in our illustration above may have had good reasons for increasing production in 19X2. For example, the company may have known that sales in 19X3 would continue at about 2,000 units, but that circumstances would be such that production in 19X3 would have to be less than 2,000 units (due to strikes, supply interruptions, etc.). The question isn't whether variations in the level of production are desirable—such variations are often unavoidable. The question is whether these variations should be permitted to influence unit costs— pushing costs up in times of low activity and pulling them down in times of high activity. Many managers would argue that the cost of a unit of product should be the same whether it is produced in 19X1 or 19X2 or any other year, so long as long-run demand for the product is reasonably stable.

How can uniformity in unit cost be attained if a firm's production is fluctuating from year to year? The answer lies in *normalized* overhead rates. A normalized overhead rate is not based on the expected activity of a single period. Rather, a normalized overhead rate is based on an average activity level that spans many periods—past, present, and future. The approach is to determine what level of activity is *normal* over the long run, and then to set predetermined overhead rates on that figure. Such rates are said to be *normalized* in the sense that they reflect what is thought to be a normal level of activity over time.

An Illustration of Normalized Overhead Rates

To illustrate the concept of a normalized overhead rate, assume that long-run average demand for a company's product is 8,000 units per year. For the next two years, however, the company expects that its production levels will vary as follows:

	Year 1	Year 2
Production in units	10,000	6,000
Sales in units.	8,000	8,000

Expected manufacturing costs for the next two years are:

Direct materials and direct labor cost per unit . . . . $	5.00
Manufacturing overhead:	
Variable cost per unit	1.00
Fixed cost in total	24,000.00

If the predetermined overhead rate is computed on a normalized basis, then an *average* production figure of 8,000 units per year should be used, rather than a figure of 10,000 units for Year 1 and a figure of 6,000 units for Year 2. On a normalized basis, the predetermined overhead rate would be:

Fixed portion:
  $24,000 ÷ 8,000 units . . . . $3.00 per unit
  Variable portion . . . . 1.00 per unit
    Total predetermined overhead rate . . . . $4.00 per unit

An overhead rate of $4.00 per unit would be used to cost production in both Year 1 and Year 2. (Rather than setting the overhead rate on a basis of the number of units produced, the company could have set it on a basis of the number of direct labor hours needed to produce these units; units of product were used in this example rather than direct labor hours simply for ease of illustration.) The total cost of a unit produced in either Year 1 or Year 2 would be:

	Per Unit
Direct materials and direct labor (given above)	$5.00
Manufacturing overhead (computed above)	4.00
Total cost per unit	$9.00

By contrast, if the company *did not* use a normalized overhead rate, then the cost per unit in the two separate years would be:

Year 1			*Year 2*		
Direct materials and			Direct materials and		
direct labor		$5.00	direct labor		$ 5.00
Manufacturing overhead:			Manufacturing overhead:		
Fixed portion:			Fixed portion:		
$24,000 ÷ 10,000			$24,000 ÷ 6,000		
units	$2.40		units	$4.00	
Variable portion	1.00	3.40	Variable portion.	1.00	5.00
Total cost per unit		$8.40	Total cost per unit		$10.00

Notice the wide variation in unit cost between the two years. Partial income statements for the two years are given below contrasting what would be reported to statement users if the company did and if the company did not use a normalized overhead rate to cost production. A selling price of $10 per unit is assumed.

If a Normalized Overhead Rate Is Used

	Year 1	Year 2	Total
Sales (8,000 units @ $10 each)	$80,000	$80,000	$160,000
Cost of goods sold (8,000 units @ $9.00 each)	72,000	72,000	144,000
Gross margin	$ 8,000	$ 8,000	$ 16,000

If a Normalized Overhead Rate Is Not Used

	Year 1	Year 2	Total
Sales (8,000 units @ $10 each)	$80,000	$80,000	$160,000
Cost of goods sold:			
Year 1: (8,000 units @ $8.40 ea.).	67,200		
Year 2: (2,000 units @ $8.40 ea.).		16,800	144,000
(6,000 units @ $10.00 ea.).		60,000	
Total cost of goods sold	67,200	76,800	144,000
Gross margin.	$12,800	$ 3,200	$ 16,000

If a normalized overhead rate is used to cost production, notice that the gross margin pattern is even over the two-year period. By contrast, if a normalized overhead rate is not used to cost production, then the gross margin pattern is erratic, even though the same number of units is sold in each year. In years when production is high (Year 1), income is also high; in years when production is low (Year 2), income is also low.

In short, normalized overhead rates largely eliminate from inventories, from cost of goods sold, and from gross margin any unfavorable impact of having production out of balance with the long-run demand for a company's products.

Overhead Variances

When normalized overhead rates are in use, the underapplied or over-applied overhead balances tend to be somewhat larger than when overhead rates are computed on the basis of a single year's activity. For this reason, when normalized overhead rates are in use, rather than closing underapplied or overapplied overhead balances out to Cost of Goods Sold, these amounts are often carried forward on the balance sheet in a permanent account. The thinking is that if the "normal" level of activity on which the predetermined overhead rate is set is carefully chosen, then the net balance in this account will tend to be nominal in amount. The underapplied balance of one period will simply be offset by the overapplied balance of a following period.

ALLOCATING SERVICE DEPARTMENT COSTS

Our discussion of product costing in the preceding chapter ignored one important dimension of the cost structure of a firm. In addition to having producing departments, firms also have service departments that carry on critical auxiliary services for the entire organization. We need now to consider how the costs of these service departments are handled under traditional product costing.

The Nature of a Service Department

Departments within a firm can be divided into two broad classes: (1) producing departments, and (2) service departments. Producing departments would include those departments where work is done directly on the product of the organization such as milling, assembly, painting, etc. Service departments do not engage directly in production. Rather, they provide services or assistance that facilitate the activities of the producing departments. Examples of such services would include internal auditing, cafeteria, personnel, cost accounting, production planning, and medical facilities.

Although service departments do not engage directly in production, the costs they incur are generally viewed as being just as much a part of the cost of a company's finished products as are materials, labor, and overhead.

The Allocation of Service Department Costs

One of the more difficult challenges of the managerial accountant is to find a way to assign the costs of service departments to finished products, and to do so in a way that is equitable between products. In the preceding chapter we found that indirect costs such as lubricants are allocated to finished products through manufacturing overhead by means of the predetermined overhead rate. Basically, the same procedure is used in the matter of service department costs. That is, before the output of a producing department is charged with overhead costs, the predetermined overhead rate is *expanded* to include a provision for the cost of services provided by the various service departments throughout the firm. This process of allocation to the producing departments, and subsequent reallocation to finished products by means of the predetermined overhead rate, can be illustrated as in Exhibit 4–1.

Should All Costs Be Allocated?

For product costing purposes, most firms allocate the bulk of all service department costs back to the producing departments for

EXHIBIT 4–1
Allocation of Service Department Costs to Finished Products

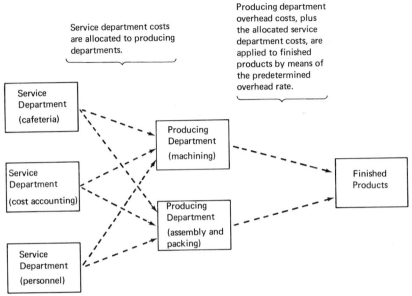

which the services were performed. There are some service department costs, however, which often are not allocated, even though they clearly benefit all parts of an organization. These are costs of services which top management wants all parts of the organization to utilize liberally.

The internal auditing department is a good example. In many firms, the managers of the various departments or divisions have considerable latitude over the extent to which the services of the internal auditing department will be utilized. Some top managers feel that charging for these services may discourage use, even though such use would clearly benefit the entire firm. To avoid discouraging use of a service that is helpful to the entire organization, some firms make no charge for the service at all. These managers feel that by making such services a "free" commodity, departments and divisions will be more inclined to take full advantage of their benefits.

Other firms take a somewhat different approach. They agree that charging according to usage may discourage utilization of such services as internal auditing, but that the service should not be free. Instead of providing free services, these firms take what is sometimes termed a "retainer fee" approach. Each department or division is charged a flat amount each year, regardless of utilization of the service. The thought is that if a department knows that it is going to be charged a certain amount for internal auditing services *regardless of usage,* then it probably will utilize the services at least to that extent.

Selecting Allocation Bases

Costs of service departments are allocated to producing departments by means of some type of allocation base. Allocation bases are selected which reflect as accurately as possible the benefits to be received by the various producing departments from the services involved. A number of such bases may be selected according to the nature of the services. Examples of allocation bases in common use include the following:

Cafeteria	Number of employees.
Medical facilities	Periodic analysis of cases handled, number of employees, hours worked.
Materials handling	Hours of service, volume handled.
Building and grounds	Square or cubic footage occupied.
Engineering	Periodic analysis of services rendered, direct labor hours.
Production planning and control	Periodic analysis of services rendered, direct labor hours.
Cost accounting	Labor hours.
Power	Metered usage, capacity of machines.
Personnel and employment	Number of employees, turnover of labor, periodic analysis of time spent.
Receiving, shipping, and stores	Units handled, number of requisition and issue slips, square or cubic footage occupied.

Once allocation bases are chosen they tend to remain unchanged for long periods of time. Selection of an allocation base represents a *major policy decision* that is reviewed normally only at very infrequent intervals, or when it appears that some major inequity exists.

The way in which service department costs are allocated to producing departments will have a heavy influence on the way in which products are costed, so the selection of an allocation base is no minor decision. Criteria for making selections may include: (1) direct, traceable benefits from the service involved, as measured, for example, by the number of service orders handled; (2) the extent of facilities provided, as measured, for example, by the square footage of space occupied; and (3) the ease of making an allocation. In regard to the latter point, complex allocation computations run the risk of yielding negative returns. That is, if allocation computations become too complex, the cost of the computation may exceed any benefits it is trying to bring about. Allocation formulas should be simple and easily understood by all involved, particularly by the managers to whom the costs are being allocated.

Allocating Reciprocal Service Department Costs

If cost allocations are to provide maximum information, they must be structured in such a way as to take into consideration the fact that some service departments provide services for each other, as well as for the producing departments of the firm. This mutual, or reciprocal, service must be taken into account if one is to know the full costs of operating a particular service department, and if these costs are to be equitably spread among the other departments which it services.

For example, if the cafeteria serves the building and grounds department as well as the producing departments, then part of the costs of the cafeteria should be allocated to the building and grounds department if one wants to know the full cost of operating the building and grounds department during a period. In like manner, if the building and grounds department provides services for the cafeteria, then a portion of the building and grounds department operating costs should be borne by the cafeteria, as well as by the producing departments of the firm.

There are two approaches to allocating costs *between* service departments. Some firms use what might be termed a sequential allocation plan. Sequential allocation begins with the service department performing the greatest amount of services to other service departments. Its costs are allocated to the other service departments as well as to the producing departments. Then, the service department performing the *second* greatest amount of services to other service departments is allocated, and so forth through all service departments in the company. The sequential allocation approach is illustrated in Exhibit 4–2. Once

XHIBIT 4–2
equential Allocation of Service Department Costs

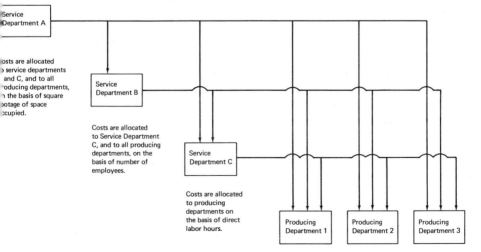

a service department's costs have been allocated to other service departments and to producing departments, no costs are subsequently reallocated back to it.

Other firms handle the reciprocal service department cost problem by use of simultaneous linear equations. This method is more accurate than the sequential allocation plan in that it makes possible cross allocations between two departments. It is a more complex allocation method, however, and its illustration would add nothing to our general understanding.

Allocating Costs by Behavior

Whenever possible, service department costs should be separated into fixed and variable classifications and allocated separately. The fixed portion should be allocated in *predetermined, lump-sum amounts* as between departments. The variable portion should then be allocated according to *whatever activity base controls its incurrence*. If, for example, the variable costs of a service department are incurred according to the number of machine hours worked in the producing departments, then they should be allocated to the producing departments on that basis.

In allocating the fixed costs of a service department, how does one proceed to break the total down into equitable lump-sum amounts for allocation to other departments? The answer lies in the long-run servicing needs of the other departments that gave rise to the organization of the service department in the first place. Fixed costs represent the costs of having long-run service capacity available. Therefore, fixed costs should be allocated to other departments according to the long-run servicing needs that were recognized in the service department's initial organization.

To illustrate, assume that Novak Company has just organized a Maintenance Department to service all machines in the Cutting, Assembly, and Finishing departments. In determining the capacity that should be built into the newly organized Maintenance Department, the company recognizes that the various producing departments will have the following long-run maintenance needs:

Department	Long-Run Maintenance Needs in Terms of Number of Hours of Maintenance Work Required	Percent of Total Hours
Cutting Department	300 hours	30%
Assembly Department	600 hours	60%
Finishing Department	100 hours	10%
	1,000 hours	100%

Therefore, in allocating the Maintenance Department fixed costs to the producing departments, 30 percent of the fixed costs should be allocated to the Cutting Department, 60 percent to the Assembly Department, and 10 percent to the Finishing Department. These lump-sum allocations *will not change* from period to period unless there is some shift in long-run servicing needs due to structural changes in the organization.

Pitfalls in Allocating Fixed Costs

Rather than allocate fixed costs in predetermined lump-sum amounts, some firms allocate them by use of a *variable* allocation base. What's wrong with this practice? The answer is that it can create serious inequities between departments. The inequities will arise from the fact that the fixed costs allocated to one department will be influenced heavily by what happens in *other departments*.

To illustrate, assume that a company has one service department and two producing departments. The service department costs are all fixed. Contrary to good practice, the company allocates these fixed costs to producing departments on the basis of machine hours (a variable base). Selected data for the two preceding years are given below:

	Year 1	*Year 2*
Service department costs (all fixed).	$30,000(a)	$30,000(a)
Producing Department A machine hours.	15,000	15,000
Producing Department B machine hours	15,000	5,000
Total machine hours	30,000(b)	20,000(b)
Allocation rate per machine hour: (a) ÷ (b)	$1.00	$1.50

Notice that Department A maintained a production level of 15,000 machine hours in both years. On the other hand, Department B allowed its production to drop off from 15,000 hours in Year 1 to only 5,000 hours in Year 2. The service department costs that would have been allocated to the two departments over the two-year span are given below:

	Department A	*Department B*
Year 1:		
Department A: 15,000 hrs. @ $1.00	$15,000	
Department B: 15,000 hrs. @ $1.00		$15,000
Year 2:		
Department A: 15,000 hrs. @ $1.50	$22,500	
Department B: 5,000 hrs. @ $1.50		$ 7,500
Total Costs Allocated	$37,500	$22,500

In Year 1 the two producing departments share the service department costs equally. In Year 2, however, the bulk of the service department costs are allocated to Department A. Department A has been forced in Year 2 to absorb the bulk of the service department costs *as a result of the inefficiency of Department B.* Even though Department A maintained the same level of efficiency in both years, the use of a variable allocation base has caused it to be penalized because of what has happened in another department.

This kind of inequity is almost inevitable when a variable allocation base is used to allocate fixed costs. The manager of Department A will be incensed at the inequity forced on his department, but he will feel powerless to do anything about it. The result will be a loss of confidence in the system, and the accumulation of a considerable backlog of ill-feeling.

Should Actual or Budgeted Costs Be Allocated?

Should a service department allocate its *actual* costs to producing departments, or should it allocate its *budgeted* costs? The answer is that budgeted costs should be allocated. What's wrong with allocating actual costs? Allocating actual costs burdens the producing departments with the inefficiencies of the service department managers. If actual costs are allocated, then any lack of cost control on the part of the service department manager is simply buried in a routine allocation to other departments.

Any variance over budgeted costs should be retained in the service department and closed out against cost of goods sold along with producing department variances. Producing department managers rarely complain about being allocated a portion of service department costs, but they complain bitterly if they are forced to absorb service department inefficiencies.

Guidelines to Allocation for Planning and Control

By way of summary, we can note five key points to remember about allocating service department costs:

1.   The distinction between variable and fixed costs in service departments should be maintained.

2.   *Beginning-of-year:* Variable costs should be allocated according to the budgeted rate, based on the budgeted level of activity (direct labor hours, etc.) in the departments which are to be serviced. This allocation will be for purposes of computing predetermined overhead rates.

End-of-Year: Variable costs should be allocated according to the budgeted rate, based on the *actual* level of activity (direct labor hours, etc.) in the departments which have been serviced. The reason for allocating according to the actual level of activity at the end of the year, rather than the budgeted level of activity, is that the actual level of activity represents the extent to which services were *actually provided* by the service department during the year.

3. Fixed costs represent the cost of having long-term service capacity available. These costs should *always* be allocated in predetermined, lump-sum amounts. The lump-sum amount going to each separate department should be in accordance with the individual long-run servicing needs of the departments that gave rise to the investment in the service department in the first place.

4. Actual service department costs should not be allocated; rather, allocations should be based on budgeted rates.

5. Reciprocal services between service departments should be recognized.

An Extended Example

The integration of these allocation guidelines can best be shown by means of an extended example.

The Proctor Company has three service departments, Building Maintenance, Cafeteria, and Inspection. The company also has two producing departments, Shaping and Assembly. The service departments provide services to each other, as well as to the producing departments. Types of costs in the service departments, and bases for allocation are:

Department	Type of Cost	Base for Allocation
Building Maintenance	Fixed costs	Square footage occupied
Cafeteria	Variable costs	Number of employees
	Fixed costs	10% to Inspection, 40% to Shaping, and 50% to Assembly.
Inspection	Variable costs	Direct labor hours
	Fixed costs	70% to Shaping, and 30% to Assembly.

The Proctor Company allocates service department costs on a sequential basis, in the following order:

1. Building Maintenance.
2. Cafeteria.
3. Inspection.

EXHIBIT 4–3

THE PROCTOR COMPANY
Beginning-of-Year Cost Allocations for Purposes of Preparing Predetermined Overhead Rates

	Building Maintenance	Cafeteria	Inspection	Shaping	Assembly
Producing department overhead costs before allocations				$220,000	$340,000
Variable costs to be allocated	$ –0–	$62,500	$ 8,520		
Cafeteria allocation @ $100 per employee:*					
30 employees × $100		(3,000)	3,000		
240 employees × $100		(24,000)		24,000	
355 employees × $100		(35,500)			35,500
Inspection allocation @ $.12 per direct labor hour:†					
40,000 DLH × $.12			(4,800)	4,800	
56,000 DLH × $.12			(6,720)		6,720
Totals	$ –0–	$ –0–	$ –0–	$248,800	$382,220
Fixed costs to be allocated	$15,000	$40,000	$20,000		
Building Maintenance allocation at $1/sq. ft.:‡					
1,000 sq. ft. × $1	(1,000)	$ 1,000			
500 sq. ft. × $1	(500)		$ 500		
4,750 sq. ft. × $1	(4,750)			$ 4,750	
8,750 sq. ft. × $1	(8,750)				$ 8,750
Cafeteria allocation:					
10% × $41,000§		(4,100)	4,100		
40% × $41,000		(16,400)		16,400	
50% × $41,000		(20,500)			20,500
Inspection allocation:					
70% × $24,600‖			(17,220)	17,220	
30% × $24,600			(7,380)		7,380
Totals	$ –0–	$ –0–	$ –0–	$ 38,370	$ 36,630
Total overhead costs	$ –0–	$ –0–	$ –0–	$287,170	$418,850(a)
Budgeted direct labor hours				40,000	56,000(b)
Predetermined overhead rate (a) ÷ (b)				$7.18	$7.48

Employees

* Inspection 30
Shaping 240
Assembly 355
Total 625

Budgeted Cost $62,500 = $100/Employee
Budgeted Employees 625

‡ Square footage of space . . . . 15,500 sq. ft.
Less Building Maintenance space . . . . 500 sq. ft.
Net space for allocation . . . . 15,000 sq. ft.

Building Maintenance Fixed Cost $15,000 = $1/sq. ft.
Net Space for Allocation 15,000 sq. ft.

|| Inspection fixed costs $20,000
Allocated from Building Maintenance 500
Allocated from Cafeteria 4,100
Total cost to be allocated $24,600

Allocation percentages are given in the problem.

† Inspection variable costs . . . . $ 8,520
Allocated from the Cafeteria 3,000
Total cost to be allocated . . . . $11,520 (a)
Direct labor hours (40,000 + 56,000) . . . . 96,000 (b)
Allocation rate per direct labor hour (a) ÷ (b). . . . . $.12

§ Cafeteria fixed costs $40,000
Allocated from Building Maintenance 1,000
Total cost to be allocated $41,000

Allocation percentages are given in the problem.

Budgeted and actual overhead costs and operating data for 19X1 are given below:

	19X1 Cost Data	
	Budgeted	*Actual*
Building Maintenance–fixed.	$ 15,000	$15,500
Cafeteria–variable	62,500	61,200
fixed	40,000	41,500
Inspection–variable.	8,520	8,875
fixed	20,000	19,800
Shaping–variable and fixed	220,000	–
Assembly–variable and fixed	340,000	–

	Number of Employees		Direct Labor Hours		Square Footage of Space Occupied (sq. ft.)
	Budgeted	*Actual*	*Budgeted*	*Actual*	
Building Maintenance.	–*	–	–	–	500
Cafeteria	–*	–	–	–	1,000
Inspection	30	30	–	–	500
Shaping	240	235	40,000	37,500	4,750
Assembly.	355	335	56,000	57,500	8,750
Totals	625	600	96,000	95,000	15,500

* Although there are employees in both of these service departments, under sequential allocation costs are only allocated *forward*—never backward. For this reason, the costs of the cafeteria will be allocated *forward* on the basis of the number of employees in the inspection, shaping, and assembly departments.

Beginning-of-Year Allocations. Allocations made at the beginning of the year will be to provide data to the producing departments so that they can prepare predetermined overhead rates. The 19X1 beginning-of-year allocations for the Proctor Company are given in Exhibit 4–3.

End-of-Year Allocations. At the end of each year, the service departments must make allocations to using departments based on the *actual* level of service provided during the year. The costs allocated to producing departments at the end of the year are added to the manufacturing overhead account by the producing departments, along with other actual manufacturing overhead costs which have been incurred.

The allocation of service department costs at the end of 19X1 by the Proctor Company is given in Exhibit 4–4.

Two things should be noted about the allocations in Exhibit 4–4. First, note that the variable costs are allocated on a basis of the *budgeted rate* developed earlier, times the *actual* level of activity in the using departments. In the case of the cafeteria, for example, notice that the

EXHIBIT 4–4

THE PROCTOR COMPANY
End-of-Year Cost Allocations

	Maintenance	Cafeteria	Inspection	Shaping	Assembly
Actual variable costs	$ –0–	$61,200	$ 8,875		
Cafeteria allocation @ $100 per *actual* employee:					
30 employees × $100	–	(3,000)	3,000	–	–
235 employees × $100	–	(23,500)	–	$23,500	–
335 employees × $100	–	(33,500)	–	–	$33,500
Inspection allocation @ $.12 per *actual* direct labor hour:					
37,500 DLH × $.12	–	–	(4,500)	4,500	–
57,500 DLH × $.12	–	–	(6,900)	–	6,900
Net variance in cost—not allocated	$ –0–	$ 1,200	$ 475		
Actual fixed costs.	$15,500	$41,500	$19,800		
Budgeted fixed costs are allocated to the using departments, according to the method and lump-sum amounts shown in Exhibit 4–3	(15,000)	(40,000)	(20,000)	38,370	36,630
Net variance in cost—not allocated	$ 500	$ 1,500	$ (200)		
End-of-year allocated costs added to actual manufacturing overhead				$66,370	$77,030

budgeted rate of $100 per employee developed earlier has been applied to the actual number of employees in each department. The reason for applying the budgeted rate times the actual level of activity in making year-end allocations is that the actual level of activity represents the extent to which servicing was *actually provided* during the year. Since the using departments had less employees working than budgeted during the period, one would expect less food to be consumed in the cafeteria. There is no reason to charge the using departments for the food that would have been consumed, had they employed the budgeted level of 625 employees. A using department should be charged at year end only for *actual usage* of service department services, so far as variable costs are concerned, and this charge should be at the *budgeted rate.*

Second, note that year-end allocations of fixed costs are the same as beginning-of-year allocations. In each case budgeted fixed costs are allocated in lump-sum amounts. Any variances between budgeted costs and actual costs are *not* allocated, but rather are kept in the service department responsible for the variance.

Beware of Sales Dollars as an Allocation Base

Over the years, sales dollars have been a favorite allocation base for service department costs. One reason is that sales dollars are simple, straightforward, and easy to work with. Another reason is that there is a tendency to feel that sales dollars indicate some measure of "ability to bear" additional costs from other parts of the organization.

Unfortunately, sales dollars often constitute a very poor allocation base. The reason is that sales dollars *vary* from period to period and the costs being allocated are often largely *fixed* in nature. As discussed earlier, if a variable base is used to allocate fixed costs, inequities can result as between departments since the costs being allocated to one department will depend in large part on what happens in *other* departments. For example, a letup in sales effort in one department would shift allocated costs off of it onto other, more productive departments. In effect, the departments putting forth the best sales efforts are penalized in the form of higher allocations, simply because of inefficiencies elsewhere that are beyond their control. The result often is bitterness and resentment on the part of the managers of the better departments.

Consider the following situation encountered by the author:

A large men's clothing store has one service department and three sales departments—suits, shoes, and accessories. The service department's costs are allocated to the three sales departments according to sales dollars. A recent period showed the following allocation:

	Suits	*Shoes*	*Accessories*	*Total*
Sales by department	$78,000	$18,000	$24,000	$120,000
Percentage of total sales	65%	15%	20%	100%
Allocation of service department costs, based on percentage of total sales	$19,500	$ 4,500	$6,000	$ 30,000

In a following period the manager of the suit department launched a very successful program to expand sales to over $100,000 in his department. Sales in the other two departments remained unchanged. Total service department costs also remained unchanged, but the allocation of these costs changed substantially, as shown below:

	Suits	*Shoes*	*Accessories*	*Total*
Sales by department	$108,000	$18,000	$24,000	$150,000
Percentage of total sales	72%	12%	16%	100%
Allocation of service department costs, based on percentage of total sales	$ 21,600	$ 3,600	$ 4,800	$ 30,000
Increase (or decrease) from prior allocation	$ 2,100	$ (900)	$ (1,200)	—

The manager of the suit department complained very bitterly that as a result of his successful effort to expand sales in his department, he was being forced to carry a larger share of the service department costs. On the other hand, the managers of the departments that showed no improvement in sales were being relieved of a portion of the costs which they had been carrying. Yet there had been no change in the amount of services provided for any department.

The manager of the suit department viewed the increased service department cost allocation to his department as a penalty for his outstanding performance, and wondered whether his efforts had really been worthwhile after all in the eyes of top management.

Sales dollars should be used as an allocation base only in those cases where there is a direct causal relationship between sales dollars and the service department costs being allocated. In those situations where service department costs are fixed in nature, they should be allocated according to the guidelines discussed earlier in the chapter.

SUMMARY

The way in which costs are allocated can have a significant impact on a firm's operating results, as well as on unit costs. In this chapter we have considered two problems in cost allocation—the first relating to fluctuating overhead rates, and the second relating to service department costs.

The problem of fluctuating overhead rates can be largely solved through use of normalized overhead rates. A normalized overhead rate is determined by looking at a *range* of activity, rather than by looking at the activity of a single period. Normalized overhead rates largely eliminate any unfavorable impact on unit costs and on reported income that might result from having current production out of balance with the long-run demand for a company's products.

A service department is a department that provides support or assistance to other departments within an organization. Although service departments do not engage directly in production, their costs are generally viewed as being part of the cost of a company's finished products. Service department costs are added in with other costs of production through allocation to the producing departments, and through the producing departments including the allocated service department costs as part of manufacturing overhead.

In order to avoid inequity in allocation, variable and fixed service department costs should be allocated separately. The variable costs should be allocated according to whatever activity measure controls their incurrence. The fixed costs should be allocated in predetermined, lump-sum amounts to the various producing departments according to the long-run servicing needs of these departments. In order to avoid the passing on of inefficiency from the service departments to the producing departments, budgeted service department costs should be allocated rather than actual costs. Any variances should be kept within the service departments themselves, and then written off to cost of goods sold.

QUESTIONS

4–1. What is the difference between a service department and a producing department? Give several examples of service departments.

4–2. How do service department costs enter into the final cost of finished products?

4–3. What are "reciprocal" service department costs? How are such costs handled for allocation purposes?

4–4. What guidelines should govern the allocation of fixed service department costs to producing and other departments? The allocation of variable service department costs?

4–5. "A variable base should never be used in allocating fixed service department costs to producing departments." Explain.

4–6. In what way are service department costs similar to costs such as lubricants, utilities, and factory supervision?

4–7. Why might it be desirable not to allocate some service department costs to producing departments?

4–8. What is the purpose of the "retainer fee" approach to cost allocation?

4–9. "Units of product can be costed equally well with or without allocations of service department costs." Do you agree? Why or why not?

4–10. What criteria are relevant to the selection of allocation bases for service department costs?

4–11. What is a normalized overhead rate?

4–12. Under what circumstances would normalized overhead rates be useful to a firm?

4–13. What advantages can be gained by using normalized overhead rates?

EXERCISES

4–1. Carter Company operates a medical services unit for its employees. The variable costs of the medical services unit are allocated to using departments on a basis of the number of employees in each department. Budgeted and actual data for 19X8 are given below:

Variable Costs—19X8

	Budgeted	*Actual*
Medical Services Unit.	$100/employee	$105/employee

Number of Employees

	Mainte- nance Depart- ment	Producing Departments		
		1	2	3
Budgeted number of employees.	20	200	700	300
Actual number of employees	21	198	704	295

Required:

Determine the amount of medical services variable cost that should be allocated to each of the four departments above at the end of 19X8.

4–2. The Bonneville Corporation has two service departments, janitorial services and cafeteria. The fixed costs of the two service departments are allocated on the following bases:

Service *Department*	*Basis for Allocation*
Janitorial Services.	Square footage of floor space occupied.

Floor space is occupied as follows:

Cafeteria . . . . 3,000 sq. ft.
Producing Department A . . . . .30,000 sq. ft.
Producing Department B . . . . .67,000 sq. ft.

Cafeteria . . . .   Producing Department A–30%
Producing Department B–70%

The fixed costs of janitorial services total $25,000 each year. The fixed costs of the cafeteria total $75,000 each year.

Required:

1. Show the allocation of the fixed costs of janitorial services.
2. Show the allocation of the fixed costs of the cafeteria.

4–3. In practice, factory service department costs are allocated to producing departments in many ways. For example, some firms allocate all service department costs, whereas other firms allocate only the variable costs. Some firms allocate only the budgeted costs, and other firms allocate full actual costs. In some cases, these allocations are made on the basis of a specified rate per unit of activity, and in other cases the allocations are in block sums. The allocation rates are sometimes computed in advance (predetermined), and at other times the rates are set only after all of the costs of the period have been accumulated.

Below are four plans for allocating service department costs to producing departments. Evaluate each plan.

1. Allocate all service department costs, based on a single rate per unit of activity. The rate is set after-the-fact, i.e., on actual costs of the period.
2. Allocate all service department costs, based on a single rate per unit of activity. The rate is predetermined.

3. Allocate only variable service department costs, based on a single rate per unit of activity. The rate is set after-the-fact, and applied at the end of the period according to the budgeted level of activity for the period.
4. Allocate all service department costs, but allocate the fixed and variable costs separately. In each case, allocate budgeted costs based on predetermined, but separate, rates per unit of activity.

4-4. The Titler Company assigns overhead cost to units of product on a basis of direct labor hours. Selected production and cost data are given below:

	Direct Labor Hours
Plant capacity per year.	100,000
Average per year utilization of capacity	90,000
Utilization planned for 19X5	75,000
Required for one unit of product.	5

	Overhead Cost
At capacity level of operations	$170,000
At average level of operations	162,000
Planned for 19X5.	150,000
Required for one unit of product.	?

Required:

1. Compute the predetermined overhead rate for 19X5 on a basis of 19X5 planned activity.
2. Compute the predetermined overhead rate for 19X5 on a normalized basis.
3. Show the differences in unit cost that would result if the overhead rate in part 1 were used as compared to the overhead rate in part 2.

4-5. The Power Services Department in a factory provides electrical power for other departments. The power budget is $9,520 per month. Of this amount, $2,500 is considered to be a fixed cost. Actual costs for the month of April amounted to $9,300.

Power consumption in the factory is measured by kilowatt hours (KWH) used. The monthly power requirements of the factory's other four departments are as follows (in KWH):

	Producing Depts.		*Service Depts.*	
	A	*B*	*X*	*Y*
Needed at capacity production	10,000	20,000	12,000	8,000
Budgeted.	8,000	15,000	8,000	5,000
Used during April.	8,000	13,000	7,000	6,000

Required:

What amount of actual power service cost should be allocated to each of these four departments for the month of April?

(AICPA, adapted)

4–6. John Holder has just been appointed production manager of Division A of White Manufacturing Company. Mr. Holder is well aware of the fact that if he does a good job as a divisional production manager he will be in line for a job in corporate headquarters. In order to familiarize himself with his new duties, Mr. Holder has requested the following data:

	Actual Data				Planned
	19X1	*19X2*	*19X3*	*19X4*	*19X5*
Sales	$20,000	$22,000	$24,000	$26,000	$28,000
Cost of goods sold	13,350	16,170	14,865	14,895	?
Gross margin	$ 6,650	$ 5,830	$ 9,135	$11,105	$?
Sales in units	5,000	5,500	6,000	6,500	7,000
Production in units	6,000	5,000	7,000	8,000	?
Ending inventory in units	1,000	500	1,500	3,000	-0-

The bulk of the manufacturing costs in Division A are fixed. The division manager commented to Mr. Holder, "We had a bad year in 19X2, but things straightened up in 19X3, and we're really moving now. We expect 19X5 to be our best year ever, profitwise. If it is, we're bound to be in line for a good bonus. But watch those inventories; corporate headquarters wants them down to zero by the end of 19X5."

Required:

1. What caused the drop in gross margin in 19X2, and the dramatic increases in gross margin in 19X3 and 19X4? No computations are necessary.
2. What dilemma is faced by Mr. Holder as production manager for 19X5?
3. What would you advise Mr. Holder to do?

PROBLEMS

4–1. *Straightforward Cost Allocation Problem.* Service Department A provides maintenance service for producing departments X and Y. The cost of this service is allocated to producing departments on a basis of machine hours. Cost and operating data for 19X5 are given below:

Service Department A

	Budget	*Actual*
Variable costs	$10,000	$13,200
Fixed costs	50,000	49,800

Producing Departments X and Y

| | Machine Hours | | |
	Long-Run Average	Budget–19X5	Actual–19X5
Department X....... 100,000		80,000	85,000
Department Y....... 150,000		120,000	135,000

Required:

1. What amount of actual variable cost should be allocated from Department A to Department X for 19X5? To Department Y?
2. What amount of fixed cost should be allocated from Department A to Department X for 19X5? To Department Y?

4–2. *Allocating Fixed and Variable Costs.* A company's factory has three producing departments, a maintenance department, and a steam electric power plant. The steam electric power plant provides electricity for the producing departments and for the maintenance department.

The 19X1 budget for the power plant shows budgeted fixed costs of $50,000, and budgeted variable costs of $.02 per kilowatt-hour produced.

The following data show the long-run demand for power in each department, the power budgeted for 19X1, and the actual power consumed during 19X1.

	Long-Run Demand (KWH)	Budgeted for 19X1 (KWH)	Actual Power Used in 19X1 (KWH)
Maintenance Department	30,000	25,000	25,000
Producing Department 1.......	280,000	250,000	160,000
Producing Department 2.......	540,000	540,000	540,000
Producing Department 3.......	150,000	85,000	75,000
Total..............	1,000,000	900,000	800,000

As shown above, the steam electric power plant actually generated 800,000 kilowatt hours of power during 19X1. Actual costs of the power plant in providing this power are given below:

Actual fixed costs............	$51,000
Actual variable costs	17,600
Total...............	$68,600

Required:

Determine how much of the $68,600 power plant cost should be allocated to each of the four departments listed above.

4–3. *Cost Allocation and Unit Costs. Focuses on the Problems Caused by Allocating a Fixed Cost on a Variable Base.* The Delta Company produces two products, awls and zones. The awls are produced in the Awl Division, and the zones are produced in the Zone Division. The company also has an M&E Division which provides maintenance and engineering services for the two producing divisions.

All costs of the M&E Division are allocated to the producing divisions on the basis of machine hours. The following data apply to operations in the various departments during 19X1:

19X1 Costs

	Variable	Fixed	Total
M&E Division	$10,000	$70,000	$80,000

19X1 Machine Hours

Awls Division	5,000
Zone Division	5,000
	10,000

Due to internal problems, production dropped off during 19X2 in the Awls Division. The following data are available for 19X2:

19X2 Costs

	Variable	Fixed	Total
M&E Division	$7,000	$70,000	$77,000

19X2 Machine Hours

Awls Division	2,000
Zone Division	5,000
	7,000

Required:

1. Compute the amount of M&E Division cost that would be allocated to each producing division for 19X1 and for 19X2. The company allocates both fixed and variable costs on the basis of actual machine hours.

2. Assume that it requires one half of a machine hour to produce one unit of product in the Zone Division. Overhead is applied to units of product on a basis of machine hours. The following costs were incurred within the Zone Division during 19X1:

Direct materials	$10,000
Direct labor	25,000
Overhead (estimated and actual)	10,000
Total.	$45,000

Compute the cost of a unit of product produced in 19X1 in the Zone Division (don't forget the allocated costs).

3. Costs incurred within the Zone Division were the same in 19X2

as in 19X1. Compute the cost of a unit of product produced in 19X2.

4. Upon seeing the per unit cost computed in Part 3 above, the president of the Delta Company gasped, "Just look at that unit cost! Why, that's as much as we can sell these things for! We had better stop producing them and turn to something more profitable!" What would be your reply?
5. What changes would you recommend that the Delta Company make in its allocation of M&E Division costs?

4–4. *The Impact of Overhead Rates on Unit Costs.* Cable Company is planning its activities for 19X4. The company projects sales and production as follows:

	5-Year Average	Planned— 19X4
Sales in units.	50,000	45,000
Production in units	50,000	42,000
Inventory in units.	8,000	5,000

Although the long-term outlook for sales is excellent, sales for 19X4 are planned to be down about 10 percent from prior years due to an economic recession which is predicted for the year.

Cable Company has just computerized its inventory control system, and as a result feels that inventories can be trimmed to a level equaling about 10 percent of long-term sales. For this reason, inventory levels will be cut back in 19X4. This cutback is reflected in the planned production for 19X4. Planned production costs for 19X4 are given below:

Direct materials	$210,000
Direct labor (168,000 hrs.)	504,000
Factory overhead:	
Variable	$1.00 per direct labor hour
Fixed.	$400,000

Overhead is assigned to production on a basis of direct labor hours.

Required:

1. Using direct labor hours as a base, compute two different predetermined overhead rates that the Cable Company might use during 19X4. Which overhead rate do you think should be used? Why?
2. What would be the overhead cost per unit of product produced in 19X4 under each of the rates you computed in Part 1 above?
3. What would be the difference in gross margin for 19X4 if one of the overhead rates computed in Part 1 is used to cost 19X4 production as compared to the other?

4–5. *Allocating Service Department Costs.* The Murray Iron Works, Inc., has two producing departments, Department A and Department B, and three service departments. The service departments, and the bases on which their costs are allocated to using departments, are listed below:

Department	Cost	Allocation Base
Building and Grounds	Fixed	Square footage occupied
Medical Services	Variable	Number of employees
	Fixed	Employee needs at full capacity
Equipment maintenance	Variable	Machine hours
	Fixed	40% to Department A
		60% to Department B

Service department costs are allocated to using departments on a sequential basis, in the order shown above. The company has developed the cost and operating data given in the following table, for purposes of preparing predetermined overhead rates in the two producing departments:

	Building and Grounds	Medical Services	Equipment Maintenance	Dept. A	Dept. B	Total
Variable costs	$ –0–	$22,200	$ 2,850	$146,000	$320,000	$ 491,050
Fixed costs.	88,200	60,000	24,000	420,000	490,000	1,082,200
Total.	$88,200	$82,200	$26,850	$566,000	$810,000	$1,573,250
Budgeted employees	6	4	30	450	630	1,120
Employee needs at capacity	8	4	45	570	885	1,512
Square footage of space occupied	600	500	1,400	12,000	15,500	30,000
Budgeted machine hours.	–	–	–	16,000	18,500	34,500

Required:

1. Show the allocation of service department costs to using departments for purposes of preparing predetermined overhead rates in departments A and B.
2. Assuming that predetermined overhead rates are set on a basis of machine hours, compute the predetermined overhead rate for each producing department.
3. Assume the following *actual* data for the year for the Medical Services Department:

Actual variable costs	$24,794
Actual employees for the year:	
Bldg & Grounds.	6
Medical Services.	4
Equipment Maintenance	32
Department A.	460
Department B.	625
	1,127

Compute the amount of end-of-year Medical Services variable cost that should be allocated to each department.

4–6. *Sales Dollars as an Allocation Base.* Lacey's Department Store allocates its fixed administrative expenses to departments on a basis of sales dollars. During 19X1, the fixed administrative expenses totaled $150,000. These expenses were allocated as follows:

	Dept. 1	Dept. 2	Dept. 3	Dept. 4	Total
Total sales— 19X1	$150,000	$375,000	$525,000	$450,000	$1,500,000
Percentage of total	10%	25%	35%	30%	100%
Allocation (based on above percentages)	$ 15,000	$ 37,500	$ 52,500	$ 45,000	$ 150,000

During 19X2, Dept. 2 launched a very successful sales campaign to double its sales volume. The sales level in all other departments remained unchanged. As a result, 19X2 sales data appeared as follows:

	Dept. 1	Dept. 2	Dept. 3	Dept. 4	Total
Total sales— 19X2	$150,000	$750,000	$525,000	$450,000	$1,875,000
Percentage of total	8%	40%	28%	24%	100%

Fixed administrative expenses of the store remained unchanged during 19X2 at $150,000.

Required:

1. Using sales dollars as an allocation base, show the allocation of the fixed administrative expenses among the four departments for 19X2.
2. Compare your allocation from part 1 to the 19X1 allocation found in the main body of the problem. As the sales manager of Dept. 2, how would you feel about the allocation which has been charged to you for 19X2?
3. Comment on the usefulness of sales dollars as an allocation base.

4–7. *Service Department Allocations, Predetermined Overhead Rates, and Unit Costs.* Apsco Company has two service departments and two producing departments. The service departments are Medical Services and Maintenance. Estimated monthly cost and operating data for the coming year are given below. These data have been prepared for purposes of computing predetermined overhead rates in the producing departments.

	Medical Services	Mainte- nance	Producing A	Producing B
Direct labor cost	—	—	$ 30,000	$ 40,000
Maintenance labor cost.	—	$ 5,000	—	—
Other indirect labor.	$ 4,500	—	4,000	5,000
Direct materials	—	—	50,000	80,000
Maintenance materials	—	7,536	—	—
Medical supplies.	3,630	—	—	—
Miscellaneous overhead costs	3,000	6,000	100,000	150,000
Total costs	$11,130	$18,536	$184,000	$275,000
Direct labor hours.	—	—	6,000	10,000
Number of employees: Presently employed.	3	8	38	64
Long-run employee needs.	3	10	60	80
Floor space occupied— sq. ft..	800	1,500	8,000	12,000

The Apsco Company allocates service department costs to producing departments for product costing purposes. The company uses a sequential allocation plan, starting with Medical Services. Allocation bases for the service departments are:

Department	Cost	Base for Allocation
Medical Services	Variable	Presently employed workers
	Fixed	Long-run employee needs
Maintenance	Variable	Direct labor hours
	Fixed	Square footage of floor space occupied

The behavior of various costs is shown below:

	Medical Services	Mainte- nance
Maintenance labor cost.	—	V
Other indirect labor.	F	—
Maintenance materials	—	V
Medical supplies.	V	—
Miscellaneous overhead costs	F	F

V = Variable
F = Fixed

Required:

1. Show the allocation of the service department costs for the purpose of computing predetermined overhead rates.
2. Compute the predetermined overhead rate to be used during the month in each of the producing departments (overhead rates are based on direct labor hours).

3. Assume that production in Department B is planned at 20,000 units for the month. Compute the planned cost of one unit of product in Department B.

4–8. *Choosing the Correct Overhead Base.* Sales and production data for Kimber Company are given below:

	19X1	19X2	19X3	19X4	19X5	Planned for 19X6
Sales in units.	30,000	30,000	30,000	30,000	30,000	30,000
Production in units	31,000	29,000	30,000	30,000	40,000	20,000

It requires three pounds of material and five direct labor hours to produce one unit of product. Total costs budgeted for 19X6 are given below (based on anticipated production of 20,000 units):

Materials	$ 240,000
Direct labor	300,000
Factory overhead	600,000
Total cost	$1,140,000

Overhead is applied to production on a basis of direct labor hours. Some $450,000 of the overhead is fixed. The company uses a normalized overhead rate.

Required:

1. Compute the predetermined overhead rate (on a normalized basis) that should be used during 19X6.
2. Compute the planned cost of a unit of product produced in 19X6.

4–9. *Case on Cost Analysis.* Bill Rolley purchased a large block of common stock in Avery Company in early 19X5. Bill had studied the company carefully for some time before making the purchase. Some of the information Bill had accumulated on the company is shown below.

AVERY COMPANY
Comparative Income Statements
For the Years Ended December 31, 19X1–19X4
(000 omitted)

	19X4	19X3	19X2	19X1
Sales	$1,300	$1,200	$1,100	$1,000
Cost of goods sold	740	696	650	600
Gross margin	560	504	450	400
Operating expenses	260	240	220	200
Net income	$ 300	$ 264	$ 230	$ 200
Earnings per share	$ 3.00	$ 2.64	$ 2.30	$ 2.00
Price/earnings ratio	13	12	11	11

Bill felt that the company's steady growth pattern, combined with its apparently sound management, industry potential, and solid earnings, made it a very attractive buy, particularly at a price/earnings ratio of only 13. Since all signs suggested that the company's prospects for growth were excellent, and since Bill was interested in long-term investment, he decided in early 19X5 to purchase the company's stock.

About a year later, in early 19X6, Bill received the Avery Company's annual report for 19X5. Selected data from this report and from other sources are given below:

	19X5 (000 omitted)
Sales	$1,300
Cost of goods sold	800
Gross margin.	500
Operating expenses	260
Net income	$ 240
Earnings per share	$2.40
Price/earnings ratio	12

Bill was stunned by what he read. He could understand why sales had remained level at $1,300,000 between 19X4 and 19X5 since a strike had occurred in the plant of Pacific Company, one of Avery Company's major suppliers, and certain key materials had been hard to get. But he couldn't understand why costs had jumped so sharply. It seemed to Bill that if sales remained constant, then profits should have remained constant, too. He was very concerned about his investment and wondered if he had made the right decision in buying the Avery Company's stock. He noticed the following report in the *Wall Street Journal*: ". . . Walter Hawkins, president of the Avery Company, states that the strike against Pacific Metals was much longer than anyone had anticipated. As a result, the Avery Company and others in its industry were forced to sharply curtail production and to rely heavily on inventories in meeting customer needs."

Bill has come to you, as an expert in cost analysis, for an explanation of what has happened in the Avery Company during 19X5. You find that the company costs inventories on a FIFO basis, and that costs have been quite stable in the industry for some time.

Required:

1. What explanation would you give Bill as to the probable cause of the sharp drop in net income for 19X5?
2. Based on the data in the problem, would you advise Bill to sell his shares of stock in the Avery Company? Explain.

4–10. *Allocation of Computer Center Costs in a University.* A large western university has a central computer system that handles the bulk of the computer needs of the administrative, teaching, and research functions of the university. The computer system is housed in a centrally located, specially constructed facility, and contains the finest in technology available both in terms of equipment and trained personnel. Virtually all costs associated with the computer system are fixed. The personnel assigned to the computer center are on flat annual salaries, and the equipment is all leased at flat monthly rates. The only variable costs associated with the computer center are paper and utilities which tend to be very nominal in comparison to the fixed costs.

Up until two years ago, the university had never attempted to allocate the use of computer time among the various university functions of administration, teaching, and research. The computer center was simply open to any users, who, after obtaining clearance for their projects (which required the approval and signature of the chairpersons, deans, etc., to whom the users were responsible) and being assigned a user number, were permitted to use the computer facilities to the extent they desired. This procedure seemed to work very well. Generally, the computer center was able to handle all user requests for computer time. In those periods when user requests exceeded the computer capacity, some projects were deferred for a day or two until the computer time became available. One factor that made the system work well was that users were willing to let the computer center supervisors schedule projects which had no particular time constraint to "slow" periods, such as between terms and in the summer months.

Two years ago, the university hired a retired, very successful businessman to develop a budgeting system for the university. One of his first steps was to set up a system of controls over the computer center. Essentially, this involved the allocation of computer time as between administration, teaching, and research uses. This allocation was made in the form of a specified dollar amount of computer time which was allocated to each prospective user for a particular year. The rate per computer hour of use was determined by taking the total costs associated with the computer center (salaries of personnel, leasing costs, estimated depreciation of the building, etc.) and dividing this figure by the maximum computer time available. Each prospective user was then allocated a certain dollar amount of computer time. This allocation was based on the user's prior-year use of computer facilities (the computer center had always kept track of the use of computer time for information and planning purposes). This pattern was to hold in future years, with each year's allocation of computer time being based on the prior year's usage. However, users had the right to petition the computer committee at any time for increases in their allocation.

Although the computer center supervisors were not happy about the thought of the new controls, they were willing to go along with the new plan. For one thing, it was argued by those setting up the allocation plan that the new plan would "put the monkey on the users' backs" in determining what was and what was not a "good" use of computer time. Since there now was a cost associated with computer use, they argued, users would be forced to evaluate each project carefully to determine which projects were justified and which were not in terms of the cost involved. As the businessman who developed the new plan explained, "This way we let the market decide how the computer should be used."

By the end of the first year under the new plan, several developments had taken place in the computer center. For the first time ever, demand for computer time far exceeded the time available. Particularly during the last few months of the year, users complained that they were unable to get adequate "turnaround" from the computer center to keep critical projects rolling. These users petitioned the computer committee for the right to take a portion of their allocated computer funds and go outside the university to process their data. Generally, these requests were denied. By the end of the year, the computer committee had received many requests from users for increases in computer allocations. In addition, grumbling was heard from some users, who complained that certain other users "thought that the computer belonged to them."

In their report to the university president at the end of the first year, those who had developed the allocation plan stated, ". . . the computer center is now under control." They pointed out the greatly increased demand for computer center services, explaining that this increased demand was a function of a growing awareness on the part of users of the value of the computer to the university community. They stated that these valuable services would continue to be controlled on a strict cost basis.

Required:

1. What do you think was the cause of the "greatly increased demand for computer center services" during the first year under the new plan?
2. Do you agree that the new plan resulted in a "cost" being associated with computer use, whereas no such cost existed before? What problems of cost justification might be encountered in a university that would not in a business firm?
3. Should the users who requested the right to take their allocated funds and go outside the university for computer services have been permitted to do so? Explain.
4. What changes, if any, would you recommend in the allocation plan?

4–11. *Allocating Costs in a Hospital.* Pleasant View Hospital has three service departments—Administrative Services, X-Ray Services, and Food Services. These service departments provide services for other departments in the hospital on the following bases:

Service Department	Costs Incurred	Base for Allocation
Administrative Services	Variable	Files processed
	Fixed	10% X-Ray, 20% Outpatient Clinic, 30% OB Care, and 40% General Hospital
X-Ray Services	Variable	X-Rays taken
	Fixed	Analysis of long-term usage
Food Services	Variable	Meals served
	Fixed	Full capacity needs

The hospital allocates costs of service departments to using departments on a sequential basis, in the order listed above. Estimated cost and operating data for all departments in the hospital for the forthcoming month are presented in the following table:

	Admin. Services	X-Ray Services	Food Services	Out-patient Clinic	OB Care	General Hospital	Total
Variable costs	$ 2,610	$39,575	$ 95,000	$18,000	$ 8,000	$ 74,000	$237,185
Fixed costs.	34,000	60,000	48,000	42,000	120,000	450,000	754,000
Total costs.	$36,610	$99,575	$143,000	$60,000	$128,000	$524,000	$991,185
Files processed	—	1,500	—	3,000	900	12,000	17,400
X-Rays taken	—	—	—	1,200	350	8,400	9,950
Long-term average X-ray needs	—	—	—	1,560	360	10,080	12,000
Meals served	—	—	—	—	7,400	42,600	50,000
Meals served at capacity	—	—	—	—	9,000	45,000	54,000

All billing in the hospital is done through the Outpatient Clinic, OB Care, or General Hospital. The hospital's administrator wants the costs of the three service departments allocated to these three billing centers.

Required:

Prepare the cost allocation desired by the hospital administrator. Include under each billing center the direct costs of the center, as well as the costs allocated from the service departments.

chapter 5

Cost Behavior Patterns— A Closer Look

IN OUR DISCUSSION of cost terms and concepts in Chapter 2, we stated that one of the ways in which costs can be classified is by behavior. Cost behavior means how a cost will change with respect to changes in levels of activity. As we stated in Chapter 2, if a cost is to be controlled by a manager, then it is necessary to know whether the cost can be expected to change under various operating conditions. If a cost can be expected to change, then it is necessary for the manager to know by how much, so that he can plan intelligently. Any attempt to make a decision without first carefully considering the impact of the decision on costs could result in disaster. A decision to double production of a particular product, for example, might result in the incurrence of far greater additional costs than the company would be able to generate in additional sales revenue.

In large part, the key to cost prediction is found in an understanding of cost behavior patterns. In this chapter we take a closer look at cost behavior patterns, and at the tools used by the manager to analyze them.

TYPES OF COST PATTERNS

In our brief discussion of cost behavior in Chapter 2 we mentioned only variable and fixed costs. There is a third behavior pattern, generally known as a *mixed* or *semivariable* cost. All three cost behavior patterns are found in most organizations.

Variable Costs

In our earlier discussion of cost behavior patterns we stated that a variable cost is so named because it varies in total in direct relationship to changes in volume or level of activity. If the level of activity doubles, then one would expect the variable costs to double as well. If the level of activity goes up only 10 percent, then one would expect the variable costs to increase by only 10 percent.

In order for variable costs to change in total in direct proportion to changes in the level of activity, they must be constant on a *per unit* basis. Assume, for example, that the Nifty Truck Company produces trucks. There is one radiator to each truck. The radiators cost $25 each. If we look at the cost of radiators on a *per truck* basis, the cost remains constant at $25 per truck. But the total cost of radiators changes in direct proportion to the number of trucks produced. These concepts are shown graphically in Exhibit 5–1.

EXHIBIT 5–1
Variable Cost Behavior

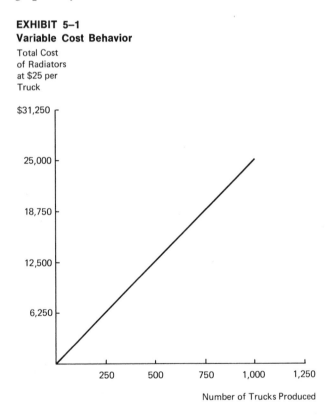

Total Cost
of Radiators
at $25 per
Truck

The Activity Base. In order for a cost to be variable, it must be variable *with something.* That "something" is the activity base. There can be many measures of activity in a firm. Two of the most common activity bases are units produced and units sold. Other activity bases used to measure variable costs might include number of miles driven by salespersons, pounds of laundry processed by a hotel, the number of letters typed by a secretary, the number of hours of machine time logged, and the number of beds in a hospital.

In order to plan and control variable costs, a manager must be well acquainted with the various activity bases within his own firm. People sometimes get the notion that if a cost doesn't vary with production and sales, then it is not really a variable cost. This, of course, is not correct. Whether a cost is variable will depend on whether its incurrence is dependent on the measure of activity under consideration. For example, if a manager is analyzing the cost of service calls under a product warranty the relevant measure of activity will be the number of service calls made. Those costs which vary in total with the number of service calls made will be variable costs.

Extent of Variable Costs. The number and type of variable costs present will depend in large part on the type of organization involved. A highly capital intensive organization such as a public utility will tend to have few variable costs. The bulk of its costs will be associated with its plant, and these costs will tend to be quite insensitive to changes in levels of service provided. A manufacturing firm, by contrast, will often have many variable costs. It will have variable costs associated with the actual manufacture of its products, as well as with their distribution to customers. A service organization or a merchandising firm will tend to fall between these extremes.

A few of the more frequently encountered variable costs are shown in the tabulation below:

Type of Organization	*Variable Costs*
Merchandising firm	Cost of merchandise sold
Manufacturing firm	Manufacturing costs:
	Prime costs:
	Direct materials
	Direct labor
	Variable portion of manufacturing overhead:
	Indirect materials
	Lubricants
	Supplies
	Utilities
	Setup time
	Indirect labor
Both merchandising and manufacturing firms	Selling and administrative costs:
	Commissions to salespersons
	Clerical costs, such as invoicing
	Freight out
Service organizations	Supplies, travel, clerical

The costs listed under "variable portion of manufacturing overhead" should not be viewed as being inclusive, but rather as being representative of the kinds of variable costs found in this classification.

True Variable versus Step-Variable Costs

Not all variable costs have exactly the same behavior pattern. Some variable costs behave in a *true variable* or *proportionately variable* pattern. Other variable costs behave in a *step-variable* pattern.

True Variable Costs. Direct materials would be a true or proportionately variable cost. Direct materials can be purchased in the exact quantity needed, and quantities used will vary directly with output. In addition, any amounts unused can be stored up and carried forward to the next period as inventory.

Step-Variable Costs. Indirect labor is also considered to be a variable cost, but it doesn't behave in quite the same way as direct materials. As an example, let us consider the labor cost of maintenance men, which would be part of indirect labor.

The time of maintenance men is obtainable only in large chunks, rather than in exact quantities. In addition, any maintenance time not utilized cannot be stored up as inventory and carried forward to the next period. Either the time is used effectively as it expires hour by hour, or it is gone forever. A further difference between these two types of variable costs is that the utilization of indirect labor time can be quite flexible, whereas the utilization of direct materials is usually quite set. A maintenance crew, for example, can work at a fairly leisurely pace if pressures are light, but then the crew can intensify its efforts if pressures build up. For this reason, somewhat small changes in the level of production may have no effect on the number of maintenance people needed to properly carry on maintenance work.

A cost (such as the labor cost of maintenance men) that is obtainable only in large chunks and which increases or decreases only in response to fairly wide changes in activity levels is known as *step-variable cost*. The behavior of a step-variable cost is illustrated in Exhibit 5–2. In order to contrast the cost behavior pattern of a step-variable cost with that of a true variable cost, the cost-behavior pattern of a true variable cost is also shown in the exhibit.

Notice that the need for maintenance help changes only with fairly wide changes in volume, and that when additional maintenance time is obtained it comes in large, indivisible pieces. The strategy of management in dealing with step-variable costs must be to obtain the highest level of utilization possible for any given step. Great care must be taken in dealing with these kinds of costs, to prevent "fat" from building up in an organization. There is a tendency to employ additional help

EXHIBIT 5–2
True Variable versus Step-Variable Costs

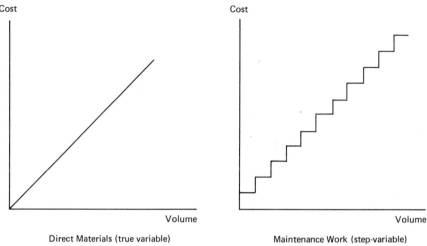

Direct Materials (true variable) Maintenance Work (step-variable)

more quickly than might be needed, and generally a reluctance to lay people off when volume declines.

The Linearity Assumption and the Relevant Range

In dealing with variable costs we have assumed a strictly linear relationship between cost and volume, except in the case of step-variable costs. Economists correctly point out that many costs which the accountant classifies as variable actually behave in a *curvilinear* fashion. The behavior of a curvilinear cost is shown in Exhibit 5–3. Notice that a strictly linear relationship between cost and volume does not exist either at very high or at very low levels of volume.

Although the accountant recognizes that many costs are not linear in their relationship to volume at some points, he concentrates on their behavior within narrow bands of activity known as the *relevant range*. The relevant range may be defined as the range over which volume is expected to fluctuate during the period of time under review. Within the relevant range the relationship of cost to volume is normally stable enough that the assumption of strict linearity can be used with insignificant loss of accuracy. The concept of the relevant range is illustrated in Exhibit 5–3.

Fixed Costs

In our discussion of cost behavior patterns in Chapter 2 we stated that fixed costs are costs which remain constant in total regardless of

EXHIBIT 5–3
Curvilinear Costs and the Relevant Range

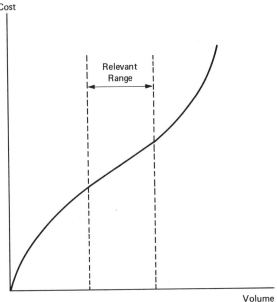

changes in the level of activity. To continue the Nifty Truck Company example, if the company rents a factory building for $50,000 per year the *total* amount of rent paid will not change regardless of the number of trucks produced in a year. This concept is shown graphically in Exhibit 5–4.

Since fixed costs remain constant in total, the amount of cost computed on a *per unit* basis will get progressively smaller the greater the number of units produced. If the Nifty Truck Company produces only 250 trucks in a year the $50,000 fixed rental cost would amount to $200 per truck. If 1,000 trucks are produced it would amount to only $50 per truck.

To summarize, a cost is fixed if its total dollar amount does not change with changes in the activity level. If a fixed cost is expressed on a per unit basis, the amount per unit will decrease as the activity level increases.

The Trend toward Fixed Costs

The trend in many companies today is toward greater fixed costs relative to variable costs. There are at least two factors responsible for this trend. First, automation is becoming increasingly important in all

EXHIBIT 5–4
Fixed Cost Behavior

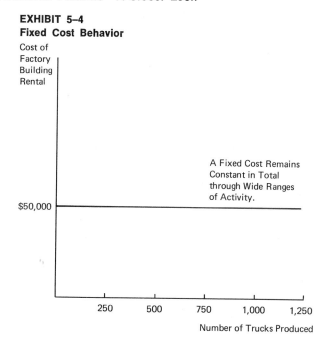

Cost of Factory Building Rental

A Fixed Cost Remains Constant in Total through Wide Ranges of Activity.

$50,000

250   500   750   1,000   1,250

Number of Trucks Produced

types of organizations. Although automation has played a significant role in factory operations for well over a century, its role continues to increase. In addition, automation is rapidly becoming a significant factor in some traditionally service-oriented industries as well. Increased automation means increased investment in machinery and equipment, with the attendent fixed depreciation or lease charges.

Second, labor unions have been increasingly successful in stabilizing employment through labor contracts. Labor leaders have set guaranteed annual salaries or guaranteed minimum weeks of work high on their list of goals for the future. Although most people would agree that a stabilization of employment is desirable from a social point of view, guaranteed salaries and work weeks do reduce the response of direct labor costs to changes in production.

This shift away from variable costs toward fixed costs has been so significant in some firms that they have become largely "fixed cost" organizations. The textile industry, for example, can be cited as one in which the bulk of firms have moved heavily toward automation with basically inflexible fixed costs replacing flexible, more responsive variable costs to a considerable extent. These shifts are very significant from a managerial accounting point of view, in that planning in many ways becomes much more crucial when one is dealing with large amounts of fixed costs. The reason is that when dealing with fixed costs the manager is much more "locked in," and generally has fewer options available to him in day-to-day decisions.

Types of Fixed Costs

Fixed costs are sometimes referred to as capacity costs, since they result from outlays made for plant facilities, equipment, etc., needed to provide the basic capacity for sustained operations. For planning purposes, fixed costs can be viewed as being either *committed* or *discretionary*.

Committed Fixed Costs. Committed fixed costs are those which relate to the investment in plant, equipment, and the basic organization of a firm. Examples of such costs would include depreciation of plant facilities (buildings and equipment), taxes on real estate, insurance, and salaries of key management and operating personnel.

The key factor about committed fixed costs is that they can't be reduced to zero even for a short period of time without impairing either profitability or the long-run goals of a firm. Even if operations are interrupted or cut back, the committed fixed costs will still continue unchanged. During a recessionary period, for example, a firm can't discharge its key executives or sell off part of the plant. Facilities and basic organizational structure must be kept intact at all times. In terms of long-run goals, the costs of any other course of action would be far greater than any short-run savings that might be realized.

Since committed fixed costs are basic to the long-run goals of a firm, their planning horizon usually encompasses many years. The commitments involved in these costs are made only after careful analysis of long-run sales forecasts, and after relating of these forecasts to future capacity needs. Careful control must be exercised by management in the planning stage to insure that a firm's long-run needs are properly evaluated. Once a decision is made to build a certain size plant, a firm becomes locked into that decision for many years to come.

After a firm becomes committed to a basic plant and organization, how are the associated costs controlled from year to year? Control of committed fixed costs comes through *utilization*. The strategy of management must be to utilize the plant and organization as effectively as possible in bringing about desired goals.

Discretionary Fixed Costs. Discretionary fixed costs (sometimes referred to as *managed* fixed costs) arise from *annual* decisions by management to spend in certain fixed cost areas. Examples of discretionary fixed costs would include advertising, research, and management development programs.

Basically, two key differences exist between discretionary fixed costs and committed fixed costs. First, the planning horizon for a discretionary fixed cost is fairly short-term—usually a single year. By contrast, we indicated earlier that committed fixed costs have a planning horizon that encompasses many years. Second, a discretionary fixed cost normally can be cut back in any given year with little or no damage to the long-run goals of a firm. For example, a firm that has been spending $1 million annually for research and development may decide in a particular year to cut its spending back somewhat due to forecasts of poor business conditions. When business conditions later improve, the research expenditures can be reinstated again, probably with little or no damage to the long-run competitive position of the firm.

The key factor about discretionary fixed costs is that management is not locked into a decision for any more than a single budget period. Each year a fresh look can be taken at the expenditure level in the various discretionary fixed cost areas. A decision can then be made on whether to continue the expenditure, increase it, reduce it, or discontinue it altogether.

Top Management Philosophy. In our discussion of fixed costs we have drawn a sharp line between committed fixed costs and discretionary fixed costs. As a practical matter, the line between these two classes of costs should be viewed as being somewhat flexible. The reason is that whether a cost is committed or discretionary will depend in large part on the philosophy of top management.

Some management groups prefer to exercise discretion as often as possible on as many costs as possible. They prefer to review costs frequently, and to adjust costs frequently, as conditions and needs warrant. Management groups who are inclined in this direction tend to view fixed costs as being largely discretionary. Other management groups are slow to make adjustments in costs (especially adjustments downward) as conditions and needs change. They prefer to maintain the status quo, and to leave programs and personnel largely undisturbed even though changing conditions and needs might suggest the desirability of adjustments. Managers inclined in this direction tend to view virtually all fixed costs as being committed.

To cite an example, during recessionary periods when the level of home building is down, many construction companies lay off their men and virtually disband operations for a period of time. Other construction companies continue large numbers of men on the payroll, even though the men have little or no work to do. In the first instance, management is viewing its fixed costs as being largely discretionary in nature. In the second instance, management is viewing its fixed costs as being largely committed. The philosophy of most management groups will fall somewhere between these two extremes.

Fixed Costs and the Relevant Range

The concept of the relevant range also has application in dealing with fixed costs, particularly those of a discretionary nature. At the beginning of a period programs are set and budgets established. The level of discretionary fixed costs will depend on the support needs of the programs which have been planned, which in turn will depend at least in part on the level of activity envisioned in the organization overall. At very high levels of activity, programs are usually broadened or expanded to include many things that might not be pursued at lower levels of activity. In addition, the support needs at high levels of activity are usually much greater than the support needs at lower levels of activity. For example, the advertising needs of a company pushing to increase sales by 25 percent probably would be much greater than if no sales increase was planned.

Fixed costs and the relevant range are shown in Exhibit 5–5.

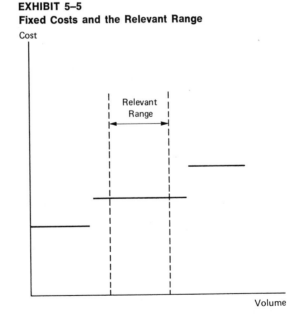

EXHIBIT 5–5
Fixed Costs and the Relevant Range

Although discretionary fixed costs are most susceptible to adjustment according to changing needs, Exhibit 5–5 also has application to committed fixed costs. As a company expands its level of activity, it may outgrow its present plant, or the key management core may need to be expanded. The result, of course, will be increased committed fixed costs as a larger plant is built, and as new key management positions are created.

One's first reaction is to say that discretionary and committed fixed costs are really just step-variable costs. To some extent this is true, since *all* costs vary in the long run. There are two major differences, however, between the step-variable costs depicted earlier in Exhibit 5–2 and the fixed costs depicted in Exhibit 5–5 above.

The first difference is that the step-variable costs can be adjusted very quickly, whereas once fixed costs have been set, even if they are discretionary fixed costs, they often can't be changed in the short run. A step-variable cost such as maintenance labor, for example, can be adjusted upward or downward very quickly by the hiring and firing of maintenance men. By contrast, once a company has committed itself to a particular program it becomes locked into the attendant fixed costs, at least for the budget period under consideration. Once an advertising contract has been signed, for example, the company is locked into the attendance costs for the contract period.

The second difference is that the *width of the steps* depicted for step-variable costs is much narrower than the width of the steps depicted for fixed costs such as those shown in Exhibit 5–5. The width of the steps relates to volume or level of activity. For step-variable costs the width of a step may be 40 hours of activity or less, if one is dealing, for example, with maintenance labor cost. By contrast, for fixed costs the width of a step may be *thousands* or even *tens of thousands* of hours of activity. In essence, the width of the steps of step-variable costs is generally so narrow that these costs can be treated essentially as variable costs. The width of the steps for fixed costs, on the other hand, is so wide that these costs generally must be treated as being entirely fixed within the relevant range.

Mixed Costs

A mixed cost (sometimes called a semivariable cost) is one that contains both variable and fixed cost elements. At certain levels of activity mixed costs may display essentially the same characteristics as a fixed cost; at other levels of activity they may display essentially the same characteristics as a variable cost.

To continue the Nifty Truck Company example, assume that the company leases a large part of the machinery used in its operations. The lease agreement calls for a flat annual lease payment of $25,000, plus $.10 for each hour that the machines are operated during the year. If during a particular year the machines are operated a cumulative total of 30,000 hours, then the lease cost of the machines will be $28,000 ($25,000 + $3,000). This cost will be a mixed cost, made up of $25,000 in fixed cost, plus $3,000 in variable cost. The concept of a mixed cost is shown graphically in Exhibit 5–6.

Even if the machines leased by the Nifty Truck Company aren't used a single hour during the year, the company will still have to pay

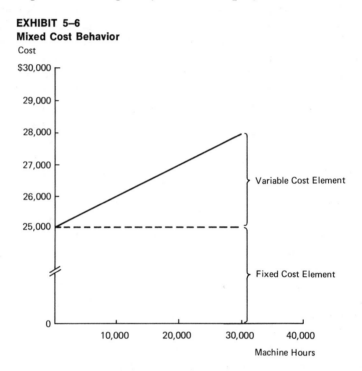

EXHIBIT 5–6
Mixed Cost Behavior

the minimum $25,000 charge. This is why the cost line in Exhibit 5–6 intersects the vertical cost axis at the $25,000 point. For each hour the machines are used, the *total* cost of leasing will increase by $.10. Therefore, the total cost line slopes upward as the variable cost element is added onto the fixed cost element.

THE ANALYSIS OF MIXED COSTS

The concept of a mixed cost is important, since mixed costs are common to a wide range of firms. Examples of mixed costs include electricity, heat, repairs, telephone, and maintenance.

The fixed portion of a mixed cost represents the basic, minimum charge for just having a service *ready and available* for use. The variable portion represents the charge made for *actual consumption* of the service. As one would expect, the variable element varies in proportion to the amount of the service which is consumed.

For planning purposes, how does management handle mixed costs? The ideal approach would be to take each invoice as it comes in and break it down into its fixed and variable elements. As a practical matter, even if this type of minute breakdown were possible the cost of doing so would probably be prohibitive. Analysis of mixed costs is normally done on an *aggregate* basis, concentrating on the *past behavior* of a cost at various levels of activity. If this analysis is done carefully, good approximations of the fixed and variable elements of a cost can be obtained with a minimum of effort.

We will examine three methods of breaking mixed costs down into their fixed and variable elements—the High-Low Method, the Scatter-graph Method, and the Least Squares Method.

The High-Low Method

This method of analyzing mixed costs requires that the cost involved (e.g., maintenance) be observed both at high and at low levels of activity within the relevant range. The difference in cost observed at the two extremes is divided by the change in level of activity in order to determine the amount of variable cost involved.

To illustrate, assume that maintenance costs for the Arco Company have been observed as follows within the relevant range of 5,000 to 8,000 direct labor hours:

Maintenance Cost Incurred	Direct Labor Hours
$ 700	5,000
800	6,000
900	7,000
1,000	8,000

Since total maintenance cost increases as the level of activity increases, it seems obvious that some variable cost is present. To separate the variable cost element from the fixed cost element, we need to relate the change in direct labor hours between the high and low points to the change which we observe in cost over that range:

	Maintenance Cost Incurred	Direct Labor Hours
High point observed	$1,000	8,000
Low point observed.	700	5,000
Change observed	$ 300	3,000

$$\text{Variable Rate} = \frac{\text{Change in Cost}}{\text{Change in Activity}} = \frac{\$300}{3,000} = \$.10 \text{ per Direct Labor Hour}$$

Having determined that the variable rate is $.10 per direct labor hour, it is now possible to determine the amount of fixed cost present:

Fixed Cost Element = Total Cost − Variable Cost Element
$$= \$1,000 \quad - (\$.10 \times 8,000 \text{ hours})$$
$$= \$200$$

Both the variable and fixed cost elements have now been isolated. The cost of maintenance within the relevant range analyzed can be expressed as being $200 plus $.10 per direct labor hour. This is sometimes referred to as a *cost formula*.

Cost Formula for Maintenance, over the Relevant Range of 5,000 to 8,000 Direct Labor Hours $\Big\} = $ $200 Fixed Cost, plus $.10 per Direct Labor Hour

As an exercise, the reader should prove this cost formula for maintenance by applying it to the 5,000, 6,000, and 7,000 direct labor hour levels of activity. If the formula is properly applied, it will result in $700, $800, and $900 respectively, for the three levels of activity. The maintenance cost used in this example is shown graphically in Exhibit 5–7.

Great care must be exercised in applying the High-Low Method to be sure that the costs being used in the analysis are representative of general business activity, and contain no distortions or unusual charges. Also, it must be kept in mind that the cost formula derived in a High-Low analysis will not be valid outside of the relevant range.

The Scattergraph Method

The High-Low Method works very well in analyzing those cost situations where the variable portion of a mixed cost varys at a constant rate per unit of activity. But many mixed costs are such that the variable portion does not vary at a constant rate, and an *average* rate of variability must be determined.

One approach to determining an average rate of variability is to construct a graph on which cost is shown on the vertical axis, and volume or rate of activity is shown on the horizontal axis. Total costs observed at various levels of activity are then plotted on the graph, and a line is fitted to the plotted points by simple visual inspection. A graph of this type is known as a *scattergraph*, and the line fitted to the plotted points is known as a *regression line*. The regression line, in effect, is a line of averages, with the average variable cost per unit of activity represented by the slope of the line, and the average fixed cost in total represented by the point where the regression line intersects the cost axis.

EXHIBIT 5–7
High-Low Method of Cost Analysis
The Arco Company—Maintenance Cost

Volume	Direct Labor Hours	Cost Observed
High	8,000	$1,000
Low	5,000	700

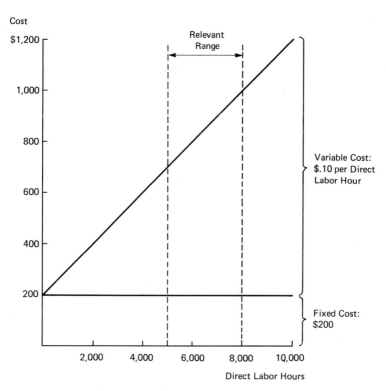

For purposes of illustration, assume that the Beach Company has recorded costs for water as follows:

Water Consumed (thousands of gallons)	Total Cost
10	$230
15	270
12	260
9	220
11	250
13	240
8	220

The total costs of water above have been plotted on the graph in Exhibit 5–8, and a regression line has been fitted to the plotted data, by visual inspection.

EXHIBIT 5–8
A Completed Scattergraph
Interpretation: The regression line begins at the $150 point, and rises at the rate of $8 per 1,000 gallons. Therefore, the fixed cost is $150, and the variable cost is $8 per 1,000 gallons of water consumed.

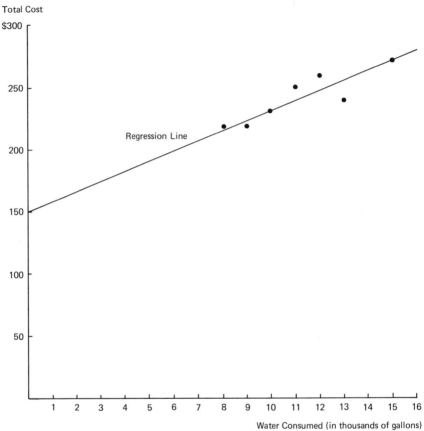

Since the regression line strikes the cost axis at the $150 point, that amount represents the fixed cost element. The variable cost element would be $8 per one thousand gallons of water consumed, since the slope of the repression line rises at that cost rate.

A scattergraph can be an extremely useful tool in the hands of an experienced analyst. Quirks in cost behavior due to strikes, bad weather, breakdowns, etc., become immediately apparent to the trained observer, and he can make appropriate adjustment to the data in fitting his regression line. Many cost analysts would argue that a scattergraph should be the beginning point in all cost analyses, due to the benefits to be gained from having the data visually available in graph form.

The Least Squares Method

The Least Squares Method is a more sophisticated approach to the scattergraph idea. Rather than fitting a regression line through the scattergraph data by simple visual inspection, the Least Squares Method fits the line by statistical analysis.

The Least Squares Method is based on computations which find their foundation in the equation for a straight line. A straight line can be expressed in equation form as

$$Y = a + bX$$

with a as the fixed element and b as the degree of variability, or the slope of the line. From this basic equation, and given a set of observations, n, two simultaneous linear equations can be developed which will fit a regression line to a linear array of data. The equations are:

$$\Sigma XY = a\Sigma X + b\Sigma X^2 \qquad (1)$$
$$\Sigma Y = na + b\Sigma X \qquad (2)$$

where a = fixed cost
     b = variable cost
     n = number of observations
     X = activity measure (hours, etc.)
     Y = total mixed cost observed

An Example of Least Squares. The application of the Least Squares Method can best be seen through a concrete example. Let us assume that a company is anxious to break its power (electrical) costs down into basic variable and fixed cost elements. Over the past year power costs (Y) have been observed as shown in the tabulation below. The number of hours of machine time logged (X) in incurring these costs is also shown in the tabulation.

Month	Machine Hours In Thousands (X)	Power Costs (Y)	XY	X²
January	9	$ 300	$ 2,700	81
February	8	250	2,000	64
March	9	290	2,610	81
April	10	290	2,900	100
May	12	360	4,320	144
June	13	340	4,420	169
July	11	320	3,520	121
August	11	330	3,630	121
September	10	300	3,000	100
October	8	260	2,080	64
November	7	230	1,610	49
December	8	260	2,080	64
	116	$3,530	$34,870	1,158

Substituting these amounts in the two linear equations given above, we have:

$$\$34,870 = 116a + 1,158b \qquad (1)$$
$$\$\ 3,530 = \ \ 12a + \ \ 116b \qquad (2)$$

In order to solve the equations, it will be necessary to eliminate one of the terms. The "*a*" term can be eliminated by multiplying equation (1) by 12, by multiplying equation (2) by 116, and then by subtracting equation (2) from equation (1). These steps are shown below:

Multiply equation (1) by 12: $\$418,440 = 1,392a + 13,896b$
Multiply equation (2) by 116: $\$409,480 = 1,392a + 13,456b$
Subtract (2) from (1): $\$\ \ \ 8,960 = \qquad\qquad 440b$
                          $\$\ \ \ 20.36 = b$

Therefore, the variable rate for power cost is $20.36 for each thousand machine hours of operating time. The fixed cost of power can be obtained by substituting the value for term *b* in equation (1):

$$\$34,870 = 116a + 1,158(\$20.36)$$
$$\$34,870 = 116a + \$23,581$$
$$\$11,289 = 116a$$
$$\$\ 97.32 = a$$

The fixed rate for power is $97.32 per month. The cost formula for the mixed cost is therefore $97.32 per month plus $20.36 per thousand machine hours worked.

Cost Formula for Power over the ⎫ $97.32 Fixed Cost, plus $20.36
Relevant Range of 7,000 to   ⎬ = per One Thousand Machine
13,000 Machine Hours.   ⎭   Hours.

In terms of the linear equation $Y = a + bX$, the cost formula can be expressed as:

$$Y = \$97.32 + \$20.36X$$

What Does "Least Squares" Mean?   The term least squares means that the sum of the squares of the deviations from the plotted points to the regession line *is smaller* than would be obtained from any other line fitted to the data. This idea can be illustrated as shown in Exhibit 5–9.

Notice from the exhibit that the deviations from the plotted points to the regression line are measured vertically on the graph. They are not measured perpendicular to the regression line. "Least squares" will have been attained when $\Sigma(Y - Y_1)^2$ is at the lowest possible figure. At the point of "least squares" the best possible fit of a regression line

EXHIBIT 5–9
The Concept of Least Squares

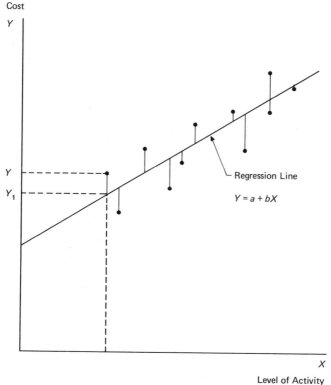

Cost

to the plotted points will have been achieved, in terms of slope and placement of the line.

The Use of Judgment in Cost Analysis

Although a cost formula has the appearance of exactness, the user should recognize that the breakdown of any mixed cost by any of the three techniques that we have discussed involves a substantial amount of estimating. The breakdowns represent *good approximations* of the fixed and variable elements involved; they should not be construed as being precise analyses. The manager must be ready to step in at any point in his analysis of a cost, and to adjust his computations for judgment factors which in his view are critical to a proper understanding of the mixed cost involved. However, the fact that computations are not exact, and involve estimates and judgment factors, does not prevent data from being useful and meaningful in decision making. The manager who waits to make a decision until he has perfect data available will rarely have an opportunity to demonstrate his decision-making ability.

Multiple Regression Analysis

In all of our computations involving mixed costs, we have assumed a single causive factor as the basis for the behavior of the variable element. That causive factor has been volume or rate of some activity, such as direct labor hours, machine hours, production, or sales. This assumption is acceptable for many mixed costs, but in some situations there may be more than one causive factor involved in the behavior of the variable element. For example, in a shipping department the cost of freight-out might depend on both the number of units shipped and the weight of the units, as dual causive factors. In a situation such as this the equation for a simple regression would have to be expanded to include the additional variable:

$$Y = a + bX + cW$$

where W = the weight of a unit, and c = the factor of variability. When dealing with an expanded equation such as this one, the simple regression analysis which we have been doing is no longer adequate. A *multiple regression analysis* is necessary. Although the added variable or variables will make the computations more complex, the principles involved are the same as in a simple regression such as we have been doing. Because of the complexity of the computations involved, multiple regression is generally done with the aid of a computer.

Engineering Approach to Cost Study

Some firms use an engineering approach to the study of cost behavior. Essentially, an engineering approach involves a quantitative analysis of what cost behavior should be, based on the industrial engineer's evaluation of the production methods to be used, the materials specifications, labor needs, equipment needs, efficiency of production, power consumption, etc. The engineering approach must be used in those situations where no past experience is available on activity and costs. In addition, it is often used in tandem with the methods we have discussed above in order to sharpen the accuracy of cost analysis. An N.A.A. research report of actual business practices describes the use of the engineering approach as follows:

> The industrial engineering approach to determination of how costs should vary with volume proceeds by systematic study of materials, labor, services, and facilities needed at varying volumes. The aim is to find the best way to obtain the desired production. These studies generally make use of past experience, but it is used as a guide or as a check upon the results obtained by direct study of the production methods and facilities. Where no past experience is available, as with a new

product, plant, or method, this approach can be applied to estimate the changes in cost that will accompany changes in volume.[1]

THE CONTRIBUTION FORMAT

The understanding of cost behavior which we have gained in this chapter will be very helpful in many of the chapters ahead. It will be particularly helpful in our study of cost-volume-profit relationships in Chapter 6. In preparation for this study it is important at this point to introduce a new format to the income statement, known as the *contribution approach*. The unique thing about the contribution approach is that it gears the income statement to cost behavior.

Why a New Income Statement Format?

The *traditional* approach to the income statement, such as illustrated in Chapter 2, and such as you studied in financial accounting, is not organized in terms of cost behavior. Rather, it is organized around what is called a "functional" approach to cost classification. The functional approach emphasizes the *functions* of production, administration, and sales as being the key factors in deciding how to classify and present costs. In a functional approach to cost classification no attempt is made to distinguish between the *behavior* of costs included under each functional heading. Under the heading "Administrative Expense" on the income statement, for example, one can expect to find *both* variable and fixed expenses lumped together.

Although an income statement prepared under functional headings, with no breakdown of costs by behavior, may be useful for external reporting purposes, it has serious limitations so far as usefulness *internally* is concerned. Internally, the manager needs cost data that will facilitate *planning* and *decision making*. Managers have found that planning and decision making are both facilitated by having costs organized and available by behavior. The contribution approach has been developed in response to this need.

The Contribution Approach

Exhibit 5–10 presents what is known as the contribution approach to the income statement. The exhibit contrasts the contribution approach with the traditional approach discussed above.

Notice that the contribution approach emphasizes cost behavior, by separating fixed and variable costs, and by segregating them on the income statement itself. Variable expenses are first deducted from sales,

---

[1] National Association of Accountants, *The Analysis of Cost-Volume-Profit Relationships*, Research Report no. 16, p. 17.

EXHIBIT 5-10
Comparison of the Contribution Income Statement with the Traditional Income Statement

Contribution Approach *(costs organized by behavior)*			*Traditional Approach* *(costs organized by function)*		
Sales		XXX	Sales		XXX
Less variable expenses:			Less cost of goods sold		XX*
Variable production	XX		Gross margin.		XX
Variable administrative.	XX		Less operating expenses:		
Variable selling	XX	XX	Administrative.	XX*	
Contribution margin		XX	Selling	XX*	XX
Less fixed expenses:			Net income		XX
Fixed production.	XX				
Fixed administrative	XX				
Fixed selling.	XX	XX			
Net income		XX			

* Contains both variable and fixed expenses.

yielding what is known as the *contribution margin*. The term "contribution margin" means what remains from total sales revenues, after deducting variable expenses, that can be used *to contribute* toward covering of fixed expenses, and then toward profits for the period.

The contribution approach to the income statement is widely used as an internal planning and decision-making tool. Its emphasis on costs by behavior facilitates cost-volume-profit analysis, such as we shall be doing in the following chapter. The approach is also very useful in appraisal of managerial performance, such as we cover in Chapter 11. Moreover, it is of considerable assistance in organizing data relevant to all kinds of special decisions, such as pricing, selection of marketing channels, adding and dropping product lines, etc. All of these topics are covered in later chapters.

SUMMARY

Managers analyze cost behavior in order to have a basis for predicting how costs will respond to changes in activity levels throughout the organization. The ability to accurately predict costs is vital to a wide range of decision making situations.

We have looked at three types of cost behavior—variable, fixed, and mixed. In the case of mixed costs, we have studied three methods of breaking a mixed cost into its basic variable and fixed elements. The High-Low Method is the simplest of the three, having as its underlying assumption that the rate of variability is constant per unit of activity. When the rate of variability in a mixed cost is not constant, an average rate of variability must be computed. This can be done by either the Scattergraph Method or the Least Squares Method. Both methods require the construction of a regression line, the slope of which represents the average rate of variability in the mixed cost being analyzed.

The Least Squares Method is the most accurate of the two, in that it uses statistical analysis to fit a regression line to a group of observed data.

As stated above, managers use costs organized by behavior as a basis for many decisions. To facilitate this use, cost are often prepared for internal use in a contribution format. The unique thing about the contribution format is that it classifies costs on the income statement by cost behavior, rather than by function of production, administration, and sales.

QUESTIONS

5–1. Distinguish between (*a*) a variable cost, (*b*) a fixed cost, and (*c*) a mixed cost.

5–2. Define the following terms: (*a*) cost behavior, and (*b*) relevant range.

5–3. What is meant by an "activity base" when dealing with variable costs? Give several examples of activity bases.

5–4. Distinguish between (*a*) a variable cost, (*b*) a mixed cost, and (*c*) a step-variable cost. Chart the three costs on a graph, with activity plotted horizontally and cost plotted vertically.

5–5. The accountant often assumes a strictly linear relationship between cost and volume. How can this practice be defended in face of the fact that many variable costs are curvilinear in form?

5–6. What are discretionary fixed costs? What are committed fixed costs? What impact does management philosophy have on these two classes of costs?

5–7. What factors are contributing to the trend toward increasing numbers of fixed costs, and why is this trend significant from a managerial accounting point of view?

5–8. Does the concept of the relevant range have application to fixed costs? Explain.

5–9. What basic assumption underlies the High-Low Method of mixed cost analysis?

5–10. What methods are available for determining the average rate of variability in a mixed cost? Which method is most accurate? Why?

5–11. What is meant by a regression line? Give the general formula for a regression line. Which term represents the variable cost? The fixed cost?

5–12. Once a regression line has been drawn, how does one determine the fixed cost element? The variable cost element?

5–13. What is meant by the term "least squares"?

5–14. What is the difference between single regression analysis and multiple regression analysis?

5–15. What is the difference between the contribution approach to the income statement and the traditional approach to the income statement?

5–16. What is meant by contribution margin? How is it computed?

EXERCISES

5-1. Darby Manufacturing Company has observed that its maintenance cost is $5,000 when operating at a level of 20,000 machine hours per period. When the operating level drops to 15,000 machine hours, maintenance cost drops to $4,000.

Required:

1. What is the cost formula for maintenance?
2. What maintenance cost would you expect to be incurred at an operating level of 18,000 machine hours?

5-2. Pleasant View Hospital normally takes between 3,000 and 4,000 X-rays each year. The hospital has determined by analysis of its costs that the cost formula for X-rays within this range is $8,000 plus $3 for each X-ray taken.

Required:

1. Plot the cost of X-rays on a graph. Make cost the vertical axis and volume the horizontal axis. Clearly show the relevant range on the graph.
2. What total cost would be incurred if 5,000 X-rays were taken during a year?

5-3. Rapid Delivery, Inc., operates a fleet of delivery trucks in a large city. The company has determined that if a truck is driven 105,000 miles during a year the operating cost per mile is 11.4¢. If a truck is driven only 70,000 miles during a year the operating cost per mile increases to 13.4¢.

Required:

1. Determine the variable and fixed cost elements of the annual cost of truck operation.
2. If a truck is driven 80,000 miles during a year what total cost would you expect to be incurred?

5-4. The 19X4 income statement for the Forde Company appeared in the company's annual report as follows:

FORDE COMPANY
Income Statement
For the Year Ending December 31, 19X4

Sales		$420,000
Less cost of goods sold		200,000
Gross margin		220,000
Less operating expenses:		
Administrative	$ 80,000	
Selling	100,000	180,000
Net Income		$ 40,000

Production costs included depreciation, supervisory salaries, and other fixed costs which totaled $90,000. The remainder of the production costs were variable. Administrative expenses were 50 percent fixed and 50 percent variable. Selling expenses were 40 percent fixed and 60 percent variable.

Required:

1. Prepare an income statement for the Forde Company for 19X4 using the contribution approach.
2. For every dollar generated in sales, what is the contribution toward covering fixed expenses and toward earning profits?

5–5. Westmore Hospital contains 450 beds. The average occupancy rate is 90 percent per month. At this level of occupancy the hospital's operating costs are $16 per occupied bed per day, assuming a 30-day month. This figure contains both fixed and variable cost elements. During June the occupancy rate was only 80 percent. The following costs were incurred during the month:

Fixed operating costs.	$ 79,350
Mixed operating costs	105,600

Required:

1. Determine the variable cost per occupied bed on a daily basis.
2. Determine the total fixed operating costs per month.
3. Assume an occupancy rate of 86 percent. What total operating costs would you expect the hospital to incur?

5–6. The data below have been taken from the cost records of the Atlanta Processing Company. The data relate to the cost of operating one of the company's processing facilities at various levels of activity.

Month	Total Cost	Level of Activity
January.	$14,000	8,000 units processed
February	16,000	10,000
March	12,500	7,000
April	15,000	9,000
May.	12,250	6,500
June	11,700	6,000
July.	11,000	5,500

Required:

1. Prepare a scattergraph by plotting the above data on a graph. Plot cost on the vertical axis and activity on the horizontal axis. Fit a line to your plotted points by visual inspection.
2. What is the approximate monthly fixed cost? The approximate variable cost per unit processed?

5–7. The Alpine House, Inc., is a large retailer of ski equipment. The company's income statement for the most recent quarter is given below:

THE ALPINE HOUSE, INC.
Income Statement
For the Quarter Ended March 31, 19XX

Sales		$247,600
Cost of goods sold		148,560
Gross margin . . . . *.*		99,040
Less operating expenses:		
Selling expenses.	$41,620	
Administrative expenses	26,200	67,820
Net income		$ 31,220

The selling expenses are 70 percent variable and 30 percent fixed. The administrative expenses are 10 percent variable.

Required:

Redo the company's income statement in the contribution format.

PROBLEMS

5–1. *Least-Squares Method of Cost Analysis.* The Carter Distributing Company is in the process of analyzing its cost structure. The company has determined that the following mixed costs exist at various levels of production:

Month	Units Produced	Total Mixed Costs
January.	25	$45
February	18	22
March	21	40
April	15	36
May.	12	32
June	19	40

The company is anxious to break the mixed costs down into their basic variable and fixed cost elements in order to assist in planning and control of operations. They have asked you, as an expert in cost analysis, to assist in this task.

Required:

Using the least squares technique, perform the desired analysis of the mixed costs.

5–2. *High-Low Method of Cost Analysis.* Barco Company has computed *total* factory overhead costs at high and at low levels of activity to be as follows:

	Level of Activity	
	Low	High
Direct labor hours.	50,000	75,000
Total factory overhead costs.	$142,500	$176,250

The *total* factory overhead costs include variable costs, fixed costs, and mixed costs. The Barco Company has analyzed these costs at the 50,000 direct labor hours level of activity, and has determined that at that level these costs exist in the following proportions:

Variable costs	$ 50,000
Fixed costs	60,000
Mixed costs	32,500
Total factory overhead costs.	$142,500

The company wants now to split the mixed costs into their variable and fixed cost elements.

Required:

1. By means of the high-low method of cost analysis, split the mixed costs into their variable and fixed cost elements. Compute the variable element in terms of its amount per direct labor hour.
2. If the Barco Company works 65,000 direct labor hours, what should be the *total* factory overhead cost?

5–3. *Scattergraph and Least Squares.* Argyris Research Corporation has a fleet of ten autos which are used by company employees on company business. All expenses of operating these autos (with the exception of depreciation) are entered into an "Automobile Expense" account on the company's books. The company also keeps a careful record of the number of miles the autos are driven each month.

The president of Arygris Research Corporation wants to know the cost of operating the fleet of cars, in terms of the fixed monthly cost and the variable cost per mile driven.

The company's records of miles driven and total auto expense by month for the past year are given below:

Month	Total Mileage (in thousands)	Total Cost
January.	8	$ 3,200
February	12	3,400
March	16	3,900
April	10	3,400
May.	13	3,700
June	15	3,700
July.	11	3,500
August	14	3,700
September	9	3,300
October	14	3,600
November	12	3,600
December	10	3,300
	144	$42,300

Required:

1. By means of a scattergraph, determine the fixed and variable elements in monthly auto expense. Fit your regression line to

the plotted data by simple visual inspection. What is the total fixed expense per month? The variable rate per mile?

2. Determine the breakdown of monthly auto expense by the least squares method. (It is not necessary to prepare a graph.)

3. From the data determined in Part 2, prepare an equation that describes the operation of the fleet of cars for one month.

5–4. *High-Low Method of Cost Analysis.* Marvel Products, Inc.'s total overhead costs at various levels of activity are presented below:

Month	Machine Hours	Total Overhead Costs
Jan.	50,000	$162,000
Feb.	40,000	140,600
Mar.	60,000	183,400
Apr.	70,000	204,800

The total overhead costs listed above contain variable costs, mixed costs, and fixed costs. The proportion of these costs at the 40,000 machine-hour level of activity is:

Variable costs	$ 42,400
Mixed costs	58,900
Fixed costs	39,300
Total overhead costs	$140,600

The company wants to break the mixed costs down into a fixed cost element and a variable rate per machine hour.

Required:

1. By means of the high-low method, break the mixed costs down into fixed and variable elements, as desired by the company.

2. Express the company's *total* overhead costs in terms of a single cost formula. Present your formula in linear equation form.

3. What total overhead costs would you expect to be incurred at an operating activity level of 55,000 machine hours?

5–5. *Least Squares Analysis of Selling Expenses.** Assume that nine monthly observations of selling expenses in a retail firm are to be used as a basis for developing a formula for total selling expenses. The company has plotted total selling expenses at various levels of sales on a graph, and the plotted points indicate that total selling expense is a mixed cost in the form $Y = a + bX$. The observations of total selling expense at various levels of sales are:

---

* Adapted from the National Association of Accountants, *Separating and Using Costs As Fixed and Variable,* Accounting Practice Report no. 10.

Month	Total Sales (in thousands)	Total Selling Expense (in thousands)
1.	$ 22	$ 23
2.	23	25
3.	19	20
4.	12	20
5.	12	20
6.	9	15
7.	7	14
8.	11	14
9.	14	16
	$129	$167

Required:

Using the least squares technique, determine the cost formula for selling expenses.

5–6. *Contribution versus Traditional Income Statement.* Marbury, Inc., is a large distributor of pianos. The company purchases its pianos from manufacturers and resells them on a retail basis. Selected information gleaned from the company's records for the month of June is presented below.

1. During June the company sold 42 pianos and delivered them to the purchasers.
2. Pianos cost Marbury, Inc., $860 each on the average, and sell for $1,250 each.
3. The company's selling expenses consist of $40 freight on each piano sold and delivered, $20 insurance on each piano sold, and a 10 percent sales commission, based on selling price. The company also has $700 each month in advertising, $350 in utilities, and $1,200 in depreciation of sales facilities.
4. The company's administrative expenses consist of executive salaries of $2,200 each month, $300 in depreciation of office equipment each month, and monthly clerical expenses of $600 plus $12 for each piano sold.

Required:

1. Prepare an income statement for Marbury, Inc., for the month of June, using the traditional format, with costs organized by function.
2. Redo Part 1, this time using the contribution format, with costs organized by behavior.

5–7. *Identifying Cost Patterns.* Below are a number of cost behavior patterns that might be found in a company's cost structure. The vertical axis on each graph represents cost, and the horizontal axis on each graph represents level of activity (volume).

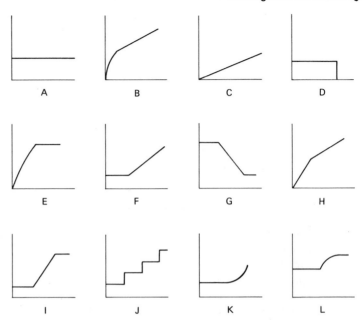

Required:

1. For each of the following situations, identify the graph which illustrates the cost pattern involved. Any graph may be used more than once.

   a. Cost of raw materials, where the cost decreases by $ .05 per unit for each of the first 100 units purchased, after which it remains constant at $2.50 per unit.

   b. Electricity bill—a flat fixed charge, plus a variable cost after a certain number of kilowatt hours are used.

   c. City water bill, which is computed as follows:

   First 1,000,000 gallons or less. . . . . $1,000 flat fee
   Next 10,000 gallons . . . .   .003 per gallon used
   Next 10,000 gallons . . . .   .006 per gallon used
   Next 10,000 gallons . . . .   .009 per gallon used
   Etc. . . . .   Etc.

   d. Depreciation of equipment, where the amount is computed by the straight-line method. When the depreciation rate was established, it was anticipated that the obsolescence factor would be greater than the wear and tear factor.

   e. Rent on a factory building donated by the city, where the agreement calls for a fixed fee payment unless 200,000 man-hours are worked, in which case no rent need be paid.

   f. Salaries of repairmen, where one repairman is needed for every 1,000 hours of machine hours or less (i.e., 0 to 1,000 hours requires one repairman, 1,001 to 2,000 hours requires two repairmen, etc.).

      g. Cost of raw material used.

      h. Rent on a factory building donated by the county, where the agreement calls for rent of $100,000 less $1 for each direct labor hour worked in excess of 200,000 hours, but a minimum rental payment of $20,000 must be paid.

      i. Use of a machine under a lease, where a minimum charge of $1,000 is paid up to 400 hours of machine time. After 400 hours of machine time, an additional charge of $2 per hour is paid up to a maximum charge of $2,000 per period.

2. How would a knowledge of cost behavior patterns such as those above be of help to a manager in analyzing the cost structure of his firm?

(AICPA, adapted)

5–8. *Scattergraph and Least Squares.* The Ferrera Company has had great difficulty in the past predicting its costs at various levels of output. The reason is that until now the company has never attempted to study its cost structure by analyzing the underlying cost behavior patterns. The president of the Ferrera Company has now become convinced that such an analysis is necessary if the company is to control its profitability and maintain its competitive position. Accordingly, an analysis of cost behavior patterns has been undertaken. The company has managed to isolate those costs which vary directly with output (variable costs), and those costs which do not vary with output (fixed costs). However, one group of costs has been isolated that does not exhibit either a strictly variable or a strictly fixed pattern. This group of costs in relation to output is shown below:

Level of Output in Units	Total Unexplained Costs Observed
20	$40
14	33
9	30
16	36
8	27
7	28

The president feels that this group of unexplained costs must contain a mixture of both variable and fixed costs. He has assigned you the responsibility of determining whether this is correct.

Required:

1. Prepare a scattergraph, using the output and cost data above. Place cost on the vertical axis and output on the horizontal axis. Fit a regression line to the plotted data, by visual inspection.

2. Is the president correct in assuming that the unexplained costs contain a mixture of fixed and variable costs? If so, what is the approximate total fixed cost, and the approximate variable cost per unit? Determine these amounts by analyzing your scattergraph.

3. Using the least squares technique, determine the approximate fixed cost and variable cost elements in the total cost observed. Notice that the variable cost and fixed cost elements obtained by a least squares analysis differ slightly from the variable cost and fixed cost elements which you worked out in part 2 above. How can you account for this difference?

5–9. *Contribution versus Traditional Income Statement.* The House of Organs, Inc., purchases organs from a well-known manufacturer and distributes them at a retail level, primarily to families for home use. The organs sell, on the average, for $3,500 each. The average cost of an organ from the manufacturer is $2,250.

The House of Organs, Inc.. has always kept careful records of its costs. The costs that the company incurs in a typical month are presented below:

Costs	Cost Formula
Selling:	
Advertising	$800 per month
Adjustment and tuning of delivered	
organs	$30 per organ sold
Freight on delivered organs	$75 per organ sold
Insurance on delivered organs. . . .	$60 per organ sold
Sales salaries.	$2,100 per month, plus 4% of sales dollars
Depreciation	$2,500 per month
Utilities	$280 per month
Administrative:	
Salaries	$2,500 per month
Depreciation	$950 per month
Clerical.	$750 per month, plus $15 per organ sold

During the month of December, 19X3, the company sold and delivered 27 organs.

Required:

1. Prepare an income statement for the month of December, 19X3, using the traditional format with costs organized by function.
2. Redo Part 1, this time using the contribution format, with costs organized by behavior.

5–10. *Multiple Choice on Cost Analysis.* Labor hours and production costs for the last four months of 19X1, which you believe are representative for the year, were as follows:

Month	Labor Hours	Total Production Costs
September	2,500	$ 20,000
October	3,500	25,000
November	4,500	30,000
December	3,500	25,000
	14,000	$100,000

Based upon the above information, select the best answer for each of questions 1 through 6.

Let a = Fixed production costs per month
b = Variable production costs per labor hour
n = Number of months
x = Labor hours per month
y = Total monthly production costs
Σ = Summation

1. The equation(s) required for applying the least squares method of computation of fixed and variable production costs could be expressed:
   a. $\Sigma xy = a\Sigma x + b\Sigma x^2$
   b. $\Sigma y = na + b\Sigma x$
   c. $y = a + bx^2$
      $\Sigma y = na + b\Sigma x$
   d. $\Sigma xy = a\Sigma x + b\Sigma x^2$
      $\Sigma y = na + b\Sigma x$

2. The cost function derived by the least squares method:
   a. Would be linear.
   b. Must be tested for minima and maxima.
   c. Would be parabolic.
   d. Would indicate maximum costs at the point of the function's point of inflection.

3. Monthly production costs could be expressed:
   a. $y = ax + b$
   b. $y = a + bx$
   c. $y = b + ax$
   d. $y = \Sigma a + bx$

4. The fixed monthly production cost in total is (use the high-low method):
   a. $10,000
   b. $9,500
   c. $7,500
   d. $5,000

5. The variable production cost per labor hour is (use the high-low method):
   a. $6.00
   b. $5.00
   c. $3.00
   d. $2.00

6. The least squares method of cost analysis must be used in those situations where:
   a. The mixed cost being analyzed consists of more than 50 per cent fixed cost.

    b. The variable portion of the mixed cost is constant per unit of activity.

    c. The fixed costs being analyzed are discretionary rather than committed.

    d. The variable portion of the mixed cost being analyzed must be determined in terms of some average amount per unit of activity.

(AICPA, adapted)

5–11. *High-Low Method of Cost Analysis.* Selected information on Appleby Company's operations at high and at low levels of activity is given below:

	Level of Activity	
	19X4–Low	*19X6–High*
Number of units produced.	10,000	15,000
Cost of goods manufactured.	$157,000	$225,000
Work in process inventory–beginning	12,000	15,000
Work in process inventory–ending	15,000	10,000
Direct material and direct labor cost per unit of product	10	10

The company's manufacturing overhead consists of both variable and fixed costs. In order to have data available for planning, the management of Appleby Company is very anxious to determine how much of the overhead is variable with units of product, and to determine how much is fixed in total.

Required:

1. By means of the high-low method of cost analysis, determine the cost formula for manufacturing overhead. Express the variable portion of the cost formula in terms of a variable rate per unit of product.

2. If 12,000 units of product are produced during a period, what would be the cost of goods manufactured, assuming that work-in-process inventories remain unchanged?

5–12. *Analysis of Cost Behavior.* Pleasant View Hospital has just hired a new chief administrator. The new chief administrator is anxious to employ sound management and planning techniques in the business affairs of the hospital. He has directed his assistant to summarize the cost structure existing in the various departments of the hospital, in terms of variable, fixed, and mixed cost present. In Department A, the assistant identified the variable and fixed costs fairly easily, but is uncertain how to classify the utilities cost of the department. He has observed utilities cost as follows over the past six months:

Month	Departmental Volume in Units	Utilities Cost Observed
January	60	$110
February	80	115
March	40	85
April	70	105
May	90	120
June	50	100

The chief administrator has informed his assistant that the utilities cost is probably a mixed cost, that will have to be broken down into its variable and fixed cost elements by use of a scattergraph. The assistant feels, however, that if an analysis of this type is necessary, then the high-low method should be used, since it is easier and quicker. The chief surgeon of the hospital, standing nearby and hearing the conversation, suggests that statistical least squares (which he heard about from his brother, who is a statistician) is the best approach.

Required:

1. Prepare a cost formula for the utilities expense of Department A, using the high-low method.
2. Repeat Part 1, this time using a scattergraph and fixing a trend line by visual inspection.
3. Repeat Part 1 again, this time using least squares analysis.

chapter 6

Cost-Volume-Profit Relationships

COST-VOLUME-PROFIT analysis involves a study of the interrelationship between the following factors:

1. Prices of products.
2. Volume or level of activity.
3. Per unit variable costs.
4. Total fixed costs.
5. Mix of products sold.

It is a key factor in many decisions, including choice of product lines, pricing of products, marketing strategy, and utilization of productive facilities. The concept is so pervasive in managerial accounting that it touches on virtually everything that a manager does. Although an understanding of cost-volume-profit relationships does not necessarily guarantee profits, it is an indispensable aid in uncovering profit potential in a firm.

THE BASICS OF COST-VOLUME-PROFIT ANALYSIS

The essence of cost-volume-profit analysis is gaining an understanding of how costs and profits change in response to changes in volume. In the preceding chapter we introduced the concept of cost/volume relationships, through our study of cost behavior. We need now to expand that discussion, and to integrate the profit dimension into it.

As a basis for discussion, let us assume the following situation:

The Barco Company leases booths at football stadiums and sells soft drinks. The company is anxious to expand the number of its outlets, and is now in the process of negotiating with State University for a booth in State University's newly completed stadium. The Barco Company has determined that the following costs and prices will probably characterize the new booth if it is opened:

Sale price per cup.		$ .25	100%
Variable expense per cup:			
Commission to State University.	$.06		
Soft drink in each cup	.05		
Cost of each paper cup.	.02	.13	52
Contribution margin per cup		$ .12	48%
Fixed expenses (per game):			
Lease cost of booth		$200	
Wages of 15 hawkers at $10 each.		150	
Liability insurance		10	
Total.		$360	

Should The Barco Company enter into a lease agreement with State University for a booth in the new stadium? In coming to a decision, the company will have to resolve questions such as the following:

1. What would be the break-even point for the booth in number of cups sold, and in dollars of sales?

2. What is the appearance of the cost-volume-profit data in graphical form?

3. If The Barco Company needs a minimum $600 in profits per game, how many cups will have to be sold? What will the dollar sales be?

4. If the booth is very successful and State University decides to double the lease cost, what will be the effect on the break-even point? How many cups will have to be sold to yield the minimum required $600 in profits?

5. Assuming the original data, if the cost of each paper cup doubles what will be the effect on the break-even point in number of cups sold? How many cups will have to be sold to yield the minimum required $600 in profits?

6. Assume that the booth is rented, and that 10,000 drinks are being sold each game. The Barco Company managers estimate that hiring five additional hawkers will result in an additional 1,000 drinks being sold each game. Should the five additional hawkers be hired?

7. Assume again that the booth is rented, and that 10,000 drinks are being sold each game. The Barco Company is contemplating increasing the sale price of each cup of drink from $.25 to $.30. The company estimates, however, that if the price is increased the number of drinks sold may decrease by as much as 30 percent. Should the price increase

be made? If the price increase is made, by how much can volume decrease and the company still earn at least the profits that were being
earned before?

8. Assume again that the booth is rented, and that 10,000 drinks
are being sold each game. The Barco Company is contemplating placing
the hawkers on a commission basis, rather than a flat $10-per-game
salary. The commission would be $.02 per cup sold. The company esti-
mates that if the hawkers are placed on a commission basis they will
sell 15 percent more drinks each game. Should the hawkers be paid
a commission rather than a flat salary?

The eight questions listed above are treated in order in the following
eight sections.

Break-Even Computations

**Question 1: What would be the break-even point for the booth in
number of cups sold, and in dollars of sales?**

Cost-volume-profit analysis is sometimes referred to simply as break-
even analysis. This is unfortunate, because break-even analysis is just
one part of the cost-volume-profit concept. However, it is often the
starting point in analytical work and can give the manager many insights
into the data at hand. Break-even analysis can be approached in two
ways—by the equation technique, and by the unit contribution
technique.

The Equation Technique. The equation technique centers on the
contribution approach to the income statement discussed in the preceding chapter. The format of the contribution income statement can be
expressed in equation form as follows:

$$\text{Sales} = \text{Variable Expenses} + \text{Fixed Expenses} + \text{Profits}$$

At the break-even point, profits will be zero. Therefore, the break-even
point can be computed by finding that point where sales just equal
the total of the variable expenses plus the fixed expenses.

To illustrate, refer to the data of The Barco Company above. If we
let X equal the number of cups of soft drink that must be sold for
the company to break even each game, the break-even point can be
computed as follows:

$$\text{Sales} = \text{Variable Expenses} + \text{Fixed Expenses} + \text{Profits}$$

$$\$.25X = \$.13X + \$360 + -0-$$
$$\$.12X = \$360$$
$$X = 3,000 \text{ cups}$$

where: X = break-even point in cups sold
  $ .25 = unit sales price
  $ .13 = unit variable expenses
  $360 = total fixed expenses

After the break-even point in *units sold* has been computed, the break-even point in *sales dollars* can be computed by multiplying the break-even level of units by the sales price per unit:

$$3,000 \text{ cups} \times \$.25 = \$750$$

At times, the *dollar* relationship between variable expenses and sales may not be known. In these cases, if one knows the *percentage* relationship between variable expenses and sales, then the break-even point can still be computed. To illustrate, notice from the original data that The Barco Company's variable expenses are 52 percent of sales. Rather than taking the dollar amount of variable expenses, we will use this percentage in the equation to compute the break-even point.

$$\text{Sales} = \text{Variable Expenses} + \text{Fixed Expenses} + \text{Profits}$$

$$X = .52X + \$360 + -0-$$
$$.48X = \$360$$
$$X = \$750$$

where: X = break-even point in sales dollars
  .52 = variable expenses as a percentage of sales
  $360 = total fixed expenses

Firms often have data available only in percentage form, and the approach we have just illustrated must be used to find the break-even point. Notice that use of percentages in the equation yields a break-even in *sales dollars*, rather than in units sold. If one has the break-even point in sales dollars, and wishes to translate it into units sold, it is necessary to divide by the sales price per unit:

$$\$750 \div \$.25 = 3,000 \text{ cups}$$

The Unit Contribution Technique. The unit contribution technique of break-even analysis is actually just a variation of the equation technique already described. The approach centers on the idea that each unit sold provides a certain amount of contribution margin that goes toward covering of fixed costs. To find how many units must be sold to break even, one must divide the total fixed costs by the contribution margin being generated by each unit sold.

$$\frac{\text{Total Fixed Expenses}}{\text{Unit Contribution Margin}} = \text{Break-even Point}$$

Each cup of drink which The Barco Company sells generates a contribution margin of $.12 ($.25 selling price, less $.13 variable expenses). Since total fixed expenses are $360, the break-even point is:

$$\frac{\text{Total Fixed Expenses}}{\text{Unit Contribution Margin}} = \frac{\$360}{\$.12} = 3{,}000 \text{ cups}$$

If only the *percentage* relationship between variable expenses and sales is known, the formula can still be used to compute the break-even point. In the case of The Barco Company, the unit contribution margin in percentage terms is 48 percent. Therefore, the break-even computation is:

$$\frac{\text{Total Fixed Expenses}}{\text{Unit Contribution Margin}} = \frac{\$360}{48\%} = \$750$$

When the "Unit Contribution Margin" is expressed in percentage form as above, it is usually referred to as the *profit/volume ratio,* or simply the *P/V ratio* for short. The P/V ratio for The Barco Company is 48 percent, since this is the percentage relationship between the company's contribution margin and sales. The formula for computing the break-even point when only percentages are known can be restructured as follows:

$$\frac{\text{Total Fixed Expenses}}{\text{P/V Ratio}} = \text{Break-even Point in Dollars}$$

The P/V ratio is discussed further in a later section of the chapter.

Cost-Volume-Profit Relationships in Graphical Form

Question 2: What is the appearance of the cost-volume-profit data in graphical form?

The data which The Barco Company has gathered on the new booth can be expressed in graphical form. Graphing of data can be very helpful, in that it highlights cost-volume-profit relationships over wide ranges of activity, and can give managers a perspective that can be obtained in no other way. Such graphing is sometimes referred to as preparing a "break-even chart." This is correct to the extent that the break-even point is clearly shown on the graph. The reader should be aware, however, that a graphing of cost-volume-profit data highlights cost-volume-profit relationships throughout the *entire* relevant range—not just at the break-even point.

Preparing the Cost-Volume-Profit Graph. Preparing a cost-volume-profit graph (sometimes called a "break-even chart") involves three steps. These steps are keyed to the graph in Exhibit 6–1.

EXHIBIT 6–1
Preparing the Cost-Volume-Profit Graph

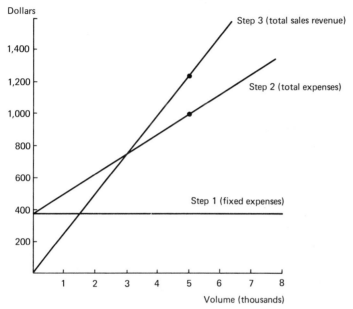

1. Draw a line parallel to the volume axis, representing total fixed expenses. For The Barco Company, total fixed expenses are $360.
2. Choose some volume of sales above zero, and plot the point representing total costs (fixed and variable) at that volume of sales. In Exhibit 6–1 we have chosen a volume of sales of 5,000 cups. Total costs for a sales volume of 5,000 cups would be:

> Fixed expenses . . . . $ 360
> Variable expenses (5,000 cups × $.13).   650
> Total $1,010

After the point is plotted, draw a line through it back to the point where the fixed expense line intersects the dollars axis.
3. Choose some volume of sales above zero, and plot the point representing total sales dollars at that volume. In Exhibit 6–1 we have again chosen a volume of sales of 5,000 cups. Total sales dollars at that volume of activity is $1,250 (5,000 cups × $.25). Draw a line through this point back to the origin.

The interpretation of the completed cost-volume-profit graph is given in Exhibit 6–2. The anticipated profit or loss at any given level of sales is measured by the vertical distance between the total revenue line (sales) and the total expense line (variable expense plus fixed expense).

EXHIBIT 6–2
The Completed Cost-Volume-Profit Graph

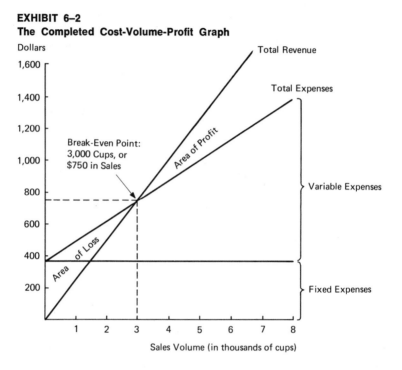

The break-even point is where these two lines cross. The break-even point of 3,000 cups in Exhibit 6–2 agrees with the break-even point obtained for The Barco Company in earlier computations.

An Alternative Approach. Another approach to the cost-volume-profit graph is presented in Exhibit 6–3. This approach, called a "profit-graph," is preferred by some managers because it focuses more directly on how profits change with changes in volume. It has the added advantage of being easier to interpret than the more traditional approach illustrated above. It has the disadvantage, however, of not showing as clearly how costs change with changes in the level of sales.

The "profit-graph" approach is constructed in two steps. These steps are illustrated in Exhibit 6–3.

1. Locate total fixed expenses on the vertical axis, assuming zero level of activity. This point will be in the "loss" area, equal to the total fixed expenses expected for the period.

EXHIBIT 6–3
Preparing the "Profit-Graph"

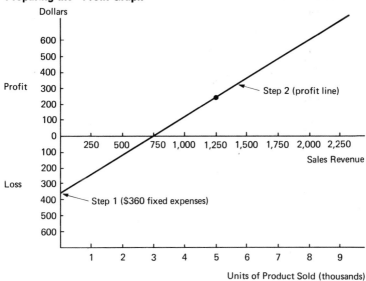

2. Plot a point representing expected profit or loss at any chosen level of sales volume. In Exhibit 6–3 we have chosen to plot the point representing expected profits at a sales volume of 5,000 cups. Expected profits at this sales volume are:

Sales (5,000 × $.25)	$1,250
Variable expenses (5,000 × $.13).	650
Contribution margin	600
Fixed expenses	360
Net income	$ 240

After this point is plotted, draw a line through it back to the point on the vertical axis representing total fixed costs.

The interpretation of the completed "profit-graph" is given in Exhibit 6–4. The break-even point is where the profit line crosses the break-even line. The vertical distance between these two lines represents the expected profit or loss at any given level of sales volume. This vertical distance can be translated directly into dollars by referring to the profit and loss figures on the vertical axis.

Working with Target Net Profit Requirements

Question 3: If The Barco Company needs a minimum $600 in profits per game, how many cups will have to be sold? What will the dollar sales be?

EXHIBIT 6–4
The Completed "Profit-Graph"

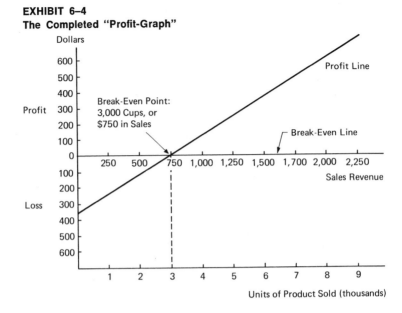

Sales needed to meet target net profit requirements can be computed in any one of several ways.

The Cost-Volume-Profit Equation. One approach would be to use the cost-volume-profit equation. The target net profit required can be added into the basic equation data. The solution to the equation will then show what level of sales is necessary to cover all expenses, *plus* yield the target net profit.

$$\text{Sales} = \text{Variable Expenses} + \text{Fixed Expenses} + \text{Profits}$$

$$\$.25X = \$.13X + \$360 + \$600$$
$$\$.12X = \$960$$
$$X = 8,000 \text{ cups.}$$

where: X = number of cups sold
 $\$.25$ = unit sales price
 $\$.13$ = unit variable expenses
 $\$360$ = total fixed expenses
 $\$600$ = target net profit

In order to realize a minimum target net profit of $600, The Barco Company must sell 8,000 cups of drink during each game. That number of cups would equal $2,000 in total sales ($8,000 \times \$.25$).

An Incremental Analysis. A second approach would be to do an *incremental* analysis, involving the target net profit alone. Each cup of drink sold *after the break-even point has been reached* will yield $.12 in contribution margin that can be applied toward covering the $600 target profit requirement. The number of cups that will have to be sold above the break-even point to generate $600 in profits can be computed as follows:

$$\frac{\$600 \text{ target net profit}}{\$.12 \text{ contribution margin per cup}} = 5,000 \text{ cups}$$

The Barco Company will have to sell 5,000 cups *above* the break-even point (a total of 8,000 cups) to yield a target net profit of $600.

The Profit-Graph. A third approach would be to refer to the "profit-graph" in Exhibit 6–4. Look on the vertical axis of the graph in Exhibit 6–4, and find the point of $600 in profits. From this point move your finger horizontally across the graph to the profit line. From the profit line move your finger downward to the sales line. You should reach a point on the sales line of 8,000 cups sold.

Fixed Cost Changes

Question 4: If the booth is very successful and State University decides to double the lease cost, what will be the effect on the break-even point? How many cups will have to be sold to yield the minimum required $600 in profits?

This question can be answered by again turning to the break-even equation. If the lease cost of the booth is doubled, total fixed expenses will increase from $360 to $560 ($360 plus $200).

Sales = Variable Expenses + Fixed Expenses + Profits

$.25X = $.13X + $560 + –0–
$.12X = $560
    X = 4,667 cups (as compared to 3,000 cups before
                    the fixed cost increase)

The break-even point has been increased from 3,000 cups to 4,667 cups, to reflect the doubling of the lease cost of the booth. If all else remains unchanged, an increase in fixed expenses will always raise the break-even point.

In order to maintain the desired $600 in profits, total sales in cups will have to be increased. Increased by how much? The answer is 1,667 cups, the same as the increase in the break-even point:

Sales = Variable Expenses + Fixed Expenses + Profits

$.25X = $.13X + $560 + $600
$.12X = $1,160
    X = 9,667 cups

Under our original assumptions, the company had to sell 8,000 cups to generate $600 in profits. It now has to sell 1,667 cups more, or a total of 9,667 cups, to generate $600 in profits.

Variable Cost Changes

Question 5: Assuming the original data, if the cost of each paper cup doubles what will be the effect on the break-even point in number of cups sold? How many cups will have to be sold to yield the minimum required $600 in profits:

A doubling of the cost of paper cups would increase total variable expenses to $.15 per cup of drink sold. It would reduce the contribution margin from $.12 to only $.10 per cup of drink sold. The new cost structure would be:

			$.25	100%
Sales price per cup			$.25	100%
Variable expense per cup:				
Commission to State University.	$.06			
Soft drink in each cup	.05			
Cost of each paper cup.	.04		.15	60
Contribution margin per cup			$.10	40%

Based on these new data, the break-even point becomes:

$$Sales = Variable\ Expenses + Fixed\ Expenses + Profits$$

$$\$.25X = \$.15X + \$360 + \text{--}0\text{--}$$
$$\$.10X = \$360$$
$$X = 3,600 \text{ cups}$$

The break-even point has gone from 3,000 cups up to 3,600 cups—an increase of 600 cups. What effect will the increase in variable cost have on the number of cups that must be sold to yield the target net profit of $600? Under our original assumptions, we determined that The Barco Company has to sell a total of 8,000 cups to generate $600 in profits. Will this figure now increase to 8,600 cups, to reflect the 600-cup increase in the break-even point? In the case of a change in fixed costs we saw that this was true, but what about the case of a change in variable costs? Try to think the answer through before you read on.

The answer is that total sales of cups will have to be increased by *more* than 600 cups. The reason is that a change in variable expenses not only changes total expenses, *but also changes the contribution margin as well*. In the case of The Barco Company, the contribution margin has been decreased from $.12 to only $.10 per cup of drink sold. *Due to the lower contribution margin,* even after the break-even point is reached it will take sales of a proportionately larger number of cups to generate the desired $600 in profits than it would have taken before the variable cost change. This can be proven by the basic cost-volume-profit equation:

$$\text{Sales} = \text{Variable Expenses} + \text{Fixed Expenses} + \text{Profits}$$

$$\$.25X = \$.15X + \$360 + \$600$$
$$\$.10X = \$960$$
$$X = 9{,}600 \text{ cups}$$

In order to generate $600 in profits The Barco Company must now sell 9,600 cups, rather than 8,000 cups as before. This represents an increase of 1,600 cups—not an increase of only 600 cups as might have been expected looking at the change in break-even point alone. The moral of this illustration is that changes in variable expenses normally carry a much greater impact on profits than a change in fixed expenses. The reason is that a change in variable expenses affects both costs *and* contribution margin, whereas a change in fixed expenses affects only costs. By means of this simple example we have been able to show rather dramatically why managers spend much more time, thought, and effort in controlling variable expenses than they do in controlling fixed expenses.

Incremental Changes in Both Costs and Revenues

Question 6: Assume that the booth is rented, and that 10,000 drinks are being sold each game. The Barco Company managers estimate that hiring five additional hawkers will result in an additional 1,000 drinks being sold each game. Should the five additional hawkers be hired?

Firms are usually anxious to increase total revenues. The only problem is that increased revenues are generally accompanied by increased expenses, and the expenses could outweigh the revenues.

Prepare an Income Statement. One approach to deciding on the additional hawkers would be to compute the expected net income from sales of 11,000 drinks, and compare it to the net income already being earned on sales of 10,000 drinks. If the net income from sales of 11,000 drinks is greater, then hire the additional hawkers.

An Incremental Analysis. A better approach would be to focus only on the *incremental* costs and revenues involved in the decision. Using the incremental approach keeps the data clearer, and permits the decision maker to focus his attention on the *specific* elements that will affect profitability.

In the case of The Barco Company, the incremental costs and revenues are:

```
Incremental revenues:
    1,000 drinks sold at $.25 each  . . . . . . . . . . .   $250

Incremental costs:
    Variable: 1,000 drinks at $.13 each  . . . . . . . .   $130
    Fixed: 5 new hawkers at $10 each  . . . . . . . . .      50
                                                           $180
```

Comparing the incremental revenues against the incremental costs shows that The Barco Company would be $70 better off each game by hiring the five additional hawkers.

Contribution Margin versus Fixed Costs. Still a third way to approach the problem would be to compare the *incremental contribution margin* from sale of 1,000 additional drinks against the *incremental fixed costs* that would be incurred in selling the drinks. The analysis is:

```
Incremental contribution margin:
    1,000 drinks sold, yielding a contribution margin of $.12 each . . . . .   $120

Incremental fixed costs:
    5 hawkers at $10 each . . . . . . . . . . . . . . . . . . . . . . . . . . . .    50
                                                                                 $ 70
```

The answer, of course, is the same—profits will increase by $70 per game if the five additional hawkers are hired.

What should the manager do in a decision situation such as this—prepare a full-blown income statement, as suggested in the first approach above, or prepare some type of incremental analysis, as suggested in the second two approaches above? Most managers would prefer an incremental analysis. The reason is that it is simpler, more direct, and, as mentioned earlier, allows the manager to focus on the *specific* items involved in the decision.

Change in Sales Price and in Sales Volume

Question 7: Assume again that the booth is rented, and that 10,000 drinks are being sold each game. The Barco Company is contemplating increasing the sale price of each cup of drink from $.25 to $.30. The company estimates, however, that if the price is increased the number of drinks sold may decrease by as much as 30 percent. Should the price increase be made? If the price increase is made, by how much can volume decline and the company still earn at least the profits that were being earned before?

If 10,000 drinks are currently being sold, then The Barco Company is realizing $1,200 in contribution margin and $840 in net income:

Sales (10,000 × $.25)	$2,500
Less variable expenses:	
(10,000 × $.13)	1,300
Contribution margin	1,200
Less fixed expenses.	360
Net income	$ 840

We have two problems to consider. First, should the price per drink be increased to $.30 if it will result in a 30 percent loss in sales volume? And second, if the price increase is made, by how much can sales volume decline and the company still earn at least $840 in profits?

Thirty Percent Loss in Sales Volume. As discussed in the preceding section, the best approach to a decision of this type is to prepare an incremental analysis, focusing on those items which change under the new operating conditions. The changes in data can be summarized as follows:

With a selling price of $.25, the contribution margin per unit is $.12, and the sales volume is 10,000 units. With an increase in the selling price to $.30, the contribution margin will increase to $.17 per unit, but the volume will drop to 7,000 units sold.

The impact on *net income* of these changes can be shown in the following form:

Old price/volume structure:
10,000 cups sold × $.12
contribution margin per cup . . . . $1,200 total contribution margin
New price/volume structure:
7,000 cups sold × $.17
contribution margin per cup . . . . 1,190 total contribution margin
Decrease in total contribution margin,
and net income . . . . $ 10

A key factor in decisions of this type is to recognize that *when fixed costs remain unchanged,* any change in contribution margin will be reflected dollar for dollar in changed net income. If contribution margin *in total* is reduced, then net income will also be reduced in total by an *equal* amount.

It appears from the data above that The Barco Company should not raise the price of its drinks to $.30 per cup. If the price is raised, and volume declines by 30 percent, then total profits will decrease by $10 per game.

Maximum Loss in Sales Volume. The second question centers on how far sales volume can decline without affecting total profits, if the selling price *is* raised to $.30 per cup of drink.

The question can be answered by returning to the basic cost-volume-profit equation:

$$\text{Sales} = \text{Variable Expenses} + \text{Fixed Expenses} + \text{Profits}$$

$$\$.30X = \$.13X + \$360 + \$840$$
$$\$.17X = \$1,200$$
$$X = 7,059 \text{ cups (rounded)}$$

where: X = number of cups sold
  $\$.30$ = unit sales price
  $\$.13$ = unit variable expenses
  $\$360$ = total fixed expenses
  $\$840$ = desired total profits (present level of profits)

In sum, if the selling price is raised from $.25 to $.30 per cup of drink sold, total sales volume in cups can drop from the present 10,000 cup level to only 7,059 cups, and the company will still earn $840 in profits. We can prove the accuracy of these figures by comparing the "old" and the "new" income statements:

$.25 Per Cup Selling Price		$.30 Per Cup Selling Price	
Sales (10,000 × $.25)	$2,500	Sales (7,059 × $.30)	$2,118
Less variable expenses:		Less variable expenses:	
(10,000 × $.13)	1,300	(7,059 × $.13)	918
Contribution margin	1,200	Contribution margin	1,200
Less fixed expenses	360	Less fixed expenses	360
Net income	$ 840	Net income	$ 840

Commission Payments versus Flat Salaries

Question 8: Assume again that the booth is rented, and that 10,000 drinks are being sold each game. The Barco Company is contemplating placing the hawkers on a commission basis, rather than on a flat $10-per-game salary. The commission would be $.02 per cup sold. The company estimates that if the hawkers are placed on a commission basis they will sell 15 percent more drinks each game. Should the hawkers be paid a commission rather than a flat salary?

If the switch to a commission basis is made, then both fixed and variable costs will change, as well as total sales volume. The changes in summary form are:

1. Sales volume will increase by 15 percent, from 10,000 to 11,500 cups sold each game.

2. Variable expenses will increase by $.02 per cup, from $.13 to $.15 per cup of drink sold.
3. As a result of the increase in variable expenses, contribution margin will decrease from $.12 to $.10 per cup of drink sold.
4. Fixed expenses will decrease by $150 per game (the salary formerly paid to the hawkers).

Using the incremental approach, the analysis as to whether the commission plan should be adopted would be:

```
Change in contribution margin:
  Old contribution margin: 10,000 cups × $.12. . . . . . . . . .   $1,200
  New contribution margin: 11,500 cups × $.10 . . . . . . . . .    1,150
  Loss in total contribution margin. . . . . . . . . . . . . . .       50
Change in fixed expenses:
  Fixed salaries avoided if a commission is paid. . . . . . . . .      150
Increased net income if the commission plan is adopted . . . . .  $  100
```

The same solution can be obtained by comparing the "old" and "new" income statements, with the new income statement incorporating the changes in cost-volume-profit data:

Flat Salary of $150 Paid to the Hawkers		Commission of $.02 per Cup Paid to the Hawkers	
Sales (10,000 × $.25)	$2,500	Sales (11,500* × $.25).	$2,875
Less variable expenses:		Less variable expenses:	
(10,000 × $.13)	1,300	(11,500 × $.15)†	1,725
Contribution margin	1,200	Contribution margin	1,150
Less fixed expenses	360	Less fixed expenses	210‡
Net income	$ 840	Net income	$ 940

* 10,000 × 115% = 11,500
† Former variable expenses of $.13 per cup, plus commission per cup added of $.02 equals new total variable expenses of $.15 per cup.
‡ Former fixed expenses of $360, less hawker salaries of $150, equals $210.

FURTHER USES OF COST-VOLUME-PROFIT ANALYSIS

The preceding sections have given us a good perspective of the variety of possible uses of the concepts involved in cost-volume-profit analysis. We need now to step away from the soft drink example and to look at some of the other ways in which managers use cost-volume-profit data in planning and decision making. The situations illustrated below are in no way intended to be inclusive of the possible applications of cost-volume-profit concepts. They are presented merely as being representative of some of the kinds of ways that cost-volume-profit data can be used in an organization.

Structuring Advertising Programs

Cost-volume-profit analysis is used widely by marketing managers in structuring advertising and promotional programs. To illustrate one such application, assume that the Dewey Company has three product lines—Line A, Line B, and Line C. Over the past several years the average performance of the lines has been as shown below:

	Line A	Line B	Line C
Sales	$300,000	$180,000	$250,000 (a)
Less variable expenses	180,000	135,000	205,000
Contribution margin	$120,000	$ 45,000	$ 45,000 (b)
Profit/volume ratio (b) ÷ (a).	40%	25%	18%

As mentioned earlier in the chapter, the percentage of contribution margin to total sales is often called the *profit/volume ratio,* or simply the *P/V ratio* for short. The P/V ratio shows how contribution margin will be affected by dollar changes in total sales. Notice, for example, that Line A has a P/V ratio of 40 percent. For each dollar increase in sales in Line A, total contribution margin will increase by $.40 ($1.00 sales × P/V ratio of 40 percent). *Net income in Line A will also increase by $.40, assuming that there are no changes in fixed costs.* Thus the term profit/volume ratio. *The impact on net income of any given dollar change in total sales can be computed in seconds by simply applying the P/V ratio to the dollar change.* If a company, for example, has a P/V ratio of 56 percent and plans a $70,000 increase in sales for the coming year, the impact will be:

$70,000 × 56% P/V ratio = $39,200 increased contribution margin.

Net income will also increase by $39,200 if the company's fixed costs do not change.

The P/V ratio is a very useful planning and decision-making tool. To show its application in marketing decisions, assume that the Dewey Company is trying to decide which product line to concentrate on in a promotional campaign over the next three months. The company has $5,000 in advertising funds available for the promotional campaign, but is unsure whether to concentrate on Line A, Line B, or Line C. Which product line does the reader think the company should concentrate on?

At first glance, one is inclined to say that the company should concentrate on Line A, since it has the highest P/V ratio. This answer would be correct if the advertising funds would yield the same total dollar sales regardless of whether they were spent in promoting Line A, Line B, or Line C. But undoubtedly some lines are nearer market saturation than others, and would not yield as much in incremental sales for the advertising dollars expended. Let us assume that the marketing division of the Dewey Company has made the following product line estimates of the incremental dollars of sales that can be realized for each advertising dollar spent:

Incremental Dollars of Sales for
Each Advertising Dollar Spent

Line A	$ 6
Line B	12
Line C	10

These incremental sales are related to the product lines' P/V ratios in Exhibit 6–5.

EXHIBIT 6–5
P/V Comparison of Product Lines

Product Line	(1) Incremental Dollars of Sales per Advertising Dollar Expended	(2) Total Advertising Dollars Available	(3) Total Incremental Sales (1) × (2)	(4) P/V Ratio	(5) Total Increased Contribution (3) × (4)
Line A	$ 6	$5,000	$30,000	40%	$12,000
Line B	12	5,000	60,000	25	15,000
Line C	10	5,000	50,000	18	9,000

The company should concentrate its advertising program on Line B. For the $5,000 expended, this product line will contribute more toward covering of fixed costs and toward profits than either of the other two product lines.

Structuring Commissions to Salespersons

Some firms base salespersons' commissions on contribution margin generated, rather than on sales generated. The reasoning goes like this: Since contribution margin represents the amount of sales revenue available to cover fixed expenses and profits, a firm's wellbeing will be maximized when contribution margin is maximized. By tying salespersons' commissions to contribution margin the salespersons are automatically encouraged to concentrate on that element which is of most importance to the firm. There is no need to worry about what mix of products the salespersons sell, because they will *automatically* sell that mix of products which will maximize the base on which their commissions are to be paid. That is, if salespersons are aware that their commissions will depend on the amount of contribution margin which they are able to generate, then they will use all of the experience, skill, and expertise which they have at their command to sell that mix of products which will maximize the contribution margin base. In effect, by maximizing their own wellbeing, they automatically maximize the wellbeing of the firm.

	Line A		Line B		Line C		Total	
	Amount	%	Amount	%	Amount	%	Amount	%.
Sales	$20,000	100%	$30,000	100%	$50,000	100%	$100,000	100%
Less variable expenses	15,000	75	18,000	60	40,000	80	73,000	73
Contribution margin	$ 5,000	25%	$12,000	40%	$10,000	20%	$ 27,000	27%
Sales mix.	20%		30%		50%		100%	

Although total sales remain unchanged at $100,000, the sales mix of Line B and Line C is exactly reversed from what it was in the preceding section. Line B now makes up 30 percent of total sales, whereas it made up 50 percent before, etc. Notice that this shift in sales mix toward the less profitable Line C has caused the average P/V ratio to drop from 31 percent in 19X1 to only 27 percent in 19X2.

The new break-even point will be:

$$\frac{\text{Total fixed costs } \$15,500}{\text{P/V ratio } 27\%} = \$57,407 \text{ sales to break even}$$

The break-even point has increased from $50,000 in 19X1 to $57,407 in 19X2, as a result of the shift in sales mix toward the less profitable Line C.

In preparing a break-even analysis, some assumption must be made concerning the sales mix. Usually, the assumption is that the sales mix will not change. However, if the manager *knows* that shifts in various factors (consumer tastes, etc.) are causing shifts in the mix of his company's sales, then these factors must be considered in any subsequent cost-volume-profit analyses. Otherwise, the manager may find himself making decisions on the basis of outmoded or faulty data.

Sales Mix and Per-Unit Contribution Margin. Sometimes the sales mix is measured in terms of the average per-unit contribution margin. To illustrate, assume that a company has two products—X and Y. During 19X1 and 19X2 sales of products X and Y were as follows:

	Contribution Margin per Unit	Total Units Sold		Total Contribution Margin	
		19X1	19X2	19X1	19X2
Product X	$5.00	1,000	2,000	$ 5,000	$10,000
Product Y	$3.00	3,000	2,000	9,000	6,000
		4,000	4,000	$14,000	$16,000
Average per-unit contribution margin ($14,000 ÷ 4,000 units)				$3.50	
Average per-unit contribution margin ($16,000 ÷ 4,000 units).					$4.00

Two things should be noted about the schedule above. First, note that the sales mix in 19X1 was 1,000 units of product X and 3,000 units of product Y. This sales mix yielded $3.50 in average per-unit contribution margin.

Second, note that the sales mix in 19X2 shifted to 2,000 units for both products, although *total* sales remained unchanged at 4,000 units. This sales mix yielded $4.00 in average per-unit contribution margin, an increase of $.50 per unit over the prior year.

What caused the increase in average per-unit contribution margin between the two years? The answer is the shift in sales mix toward the more profitable product X. Although total volume (in units) did not change, total and per-unit contribution changed simply because of the change in sales mix.

LIMITING ASSUMPTIONS IN COST-VOLUME-PROFIT ANALYSIS

Several limiting assumptions must be made when using data for cost-volume-profit analysis. These assumptions are:

1. That the behavior of both revenues and expenses is linear throughout the entire relevant range. The economist would differ from this view. He would say that changes in volume will trigger changes in both revenues and expenses in such a way that relationships will not remain linear.
2. That expenses can be accurately divided into variable and fixed categories.
3. That the sales mix is constant.
4. That inventories do not change in break-even computations (this assumption is considered further in Chapter 7).
5. That worker productivity and efficiency do not change throughout the relevant range.

SUMMARY

The least desirable of all worlds is one in which the manager is faced with high fixed costs, low contribution margin, and low volume. On the other hand, a manager would love to have low fixed costs, high contribution margin, and unlimited demand generating a high volume of sales. Most firms have to be content to fall somewhere between these two extremes. It is the responsibility of the manager to plan and control the mix of these factors in a way that will generate the maximum profitability for his firm.

QUESTIONS

6–1. What five factors are involved in a study of cost-volume-profit relationships?

6–2. How is the contribution approach to the income statement useful in break-even analysis?

6–3. Why is the term "break-even analysis" a misnomer?

6–4. What is meant by the term "break-even point"?

6–5. Name three approaches to break-even analysis. Briefly explain how each approach works.

6–6. Beta Company's total contribution margin just equals the company's total fixed costs. Is Beta Company operating at a profit or at a loss? Explain.

6–7. The equation for total expenses in the Carson Company is:

$$Y = \text{total expenses}$$
$$Y = 50,000 + 0.4X$$

If X represents dollars of sales, explain the significance of the 50,000 and the 0.4 items in the equation above.

6–8. What is meant by the term "sales mix"? Explain how a shift in the sales mix could result in a higher break-even point, and at the same time in a lower net income.

6–9. In response to a request from your immediate supervisor, you have prepared a cost-volume-profit graph portraying the cost and revenue characteristics of your company's product and operations. Explain how the lines on the graph would change if (*a*) the selling price per unit decreased, (*b*) fixed costs increased throughout the entire range of activity portrayed on the graph, and (*c*) variable costs per unit increased.

6–10. Al's Auto Wash charges $2 to wash a car. The variable costs of washing a car are 15 percent of sales. Fixed costs total $1,020 monthly. How many cars must be washed each month in order for Al to break even?

6–11. Often the most direct route to a business decision is to make an incremental analysis based on the information available. What is meant by an "incremental analysis"?

6–12. What is meant by a product's "profit/volume ratio"? How is this ratio useful in planning of business operations?

6–13. Able Company and Baker Company are competing firms. Each company sells a single product, Widgets, in the same market at a price of $50 per Widget. Variable costs are the same in each company—$35 per Widget. Able Company has discovered a way to reduce its variable costs by $4 per unit, and has decided to pass half of this cost savings on to its customers in the form of a lower price. Although Baker Company has not been able to reduce its variable costs, it also is thinking about lowering its selling price in order to remain competitive with Able Company. If each company sells 10,000 units each year, what will be the effect of the changes on each company's profits?

6–14. "Changes in fixed costs are much more significant to a company than changes in variable costs." Discuss.

6–15. Explain how the so-called "break-even formula" can be used as a profit-planning device.

EXERCISES

6–1. Spaceage Toys, Inc. sells a toy rocket at a price of $12. The variable costs of producing and selling the rocket are $8 per unit. Fixed costs associated with the rocket total $24,000 annually.

Required:

1. Assume that next year sales are projected to total 7,000 rockets nationally. Prepare an income statement, using the contribution format.
2. Prepare a cost-volume-profit graph, with units ranging from a volume of 1,000 to 10,000 units.
3. Prepare a "profit-graph" using the same volume range of 1,000 to 10,000 units.

6–2. The Baker Company manufactures and sells pre-hung doors to home builders. The doors are sold for $30 each. Variable costs are $20 per door, and fixed costs total $150,000 per year. Last year the firm reported a profit of $50,000.

Required:

1. Using the equation technique:
   a. What is the break-even point in units and in dollar sales?
   b. What was the volume in units and in dollar sales last year?
2. Repeat Part 1 using the unit contribution technique.

6–3. Fill in the missing amounts in each of the eight case situations below. Each case is independent of the others.
   a. Assume that only one product is being sold in each of the four following case situations:

Case	Units Sold	Sales	Variable Expenses	Contribution Margin per Unit	Fixed Expenses	Net Income
1	?	$50,000	$?	$4	$10,000	$10,000
2	8,000	?	40,000	3	?	9,000
3	3,000	45,000	?	?	18,000	(3,000
4	9,000	81,000	45,000	?	20,000	?

   b. Assume that more than one product is being sold in each of the four following case situations:

Case	Sales	Variable Expenses	Average Contribution Margin %	Fixed Expenses	Net Income
1	$180,000	$?	40%	$?	$12,000
2	300,000	165,000	?	100,000	?
3	?	?	30	80,000	(5,000)
4	400,000	260,000	?	?	30,000

6–4. A "break-even" chart, as illustrated below, is a useful technique for showing relationships between costs, volume, and profits.

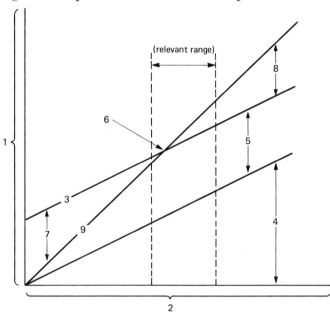

Required:

1. Identify the numbered components of the "break-even" chart.
2. Discuss the significance of the concept of the "relevant range" to break-even analyses.

(AICPA, adapted)

6–5. Dupler Company manufactures and sells a single product. Cost and revenue data on the product are given below:

Selling price per unit		$15.00
Variable costs per unit:		
Direct materials.	$1.00	
Direct labor	3.00	
Manufacturing overhead	2.00	
Selling and administrative expenses.	3.00	9.00
Contribution margin per unit		$ 6.00

Required:

1. Assume that the annual break-even volume of sales is $200,000. Compute the annual fixed costs of the Dupler Company.
2. The labor contract covering the Dupler Company's employees has just been renegotiated. The new contract calls for a wage increase of 8 percent on direct labor employees. By how much will the Dupler Company have to raise the selling price of its product in order to cover the wage increase and still realize a contribution margin ratio of 40 percent of sales?

6–6. The Roberts Company manufacturers and sells a single product. The product sells for $40. The contribution margin is 30 percent and fixed expenses are $120,000 per year.

Required:

1. What are the variable expenses per unit?
2. Using the equation technique:
    a. What is the break-even point in units and in dollar sales?
    b. What sales level in units and in dollar sales is required to earn a profit of $24,000?
    c. If the contribution margin is raised to 40 percent, what is the new break-even point in units and in dollar sales?
3. Repeat Part 2 using the unit contribution approach.

6–7. In each of the situations below, compute the number of units of product that must be sold to break even.

1. Theta Company's contribution margin is 60 percent of sales revenue. The company's products sell for $8 each. Fixed costs total $48,000 per year.
2. Beta Company's fixed costs total $90,000 annually. Each unit of product sold contributes $5 toward recovery of the company's fixed costs and to profits.
3. Alpha Company's variable costs as a percentage of sales revenue are:

Production.	35%
Selling	25
Administrative.	10
Total.	70%

Fixed costs total $105,000 each year, and units of product sell for $50 each.

4. Gamma Company's annual fixed costs are given below:

Production.	$60,000
Selling	10,000
Administrative.	14,000
Total.	$84,000

Units of product sell for $18 each, and variable expenses total $12 per unit.

5. Sigma Company's present sales total $150,000 annually, from which the company is reporting $12,000 in net income. For next year, sales volume is expected to drop by 10 percent. This 10 percent drop in sales volume will cause net income to decrease by 75 percent. The selling price per unit will remain unchanged at $40. Unit variable costs will also remain unchanged. What is Sigma Company's break-even point in units of product?

6. Last year Kappa Company reported net income of $18,000. Variable expenses totaled $84,000, or $6 per unit sold. For next year, the company expects sales volume to increase by 15 percent. However, the sales price per unit will remain unchanged, and variable expenses will remain unchanged at 40 percent of sales. What is the break-even point in units of product?

6–8. Carrier Company is one of several producers of a part used in the small appliance industry. The company is presently producing and selling 130,000 parts a year. Profits are $45,000 per year, based on a selling price of $4.00 per part. Fixed costs total $150,000 annually.

After a study of the market, the president is convinced that a 5 percent reduction in Carrier Company's selling price will result in a 20 percent increase in number of parts sold. Unit variable costs and total fixed costs will not be affected.

Required:

1. What will be the effect on net income if the price change is made?

2. How many units will have to be sold at the new selling price to yield the present $45,000 annual income?

6–9. Arbor Company produces and distributes vinegar at the retail level. The company's income statement for the most recent year is given below:

Sales (500,000 gal. @ $2.50).	$1,250,000
Variable expenses.	800,000
Contribution margin	450,000
Less fixed expenses.	460,000
Net loss.	$ (10,000)

Another manufacturing company that uses vinegar as an ingredient in its product has offered to buy 100,000 gallons of vinegar a year "if the price is right". Arbor Company would not have to pay the regular sales commission of 25¢ per gallon on this business. Regular business would be undisturbed by the manufacturing company sales.

Required:

What price per gallon should be quoted to the manufacturing company in order for Arbor Company to earn a net income of $15,000 per year on *total* vinegar sales?

PROBLEMS

6–1. *Straightforward Break-Even Computation, Graphing of Data, and Incremental Analysis.* Mr. Egon, president of the Tic-Tok Clock Company, recently completed a course in managerial accounting at the state university. He believes he can apply certain aspects of the course to his business. He is particularly interested in adopting the cost-volume-profit approach to decision-making. Thus, he has prepared the following analysis:

Sales price per clock		$8.00	100%
Variable expenses per clock:			
Materials	$2.00		
Labor	1.80		
Variable overhead	1.00	4.80	60%
Contribution margin		$3.20	40%
Fixed expenses (per year):			
Depreciation–equipment	$12,000		
Rental of building	24,000		
Selling	16,000		
Administrative	20,000		
	$72,000		

Required:

1. What is the break-even point in units and in dollar sales?
2. What is the appearance of the cost-volume-profit data in graphical form?
3. If net income was $19,200 last year, how many clocks were sold?
4. Mr. Egon presently has one full-time and one part-time salesperson working for him. It will cost Mr. Egon an additional $8,000 per year to convert the part-time position to a full-time position. He believes the move will bring in an additional $24,000 in sales each year. Should Mr. Egon convert the position? Show all calculations.

6–2. *Basics of CVP Analysis.* Harlow Company produces a product which sells for $15 per unit. Variable costs are $9 per unit, and fixed costs total $90,000 annually.

Required:

Answer the following independent questions:

1. What is the P/V ratio for the product?
2. Use the P/V ratio to determine the break-even point in sales dollars.
3. The company estimates that sales will increase by $25,000 during the coming year. By how much should net income increase?
4. The president would like to increase profits by $15,000. How much would sales have to increase in dollars?

  5. The sales manager is confident he can increase sales by $30,000 if he is given a greater advertising budget. What is the maximum amount the advertising budget could be increased with profits remaining unchanged?

  6. An order has been received from a wholesale distributor who wants to purchase 2,000 units. What price would have to be quoted to the distributor on these units if Harlow company wants to increase its overall profits by $3,000 per year?

  7. Assume that the company is presently selling 18,000 units annually. The sales manager would like to cut the selling price by 10 percent and increase the advertising budget by $21,500 annually. How many additional units would have to be sold each year to justify the changes?

6–3. *Rental Policy in a Motel.* The Kamver Corporation owns and operates a luxurious motel in a famous resort area. The corporation presently rents rooms to singles and groups of two or more people. The following data are representative of the past two years:

Average room rate.	$30.00 per night
Average variable expenses	4.00 per night
Average contribution margin	$26.00 per night
Fixed expenses	$1,170 per night

The motel has 120 rooms and an average occupancy rate of 90 percent.

Required:

  1. Prepare a contribution-type income statement, showing the average net income per night.

  2. What is the break-even point in rooms per night?

  3. The management is considering not renting rooms to singles. If this is done, it is believed that the average room rate will be $34.00 per night, average variable expenses will be $5.00 per night, and fixed costs will remain the same. It is expected that the occupancy rate will decline to 85 percent. Should this change be made? Show computations.

6–4. *Impact of a Manager's Salary on Contribution Margin and Net Income.* The Inrol Lamp Shop sells lamps to retail customers. The shopowner, Mr. Inrol, purchases the lamps from various sources and sells the lamps at a 60 percent markup over the purchase price. The lamps cost, on the average, $18 each. In addition to the cost of the lamps, other variable expenses are $2.80 per lamp. Fixed expenses are $360 per month.

Required:

  1. What is the break-even point in units and in dollar sales?

  2. What level of sales is required (in units and in dollars) in order to make a profit of $1,000 per month?

3. Mr. Inrol is going to hire a manager to run the shop. The manager will be paid $500 per month, plus a commission of $1 per lamp for the first 150 lamps sold each month, and $2 for each additional lamp sold. How many lamps must be sold each month for the shop to show a monthly profit of $400?

4. What possible problems might arise with the compensation plan for the manager? How can these problems be solved?

6–5. *Impact of Cost-Volume Changes on Net Income.* The following data pertain to the budget of Stuart & Adams for the next year:

Sales	200,000 units
Sales price	$1.50 per unit
Variable expenses.	$1.00 per unit
Fixed expenses	$50,000

Required:

1. What is the projected net income?
2. What would be the net income under each of the following independent cases?
   a. Sales volume increases by 10 percent.
   b. Sales volume decreases by 10 percent.
   c. Sales price increases by 10 percent.
   d. Sales price decreases by 10 percent.
   e. Variable expenses increase by 10 percent.
   f. Variable expenses decrease by 10 percent.
   g. Fixed expenses increase by 10 percent.
   h. Fixed expenses decrease by 10 percent.
   i. Sales volume increases by 10 percent, and sales price decreases by 10 percent.
   j. Variable expenses decrease by 10 percent, and fixed expenses increase by 10 percent.
   k. Sales volume increases by 10 percent, sales price decreases by 10 percent, variable expenses decrease by 10 percent, and fixed expenses increase by 10 percent.

6–6. *Changing Levels of Fixed and Variable Costs.* The Edman Company is considering a new product line which will require a fixed cost of $20,000 per month in order to manufacture 18,000 units. To manufacture over 18,000 units, the firm will have to spend an additional $12,000 in fixed costs per month. The product will sell for $2.50 per unit. Variable costs will be $1.60 per unit for the first 18,000 units, and $1.70 per unit for anything over 18,000 units.

Required:

1. What is the monthly break-even point in units and in dollar sales?
2. How many units must be sold in order to make a profit of $11,200 each month?
3. If the sales manager receives a bonus of $.10 per unit sold in excess of the break-even point, how many units must be sold in order to make a profit of $11,200 per month?

6–7. *The Case of the Suddenly-Appearing Fixed Costs.* The Denon Stein Shop sells steins from all parts of the world. The owner of the shop, Mr. Denon, is thinking of expanding his operations by hiring local college students, on a commission basis, to sell steins bearing the school emblem at the local college.

These steins must be ordered from the manufacturer three months in advance and cannot be returned because of the unique emblem of each college. The steins would cost Mr. Denon $2.50 each with a minimum order of 24 steins. Any number above 24 would have to be ordered in increments of 12.

Since this expansion plan would not require additional facilities, Mr. Denon's only costs for the project would be the costs of the steins and the costs of the sales commissions. The selling price of the steins would be $6.00. The sales commission would be $1.00 per stein.

Required:

1. In order to make the investment worthwhile, Mr. Denon would require a $300 profit for the first three months of the venture. What level of sales in units and in dollars would be required to reach this target net income?
2. Assuming that the venture is undertaken and that an order is placed, what would be the break-even point in units and in dollar sales? Explain the reasoning behind your answer. Assume an order of 24 steins.

√ 6–8. *Basics of CVP Analysis.* The Palumbo Company has been experiencing difficulty for some time. The company's income statement for the most recent period is given below:

Sales (6,000 units @ $12)	$72,000
Less variable expenses	54,000
Contribution margin	18,000
Less fixed expenses	22,000
Net loss	$ (4,000)

Required:

Answer each of the following independent questions:
1. What is the company's P/V ratio?
2. What increase in sales dollars would be necessary to change the company's net loss to a net income of $5,000 per period?
3. The sales manager is convinced that a one-dollar reduction in the selling price, combined with an increase of $8,000 in the advertising budget, would cause unit sales to double. What would the new income statement look like if these changes were adopted?
4. The president is certain that a $4,000 increase in the advertising budget, combined with an intensified effort by the salespersons, will result in a $25,000 increase in sales. If the president is right, what would the company's overall net income be in each period? Do not prepare an income statement.

5. Another company has offered to purchase 2,000 units on a special price basis. Variable selling expenses of $2 per unit could be avoided on these sales. What price per unit should be quoted by the Palumbo Company if it desires to make an overall net income of $3,000 for the company as a whole?

6. The company can reduce variable expenses by one third by using less costly inputs. Even though advertising would be increased by $4,000 per period, the lower overall quality of the product could result in a 25 percent loss in sales volume. Would you recommend that the changes be made? Do not prepare an income statement.

6–9. *Sensitivity Analysis of Net Income and Changes in Volume.* The Gerald Company's marketing expert, Mr. Rand, believes that the firm can increase sales by 5,000 units for each $2.00 per unit reduction in selling price. The company's present selling price is $80 per unit, and variable expenses are $50 per unit. Fixed expenses are $600,000 per year. Present sales volume is 30,000 units.

Required:

1. *a.* What is the present yearly net income?
   b. What is the present break-even point in units and in dollar sales?
2. *a.* Assuming that Mr. Rand is correct, what is the *maximum* profit that the firm could generate yearly? At how many units and at what selling price per unit would the firm generate this profit?
   b. What would be the break-even point in units and in dollar sales using the selling price you have determined above?

6–10. *Sales Mix.* Alpine, Inc., is a producer of recreational equipment. The company's sleeping bag division produces three types of sleeping bags—the Backpacker, the Regular, and the Economy. Selected information on the bags is given below:

	Backpacker	Regular	Economy
Selling price per bag	$60.00	$45.00	$32.00
Variable expenses per bag:			
Production	23.00	19.00	16.50
Selling	2.40	2.10	1.80
Administrative	1.10	1.10	1.10

The company operates on a regional basis, with sales restricted to the western United States. All sales are made through the company's own retail outlets. The cost records show that the following fixed costs are assignable to the sleeping bag division:

	Per Month
Fixed production costs	$43,250
Fixed selling costs	24,600
Fixed administrative costs	16,500
Total	$84,350

Sales of sleeping bags over the past two months have been:

	Backpacker	Regular	Economy	Total
May.	1,650	1,220	1,540	4,410
June	1,050	950	3,280	5,280
Total	2,700	2,170	4,820	9,690

Required:

1. Prepare an income statement for May, and an income statement for June. Use the contribution approach, with the following headings:

Total		Backpacker		Regular		Economy	
Amount	%	Amount	%	Amount	%	Amount	%

Sales
Etc.

Place the fixed expenses only in the "total" column. Do not show percentages for the fixed expenses.

2. Upon seeing the May and June income statements, one of the stockholders exclaimed, "The company needs a new manager in that sleeping bag division. Just look at these income statements. June sales are up, but net income is down. That manager just can't control costs." What other explanation can you give for the drop in net income?

3. Compute the division's break-even point in dollars for the month of May.

4. Has June's break-even point in dollars gone up or down from May's break-even point? Explain without computing a break-even point for June.

5. Assume that sales of the Backpacker bag increase by $10,000. What would be the effect on net income? What would be the effect if Regular bag sales increased by $10,000? Economy bag sales increased by $10,000? Do not prepare income statements.

6–11. *CVP Analysis.* (This problem requires a maximum of thought and a minimum of pencil-pushing.) An income statement for Deseret Company is given below:

Sales	$96,000
Less variable expenses	60,000
Contribution margin	36,000
Less fixed expenses.	30,000
Net income	$ 6,000

The Deseret Company has ample unused capacity, and is anxious to increase its overall net income.

Required:

Each of the situations below is independent of the others. Provide the information requested.

1. The company's marketing staff is certain that total sales can be increased by $20,000 each period if the advertising budget is increased by $8,000. If the staff is correct, what would the new net income be each period? Per-unit variable costs would not be affected by the sales increase. Do not prepare an income statement.

2. The company is thinking about changing its marketing method. Under the new method sales would increase by 15 percent, and net income would increase by one third. Fixed costs could be slashed to only $25,120 each period. Compute the break-even point for the company before and after the change in marketing method.

3. Due to a sudden and unprecedented surge in demand, the company's sales increased by 25 percent during one period. During that period net income doubled. Would you congratulate management for an outstanding performance, or would you chastise management for not doing its job well during the period? Explain.

√ 6–12. *Changing Sales Mix, Commission Structure, and the Break-Even Point.* The Calvin Pipe Company produces quality pipes out of carbon in a revolutionary manner. The company makes a standard model pipe and a deluxe model pipe, and sells them to retail tobacco shops throughout the country. The standard model pipes are sold to retailers for $10 each. The deluxe model pipes are sold to retailers for $12 each. The variable costs associated with each model of pipe are given below (in cost per pipe):

	Standard	Deluxe
Materials	$1.25	$1.25
Labor.	2.40	3.80
Variable factory overhead	1.20	1.90
Sales commissions (10% of sales price)	1.00	1.20
Total.	$5.85	$8.15

The Calvin Pipe Company's fixed expenses for each month are:

Depreciation–equipment	$ 3,600
Depreciation–building	3,200
Selling	2,000
Administrative	3,200
Total.	$12,000

Sales, in units, for the previous two months are as follows:

	Standard	Deluxe	Total
September	4,000	2,000	6,000
October	3,000	3,000	6,000

Required:

1. *a.* What was the net income for September and for October?
   b. Explain why there was a difference in net income between the two months, even though the same *total* number of pipes was sold in each month.
2. *a.* What might account for the shift in sales to the deluxe model in October?
   b. What can be done to the sales commissions to optimize the sales mix?
3. *a.* Using October's figures, what was the unit break-even point for the month?
   b. Has October's break-even point gone up or down from that of September? Explain your answer without resorting to calculating the break-even point for September.

part two
Uses of Managerial Accounting Data

chapter 7

Segmented Reporting, and the Contribution Approach to Costing

ONE ASPECT of the accountant's work centers on the problem of allocating costs to various parts of an organization. Cost allocation is necessary to provide useful and relevant data for three purposes:

1. For product costing and for pricing.
2. For appraisal of managerial performance.
3. For making special decisions.

There are two basic approaches to costing in use today. One is known as the absorption approach, and the other is known as the contribution approach. The absorption approach to costing was discussed at length in chapters 3 and 4. The contribution approach was discussed briefly in chapters 5 and 6. We need now to look more closely at the contribution approach to costing, to see what benefits it may have to offer in meeting the data needs listed above. Since the contribution approach emphasizes costs by behavior, many persons feel that it provides insights into cost data that are often obscured by the absorption approach.

COST ALLOCATION THROUGH THE CONTRIBUTION APPROACH

Segments of an Organization

To illustrate the contribution approach to costing it will be helpful to focus on the concept of *segments* of an organization. A segment can be defined as any portion or activity of an organization about which a manager seeks cost data. A single unit of product, a group or line of products, an operation, a department, a division, or a territory would all be examples of segments of an organization.

The contribution approach to costing attempts to assign costs to various segments of an organization according to:

1. Underlying cost behavior patterns, and
2. Whether the costs are *directly traceable* to the particular segment involved.

Under the contribution approach, no costs are arbitrarily assigned to a segment. If a cost cannot be traced *directly* to some segment, then it is treated as a *common cost* and kept separate from the segments themselves.

Exhibit 7–1 illustrates the contribution approach to costing, when segments of an organization are involved. We have chosen three ways to define the segments in this exhibit. We have defined the segments, first, as the divisions of the company. We have defined the segments, second, as the product lines in Division 2 alone. And third, we have defined the segments as the sales territories for one product line in Division 2.

Exhibit 7–1 should be studied with great care. A thorough understanding of the concepts on which it is constructed is critical to an understanding of the contribution approach to costing. We will now consider various parts of the exhibit in greater depth.

Contribution Margin

To obtain the contribution margin by segments, sales revenues and variable expenses must be allocated to the segments responsible for them. This is normally a simple task, since records are generally kept by segment showing sales and other activity.

Variable expenses deducted from sales revenue yields contribution margin. The concept of contribution margin is unique to the contribution approach to costing. No such concept exists in absorption costing. The reader will recall that the absorption approach to costing is based on a *functional* classification of costs, as illustrated in Exhibit 7–2, rather than on a classification by cost behavior.

Using the Contribution Margin. The contribution margin yielded by the contribution approach to costing is an extremely useful piece of data. It is particularly useful for determining the effect on net income of short-run changes in sales volume, as discussed in Chapter 6. If sales volume goes up or down, the impact on net income can be quickly computed by simply multiplying the per-unit contribution margin by the change in units sold, or by multiplying the change in sales dollars by the P/V ratio.

EXHIBIT 7–1
Cost Allocation through the Contribution Approach

Segments Defined as Divisions:

	Total Company	*Segments*	
		Division #1	Division #2
Sales	$90,000	$50,000	$40,000
Less variable expenses:			
Cost of goods sold	40,000	27,000	13,000
Other variable expenses	10,000	7,000	3,000
Total variable expenses	50,000	34,000	16,000
Contribution margin	40,000	16,000	24,000
Less direct fixed expenses	15,000	8,000	7,000
Divisional segment margin	25,000	$ 8,000	$17,000
Less common fixed expenses	16,000		
Net income	$ 9,000		

Segments Defined as Product Lines of Division #2:

	Division #2	*Segments*	
		Deluxe Model	Regular Model
Sales	$40,000	$15,000	$25,000
Less variable expenses:			
Cost of goods sold	13,000	5,000	8,000
Other variable expenses	3,000	2,000	1,000
Total variable expenses	16,000	7,000	9,000
Contribution margin	24,000	8,000	16,000
Less direct fixed expenses	3,000	1,000	2,000
Product line segment margin	21,000	$ 7,000	$14,000
Less common fixed expenses	4,000		
Divisional segment margin	$17,000		

Segments Defined as Sales Territories for One
Product Line of Division #2:

	Regular Model	*Segments*	
		Home Sales	Foreign Sales
Sales	$25,000	$18,000	$ 7,000
Less variable expenses:			
Cost of goods sold	8,000	6,000	2,000
Other variable expenses	1,000	300	700
Total variable expenses	9,000	6,300	2,700
Contribution margin	16,000	11,700	4,300
Less direct fixed expenses	1,000	700	300
Territorial segment margin	15,000	$11,000	$ 4,000
Less common fixed expenses	1,000		
Product line segment margin	$14,000		

EXHIBIT 7–2
Income Statement—Absorption Costing Basis

Sales		XXX
Less cost of goods sold:*		
Opening inventory	XX	
Cost of goods manufactured	XX	
Goods available for sale	XX	
Ending inventory	XX	XX
Gross margin		XX
Less operating expenses:*		
Selling expenses.	XX	
Administrative expenses	XX	XX
Net income		XX

* Includes both variable and fixed expenses.

Since the contribution margin is basically a short-run planning tool, it is especially valuable in decisions relating to temporary uses of capacity, to special orders, to short-term product line promotion, and to related kinds of activities. Decisions relating to the short-run usually involve only variable costs and revenues, which of course are the very elements involved in contribution margin. Thus, the contribution margin provides the manager with the exact tool he needs to make the decision that will maximize short-run benefits.

The Impact of Fixed Costs. If a short-run increase in sales results in increased fixed costs, the manager can readily relate the increased fixed costs to any anticipated increase in contribution margin, to see if the increase in sales is worthwhile. An increase in sales would be worthwhile only if the increased contribution margin exceeded the increased fixed costs. Computations of this type were illustrated in the preceding chapter. The point to be made here is that these kinds of analyses are not easily done when absorption costing is in use. The mingling of fixed and variable costs together under absorption costing often obscures the impact of short-run changes in volume on net income. The result is that managers may be forced to make "seat of the pants" estimates which can lead to costly errors in planning, and to misallocation of resources.

The Importance of Fixed Costs. The emphasis which we have placed on the usefulness of the contribution margin should not be taken as a suggestion that fixed costs are not important. *Fixed costs are very important in any organization.* What the contribution approach does imply is that *different costs are needed for different purposes.* For one purpose, variable costs and revenues alone may be adequate for a manager's needs; for another purpose his needs may encompass the fixed costs as well.

The breaking apart of fixed and variable costs also emphasizes to management that the costs are controlled differently, and that these differences must be kept clearly in mind for both short-run and long-run planning. Moreover, the grouping of fixed costs together under the contribution approach highlights the fact that net income emerges only after the fixed costs have been covered. It also highlights the fact that after the fixed costs have been covered, net income will increase to the extent of the contribution margin generated on each additional unit sold. All of these concepts are useful to the manager *internally*, for planning purposes.

Direct and Common Costs

Direct costs can be defined as those costs which can be identified directly with a particular segment, and which arise either because of the existence of the segment, or because of the activity within it. As stated in Chapter 2, direct costs can be *obviously* and *physically* traced to the unit (segment) under consideration.

Common costs can be defined as those costs which cannot be identified directly with a particular segment, but rather are identified in common with *all* segments of an organization. Common costs are costs that cannot be allocated to segments except on some highly arbitrary basis. They are also known as *indirect costs*.

In Chapter 2 the following guidelines were given in distinguishing between direct and indirect (or common) costs:

1. If a cost can be conveniently, obviously, and physically traced to a segment, then it is a direct cost with respect to that segment.
2. If a cost must be allocated in order to be assigned to a segment, then it is an indirect (common) cost with respect to that segment.

Examples of direct costs would include individual segment advertising and promotional outlays, salaries of segment supervisors, and depreciation of segment fixed assets. Examples of common costs would include salaries of top corporate administrative officers, corporate image advertising, and depreciation of facilities *shared by several* segments.

Classification Guidelines. As the reader may suppose, the distinction between direct and common costs is not always easy to maintain. One widely used rule of thumb is to treat as direct costs *only those costs that would disappear if the segment itself disappeared.* For example, if Division #1 in Exhibit 7–1 was discontinued, then it is unlikely that the division manager would be retained either. Since he would disappear with his division, then his salary should be classified as a direct fixed cost of Division #1. On the other hand, the president of the company very likely would continue even if Division #1 was dropped. There-fore, the cost of his salary is common to both divisions. The same idea can be expressed another way: treat as *direct costs* only those costs that are *added* as a result of the creation of a segment.

There will always be some costs that fall between the direct and common categories, which will require considerable care and good judg-ment for proper classification. The important point is to resist the tempta-tion to allocate arbitrarily. *Any arbitrary allocation of common costs would simply destroy the value of the segment margin as a guide to long-run individual segment profitability.*

Classifications Are Not Static. The reader should take particular note from Exhibit 7–1 that costs that are direct under one segment ar-rangement may be common under another segment arrangement. This is due to the fact that there are limits to how finely a cost may be separated. The more finely segments are defined, the more costs there are that become common.

To illustrate, notice from Exhibit 7–1 that when segments are defined as divisions, Division #2 has $7,000 in direct fixed costs. Only $3,000 of this amount *remains* direct, however, when we narrow our definition of a segment from divisions to that of product lines in Division #2 alone. Notice that the other $4,000 then becomes a *common* cost of Division #2 product lines.

	Total Company	Segments	
		Division #1	Division #2
Direct fixed costs	$15,000	$8,000	$ 7,000

	Division #2	Segments	
		Deluxe Model	Regular Model
Direct fixed costs	$ 3,000	$1,000	$ 2,000
Product line segment margin	21,000	$7,000	$14,000
Common fixed costs	4,000		
Divisional segment margin	$17,000		

Why would $4,000 of direct fixed costs become common costs when the division is broken down into product line segments? The $4,000 could be the monthly salary of the manager of Division #2. His salary would be a *direct* cost when we are speaking of the division as a whole. But his salary would be *common* to the separate product lines within the division, since it could be allocated to the product lines only on some arbitrary basis.

What about the $3,000 that remained a direct fixed cost even after Division #2 was broken down into product line segments? This amount could be advertising expended directly for the *individual* promotion of the Deluxe and Regular product lines. The amount would be a direct cost of the division as a whole, and would *remain* a direct cost when the division was broken down into its product line segments, since it could be physically traced in distinct amounts to the separate lines themselves.

A Company Can Be Viewed from Many Directions. The contribution approach to cost allocation gives a company the ability to look at itself from many different directions. Some of the ways in which cost and profitability data can be generated include:

1. By division.
2. By product lines.
3. By sales territory.
4. By region of the country.
5. By domestic and foreign operations.

In turn, each of these segments can be broken down into many parts. For example, data by sales territories could include: by individual salesperson, by sales district, by product lines within the territories, etc. The number of possible directions in which segments can be defined is limited only by one's imagination or by the needs of his firm.

Segment Margin

The divisional segment margin, the product line segment margin, and the territorial segment margin in Exhibit 7–1 were all obtained by deducting the direct fixed costs from the contribution margin of the segment. *The segment margin is viewed as being the best gauge of the long-run profitability of a segment.* It represents what remains after a segment has covered all of its own direct costs, that may be applied toward covering of common costs, and finally toward the net income of the firm as a whole.

The segment margin is especially useful in those decisions relating to long-run capacity, and to allocation of resources between various segments of an organization. For example, assume that the firm in Exhibit 7–1 is contemplating adding a new product line to Division #2 that would be known as the Special Deluxe Model. According to the best estimates of the accounting, marketing, and engineering staffs, the

following costs and revenues probably would characterize the new line
if it was introduced:

Sales	$10,000
Less variable expenses	5,000
Contribution margin	5,000
Less direct fixed expenses	2,000
Product line segment margin	$ 3,000

Should the decision to either add or reject the new line be based
on its projected contribution margin of $5,000, or on its projected seg-
ment margin of $3,000? The segment margin would clearly form the
basis for the decision. The contribution margin would not be an adequate
basis for a decision, since the question at hand relates to long-run capacity and involves the incurrence of direct fixed costs as well as variable
costs. Generally speaking, the contribution margin will be most useful
in those situations involving short-run decisions, such as pricing of special orders and special promotional campaigns. By contrast, the segment
margin will tend to be most useful in those situations involving long-run
capacity changes, and evaluation of long-run segment performance.

Common Costs and Net Income

Notice from Exhibit 7–1 that no attempt has been made to allocate
any of the costs falling below the segment margin line. Common costs
are not allocated, but simply deducted in total to arrive at the net
income for the company as a whole. Advocates of the contribution approach to cost allocation contend that nothing is added to the overall
usefulness of data by allocating common costs among the segments of
an organization. Rather, they would argue that such allocations tend
to *reduce* the usefulness of data. The reason is that arbitrary allocations
draw attention away from the costs over which a segment manager
has control, and which should form the basis for an appraisal of his
performance.

In addition, it is argued that any attempt to allocate common fixed
costs among segments of an organization may result in misleading data,
or may obscure important relationships between segment revenues and
segment earnings. Backer and McFarland state the problem as follows:

> A characteristic of all arbitrary allocations is that they lack universality.
> Sooner or later circumstances arise in which allocation procedures break
> down and yield misleading or even absurd results.[1]

---

[1] Morton Backer and Walter B. McFarland, *External Reporting for Segments of
a Business* (New York: National Association of Accountants, 1968), p. 23.

Backer and McFarland point out that arbitrary allocations of common fixed costs often result in a segment *appearing* to be unprofitable, whereas it may be contributing substantially above its own direct costs toward the overall profitability of the firm. In such cases, the arbitrary allocation of common fixed costs may lead to the unwise elimination of a segment, and to a *decrease* in total profits for the firm.

A General Model

In Exhibit 7–3 a general model is presented of the contribution approach to allocating costs in a firm.

EXHIBIT 7–3
The Contribution Approach to Cost Allocation—A General Model

	Total	*A*	*B*	*C*	*D*
			Segment		
Sales, tuition, fees, etc.	$XXX	$XX	$XX	$XX	$XX
Less variable expenses	XX	X	X	X	X
Contribution margin	XX	X	X	X	X
Less direct fixed expenses:					
Production	XX	X	X	X	X
Selling	XX	X	X	X	X
Administrative	XX	X	X	X	X
Total direct fixed expenses	XX	X	X	X	X
Segment margin	XX	$ X	$ X	$ X	$ X
Less common fixed expenses:					
Production	XX				
Selling	XX				
Administrative	XX				
Total common fixed expenses	XX				
Net income	$ XX				

The approach to cost allocation illustrated in this exhibit has wide application among many different kinds of organizations. It is equally applicable to the non-profit organization as it is to the profit-seeking organization. Hospitals, for example, are finding this approach to cost allocation to be extremely useful as a guide to assessing program effectiveness, and as an assist in overall decision-making and planning. Universities use the approach in such decision areas as planning evening and extension program offerings, and assessing program effectiveness through cost-benefit studies.

In a hospital the segments might be laboratory, X-ray, outpatient service, private rooms, semi-private rooms, therapy services, etc. In a university the segments might be by college or by department or by program. In an evening program of a university the segments might be by course offering, such as English Composition, Chemistry, Introductory Accounting, Business Finance, Music Appreciation, etc. The tuition yielded by each course could be compared against the direct costs of offering the course, as an assist to the administrator in his overall direction of the program. In a nonprofit organization such as a university the fact that a segment did not cover all of its own direct costs would be no necessary reason to eliminate the segment (course, department, etc.). But such information would be vital to intelligent cost-benefit studies, and to overall direction of the university.

Review Problem on Segmented Reporting

To pull together the concepts developed in this section, a review problem on segmented reporting is presented below.

1. Fairfield Company sells two products, X and Y:

	X	*Y*
Selling price per unit	$10	$6
Variable cost per unit	6	4
Contribution margin per unit	$ 4	$2

2. Sales in units during 19X1 were:

	East Division	*West Division*	*Total Sales*
Product X sales	3,000	7,000	10,000
Product Y sales	6,000	9,000	15,000

3. Fixed costs incurred during 19X1 were:

Production costs—Product X	$ 8,000
Production costs—Product Y	6,000
Selling costs—East Division	12,000
Selling costs—West Division	10,000
Administration costs—Product X	2,000
Administration costs—Product Y	1,500
Administration costs—East Division	2,200
Administration costs—West Division	2,300
General administrative costs	9,000

An income statement for the company for 19X1, with segments organized as product lines, would be prepared as follows:

	Total Firm	Product X	Product Y
Sales	$190,000	$100,000	$90,000
Less variable expenses	120,000	60,000	60,000
Contribution margin	70,000	40,000	30,000
Less direct fixed expenses:			
Production	14,000	8,000	6,000
Administration–Product lines	3,500	2,000	1,500
Total direct fixed expenses	17,500	10,000	7,500
Product line segment margin	52,500	$ 30,000	$22,500
Less common fixed expenses:			
Selling–Divisions	22,000		
Administration–Divisions	4,500		
General administrative	9,000		
Total common fixed expenses.	35,500		
Net income	$ 17,000		

If the company wanted to know its profitability by divisions, it could prepare an income statement as shown below, this time breaking total sales down by division, rather than by product line:

	Total Firm	Division	
		East	West
Sales	$190,000	$66,000[1]	$124,000[1]
Less variable expenses	120,000	42,000[2]	78,000[2]
Contribution margin	70,000	24,000	46,000
Less direct fixed expenses:			
Selling–divisions	22,000	12,000	10,000
Administration–divisions	4,500	2,200	2,300
Total direct fixed expenses	26,500	14,200	12,300
Divisional segment margin	43,500	$ 9,800	$ 33,700
Less common fixed expenses:			
Production.	14,000		
Administration–product lines.	3,500		
General administrative	9,000		
Total common fixed expenses.	26,500		
Net income	$ 17,000		

[1] Sales by division:

	East	West
Product X @ $10 per unit sold	$30,000	$ 70,000
Product Y @ $ 6 per unit sold	36,000	54,000
Total sales, as above	$66,000	$124,000

[2] Variable expenses by division:

	East	West
Product X @ $6 per unit sold	$18,000	$ 42,000
Product Y @ $4 per unit sold	24,000	36,000
Total variable expenses, as above.	$42,000	$ 78,000

INVENTORY VALUATION UNDER THE CONTRIBUTION APPROACH—DIRECT COSTING

As discussed in Chapter 3, absorption costing allocates a portion of fixed manufacturing overhead to each unit produced during a period, along with variable manufacturing costs. Since absorption costing mingles variable and fixed costs together, units of product costed by that method are not well suited for inclusion in a contribution-type income statement. This has led to the development of an alternative unit costing method that has come to be known as *direct costing*.

Direct Costing

Under direct costing, only variable manufacturing costs are included as part of the cost of a unit of product. Fixed manufacturing overhead is not viewed to be an inventoriable item; that is, it is not included as part of a product's cost of production. Rather, fixed manufacturing overhead is charged off against income each period in total as a *period cost*, much as are selling and administrative expenses.

To illustrate, assume the following data:

The Boley Company produces a single product. The cost characteristics of the product and of the manufacturing plant are given below:

```
Direct materials cost per unit . . . . . . . . . . . . . . . $3
Direct labor cost per unit  . . . . . . . . . . . . . . . . . $2
Variable manufacturing overhead cost per unit . . . . . $3
Fixed manufacturing overhead (total) . . . . . . . . . . $15,000
Number of units produced each year . . . . . . . . . . . 3,000
```

Required:

1. Compute the cost of a unit of product under absorption costing.
2. Compute the cost of a unit of product under direct costing.

Absorption Costing

```
Direct materials . . . . . . . . . . . . . . . . . . . . . . . . . . . $ 3
Direct labor . . . . . . . . . . . . . . . . . . . . . . . . . . . . . .   2
Variable overhead . . . . . . . . . . . . . . . . . . . . . . . . . .   3
    Total variable production cost . . . . . . . . . . . . . .   8
Fixed overhead ($15,000 ÷ 3,000 units of product) . . . . .   5
Total cost per unit . . . . . . . . . . . . . . . . . . . . . . . . $13
```

Direct Costing

```
Direct materials . . . . . . . . . . . . . . . . . . . . . . . . . . . $ 3
Direct labor . . . . . . . . . . . . . . . . . . . . . . . . . . . . . .   2
Variable overhead . . . . . . . . . . . . . . . . . . . . . . . . . .   3
Total cost per unit . . . . . . . . . . . . . . . . . . . . . . . . $ 8
```

(The $15,000 fixed overhead will be charged off in total against income as a period expense.)

If the Boley Company sells a unit of product, and absorption costing is being used, then $13 will be deducted on the income statement as cost of goods sold. If the company sells a unit of product, and direct costing is being used, then only $8 will be deducted as cost of goods sold. In a similar manner, under absorption costing, units of inventory on the balance sheet will be valued at $13 each. Under direct costing, units of inventory on the balance sheet will be valued at only $8 each.

The Controversy over Fixed Costs

The term "direct costing" is really a misnomer. Direct costing could more accurately be called variable or marginal costing, since it centers on the notion that only variable production costs should be added to the cost of goods produced. The term direct costing is so firmly imbedded in the literature, however, that it seems unlikely that any change in terminology will be made.

Probably no subject in all of managerial accounting has created as much controversy among accountants as direct costing. The controversy isn't over whether costs should be separated as between variable and fixed in matters relating to planning and control. Rather, the controversy is over the theoretical justification of excluding fixed production costs from inventory.

Advocates of direct costing take the position that fixed costs of production relate to the *capacity* to produce rather than to the production of specific units of product in any given year. That is, fixed costs of production such as depreciation and supervisory salaries are viewed as being costs that will be incurred regardless of whether any actual production takes place. For this reason, it is felt that they should be charged against the *period*, rather than against the *product*.

Advocates of absorption costing view the matter differently. They feel that the distinction between variable and fixed costs is immaterial so far as product costing is concerned. Since both fixed and variable costs are required in the production of goods, it is argued that both should be included in costing individual units of product.

Comparison of Absorption and Direct Costing

Income statements prepared under the absorption and direct costing approaches are shown in Exhibit 7–4. In preparing these statements the following data have been assumed:

		Cost of producing one unit of product:
Beginning inventory	-0-	
Units produced	5,000	Under direct costing:
Units sold	4,000	Variable cost of production
Sales price per unit	$ 10	only (all $10,000 of fixed
Selling and administrative expense:		production cost is charged against the period) $4
Variable per unit	$ 1	Under absorption costing:
Fixed (total)	$ 2,000	Variable cost of production . . . $4
Costs of production:		Fixed cost of production
Variable (direct materials, direct labor, and variable overhead) per unit	$ 4	($10,000 ÷ 5,000 units produced) 2
Fixed (total)	$10,000	Total $6

EXHIBIT 7–4
Comparison of Direct and Absorption Costing

Absorption Costing

Sales (4,000 units × $10)		$40,000
Cost of goods sold:		
Beginning inventory	$ -0-	
Cost of goods produced (5,000 units × $6)	30,000	
Goods available for sale	30,000	
Less ending inventory (1,000 units × $6)	6,000	24,000
Gross margin		$16,000
Less selling and administrative expense ($4,000 total variable, plus $2,000 fixed)		6,000
Net income		$10,000

Direct Costing

Sales (4,000 units × $10)		$40,000
Less variable expenses:		
Variable production costs (5,000 units × $4)	$20,000	
Less ending inventory (1,000 units × $4)	4,000	
Variable cost of goods sold	16,000	
Variable selling and administrative expense (4,000 units × $1)	4,000	20,000
Contribution margin		20,000
Less period costs:		
Fixed production costs	10,000	
Fixed selling and administrative expenses	2,000	12,000
Net income		$ 8,000

Note the difference in ending inventories $2 per unit fixed production cost is included under the absorption approach This explains the difference in ending inventory and in net income (1,000 units $2 = $2,000).

Several points should be noted from the statements in this exhibit:

1. Under absorption costing, the fixed costs of production are unitized (at $2 per unit) and added to the cost of the units produced. As units of product are sold, these fixed costs of production are released to expense as part of cost of goods sold. Units remaining unsold at

the end of a period carry a portion of these fixed costs of production *forward with them* to the next period. In Exhibit 7–4 1,000 units remain unsold at the end of the period. The $6,000 inventory value of these units is computed as follows:

Variable costs of production: 1,000 units × $4	$4,000
Fixed costs of production: 1,000 units × $2	2,000
Total inventory value.	$6,000

The $2,000 in fixed production costs carried forward in inventory to the next period will become an expense in that period as the units of product making up the inventory are sold. In summary, of the $10,000 total fixed costs of production incurred for the year, only $8,000 is charged against revenues as part of cost of goods sold. The remaining $2,000 has been *deferred* in inventory as part of the cost of unsold units of product.

2. Under direct costing, fixed costs of production are not included as part of the cost of units produced, but rather are expensed in total ($10,000) as a period cost, along with selling and administrative expenses. The expensing of all fixed costs of production explains the reason for the ending inventory value under direct costing being $2,000 lower than it is under absorption costing. Under direct costing, only the variable production costs have been inventoried:

Variable costs of production: 1,000 units × $4 . . . . $4,000

The difference in ending inventories also explains the difference in net income reported under the two costing approaches. Since under absorption costing we have *deferred* $2,000 of fixed costs in inventory, net income is $2,000 *higher* under that approach than it is under direct costing.

3. Since the absorption costing income statement makes no distinction between fixed and variable costs it is not well suited for cost-volume-profit computations, which we have emphasized as being important to good planning and control. In order to generate data for cost-volume-profit analysis, it would be necessary to spend considerable time reworking and reclassifying the absorption statement.

4. The direct costing approach to costing units of product blends very well with the contribution approach to the income statement, since both concepts are based on the idea of classifying costs by behavior. The direct costing data in Exhibit 7–4 could be used immediately in cost-volume-profit computations.

The Definition of an Asset

Essentially, the difference between the absorption and the direct costing approaches centers on the matter of timing. Direct costing advocates say that fixed manufacturing costs should be released against revenues immediately in total, whereas absorption costing advocates say that fixed manufacturing costs should be released against revenues bit by bit as units of product are sold. Any units of product not sold under absorption costing result in fixed costs being inventoried and carried forward *as assets* to the next period. The solution to the controversy as to which costing method is "right" should therefore rest in large part on whether fixed costs added to inventory fall within the definition of an asset as this concept is generally viewed in accounting theory.

What Is an Asset? A cost is normally viewed as being an asset if it can be shown that it has revenue producing powers, or if it can be shown that it will be beneficial in some way to operations in future periods. In short, a cost is an asset if it can be shown that it has *future service potential* that can be identified. For example, insurance prepayments are viewed as being assets, since they have future service potential. The prepayments acquire protection that can be used in future periods to guard against losses that might otherwise hinder operations. If fixed production costs added to inventory under absorption costing are indeed properly called assets, then they, too, must meet this test of service potential.

The Absorption Costing View. Advocates of absorption costing argue that fixed production costs added to inventory do, indeed, have future service potential. They take the position that if production exceeds sales then a benefit to future periods is created in the form of an inventory that can be carried forward and sold, resulting in a future inflow of revenue. They argue that *all costs* that are involved in the creation of inventory should be carried forward as assets—not just the variable costs. The fixed costs of depreciation, taxes, insurance, supervisory salaries, etc., are just as essential to the creation of units of product as are the variable costs. It would be just as impossible to create units of product in the absence of equipment as it would be to create them in the absence of raw materials, or in the absence of workers to operate the machines. In sum, until the fixed production costs have been recognized and attached, units of product have not been fully costed. Both variable and fixed costs become inseparably attached as units are produced, and *remain* inseparably attached regardless of whether the units are sold immediately, or carried forward as inventory to generate revenue in future periods.

The Direct Costing View. Direct costing advocates argue that a cost has service potential and is therefore an asset *only if its incurrence now will make it unnecessary to incur the same cost again in the future.* Service potential, therefore, is said to hinge on the matter of *future cost avoidance.* If the incurrence of a cost now will have no effect on whether or not the same cost will be incurred again in the future, then that cost is viewed as having no relevance to future events. It is argued that such a cost can in no way represent a future benefit or service.

For example, the prepayment of insurance is viewed as being an asset because the cash outlays made when the insurance is acquired make it unnecessary to sustain the same outlays again in the future periods for which insurance protection has been purchased. In short, by making insurance payments now, a company *avoids* having to make payments in the future. Since prepayments of insurance result in *future cost avoidance*, the prepayments qualify as assets.

This type of cost avoidance does not exist in the case of fixed production costs. The incurring of fixed production costs in one year in no way reduces the necessity to incur the same costs again in the following year. Since the incurring of fixed production costs does not result in *future cost avoidance*, the costs of one year can have no relevance to future events, and therefore cannot possibly represent a future benefit or service. Direct costers argue, therefore, that no part of the fixed production costs of one year should ever be carried forward as an asset to the following year. Such costs do not result in future cost avoidance—the key test for any asset.[2]

Extended Comparison of Income Data

Having gained some insights into the conceptual differences between absorption and direct costing, we are now prepared to take a more detailed look at the differences in income data generated by these two approaches to cost allocation. Exhibit 7–5 presents data covering a span of three years. In the first year, production and sales are exactly equal. In the second year production exceeds sales. In the third year the tables are reversed, with sales exceeding production.

Certain generalizations can be drawn from the data in this exhibit:

1. When production and sales are equal, the same net income will be produced regardless of whether absorption or direct costing is being used (see Year 1 in Exhibit 7–5). The reason is that when production and sales are equal there is no chance for fixed costs to be deferred in inventory or released from inventory under absorption costing.

2. When production exceeds sales, the net income reported under absorption costing will be greater than the net income reported under direct costing (see Year 2 in Exhibit 7–5). The reason is that when more is produced than is sold, a portion of the fixed production costs are deferred in inventory under absorption costing. For example, in

---

[2] For further discussion, see David Green, Jr., "A Moral to the Direct Costing Controversy?" *Journal of Business*, vol. 33, no. 3 (July 1960), p. 218–26; and Charles T. Horngren and George H. Sorter, "Direct Costing for External Reporting," *Accounting Review*, vol. 36, no. 1 (January 1961), p. 88–93.

EXHIBIT 7-5
Absorption Costing versus Direct Costing—Extended Income Data

Basic Data

Sales price per unit	$	12
Variable production costs per unit (direct materials, direct labor, and variable overhead)	$	5
Fixed production costs (total).	$24,000	

Cost of producing one unit of product:
  Under direct costing:

Variable production costs	$	5

  Under absorption costing:

Variable production costs	$	5
Fixed production costs (based on a normal production volume of 8,000 units per year—$24,000 ÷ 8,000)		3
Total absorption costs	$	8

Selling and administrative expenses are assumed to be all fixed, for simplicity, at $25,000 per year.

	Year 1	Year 2	Year 3	Three Years Together
Opening inventory in units.	–0–	–0–	1,000	–0–
Units produced during the year	8,000	8,000	8,000	24,000
Units sold during the year	8,000	7,000	9,000	24,000
Ending inventory in units	–0–	1,000	–0–	–0–
Direct Costing				
Sales	$96,000	$84,000	$108,000	$288,000
Less variable expenses	40,000*	35,000*	45,000*	120,000
Contribution margin	56,000	49,000	63,000	168,000
Less fixed expenses:				
Production	24,000	24,000	24,000	72,000
Selling and administrative	25,000	25,000	25,000	75,000
Total fixed expenses	49,000	49,000	49,000	147,000
Net income	$ 7,000	$ –0–	$ 14,000	$ 21,000
Absorption Costing				
Sales	$96,000	$84,000	$108,000	$288,000
Opening inventory	–0–	–0–	8,000	8,000
Cost of goods produced	64,000	64,000	64,000	192,000
Goods available for sale	64,000	64,000	72,000	200,000
Ending inventory	–0–	8,000	–0–	8,000
Cost of goods sold	64,000	56,000	72,000	192,000
Gross margin	32,000	28,000	36,000	96,000
Selling and administrative expenses. . . .	25,000	25,000	25,000	75,000
Net income	$ 7,000	$ 3,000	$ 11,000	$ 21,000

* Variable expenses: Year 1: 8,000 units sold × $5 = $40,000
                     Year 2: 7,000 units sold × $5 = $35,000
                     Year 3: 9,000 units sold × $5 = $45,000

EXHIBIT 7–6

Reconciliation of Direct Costing and Absorption Costing, Net Income Data from Exhibit 7–5

	Year 1	Year 2	Year 3
Direct costing net income	$7,000	$ –0–	$14,000
Add: Fixed production costs deferred in inventory under absorption costing (1,000 units × $3 per unit).	–	3,000	–
Deduct: Fixed production costs released from inventory under absorption costing (1,000 units × $3 per unit)	–	–	(3,000)
Absorption costing net income	$7,000	$3,000	$11,000

Year 2 $3,000 of fixed costs (1,000 units × $3/unit) have been deferred in inventory under the absorption approach. Only that portion of fixed production costs not deferred in inventory has been charged against income.

By contrast, under direct costing all of the fixed production costs have been charged against income. The result is that net income is $3,000 lower under direct costing than it is under absorption costing. Exhibit 7–6 contains a reconciliation of the direct costing and absorption costing net income figures.

3. When sales exceed production, the net income reported under the absorption costing approach will be less than the net income reported under the direct costing approach (see Year 3 in Exhibit 7–5).

The reason is that when more is sold than is produced, inventories are drawn down, and fixed costs that were previously deferred in inventory under absorption costing are released and charged against income. For example, in Year 3 the $3,000 fixed costs deferred in inventory under the absorption approach in the prior years are released from inventory through the sales process and charged against income. As a result, cost of goods sold for Year 3 contains not only all of the fixed production costs for Year 3 (since all that was produced in Year 3 was sold in Year 3), but also $3,000 of the fixed production costs of Year 2 as well.

By contrast, under direct costing only the fixed production costs of Year 3 have been charged against Year 3. The result is that net income under direct costing is $3,000 higher than it is under absorption costing. Exhibit 7–6 contains a reconciliation of the direct costing and the absorption costing net income figures.

4. Over an *extended* period of time the net income figures reported under absorption costing and direct costing will tend to be the same. The reason is that over the long run sales can't exceed production, nor can production much exceed sales. The shorter the time period, the more the net income figures will tend to vary.

Sales Constant, Production Fluctuates

Exhibit 7–7 presents a reverse situation from that depicted in Exhibit 7–5. In Exhibit 7–5 we made production constant, and allowed sales to fluctuate from period to period. In Exhibit 7–7, sales are constant, and production fluctuates. Our purpose in Exhibit 7–7 is to observe

EXHIBIT 7–7
Sensitivity to Changes in Production and Sales

	Basic Data		
Sales price per unit			$ 10
Variable production costs per unit			$ 4
Fixed production costs (total)			$24,000
Selling and administrative expense (all assumed, for simplicity, to be fixed)			$ 5,000

	Year 1	*Year 2*	*Year 3*
Number of units produced	6,000	8,000	4,000
Number of units sold	6,000	6,000	6,000
Cost of producing one unit:			
Under direct costing (variable production costs only)	$4	$4	$4
Under absorption costing:			
Variable production costs	$4	$4	$4
Fixed production costs ($24,000 total spread in each year over the number of units produced)	4	3	6
Total cost per unit	$8	$7	$10
Direct Costing			
Sales (6,000 units)	$60,000	$60,000	$60,000
Less variable expenses (6,000 units)	24,000	24,000	24,000
Contribution margin	36,000	36,000	36,000
Less fixed expenses:			
Fixed production expenses	24,000	24,000	24,000
Fixed selling and administrative expense	5,000	5,000	5,000
Total fixed	29,000	29,000	29,000
Net income	$ 7,000	$ 7,000	$ 7,000
Absorption Costing			
Sales (6,000 units)	$60,000	$60,000	$60,000
Opening inventory	–0–	–0–	14,000
Cost of goods produced	48,000	56,000	40,000
Goods available for sale	48,000	56,000	54,000
Ending inventory	–0–	14,000	–0–
Cost of goods sold (6,000 units)	48,000	42,000	54,000
Gross margin	12,000	18,000	6,000
Less selling and administrative expense	5,000	5,000	5,000
Net income	$ 7,000	$13,000	$ 1,000

the effect of changes in production on net income under both absorption and direct costing.

Direct Costing. Net income is not affected by changes in production under direct costing. Notice from Exhibit 7–7 that net income is the same for all three years under the direct costing approach, although production exceeds sales in one year, and is less than sales in another year. In short, the only thing that can affect net income under direct costing is a change in sales—a change in production has no impact when direct costing is in use.

Absorption Costing. Net income *is* affected by changes in production when absorption costing is in use. Notice from Exhibit 7–7 that net income goes up in Year 2, in response to the increase in production for that year, and goes down in Year 3, in response to the drop in production for that year. The reason for this effect can be traced to the shifting of fixed overhead between periods through the inventory account under absorption costing.

When production exceeds sales, then units of product are carried forward as inventory to the next period. These units of product take a portion of the current period's fixed costs forward to the next period with them, thereby relieving the current period of costs, and causing its income to rise in comparison with past periods. This effect can be observed in Year 2 in Exihibit 7–7. Even though Year 2 sold the same number of units as Year 1, its net income was substantially higher, due to the shifting of part of its fixed costs into Year 3.

The reverse effect occurs in Year 3. Since sales exceed production in Year 3, that year is forced to cover all of its own fixed overhead costs as well as the fixed overhead costs carried forward in inventory from Year 2. The result is a substantial drop in net income during Year 3, as shown in Exhibit 7–7.

Opponents of absorption costing argue that this shifting of fixed overhead between periods can be confusing to a manager, and can cause him either to misinterpret data or to make faulty decisions. The reader may recall from Chapter 4 that one way to overcome problems of this type is to use *normalized* overhead rates. Even if normalized overhead rates are used, the same problems can arise if the under- or overapplied overhead resulting from production being out of balance with sales is taken to cost of goods sold. The only way to avoid the problems entirely is to use normalized overhead rates, and to place any under- or over-absorbed overhead in a balance-sheet clearing account of some type.

Cost-Volume-Profit Analysis and Absorption Costing

Absorption costing is widely regarded as a product costing method. Many firms use the absorption approach exclusively because of its focus on "full" costing of units of product. If the approach has a weakness, it is to be found in its inability to dovetail well with cost-volume-profit analysis under certain conditions.

To illustrate, refer again to Exhibit 7–5. Let us compute the break-even point for the firm represented by the data in this exhibit. To obtain the break-even point, we divide total fixed costs by the contribution margin per unit:

Sales price per unit	$12
Variable costs per unit	5
Contribution margin per unit	$ 7
Fixed production costs	$24,000
Fixed selling and administrative costs	25,000
Total fixed costs	$49,000

$$\frac{\text{Total Fixed Costs}}{\text{Contribution Margin per Unit}} = \frac{\$49,000}{\$7} = 7,000 \text{ Units}$$

We have computed the break-even point to be 7,000 units sold. Notice from Exhibit 7–5 that in Year 2 the firm sold exactly 7,000 units, the break-even volume. Under the contribution approach, using direct costing, the firm does exactly break even in Year 2, showing zero net income or loss. *Under the absorption approach, however, the firm shows a positive net income of $3,000 for Year 2.* How can this be so? How can absorption costing produce a positive net income when the firm sold exactly the break-even volume of units?

The answer lies in the fact that in Year 2 under absorption costing $3,000 in fixed costs were deferred in inventory and did not appear as charges against income. By deferring these fixed costs in inventory, the firm was able to show a profit even though it sold exactly the break-even volume of units. This leads us to a general observation about absorption costing. The only way that absorption costing data can be used in a break-even analysis is to assume that inventories will not change. Unfortunately, such an assumption often falls far short of reality.

Absorption costing runs into similar kinds of difficulty in other areas of cost-volume-profit analysis, and often requires considerable manipulation of data before figures are available that are useable for decision-making purposes.

External Reporting and Income Taxes

For external reporting on financial statements, a company is required to cost units of product by the absorption costing method. In like manner, the absorption costing method must be used in preparing tax returns. In short, the contribution approach is limited to *internal* use, by the managers of a company.

The majority of accountants would agree that absorption costing *should* be used in external reporting. That is, most accountants feel that for *external reporting* purposes, units of product *should* contain a portion of fixed manufacturing overhead, along with variable manufacturing costs. The absorption costing argument that a unit of product is not fully costed until it reflects a portion of the fixed costs of production is difficult to refute, particularly as it applies to the preparing of information to be reported to stockholders and others.

The contribution approach finds its greatest application internally, as an assist to the manager in those situations where the absorption costing data are not well suited for cost-volume-profit analysis, or are not well suited for a segment-type analysis, such as covered earlier in the chapter. No particular problems are created by using *both* costing methods—the contribution method internally, and the absorption method externally. As we demonstrated earlier in Exhibit 7–6, the adjustment from direct costing net income to absorption costing net income is a simple one, and can be made in a few hours' time at year end, in order to produce an absorption costing net income figure for use on financial statements.

ADVANTAGES OF THE CONTRIBUTION APPROACH

As stated in the preceding section, many accountants feel that under the appropriate circumstances there are certain advantages to be gained from using the contribution approach (with direct costing) internally, even if the absorption approach is used externally for reporting purposes. These advantages have been summarized by the National Association of Accountants as follows:[3]

1. Cost-volume-profit relationship data wanted for profit planning purposes is readily obtained from the regular accounting statements. Hence management does not have to work with two separate sets of data to relate one to the other.
2. The profit for a period is not affected by changes in absorption of fixed expenses resulting from building or reducing inventory. Other things remaining equal (e.g., selling prices, costs, sales mix) profits move in the same direction as sales when direct costing is in use.
3. Manufacturing cost and income statements in the direct cost form follow management's thinking more closely than does the absorption cost form for these statements. For this reason, management finds it easier to understand and to use direct cost reports.
4. The impact of fixed costs on profits is emphasized because the total amount of such cost for the period appears in the income statement.

[3] *Direct Costing*, Research Series No. 23 (New York: National Association of Accountants, 1953), p. 55.

5. Marginal income figures facilitate relative appraisal of products, territories, classes of customers, and other segments of the business without having the results obscured by allocation of joint fixed costs.
6. Direct costing ties in with such effective plans for cost control as standard costs and flexible budgets.[4] In fact, the flexible budget is an aspect of direct costing and many companies thus use direct costing methods for this purpose without recognizing them as such.
7. Direct cost constitutes a concept of inventory cost which corresponds closely with the current out-of-pocket expenditure necessary to manufacture the goods.

SUMMARY

Cost allocation problems exist in every company. The contribution approach attempts to handle these problems by defining segments of an organization, and by classifying costs as being either direct or common to the segments. Only those costs that are direct to the segments are allocated. Costs that are not direct to the segments are treated as common costs, and are not allocated.

The contribution approach also classifies costs by behavior. For this reason those costs traceable *directly* to a segment are classified as between variable and fixed. Total variable costs deducted from sales yields a contribution margin, which is highly useful in short-run planning and decision making. The direct fixed costs of a segment are then deducted from the contribution margin, yielding a segment margin. The segment margin is highly useful in long-run planning and decision making. Segments can be arranged in many ways, including by sales territory, by division, by product line, by salesperson, etc.

In costing units of product in a manufacturing firm, the contribution method with direct costing adds only the variable manufacturing costs to units of product. The fixed manufacturing costs are taken directly to the income statement as expenses of the period.

Although the contribution approach cannot be used externally either for financial reporting or for tax purposes, it is often used internally by management. Its popularity internally can be traced in large part to the fact that it dovetails well with cost-volume-profit concepts that are often indispensable in profit planning and decision making.

QUESTIONS

7–1. Define a segment of an organization. Give several examples of segments.

7–2. How does the contribution approach attempt to assign costs to segments of an organization?

---

[4] Standard costs and flexible budgets are covered in Chapters 9 and 10 following.

7-3. Distinguish between a direct and a common cost. Give several examples of each.

7-4. Explain why the concept of a contribution margin is important to management.

7-5. Explain how the segment margin differs from the contribution margin. Which concept is most useful to the manager? Why?

7-6. In Chapter 4 we found that costs that were common to several departments (segments) were allocated to these departments on some basis, such as square footage of floor space. Why aren't common costs allocated to segments under the contribution approach to costing?

7-7. How is it possible for a direct cost under one segment arrangement to become a common cost under another segment arrangement?

7-8. In what way does absorption costing differ from direct costing?

7-9. Explain how fixed overhead costs are shifted from one period to another under absorption costing.

7-10. If production exceeds sales, which method would you expect to show the highest net income, direct costing or absorption costing? Why?

7-11. If sales and production are equal, which method would you expect to show the highest net income, direct costing or absorption costing? Why?

7-12. What arguments can be advanced in favor of adding fixed overhead to the cost of production?

7-13. What arguments can be advanced in favor of treating fixed overhead as a period cost, rather than as a cost of production?

7-14. What special assumption must be made in order to compute a break-even point under absorption costing?

7-15. What limitations are there to the use of the contribution approach (with direct costing)?

7-16. "One of the main objections to the contribution approach to costing is that it ignores fixed costs." Do you agree? Explain.

EXERCISES

7-1. The Fitz Company has two divisions, Division A and Division B. Operating data for a recent period are given below:

| | Total Company | Segments | |
		Division A	Division B
Sales	$140,000	$60,000	$80,000
Less variable expenses	100,000	40,000	60,000
Contribution margin	40,000	20,000	20,000
Less direct fixed expenses	16,000	8,000	8,000
Divisional segment margin	24,000	$12,000	$12,000
Less common fixed expenses	10,000		
Net income	$ 14,000		

Required:

1. How much would net income increase if Division A increased sales by $6,000?
2. How much would net income increase if Division B increased sales by $6,000?
3. How much would net income increase if Division A increased sales by $6,000 and increased fixed expenses by $800?

7–2. Refer to Exercise 7–1. Assume that Division A's sales by product are:

		Segments	
	Division A	*Product X*	*Product Y*
Sales	$60,000	$40,000	$20,000
Less variable expenses	40,000	30,000	10,000
Contribution margin	20,000	10,000	10,000
Less direct fixed expenses	5,000	2,000	3,000
Product line segment margin	15,000	$ 8,000	$ 7,000
Less common fixed expenses	3,000		
Divisional segment margin	$12,000		

The Fitz Company plans to spend $1,000 in direct advertising in Division A on either Product X or Product Y. If spent on Product X, sales of Product X will increase by $4,000. If spent on Product Y, sales of Product Y will increase by $3,500.

Required:

1. On which product line should the company spend the advertising funds? Show your calculations.
2. In Exercise 7–1, Division A shows $8,000 in direct fixed expenses. What happened to the $8,000 in this exercise?

7–3. The Virgil Company produces and sells a single product. The following cost data are available:

Direct materials cost per unit	$4
Direct labor cost per unit	$3
Variable manufacturing overhead cost per unit	$4
Fixed manufacturing overhead (total)	$20,000
Number of units produced each year	5,000

The selling price is $20 per unit. Selling and administrative expenses are $10,000 per year, and are all fixed.

Required:

1. Compute the cost of a unit of product under absorption costing.
2. Compute the cost of a unit of product under direct costing.
3. If 4,000 units are sold during a particular year, what is the net income under absorption costing? Assume there is no beginning inventory.

4. If 4,000 units are sold during a particular year, what is the net income under direct costing? Assume there is no beginning inventory.

7–4. Selected information on the operations of Gary Company for 19X4 is given below:

Units produced	4,000
Units sold	3,500
Units in beginning inventory.	-0-
Contribution margin ratio	50%
Direct materials used	$20,000
Direct labor	32,000
Selling and administrative expenses:	
Variable	16,000
Fixed.	21,000
Manufacturing overhead:	
Variable	24,000
Fixed.	28,000

The company maintains no work-in-process inventories.

Required:

1. Assume the company uses absorption costing. What is the ending finished goods inventory?
2. Assume the company uses direct costing. What is the ending finished goods inventory?
3. Which costing method would show the highest net income for 19X4? By how much?

7–5. The Porter Company sells Trinkets and Gadgets. An income statement for a recent period is given below:

	Total Sales	Trin- kets	%	Gad- gets	%
			Product Lines		
Sales	$500	$200	100%	$300	100%
Less variable expenses	240	90	45	150	50
Contribution margin	260	110	55%	150	50%
Less direct fixed expenses	150	80		70	
Segment margin.	110	$ 30		$ 80	
Less common fixed expenses	60				
Net income	$ 50				

The Trinkets and Gadgets are sold in a home market and in a foreign market, as follows:

	Home	Foreign
Trinket sales.	$120	$ 80
Gadget sales	190	110
Total sales	$310	$190

The common fixed expenses above are partly traceable to the home market, partly traceable to the foreign market, and partly traceable to general administration:

Home market fixed expenses	$20
Foreign market fixed expenses	25
General administration fixed expenses	15
Total common fixed expenses (above)	$60

Required:

Prepare a segmented income statement, as above, but this time with the segments defined as the home and foreign markets. (It is *not* necessary to state segment sales, variable expenses, etc., in percentage terms.)

7–6. Starco, Inc., uses absorption costing for external reporting purposes. The company's income statements for the last three years are given below:

	19X3	19X4	19X5
Sales	$80,000	$48,000	$96,000
Cost of goods sold	50,000	30,000	60,000
Gross margin	30,000	18,000	36,000
Selling and administrative expenses	15,000	15,000	15,000
Net income	$15,000	$ 3,000	$21,000

Sales and production data for these three years are:

Units produced	10,000	10,000	10,000
Units sold	10,000	6,000	12,000

Variable manufacturing costs total $3 per unit. Fixed overhead is applied to units of product on a basis of $2 per unit. Assume a Fifo inventory flow.

Required:

1. Prepare income statements for the three years, using direct costing.
2. Reconcile the absorption costing and direct costing net income figures for each year.

7–7. Income statements for Hal Company for 19X1 and 19X2 are given below (absorption costing basis):

	19X2	19X1
Sales	$120,000	$120,000
Cost of goods sold	83,200	88,000
Gross margin	36,800	32,000
Selling and administrative expense	20,000	20,000
Net income	$ 16,800	$ 12,000

Sales and production data are:

	19X2	19X1
Sales in units	8,000	8,000
Production in units	10,000	8,000
Variable production cost per unit.	$ 8	$ 8
Fixed overhead cost	$24,000	$24,000

Fixed overhead costs are applied to units of product on a basis of each year's production. Variable selling and administrative expenses are $1 per unit sold.

Required:

1. Compute the cost of producing one unit of product in 19X1 and in 19X2 by the absorption approach.
2. Explain why the net income for 19X2 was higher than the net income for 19X1, when the same number of units was sold in 19X2 as in 19X1. No computations are necessary.
3. Prepare income statements for 19X1 and 19X2 by the contribution approach, using direct costing.
4. Reconcile the 19X2 absorption costing and direct costing net income figures.

PROBLEMS

7-1. *Product Line Analysis.* Mr. Jayton, president of the Martin Company, wants a contribution-type income statement prepared by products. The following data are available for the firm:

Sales	$140,000
Less variable expenses	93,000
Contribution margin	47,000
Less fixed expenses.	25,000
Net income	$ 22,000

The firm produces three products. Sales, contribution margin ratios, and direct fixed expenses for the three products are as follows:

	Product A	*Product B*	*Product C*
Sales	$60,000	$50,000	$30,000
Contribution margin ratio	30%	40%	30%
Direct fixed expenses.	$ 8,000	$ 7,000	$ 5,000

Required:

1. Prepare a contribution-type income statement by products, as desired by Mr. Jayton. Include the net income for the entire firm in your statement.
2. The firm has an opportunity to increase sales of Product B by 50 percent. However, this would require an additional outlay

for fixed expenses of $8,000 per period. Prepare an analysis to determine whether the firm should undertake this expansion program.

7–2. *Prepare Contribution Income Statements.* The Michman Company sells its products in two markets. The firm sells to local retailers and sells to retailers outside the local area. Local sales are made through a salaried office force. All other sales are made through salespersons, who are paid a commission based on dollar sales. The following data are available for 19X8:

	Sales Area	
	Local	*Other*
Sales in units	15,000	30,000
Average sales price per unit	$ 20	$ 22
Average variable manufacturing expenses per		
unit.	$ 12	$ 14
Sales commissions		10% of sales
Direct fixed selling expenses.	$25,000	

Fixed manufacturing expenses are common, and total $100,000 per year. All other selling and administrative expenses are common, and total $140,000 per year.

Required:

1. Prepare a contribution-type income statement by sales area and in total for the firm.
2. What would the net income for 19X8 have been if the average selling price for each market had been reduced by $1 per unit, and the sales volume increased by 3,000 units in the local market and 7,000 units in the other market? Assume that the average variable manufacturing expenses per unit, and the total fixed expenses, do not change.

7–3. *A Comparison of Costing Methods.* The Staub Company manufactures and sells bus token boxes to a number of bus manufacturing companies. The Staub Company has used absorption costing for both financial and managerial purposes in the past, but now wants to use direct costing internally. The following data are available for the month of October:

Beginning inventory	$ –0–
Units produced	5,000
Units sold	4,500
Sales price per unit	$ 300
Selling and administrative expenses (all fixed)	50,000
Costs of production:	
Direct materials cost per unit	50
Direct labor cost per unit	60
Variable manufacturing overhead per unit.	30
Fixed manufacturing overhead (total)	50,000

Required:

1. Compute the cost of a unit of product under absorption costing.
2. Compute the cost of a unit of product under direct costing.
3. What is the net income for the month under absorption costing?
4. What is the net income for the month under direct costing?
5. Explain the reason for the difference in net income under absorption costing and direct costing.

7–4. *A Comparison of Costing Methods.* The Denall Company is a major manufacturer and seller of slot machines in Nevada. The firm's accounting department is preparing an income statement for 19X4, and has gathered the following data:

Beginning inventory	–0–
Units produced	10,000
Units sold	9,600
Sales price per unit	$ 1,300
Selling and administrative expenses:	
Variable per unit	60
Fixed (total)	700,000
Costs of production:	
Direct materials cost per unit	65
Direct labor cost per unit	140
Variable manufacturing overhead per unit	25
Fixed manufacturing overhead (total)	3,800,000

Required:

1. Prepare an income statement for the year, using absorption costing.
2. Prepare an income statement for the year, using direct costing.
3.   *a.* What is the value of the ending inventory under absorption costing?
     b. What is the value of the ending inventory under direct costing?
     c. Explain the reason for the difference in ending inventory under absorption costing and direct costing.

7–5. *Contribution Income Statement Prepared from Absorption Costing Data.* The income statement (using absorption costing) for the Swinson Company for the year ending December 31, 19X7, is presented below:

THE SWINSON COMPANY
Income Statement
for the year ending December 31, 19X7

Sales (14,000 units × $30 selling price)		$420,000
Less cost of goods sold:		
Beginning inventory	$ –0–	
Cost of goods produced (15,000 units × $20)	300,000	
Goods available for sale	300,000	
Less ending inventory (1,000 units × $20)	20,000	280,000
Gross margin		140,000
Less selling and administrative expenses		90,000
Net income		$ 50,000

Total fixed manufacturing expenses are $75,000 per year. The firm's contribution margin ratio is 40%. Some of the selling and administrative expenses are variable, and some are fixed.

Required:

1. Prepare an income statement for 19X7 using direct costing.
2. Mr. Calvin, president of the firm, has an opportunity to sell the remaining 1,000 units of the year's output at a price of $20 per unit. Assuming that the Swinson Company will not encounter any legal problems or loss of customer goodwill, should Mr. Calvin accept this offer? Show your calculations.

7-6. *Cost Allocation by Product Line and by Sales Territory.* Selected information relating to the operations of National Company for a recent period is given below:

	Product Line			
	A	B	C	Total
Sales in units	10,000	20,000	15,000	45,000
Selling price per unit	$ 15	$ 12	$ 7	$ –
Variable cost per unit for production, administration, and sales	9	9	5	–
Depreciation of production equipment	3,000	4,000	2,000	9,000
Product line supervisor	12,000	14,000	10,000	36,000
General factory overhead- fixed	–	–	–	10,000
Administrative expense- fixed	–	–	–	25,000
Selling expense–fixed	–	–	–	60,000

National Company products are sold throughout the United States, in three sales territories—the East, the Midwest, and the West. $20,000 of the $25,000 administrative expense above, and all of the $60,000 selling expense above is traceable to these three sales territories, as shown below. The percentage of product line sales made in each of the three sales territories is also shown below.

	Sales Territory			
	East	Midwest	West	Total
Administrative expense	$ 5,000	$ 5,000	$10,000	$20,000
Selling expense	14,000	16,000	30,000	60,000
Product line A.	40%	50%	10%	100%
Product line B	40%	40%	20%	100%
Product line C	20%	20%	60%	100%

Required:

1. Prepare a contribution-type income statement from the data above, by product line and for the company in total.
2. Prepare a contribution-type income statement from the data above, by sales territory and for the company in total.
3. Comment on the profitability of the various sales territories.

7-7. *Preparing and Using Segmented Data.* The Mitchfield Corporation manufactures and sells two types of electric room air freshners in its Special Products Division. The standard model sells for $20 per unit, and the executive model sells for $30 per unit. The contribution margin ratios for the standard model and the executive model are 30 percent and 40 percent, respectively.

Variable production costs are 40 percent of the selling price for the standard model, and 30 percent of the selling price for the executive model. All other variable costs are included as part of the selling and administrative expenses. Direct fixed expenses are $5,000 and $8,000 for the standard model and the executive model, respectively. An additional $6,000 in fixed expenses are considered to be common to the two product models.

An income statement is presented below for the fiscal year ending January 31, 19X6, using the contribution approach, and allocating costs by divisions:

| | | Division | |
	Total Company	Small Appliances	Special Products
Sales	$256,000	$130,000	$126,000
Less variable expenses:			
Variable production	82,800	39,000	43,800
Other variable expenses	72,800	35,000	37,800
Total variable expenses	155,600	74,000	81,600
Contribution margin	100,400	56,000	44,400
Less direct fixed expenses	45,000	26,000	19,000
Division segment margin	55,400	$ 30,000	$ 25,400
Less common fixed expenses	20,000		
Net income	$ 35,400		

Required:

1. Assuming that 3,000 standard models were sold during the fiscal year, prepare a segmented income statement for the Special Products Division. Use the contribution approach, where the segments are defined as the Standard Model and the Executive Model.
2. Determine the change in profits in each of the following independent situations:
   a. Standard model sales increase by 1,000 units.
   b. Executive model sales decrease by 1,000 units.

    c. Standard model sales increase by 1,000 units and direct fixed
expenses increase by $8,000.

    d. Executive model sales decrease by 1,000 units and direct fixed
expenses decrease by $6,000.

7–8. *Segmented Reporting and Analysis.* The Mast Corporation manufactures and sells three products, A, B, and C in two regional markets, X and Y. For the fiscal year just ended, the following absorption costing income statement was prepared:

	Total	Region X	Region Y
Sales	$2,600,000	$2,100,000	$500,000
Cost of goods sold	1,940,000	1,550,000	390,000
Gross margin.	$ 660,000	$ 550,000	$110,000
Selling and administrative expenses.	500,000	403,000	97,000
Net income	$ 160,000	$ 147,000	$ 13,000
Ratio of net income to sales.	6.2%	7.0%	2.6%

After reviewing the above results, Mr. Brothers, the president of the Mast Corporation, requested additional information on Region Y, because of the region's poor ratio of net income to sales. Mr. Brothers has suggested that it may be necessary to eliminate Region Y. In response to the president's request, the following additional information has been assembled for the current year:

1. Sales by product, and selected variable expense data:

	Products		
	A	B	C
Sales	$1,000,000	$1,000,000	$600,000
Variable manufacturing expenses as a percentage of sales	50%	50%	70%
Variable selling expenses.	$40,000	$40,000	$30,000
Variable selling expenses as a percentage of sales	4%	4%	5%

2. Sales of product by region:

Product	Region X	Region Y	Total
A	$ 800,000	$200,000	$1,000,000
B	900,000	100,000	1,000,000
C	400,000	200,000	600,000
	$2,100,000	$500,000	$2,600,000

3. Fixed selling expenses total $260,000 per year. $210,000 of this amount is incurred in Region X and $50,000 is incurred in Region Y.
4. Fixed administrative expenses total $130,000 per year. These expenses are common to the two sales regions. However, in the income statement above the fixed administrative expenses were allocated to the two regions on a basis of sales dollars. This allocation resulted in $105,000 being allocated to Region X and $25,000 being allocated to Region Y.
5. Fixed manufacturing overhead is common to the two regions.

Required:

1. Prepare a contribution-type income statement by region and in total for the company, for the current year.
2. Based on the data available, would you recommend elimination of Region Y? Explain.

7-9. *Preparing Segmented Income Statements.* The Philstor Company's income statement for 19X5, using the contribution approach, is as follows:

	Total Company	Segments	
		Division A	Division B
Sales	$190,000	$80,000	$110,000
Less variable expenses:			
Manufacturing	87,000	32,000	55,000
Other	9,500	4,000	5,500
Total	96,500	36,000	60,500
Contribution margin	93,500	44,000	49,500
Less direct fixed expenses	35,000	15,000	20,000
Divisional segment margin	58,500	$29,000	$ 29,500
Less common fixed expenses	25,000		
Net income	$ 33,500		

Selected additional information on Division B is presented below:

	Product		
	X	Y	Z
Sales	$40,000	$40,000	$30,000
Variable manufacturing expenses as a percentage of sales	60%	40%	50%
Other variable expenses as a percentage of sales	5%	5%	5%
Direct fixed expenses	$5,000	$5,000	$5,000

Product X is sold in a local market and in a regional market. Sales and other data on Product X are given below:

	Product X	Sales Market Local	Regional
Sales	$40,000	$30,000	$10,000
Variable manufacturing expenses as a percentage of sales	60%	60%	60%
Other variable expenses as a percentage of sales........................	5%	2%	14%

Direct fixed expenses of $4,000 are divided equally between the Local and Regional markets. Common fixed expenses total $1,000 for the two markets.

Required:

1. Prepare a segmented income statement for Division B using the contribution approach, with segments defined by product.
2. Prepare a segmented income statement for Product X using the contribution approach with segments defined by markets.
3. Mr. Stor, president of the company, wants to spend $1,000 on advertising of Product X in Division B. If he spends it in the local market, sales of Product X in the local market will increase by $3,000. If he spends it in the regional market, sales of Product X in that market will increase by $3,500. In which market should he spend the $1,000? Explain.

7–10. *Segmented Reporting.* Deseret College is located in a large metropolitan area. The school offers three courses to both day and night students. Selected information on the courses for the most recent term is given below:

	Executive Secretary	Sales Management	Commercial Art	Total
Number of students enrolled	400	250	200	850
Tuition per student..........	$ 350	$ 380	$ 400	$ —
Cost of supplies, etc., per student provided by the school each term	150	120	220	—
Course instruction cost—day program	10,000	15,000	13,000	38,000
Course instruction cost—night program	15,000	18,000	15,000	48,000
Depreciation of special equipment.............	10,000	2,000	12,000	24,000
Program advertising.........	—	—	—	20,000
Program supervision	—	—	—	15,000
Administration	—	—	—	18,000

Of the program advertising above, 25 percent is for the night program alone. The remainder is advertising for the school in general. Two thirds of the program supervision cost above relates to the day program, and the remainder to the night program. The portion of students attending the day program and the night program is given below for each course:

	Day Program	Night Program	Total
Executive Secretary course	70%	30%	100%
Sales Management course	20%	80%	100%
Commercial Art course.........	40%	60%	100%

Required:

1. Prepare a contribution-type income statement from the data above, by course and for the school in total.
2. Prepare a contribution-type income statement from the data above, by program and for the school in total.

7–11. *Absorption Costing, Direct Costing, and Shifting of Fixed Overhead.* Rayco, Inc., was organized on January 2, 19X1. Operating results for the first three years of activity were as follows:

	19X3	19X2	19X1
Sales	$75,000	$60,000	$75,000
Cost of goods sold:			
Opening inventory	20,000	–0–	–0–
Cost of goods produced	52,000	60,000	56,000
Goods available for sale	72,000	60,000	56,000
Less ending inventory	13,000	20,000	–0–
Cost of goods sold	59,000	40,000	56,000
Gross margin	16,000	20,000	19,000
Selling and administrative expenses.....	15,000	13,000	15,000
Net income	$ 1,000	$ 7,000	$ 4,000

Additional information on the operations of these three years is given below:

1. Sales and production data for the three years:

	19X3	19X2	19X1
Sales in units............	10,000	8,000	10,000
Production in units	8,000	12,000	10,000

2. Variable manufacturing costs were $2 per unit in each year. Fixed manufacturing costs totaled $36,000 in each year.
3. Variable selling and administrative expenses were $1 per unit in each year. The remainder of the selling and administrative expenses are fixed.

4. The company applies fixed manufacturing costs to units of product on a basis of each year's actual production.

5. Assume a Fifo inventory flow.

Required:

1. Explain why net income is higher in 19X2 than it is in 19X1, in light of the fact that less units were sold in 19X2 than in 19X1.

2. Explain why net income is lower in 19X3 than it is in 19X1, in light of the fact that the same number of units was sold in each year.

3. Prepare income statements for each year, using the contribution approach with direct costing.

4. Reconcile the absorption costing and direct costing net income figures for each year.

7-12. *The Case of the Perplexed President.* Budgeted sales for Advance Products, Inc., for the four quarters of 19X3 are given below, along with actual sales for the first two quarters of the year:

	First	Second	Third	Fourth
Budgeted sales in units	10,000	12,000	12,000	14,000
Actual sales in units.	10,000	12,000	—	—

The income statements for the first two quarters are presented below:

	First Quarter		Second Quarter	
Sales		$200,000		$240,000
Cost of goods sold:				
Opening inventory	$ 40,000		$ 60,000	
Cost of goods produced	120,000		80,000	
Goods available for sale.	160,000		140,000	
Less ending inventory. . . .	60,000		20,000	
Cost of goods sold	100,000		120,000	
Add underapplied overhead.	—	100,000	24,000	144,000
Gross margin		100,000		96,000
Less selling and administrative expenses.		80,000		90,000
Net income		$ 20,000		$ 6,000

Mr. Walter Ovard, the president of Advance Products, Inc., was looking forward to receiving the second quarter income statement. He knew that the sales budget of 12,000 units sold had been met during the second quarter, and that this represented a substantial increase in sales over the first quarter. Mr. Ovard was especially happy about the increase in sales, since Advance Products, Inc., was about to approach its bank for additional loan money for expansion purposes. Mr. Ovard anticipated that the strong second-quarter showing would be a real plus in persuading the bank to extend the additional credit.

For this reason, Mr. Ovard was shocked when he received the second-quarter income statement above, which showed a substantial drop in net income from the first quarter. Mr. Ovard was sure that there had to be an error somewhere, and immediately called the controller into his office to find the problem. The controller stated, "That net income figure is correct, Chief. I agree that sales went up during the quarter, but the problem is in production. You see, we budgeted to produce 12,000 units each quarter, but a strike in one of our supplier's plants forced us to cut production back to only 8,000 units in the second quarter. That's what caused the drop in net income."

Mr. Ovard was angered by the controller's explanation. "I call you in here to find out why income dropped when sales went up, and you talk about production! So what if production was off? What does that have to do with the sales that we made? If sales go up, then income ought to go up. If your statements can't show a simple thing like that, then we're spending too much money in your area!"

Fixed manufacturing overhead amounts to $72,000 each quarter. Variable manufacturing costs are $4 per unit. The fixed overhead is applied to units of product at a rate of $6 per unit, based on budgeted production of 12,000 units each quarter. Any under-or over-applied overhead is taken to cost of goods sold. Variable selling and administrative expenses are $5 per unit sold.

Required:

1. How would you have explained the drop in net income to Mr. Ovard?
2. Prepare income statements for each quarter using the contribution approach with direct costing.
3. Reconcile the absorption costing and direct costing net income figures for each quarter.

chapter 8

Profit Planning

IN THIS CHAPTER we are interested in looking at the planning that businesses do for profits—generally called *profit planning*. We shall see that profit planning is accomplished through the preparation of a number of *budgets*, which combined together form an integrated business plan known as the *master budget*. We shall find that the data going into the preparation of the master budget focus heavily on the *future*, rather than on the past.

THE BASIC FRAMEWORK OF BUDGETING

Definition of Budgeting

A budget is a detailed plan showing how resources will be acquired and used over some specific time interval. It represents a plan for the future expressed in formal quantitative terms. The act of preparing a budget is called *budgeting*. The use of budgets to control a firm's activities is known as *budgetary control.*

The *master budget* is a summary of all phases of a company's plans and goals for the future. It sets specific targets for sales, production, distribution, and financing activities, and generally culminates in a projected statement of net income and a projected statement of cash position. In short, it represents a comprehensive expression of management's plans for the future, and how these plans are to be accomplished.

Nearly Everyone Budgets

Nearly everyone prepares and uses budgets of some sort, even though they may not recognize what they are doing as budgeting. For example, most people make estimates of the income to be realized over some future time period, and plan expenditures for food, clothing, housing, etc., accordingly. As a result of this planning, spending will usually be restricted by limiting it to some predetermined, allowable amount. This type of action is using a budget as a control device. At other times, individuals will use estimates of income and expenditures to predict what their financial condition will be at some specific future time. The budgets involved here may exist only in the mind of the individual, but they are budgets nonetheless in that they involve plans of how resources will be acquired and used over some specific time period.

The budgets of a business firm serve much the same functions as the budgets prepared informally by individuals. Business budgets tend to be much more detailed and involve much more work in preparation (mostly because they are formal, rather than informal), but are similar in most other respects. As in the case of the individual, they assist in planning and controlling expenditures, and they assist in predicting operating results and financial condition in future periods.

Difference between Planning and Control

The terms planning and control are often confused, and occasionally used in such a way as to suggest that they are the same thing. Actually they are two quite distinct concepts. Planning involves the development of future objectives, and the formulation of steps to achieve these objectives. Control involves the means by which management assures that all parts of the organization function properly, and attain the objectives set down in the planning stage. To be completely effective, a good budgeting system must provide for *both* planning and control. Good planning without effective control is time wasted. On the other hand, unless plans are laid down in advance, there are no objectives toward which control can be directed.

Advantages of Budgeting

There is an old saying to the effect that "A man is usually down on what he isn't up on." A manager who has never tried budgeting or attempted to find what benefits might be available through the budget process is usually quick to state that budgeting is a waste of time. He may argue that even though budgeting may work well in *some* situations, it would never work well with his company because there are too many complexities and too many uncertainties involved. Yet this same man invariably will be constantly planning (albeit on an informal basis). He will have well-defined thoughts about what he wants to accomplish, and when he wants it accomplished. The difficulty is that unless he has some way of communicating his thoughts and plans to others, the only way the company will ever attain the desired objectives will be through accident. Even though such companies may attain a certain degree of success, they never attain the heights that could have been reached had the efforts of the entire organization been coordinated by means of a detailed system of budgets.

One of the great values of budgeting is that it requires managers to bring planning to the forefront of their minds. Moreover, it provides a vehicle for communicating these plans in an orderly way throughout an entire organization. No one has any doubt about what the boss wants to accomplish, or how he wants it done. Other benefits of budgeting:

1. It forces managers to think ahead by requiring them to formalize their planning efforts.
2. It provides definite goals and objectives which serve as *benchmarks* for evaluating subsequent performance.
3. It uncovers potential *bottlenecks* before they occur.
4. It *coordinates* the activities of the entire organization by *integrating* the plans and objectives of the various parts. By so doing, the budget insures that the plans and objectives of the parts are consistent with the broad goals of the entire organization.

Consider the following situation encountered by the author:

Company X is a mortgage banking firm. For years the company operated with virtually no system of budgets whatever. Management contended that budgeting wasn't well suited to their type of operation. Moreover, management pointed out that the firm was already profitable. Indeed, outwardly the company gave every appearance of being a well-managed, smoothly operating organization. If one took a careful look within, however, he found that day-to-day operations were far from smooth, and often approached chaos. The average day was nothing more than an exercise in putting out one brush fire after another. The cash account was always at crisis levels. At the end of a day no one ever knew if enough cash would be available the next day to cover required loan closings. Departments were uncoordinated, and it was not uncommon to find that one department was pursuing a course that conflicted with the course of another department. Employee morale was low and turnover was high. Employees complained bitterly that when a job was well done, nobody ever knew about it.

Company X was bought out by a new group of stockholders who required that the company establish an integrated budgeting system to control operations. Within one year's time, significant changes were evident. Brush fires were rare. Careful planning virtually eliminated the problems that had been experienced with cash, and departmental efforts were coordinated and directed toward predetermined overall company goals. Although they were very wary of the new budgeting program initially, employees became "converted" when they saw the positive effects that it brought about. The more efficient operations caused profits to jump dramatically. Communication increased throughout the organization. When a job was well done, everybody knew about it. As one employee stated, "For the first time we know what the company expects of us."

Choosing a Budget Period

Budgets covering acquisition of capital equipment (often called *capital budgets*) generally have quite long time horizons, and may extend 30 years or more into the future. The later years covered by such budgets may be quite indefinite, but at least management is kept planning ahead sufficiently to insure that funds will be available when purchases of equipment become necessary. As time passes, capital equipment plans that were once somewhat indefinite come more sharply into focus, and the capital budget is updated accordingly. Without such long-term planning, an organization can suddenly come to the realization that substantial purchases of capital equipment are needed, but find that no funds are available to make the acquisitions.

Operating budgets are ordinarily set to cover a one-year period. This one-year period should correspond to whatever fiscal year the company is following so that comparisons of budget to actual results can be made. Many companies divide their budget year into four quarters. The first quarter is then subdivided into months, and monthly budget figures are established. These near-term figures can usually be established with considerable accuracy. The last three quarters are carried in the budget at quarterly totals only. As the year progresses, the figures for the second quarter are broken down into monthly amounts, then the third quarter figures are broken down, etc. This approach has the advantage of requiring a constant review and reappraisal of budget data.

Continuous or perpetual budgets are becoming very popular. A continuous or perpetual budget is one which covers a 12-month period, but which is constantly adding a new month on the end as the current month is completed. Advocates of continuous budgets state that this approach to budgeting is superior to other approaches in that it keeps management thinking and planning a full 12 months ahead. Thus, it stabilizes the planning horizon. Under other budget approaches, the planning horizon becomes shorter as the year progresses.

The Self-Imposed Budget

The success of any budget program will be determined in large part by the way in which the budget itself is developed. Generally, the most

EXHIBIT 8–1
The Initial Flow of Budget Data
The initial flow of budget data is from lower levels of responsibility to higher levels of responsibility. Each person with responsibility for cost control will prepare his own budget estimates and submit them to his superior. These estimates are consolidated as they move upward in the organization.

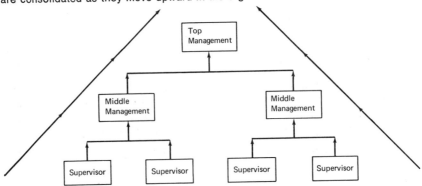

successful budget programs are those that permit persons with responsibility over cost control to prepare their own budget estimates, as illustrated in Exhibit 8–1. This approach to preparing budget data is particularly important if the budget is to be used in controlling a person's activities after it has been developed. If a budget is forced on a person from above, it likely will generate resentment and ill will rather than cooperation and increased productivity.

When a person prepares his own budget estimates, the budget which he prepares becomes *self-imposed* in nature. Certain distinct advantages arise from the self-imposed budget:

1. Individuals on all levels of the organization are recognized as members of the team, whose views and judgments are valued by top management.
2. The person in direct contact with an activity is in the best position to make budget estimates. Therefore, budget estimates tend to be more accurate and reliable.
3. A person is much more apt to work at fulfilling a budget which he has set himself than he is to work at fulfilling a budget imposed on him from above.
4. A self-imposed budget contains its own unique system of control, in that if an individual is not able to meet budget specifications he only has himself to blame. On the other hand, if a budget is imposed on him from above, he can always say that the budget was unreasonable or unrealistic to start with, and therefore was impossible to meet.

Once self-imposed budgets are prepared, are they subject to any kind of review? The answer is yes. Even though individual preparation of budget estimates is critical to a successful budgeting program, such budget estimates cannot necessarily be accepted without question by higher levels of management. If no system of checks and balances is present, the danger exists that self-imposed budgets will be too loose, and allow too much freedom in activities. The result will be inefficiency and waste. Therefore, before budgets are accepted, they must be carefully reviewed by immediate superiors. If changes from the original budget seem desirable, the items in question are discussed, and compromises reached that are acceptable to all concerned.

In essence, all levels of an organization work together to produce the budget. Since top management is generally unfamiliar with detailed, day-to-day cost matters, they will rely on subordinates to provide detailed budget information. On the other hand, top management has a perspective on the company as a whole that is vital in making broad policy decisions in budget preparation. Each level of responsibility in an organization contributes in the way that it best can in a *cooperative* effort to develop an integrated budget document.

The Matter of Human Relations

The attitudes of lower management personnel toward the budget program will in large part be a reflection of the attitude of top management, and a reflection of the way in which top management *uses* budgeted data.

If a budget program is to be successful, it must have the wholehearted support of top management. Moreover, the budget should never be used as an excuse to conduct "witch hunts" or to find someone to "blame" for a particular problem. Employees are rarely excited about any technique that makes it possible for a superior to "check up" on their performance. If the technique is used as a device to beat them over the head, or to hold them up in shame to their peers, then it becomes all but intolerable, and will be destined for almost certain failure.

The budget should never be used in any way as a tool for harassing an employee. Rather, it should be used as a positive instrument to aid the company in setting standards of performance, in measuring results, in working toward short- and long-range goals, and in isolating areas that are in need of extra effort or attention. Any misgivings that employees have about a budget program can be overcome by careful salesmanship from the top management level, and by proper use of the program over a period of time. Administration of a budget program is a sensitive and delicate task. The ultimate objective must be to develop the realization that the budget is designed to be a positive aid on both an individual and a collective basis.

The paramount importance of the human relations dimension in budgeting cannot be overemphasized. Too often managers have become preoccupied with the technical aspects of the budget program to the exclusion of the human aspects. Accountants particularly are open to criticism in this regard. Unfortunately, preoccupation with the dollars and cents in the budget can lead to insensitivity to the purposes which the budget program is designed to accomplish, in terms of human motivation and coordination of efforts.

The Budget Committee

A standing budget committee will usually be responsible for overall policy matters relating to the budget program and for coordination in preparation of the budget itself. This committee generally consists of the president; vice presidents in charge of various functions such as sales, production, and purchasing; and the controller. Difficulties and disputes between segments of the organization in matters relating to the budget are resolved by the budget committee. In addition, the budget committee approves the final budget, and receives periodic reports on the progress of the company in attaining budgeted goals.

The Master Budget—A Network of Interrelationships

The master budget is a network consisting of many separate budgets that are interdependent. This network is illustrated in Exhibit 8–2.

The Sales Budget. Nearly all other parts of the master budget are dependent in some way on the sales budget. Once the sales budget has been set, a decision can be made on the level of production that will be needed to support sales, and the production budget can be set as well. The production budget then becomes a key factor in the determination of other budgets, including the direct materials budget, the direct labor budget, and the manufacturing overhead budget. These budgets, in turn, are needed to assist in formulating a cash budget for the budget period. In essence, the sales budget triggers a chain reaction that leads to the development of many other budget figures in an organization.

As shown in the exhibit, the selling and administrative expense budget is both dependent on and a determinant of the sales budget. This reciprocal relationship arises from the fact that sales will in part be determined by the funds available for advertising and sales promotion.

The Cash Budget. Once the operating budgets (sales, production, etc.) have been established, the cash budget and other financial budgets

EXHIBIT 8–2
The Master Budget Interrelationships

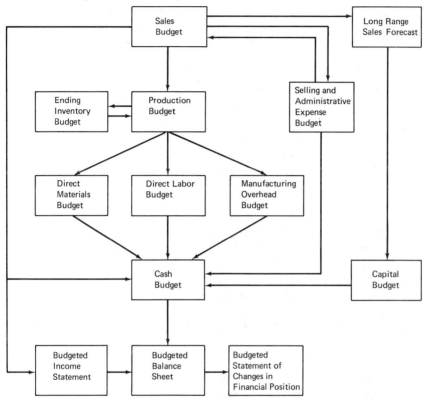

can be prepared. Notice from Exhibit 8–2 that all of the operating budgets, including the sales budget, have an impact of some type on the cash budget. In the case of the sales budget, the impact comes from the planned cash receipts to be received on sales. In the case of the other budgets, the impact comes from the planned cash expenditures within the budgets themselves.

Sales Forecasting—A Critical Step

Since nearly all budgets are derived from it in some way, the sales budget is the key to the entire budgeting process. If the sales budget is sloppily done, then the entire master budget will be worthless, and a waste of time and effort.

The sales budget is prepared from the *sales forecast*. A sales forecast is broader than a sales budget, generally encompassing potential sales for the entire industry, as well as potential sales for the firm preparing the forecast. Factors which are considered in making a sales forecast include:

1. Past experience in terms of sales volume.
2. Prospective pricing policy.
3. Unfilled order backlogs.
4. Market research studies.
5. General economic conditions.
6. Industry economic conditions.
7. Movements of economic indicators such as gross national product, employment, prices, and personal income.
8. Advertising and product promotion.
9. Industry competition.
10. Market share.

Previous sales volume is usually the starting point in preparing a sales forecast. Forecasters examine sales data in relation to various factors, including prices, competitive conditions, availability of supplies, general economic conditions, etc. Projections are then made into the future, based on those factors which the forecasters feel will be significant over the budget period. In-depth discussions generally characterize the gathering and interpretation of all data going into the sales forecast. These discussions, held on all levels of the organization, develop perspective, and assist in assessing the significance and usefulness of data.

Statistical tools such as regression analysis, trend and cycle projection, and correlation analysis are widely used in sales forecasting. In addition, some firms have found it useful to build econometric models of their industry or of the nation to assist in forecasting problems. Such models hold great promise for improving the overall quality of budget data.

PREPARING THE MASTER BUDGET

To show how the separate budgets making up the master budget are developed and integrated, we focus now on the The Able Company. The Able Company produces and sells a single product, which we will call Product A. Each year the company prepares the following budget documents:

1. A sales budget, including a computation of expected cash receipts.
2. A production budget.
3. A direct materials budget, including a computation of expected cash payments for raw materials.
4. A direct labor budget.
5. A manufacturing overhead budget.

6. An ending finished goods inventory budget.
7. A selling and administrative expense budget.
8. A cash budget.
9. A budgeted income statement.
10. A budgeted balance sheet.

These budgets for the year 19X1 are illustrated in schedules 1 through 10 following.

The Sales Budget

The sales budget is the starting point in preparing the master budget. As shown earlier in Exhibit 8–2, nearly all other items in the master budget, including production, purchases, inventories, and expenses, depend on it in some way.

The sales budget is constructed by multiplying the expected sales in units by the sales price. Schedule 1 following contains the sales budget for The Able Company for 19X1, by quarters.

Generally the sales budget is accompanied by a computation of expected cash receipts for the forthcoming budget period. This computation is needed to assist in preparing the cash budget for the year. Expected cash receipts are composed of collections on sales made to customers in prior periods, plus collections on sales made in the current budget period. Schedule 1 below contains a computation of expected cash collections for The Able Company.

SCHEDULE 1

THE ABLE COMPANY
Sales Budget
For the Year Ended December 31, 19X1

| | Quarter | | | | |
	1	2	3	4	Year
Expected sales in units	1,000	1,500	2,000	1,500	6,000
Selling price per unit	× $75	× $75	× $75	× $75	× $75
Total sales.	$75,000	$112,500	$150,000	$112,500	$450,000

Schedule of Expected Cash Collections

Accounts receivable, 12/31/X0	$24,000				$ 24,000
1st quarter sales ($75,000).	30,000	$ 45,000			75,000
2nd quarter sales ($112,500)		45,000	$ 67,500		112,500
3rd quarter sales ($150,000).			60,000	$ 90,000	150,000
4th quarter sales ($112,500).				45,000	45,000
Total cash collections	$54,000	$ 90,000	$127,500	$135,000	$406,500

Note: 40 percent of a quarter's sales are collected in the quarter of sale; the remaining 60 percent is collected in the quarter following.

The Production Budget

After the sales budget has been prepared, the production requirements for the forthcoming budget period can be determined. Sufficient goods will have to be available to meet sales needs, plus provide for the desired ending inventory. A portion of these goods will already exist in the form of a beginning inventory. The remainder will have to be produced. Therefore, production needs can be determined by adding budgeted sales (in units or in dollars) to the desired ending inventory (in units or in dollars), and deducting the beginning inventory (in units or in dollars) from this total. Schedule 2 below contains a production budget for The Able Company.

SCHEDULE 2

THE ABLE COMPANY
Production Budget, In Units
For the Year Ended December 31, 19X1

	Quarter				
	1	*2*	*3*	*4*	*Year*
Expected sales (Schedule 1)	1,000	1,500	2,000	1,500	6,000
Add: Desired ending inventory of finished goods*.	150	200	150	110‡	110
Total needs	1,150	1,700	2,150	1,610	6,110
Less: Beginning inventory of finished goods†.	100	150	200	150	100
Units to be produced	1,050	1,550	1,950	1,460	6,010

* Ten percent of the next quarter's sales.
† The same as the prior quarter's *ending* inventory.
‡ Estimated.

Students are often surprised to learn that firms budget the level of their ending inventories. Budgeting of inventories is a common practice, however. If inventories are not carefully planned, the levels remaining at the end of a period may be excessive, causing an unnecessary tie-up of funds and an unneeded expense of carrying the unwanted goods. On the other hand, without proper planning, inventory levels may be too small, thereby requiring crash production efforts in following periods, and perhaps loss of sales due to inability to meet shipping schedules.

The Direct Materials Budget

After production needs have been computed, a direct materials budget should be prepared to show the materials that will be required in the production process. Sufficient raw materials will have to be available to meet production needs, plus provide for the desired ending raw materials inventory for the budget period. Part of this raw materials requirement will already exist in the form of a beginning raw materials inventory. The remainder will have to be purchased from suppliers. Therefore, the budget should show raw material needs for production, plus raw material needs for ending inventory. The beginning inventory will be deducted from this total. In sum, the format for computing raw materials needs is:

Raw materials needed to meet the production schedule	XXXXX
Plus desired ending inventory of raw materials	XXXXX
Total raw materials needs	XXXXX
Less beginning inventory of raw materials	XXXXX
Raw materials to be purchased	XXXXX

In order to determine the *cost* of the raw materials to be purchased, the total "raw materials to be purchased" above is multiplied by the cost per unit (pound, gallon, etc.). These computations for The Able Company are shown on Schedule 3 following.

The direct materials budget is usually accompanied by a computation of expected cash disbursements for raw materials. This computation is needed to assist in developing a cash budget. Disbursements for raw materials will consist of payments for prior periods, plus payments for current budget-period purchases. Schedule 3 contains a computation of expected cash disbursements for The Able Company.

The Direct Labor Budget

The direct labor budget is also developed from the production budget. Direct labor requirements must be computed so that the company will know if sufficient labor time is available to meet production needs. By knowing in advance just what will be needed in the way of labor time throughout the budget year, plans can be developed to adjust the labor force as the situation may require. Firms that neglect to budget run the risk of facing labor shortages or having to hire and fire at awkward times. Erratic labor policies lead to insecurity and inefficiency on the part of employees.

To compute direct labor requirements, the number of units of finished product to be produced each period (month, quarter, etc.) is multiplied by the number of direct labor hours required to produce a single unit. Many different types of labor may be involved. If so, then computations should be by type of labor needed. The hours of direct labor time resulting from these computations can then be multiplied by the direct labor cost per hour to obtain budgeted total direct labor costs. Schedule 4 following contains such computations for The Able Company.

SCHEDULE 3

THE ABLE COMPANY
Direct Materials Budget
For the Year Ended December 31, 19X1

	Quarter				
	1	*2*	*3*	*4*	*Year*
Units to be produced (Schedule 2)............	1,050	1,550	1,950	1,460	6,010
Raw material needs per unit.................	X 2 lbs.	X 2 lbs.	X 2 lbs.	X 2 lbs.	X 2 lbs.
Production needs........	2,100 lbs.	3,100 lbs.	3,900 lbs.	2,920 lbs.	12,020 lbs.
Desired ending inventory of raw materials*.........	620 lbs.	780 lbs.	584 lbs.	460 lbs.	460 lbs.
Total needs...........	2,720 lbs.	3,880 lbs.	4,484 lbs.	3,380 lbs.	12,480 lbs.
Beginning inventory of raw materials.........	420 lbs.	620 lbs.	780 lbs.	584 lbs.	420 lbs.
Raw materials to be purchased...........	2,300 lbs.	3,260 lbs.	3,704 lbs.	2,796 lbs.	12,060 lbs.
Raw material cost per pound.............	X $5	X $5	X $5	X $5	X $5
Cost of raw materials to be purchased.........	$11,500	$16,300	$18,520	$13,980	$60,300

Schedule of Expected Cash Disbursements

Accounts payable 12/31/X0............	$ 6,000				$ 6,000
1st quarter purchases ($11,500)............	5,750	$ 5,750			11,500
2nd quarter purchases ($16,300)............		8,150	$ 8,150		16,300
3rd quarter purchases ($18,520)............			9,260	$ 9,260	18,520
4th quarter purchases ($13,980)............				6,990	6,990
Total cash disbursements....	$11,750	$13,900	$17,410	$16,250	$59,310

Note: 50 percent of a quarter's purchases are paid for in the quarter of purchase; the remaining 50 percent are paid for in the quarter following.

* Twenty percent of the next quarter's production needs. For example, the second quarter production needs are 3,100 lbs. Therefore, the desired ending inventory for the first quarter would be 20 percent X 3,100 lbs. = 620 lbs. The ending inventory of 460 lbs. for the fourth quarter is estimated.

The Manufacturing Overhead Budget

The manufacturing overhead budget should provide a schedule of all costs of production other than direct materials and direct labor. These costs should be broken down by cost behavior for budgeting purposes, and a predetermined overhead rate developed. This rate will be used to apply manufacturing overhead to units of product throughout the budget period. In the case of The Able Company, the contribution ap-

SCHEDULE 4

THE ABLE COMPANY
Direct Labor Budget
For the Year Ended December 31, 19X1

	Quarter				
	1	2	3	4	Year
Units to be produced (Schedule 2)	1,050	1,550	1,950	1,460	6,010
Direct labor time per unit	× 5 hrs.	× 5 hrs.	× 5 hrs.	× 5 hrs.	× 5 hrs.
Total hours of direct labor time needed	5,250 hrs.	7,750 hrs.	9,750 hrs.	7,300 hrs.	30,050 hrs.
Direct labor cost per hour	× $4	× $4	× $4	× $4	× $4
Total direct labor cost	$21,000	$31,000	$39,000	$29,200	$120,200

proach to costing is being used internally for planning purposes, and so only variable overhead is included in the predetermined overhead rate.

A computation showing budgeted cash disbursements for manufacturing overhead should be made for use in developing the cash budget. The critical thing to remember in making this computation is that depreciation is a noncash charge. Therefore, any depreciation charges included in manufacturing overhead must be deducted from the total in computing expected cash payments. These computations are shown in Schedule 5.

SCHEDULE 5

THE ABLE COMPANY
Manufacturing Overhead Budget
For the Year Ended December 31, 19X1

Manufacturing Overhead Costs:
Variable:

Indirect labor	$12,000
Indirect materials	18,000
Maintenance	8,000
Utilities	15,000
Lubricants	7,100
Total	$60,100

Fixed:

Maintenance	$14,000
Depreciation	15,000
Supervision	25,000
Insurance	4,000
Property taxes	2,000
Total	$60,000

Since the Able Company uses the contribution approach internally for budgeting and planning purposes, only the variable manufacturing overhead is inventoried. The fixed manufacturing overhead is taken directly to the income statement as a charge against the period. The predetermined overhead rate for the variable manufacturing overhead would be $2 per direct labor hour, computed as follows:

$$\frac{\text{Total Variable Manufacturing Overhead Costs}}{\text{Total Direct Labor Hours}} = \frac{\text{Manufacturing Overhead}}{\text{Cost per Direct Labor Hour}}$$

$$\frac{\$60,100 \text{ (see above)}}{30,050 \text{ hrs. (see Schedule 4)}} = \$2 \text{ per direct labor hour}$$

Cash disbursements for manufacturing overhead are estimated to be equal over the four quarters of the year:

Variable manufacturing overhead		$ 60,100
Fixed manufacturing overhead	$60,000	
Less depreciation	15,000	45,000
Total cash disbursements for overhead		$105,100
$105,100 ÷ 4 quarters = $26,275 per quarter		

Cost of a Unit of Product

After completing schedules 1–5, sufficient data will have been generated to compute the cost of a unit of finished product. This computation is needed for two reasons. First, to know how much to charge as cost of goods sold on the budgeted income statement. And second, to know what value to place on the balance sheet for the ending finished goods inventory.

For the Able Company, the cost of a unit of finished product is $40, consisting of $10 of direct materials, $20 of direct labor, and $10 of variable manufacturing overhead. The computations behind these figures are shown below in Schedule 6.

The Selling and Administrative Expense Budget

The selling and administrative expense budget contains a listing of anticipated expenses for the budget period that will be incurred in areas other than manufacturing. The budget will be made up of many smaller, individual budgets submitted by various persons having responsibility for cost control in selling and administrative matters. If the number

SCHEDULE 6

THE ABLE COMPANY
Ending Finished Goods Inventory Budget
For the Year Ended December 31, 19X1

Variable Production Cost per Unit:

Item	Quantity	Cost	Total
Raw materials	2 lbs.	$5/lb.	$10
Direct labor	5 hrs.	$4/hr.	20
Variable manufacturing overhead	5 hrs.	$2/hr.	10
			$40

Budgeted Finished Goods Inventory:

Ending finished goods inventory in units (Schedule 2) 110
Total variable production cost per unit (see above) . . . . × $40
Ending finished goods inventory in dollars $4,400

of expense items is very large, separate budgets may be needed for the selling and administrative functions.

This budget should be accompanied by a schedule showing the anticipated cash payments associated with the budgeted items. Schedule 7 below contains the selling and administrative expense budget for The Able Company for 19X1.

SCHEDULE 7

THE ABLE COMPANY
Selling and Administrative Expense Budget
For the Year Ended December 31, 19X1

Selling and administrative expense:
Variable:

Sales commissions	$12,000
Clerical.	2,500
Freight out	15,500
Total	30,000

Fixed:

Advertising	9,000
Executive salaries.	25,000
Insurance	6,000
Property taxes	2,000
Total	42,000
Total	$72,000

Cash disbursements for selling and administrative expenses are estimated to be equal over the four quarters of the year:

$72,000 ÷ 4 quarters = $18,000 per quarter

The Cash Budget

The cash budget pulls together much of the data developed in the preceding steps, as illustrated earlier in Exhibit 8–2. The reader should restudy this exhibit before reading on.

The cash budget is composed of four major sections:

1. The receipts section.
2. The disbursements section.
3. The cash excess or deficiency section.
4. The financing section.

The receipts section consists of the opening cash balance added to whatever is expected in the way of cash receipts during the budget period. Generally the major source of receipts will be from sales, as discussed earlier.

The disbursements section consists of all cash payments that are planned for the budget period. These payments will include raw materials purchases, direct labor payments, manufacturing overhead costs, etc., as contained in their respective budgets. In addition, other cash disbursements such as income taxes, capital equipment purchases, and dividend payments will also be included.

The cash excess or deficiency section consists of the difference between the cash receipts section totals and the cash disbursements section totals. If a deficiency exists, the company will need to arrange for borrowed funds from its bank. If an excess exists, funds borrowed in previous periods can be repaid, or the idle funds can be placed in short-term investments.

The financing section provides a detailed account of the borrowings and repayments projected to take place during the budget period. It also includes a detail of interest payments that will be due on money borrowed. Banks are becoming increasingly insistent that firms in need of borrowed money give long advance notice of the amounts and times that funds will be needed. This permits the banks to plan, and helps to assure that funds will be ready when needed. Moreover, careful planning of cash needs via the budgeting process avoids unpleasant surprises for companies as well. Few things are more disquieting to an organization than to run into unexpected difficulties in the cash account. A well-coordinated budgeting program eliminates the uncertainty as to what the cash situation will be two months, six months, or a year from now.

The cash budget should be broken down into time periods that are as short as feasible. Many firms budget cash on a weekly basis, and some larger firms go so far as to plan daily cash needs. The more common planning horizons are geared to monthly or quarterly figures. The

THE ABLE COMPANY
Cash Budget
For the Year Ended December 31, 19X1

	Schedule	Quarter 1	Quarter 2	Quarter 3	Quarter 4	Total Year
Cash balance, beginning		$12,000	$ 10,975	$ 10,800	$ 10,115	$ 12,000
Add receipts:						
Collections from customers	1	54,000	90,000	127,500	135,000	406,500
Total cash available before current financing . . .		66,000	100,975	138,300	145,115	418,500
Less disbursements:						
Direct materials.	3	11,750	13,900	17,410	16,250	59,310
Direct labor	4	21,000	31,000	39,000	29,200	120,200
Manufacturing overhead	5	26,275	26,275	26,275	26,275	105,100
Selling and administrative	7	18,000	18,000	18,000	18,000	72,000
Income taxes		4,000	4,000	4,000	4,000	16,000
Equipment purchases.	9		16,000			16,000
Dividends		2,000	2,000	2,000	2,000	8,000
Total disbursements		83,025	111,175	106,685	95,725	396,610
Excess (deficiency) of cash available over disbursements		(17,025)	(10,200)	31,615	49,390	21,890
Financing:						
Borrowings (at beginning)		28,000*	21,000			49,000
Repayments (at ending)				(20,000)	(29,000)	(49,000)
Interest (at 10% per annum). . . .				(1,500)†	(2,375)	(3,875)
Total financing		28,000	21,000	(21,500)	(31,375)	(3,875)
Cash balance, ending		$10,975	$ 10,800	$ 10,115	$ 18,015	$ 18,015

* The company requires a minimum cash balance of $10,000. Therefore, borrowing must be sufficient to cover the cash deficiency of $17,025 plus provide for the minimum cash balance of $10,000.

† The interest payments relate only to the principle being repaid at the time it is repaid. For example, the interest in quarter 3 relates only to the $20,000 principle being repaid at that point in time ($20,000 × 10% × 9 months = $1,500 interest).

cash budget for The Able Company for 19X1 is shown on a quarterly basis in Schedule 8 on page 261.[1]

The Budgeted Income Statement

A budgeted income statement can be prepared from the data developed in schedules 1–8. *The budgeted income statement is one of the key schedules in the budget process.* It is the document that tells how profitable operations are anticipated to be in the forthcoming period. After it is developed it stands as a benchmark against which subsequent company performance can be measured.

Schedule 9 below contains a budgeted income statement for The Able Company for 19X1.

SCHEDULE 9

THE ABLE COMPANY
Budgeted Income Statement
For the Year Ended December 31, 19X1

	Schedule		
Sales (6,000 units @ $75)	1		$450,000
Less variable expenses:			
Variable cost of goods sold (6,000 units			
@ $40).	6	$240,000	
Variable selling and administrative	7	30,000	270,000
Contribution margin			180,000
Less fixed expenses:			
Manufacturing overhead	5	60,000	
Selling and administrative	7	42,000	102,000
Net operating income.			78,000
Less interest expense	8		3,875
Net income before taxes			74,125
Less income taxes.	*		16,000
Net income			$ 58,125

   * Estimated.

The Budgeted Balance Sheet

The budgeted balance sheet is developed by beginning with the current balance sheet and adjusting it for the data contained in the other budgets. A budgeted balance sheet for The Able Company for 19X1

---

[1] The Able Company has an open line of credit with its bank, which can be used as needed to bolster the cash position. Borrowings must be in round $1,000 amounts, and interest is 10 percent per annum. Interest is computed and paid on principle as the principle is repaid. All borrowings take place at the beginning of a quarter, and all repayments are made at the end of a quarter.

is presented in Schedule 10 following. The company's beginning-of-year balance sheet, from which the budgeted balance sheet in Schedule 10 has been derived in part, is presented below:

THE ABLE COMPANY
Balance Sheet
December 31, 19X0
Assets

Current Assets:
Cash	$12,000	
Accounts receivable	24,000	
Raw materials inventory (420 lbs.)	2,100	
Finished goods inventory (100 units)	4,000	
		$ 42,100

Fixed Assets:
Land	40,000	
Buildings and equipment	60,000	
Accumulated depreciation	(40,000)	
		60,000
Total Assets		$102,100

Equities

Current Liabilities:
Accounts payable (raw material)		$ 6,000

Stockholders' Equity:
Common stock, no par	$40,000	
Retained earnings	56,100	
		96,100
Total Equities		$102,100

THE NEED FOR FURTHER BUDGETING MATERIAL

The material covered in this chapter represents no more than an introduction into the vast area of budgeting and profit planning. Our purpose has been to present an overview of the budgeting process, and to show how the various operating budgets build on each other in guiding a firm toward its profit objectives. However, the matter of budgeting and profit planning is so critical to the intelligent management of a firm in today's business environment that we can't stop with simply an overview of the budgeting process. We need to look more closely at budgeting to see how it helps managers in the day-to-day conduct of business affairs. We will do this by studying standard costs and flexible budgets in the following two chapters, and by introducing the concept of performance reporting. In Chapter 11 we will expand on these ideas by looking at budgeting and profit planning as tools for control of decentralized operations, and as facilitating factors in judging managerial performance.

SCHEDULE 10

THE ABLE COMPANY
Budgeted Balance Sheet
December 31, 19X1

Assets

Current Assets:
Cash .... $ 18,015 (*a*)
Accounts receivable .... 67,500 (*b*)
Raw materials inventory.................. 2,300 (*c*)
Finished goods inventory .... 4,400 (*d*)
                                                            $ 92,215

Fixed Assets:
Land .... 40,000 (*e*)
Buildings and equipment .... 76,000 (*f*)
Accumulated depreciation................ (55,000) (*g*)
                                                              61,000

Total Assets......................... $153,215

Equities

Current Liabilities:
Accounts payable (raw materials)............ $ 6,990 (*h*)
Stockholders' Equity:
Common stock, no par.................. $ 40,000 (*i*)
Retained earnings..................... 106,225 (*j*)   146,225

Total Equities...................... $153,215

Explanation of December 31, 19X1, balance sheet figures:
(*a*) The ending cash balance, as projected by the cash budget in Schedule 8.
(*b*) 60 percent of fourth-quarter sales, from Schedule 1 ($112,500 × 60 percent = $67,500).
(*c*) From Schedule 3, the ending raw materials inventory will be 460 lbs. This material costs $5 per lb. Therefore, the ending inventory in dollars will be 460 lbs. × $5 = $2,300.
(*d*) From Schedule 6.
(*e*) From the December 31, 19X0, balance sheet (no change).
(*f*) The December 31, 19X0, balance sheet indicated a balance of $60,000. During 19X1, $16,000 additional equipment will be purchased (see Schedule 8), bringing the December 31, 19X1, balance to $76,000.
(*g*) The December 31, 19X0, balance sheet indicated a balance of $40,000. During 19X1 $15,000 of depreciation will be taken (see Schedule 5), bringing the December 31, 19X1, balance to $55,000.
(*h*) One half of the fourth-quarter raw materials purchases, from Schedule 3.
(*i*) From the December 31, 19X0, balance sheet (no change).
(*j*) December 31, 19X0, balance .... $ 56,100
         Add net income, from Schedule 9   58,125
                                                                        114,225
         Deduct dividends paid, from Schedule 8.   8,000
         December 31, 19X1, balance $106,225

In sum, the materials in the following two chapters build on the budgeting and profit planning foundation which has been laid in this chapter, by expanding on certain concepts which have been introduced, and by refining others. The essential thing to keep in mind at this point is that the material covered in the current chapter does not conclude our study of budgeting and profit planning, but rather just introduces the ideas.

QUESTIONS

8–1. What is a budget? What is budgetary control?

8–2. Discuss some of the major benefits to be gained from budgeting.

8–3. What is a master budget? Briefly describe its contents.

8–4. Which is a better basis for judging actual results, budgeted performance or past performance? Why?

8–5. Why is the sales forecast always the starting point in budgeting?

8–6. Is there any difference between a sales forecast and a sales budget? Explain.

8–7. "As a practical matter, planning and control mean exactly the same thing." Do you agree? Explain.

8–8. Describe the flow of budget data in an organization. Who participates in the budgeting process, and how do they participate?

8–9. "To a large extent, the success of a budget program hinges on education and good salesmanship." Do you agree? Explain.

8–10. What is a self-imposed budget? What are the major advantages of self-imposed budgets? What caution must be exercised in their use?

8–11. In structuring a cash budget, what important factors must be considered in planning cash collections from sales? In planning cash disbursements to suppliers?

8–12. What is the general approach used in determining how many units of product must be produced during a period?

8–13. What is the general approach used in determining the dollar amount of raw materials which must be purchased to support anticipated production?

8–14. How can budgeting assist a firm in its employment policies?

8–15. "The principal purpose of the cash budget is to see how much cash the company will have in the bank at the end of the year." Do you agree? Explain.

EXERCISES

8–1. Harper Products, Ltd. has budgeted sales for the next four months as follows:

Sales in Units

April	50,000
May.	60,000
June.	80,000
July.	70,000

The company is now in the process of preparing a production budget for the second quarter. Past experience has shown that end-of-month inventory levels must equal 15 percent of the following month's sales. The inventory at the end of March was 7,500 units.

Required:

How many units must be produced during each month of the second quarter, and for the quarter in total?

8–2. Crestline Corporation manufactures and sells camping equipment. Included in the company's line of products are two types of backpacks, type A and type B. Sales of the backpacks for the next quarter are budgeted as follows:

	Sales in Units	
	A	*B*
July.	8,000	15,000
August	9,000	17,000
September	6,000	12,000

Type A backpack sells for $15. Type B sells for $10. Past experience shows that sales returns, allowances, and losses on uncollectible accounts average 1 percent of sales.

Required:

Prepare a sales budget for the quarter, by month, and in total. Sales should be detailed by product and in total.

8–3. The sales budget for Briggs Sales Company for the first quarter of 19X4 is given below:

	Jan.	Feb.	Mar.	Total
Budgeted sales.	$50,000	$75,000	$90,000	$215,000

In order to have data available for preparing a cash budget, the company is anxious to determine the budgeted cash collections from sales. To this end, the following information has been assembled:

Collections on sales
$\begin{cases} \text{60\% in month of sale} \\ \text{30\% in month following sale} \\ \text{8\% in second month following sale} \\ \text{2\% uncollectible} \end{cases}$

Briggs Sales Company gives a 2 percent cash discount for payments made by customers during the month of sale. The accounts receivable balance to start the year is $22,000, of which $4,000 represents uncollected November sales, and $18,000 represents uncollected December sales.

Required:

1. What were the total sales for November? For December?
2. Prepare a schedule showing the budgeted cash collections from sales, by month and in total, for the three-month period.

8-4. Three ounces of musk oil are required for each bottle of "allure," a very popular perfume. The cost of the musk oil is $3 per ounce. Scheduled production of "allure" for 19X5 is given below, by quarters:

	First	Second	Third	Fourth
Production in bottles.	8,000	10,000	18,000	6,000

Musk oil has become so popular as a perfume base that it has become necessary to carry large inventories as a precaution against stock-outs. For this reason, the inventory of musk oil at the end of any quarter must not be less than 25 percent of the following quarter's production needs.

Required:

Compute the budgeted purchases of musk oil for the third quarter.

8-5. A cash budget, by quarters, is given below. Fill in the missing amounts (000 omitted). The company requires a minimum cash balance of at least $5,000 to start each quarter.

	1	2	3	4	Year
Cash balance, beginning	$ 8	$?	$?	$?	$?
Add collections from customers	?	?	96	?	321
Total cash available	68	?	?	?	?
Less disbursements:					
Purchase of inventory	35	45	?	35	?
Operating expenses.	?	30	30	?	113
Equipment purchases	8	8	10	?	36
Dividends	2	2	2	2	?
Total disbursements	?	85	?	?	?
Excess (deficiency) of cash available over disbursements	(2)	?	11	?	?
Financing:					
Borrowings	?	15	–	–	?
Repayments (with interest)	–	–	(?)	(17)	(?)
Total financing	?	?	?	?	?
Cash balance, ending	$?	$?	$?	$?	$?

8-6. Marchant Products, Inc., produces a small circuit that is used as a component part in two different products sold in two different markets. The product sold in market A requires three circuits per unit, and the product sold in market B requires five circuits per unit. Market studies indicate that sales of the market A product should total 5,000,000 units during 19X5. These studies indicate that sales of the market B product should be up about 15 percent over 19X4 sales of 10,000,000 units of product.

Marchant Products, Inc., also sells circuits to retail electronic houses around the nation for over-the-counter sales to electronic buffs. Over the past four years, these sales have been as follows:

19X1 1,400,000 circuits	19X3 1,499,680 circuits
19X2 1,442,000	19X4 1,574,664

The company expects the trend in sales to the retail electronic houses to continue. The company also expects to capture 25 percent of the market A circuit needs, and to capture 10 percent of the market B circuit needs. Marchant Products, Inc., sells its circuits for $4 each.

Required:

Compute Marchant Products, Inc.'s expected sales of circuits for 19X5, in units and in dollars of sales revenue.

8–7. Barker Baskets, Inc. produces three styles of baskets—one for laundry, one for shopping, and one for bicycles. The production budget for each style of basket for January, February, and March is given below:

	Laundry	Shopping	Bicycle
January	4,000	6,000	12,000
February	4,500	6,400	14,000
March	4,800	6,600	15,000

Careful records have been kept of the direct labor time required in the production of each type of basket. This time per basket follows:

Laundry	30 minutes
Shopping	24
Bicycle	12

Barker Baskets, Inc. pays direct labor employees $3.50 per hour.

Required:

Prepare a direct labor budget for each of the months, January, February, and March. Show the budget in both hours and dollars of cost.

8–8. The CEJ Company needs a cash budget for the month of September, 19X4. The following information is available:
1. The cash balance on September 1 is $6,600.
2. Actual sales for July and August, and expected sales for September, are:

	July	August	September
Cash sales	$ 4,500	$ 4,800	$ 5,500
Credit sales	20,000	30,000	35,000
Total sales	$24,500	$34,800	$40,500

Credit sales are collected over a three-month period, in the ratio 60%, 30%, 10%.

3. Purchases of inventory will total $18,000 for September. Seventy percent of a month's purchases are paid for during the month of purchase. Accounts payable for August purchases total $5,000, which will be paid in September.

4. Selling and administrative expenses are budgeted at $14,000 for September. Five thousand dollars of this amount is depreciation.

5. Dividends of $4,000 will be paid during September, and equipment costing $12,000 will be purchased.

6. The company must maintain a minimum cash balance of $5,000. An open line of credit is available from the company's bank to bolster the cash position as needed.

Required:

Prepare a cash budget for the month of September. Indicate in the financing section any borrowing that will be necessary during the month.

PROBLEMS

8–1. *Production and Purchases Budgets.* Vincent Products, Inc., manufactures and distributes a number of products to retailers. One of these products, Playclay, requires 3 lbs. of Material A in its manufacture. In order to keep production moving smoothly, the company wants raw materials on hand at the beginning of each month equal to one-half of the month's production needs. This requirement was met on July 1, the start of the third quarter, 19X5. The company maintains no work-in-process inventories. A sales budget for Playclay for the last six months of 19X5 is given below:

	Budgeted Sales in Units
July	18,000
August	20,000
September	24,000
October	26,000
November	19,000
December	16,000

Vincent Products, Inc. has found that the finished goods inventory at the end of each month must be equal to 5,000 units plus 10 percent of the next month's sales. On June 30, the finished goods inventory totaled 6,800 units.

Required:

Prepare a budget showing the quantity of Material A to be purchased for July, August, and September 19X5. (Hint: In order to prepare a materials purchases budget, it will be necessary first to prepare a production budget for each of the months July–October.)

8–2. *Cash Budget.* Bill Greer, president of Driftwood Products, has just approached the company's bank with a request for a short-term loan of $16,000. The purpose of the loan is to assist the company in building inventories in support of peak April sales. Although Driftwood Products has borrowed from the bank before for this purpose, the amount of the present loan is considerably more than has been needed in prior years. For this reason, the bank's loan officer is somewhat concerned over Driftwood Products's ability to repay the loan as planned. The company's plan is to borrow the money on March 1, repayable at 10 percent interest three months later, on May 31.

The loan officer has asked Mr. Greer to submit a cash budget covering the loan period, to see what Driftwood Products's cash balance will be on May 31, assuming the loan is made as planned. Accordingly, Mr. Greer's staff has assembled the following budgeted information for the next three months:

	March	April	May
Sales	$30,000	$40,000	$20,000
Merchandise purchases	24,000	12,000	8,000
Payroll	4,000	4,500	3,000
Lease payments	3,000	3,000	3,000
Other cash payments	4,000	6,000	3,000
Depreciation expense	1,000	1,000	1,000
Net income	3,000	6,000	1,000
Equipment purchases	2,000	–	–

On March 1, the company plans to have a cash balance of $4,000. Accounts receivable on that date are planned at $16,800, of which $15,600 will be collected during March, and $800 will be collected during April. The remainder probably will be uncollectible. The company's collection pattern for sales is 20 percent during the month of sale, 75 percent in the month following sale, and 4 percent in the second month following sale. On March 1, the accounts payable balance will be $18,000, representing February purchases of merchandise inventory. All purchases are paid for in the month following purchase.

Required:

1. Prepare a schedule of budgeted cash collections on sales and accounts receivable.
2. Prepare a cash budget, by month and in total, for the loan period assuming that the loan is made and repaid as planned.
3. If the company needs a minimum cash balance of $4,000 at the beginning of each month, can the loan be repaid as planned? Explain.

8–3. *Integrating the Sales, Production, Direct Materials, and Direct Labor Budgets.* Selected budgets for Avery Products are given below:

Sales Budget

	April	May	June	Quarter
Expected sales in units	500	600	800	?
Selling price per unit	X $12	X $12	X $12	X ?
Total sales	$?	$?	$?	$?
Expected cash collections:*				
From accounts receivable	$1,375			$?
From April sales	?	?		?
From May sales		?	?	?
From June sales			?	?
Total collections	$?	$?	$?	$?

Production Budget

	April	May	June	Quarter
Expected sales in units	?	?	?	?
Desired ending inventory†	?	?	?	180
Total needs	?	?	?	?
Less: Beginning inventory	?	?	?	110
Units to be produced	?	?	?	?

Direct Materials Budget

	April	May	June	Quarter
Units to be produced	?	?	?	?
Raw materials needs per unit	X 4 ozs	X 4 ozs	X 4 ozs	?
Total production needs	?	?	?	?
Desired ending inventory in ozs.‡	?	?	?	360 ozs
Total needs	?	?	?	?
Less beginning inventory in ozs.	?	?	?	220 ozs
Raw materials to be purchased	?	?	?	?
Raw material cost per ounce	X $?	X $?	X $?	X $?
Total raw materials cost	$?	$1,316	$?	$?
Expected cash disbursements: §				
Accounts payable	$ 600			$?
April purchases	?	$?		?
May purchases		?	$?	?
June purchases			?	?
Total disbursements	$?	$?	$?	$?

Direct Labor Budget

	April	May	June	Quarter
Units to be produced.	?	?	?	?
Direct labor time per unit	X ?hrs	X ?hrs	X ?hrs	X ?hrs
Total direct labor time needed	?	?	?	3,940 hrs
Direct labor cost per hour	X $?	X $?	X $?	X $?
Total direct labor cost	$3,060	$?	$?	$?

* Note: 75 percent of a month's sales are collected by month end; the remaining 25 percent is collected in the month following.
† Twenty percent of the next month's sales.
‡ Ten percent of the next month's production needs.
§ Note: 50 percent of a month's purchases are paid for immediately; the other 50 percent is paid in the month following.

Required:

Provide the missing data.

8–4. *Planning Bank Financing by Means of a Cash Budget.* When the treasurer of Susan Company approached the company's bank late in 19X1 seeking short-term financing, he was told that money was very tight, and that any borrowing over the next year would have to be supported by a detailed statement of cash receipts and disbursements. The treasurer also was told that it would be very helpful to the bank if borrowers would indicate the quarters in which they would be needing funds, as well as the amounts that would be needed and the quarters in which repayments could be made.

Since the treasurer is unsure as to the particular quarters in which the bank financing will be needed, he has assembled the following budgeted data for 19X2, as well as selected actual data for the last quarter of 19X1:

	Sales	Merchandise Purchases
19X1–Fourth quarter actual	$200,000	$126,000
19X2–First quarter estimated	300,000	186,000
Second quarter estimated	400,000	246,000
Third quarter estimated	500,000	282,000
Fourth quarter estimated	200,000	126,000

Operating expenses for 19X2 are budgeted quarterly at $50,000 plus 15 percent of sales. Of the fixed amount, $20,000 each quarter is depreciation. Susan Company plans to pay $10,000 in dividends each quarter. The company also plans to make equipment purchases of $75,000 in the second quarter and $67,000 in the third quarter.

The company normally collects 65 percent of a quarter's sales before the quarter ends, and another 33 percent in the following quarter. The remainder is uncollectible. Eighty percent of a quarter's purchases are paid for within the quarter. The remainder is paid in the quarter following. This pattern of collections and payments is now being experienced in the 19X1 fourth quarter actual data.

The cash account at the end of 19X1 contains $10,000. The treasurer of Susan Company feels that this represents a minimum cash balance that must be maintained. Any borrowing will take place at the beginning of a quarter, and any repayments will be made at the end of a quarter at an annual interest rate of 10 percent. All borrowings and repayments must be in round thousand-dollar amounts.

Required:

1. Prepare schedules of budgeted cash collections on sales and budgeted cash payments for merchandise purchases.
2. Prepare a cash budget for 19X2, by quarter and in total for the year. Show clearly in your budget the quarter(s) in which borrowing will be necessary, and the quarter(s) in which repayments can be made, as requested by Susan Company's bank.

8–5. *Master Budget.* The balance sheet of Darby Sales Company as of May 31, 19X4, is given below:

DARBY SALES COMPANY
Balance Sheet
May 31, 19X4

Assets

Cash	$ 19,000
Accounts receivable, customers	35,000
Inventory	50,000
Plant and equipment, net of depreciation	140,000
Total assets	$244,000

Liabilities and Equity

Accounts payable, suppliers	$ 38,000
Note payable	8,000
Capital stock, no par	120,000
Retained earnings	78,000
Total liabilities and equity	$244,000

Darby Sales Company has never budgeted before, and for this reason is limiting its master budget planning horizon to just one month—June, 19X4. The company has assembled the following budgeted information relating to the month of June:

1. Sales are budgeted at $130,000. Of these sales, $30,000 will be for cash; the remainder will be credit sales. Fifty percent of credit sales are collected in the month the sales are made, and the remainder is collected in the following month. All of the May 31 accounts receivable will be collected during June.
2. Purchases of inventory are expected to total $80,000 during the month, all on account. Forty percent of all purchases are paid for in the month of purchase; the remainder is paid in the following month. All of the May 31 accounts payable to suppliers will be paid during June.

3. The June 30 inventory balance is budgeted at $60,000.
4. Operating expenses for June are budgeted at $35,000, exclusive of depreciation. These expenses will all be paid in cash. Depreciation is budgeted at $2,000 for the month.
5. Equipment costing $15,000 will be acquired during June. The company will give a note payable covering the equipment cost, due in one year.
6. The note payable at May 31 will be paid in June, with $500 interest.

Required:

1. Prepare a cash budget for the month of June 19X4.
2. Prepare a budgeted income statement for the month of June 19X4. Use the traditional income statement format. Ignore income taxes.
3. Prepare a budgeted balance sheet as of June 30, 19X4.

8–6. *Production Budget, Purchase Budget, and Income Statement.* The sales budget of Marvel Glue Products calls for sales of 200,000 bottles of Formula 7, one of the company's glue products, during the second quarter of 19X8. The sales budget calls for a selling price of $5 per bottle. Since sales of this product tend to fall off during the summer months, the finished goods inventory at the end of the second quarter is planned to be down by 20 percent from its present level of 20,000 bottles.

Only six minutes of direct labor time is required to produce each bottle of Formula 7. The direct labor rate is $4 per hour. Two different raw materials ingredients go into the production of Formula 7. Material X costs 15 cents per ounce, and four ounces are required per bottle of Formula 7. Material Y costs 80 cents per ounce, but only two ounces are required per bottle. The following inventory levels are existing or planned for the second quarter:

	Beginning Actual	Planned Ending
Material X	80,000 ozs	60,000 ozs
Material Y	45,000 ozs	60,000 ozs

Material Y is sometimes hard to find; therefore, inventory levels of Material Y are being increased. Other variable costs include manufacturing overhead of 25 cents per bottle of Formula 7, and selling and administrative expenses of 20 cents per bottle. Fixed costs are given below per quarter:

Manufacturing overhead	$90,000
Selling and administrative	60,000

Required:

1. Prepare a production budget for Formula 7 for the second quarter.
2. Prepare a raw materials purchases budget for both Material X

and Material Y for the second quarter. Show the budgeted purchases in both ounces and dollars.

3. Prepare a budgeted income statement for the third quarter. Show sales revenue and variable expense data per unit and in total.

8–7. *Budgeting in a Hospital.* The X-ray department of Valley Hospital expects to take 2,520 X-rays during the coming quarter. The charge for X-rays is $15 each. The salary of technicians is $600 per month. There are two technicians assigned to X-ray. Fixed overhead costs of the department are $5,200 monthly, exclusive of the technicians. Of this amount, $2,500 is depreciation.

Variable costs per X-ray are $7. The bulk of the variable costs consists of the cost of film, which is $4 per X-ray. The department has sufficient film on hand at the start of the quarter to take 800 X-rays. By the end of the quarter, this inventory should consist of sufficient film to take 1,000 X-rays. Only half of the cost of any purchases of film will be paid for during the quarter; $4,000 will be paid during the quarter on the prior quarter's film purchases. All other variable costs are paid for as incurred each month.

The X-ray department expects to collect about 80 percent of the revenues due on X-rays taken during the quarter. In addition, about $6,000 will be collected on accounts receivable from the prior quarter.

Required:

1. Prepare a budgeted income statement for the quarter. Use the contribution format. Assume that all fixed costs are direct.
2. Compute net cash inflow or outflow during the quarter as a result of activities in the X-ray department.
3. What is the *primary* reason why the net cash flow for the quarter differs from the net income for the quarter?

8–8. *Defending a Budget Proposal.* Kendall Corporation is a medium-sized manufacturer of a number of consumer products. You have been working for the company for only a few months. In order for you to become familiar with the company's operations, the president assigned you to do a general study of its manufacturing and financing activities. You were instructed to prepare a memo for the president outlining any new programs or changes that seemed desirable for the company to consider.

In your study, you have found that the company is experiencing certain operating difficulties, particularly in controlling costs and co-ordinating operations. You have recommended to the president in your memo that the company give serious consideration to implementing a comprehensive budgeting program as one step toward overcoming these difficulties. The president is very much interested in your suggestion, and has brought the matter before the company's executive committee, with you present for the purpose of answering any questions. Upon hearing the president's comments, one of the senior members of the committee replies, "I just can't see trying to budget in our size of operation. I don't doubt that it works well in the giants, like General Motors, but we're just a drop in the bucket compared to them. Besides, we have special problems, like reliance on a couple of foreign suppliers, and concentration of sales on the coast. If we were nationwide, it might be different. And I seriously question whether the accounting people would ever be able to guess our expenses in advance—there are just too many variables involved. Besides, when would Bill (the controller) find time to make up a lot of budgets? It's all he can do to get out the monthly statements as it is. Even if Bill did get the time to make budgets, who would follow them?"

As you glance around the table, you notice that several heads are nodding affirmatively to the committee member's comments. The president turns to you for a reply.

Required:

Write your reply out in narrative form, keeping in mind that all eyes are on you as you speak.

8–9. *Cash Budget.* Holman Hardware, Inc., is planning its cash needs for the first quarter of 19X2. The company usually has to borrow money during this quarter to support peak sales of gardening equipment, which occur during February. The following information has been assembled to assist in preparing a cash budget for the quarter:

1. Budgeted monthly income statements for the first four months of 19X2 are:

	January	February	March	April
Sales	$16,000	$24,000	$18,000	$16,000
Cost of goods sold	9,600	14,400	10,800	9,600
Gross margin	6,400	9,600	7,200	6,400
Less operating expenses:				
Selling expense	2,200	3,000	2,400	2,200
Administrative expense*	2,600	3,080	2,720	2,600
Total...............	4,800	6,080	5,120	4,800
Net income	$ 1,600	$ 3,520	$ 2,080	$ 1,600

* Includes $1,200 depreciation.

2. Sales are 20 percent for cash and 80 percent on credit.
3. Credit sales are collected over a three-month period, in the ratio 10%, 70%, 20%. November's sales totaled $14,000 and December's sales totaled $15,000.
4. Inventory purchases are paid for within 15 days. Therefore, approximately 50 percent of a month's inventory purchases are paid for in the month of purchase. The remaining 50 percent is paid in the following month. Accounts payable for inventory purchases at December 31 total $4,575.
5. The company maintains its ending inventory levels at $5,000 plus 25 percent of the cost of the merchandise to be sold in the follow-

ing month. The merchandise inventory at December 31 is $7,200.

6. Dividends of $2,000, declared in December, will be paid in January.

7. Equipment costing $7,500, received in November 19X1, is being paid in three equal payments, starting in December 19X1.

8. The company must maintain a cash balance of at least $5,000. The cash balance on December 31, 19X1, is $5,155.

9. The company can borrow from its bank as needed to bolster the cash account. Borrowings must be in multiples of $500. All borrowings take place at the beginning of a month, and all repayments are made at the end of a month. The interest rate is 12 percent per annum. Compute interest on whole months (e.g., 1/12, 2/12, etc.).

Required:

1. Prepare a schedule of budgeted cash collections from sales for each of the months January, February, and March.

2. Prepare a schedule of budgeted cash payments for inventory purchases for each of the months January, February, and March.

3. Prepare a cash budget for the first quarter, 19X2. Show figures by month as well as for the quarter in total. Show borrowings from the company's bank and repayments to the bank as needed to maintain the minimum cash balance.

8–10. *Budgeting Selling and Administrative Expenses.* Soylent Corporation is preparing its master budget for 19X9. The following information has been accumulated on selling and administrative expenses for the coming budget year:

1. Payments of salaries to administrative personnel will total $75,400 during the year. The liability for administrative salaries at the beginning of the year is $12,400 and will amount to $10,500 at the end of the year.

2. The cost of executive expense accounts is budgeted at $30,000 for 19X9. Expense advances of $8,000 are outstanding on January 1, and advances will probably amount to at least $5,000 at the end of the year.

3. The inventory of office supplies on hand to start the year stands at $5,500 and probably will increase by $1,000 during the year. Payments for office supplies are estimated at $32,300 for the year.

4. Miscellaneous administrative expenses, exclusive of depreciation, are planned at $33,000. Payments of these expenses are planned at $31,500.

5. Net sales for 19X9 are budgeted at $5,500,000. These sales are subject to sales commissions of 12 percent. The liability for sales commissions at the beginning of the year amounts to $43,000 and the liability at the end of the year probably will amount to $30,000.

6. The liability for unpaid travel and entertainment expense to start the year is $7,400. This liability is expected to decline by at least $2,000 by year-end. Travel and entertainment expense chargeable to operations is budgeted at $63,000 for 19X9. These expenses relate to the Sales Division.

7. The Sales Division rents certain warehouse facilities. Prepaid rent on these warehouses totals $2,000 at the start of the year. The warehouses are rented at a monthly charge of $4,000. Unpaid rent of $3,000 will be owed at year-end.

8. Payments to advertising agencies during the year will total $425,000. Prepaid advertising will decrease by $20,000 during the year.

9. Miscellaneous selling expenses, exclusive of depreciation, are budgeted at $18,000, of which $16,500 will be paid in cash during the year.

10. The sales and administrative divisions occupy the same building. Depreciation on the building is budgeted at $90,000 for 19X9. Administrative offices occupy 35 percent of the building space, and the sales offices occupy the remaining 65 percent.

11. Depreciation budgeted for furniture, fixtures, and equipment is:

Administrative.	$ 8,500
Selling	16,500

Required:

1. Prepare expense budgets for the Sales Division and for the Administrative Division for 19X9.
2. Prepare budgets of expected cash payments for the Sales Division and for the Administrative Division for 19X9.
3. What use would be made of the budgets prepared in Part 1? Part 2?

8–11. *Budgeting in a University.* Baldwin College has asked your assistance in developing its budget for the coming academic year. You have been supplied with the following data for the current year for the lower and upper divisions. The lower division is composed of the freshman-sophomore classes, and the upper division is composed of the junior-senior classes.

	Lower Division	Upper Division
Average number of students per class.	25	20
Average salary of faculty member.	$15,000	$15,000
Average number of credit hours carried each year by each student	33	30
Enrollment (including students on scholarships).	2,500	1,700
Average faculty teaching load in credit hours a year (10 classes of 3 credit hours each)	30	30

1. Lower division enrollment in the coming year is expected to increase by 10 percent, while the upper division's enrollment is expected to remain at the current year's level.
2. Faculty salaries will be increased by a standard 5 percent, and additional merit increases to be awarded to individual faculty members will be $90,750 for the lower division and $85,000 for the upper division.
3. The budget for the remaining expenditures for the coming year contains the following:

Administrative and general.	$440,000
Library.	160,000
Health and recreation.	75,000
Athletics.	320,000
Insurance and retirement.	365,000
Interest.	48,000
Operation and maintenance of plant and equipment	223,500
Capital outlays (new buildings and equipment)	300,000

4. The college expects to award 25 tuition-free scholarships to lower-division students and 15 to upper-division students. Tuition is $31 per credit hour. No other fees are charged.
5. Budgeted revenues for the coming year from sources other than tuition are as follows:

From endowment fund.	$114,000
From auxiliary services.	235,000
From athletics.	280,000
From the annual support campaign.	?

The college holds the "annual support campaign" each spring. Enough funds must be raised in this campaign each spring to permit the college to at least break even for the year.

Required:

1. Compute the following for the coming year:
    a. The anticipated enrollment.
    b. The total credit hours to be carried by students.
    c. The number of faculty members needed for each division.
    d. The budgeted cost of faculty salaries.
    e. The budgeted revenues from tuition.
2. How much in funds must be raised during the "annual support campaign" in the coming spring? Present your computations in contribution format, to the extent possible.*

(AICPA, adapted)

---

* Note to the instructor: This problem has been adapted from a problem which appeared on the CPA exam. As adapted, the problem is quite straightforward, but very instructive in terms of showing how budgeting concepts can be applied in not-for-profit situations.

8–12. *Master Budget, with Supporting Budgets.* You have just been hired as a new management trainee by Super Sales Company, a nationwide distributor of a revolutionary new type of cigarette lighter. The company has an exclusive franchise on distribution of the lighter, and sales have grown so rapidly over the last few years that it has become necessary to add new members to the management team. You have been given direct responsibility for all planning and budgeting. Your first assignment is to prepare a master budget for the next three months, starting April 1. You are anxious to make a favorable impression on the president, and have assembled the information below.

The company desires a minimum ending cash balance each month of $10,000. The lighters are forecasted to sell for $8 each. Recent and forecasted sales in units are:

January (actual). 20,000	April 35,000	July. 40,000
February (actual). 24,000	May. 45,000	August 36,000
March (actual). 28,000	June 60,000	September 32,000

The large buildup in sales before and during the month of June is due to Father's Day. Ending inventories are supposed to equal 90 percent of the next month's sales in units. The lighters cost the company $5 each.

Purchases are paid for as follows: 50 percent in the month of purchase, the remaining 50 percent in the following month. All sales are on credit, with no discount, and payable within 15 days. The company has found, however, that only 25 percent of a month's sales are collected by month-end. An additional 50 percent is collected in the month following, and the remaining 25 percent collected in the second month following. Bad debts have been negligible.

The company's monthly operating expenses are given below:

Variable:
    Sales commissions . . . . $1 per
                                    lighter

Fixed:
    Wages and salaries. $36,000
    Utilities   1,000
    Insurance expired.   1,200
    Depreciation.   1,500
    Miscellaneous   2,000

All operating expenses are paid during the month, in cash, with the exception of depreciation and insurance expired. New fixed assets will be purchased during May, for $25,000 cash. The company declares dividends of $12,000 each quarter, payable in the first month of the following quarter. Super Sales Company's balance sheet at March 31 is given below:

Assets

Cash	$ 14,000
Accounts receivable ($48,000 February sales;	
$168,000 March sales)	216,000
Inventory (31,500 units).	157,500
Unexpired insurance	14,400
Fixed assets, net of depreciation	172,700
Total assets	$574,600

Liabilities and Equity

Accounts payable, purchases	$ 85,750
Dividends payable.	12,000
Capital stock, no par	300,000
Retained earnings.	176,850
Total liabilities and equity	$574,600

Super Sales Company can borrow money from its bank at 10 percent annual interest. All borrowing must be made at the beginning of a month, and repayments must be made at the end of a month. Interest is computed and paid only when the principle is repaid. Repayments of principle must be in round $1,000 amounts. Borrowing can be in any amount.

Required:

Prepare a master budget for the three-month period ending June 30. Include the following detailed budgets:

1. *a.* A sales budget, by month and in total.
   b. A schedule of budgeted cash collections from sales and accounts receivable, by month and in total.
   c. A purchases budget in units and in dollars. Show the budget by month and in total.
   d. A schedule of budgeted cash payments for purchases, by month and in total.
2. A cash budget. Show the budget by month and in total.
3. A budgeted income statement for the three-month period ending June 30.
4. A budgeted balance sheet as of June 30.

chapter 9

Control through Standard Costs

In ATTEMPTING to control costs, managers have two types of decisions to make—decisions relating to prices paid, and to quantities used. A manager is expected to pay the lowest possible prices, consistent with the quality of output desired, in attaining the objectives of his firm. In attaining these objectives he is also expected to consume the minimum quantity of whatever resources he has at his command, again consistent with the quality of output desired. Breakdowns in control over either price or quantity will lead to excessive costs and to deteriorating profit margins.

How does a manager attempt to control price paid and quantity used? He could personally examine every transaction that takes place, but this obviously would be an inefficient use of management time. The answer to the control problem lies in *standard costs*.

STANDARD COSTS—MANAGEMENT BY EXCEPTION

A standard may be defined as a benchmark for measuring achievement. It represents a certain degree of excellence to be attained, and stands as the basis for measuring the adequacy of results that have been accomplished. Standards are used in cost control to measure how well operations are being kept within the price and quantity limits that are necessary if optimum profit levels are to be attained.

Standards are set for all three elements in the cost of a manufactured product—materials, labor, and overhead—and in terms of both *quantity* and *cost*. Quantity standards say *how much* of a cost element, such as materials, should be used in producing a single unit of product. Cost standards say what the cost of this quantity of materials should be. Actual quantities and actual costs of inputs are measured against these standards to see if operations are proceeding within the limits that management has set. If either quantity or cost of inputs exceeds the bounds which management has set, attention is directed to the difference, thereby permitting the manager to focus his efforts where they will do the most good.

How Are Standard Costs Set?

The setting of standard costs is more of an art than a science. It involves the combined thinking and expertise of several persons, including the managerial accountant, the industrial engineer, and the line managers who will be working under the standard costs that are set.

The beginning point in setting standard costs in a rigorous look at past experience. The managerial accountant can be of great help in this task by preparing data on the cost characteristics of prior years' activities at various levels of operations. A standard for the future must be more than simply a projection of the past, however, Data must be adjusted and modified in terms of changing economic patterns, demand and supply characteristics, and changing technology. Past experience in certain costs may be distorted due to inefficiencies. To the extent that such inefficiencies can be identified, the data must be appropriately adjusted. The manager must realize that the past is of value only insofar as it helps to predict the future. Standards must be reflective of what costs *should be,* not just what they *have been.*

The industrial engineer plays a key role in setting standard costs through his studies of plant layout, flow of goods, and measurement of work tasks. The measurement of work tasks is of particular importance. The tasks associated with each operation must be carefully timed and evaluated. The resulting measures are then used to assist in determining the acceptable level of efficiency for each operation.

Although both the managerial accountant and the industrial engineer play key roles in the setting of standard costs, the final decisions on what standards will prevail must come about through face-to-face meetings between the line manager who will have to work under the standard being set, and his immediate superior. A key concept in the budgeting and control process is that no person should be measured against a cost over which he has no control. Therefore, the basic, final responsibility for standard setting must fall on the person who will be working under the standard itself. Any other approach to standard setting will almost certainly breed deep resentment on the part of line personnel, and probably lead to failure of the control function.

Ideal versus Practical Standards

How should standards be set? Should they be attainable all of the time, or only part of the time; or should they be so tight that they become, in effect, "the impossible dream"? Opinions among managers vary, but standards tend to fall into one of two categories—either ideal or pratical.

Ideal standards are those that can be attained only under the best circumstances. They allow for no machine breakdowns, work interruptions, etc., and call for a level of effort that can be attained only by the most skilled and efficient employee working at peak effort 100 percent of the time. Some managers feel that such standards have a motivational value. These managers argue that even though an employee knows he will never stay within the standard set, it is a constant reminder to him of the need for ever-increasing efficiency and effort. Few firms use ideal standards. Most managers are of the opinion that ideal standards tend to discourage even the most diligent workers. Moreover, when ideal standards are used, variances from standards have little meaning. The reason is that they contain elements of "normal" inefficiency, not just the abnormal inefficiencies that managers would like to have isolated and brought to their attention.

Practical standards can be defined as standards that are "tight, but attainable." They allow for normal machine breakdown time, pauses by employees, etc. They can be attained through reasonable, though highly efficient, efforts by the average worker at a particular task. Variances from such a standard are very useful to management in that they represent deviations that fall outside of normal, recurring inefficiencies, and signal a need for management attention. Furthermore, practical standards can serve multiple purposes. In addition to signaling abnormal deviations in costs, they can also be used in forecasting cash flows and in inventory planning. By contrast, ideal standards cannot be used in forecasting and planning; they do not allow for normal inefficiencies, and therefore result in unrealistic planning and forecasting figures.

Advantages of Standard Costs

A number of distinct advantages can be cited in favor of using standard costs in an organization.

1. The use of standard costs makes possible the concept of "management by exception." So long as costs remain within the standards set, no attention by management is needed. When costs fall outside of the standards set, then the matter is brought to the attention of management at once as an "exception." "Management by exception" makes possible more productive use of management time.

2. Standard costs facilitate cash planning and inventory planning.

3. So long as standards are set on a "practical" basis, they promote economy and efficiency in that employees normally become very cost conscious. In addition, wage incentive systems can be tied to a system of standard costs once the standards have been set.

4. In income determination, a system of standard costs may be more economical and simpler to operate than a historical cost system. Standard cost cards can be kept for each product or operation, and costs for material, labor, and manufacturing overhead charged out according to the standards set. Any costs above the standards allowed can be added through the use of some type of "excess requisition" slip, thereby pinpointing any variance in cost as soon as it occurs.

5. Standard costs can assist in the implementation of "responsibility accounting," in which responsibility over cost control is assigned, and the extent to which that responsibility has been discharged can be evaluated through performance reports.

Are Standards the Same as Budgets?

Essentially standards and budgets are the same thing. The only distinction between the two terms is that a standard is a *unit* concept, whereas a budget is a *total* concept. That is, the standard cost for materials in a unit of product may be $5. If 1,000 units of the product are to be produced during a period, then the budgeted cost of materials is $5,000. In effect, a standard may be viewed as being the *budget for a single unit of product.*

In most firms, direct labor and raw materials are controlled through use of standard costs, whereas manufacturing overhead is controlled through use of departmental overhead budgets. The reason for this is that direct labor and raw material costs tend to be very large in dollar amount per unit of product, and therefore are easy to isolate and control individually through use of standard costs. By contrast, manufacturing overhead is made up of many *small cost* items that are more easily controlled through working with the *total* budgeted amounts for a particular period.

In the remaining sections of this chapter we first consider the use of standard costs in controlling raw materials and direct labor. We then briefly examine methods of analyzing variable manufacturing overhead. The bulk of our discussion of overhead control will be reserved until the following chapter.

A GENERAL MODEL FOR VARIANCE ANALYSIS

Earlier in the chapter the point was made that managers have two types of decisions to make in their attempts to control costs—decisions relating to prices paid, and decisions relating to quantities used. Generally, these decisions will fall at different points in time.

For example, in the case of raw materials, the price decision will be made at the time of purchase. By contrast, the quantity decision will be made at the time the raw materials are used in production, which may be many weeks or months after the purchase date. In addition, the price and quantity decisions will very likely be made by different managers, and will therefore need to be assessed independently. As we stressed earlier, a basic concept of cost control is that no person should be held responsible for a cost over which he has no control. It is important, therefore, that we separate price considerations from quantity considerations in our approach to the control of costs.

The General Model

A general model exists that is very useful in variance analysis. A *variance* is the difference between *standard* prices and quantities and *actual* prices and quantities. This model helps to distinguish between *price* variances and *quantity* variances, as well as showing how each of these variances is computed. The model is presented in Exhibit 9–1.

Two things should be noted from the exhibit. First, that a price variance and a quantity variance can be computed for all three variable cost elements—materials, labor, and variable overhead—even though the variance is not called by the same name in all cases. For example,

EXHIBIT 9–1
A General Model for Variance Analysis

(1) Actual Quantity × Actual Price

Price Variance
(1) – (2)

Materials Price Variance
Labor Rate Variance
Variable Overhead Spending Variance

(2) Actual Quantity × Standard Price

Quantity Variance
(2) – (3)

Materials Quantity Variance
Labor Efficiency Variance
Variable Overhead Efficiency Variance

(3) Standard Quantity × Standard Price

Total Budget Variance (1) – (3)

a price variance is called a "materials price variance" in the case of materials, but a "labor rate variance" in the case of direct labor and an "overhead spending variance" in the case of variable manufacturing overhead.

Second, even though a price variance may be called by different names, it is computed in exactly the same way regardless of whether one is dealing with materials, labor, or variable overhead. The same is true with the quantity variance. With this general model as a foundation, we will now examine the price and quantity variances in more detail.

USING STANDARD COSTS—PRICE VARIANCES

Materials Price Variance

A materials price variance measures the difference between what is paid for a given quantity of materials and what should have been paid according to the standard that has been set. From Exhibit 9–1 this difference can be expressed by the following formula:

$$\left(\begin{array}{c}\text{Actual} \\ \text{Quantity}\end{array} \times \begin{array}{c}\text{Actual} \\ \text{Price}\end{array}\right) - \left(\begin{array}{c}\text{Actual} \\ \text{Quantity}\end{array} \times \begin{array}{c}\text{Standard} \\ \text{Price}\end{array}\right) = \text{Price Variance}$$

or, in terms of symbols only,

$$(AQ \times AP) - (AQ \times SP) = \text{Price Variance}$$

The formula can be factored into simpler form as:

$$AQ(AP - SP) = \text{Price Variance}$$

The Price Variance Illustrated. Assume that the production superintendent of Gates Corporation has instructed the purchasing agent to acquire 2,000 lbs. of Material X and 500 gallons of Material Y. The standard cost of Material X is $2 per pound, and the standard cost of Material Y is $8 per gallon. If the purchasing agent actually acquires Material X for $2.20 per pound, and Material Y for $7.80 per gallon, the acquisitions will be evaluated as follows:

$$AQ(AP - SP) = \text{Price Variance}$$

Material X: 2,000 lbs. ($2.20 − $2.00) = $400 U
Material Y: 500 gals. ($7.80 − $8.00) = $100 F

For Material X the variance is unfavorable (U), while for Material Y the variance is favorable (F). The Gates Corporation could place its variance analysis into performance report form, as follows:

GATES CORPORATION
Performance Report–Purchasing Department

Item Purchased	(1) Quantity Purchased	(2) Actual Price	(3) Standard Price	(4) Difference In Price (2) – (3)	Total Price Variance (1) × (4)
Material X	2,000 lbs.	$2.20/lb.	$2/lb.	$.20/lb. U	$400 U
Material Y	500 gals.	$7.80/gal.	$8/gal.	$.20/gal. F	$100 F

F = Favorable   U = Unfavorable

A variance is unfavorable if the actual exceeds the standard, as in the case of Material X above. A variance is favorable if the actual is less than the standard, as in the case of Material Y above.

At what point should variances be isolated and brought to the attention of management? The answer is, the earlier the better. One of the basic reasons for utilizing standard costs is to facilitate cost control. Therefore, the sooner deviations from standard are brought to the attention of management, the sooner problems can be evaluated and corrected. If long periods are allowed to elapse before variances are computed, costs that otherwise could have been controlled may accumulate to the point that significant damage may be done to profits. Many firms compute materials price variances, for example, at the time that purchase orders are placed with suppliers, rather than waiting until an actual invoice is received. This permits early recognition of any potential price variances, and makes possible adjustment of purchase plans, if necessary.

How Are Variances Used? Once a performance report as been prepared, what does management do with the price variance data? The variances should be viewed as "red flags," calling attention to the fact that an exception has occurred which will require some follow-up effort. Normally the performance report itself will contain some explanation of the underlying cause of each variance and a statement as to what action is recommended to keep the variance from reoccurring in the future.

The essential point is that variances signal to management some particular area of operations to which attention must be directed if cost control is to be maintained.

Responsibility for the Variance. Who is responsible for the materials price variance? Generally speaking, the purchasing agent has control over the price to be paid for goods, and therefore is responsible for any price variances. Many factors control the price paid for goods, including size of lots purchased, delivery method used, quantity discounts available, rush orders, quality of materials purchased, etc. To the extent that the purchasing agent can control these factors, he is responsible for seeing that they are kept in agreement with the factors anticipated when the standard costs were initially set. A deviation in any factor from what was intended in the initial setting of a standard cost can result in a price variance. For example, delivery by air freight, rather than by truck as intended in the standard cost, would result in an unfavorable price variance.

There may be times, however, when someone other than the purchasing agent is responsible for a materials price variance. Production may be scheduled in such a way, for example, that the purchasing agent is required to obtain delivery of goods by air freight, or he may be forced to buy in uneconomical quantities. In these cases, the production superintendent will bear responsibility for variances that develop.

A word of caution is in order. Variance analysis should not be used as an excuse to conduct witch hunts, or as a means of beating line managers over the head. The emphasis must be on the control function in the sense of *supporting* the line managers, and *assisting* them in meeting the goals they have participated in setting for the company. In short, the emphasis must be positive, rather than negative. Excessive dwelling on what has already happened, particularly in terms of trying to find someone to "blame," can often be destructive to the goals of an organization.

Labor Rate Variances

The price variance for labor is commonly termed a *rate* variance. The variance is computed in exactly the same way as the materials price variance except that in place of the terms "quantity" and "price," the terms "hours" and "rate" are used.

$$\begin{pmatrix} \text{Actual} \\ \text{Hours} \end{pmatrix} \times \begin{pmatrix} \text{Actual} \\ \text{Rate} \end{pmatrix} - \begin{pmatrix} \text{Actual} \\ \text{Hours} \end{pmatrix} \times \begin{pmatrix} \text{Standard} \\ \text{Rate} \end{pmatrix} = \text{Rate Variance}$$

In terms of symbols only, the formula is:

$$(AH \times AR) - (AH \times SR) = \text{Rate Variance}$$

It can be factored into simpler form as:

$$AH(AR - SR) = \text{Rate Variance}$$

In many firms the rates paid workers are set by union contract; therefore, rate variances, in terms of amounts paid to workers, tend to be almost nonexistant. Rate variances can arise, though, through the way labor is used. Skilled workmen with high hourly rates of pay can be given duties that require little skill and call for low hourly rates of pay. This type of misallocation of the work force will result in unfavorable labor rate variances since the actual hourly rate of pay will exceed the standard rate authorized for the particular task being performed. A reverse situation exists when unskilled or untrained workers are paid hourly rates rather than piecework rates. The low productivity of the unskilled workers will result in unfavorable rate variances. Unfavorable rate variances can also arise from overtime work at premium rates.

Who is responsible for controlling the labor rate variance? Since rate variances generally arise as a result of how labor is used, those supervisors in charge of effective utilization of labor time bear responsibility for seeing that labor rate variances are kept under control.

The Rate Variance Illustrated. Let us assume that Gates Corporation has two labor tasks, grinding and assembly, in a particular operation. The standard labor cost for grinding is $4 per direct labor hour. The standard labor cost for assembly is $9 per completed unit. Assume that during the preceding period 500 hours were worked in grinding at an average rate of $3.90 per direct labor hour. Also assume that during the same period 400 units were completed in assembly at a labor cost of $9.25 per unit. The rate variances would be:

$$AH(AR - SR) = \text{Rate Variance}$$

Grinding: 500 hrs ($3.90 − $4.00) = $50 F
Assembly: 400 units ($9.25 − $9.00) = $100 U

If the company wanted to place the rate varaince data into a more formal form, the following performance report could be prepared:

GATES CORPORATION
Performance Report—Grinding and Assembly Operation

Task	(1) Actual Hours Worked or Units Completed	(2) Actual Rate	(3) Standard Rate	(4) Difference In Rate (2) − (3)	Total Rate Variance (1) × (4)
Grinding	500 hrs.	$3.90/DLH	$4/DLH	$.10/DLH F	$50 F
Assembly	400 units	$9.25/Unit	$9/Unit	$.25/Unit U	$100 U

F = Favorable   U = Unfavorable

USING STANDARD COSTS—QUANTITY VARIANCES

Standards are set on the *quantity* of raw materials and on the *amount* of direct labor time going into a finished product, the same as standards are set on the costs of these items. The standard quantities and amounts to be used are detailed on a *bill of materials* and on a *standard time sheet* for materials and labor, respectively. These forms are illustrated in Exhibits 9–2 and 9–3.

EXHIBIT 9–2
Bill of Materials

Department ___5___   Operation ___Assembly___   Description ___Chair___

Part Number	Quantity	Description
Q446	1	Padded back
R2834	1	Padded seat
LG19	2	Tubular support legs
LG20	2	Tubular support legs
BT88	1	Bolt kit
P8	4	Leg plugs
BR90	2	Braces

EXHIBIT 9–3
Standard Time Sheet

Department ___5___   Operation ___Assembly___   Description ___Chair___

Task	Time	Rate/DLH
Weld tubular legs	8 min.	$3.00
Bolt back and seat	2 min.	$3.00
Attach leg plugs and weld braces	2 min.	$3.00
	12 min.	

Materials Quantity Variance

The materials quantity variance is best isolated at the time that materials are placed into production. Materials are drawn for the number of units to be produced, according to the standard bill of materials for each unit. Any additional materials are usually drawn on an excess materials requisition slip, which is different in color from the normal requisition slips. This procedure calls attention to the excessive usuage of materials *while production is still in process,* and permits opportunity for early control of any developing problem.

Although the materials quantity variance is concerned with the physical usage of materials, the variance is generally stated in dollar terms. From Exhibit 9–1, the formula for the materials quantity variance is:

$$\left(\begin{array}{c} \text{Actual} \\ \text{Quantity} \end{array} \times \begin{array}{c} \text{Standard} \\ \text{Price} \end{array}\right) - \left(\begin{array}{c} \text{Standard} \\ \text{Quantity} \end{array} \times \begin{array}{c} \text{Standard} \\ \text{Price} \end{array}\right) = \text{Quantity Variance}$$

In terms of symbols only, the formula is:

$$(AQ \times SP) - (SQ \times SP) = \text{Quantity Variance}$$

Again, the formula can be factored into simpler terms:

$$SP(AQ - SQ) = \text{Quantity Variance}$$

Computing the Materials Quantity Variance. To illustrate the computation of the materials quantity variance, we shall return to the example of Gates Corporation used earlier. In the earlier example we assumed the following data:

Item	Quantity Available	Standard Price
Material X	2,000 lbs.	$2/lb.
Material Y	500 gallons	$8/gal.

Let us assume that it takes 4 pounds of Material X and 1 gallon of Material Y to make a finished unit of product. All 2,000 pounds of Material X and all 500 gallons of Material Y are used in producing 450 units of finished product. The quantity variances would be:

$$SP(AQ - SQ) = \text{Quantity Variance}$$

Material X: $2/lb. (2,000 lbs. − 1,800 lbs.[1]) = $400 U
Material Y: $8/gal. (500 gals. − 450 gals.[2]) = $400 U

The same data placed in performance report format would be:

GATES CORPORATION
Performance Report–Production Department

Types of Materials	(1) Standard Price	(2) Actual Quantity	(3) Standard Quantity	(4) Difference In Quantity (2) – (3)	Total Quant Varian (1) ×
Material X	$2/lb.	2,000 lbs.	450 finished units × 4 lbs. = 1 800 lbs.	200 lbs. U	$400
Material Y	$8/gal.	500 gals.	450 finished units × 1 gal. = 450 gals.	50 gals. U	$400

U = Unfavorable   F = Favorable

Notice the use of the term *standard quantity* above. Standard quantity can be defined as the quantity of materials that *should have been used* to complete the output of the period.

Using the Variance Report. What does the manager do with this information? He seeks to find the *cause* of the variances, as explained earlier. Excessive usage of raw materials can result, for example, from inferior quality purchased, from untrained workers, or from faulty machines. It is the responsibility of the production department to see that material usage is kept in line with standards. There may be times, however, when the *purchasing* department may be responsible for an unfavorable material quantity variance. If the purchasing department obtains

---

[1] 450 units × 4 lbs./unit = 1,800 lbs.
[2] 450 finished units × 1 gal. of Material Y each = 450 gals.

materials of inferior quality in an effort to economize on price, the materials may prove to be unsuitable for use on the production line and may result in excessive waste. In such situations, the purchasing department would have to bear responsibility for the materials quantity variance.

Labor Efficiency Variance

The labor quantity variance, more commonly called the labor *efficiency* variance, measures the productivity of labor time. No variance is more closely watched by management since increasing productivity of labor time is a vital key to reducing unit costs of production.

The labor efficiency variance is computed using the same basic formula used in computing the materials quantity variance. In place of the terms "price" and "quantity" the terms "rate" and "hours" are used:

$$\left(\begin{array}{c}\text{Actual}\\\text{Hours}\end{array} \times \begin{array}{c}\text{Standard}\\\text{Rate}\end{array}\right) - \left(\begin{array}{c}\text{Standard}\\\text{Hours}\end{array} \times \begin{array}{c}\text{Standard}\\\text{Rate}\end{array}\right) = \text{Efficiency Variance}$$

or, in terms of symbols only,

$$(AH \times SR) - (SH \times SR) = \text{Efficiency Variance}$$

Factored into simpler terms, the formula is:

$$SR(AH - SH) = \text{Efficiency Variance}$$

Computing the Labor Efficiency Variance. To illustrate the computation of the labor efficiency variance, we will again return to the data of Gates Corporation. In our earlier example dealing with direct labor, we assumed the following:

Task	Standard Labor Time Per Unit	Standard Rate	Units Completed
Grinding	1 hr.	$4/DLH	400
Assembly	2¼ hr.*	$4/DLH	400

* $9/unit ÷ $4/DLH = 2¼ hrs.

Let us assume that 500 hours of grinding time and 800 hours of assembly time were used to produce the 400 completed units of product listed above. The labor efficiency variances would be:

$$SR(AH - SH) = \text{Efficiency Variance}$$

Grinding: $4/DLH (500 hrs. − 400 hrs.[3]) = $400 U
Assembly: $4/DLH (800 hrs. − 900 hrs.[4]) = $400 F

---

[3] 400 units × 1 hr. = 400 hrs.
[4] 400 units × 2¼ hrs. = 900 hrs.

These same data in performance report format would be:

GATES CORPORATION
Performance Report—Production Department

Task	(1) Standard Labor Rate	(2) Actual Hours	(3) Standard Hours	(4) Difference In Hours (2) – (3)	Total Efficiency Variance (1) × (4)
Grinding	$4/DLH	500 hrs.	400 units × 1 hr. = 400 hrs.	100 hrs. U	$400 U
Assembly	$4/DLH	800 hrs.	400 units × 2¼ hrs. = 900 hrs.	100 hrs. F	$400 F

F = Favorable   U = Unfavorable

Notice the use of the term *standard hours* above. Standard hours can be defined as the time that *should have been taken* to complete the output of the period.

GRAPHICAL ANALYSIS OF THE PRICE AND QUANTITY VARIANCES

The way in which the price and quantity variances are computed can lead to a problem between the purchasing and production departments. The problem can be illustrated by graphing the price and quantity variances that we computed earlier for Material X of Gates Corporation. The variances are summarized below, and then presented in graphical form in Exhibit 9–4.

Summary of Data—Material X

Standard price per lb	$2.00
Actual price per lb	$2.20
Standard quantity for production of 450 units of product (4 lbs. per unit × 450 units)	1,800 lbs.
Actual quantity used in production of 450 units of product	2,000 lbs.

Summary of Variances—Material X:

$$AQ(AP - SP) = \text{Price Variance}$$
$$2{,}000 \text{ lbs. } (\$2.20 - \$2.00) = \$400 \text{ U}$$
$$SP(AQ - SQ) = \text{Quantity Variance}$$
$$\$2.00(2{,}000 \text{ lbs. } - 1{,}800 \text{ lbs.}) = \$400 \text{ U}$$

The problem referred to can arise from the upper right corner of the graph in Exhibit 9–4. This corner represents a *mutual price-quantity variance,* although we have shown it to be part of the price variance in our computations above. The purchasing agent may contend that it us unfair to charge him for the $40 mutual price-quantity variance

EXHIBIT 9–4
Graphical Analysis of Price and Quantity Variances

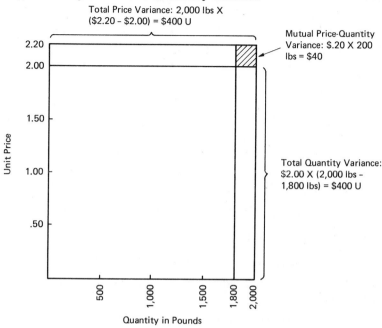

Total Price Variance: 2,000 lbs X
($2.20 – $2.00) = $400 U

Mutual Price-Quantity
Variance: $.20 X 200
lbs = $40

Total Quantity Variance:
$2.00 X (2,000 lbs –
1,800 lbs) = $400 U

Unit Price

Quantity in Pounds

represented in this corner since it has arisen only because of the inefficient use of materials by the production department. If the production department had produced at standard and used only the 1,800 lbs. of materials called for, then the extra 200 lbs. of materials wouldn't have been purchased in the first place, and the extra $40 of variance would not have arisen. The purchasing agent may argue, therefore, that the $40 mutual price-quantity variance should be charged to production, not to purchasing.

Whether the mutual price-quantity variance is computed as part of the price variance, as we have done, or as part of the quantity variance, will depend on which variance management feels is most important. Generally speaking, the quantity variance is viewed as being the most important of the two since quantity used tends to be more controllable than price paid. For this reason, most firms will consider the mutual price-quantity variance to be part of the price variance in an effort to keep the quantity variance as "clean" as possible.

VARIABLE OVERHEAD VARIANCES

The variable portion of manufacturing overhead can be analyzed and controlled using the same basic variance formulas as in analyzing materials and labor. In order to lay a foundation for the following chapter, where we discuss overhead control at length, it will be helpful at this time to illustrate the analysis of variable overhead using these basic formulas. As a basis for discussion, assume the following information:

Standard variable overhead rate per direct labor hour $6
Standard direct labor hours per unit of finished product.   3
Number of finished units for the period   300
Actual direct labor hours worked   960
Actual variable overhead cost $6,048

The Spending Variance

As illustrated earlier in Exhibit 9–1, the variable overhead spending variance is computed the same way as the material price variance and the labor rate variance. The formula is:

$$(AH \times AR) - (AH \times SR) = \text{Spending Variance}$$

or, factored into simpler terms:

$$AH(AR - SR) = \text{Spending Variance}$$

Using this formula, the spending variance computed on the data above would be:

$$960 \text{ hrs. } (\$6.30^5 - \$6.00) = \$288 \text{ U}$$

The Efficiency Variance

Based on the data in Exhibit 9–1, the formula for the variable overhead efficiency variance is:

$$(AH \times SR) - (SH \times SR) = \text{Efficiency Variance}$$

or, factored into simpler terms:

$$SR(AH - SH) = \text{Efficiency Variance}$$

Using this formula, the efficiency variance computed from the data above would be:

$$\$6(960 \text{ hrs. } - 900 \text{ hrs.}^6) = \$360 \text{ U}$$

VARIANCE ANALYSIS AND MANAGEMENT BY EXCEPTION

Variance analysis and performance reports provide a vehicle for implementation of the concept of management by exception. Simply put, management by exception means that the manager's attention must be directed toward those parts of the organization where things are not

---

[5] $6,048 ÷ 960 hrs. = $6.30.

[6] 3 hrs. × 300 units = 900 hrs.

proceeding according to plans. Since a manager's time is limited, he must use every hour as effectively as possible, and not waste time and effort looking after those parts of the organization where things are going smoothly.

The budgets and standards discussed in this and in the preceding chapter represent the "plans" of management. If all goes smoothly then it would be expected that costs will fall within the budgets and standards that have been set. To the extent that this happens, the manager is free to spend his time elsewhere with the assurance that, at least in the budgeted areas, all is proceeding according to expectations. To the extent that actual costs and revenues do not conform to the budget, however, a signal comes to the manager that an "exception" has occurred. This exception comes in the form of a variance from the budget or standard that was originally set.

The major question at this point is, "Are *all* variances to be considered exceptions that will require the attention of management?" The answer is no. If every variance was considered to be an exception, then management would get little else done other than chasing down nickle-and-dime differences. Obviously, some criteria are needed to determine when a variance has occurred that can properly be called an exception. We consider some of these criteria below.

Criteria for Determining "Exceptions"

It is probably safe to say that only by the rarest of coincidences will actual costs and revenues ever conform exactly to the budgeted pattern. The reason is that even though budgets may be prepared with the greatest of care, it will never be possible to develop budgeted data that contain the precise allowances necessary for each of the multitude of variables that can affect actual costs and revenues. For this reason, one can expect that in every period virtually every budgeted figure will produce a variance of some type when compared to actual cost data. How do managers decide which of all of these variances are worthy of their attention? We can identify at least four criteria that are used in actual practice: materiality, consistency of occurrence, ability to control, and nature of the item.

Materiality. Ordinarily, management will be interested only in those variances that are material in amount. To separate the material variances from the immaterial variances, firms often set guidelines, such as stating that any variance that differs from the budget by 10 percent or more will be considered a material variance. Notice that we said "differs" from the budget, not "exceeds" the budget. We say "differs" because management will be just as interested in those material variances that are *under* the budget as they are in those that exceed it. The reason is that a level of spending that is under the budget can be just as critical to profitability as a level of spending that exceeds the budget. For example, if advertising is budgeted to be $100,000 during a period and only $80,000 is spent, this favorable spending variance could be damaging to profits because of insufficient promotion of the firm's products.

Generally, a guideline such as a 10 percent deviation from budget will not be sufficient to judge whether a variance is material. The reason is that a 5 percent variance in some costs could be far more critical to profits than a 20 percent variance in other costs. For this reason, a firm will often supplement the percentage guideline with some minimum absolute dollar figure, stating that even if a variance doesn't exceed the percentage guideline it will still be considered material if it exceeds the minimum dollar figure. To illustrate, a firm might state that any variance will be considered material if it differs from the budget by 10 percent or more, or $1,000.

Consistency of Occurrence. Even if a variance never exceeds the minimum stated percentage or the minimum dollar amount, many firms want it brought to the attention of management if it comes *close* to these limits period after period. The thinking here is that the budget or standard could be out of date, and adjustment to more current levels might improve overall profit planning. Or, that some laxness in cost control may be present, warranting an occasional check by the relevant supervisor.

Ability to Control. Some costs are largely out of the control of management, and in such cases even though variances may occur that are material in amount, no follow-up action on management's part is necessary. For example, utility rates and local tax rates are generally not controllable internally, and large variances resulting from rate increases will require little or no follow-up effort, even though they may be presented on the variance report for information purposes.

Nature of the Item. By their very nature, some costs are much more critical to long-run profitability than others. One such cost is advertising. As mentioned above, underutilization of the advertising budget can have a severe adverse impact on sales, with a resulting loss of revenue that greatly outweighs any saving in advertising dollars. Another such cost is maintenance. Although inadequate maintenance may produce short-run savings in costs, these savings will likely be more than offset by future breakdowns, repairs, and loss of revenue from reduced productivity and efficiency.

Because of the critical nature of costs such as advertising and maintenance, the guidelines for determining whether a variance is material are usually much more stringent for them than for other costs. That is, these variances are generally watched more closely by management than those in other, less critical, areas. It may be that management will want to see *any* variance in certain key areas such as advertising and promotion. In addition, the normal guidelines may be reduced by half in other key areas such as maintenance and certain critical component parts.

Statistical Analysis of Random Variances

The purpose of establishing criteria for separating material from immaterial variances is to isolate those variances which are *not* due to random causes, and which can and should be controlled by the company. The "10 percent of budget, or $1,000" approach described in the preceding section is a somewhat crude way of accomplishing this objective, although it is used widely in practice. The approach is crude because it really is based on rough guessing and on rules of thumb rather than on precise analysis.

A much more dependable way of separating random variances from those variances which are controllable can be found in statistical analysis. This approach to segregating random variances has its basis in the idea that a budget or standard represents a *range* of acceptability, rather than a single point. Any variance falling within this range is considered to be due solely to random causes which either are not within the ability of management to control or which would be impractical to control. One author puts the idea this way:

> Measured quality of manufactured product is always subject to a certain amount of variation as a result of chance. Some stable "system of chance causes" is inherent in any particular scheme of production and inspection. Variation within this stable pattern is inevitable. The reasons for variation outside this stable pattern [should] be discovered and corrected.[7]

How does a firm isolate the range within which variances from budget will be due to chance or random causes? This is done by means of statistical sampling of the population represented by the budgeted data. Random samples of the population are drawn, and the variances found in these samples are plotted on a *control chart*, such as illustrated in Exhibit 9–5. In effect, the upper and lower limits on the chart represent the normal distribution (bell-shaped curve), with the upper and lower limits generally being three standard deviations from the grand mean. Any variances falling within the upper and lower control limits will be due simply to chance occurrences and, therefore, will not be within the ability of management to control. Any variances falling outside of these limits will not be due to random or chance causes, and will be

[7] Eugene L. Grant and Richard L. Leavenworth, *Statistical Quality Control*, 4th Edition (New York: McGraw-Hill Book Company, 1972), page 3. Used with permission of McGraw-Hill Book Company.

EXHIBIT 9–5
A Statistical Control Chart

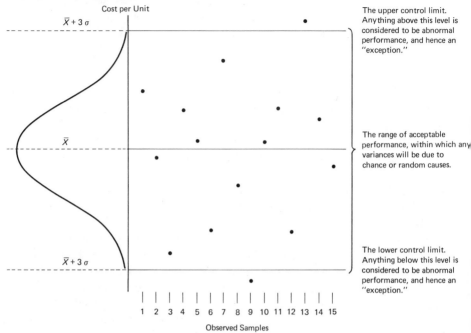

considered "exceptions" toward which management attention will need to be directed.

The value of a budgeting system is greatly increased if variances are analyzed by a statistical approach such as that described above, rather than by the "10 percent or $1,000" approach described earlier. The reason, of course, is that the statistical approach eliminates guesswork and zeros management in on those cost variations that are indeed within its ability to control.[8]

SUMMARY

Cost control centers in two areas—price paid, and quantity used. The best way to effect control in these two areas is through use of standard costs. A standard can be viewed as being the budget for a single unit of product expressed in terms of either price or quantity.

Generally, standards are set by the cooperative effort of many people in an organization, including the accountant, the industrial engineer, and various levels of management. Standards are normally "practical"

---

[8] For further discussion of this and other statistical uses in cost analysis, see Joel S. Demski, *Information Analysis* (Reading, Mass: Addison-Wesley Publishing Company, Inc., 1972), chapter 6.

in nature, meaning that they can be attained by reasonable, though highly efficient, efforts. Such standards are generally felt to have a favorable motivational impact on employees.

Comparing standards against actual performance results in variances. If a variance falls outside of the limits set by management, it is considered to be an exception toward which management time and attention must be directed. Ordinarily, the accounting system will be organized in such a way as to bring exceptions to the attention of management as early in time as possible in order that control may be maintained, and corrections made before significant damage is done to profits.

REVIEW PROBLEM ON STANDARD COSTS

Xavier Company produces a single product. The standard costs for one unit of product are:

Direct material: 6 oz. at $.50 per oz.	$ 3.00
Direct labor: 2 hrs. at $5.00 per hr.	10.00
Variable overhead: 2 hrs. at $2.00 per hr.	4.00
Total standard variable cost per unit	$17.00

During June, 400 units were produced. The costs associated with the month were:

Material purchased: 4,000 oz. at $.55	$2,200
Material used in production: 2,800 oz.	—
Direct labor: 890 hrs. at $4.70	4,183
Variable overhead costs incurred	2,047

Materials Variances

Actual Quantity
  × Actual Price
4,000 oz. × $.55
  = $2,200

Price variance, $200 U

4,000 oz. × $.50
  = $2,000
Actual Quantity
  × Standard Price
2,800 oz. × $.50
  = $1,400

Quantity variance, $200 U

Standard Quantity
  × Standard Price
2,400[9] oz. × $.50
  = $1,200

A total budget variance can't be computed in this situation, since the amount of materials purchased (4,000 ozs.) differs from the amount of materials used in production (2,800 ozs.).

[9] 400 units × 6 oz. = 2,400 oz.

The same variances in shortcut format would be:

$$AQ(AP - SP) = \text{Price Variance}$$
$$4{,}000 \text{ oz. (\$.55} - \$.50) = \$200 \text{ U}$$
$$SP(AQ - SQ) = \text{Quantity Variance}$$
$$\$.50 \text{ (2,800 oz.} - 2{,}400 \text{ oz.)} = \$200 \text{ U}$$

Notice that the price variance is computed on the entire amount of material purchased (4,000 oz.), whereas the quantity variance is computed only on the portion of this material used in production during the period (2,800 ozs.). This is a common situation. The price variance is always computed on whatever materials have been purchased. The quantity variance, however, can only be computed on that portion of the purchased materials *actually used* during the period.

Labor Variances

Actual Hours
 × Actual Rate
890 hrs. × $4.70
 = $4,183

Rate variance, $267 F

Actual Hours
 × Standard Rate
890 hrs. × $5.00
 = $4,450

Budget variance, $183 U

Efficiency variance, $450 U

Standard Hours
 × Standard Rate
800[9] hrs. × $5.00
 = $4,000

The same variances in shortcut format would be:

$$AH(AR - SR) = \text{Rate Variance}$$
$$890 \text{ hrs (\$4.70} - \$5.00) = \$267 \text{ F}$$
$$SR(AH - SH) = \text{Efficiency Variance}$$
$$\$5.00 \text{ (890 hrs.} - 800 \text{ hrs.)} = \$450 \text{ U}$$

---

[9] 400 units × 2 hrs. = 800 hrs.

Variable Overhead Variances

Actual Hours
  × Actual Rate
890 hrs. × $2.30[10]
  = $2,047

Spending variance, $267 U

Actual Hours
  × Standard Rate
890 hrs. × $2.00
  = $1,780

Budget variance, $447 U

Efficiency variance, $180 U

Standard Hours
  × Standard Rate
800[11] hrs. × $2.00
  = $1,600

The same variances in shortcut format would be:

$$AH(AR - SR) = \text{Spending Variance}$$
$$890 \text{ hrs. } (\$2.30 - \$2.00) = \$267 \text{ U}$$
$$SR(AH - SH) = \text{Efficiency Variance}$$
$$\$2.00 \ (890 \text{ hrs. } - 800 \text{ hrs.}) = \$180 \text{ U}$$

QUESTIONS

9–1. What is the difference between a budget and a standard?

9–2. Why must a standard for the future be more than simply a projection of the past?

9–3. Distinguish between ideal and practical standards.

9–4. What is meant by the term "variance"?

9–5. What is meant by the term "management by exception"?

9–6. Why are variances generally segregated in terms of a price variance and a quantity variance?

9–7. Who generally is responsible for the materials price variance? The materials quantity variance? The labor efficiency variance?

9–8. "Our workers are all under labor contracts; therefore, our labor rate variance is bound to be zero." Discuss.

9–9. Why is the mutual price-quantity variance generally buried in the price variance, rather than in the quantity variance?

9–10. What factors are considered by management in determining whether a variance is properly called an exception?

9–11. Who is responsible for developing standards?

9–12. What is a statistical control chart, and how is it used?

---

[10] $2,047 ÷ 890 hrs. = $2.30.

[11] 400 units × 2 hrs. = 800 hrs.

EXERCISES

9–1. Arnett Products has just completed operations for the month of June. The total standard costs for all activity during June are given below.

	Total Standard Cost
Direct materials	$50,000
Direct labor	90,000
Variable factory overhead	60,000

Variances from standard:

	Favorable	*Unfavorable*
Materials price variance	$2,000	
Materials quantity variance	1,000	
Labor rate variance		$1,500
Labor efficiency variance		3,000
Overhead spending variance	3,000	
Overhead efficiency variance		2,000

Required:

Compute the actual cost incurred during June for direct materials, direct labor, and variable factory overhead. There were no beginning or ending inventories of materials.

9–2. Rosewood Household Products, Inc., manufactures a number of consumer items for general household use. One of these products, a chopping board, requires an expensive hardwood in its manufacture. During a recent month, the company manufactured 4,000 chopping boards, using 10,400 board feet of hardwood in the process. The hardwood cost the company $11,648.

The company's standards for one chopping board are 2.5 board feet of hardwood, at a cost of $1.05 per board foot.

Required:

1. What cost should have been incurred in the manufacture of the 4,000 chopping blocks? How much greater or less is this than the cost that was incurred?
2. Break the difference computed in Part 1 above down in terms of a material price variance and a material quantity variance.

9–3. Brinson Corporation produces machine tools for industry. The company uses standards to control its costs. The labor standards which have been set for one very popular machine tool are:

Direct labor time per tool	15 minutes
Direct labor rate per hour	$5.20

During 19X5, the company worked 7,750 hours in order to produce 30,000 of these tools. The direct labor cost amounted to $39,525.

Required:

1. What direct labor cost should have been incurred in the manufacture of the 30,000 machine tools? By how much does this cost differ from the cost that was incurred?
2. Break the difference in cost from Part 1 down in terms of a labor rate variance and a labor efficiency variance.
3. For each direct labor hour worked, the company expects to incur $5 in variable overhead cost. This rate was experienced in 19X5. What effect did the efficiency (or inefficiency) of labor have on variable overhead cost in 19X5?

9–4. The direct materials and direct labor standards for one bottle of Product 412 are given below:

	Standard Quantity	Price or Rate	Standard Cost
Direct materials	8 ozs.	$1.20/oz.	$9.60
Direct labor	.5 hrs.	$6/hr.	3.00

During a recent period, the following activity took place:
a. 15,000 ozs. of material were purchased at a cost of $18,750.
b. All of the material purchased was used to produce 1,760 bottles of Product 412.
c. 835 hours of direct labor time were recorded during the period at a total labor cost of $5,177.

Required:

1. Compute materials price and quantity variances for the period.
2. Compute labor rate and efficiency variances for the period.

9–5. The direct material and direct labor standards per unit of Product A are given below:

	Standard Quantity	Price or Rate	Standard Cost
Direct material	8 feet	$.50/ft	$4
Direct labor	2 hours	$4/hr	8

During the month of June, the following activity occurred:
a. 6,000 feet of material were purchased at a cost of $.48 per foot.
b. 5,400 feet of material were used to produce 650 units of Product A.
c. 1,365 hours of direct labor time were worked to produce the 650 units of Product A. The cost of labor time averaged $3.90 per hour.

Required:

1. Compute the material price and quantity variances that would have resulted from the June activities.
2. Compute the labor rate and efficiency variances that would have resulted from the June activities.

9–6. Diehl Company produces a powerful cleaning solvent. Each quart of solvent requires 1.2 quarts of material X and 2 pounds of material Y.

Material X is purchased in 15-gallon containers, at a cost of $30 per container. Discount terms of 2/10, n/30 are offered by the supplier. Diehl Company takes all discounts available. Freight is paid by the supplier.

Material Y is purchased in 100-pound cartons, at a cost of $40 per carton. No discount terms are available. Diehl Company must pay all freight charges, which amount to $58 for an average shipment of 50 cartons.

About 2 percent of material Y is wasted in the production process.

Required:

Compute the standard material cost for one quart of cleaning solvent.

PROBLEMS

9–1. *Routine Variance Analysis.* Super Surf Boards manufactures a single product. The standard costs of one unit of this product are:

Direct material: 6 feet @ $1.00	$6.00
Direct labor: 1 hour @ $4.50	4.50
Variable overhead: 1 hour @ $3.00.	3.00
Total standard variable cost per unit	$13.50

During the month of October 6,000 units were produced. The costs associated with this production were as follows:

Material purchased: 60,000 feet @ $.95	$57,000
Material used in production: 38,000 feet	
Direct labor: 6,500 hours @ $4.30	27,950
Variable overhead cost incurred.	20,475

There was no beginning inventory of raw materials. The variable overhead rate is based on direct labor hours.

Required:

1. Compute the materials price and quantity variances.
2. Compute the direct labor rate and efficiency variances.
3. Compute the variable overhead spending and efficiency variances.

9–2. *Standard Unit Cost Computation, and Variance Analysis.* Dupler Company uses a standard cost system and a flexible budget as assists in controlling costs. The company normally produces 15,000 units each period, working 45,000 direct labor hours. The standard variable costs associated with this level of production are:

Direct material	$ 75,000
Direct labor	180,000
Variable factory overhead	135,000
Total variable cost	$390,000

Variable overhead is applied to production on a basis of direct labor hours.

Required:

1. Compute the standards associated with one unit of product for materials, labor, and overhead.
2. Assume that during a recent period the company worked 49,000 direct labor hours and produced 16,000 units of product. The actual costs of this production included the following:

Direct labor	$191,100
Variable factory overhead	156,800

   a. Compute the direct labor variances from standard.
   b. Compute the overhead variances from standard.

9–3. *Setting Materials and Labor Standards.* The Scera Company manufactures trivets. The company is just starting to use standard costs. From accounting records, industrial engineering studies, and other sources the following information has been developed:

1. The clocked labor time to produce one trivet (good or defective) is 1.5 hrs.
2. Ten percent of all completed trivets are scrapped as defective. The scrapped trivets have no monetary value.
3. The materials consumed in the production of one trivet (good or defective) are:

Material	Quantity Required Per Trivet	Invoice Cost	Freight
H–4	3.6 qts.	$3/qt.	$.10/qt.
H–11	2.7 lbs.	$4/lb.	$.20/lb.

4. All materials are purchased subject to a 2 percent cash discount if paid within 10 days. All discounts are taken.
5. Only 80 percent of Material H-4 finds its way into a trivet. The remainder is lost through spillage or evaporation.
6. The labor rate is $6 per hour.
7. Coffee breaks, clean-up, etc., consumes about 0.8 hours of labor time each eight-hour day. The company works a 40-hour week.

Required:

1. Compute the standard quantity of Material H-4 and the standard quantity of Material H-11 for each acceptable trivet, allowing for the normal loss factors mentioned above.
2. Compute the standard cost of each type of material per acceptable trivet.
3. Compute the standard amount of labor time per acceptable trivet, again allowing for normal loss factors.
4. Compute the standard labor cost per acceptable trivet.

9–4. *Overhead Standards and Variances.* Kimber Company has a standard cost system in operation. The standard direct labor time required to produce one unit of Formula B, one of the company's products, is two hours. At a normal activity level of 4,000 units of Formula B, the standard costs are:

Direct materials	$ 8,000
Direct labor	24,000
Variable factory overhead	12,000

During a recent period, a shortage in raw materials forced a sharp cutback in production of Formula B, so that only 3,000 units were produced. This production required 6,500 direct labor hours and $9,100 in variable overhead cost. Overhead is applied to production on a basis of direct labor hours.

Required:

1. What is Kimber Company's standard variable overhead rate per hour?
2. What variable overhead cost should have been incurred in the production of the 3,000 units of Formula B? By how much does this differ from the actual cost incurred?
3. Break the difference in Part 2 down in terms of an overhead spending variance and an overhead efficiency variance.
4. If overhead is applied to production on the basis of direct labor hours, is it possible to have a favorable direct labor efficiency variance and an unfavorable overhead efficiency variance? Explain.

9–5. *Straightforward Variance Analysis.* The standard cost sheet for one of the products produced by Advance Template Design, Inc., is presented below:

Materials	8 feet @ $3	$24
Direct labor	2 hrs @ 4.50	9
Variable overhead.	2 hrs @ 4	8
Total standard cost per unit		$41

During a recent month, the following activity occurred:
1. Actual production, 800 units.
2. Materials purchased and used, 6,800 feet @ $3.12.
3. Direct labor cost incurred (1,550 hrs.), $7,285. $4.70
4. Variable overhead cost incurred, $6,045.

Required:

Compute three variances each (one of the variances will be the total budget variance) for materials, labor, and variable overhead. The variable overhead rate is based on direct labor hours.

9–6. *Comprehensive Problem on Standard Costs.* Olmo Company has used a standard cost system for planning and control purposes for many years. One month's data for one of the company's products are given below:

Standard direct labor cost: $5 per hour.
Standard direct materials cost: $1.50 per yard.

Standard yards of material in a finished unit of product: 6.
Standard hours of direct labor time per finished unit of product: 2.
Variable overhead budget per direct labor hour: $2.
Direct materials purchased (18,000 yards): $26,100.
Direct materials used in production: 16,000 yards.
Direct labor cost incurred (5,200 hrs): $24,960.
Variable overhead costs incurred: $10,920.
Budgeted production in units: 3,000.
Actual production in units: 2,500.

Required:

1. Compute the materials price and quantity variances.
2. How much direct labor cost should have been incurred for the month's production?
   a. By how much does this differ from the cost that was incurred? What would you call this variance?
   b. Show how much of the difference in Part 2a is due to a labor rate variance, and how much is due to a labor efficiency variance.
3. How much variable overhead cost should have been incurred for the month's production?
   a. By how much does this differ from the cost that was incurred? What would you call this variance?
   b. Show how much of the difference in Part 3a is due to an overhead spending variance, and how much is due to an overhead efficiency variance.

9–7. *Standards and Variances from Incomplete Data.* The following information is available on the single product produced by Carbo-Weld, Inc., for the month of March:

	Materials Used	Direct Labor	Variable Overhead
Standard costs	$200	$1,200	$750
Actual costs incurred	209	?	782
Materials price variance	?		
Materials quantity variance	10 F		
Labor rate variance		?	
Labor efficiency variance		?	
Overhead spending variance			?
Overhead efficiency variance			?

The following additional information is available for March production:

Number of units produced	100
Actual direct labor hours	340
Standard overhead rate per hour	$2.50
Standard price of one pound of materials	$ .50
Overhead is based on	Direct labor hours
Difference between standard and actual cost per unit produced during March	$2.52 U

Required:

1. What is the standard cost of a single unit of product?
2. What was the actual cost of a unit of product produced during March?
3. How many pounds of material are required at standard per unit of product?
4. What was the materials price variance for March?
5. What was the labor rate variance? The labor efficiency variance?
6. What was the overhead spending variance? The overhead efficiency variance?

9–8. *Variances and Unit Costs.* Wickingham Mills, Inc., is a large producer of men and women's clothing. The company uses standard costs for all of its products. The standard costs and actual costs for a recent period are given below for one of the company's product lines (per unit of product):

	Standard Cost	Actual Cost
Materials:		
Standard: 4.0 yards @ $2.10 per yard	$ 8.40	
Actual: 4.4 yards @ $2.00 per yard		$ 8.80
Labor:		
Standard: 1.6 hours @ $4.50 per hour	7.20	
Actual: 1.4 hours @ $4.85 per hour		6.79
Variable overhead:		
Standard: 1.6 hours @ $1.80 per hour	2.88	
Actual: 1.4 hours @ $2.15 per hour		3.01
Total cost	$18.48	$18.60

During this period the company produced 4,800 units of product. A comparison of standard and actual costs for the period on a total cost basis is given below:

Actual costs: 4,800 units @ $18.60.	$89,280.00
Standard costs: 4,800 units @ $18.48	88,704.00
Difference in cost	$ 576.00

Required:

Determine how much of the $576.00 excess cost for the period is due to:

1. The materials price variance and the materials quantity variance.
2. The labor rate variance and the labor efficiency variance.
3. The variable overhead spending variance and the variable overhead efficiency variance.

Prove your answer by showing that the total of your variances is $576.00.

9–9. *The Impact of Variances on Unit Costs; Variance Analysis.* Metal Specialties, Inc., produces a number of products. The standards relating to one of these products are shown below, along with actual cost data for the month of May (per unit):

	Standard Cost	Actual Cost
Direct materials:		
Standard: 1.5 pounds at $1.40 per pound	$2.10	
Actual: 1.48 pounds at $1.50 per pound . . . . : .		$2.22
Direct labor:		
Standard: .40 hours at $4.50 per hour	1.80	
Actual: .45 hours at $4.40 per hour		1.98
Variable overhead:		
Budget: .40 hours at $3.00 per hour	1.20	
Actual: .45 hours at $2.80 per hour		1.26
Total per unit cost	$5.10	$5.46
Increase in per unit cost over standard		$.36

When the production superintendent saw these unit cost figures, he stated, "This is no good. We sell these units for only $5.50 each. If they are costing us $5.46 each to produce, that leaves a contribution margin of only $.04. We've got to isolate and correct the cost problem. We can't stay in business with a four-cent contribution margin."

Budgeted production during May was 12,000 units. Actual production was 11,000 units.

Required:

1. Compute the following variances for the month of May:
    a. Material price and quantity.
    b. Labor rate and efficiency.
    c. Overhead spending and efficiency.
2. Show how much of the $.36 excessive unit cost is traceable to each of the variances computed in Part 1 above.
3. Show how much of the $.36 excessive unit cost is traceable to the inefficient use of labor time.

9-10. *Reports for Management; Preparation of a Variance Report.* Quality Plastic Products uses a standard cost system for planning and control purposes. Management has been unhappy with the system in that great difficulty has been experienced in trying to interpret the reports coming from the accounting department, and in trying to determine how to control the variances being reported. A typical report is shown below. This report contains cost variance data for the month of July on one of the company's products:

	Total	Per Unit
Excess plastic used in production	$ 370	$ .74
Excess direct labor cost incurred	600	1.20
Excess variable overhead cost incurred	240	.48
Total excess cost incurred	$1,210	$2.42

During July, 500 units of this product were produced. The per unit actual costs of production were:

Plastic: 3.8 lbs. at $4.30 per lb. $16.34
Direct labor: .8 hr at $5.25 per hr. 4.20
Variable overhead: .8 hr at $3.60. . . . .   2.88

Total actual per unit cost $23.42

The standard cost of one unit of product is given below:

Plastic: 3.9 lbs at $4.00 per lb. $15.60
Direct labor: .6 hr at $5.00 per hr. 3.00
Variable overhead: .6 hr at $4.00 per hr. 2.40

Total standard per unit cost $21.00

Quality Plastic Products has hired you, as an expert in cost analysis, to help management clarify the reports coming from accounting.

Required:

1. What criticisms can be made of the cost variance reports presently being prepared by accounting?
2. Prepare a report which will give management better insight into the causes of the $1,210 excess cost incurred during July. This report should include detailed variances for materials, labor, and overhead.

9–11. *Standard Costs and Variance Analysis.* Hobart Company produces a single product in its factory, and uses a standard cost system. According to the standards which have been set, the factory should work 145 direct labor hours each week, and produce 2,900 units of product. The standard costs associated with this level of production activity are:

	Total	Per Unit of Product
Direct materials	$3,770	$1.30
Direct labor	696	.24
Variable overhead (based on direct labor hours)	435	.15
		$1.69

During the first week of June, the factory worked 140 direct labor hours, and produced 2,940 units of product. The following actual costs were recorded during the week:

	Total	Per Unit of Product
Direct materials (1,500 yds.)	$3,969	$1.35
Direct labor	735	.25
Variable overhead	294	.10
		$1.70

Each unit of product should require only 0.5 yds. of material.

Required:

For the first week of June, compute:

1. The materials price and quantity variances.
2. The labor rate and efficiency variances.
3. The variable overhead spending and efficiency variances.

(Hint: Take care that you don't try to mix apples and oranges in your variance analysis!!)

chapter 10

Flexible Budgets and Overhead Analysis

THERE ARE FOUR problems involved in overhead cost control. First, manufacturing overhead is usually made up of many (perhaps scores) of separate costs. Second, these separate costs are often very small in dollar amount, making it highly impractical to control the costs the same way that direct materials and direct labor are controlled. Third, these small, separate costs are often the responsibility of different managers. And fourth, manufacturing overhead costs vary in behavior, some being variable, some fixed, and some mixed in nature.

Most of these problems can be overcome by use of a *flexible budget*. In this chapter we study flexible budgets, and their use in overhead cost control. We also expand the study of overhead variances which we started in Chapter 9.

FLEXIBLE BUDGETS

Characteristics of a Flexible Budget

The budgets we studied in Chapter 8, including the sales budget, the production budget, the cash budget, etc., all have two points in common:

1. They are geared toward a single level of activity.
2. They are *static* in nature. Comparison of actual results is made against the original single level of activity.

The flexible budget is different from other budgets on both of these points. It does not confine itself to a single level of activity, but rather is geared toward a *range* of activity. Also, the flexible budget is *not* static in nature. A budget can be constructed, *even after the fact*, to compare against any level of actual activity and costs within the relevant range. Hence, the term "flexible" budget. In sum, the characteristics of a flexible budget are:

1. It is geared toward a *range* of activity rather than toward a single level of activity.
2. It is *dynamic* in nature rather than static. A budget can be tailored for any level of activity, even after the period's activity is over. That is, a manager can look at what activity level *was attained* during a period, and then turn to his flexible budget to determine what costs *should have been* at that activity level.

Deficiencies of the Static Budget

To illustrate the difference between a static budget and a flexible budget, let us assume that the Assembly Operation of Rocco Company has budgeted to produce 10,000 units during March. The variable overhead budget which has been set is shown in Exhibit 10–1.

EXHIBIT 10–1

ROCCO COMPANY
Static Budget
Assembly Operation
For the Month of March 19X1

Budgeted production in units 10,000

Budgeted variable overhead costs:
Indirect materials $1,000
Lubricants   800
Power   500
Total $2,300

Let us assume that the production goal of 10,000 units is not met. The company is able to produce only 9,000 units during the month. *If a static budget approach is used,* the performance report for the month will appear as shown in Exhibit 10–2.

What's wrong with this report? The deficiencies of the static budget can be explained as follows. A production manager has two prime responsibilities to discharge in the performance of his duties—*production control* and *cost control*. Production control is involved with seeing that production goals in terms of output are met. Cost control is involved with seeing that output is produced at the least possible cost, consistent with quality standards. These are different responsibilities, and must

EXHIBIT 10-2

ROCCO COMPANY
Static Budget Performance Report
Assembly Operation
For the Month of March 19X1

	Budget	*Actual*	*Variance*
Production in units	10,000	9,000	1,000 U
Variable overhead costs:			
Indirect materials.	$1,000	$ 910	$ 90 F*
Lubricants.	800	730	70 F*
Power	500	475	25 F*
Total	$2,300	$2,115	$185 F*

* These cost variances are useless, since they have been derived by comparing actual costs at one level of activity against budgeted costs at a *different*
level of activity.

be kept separate in attempting to assess how well the production manager is doing his job. The main difficulty with the static budget is that
it fails completely to distinguish between the production control and
the cost control dimensions of a manager's performance.

Of the two, the static budget does a good job of measuring only
whether production control is being maintained. Look again at the data
in Exhibit 10–2. The data on the top line relate to the production superintendent's responsibility for production control. These data for Rocco
Company properly reflect the fact that production control was not maintained during the month. The company failed to meet its production
goal by 1,000 units.

The remainder of the data on the report deal with cost control. These
data are useless in that they are comparing apples to oranges. Although
the production manager may be very proud of his favorable cost variances, they tell nothing about how well costs were controlled during
the month. The problem is that the budget costs are based on an
activity level of 10,000 units, whereas actual costs were incurred at an
activity level substantially below this (only 9,000 units). From a cost
control point of view, it is total nonsense to try to compare costs at one
activity level to costs at a different activity level. Such comparisons will
always make a production manager look good so long as his actual
production is less than his budgeted production.

How the Flexible Budget Works

The basic idea of the flexible budget approach is that, through a
study of cost behavior patterns, a budget can be prepared that is geared

to a *range* of activity rather than to a single level. The basic steps in preparing a flexible budget are:

1. Determine the relevant range over which activity is expected to fluctuate during the coming period.
2. Analyze costs that will be incurred over the relevant range in terms of determining cost behavior patterns (variable, fixed, mixed).
3. Separate costs by behavior, determining the formula for variable and mixed costs, as discussed in Chapter 5.
4. Using the formula for the variable portion of the costs, prepare a budget showing what costs will be incurred at various points throughout the relevant range.

To illustrate, let us assume that Rocco Company's production normally fluctuates between 8,000 and 11,000 units each month. A study of cost behavior patterns over this relevant range has revealed the following formulas for the variable portion of overhead:

Cost	Variable Cost Formula
Indirect materials.	$.10 per unit
Lubricants	$.08 per unit
Power	$.05 per unit

Based on these cost formulas, a flexible budget for Rocco Company would appear as follows:

EXHIBIT 10–3

ROCCO COMPANY
Flexible Budget
Assembly Operation
For the Month of March 19X1

Budgeted production in units 10,000

	Cost Formula	Range of Production in Units			
		8,000	9,000	10,000	11,000
Variable Overhead Costs:					
Indirect materials.	$.10/unit	$ 800	$ 900	$1,000	$1,100
Lubricants.	$.08/unit	640	720	800	880
Power	$.05/unit	400	450	500	550
Total	$.23/unit	$1,840	$2,070	$2,300	$2,530

Using the Flexible Budget. Once the flexible budget is prepared, the manager is ready to compare actual results for a period against the comparable budget level anywhere throughout the relevant range. He isn't limited to a single budget level as with the static budget. To illustrate, let us again assume that Rocco Company is unable to meet its production goal of 10,000 units during the month of March. As before, we will assume that only 9,000 units are produced. Under the flexible budget approach, the performance report would appear as follows:

EXHIBIT 10–4

ROCCO COMPANY
Performance Report
Assembly Operation
For the Month of March 19X1

Budgeted production in units 10,000
Actual production in units 9,000

	Budget 9,000 units	*Actual 9,000 units*	*Spending Variance*
Variable overhead costs:			
Indirect materials.	$ 900	$ 910	$10 U*
Lubricants.	720	730	10 U*
Power	450	475	25 U*
Total.	$2,070	$2,115	$45 U*

* These cost variances are useable in evaluating cost control, since they have been derived by comparing actual costs and budgeted costs at the *same* level of activity.

In contrast to the performance report prepared earlier under the static budget approach (Exhibit 10–2), this performance report distinguishes clearly between production control and cost control. The production data at the top of the report indicate whether the production goal was met. The cost data at the bottom of the report tell how well costs were controlled for the 9,000 units that actually were produced.

Notice that all cost variances are *unfavorable,* as contrasted to the *favorable* cost variances on the performance report prepared earlier under the static budget approach. The reason for the change in variances is that by means of the flexible budget approach we are able to compare budgeted and actual costs at *the same level of activity* (9,000 units produced), rather than compare budgeted costs at one level of activity against actual costs at a different level of activity as was necessary under the static budget approach. In effect, using a flexible budget makes it possible for us to compare apples to apples, rather than forcing us to compare apples to oranges. The result shows up in more usable variances.

A Dynamic Tool. Even if actual activity results in some odd figure that does not appear in the flexible budget, such as 9,200 units, budgeted costs can still be prepared to compare against actual costs. One simply develops a budget at the 9,200-unit level by using the cost formulas contained in the flexible budget. Herein lies the strength and dynamic nature of the flexible budget approach. It is possible to develop a budget, *after the fact,* for *any* activity level within the relevant range by simply applying the cost formulas.

The Measure of Activity—a Critical Choice

In the Rocco Company example we chose to use units of production as the activity base for developing a flexible budget. Rather than units of production we could have used some other base such as direct labor hours or machine hours. What is "best" in terms of an activity base will vary from firm to firm. At least three factors should be considered in the activity base decision:

1. The existence of a causative relationship between the activity base and overhead costs.
2. The avoidance of dollars in the activity base itself.
3. The selection of an activity base that is simple and easily understood.

Causative Relationship. There should be a direct causative relationship between the activity base and a company's variable overhead costs. That is, the variable overhead costs should vary as a result of changes in the activity base. In a machine shop, for example, one would expect that power usage and other variable overhead costs would vary in relationship to the number of machine hours worked. Machine hours would therefore be the proper base to use in the flexible budget.

Other common activity bases include direct labor hours, miles driven by salesmen, contacts made by salesmen, number of invoices processed, number of beds in a hospital, and number of X-rays given. Any one of these could be used as the base for preparing a flexible budget in the proper situation.

Do Not Use Dollars. The activity base should be expressed in units rather than in dollars, whenever possible. If dollars are used, they should be standard dollars rather than actual dollars.

The problem with dollars is that they are subject to price-level changes, which can cause a distortion in the activity base if it is expressed in dollar terms. A similar problem arises when wage-rate changes take place, if direct labor cost is being used as the activity base in a flexible budget. The change in wage rates will cause the activity base to change, even though no change will have taken place in the overhead costs themselves. These types of fluctuations generally make dollars difficult to work with, and argue strongly for units rather than dollars in the activity base. The use of *standard* dollar costs, rather than *actual* dollar costs, overcomes the problem to some degree, but standard costs still have to be adjusted from time to time as changes in actual costs take place. On the other hand, *units* as a measure of activity (beds, hours, miles, etc.) are subject to few distorting influences, and are less likely to cause problems in preparing and using a flexible budget.

Keep the Base Simple. The activity base should be simple and easily understood. A base that is not easily understood by the manager who works with it day by day will probably result in confusion and misunderstanding rather than serve as a positive means of cost control.

THE OVERHEAD PERFORMANCE REPORT—
A CLOSER LOOK

A special problem arises in preparing overhead performance reports when the flexible budget is based on *hours* of activity such as direct labor hours, rather than on units of product. The problem relates to what hour base to use in constructing budget allowances on the performance report.

The Problem of Budget Allowances

The nature of the problem can best be seen through a specific example. Assume that the Packaging Operation of the Condor Corporation is budgeting its activities for the month of June. The flexible budget which has been prepared is shown in Exhibit 10–5.

EXHIBIT 10–5

CONDOR CORPORATION
Flexible Budget
Packaging Operation

Budgeted machine hours. 6,500

	Cost Formula	Machine Hours			
		5,000	5,500	6,000	6,500
Variable overhead costs:					
Indirect labor	$.12/MH	$ 600	$ 660	$ 720	$ 780
Lubricants.	$.08/MH	400	440	480	520
Maintenance	$.02/MH	100	110	120	130
Total variable.	$.22/MH	$1,100	$1,210	$1,320	$1,430

As shown in Exhibit 10–5, the company uses machine hours as an activity base in its flexible budget. Two machine hours are required to produce one unit of output. For the month of June, the company has budgeted to work 6,500 machine hours in the Packaging Operation, and to product 3,250 units of output (6,500 hrs. ÷ 2 hrs./unit = 3,250 units). Let us assume that after the month is over the company finds that only 6,000 machine hours were worked, and that only 2,900 units were produced. A summary of actual activity and costs for the month is given below:

Number of machine hours worked	6,000
Number of units produced.	2,900

	Actual Costs Incurred
Indirect Labor	$ 780
Lubricants	360
Maintenance.	300
Total actual costs.	$1,440

In preparing a performance report for the month, what hour base should the Condor Corporation use in computing budget allowances to compare against actual results? There are two possibilities. The company could use:

1. The 6,000 hours *actually worked* during the month.
2. The 5,800 hours that *should have been worked* during the month to produce 2,900 units of output (since it should take 2 hours to produce one unit).

Which base the company chooses will depend on how much detailed variance information it wants. As we learned in the preceding chapter, variable overhead can be analyzed in terms of a *spending* variance and an *efficiency* variance. The two bases provide different variance output.

Spending Variance Alone

If the Condor Corporation chooses alternative #1, and bases its performance report on the 6,000 hours actually worked during the period, then the performance report will show only a spending variance for overhead. A performance report prepared this way is shown in Exhibit 10–6.

The formula behind the spending variance was introduced in the preceding chapter. For review, that formula is:

$$(AH \times AR) - (AH \times SR) = \text{Spending Variance}$$

or, in factored form:

$$AH(AR - SR) = \text{Spending Variance}$$

The report in Exhibit 10–6 is prepared around the first, or unfactored, format.

EXHIBIT 10-6

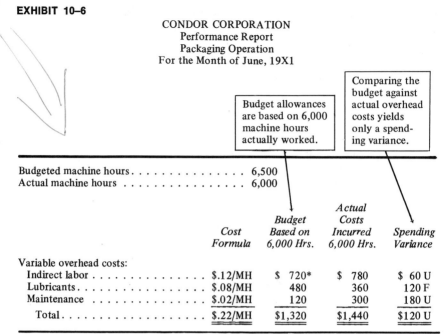

CONDOR CORPORATION
Performance Report
Packaging Operation
For the Month of June, 19X1

	Budget allowances are based on 6,000 machine hours actually worked.	Comparing the budget against actual overhead costs yields only a spending variance.

Budgeted machine hours 6,500
Actual machine hours 6,000

	Cost Formula	Budget Based on 6,000 Hrs.	Actual Costs Incurred 6,000 Hrs.	Spending Variance
Variable overhead costs:				
Indirect labor	$.12/MH	$ 720*	$ 780	$ 60 U
Lubricants	$.08/MH	480	360	120 F
Maintenance	$.02/MH	120	300	180 U
Total	$.22/MH	$1,320	$1,440	$120 U

* 6,000 hrs. × $.12 = $720. Other budget allowances are computed in the same way.

Interpreting the Spending Variance. The overhead spending variance is affected by two things. First, a spending variance may occur simply because of price increases over what is shown in the flexible budget. For the Condor Corporation this means that prices paid for overhead items may have gone up during the month, resulting in unfavorable spending variances. This portion of the overhead spending variance is just like the price variance for raw materials.

Second, the overhead spending variance is affected by waste or excessive usage of overhead materials. A first reaction is to say that waste or excessive usage of materials ought to show up as part of the efficiency variance. But this isn't true so far as overhead is concerned. Waste or excessive usage will show up as part of the spending variance. The reason is that the overhead spending variance measures more than just deviations in price paid; it measures deviations in the amount *spent* for overhead items. Total spending can be affected as much by waste as it can by higher than expected prices.

In sum, the overhead spending variance contains both price and quantity (waste) elements. These two elements could be broken out and shown separately on the performance report, but this is rarely done in actual practice.

Usefulness of the Spending Variance. Most firms consider the overhead spending variance to be highly useful. Generally the price element in this variance will be small, so the variance permits a focusing of attention on that thing over which the supervisor probably has the greatest control—usage of overhead in production. In many cases, firms will limit their overhead analysis to the spending variance alone, feeling that the information it yields is sufficient for overhead cost control.

In those cases where the performance report is prepared on a basis of *units of output,* no overhead variances are possible other than the spending variance. For example, turn back to the performance report in Exhibit 10–4. Notice that only one variance is shown on the report, and that this variance is a spending variance.

Both Spending and Efficiency Variances

If the Condor Corporation wants both a spending and an efficiency variance for overhead, then it should compute budget allowances for *both* 5,800 machine-hour and 6,000 machine-hour levels of activity. The 5,800 machine hours would be the *standard hours of production* for the month. As defined in the preceding chapter, standard hours represent the time that should have been taken to complete the period's output:

2,900 units $\times$ 2 standard hours per unit = 5,800 standard hours

A performance report prepared this way is shown in Exhibit 10–7.

Notice from the exhibit that the spending variance is the same as the spending variance shown earlier in Exhibit 10–6. The performance report in Exhibit 10–7 has simply been expanded to include an efficiency variance as well. Together, the spending and efficiency variances make up the total budget variance, as explained in the preceding chapter.

Interpreting the Efficiency Variance. The term "overhead efficiency variance" is a misnomer, since this variance has nothing to do with efficiency in the use of overhead. What the variance really measures is how efficiently the *base* underlying the flexible budget is being utilized in production. Recall from the preceding chapter that the variable overhead efficiency variance is a function of the difference between the actual hours utilized in production, and the hours that should have been taken to produce the period's output:

$$(AH \times SR) - (SH \times SR) = \text{Efficiency Variance}$$

or, in factored form:

$$SR(AH - SH) = \text{Efficiency Variance}$$

If more hours are worked than allowed at standard, then the overhead efficiency variance will be unfavorable to reflect this inefficiency. As a practical matter, however, the inefficiency isn't in the use of overhead, *but rather in the use of the base itself.*

EXHIBIT 10–7

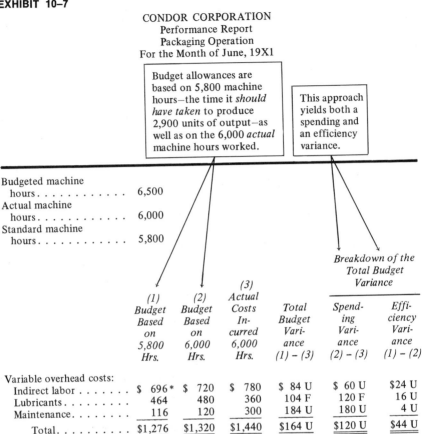

CONDOR CORPORATION
Performance Report
Packaging Operation
For the Month of June, 19X1

Budget allowances are based on 5,800 machine hours—the time it *should have taken* to produce 2,900 units of output—as well as on the 6,000 *actual* machine hours worked.

This approach yields both a spending and an efficiency variance.

Budgeted machine hours 6,500
Actual machine hours 6,000
Standard machine hours 5,800

Breakdown of the Total Budget Variance

	(1) Budget Based on 5,800 Hrs.	*(2)* Budget Based on 6,000 Hrs.	*(3)* Actual Costs In- curred 6,000 Hrs.	Total Budget Vari- ance *(1) – (3)*	Spend- ing Vari- ance *(2) – (3)*	Effi- ciency Vari- ance *(1) – (2)*
Variable overhead costs:						
Indirect labor	$ 696*	$ 720	$ 780	$ 84 U	$ 60 U	$24 U
Lubricants	464	480	360	104 F	120 F	16 U
Maintenance	116	120	300	184 U	180 U	4 U
Total	$1,276	$1,320	$1,440	$164 U	$120 U	$44 U

* 5,800 hrs. × $.12 = $696. Other budget allowances are computed in the same way.

This point can be illustrated by looking again at Exhibit 10–7. Two hundred more machine hours were used during the period than should have been used to produce the period's output. Each of these hours required the incurrence of $.22 of variable overhead, resulting in an unfavorable variance of $44 (200 hours × $.22). Although this $44 variance is called an overhead efficiency variance, it could better be called a "machine hours efficiency variance," since it measures the efficiency of utilization of machine time. The term "overhead efficiency variance" is so firmly engrained in day-to-day use that a change is unlikely, however. Even so, the user must be careful to interpret the variance with a clear understanding of what it really measures.

Control of the Efficiency Variance. Who is responsible for control of the overhead efficiency variance? Since the variance really measures efficiency in the utilization of the base underlying the flexible budget, whoever is responsible for control of this base is responsible for control of the variance. If the base is direct labor hours, then the supervisor responsible for the use of labor time will be chargeable for any overhead efficiency variance.

FIXED COSTS AND THE FLEXIBLE BUDGET

Should the flexible budget contain fixed costs as well as variable costs? The term "flexible budget" implies variable costs only. As a practical matter, however, many firms include fixed overhead costs in the budget as well.

Exhibit 10–8 illustrates a flexible budget that contains fixed overhead costs as well as variable overhead costs. Actually, the fixed cost portion

EXHIBIT 10–8

DONNER COMPANY
Flexible Budget
Stamping Department

Budgeted Machine Hours. 5,000

	Cost Formula	Machine Hours			
		4,500	5,000	5,500	6,000
Variable overhead costs:					
Indirect labor	$.10/MH	$ 450	$ 500	$ 550	$ 600
Lubricants.	$.20/MH	900	1,000	1,100	1,200
Total.	$.30/MH	$1,350	$1,500	$1,650	$1,800
Fixed overhead costs:					
Depreciation.		$4,000	$4,000	$4,000	$4,000
Supervisory salaries.		3,000	3,000	3,000	3,000
Taxes.		350	350	350	350
Total.		$7,350	$7,350	$7,350	$7,350
Total overhead costs, variable and fixed.		$8,700	$8,850	$9,000	$9,150

of the budget is a *static budget* in that the amounts remain unchanged throughout the relevant range.

Whether or not fixed overhead should be included in the flexible budget will vary from company to company. As we have mentioned before, no manager should be held responsible for a cost over which he has no control. The guiding factor, therefore, on whether fixed costs should be included in the flexible budget will be whether the manager involved *has control* over the fixed costs. If he has control, they can be included; if not, they should be omitted.[1]

---

[1] Fixed costs are often included in the flexible budget for purposes of computing the predetermined overhead rate. This point is covered in the next part of the chapter.

FIXED OVERHEAD ANALYSIS

Fixed costs come in large indivisible chunks that by definition do not change with changes in the level of activity. This creates a problem in product costing, since a given level of fixed overhead cost spread over a small number of units produced will result in a higher cost per unit than if the same amount of cost is spread over a large number of units. Consider the data in the table below:

Month	(1) Fixed Overhead Cost	(2) Number of Units Produced	Unit Cost (1) ÷ (2)
Jan.	$6,000	1,000	$6.00
Feb.	6,000	1,500	4.00
Mar.	6,000	800	7.50

This problem doesn't arise with variable overhead, since by definition it remains *constant* per unit, changing in total amount in direct relation to changes in the level of activity. For pricing and other reasons, managers need to have a *stable* unit cost figure that can be used throughout the year without regard to month-by-month changes in activity levels. An *artificial stability* in unit costs can be created so far as fixed overhead is concerned, by using a predetermined overhead rate, as discussed in Chapter 3.

Denominator Activity

The activity level on which the predetermined overhead rate is set is known as the *denominator* activity. It is so named because it appears as the denominator in the predetermined overhead rate formula:

$$\frac{\text{Estimated Total Manufacturing Overhead Costs}}{\substack{\text{Estimated Direct Labor Hours, Etc.} \\ \text{(denominator activity)}}} = \text{Predetermined Overhead Rate}$$

The denominator activity level is generally set on a basis of the expected activity (e.g., budgeted hours) for the entire year. Thus month-by-month fluctuations in activity will not affect unit costs. Once a denominator activity level has been chosen, it remains unchanged throughout the year, even if *actual* activity later proves the denominator to be somewhat in error. This provides the manager with the distinct advantage of a stable unit cost figure so far as overhead is concerned, regardless of when a unit is produced during the year, and regardless of whether actual production turns out to be more or less than planned.

Refer again to the flexible budget of the Donner Company in Exhibit 10–8. The company's denominator activity for the period is 5,000 machine hours. According to the flexible budget, $8,850 in overhead costs will be incurred during the period at that activity level. Therefore, the predetermined overhead rate is:

$$\frac{\$8,850}{5,000 \text{ MH}} = \$1.77 \text{ per machine hour}$$

Or, the company can break its predetermined overhead rate down into variable and fixed elements rather than using a single combined figure:

$$\text{Variable Element} \quad \frac{\$1,500}{5,000 \text{ MH}} = \$.30 \text{ per machine hour}$$

$$\text{Fixed Element} \quad \frac{\$7,350}{5,000 \text{ MH}} = \$1.47 \text{ per machine hour}$$

For every machine hour of operation, work in process will be charged with $1.77 of overhead, of which $.30 will be variable overhead and $1.47 will be fixed overhead. If a unit of product takes five machine hours to complete, then its cost will include $8.85 of overhead, of which $1.50 will be variable and $7.35 will be fixed. Thus by means of the denominator activity concept we are able to *artificially* stabilize the fixed element of unit cost.

The Fixed Overhead Variances

If the Donner Company works *exactly* 5,000 machine hours (the denominator activity) then it will charge production with all of the fixed costs contained in the flexible budget:

$$5,000 \text{ MH} \times \$1.47 \text{ per MH} = \$7,350$$

But what if the company works *more* or *less* than the 5,000 hours planned? It it works *more* than 5,000 hours, then *more* than $7,350 will be charged to production, which will exceed the *actual* fixed overhead costs. The opposite will be true if less than 5,000 hours is worked. Assume the following actual operating results for the Donner Company:

Actual machine hours	4,200
Standard machine hours	4,000
Actual fixed overhead costs	$7,540
Fixed overhead applied to work in process (4,000 standard hours × $1.47)	$5,880

From these data two variances can be computed for fixed overhead—a *budget variance* and a *volume variance.*

The Budget Variance. The budget variance represents the difference between actual fixed overhead costs and budgeted fixed overhead costs. For the Donner Company, the variance would be:

Actual fixed overhead costs $7,540
Budgeted fixed overhead costs (from the
flexible budget in Exhibit 10–8)   7,350
Budget variance . . . . $ 190 U

The variance measures the deviation from the budget in the amount spent for fixed overhead items. In this sense it is similar to the variable overhead spending variance.

The Volume Variance. The volume variance is a rough measure of *utilization* of planned capacity.[2] If a company works more hours than planned in the denominator activity, then it will have overutilized capacity, and the volume variance will be favorable. If it works less hours than planned, then capacity will be underutilized, and the volume variance will be unfavorable.

The formula for the variance is:

Fixed Portion of the Predetermined Overhead Rate
$$\times \left(\frac{\text{Denominator}}{\text{Hours}} - \frac{\text{Standard Hours}}{\text{Allowed}} \right) = \text{Volume Variance}$$

Applying this formula to the Donner Company, the volume variance would be:

$$\$1.47 \, (\, 5,000 \text{ MH} - 4,000 \text{ MH}) = \$1,470 \text{ Unfavorable}$$

Now stop and think for a minute about what this variance means. If the company had worked the 5,000 hours planned, it would have charged production with the full $7,350 in planned fixed costs as we stated earlier:

$$5,000 \text{ MH} \times \$1.47 = \$7,350$$

But only 4,000 hours were worked at standard, so *even though $7,350 in fixed costs would have been incurred, less than this amount would have been charged to production:*

$$4,000 \text{ MH} \times \$1.47 = \$5,880$$

The difference between the two figures is the volume variance:

$$\$7,350 - \$5,880 = \$1,470$$

The volume variance does not measure over- or underspending. A company would normally incur the *same* dollar amount of fixed overhead regardless of whether actual activity was above or below the denominator level. The variance is a measure of *utilization* of planned capacity. It is explainable only by activity, and is controllable only through activ-

---

[2] The term *planned capacity* refers to the level of activity *planned* for a period. It is not necessarily the same as *full* capacity.

ity. In the case of the Donner Company, management should seek an explanation as to why denominator activity was not reached during the period, since the result was an underutilization of capacity.

To summarize:

1. If the denominator activity and the standard hours allowed are the same, then there is no volume variance.
2. If the denominator activity is greater than the standard hours allowed, then the volume variance is unfavorable, signifying an underutilization of planned capacity.
3. If the denominator activity is less than the standard hours allowed, then the volume variance is favorable, signifying an overutilization of planned capacity.

Graphical Analysis. Some insights into the budget and volume variances can be gained through graphical analysis. The needed graph is presented in Exhibit 10–9.

EXHIBIT 10–9
Graphical Analysis of Fixed Overhead Variances

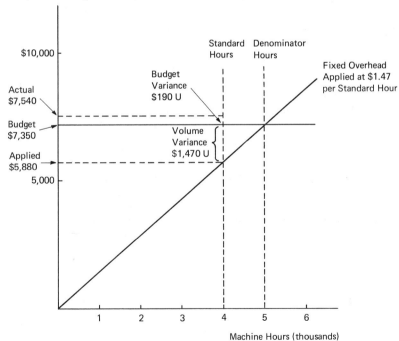

Notice from the graph that the budget variance and the volume variance taken together explain the difference between the *actual fixed overhead cost incurred* and the *fixed overhead applied to production.*

Actual fixed overhead cost incurred		$7,540
Less:		
Unfavorable budget variance	$ 190	
Unfavorable volume variance	1,470	1,660
Fixed overhead applied to production		$5,880

Cautions in Fixed Overhead Analysis

There can be no volume variance for variable overhead, since budgeted costs and applied costs are *both* dependent on activity and will always coincide. The reason we get a volume variance for fixed overhead is that budgeted costs *do not* depend on activity, but yet when applying the costs we treat them *as if* they were variable. This point can be seen from the graph in Exhibit 10–9. This *as if* treatment is necessary for product costing purposes, as explained earlier, but there are some real dangers here. The manager can easily become misled, and start thinking of his fixed overhead costs as if they were in fact variable. The manager must keep clearly in mind that fixed overhead costs come in *large, indivisable chunks* that cannot be broken down. Any breakdown of such costs, though necessary for product costing purposes, is *artificial* in nature. That is why the volume variance is not a controllable variance from a spending point of view. The per-hour dollar figure used to compute the variance is simply a derived figure needed for product costing purposes, but which has no significance from a cost control viewpoint.

Because of these factors, some companies present the volume variance in terms of physical units (e.g., hours) only. Whichever method is used to present the variance should depend on which will provide management with the clearest insights and the most usable data in directing operations.

SUMMARY PROBLEM ON OVERHEAD ANALYSIS

A flexible budget for Carey Company is given below:

Overhead Costs	Cost Formula	Direct Labor Hours		
		4,000	6,000	8,000
Variable costs:				
Supplies	$.20/DLH	$ 800	$ 1,200	$ 1,600
Indirect labor	$.30/DLH	1,200	1,800	2,400
Total.	$.50/DLH	2,000	3,000	4,000
Fixed costs:				
Depreciation.		4,000	4,000	4,000
Supervision		5,000	5,000	5,000
Total.		9,000	9,000	9,000
Total overhead costs		$11,000	$12,000	$13,000

The company has set denominator activity for the coming period at 6,000 hours. The computation of the predetermined overhead rate would be:

$$\text{Total } \frac{\$12,000}{6,000 \text{ DLH}} = \$2.00/\text{DLH}$$

$$\frac{\text{Variable}}{\text{Element}} \frac{\$3,000}{6,000 \text{ DLH}} = \$.50/\text{DLH}$$

$$\frac{\text{Fixed}}{\text{Element}} \frac{\$9,000}{6,000 \text{ DLH}} = \$1.50/\text{DLH}$$

Assume the following actual results for the period:

Actual direct labor hours.	6,800
Standard direct labor hours	6,500
Actual variable overhead cost	$ 4,080
Actual fixed overhead cost	$ 9,450
Overhead applied to production	
(6,500 standard hours × $2.00).	$13,000

Therefore, the company's manufacturing overhead account would appear as follows at the end of the period:

Manufacturing Overhead

Actual Overhead Costs	13,530	13,000	Overhead Costs Applied
Underapplied Overhead	530		

Required:

Analyze the $530 underapplied overhead in terms of:
1. A variable overhead spending variance.
2. A variable overhead efficiency variance.
3. A fixed overhead budget variance.
4. A fixed overhead volume variance.

Variable overhead spending variance:

$$AH(AR - SR) = \text{Spending Variance}$$
$$6,800 (\$.60^3 - \$.50) = \$680 \text{ U}$$

---

[3] $\$4,080 \div 6,800 \text{ hrs.} = \$.60$.

Variable overhead efficiency variance:

$$SR(AH - SH) = \text{Efficiency Variance}$$
$$\$.50 \ (6,800 \text{ hrs.} - 6,500 \text{ hrs.}) = \$150 \text{ U}$$

Fixed overhead budget variance:

Actual fixed overhead	$9,450
Budgeted fixed overhead.	9,000
Budget variance.	$ 450 U

Fixed overhead volume variance:

$$\begin{pmatrix} \text{Fixed Portion of} \\ \text{the Predetermined} \\ \text{Overhead Rate} \end{pmatrix} \times \begin{pmatrix} \text{Denominator} \\ \text{Hours} \end{pmatrix} - \begin{pmatrix} \text{Standard} \\ \text{Hours} \end{pmatrix} = \text{Volume Variance}$$

$$\$1.50 \ (6,000 \text{ hrs.} - 6,500 \text{ hrs.}) = \$750 \text{ F}$$

Summary of variances:

Variable overhead:	
Spending variance	$680 U
Efficiency variance	150 U
Fixed overhead:	
Budget variance.	450 U
Volume variance	750 F
Underapplied overhead.	$530

Notice that the $530 summary variance figure agrees with the under-applied balance in the company's manufacturing overhead account. This agreement stands as proof of the accuracy of our variance analysis. *Each period* the under- or overapplied overhead balance should be analyzed as we have done above. These variances will help the manager to see where his time and the time of his subordinates should be directed for better control of costs and operations.

QUESTIONS

10–1. What is a static budget?

10–2. What is a flexible budget, and how does it differ from a static budget? What is the main deficiency of the static budget?

10–3. What are the two prime responsibilities of the production manager? How do these two responsibilities differ?

10–4. Name three criteria that should be considered in choosing an activity base on which to construct a flexible budget.

10–5. In comparing budgeted data to actual data in a performance report for variable manufacturing overhead, what variance(s) will be produced if the budgeted data are based on actual hours worked? On both actual hours and standard hours worked?

10–6. What is meant by the term "standard hours of production?"

10–7. How does the variable manufacturing overhead spending variance differ from the materials price variance?

10–8. Why is the term "overhead efficiency variance" a misnomer?

10–9. "Fixed costs have no place in a flexible budget." Discuss.

10–10. What problem is created by the fact that fixed overhead costs come in large indivisable chunks?

10–11. What is meant by the term "denominator level of activity?"

10–12. What does the fixed overhead budget variance measure?

10–13. Does the fixed overhead volume variance measure deviations in spending for fixed overhead items? Explain.

10–14. In Chapter 3 you became acquainted with the concept of under- or overapplied overhead. What four variances can be computed from the under- or overapplied overhead total?

EXERCISES

10–1. The cost formulas for Rider Company's overhead costs are given below. The costs cover a range of 4,000 to 6,000 direct labor hours (DLH).

Cost	Cost Formula
Indirect labor	$1,500 plus $.20 per DLH
Supplies	$.15 per DLH
Maintenance	$1,800 plus $.10 per DLH
Depreciation	$2,000
Utilities	$.08 per DLH

Required:

Prepare a flexible budget in increments of 1,000 direct labor hours. Include the fixed costs in your flexible budget.

10–2. Budgeted and actual overhead cost data for 19X5 are presented below for the Brandon Company:

	Budgeted Costs	Actual Costs
Variable overhead.........	$16,500	$14,342
Fixed overhead	30,000	30,850

Budgeted and actual operating figures for the year were:

Budgeted direct labor hours 15,000*
Actual direct labor hours. 14,200
Standard direct labor hours 13,700
    * Denominator activity.

Required:

Compute the fixed overhead budget and volume variances.

10–3. Selected operating information on four different companies for the year 19X8 is given below:

	A	B	C	D
Full capacity direct labor hours	12,000	14,000	9,000	16,000
Budgeted direct labor hours*	10,000	14,000	6,000	15,000
Actual direct labor hours	11,000	13,500	6,000	15,500
Standard direct labor hours for actual production	9,500	14,000	6,500	14,000

      * Denominator activity.

Required:

In each case, state whether the company would have
a. No volume variance.
b. A favorable volume variance.
c. An unfavorable volume variance.
Also state in each case why you chose *a*, *b*, or *c*.

10–4. Redfern Company has analyzed its monthly costs within the relevant range of 5,000 to 7,000 machine hours. The cost formulas which have been computed for overhead are given below:

Cost	Cost Formula
Indirect materials	$2,000 plus $.80 per machine hour
Maintenance	$4,000 plus $.50 per machine hour
Machine setup	$.20 per machine hour
Utilities	$1,500 plus $.10 per machine hour
Depreciation	$3,500

Required:

Prepare a flexible budget in increments of 1,000 hours. Include the fixed costs in your budget.

10–5. Archer Machine Company's flexible budget is given below.

ARCHER MACHINE COMPANY
Flexible Budget

Overhead Costs	Cost Formula	Number of Units		
		10,000	11,000	12,000
Maintenance	$1.00/unit	$10,000	$11,000	$12,000
Indirect materials	.80/unit	8,000	8,800	9,600
Rework time	.50/unit	5,000	5,500	6,000
Total	$2.30/unit	$23,000	$25,300	$27,600

During a recent period the company produced 11,400 units. The overhead costs incurred were:

Maintenance	$10,146
Indirect materials	9,804
Rework time	7,068

The production budgeted for the period had been 11,500 units.

Required:

Prepare a performance report for the period. Indicate whether variances are favorable (F) or unfavorable (U).

10–6. Maravich Company's predetermined overhead rate for 19X1 is computed below:

Budgeted variable overhead	$10,000
Budgeted fixed overhead.	24,800
Total overhead	$34,800

$$\frac{\$34,800}{8,000 \text{ DLH}} = \$4.35/\text{DLH}$$

In working 8,000 standard direct labor hours, the company should produce 3,200 units of product. During 19X1, the company produced 3,500 units of product. Actual operating results were:

Actual direct labor hours.	8,500
Actual variable overhead costs.	$ 9,860
Actual fixed overhead costs	$25,100

Required:

1. What were the standard hours worked for 19X1?
2. Compute the variable overhead spending and efficiency variances for 19X1, and the fixed overhead budget and volume variances.

10–7. An incomplete flexible budget is given below:

		Direct Labor Hours			
Overhead Costs	Cost Formula	2,000	4,000	6,000	8,000
Variable:					
Maintenance.			$ 600		
Supplies			320		
Rework time			360		
Total.					
Fixed:					
Depreciation.			1,400		
Taxes.			800		
Supervision			3,500		
Total.					
Total overhead costs					

Required:

Provide the missing information in the budget.

10–8. Operating at a normal level of 24,000 direct labor hours, the ABC Company produces 8,000 units of product. Fixed overhead costs total $84,000 per year. Variable overhead costs are budgeted at $38,400 at the normal activity level. The direct labor wage rate is $6.30 per hour. Two pounds of raw materials go into each unit of product, at a cost of $3.40 per pound.

Required:

Complete the standard cost sheet below for one unit of product:

Direct materials, 2 lbs. @ $3.40	$6.80
Direct labor, ?	?
Variable overhead, ?	?
Fixed overhead, ?	?
Total standard cost per unit.	$?

PROBLEMS

10–1. *Volume Variance, with Explanation.* Hoover Company's budgeted and actual fixed overhead costs for 19X6 are given below:

	Budgeted	*Actual*
Fixed overhead costs	$90,000	$91,300

Other information on the company is given below:

	Direct Labor Hours
Full capacity.	40,000
Budgeted for 19X6	30,000
Actual hours worked during 19X6	35,000
Standard hours for work completed during 19X6.	32,000

Required:

1. Assume that the company uses budgeted hours as the denominator activity. Compute the fixed overhead budget and volume variances.
2. Assume that the company uses full capacity hours as the denominator activity. Compute the fixed overhead budget and volume variances.
3. Explain why the budget variances computed in 1 and 2 are the same, and why the volume variances are different.

10–2. *Overhead Analysis.* The FAB Company operates with a standard cost system, and produces a single product. Selected information from the company's flexible budget for 19X4 follows:

Budgeted direct labor hours	12,000*
Budgeted variable overhead	$18,600
Budgeted fixed overhead.	$45,000
* Denominator activity level.	

During 19X4, the following operating results were recorded:

Actual direct labor hours worked	10,800
Standard direct labor hours worked	11,000
Actual variable overhead	$18,360
Actual fixed overhead	$44,500

At the end of 19X4, the company's manufacturing overhead account contained the following items:

Manufacturing Overhead

Actual 62,860	58,300 Applied
4,560	

Required:

1. Compute the predetermined overhead rate that would have been used during 19X4. Break it down into variable and fixed cost elements.
2. How was the $58,300 "applied" figure in the manufacturing overhead account computed?
3. Analyze the $4,560 underapplied overhead figure in terms of variable overhead spending and efficiency variances, and fixed overhead budget and volume variances.

10–3. *Overhead Analysis.* According to the CSJ Company's flexible budget, the company should incur the following overhead costs at a denominator activity level of 15,000 machine hours per month:

Variable overhead costs	$24,000
Fixed overhead costs	52,500
Total overhead costs	$76,500

[handwritten: % 15,000 = 1.60]

During 19X5, the company recorded the following actual operating results:

Actual machine hours worked.	16,200
Standard machine hours worked	15,800
Actual variable overhead costs.	$23,490
Actual fixed overhead costs	$52,950

Required:

1. Compute the predetermined overhead rate that the company would have used during 19X5. Break it down into fixed and variable elements.
2. Prepare a T-account for manufacturing overhead.
   a. Enter the actual overhead costs for 19X5 into the T-account.
   b. Compute the applied overhead for 19X5, and enter the amount into the T-account.
   c. Compute the under- or overapplied overhead for 19X5, and enter the amount into the T-account.
3. Analyze the under- or overapplied overhead figure in terms of variable overhead spending and efficiency variances, and fixed overhead budget and volume variances.
4. Explain the meaning of each variance which you computed in part 3.

10–4. *Overhead Analysis, with Graphing.* For 19X5, the Durrant Company has planned a denominator activity level of 16,000 direct labor hours. At this level of activity, the following overhead costs are budgeted:

Variable overhead.	$28,800
Fixed overhead	44,800

The company produces a single product, that requires 2.5 hours to complete. The direct labor rate is $6.50 per hour. The product requires 4 pounds of raw materials, at $3.20 per pound.

Required:

1. Compute the predetermined overhead rate that the company will use during 19X5. Break the rate down into fixed and variable cost elements.
2. Prepare a standard cost sheet for one unit of product, using the following format:

Direct materials, 4 lbs. @ $3.20	$12.80
Direct labor, ?	?
Variable overhead, ?	?
Fixed overhead, ?	?
Total standard cost per unit.	$?

3. Graph the following costs from an activity level of zero to 18,000 direct labor hours:
   a. Budgeted fixed overhead (in total).
   b. Applied fixed overhead (applied at the hourly rate computed in part 1).
4. Assume that during 19X5 the company works 15,500 actual direct labor hours and produces 6,000 units of product. Actual fixed overhead costs are $45,100.
   a. Compute the fixed overhead budget and volume variances.
   b. Show the volume variance on the graph which you prepared in part 3.
5. Assume that during 19X5 the company works 16,400 actual direct labor hours and produces 6,600 units of product. Actual fixed overhead costs are again $45,100.
   a. Compute the fixed overhead budget and volume variances.
   b. Show the volume variance on the chart which you prepared in part 3.

10–5. *Comprehensive Problem—Overhead Costing and Analysis.* The condensed flexible budget of KEN Company is given below for 19X2:

		Direct Labor Hours		
Overhead Costs	Cost Formula	4,000	6,000	8,000
Variable costs	$2.30/DLH	$ 9,200	$13,800	$18,400
Fixed costs		36,000	36,000	36,000
Total overhead costs		$45,200	$49,800	$54,400

The company produces a single product that requires 3.5 direct labor hours to complete. The direct labor wage rate is $5.80 per hour. Three yards of raw material are required for each unit of product at a cost of $4.50 per yard.

Required:

1. Assume that the company chooses 6,000 direct labor hours as the denominator level of activity. Compute the predetermined overhead rate, breaking it down into fixed and variable cost elements.
2. Assume that the company chooses 8,000 direct labor hours as the denominator level of activity. Repeat the computations in part 1.
3. Complete two standard cost sheets, as outlined below. Each sheet should relate to a single unit of product.

Denominator Activity: 6,000 DLH

Direct materials, 3 yds. @ $4.50. . . . . $13.50
Direct labor,   ? . . . .   ?
Variable overhead, ? . . . .   ?
Fixed overhead,   ? . . . .   ?
    Total standard cost per unit. . . . . $?

Denominator Activity: 8,000 DLH

Direct materials, 3 yds. @ $4.50. . . . . $13.50
Direct labor,   ? . . . .   ?
Variable overhead, ? . . . .   ?
Fixed overhead,   ? . . . .   ?
    Total standard cost per unit. . . . . $?

4. Assume that 6,400 actual hours are worked during 19X2, and that 1,900 units are produced. Actual overhead costs for the year are:

Variable overhead. $15,960
Fixed overhead   36,875
    Total. $52,835

  a. Compute the standard hours allowed for 19X2 production.
  b. Compute the missing items from the manufacturing overhead account below. Assume that denominator activity is 6,000 direct labor hours, as used in part 1.

Manufacturing Overhead

Actual Costs	52,835	?	Applied Costs
Under-Applied Overhead	?	?	Over-Applied Overhead

c. Analyze your under- or overapplied overhead balance in terms of variable overhead spending and efficiency variances and fixed overhead budget and volume variances.

10–6. *Incomplete Data.* Each of the cases below is independent. You may assume that each company uses a standard cost system, and that each company's flexible budget is based on standard direct labor hours.

Item	Company A	Company B
1. Denominator activity in hours.	?	6,500
2. Standard hours allowed for units produced.	5,250	?
3. Actual hours worked	5,600	?
4. Flexible budget variable overhead per DLH	$?	$ 1.70
5. Flexible budget fixed overhead (total)	?	?
6. Actual variable overhead	8,000	12,960
7. Actual fixed overhead	20,500	24,000
8. Variable overhead applied to production*	?	11,730
9. Fixed overhead applied to production*	21,000	?
10. Variable overhead spending variance	?	?
11. Variable overhead efficiency variance.	525 U	510 F
12. Fixed overhead budget variance.	?	1,250 U
13. Fixed overhead volume variance	1,000 F	?
14. Variable portion of predetermined overhead rate	?	?
15. Fixed portion of predetermined overhead rate	?	?
16. (Underapplied) or Overapplied overhead (total).	?	?

* Based on standard hours allowed for units produced.

Required:

Compute the unknown amounts.

10–7. *Performance Report for Variable Overhead, with Interpretation.* The budgeted variable overhead costs per machine hour in the cutting department of Builtrite Shoes, Inc., are:

Material handling	$ .60
Machine setup	.20
Rework time	.05
Supplies	.40
Maintenance	.15
Total variable cost	$1.40

The following data are available for the month of October in the cutting department:

Budgeted machine hours	18,000
Standard machine hours worked	20,000
Actual machine hours worked	19,000

The actual variable overhead costs incurred during October were:

Material handling	$12,540
Machine setup	5,320
Rework time	1,140
Supplies	7,790
Maintenance	1,900
Total actual variable cost	$28,690

Required:

1. Prepare a performance report for the month of October for the cutting department. Management is interested only in a spending variance for overhead.
2. Of the five spending variances computed in part 1 above, over which two would management probably be most concerned? Why?

10–8. *Flexible Budget and Performance Report.* The Lanier Company has had great difficulty controlling overhead costs. At a recent convention, the president heard about a control device for overhead costs known as a flexible budget, and has hired you to implement this budgeting program in the Lanier Company. After some effort, you develop the following cost formulas for the company's machining department. These costs are based on a normal operating range of 8,000 to 10,000 machine hours per month:

Cost	*Cost Formula*
Machine setup	$.20 per machine hour
Lubricants	$500 plus $.10 per machine hour
Utilities	$300 plus $.08 per machine hour
Supplies	$.30 per machine hour
Indirect labor	$2,000 plus $.80 per machine hour

The manager of the machining department has no control over the fixed utilities cost; however, he has control over the other fixed costs incurred in his department.

During March, the first month after your preparation of the above data, the machining department worked 9,400 machine hours and produced 18,000 units of product. The actual costs of this production were:

Machine setup	$ 2,068
Lubricants	1,346
Utilities	1,052
Supplies	3,290
Indirect labor	9,050
Total costs	$16,806

There were no variances in the fixed costs. The department had originally budgeted to work 10,000 machine hours during March.

Required:

1. Prepare a flexible budget for the machining department in increments of 1,000 hours.
2. Prepare a performance report for the machining department for the month of March. Show only a spending variance on the report.
3. What additional information would you need to have in order to compute an overhead efficiency variance for the department?

10–9. *Evaluating and Interpreting a Performance Report.* Several years ago Boudine Company developed a comprehensive budgeting system for profit planning and control purposes. The line foremen have been very happy with the budgeting system, but considerable dissatisfaction has been expressed on the part of middle and upper management. A typical performance report for a recent period is shown below:

BOUDINE COMPANY
Performance Report
Assembly Operation
For the Month of August

	Budget	*Actual*	*Variance*
Units produced	14,000	12,000	
Variable overhead:			
Indirect materials	$14,000	$13,800	$200 F
Rework time	2,800	2,880	80 U
Machine setup	1,400	1,380	20 F
Utilities	5,600	5,400	200 F
Total variable costs	23,800	23,460	340 F
Fixed overhead:			
Maintenance	12,000	11,800	200 F
Inspection	15,000	15,000	–
Total fixed costs	27,000	26,800	200 F
Total overhead costs	$50,800	$50,260	$540 F

Upon receiving a copy of this performance report, the foreman of the assembly operation stated, "These reports are great. It makes me feel really good to see how well things are going in my part of the shop. I can't understand why those guys upstairs complain so much."

Required:

1. If you were the immediate superior of the foreman of the assembly operation, how would you feel about the performance report above?
2. What changes, if any, would you recommend be made in the performance report, in order to give you better insight into how well the foreman is doing his job?

3. Prepare a new performance report for the month of August, incorporating any changes you suggested in part 2 above.

10–10. Detailed Performance Report. The UAL Company produced 4,200 units of product during May 19X2. The standard cost sheet shows that the standard direct labor time is 2 hours per unit, or a total of 8,400 direct labor hours for May. The company actually worked 9,000 direct labor hours during the month. The company's actual variable overhead costs for the month are given below, along with the standard cost per direct labor hour, as shown in the flexible budget:

Actual Costs Incurred	Variable Overhead Item	Cost Formula (per direct labor hour)
$1,080	Supplies	$.15
900	Power.	.08
810	Maintenance	.12
1,350	Setup time	.20
$4,140	Total variable overhead	$.55

Required:

Prepare a performance report for the month, using the following column headings in your report:

			Actual		Breakdown of the Total Budget Variance	
	Budget Based	Budget Based	Costs In-	Total	Spend-	Effi-
Overhead Item	on 8,400 Hrs.	on 9,000 Hrs.	curred 9,000 Hrs.	Budget Variance	ing Variance	ciency Variance

10–11. Detailed Performance Report. The cost formulas for variable overhead costs in a machining operation are given below:

Variable Overhead Cost	Cost Formula (per machine hour)
Power.	$.30
Setup time	.20
Polishing wheels	.16
Maintenance	.18
Total variable overhead	$.84

During the month of August the machining operation was scheduled to work 8,500 machine hours, and to produce 3,400 units of product. The standard machine time per unit of product is 2.5 hours. A strike near the end of the month forced a curtailment of production. Actual results for the month were:

Actual machine hours worked. 6,500
Actual number of units produced. 2,500

Actual costs for the month were:

	Total Actual Costs	Per Machine Hour
Power.	$1,690	$.26
Setup time.	1,365	.21
Polishing wheels.	845	.13
Maintenance.	1,690	.26
	$5,590	$.86

Required:

Prepare a performance report for the machining operation for the month of August. Use column headings in your report as shown in Exhibit 10–7.

10.12. *Comprehensive Problem, Flexible Budget and Performance Reports.* Pacific States Fabricating, Inc., has recently introduced budgeting as an integral part of its corporate planning process. The company's first effort at constructing a flexible budget for overhead is shown below.

Percentage of capacity	80%	100%
Direct labor hours.	4,000	5,000
Maintenance.	$1,400	$1,500
Supplies	1,600	2,000
Utilities.	1,700	2,000
Supervision	3,000	3,000
Machine Setup.	800	1,000
Total overhead cost	$8,500	$9,500

The budgets above are for costs over a relevant range of 80 percent to 100 percent of capacity on a monthly basis. The managers who will be working under these budgets have control over both fixed and variable costs.

Required:

1. Redo the company's flexible budget, presenting it in better format. Show the budget at 80 percent, 90 percent, and 100 percent levels of capacity.
2. Express the budget prepared in part 1 in cost formula form, using a single cost formula to express all overhead costs.
3. During the month of April, the company operated at 88 percent of capacity, and produced 12,000 units of product. The company had budgeted to operate at 90 percent of capacity. The standard

hours of production were 4,200 direct labor hours. The actual costs incurred were:

Maintenance	$1,308
Supplies	1,804
Utilities	1,864
Supervision	3,000
Machine setup	1,232
Total costs	$9,208

Prepare a performance report for the month of April. Management is interested only in a spending variance for overhead.

chapter 11

Control of Decentralized Operations

IN THIS CHAPTER we expand our knowledge of performance reports through introduction of a concept known as *responsibility accounting*. this concept permits us to tie together a number of ideas developed in preceding chapters, and to extend the technique of performance reporting to the company as a whole.

RESPONSIBILITY ACCOUNTING

Responsibility accounting centers on the idea that an organization is simply a group of individuals working toward common goals. The more each individual can be assisted in the performance of his or her tasks, then the better chance the organization has of reaching the goals it has set. Responsibility accounting recognizes each person in an organization who has any control over cost or revenue to be a *separate responsibility center*, whose stewardship must be defined, measured, and reported upward in the organization. One author expresses the idea this way:

> In effect, the system personalizes the accounting statements by saying, "Joe, this is what you originally budgeted and this is how you performed for the period with actual operations as compared against your budget." By definition it [responsibility accounting] is a system of accounting which is tailored to an organization so that costs are accumulated and reported by levels of responsibility within the organization. Each supervisory area in the organization is charged *only* with the cost for which it is responsible and over which it has control.[1]

---

[1] John A. Higgins, "Responsibility Accounting," *The Arthur Andersen Chronicle* (April 1952), p. 94.

Although the idea behind responsibility accounting is not new, the implementation of the idea on a widespread basis is quite recent, and has come about in response to the manager's need for better and more efficient ways to control operations.

The Functioning of the System

To gain insight into the functioning of a responsibility accounting system we will consider data of the Potter Company, a part of the Western Division of the National Corporation. A partial organization chart for Potter Company is shown in Exhibit 11–1. The data in this chart form the basis for exhibits found on the following pages.

EXHIBIT 11–1
Organization Chart—Potter Company

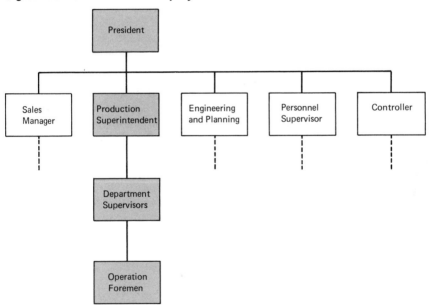

Although the concepts underlying responsibility accounting apply equally well to all parts of an organization, we will concentrate our discussion on the shaded area of Potter Company's organization chart. It depicts the line of responsibility for the production activities of the firm. This line of responsibility begins with the foreman, and moves upward in the organization, with each successive level having greater overall responsibility than the level which preceded it. To see how this concept of an upward flowing, broadening line of responsibility can be integrated into the accounting statements, refer to Exhibit 11–2.

EXHIBIT 11-2

POTTER COMPANY
An Overview of Responsibility Accounting*

President's Report

The president's performance report summarizes all company data. Since variances are given, the president can trace the variances downward through the company as needed to determine where his and his subordinates' time can best be spent.

Responsibility Center:	Budget	Actual	Variance
Sales Manager	X	X	X
Production Supt.	$26,000	$29,000	$3,000 U
Engineering and Pln.	X	X	X
Personnel Supervisor	X	X	X
Controller	X	X	X
	$54,000	$61,000	$7,000 U

Production Superintendent

The performance of each department supervisor is summarized for the Production Superintendent. The totals on the Superintendent's performance report are then passed upward to the next level of responsibility.

Responsibility Center:	Budget	Actual	Variance
Cutting Department	X	X	X
Machining Department	X	X	X
Finishing Department	$11,000	$12,500	$1,500 U
Packaging Department	X	X	X
	$26,000	$29,000	$3,000 U

Finishing Department Supervisor

The performance report of each foreman is summarized on the performance report of the departmental supervisor. The department totals are then summarized upward to the Production Superintendent.

Responsibility Center:	Budget	Actual	Variance
Sanding Operation	X	X	X
Wiring Operation	$5,000	$5,800	$800 U
Assembly Operation	X	X	X
	$11,000	$12,500	$1,500 U

Wiring Operation Foreman

The foreman of each operation receives a performance report on his center of responsibility. The totals on these reports are then communicated upward to the next higher level of responsibility.

Variable costs:	Budget	Actual	Variance
Direct materials	X	X	X
Direct labor	X	X	X
Manufacturing overhead	X	X	X
	$5,000	$5,800	$800 U

* Adapted from an illustration prepared by John A. Higgins, "Responsibility Accounting," *The Arthur Andersen Chronicle* (April 1952), p. 105.

Exhibit 11–2 provides us with a bird's eye view of the structuring of reports in a responsibility accounting system. Notice that the performance reports *start at the bottom and build upward* with each manager receiving information on his own performance as well as on the performance of each manager under him in the chain of responsibility. We will now start at the bottom of this chain and follow it upward to discuss in more detail the upward flow of information in a responsibility accounting system.

The Flow of Information

The responsibility accounting system depicted in Exhibit 11–2 is structured around four levels of responsibility. The number of levels of responsibility will vary from company to company, according to organizational structure and needs. The key point to remember is that *each level* within an organization having control over costs must be recognized as a *separate* responsibility center.

Fourth Level of Responsibility. The fourth, or lowest, level of responsibility is that of the Wiring Operation Foreman. The performance report prepared for the foreman will be similar to the performance reports discussed in the preceding chapter. This report will show budgeted data, actual data, and variances in terms of materials, labor, and overhead. This information will be communicated upward to the Department Supervisor, along with detailed variance analyses.

Third Level of Responsibility. The third level of responsibility is the Finishing Department Supervisor, who oversees the work of the Wiring Operation foreman as well as the work of the other foremen in his department. Notice from Exhibit 11–2 that the supervisor will receive summarized data from each of the operations within his department. If he desires to know the reasons behind the variances reported in these summaries (such as the $800 variance in the Wiring Operation), he can look at the detailed, individual performance reports prepared on the separate operations.

Second Level of Responsibility. The second level of responsibility is the Production Superintendent who has responsibility for all producing department activities. Notice from Exhibit 11–2 that the summarized totals from the Finishing Department Supervisor's performance report are reported upward to the Production Superintendent, along with summarized totals from the performance reports of other departments. In addition to the summarized totals, the Production Superintendent undoubtedly will also require that detailed copies of the performance reports themselves be furnished to him, as well as detailed copies of the performance reports from all separate operations within the departments. Availability of these reports will permit the Production Superintendent to go right to the heart of any problem in cost control. This, of course, is the implementation of the "management by exception" principle discussed in earlier chapters. By having variances from budget highlighted on each performance report, the Production Superintendent is able to see where his time and the time of his supervisors and foremen can best be spent.

First Level of Responsibility. The president of a company has ultimate responsibility for all costs and revenues. On his performance report, therefore, the activities of all phases of the business must be summarized for review.

The president may require that the detailed copies of the performance reports from *all* levels of responsibility be supplied to him. On the other hand, he may concern himself only with broad results, leaving the more detailed data for the scrutiny of the managers of the lower responsibility centers such as the Production Superintendent. The point is that the system provides a great deal of flexibility, and can be expanded or contracted in terms of data provided to suit the needs and interests of the particular manager involved.

In the absence of a responsibility accounting system, managers are left with little more than a "seat-of-the-pants" feel for what is going on in their own areas of responsibility, as well as that of their subordinates. In today's highly competitive business environment, a "seat-of-the-pants" feel for how well costs are being controlled is rarely sufficient to sustain profitable operations.

Expanding the Responsibility Accounting Idea

We indicated earlier that the Potter Company is a part of the Western Division of National Company. Exhibit 11–3 shows more clearly just how Potter Company fits into the structure of the National Company organization.

Exhibit 11–3 illustrates a further expansion of the responsibility accounting idea. Notice from the exhibit that contribution income statements are used to report company level performance to the division manager, and to report divisional performance to corporate headquarters.

On a corporate headquarters level, all data are summarized into various segment arrangments for an overall performance evaluation of the entire corporate structure. (See Exhibit 11–3.) Since variances from budgeted sales and costs are shown on the contribution income statements, managers at the various levels of responsibility can see clearly where profit objectives are not being met. An illustration of a contribution income statement with variances is presented in Exhibit 11–4. Income statements of this type are prepared at both the company and division levels, and then consolidated on a corporate level.

EXHIBIT 11–3
The National Company Organization—An Expansion of the Responsibility Accounting Concept

Corporate headquarters will summarize all data on contribution income statements, according to relevant segments. Segment data may be presented, for example, by division, by company within divisions, by product line, etc. In each case the actual data will be compared against the budgeted sales and costs. Variances from budget can be traced downward through the organization as needed to show where management time should be spent to improve profitability.

Separate division performance is reported upward by means of contribution income statements. The statements will be arranged according to relevant segments, such as individual companies, product lines by companies, sales territories by companies, etc. The actual performance will be compared against the budget in terms of sales and costs.

Individual company performance is reported upward by means of contribution income statements. These statements will be prepared under various segment arrangements, such as product line, sales territory, etc. The actual performance on the statements is compared against the budget in terms of sales and costs.

Discharge of responsibility is reported upward through an integrated set of performance reports, such as illustrated in Chapter 10, and in Exhibit 11-2. Responsibility centers are clearly defined and performance is evaluated in light of standards and flexible budget allowances. All managers participate in the setting of the standards against which their performance is measured.

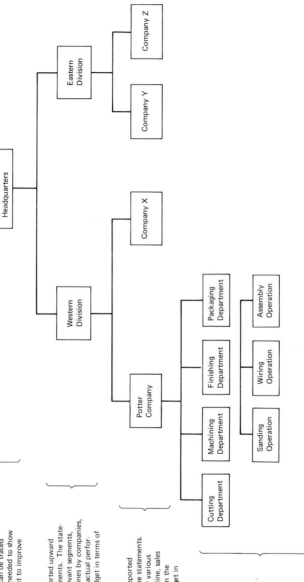

EXHIBIT 11–4

NATIONAL COMPANY
Contribution Income Statement Comparing
Budgeted Data to Actual Data
(000 omitted)

	Budget	Actual	Variance
Sales	$100,000	$97,000	$3,000 U
Variable expenses:			
Variable cost of sales.	45,000	46,000	1,000 U
Other variable expenses	15,000	14,500	500 F
Total variable expenses	60,000	60,500	500 U
Contribution margin	40,000	36,500	3,500 U
Less fixed expenses:			
Selling	13,000	13,000	–
Administrative	4,000	4,300	300 U
Manufacturing.	13,000	13,700	700 U
Total fixed expenses.	30,000	31,000	1,000 U
Net income	$ 10,000	$ 5,500	$4,500 U

Investment, Profit, and Cost Centers

In a responsibility accounting system, the structure of an organization such as National Company is visualized as consisting of various centers, such as shown in Exhibit 11–5.

EXHIBIT 11–5
The National Company Organization

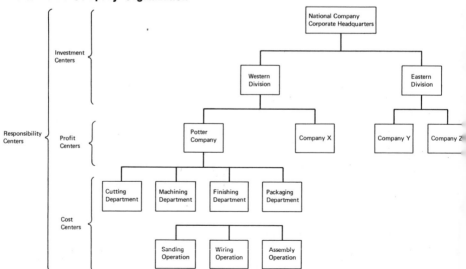

Responsibility Center. A *responsibility center* is any point within an organization where control over incurrence of cost or generating of revenue is found. Such a point could be an individual, an operation, a department, a company, a division, or the entire organization itself.

Cost Center. A *cost center* is any responsibility center that has control over the incurrence of cost. A cost center has no control over sales or over the generating of revenue.

Profit Center. By contrast to a cost center, a *profit center* has control over both cost and revenue. Potter Company, for example, would be a profit center in the National Company organization since it would be concerned with marketing its goods as well as producing them.

Investment Center. An *investment center* is any responsibility center within an organization that has control over cost and revenue, and also over investment funds. The corporate headquarters of National Company would clearly be an example of an investment center. Corporate officers have ultimate responsibility for seeing that production and marketing goals are met. In addition, they have responsibility for seeing that adequate facilities are available to carry out the production and marketing functions, and for seeing that adequate working capital is available for operating needs. Whenever a segment of an organization has control over the making of investment in such areas as physical plant and equipment, receivables, inventory, and entry into new markets, then it is termed an investment center.

The separate divisions of the National Company would also qualify as investment centers if they have control over the use of investment funds, in terms of working capital management, facility procurement, and entry into new markets. Potter Company itself could also be an investment center if it were given control over investment funds for some of these purposes. In the more usual situation, however, Potter Company would be a profit center within the larger organization.

Measuring Management Performance

These concepts of responsibility accounting are very important since they not only assist in defining a manager's sphere of responsibility, but in determining how his performance will be evaluated as well.

Cost centers are evaluated by means of performance reports, in terms of meeting cost standards that have been set. Profit centers are evaluated by means of contribution income statements, in terms of meeting sales and cost objectives. Investment centers are also evaluated by means of contribution income statements, but normally in terms of the *rate of return* they are able to generate on *invested funds*. We are now prepared to discuss the measurement of rate of return, and to consider some of the strengths and weaknesses of this tool as a means of measuring managerial performance.

RATE OF RETURN FOR MEASURING
MANAGERIAL PERFORMANCE

The development of concepts such as investment centers, profit centers, and cost centers is largely a result of the rapid growth of decentralization in corporate structures. Managers of investment centers and profit centers are generally given large amounts of autonomy in directing the affairs in their areas of responsibility. So great is this autonomy that the various profit and investment centers are often viewed as being independent businesses, with the managers having about the same control over decisions as if they were running their own independent firms. With this autonomy, fierce competition often develops between the various profit and investment centers within an organization such as National Company.

Competition is particularly keen when it comes to passing out funds for expansion of product lines, or for introduction of new product lines. How do top managers in corporate headquarters go about deciding who gets new investment funds as they become available, and how do these managers decide which investment centers are most profitably using the funds which have already been entrusted to their care? One of the most popular tools for making these judgments is rate of return on invested capital.

The Rate of Return Formula

To understand the concepts behind the rate of return formula, refer to the funds flow model illustrated in Exhibit 11–6.

EXHIBIT 11–6
The Funds Flow Model
CS = Capital Stock; LTL = Long-Term Liabilities; CL = Current Liabilities; FA = Fixed Assets; OA = Other Assets; I = Inventory; AR = Accounts Receivable.

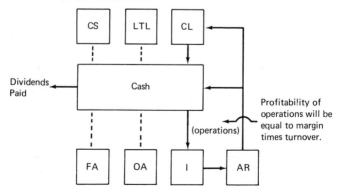

As a dollar leaves the central pool of cash in Exhibit 11-6, it is invested in inventory. The inventory is then sold, and an account receivable is created, which is subsequently collected from the customer. Upon collection from the customer, the dollar which was started through the system is returned back into the central pool of cash from which it began its journey. This dollar will bring back with it whatever additional pennies the customer has been willing to pay above the cost of the goods which he purchased. Thus, the seller's profitability will at least in part be measured by the number of these additional pennies, which we may call the *margin* earned.

But a moment's reflection will indicate that a firm's profitability is also dependent on another factor. Realizing that a dollar going through the system will bring back a certain number of additional pennies with it, we will be anxious to send that dollar through the system as many times during the period as we possibly can. The number of trips a dollar makes through the system during a period is known as the *turnover*. Thus, we can see that a firm's profitability will be a product of the margin (number of pennies brought back by a dollar in one trip through the system), multiplied by the turnover (number of times a dollar makes the trip through the system during the period). This line of reasoning gives rise to the rate of return formula:

$$\text{Margin} \times \text{Turnover} = \text{Profitability, or Rate of Return}$$

Factors Underlying Rate of Return

Armed with a conceptual perspective of the rate of return formula, we can now examine the detailed factors making up the margin and the turnover elements:

$$\text{Margin} \times \text{Turnover} = \text{Rate of Return}$$

$$\text{Margin} = \frac{\text{Net Operating Income}}{\text{Sales}} \qquad \text{Turnover} = \frac{\text{Sales}}{\text{Operating Assets}}$$

therefore,

$$\frac{\text{Net Operating Income}}{\text{Sales}} \times \frac{\text{Sales}}{\text{Operating Assets}} = \text{Rate of Return}$$

In the past, managers have tended to focus only on the margin earned and have ignored the turnover of assets. To some degree, at least, the margin earned can be a valuable measure of a manager's performance. But standing alone it overlooks one very crucial area of a manager's responsibility—the control of investment in operating assets. Excessive funds tied up in operating assets can be just as much of a drag on profitability as excessive operating expenses. One of the real advantages of the rate of return formula is that it forces the manager to control his investment in operating assets as well as expenses, the gross profit rate, and sales volume.

The DuPont Company was the first major corporation to recognize the importance of looking at both margin *and* turnover in assessing the performance of a manager. To them must go the credit for pioneering the rate of return concept. Monsanto Chemical Company and other major corporations have followed the DuPont lead, and the rate of return formula is now recognized as one of the best single measures of a manager's performance when that manager has control of an investment center. It blends together many aspects of his responsibilities into a single figure that can be compared against competing investment centers, as well as against other firms in the industry.

Operating Income and the Asset Base

The reader may have noticed in the rate of return formula above that net *operating* income was used rather than simply net income. The reason is that the definition of income used in the formula should be consistent with the asset base to which it is related. When dealing with *operating* assets as a base, it is common practice to use *net operating* income. Net operating income is income before interest and taxes. In business jargon it is sometimes referred to as EBIT (earnings before interest and taxes). The reader should become familiar with this term.

The operating asset base used in the formula is computed as the *average* between the beginning and the end of the year.

CONTROLLING THE RATE OF RETURN

When being measured by the rate of return formula, a manager can improve his profitability in three ways:

1. By increasing sales.
2. By reducing expenses.
3. By reducing assets.

To illustrate how the rate of return can be controlled by each of these three actions, let us assume the following data for an investment center:

Net operating income.	$ 10,000
Sales	100,000
Operating assets.	50,000

The rate of return generated by the investment center would be:

$$\frac{\text{Net Operating Income}}{\text{Sales}} \times \frac{\text{Sales}}{\text{Operating Assets}} = \text{Rate of Return}$$

$$\frac{\$10,000}{\$100,000} \times \frac{\$100,000}{\$50,000} = \text{Rate of Return}$$

$$10\% \quad \times \quad 2 \quad = 20\%$$

Approach #1: Increase Sales. Assume that the center above is able to increase sales from $100,000 to $110,000. Assume that net operating income increases from $10,000 to $12,000. The operating assets remain constant.

$$\frac{\$12,000}{\$110,000} \times \frac{\$110,000}{\$50,000} = \text{Rate of Return}$$

$$10.9\% \times 2.2 = 23.98\%$$

Approach #2: Reduce Expenses. Assume that the center above is able to reduce expenses by $1,000, so that net operating income increases from $10,000 to $11,000. Both sales and operating assets remain constant.

$$\frac{\$11,000}{\$100,000} \times \frac{\$100,000}{\$50,000} = \text{Rate of Return}$$

$$11\% \times 2 = 22\%$$

Approach #3: Reduce Assets. Assume that operating assets can be reduced from $50,000 to $45,000. Sales and net operating income remain unchanged.

$$\frac{\$10,000}{\$100,000} \times \frac{\$100,000}{\$45,000} = \text{Rate of Return}$$

$$10\% \times 2.22 = 22.2\%$$

Increase Sales

In first looking at the rate of return formula one is inclined to think that the sales figure is neutral, since it appears as the denominator in the margin computation and as the numerator in the turnover computation. The sales figure *could* be cancelled out, but we don't do so for two reasons. First, it would tend to draw attention away from the fact that rate of return is a function of two variables, margin and turnover. And second, it would tend to conceal the fact that control of sales is one way in which to control profitability. If a manager can either (1) increase sales proportionately faster than expenses, or (2) increase sales while holding the investment in assets relatively constant, he can increase his rate of return.

How can sales be increased proportionately faster than expenses? This is often possible in those situations where fixed expenses are high relative to variable expenses. Once the break-even point is reached, net operating income will increase very rapidly for each additional unit sold. This explains how the net operating income could increase so much more rapidly than sales in Approach #1 above.

Reduce Expenses

Often the easiest route to increased profitability is simply to cut the "fat" out of an organization through a concerted effort to control expenses. When profit margins begin to be squeezed, this is generally the first line of attack by a manager. The discretionary fixed costs usually come under scrutiny first, with various programs either curtailed or eliminated in an effort to cut costs. Firms under extreme pressures to reduce expenses have gone so far as to eliminate coffee breaks, under the reasoning that nothing could more emphatically impress the staff with the need to be cost conscious.

One of the most common ways to reduce variable expenses is to use less costly inputs of materials. Another way is to automate processes as much as possible, particularly where large volumes of units are involved.

Reduce Operating Assets

Managers have always been sensitive to the need to control operating expenses and operating margins. They have not always been equally as sensitive, however, to the need to control investment in operating assets. Firms that have adopted the rate of return approach to measuring managerial performance report that one of the first reactions on the part of investment center managers is to trim down their investment in operating assets. The reason, of course, is that these managers quickly realize that an excessive investment in operating assets will reduce the asset turnover, and hurt the rate of return. As these managers pare down their investment in operating assets, funds are released that can be used elsewhere in the organization. Consider the following actual situation:

X Company, a firm located in a western state, is a manufacturer of high quality cast iron pipe. A few years ago, a large conglomerate acquired a controlling interest in the stock of X Company. X Company became an investment center of the larger organization. The parent company measured the performance of the investment center managers by the rate of return formula. X Company managers quickly found that their performance was below that of other investment centers within the organization. With their mediocre performance, X Company managers realized that they were in a poor position to compete for new investment funds. As one step in an effort to improve the rate of return, the company took a hard look at its investment in operating assets. As a result, it was able to reduce inventory alone by nearly 40 percent. This resulted in several million dollers becoming available for productive use elsewhere in the company. Within two years' time, the rate of return being generated by X Company improved dramatically. The controller of X Company, speaking at a management development conference, stated that the company had always been profitable in terms of net income to sales, so there really had been no incentive to watch the investment in operating assets prior to being put under the rate of return microscope.

What avenues are open to an investment center manager in his attempts to control the investment in operating assets? One approach is to pare out obsolete and redundant inventory. The computer has been extremely helpful in this regard, making perpetual inventory methods more feasible as well as facilitating the use of statistical methods of inventory control, such as discussed in Chapter 16. Another approach is to devise various methods of speeding up the collection of receivables. For example, many firms now employ the lock box technique by which customers in distant states remit directly to local post office boxes. The funds are received and deposited by a local banking institution in behalf of the payee firm. This can greatly speed up the collection process, and thereby increase the turnover of assets.

The Problem of Allocated Expenses and Assets

In companies such as National Company, mentioned in the early part of the chapter, it is common practice to allocate the expenses of operating corporate headquarters out to the separate divisions. When such allocations are made, a very thorny question arises as to whether these expenses should be considered in rate of return computations.

It can be argued on the one hand that allocated expenses should be included in rate of return computations, since they represent the value of services rendered to the divisions by central headquarters. On the other hand, it can be argued that they should not be included, since the divisional managers have no control over the incurrence of the expenses, and since the "services" involved are often of questionable value, or are hard to pin down.

At the very least, *arbitrary* allocations should be avoided in rate of return computations. If arbitrary allocations are made, great danger exists of creating a bias for or against a particular division. Expense allocations should be limited to the cost of those *actual* services provided by central headquarters which the divisions *otherwise* would have had to provide for themselves. The amount of expense allocated to a division should not exceed the cost which the division would have incurred if it had provided the service for itself.

The same guidelines apply to asset allocations from central corporate headquarters to the separate divisions.

THE CONCEPT OF RESIDUAL INCOME

Up to this point we have assumed that the purpose of an investment center should be to maximize the rate of return which it is able to generate on operating assets. There is another approach to measuring performance in an investment center which focuses on a concept known as *residual income*. Residual income is the net operating income which an investment center is able to earn *above* some minimum rate of return on operating assets. When residual income is used to measure performance, the purpose is to maximize the amount of the residual income, *not* to maximize the overall rate of return.

Consider the following data for two comparable divisions:

	Performance Measured By	
	Rate of Return	*Residual Income*
	Division A	*Division B*
Average operating assets	$100,000 (a)	$100,000
Net operating income.	$ 20,000 (b)	$ 20,000
Rate of return (b) ÷ (a).	20%	
Minimum required rate of return is assumed to be 15%. 15% × $100,000		15,000
Residual income.		$ 5,000

Many companies view residual income as being a better measure of performance than rate of return. They argue that the residual income approach encourages managers to make profitable investments that would be rejected by managers being measured by the rate of return formula. To illustrate, assume that each of the divisions above is presented with an opportunity to make an investment in a new project that would generate a rate of return on invested assets of 18 percent. The manager of Division A would probably reject this opportunity. Note from the tabulation above that his division is already earning a rate of return of 20 percent. If he takes on a new project that provides a return of only 18 percent, then his overall rate of return will be *reduced*. Since his performance is being measured according to the *maximum* rate of return which he is able to generate on invested assets, he will be unenthused about any investment opportunity which reduces his current rate of return. The manager of Division A will tend to think and act along these lines, even though a rejected investment opportunity may have benefited the company *as a whole*.

On the other hand, the manager of Division B will be very anxious to accept the new investment opportunity. The reason is that he isn't concerned about maximizing his rate of return. He is concerned about maximizing his residual income. Any project that provides a return greater that the minimum required 15 percent will be attractive since it will add to the *total amount* of the residual income figure. Under these circumstances, the new investment opportunity with its 18 percent return will clearly be attractive to the manager of Division B. In effect, by maximizing his own well-being, he automatically maximizes the well-being of the company as a whole.

TRANSFER PRICING

Special problems arise in applying the rate of return or residual income approaches to performance evaluation whenever one segment of a company supplies goods or services to another. The problems revolve around the question of what *transfer price* to charge for the transfer of goods or for the exchange of services.

The Need for Transfer Prices

Assume that a vertically integrated firm has four divisions. The four divisions are:

Mining Division.
Processing Division.
Fabricating Division.
Manufacturing Division.

The Mining Division mines raw materials that are transferred to the Processing Division. After processing, the Processing Division transfers the processed materials to the Fabricating Division which makes fabricated parts and then transfers them to the Manufacturing Division. The Manufacturing Division then includes the fabricated parts as part of its finished product.

In this example we have three transfers of goods between divisions within the same company. What price should control these transfers? The choice of a transfer price can be complicated by the fact that each division may be supplying portions of its output to outside customers, as well as to sister divisions.

The price charged to outside customers will be dictated largely by the competitive conditions of the market. But should this same price be used in pricing transfers *between* divisions? This is a key question since the price charged by one division becomes a cost to the other division. The higher this cost, the lower will be the purchasing division's net operating income and overall rate of return (or residual income).

As the reader may guess, the problem of what transfer price to set between segments of a company has no easy solution, and often leads to protracted and heated disputes between investment center managers. Yet some transfer price *must* be set if data are to be available for performance evaluation of the various parts or divisions of a company. In practice, four general approaches are used in setting transfer prices:

1. Setting transfer prices at cost.
2. Setting transfer prices at variable cost.
3. Setting transfer prices at market price.
4. Setting transfer prices at negotiated market price.

Transfer Prices at Cost

Many firms make transfers between divisions on the basis of the accumulated cost of the goods being transferred. One problem with this approach is that the only division that will show any profits is the one that makes the final sale to an outside party. Other divisions will show no returns for their efforts, and evaluation by the rate of return formula, or by the residual income approach, will not be possible. A further problem arises in defining just what should be included in "cost," and whether this figure should be allowed to fluctuate from period to period according to changes in production levels, etc. Arguments pro and con can be almost endless, and the source of considerable friction and ill-feeling.

The most serious criticism of cost-based transfer prices lies in their general inability to provide incentive for control of costs. If the costs of one division are simply passed on to the next, then there is little incentive for anyone to control costs. The final selling division is simply burdened with the accumulated waste and inefficiency of intermediate processors, and will be penalized with a rate of return that is deficient in comparison to competitors. Experience has shown that unless costs are subject to some type of competitive pressures at transfer points, waste and inefficiency almost invariably develop.

Despite these shortcomings, cost-based transfer prices are in fairly common use. Advocates argue that they are easily understood and highly convenient to use. If transfer prices are to be based on cost, then the costs should be standard costs, rather than actual costs. This will at least avoid the passing on of inefficiency from one division to another.

Transfer Prices at Variable Cost

Basically the same comments can be made about pricing transfers at variable cost as those made above about pricing transfers at full cost. Variable costs do have one advantage, however, in that *so far as the short run is concerned* their use may tend to insure the best utilization of total corporate facilities. The reason is that, in the short run, fixed costs don't change. Any use of facilities, therefore, that brings in revenues in excess of variable costs will increase short-run profitability. The danger lies in becoming locked into what was intended to be a short-run arrangement but which proves to be unprofitable over the longer term when full costs are considered.

Transfer Prices at Market Price

Some form of competitive market price is generally regarded as the best approach to the transfer pricing problem. The reason is that it dovetails very well with the profit center concept, and makes profit-based performance evaluation feasible at many levels of an organization. This approach also tends to lead to the best decisions involving transfer questions that may arise on a day-to-day basis, as we shall illustrate.

The market price approach to transfer pricing views individual divisions as if they were completely separate, autonomous companies. That is, each divisional manager is considered to be running his own independent firm. The idea in using market prices to control transfers is to create the competitive market conditions that would exist if the various divisions were *indeed* separate firms, and engaged in arm's length, open-market bargaining. To the extent that the resulting transfer prices reflect actual market conditions, the operating results provide an excellent basis for evaluating performance. The National Association of Accountants has described the operation of the approach as follows:

> Internal procurement is expected where the company's products and services are superior or equal in design, quality, performance, and price, and when acceptable delivery schedules can be met. So long as these conditions are met, the receiving unit suffers no loss and the supplier unit's profit accrues to the company. Often the receiving division gains

advantages such as better control over quality, assurance of continued supply, and prompt delivery.[2]

The guidelines that should be followed in using market prices to control transfers between divisions are:

1. The buying division must purchase internally so long as the selling division meets all bona fide outside prices, and wants to sell internally.
2. If the selling division does not meet all bona fide outside prices, then the buying division is free to purchase outside.
3. The selling division must have the option of not selling internally if it prefers to sell outside.[3]
4. An impartial board must be established to arbitrate disputes over prices.

Illustrating the Market Price Approach

To illustrate the operation of the market price approach, let us assume that the Processing Division of International Company has a product that can be sold either to the Fabricating Division or to outside customers. The cost structures of the processing and fabricating divisions are given below:

Processing Division	*Fabricating Division*
Intermediate market price if sold outside $5	Final market price outside $10
Variable costs $3	Transfer price from Processing Division . . . . $ 5
	Variable costs added in Fabricating Division . . . . $ 2

The choices facing the processing and fabricating divisions are shown graphically in Exhibit 11–7.

So long as the Processing Division can get a transfer price of $5 per unit out of the Fabricating Division, it will be completely willing to sell all of its output internally. In selling to the Fabricating Division, the Processing Division will be just as well off as if it had sold its product outside at the $5 price. In like manner, so long as the price charged by outside suppliers is not less than $5 per unit, the Fabricating Division will be willing to pay that price to the Processing Division.

[2] *Accounting for Intra-Company Transfers,* Research Series No. 30 (New York: National Association of Accountants, June 1956), pp. 13–14.

[3] The reason for this guideline is that the selling division may have opportunities for using its facilities to produce and sell other, more profitable, products.

EXHIBIT 11–7
Illustration of Transfers at Market Price

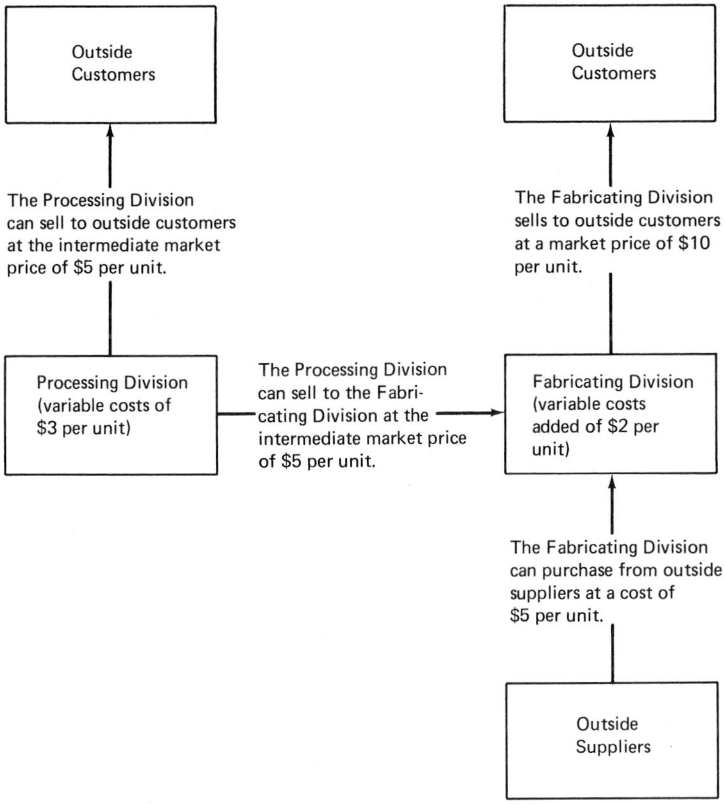

The $5 per unit intermediate market price, therefore, serves as an acceptable transfer price between the two divisions. The results of transfers at this price can be summarized as follows:

	Processing Division	Fabricating Division	Entire Company
Sales price per unit	$5	$10	$10
Variable costs added per unit	3	2	5
Transfer cost per unit.	—	5	—
Contribution margin per unit	$2	$ 3	$ 5

The contribution margin realized for the entire company is $5 per unit. By using market prices for intracompany transfers, the firm is able to show that a portion of this margin accrues from the processing activity and that a portion accrues from the fabricating activity. These data will then serve as an excellent basis for evaluating managerial performance using the rate of return or residual income approaches.

The Problem of a Change in Market Price

But what happens if the Fabricating Division finds an outside supplier who is willing to supply units at only $4 each? The answer is that the Processing Division should be given an opportunity to meet this price. If it meets the $4 price, then the Fabricating Division should continue to purchase from the Processing Division, as indicated in the guidelines given earlier. But is the Processing Division *required* to meet the $4 price? The answer is no. The guidelines given earlier indicate that the selling division is not required to sell internally. In this case, the Processing Division would *not* cut its price to $4 to retain the internal sales, so long as sufficient sales could be made to outside customers at $5.[4]

If the Processing Division decided not to reduce its price to $4 to meet outside competition, should the Fabricating Division be forced to continue to pay $5 and to buy internally? The answer again is no. The guidelines given earlier state that if the selling division is not willing to meet all bona fide outside prices, then the buying division is free to go outside to get the best price it can.

Transfers at Negotiated Market Prices

The market price at transfer points represents an *upper limit* on the charge that can be made on transfers between divisions. In many situations a lesser price can be justified. For example, selling and administrative expenses may be less when intracompany sales are involved, or the *volume* of units may be sufficiently large to justify quantity discounts. In other cases, the selling division may have substantial excess capacity, which may justify a price below the prevailing market.

Situations such as those just described can probably best be served by some type of *negotiated* market price. A negotiated market price is one agreed upon between the selling and buying divisions that reflects unusual or mitigating circumstances. Negotiated market prices are also required in those situations where no independent market prices are available. For example, one division may produce an item that is not available from any other source. Some type of negotiated market price would be required to establish the price to be paid by the buying division.

---

[4] If sufficient business could not be obtained outside at the $5 price, then the Processing Division might want to turn its facilities over to other, more profitable products.

The Matter of Opportunity Cost

The use of market price in transfer pricing helps to guard against setting transfer prices below the selling division's opportunity costs. An opportunity cost is the benefit that one foregoes in rejecting some course of action.

Selling Division at Full Capacity. If the selling division is already selling all that it can produce to outside customers, then the division's opportunity cost is the purchase price which these outside customers are willing to pay. The reason is that in accepting inside business, the selling division would have to reject outside business, and *forego* the revenues that could have been received on this business. *Thus, the transfer price inside should never be less than this opportunity cost (reduced by any costs that are avoided as a result of inside sales, as discussed earlier), or the selling division will suffer, and the company as a whole may suffer as well.*

Selling Division with Excess Capacity. If the selling division has substantial excess capacity, then a different situation exists. Under these conditions opportunity costs *may* be zero (depending on what alternative uses the seller has for his excess capacity). Even if opportunity costs are zero, many managers would argue that the transfer price should still be based on prevailing market prices, to the extent that they can be determined accurately and fairly. Other managers would argue that excess capacity combined with zero, or near zero, opportunity costs calls for a negotiation of the transfer price downward from prevailing market rates, so that both the buyer and the seller can profit from the intracompany business.

Under excess capacity conditions, so long as the selling division can receive a price greater than its variable costs (at least in the short run) all parties will benefit by keeping business inside rather than having the buying division go outside. If the selling division has excess capacity and the buying division purchases from an outside supplier then *suboptimization*[5] will result for the selling division, possibly for the buying division, and certainly for the company as a whole. In short, if excess capacity exists every effort should be made to negotiate a price acceptable to both buyer and seller that will keep business within the company as a whole.

Divisional Autonomy and Suboptimization

A question often arises as to how much autonomy should be granted to divisions in setting their own transfer prices, and in making decisions

---

[5] By *suboptimization* we mean that overall profitability will be less than it could have been.

concerning whether to sell internally or to sell outside. Should the divisional heads have complete authority to make these decisions, or should top corporate management step in if it appears that a decision is about to be made that would result in suboptimization? For example, if excess capacity exists in the selling division and divisional managers are unable to agree on a transfer price, should top corporate management step in and *force* settlement of a dispute?

Effort should always be made, of course, to bring disputing managers together. But the almost unanimous feeling among top corporate managers is that divisional heads should not be forced into an agreement over a transfer price. That is, if a particular divisional head flatly refuses to change his position in a dispute, *then his decision should be respected,* even if this results in suboptimization. This is simply the price that is paid for the concept of divisional autonomy. If top corporate management steps in and forces the decisions in difficult situations, then the concepts which we have been developing in this chapter largely evaporate and the company simply becomes a centralized operation, with decentralization of only minor decisions and responsibilities. In short, if a division is to be viewed as an autonomous unit with independent profit responsibility, then it must have control over its own destiny—even to the extent of the right to make bad decisions.

We should note, however, that if a division consistently makes bad decisions, the results will soon have an impact on its rate of return, and the divisional manager may find himself having to defend his division's performance. Even so, his right to get himself into an embarrassing situation must be respected if the divisional concept is to operate successfully. The overwhelming experience of multidivisional companies is that divisional autonomy and independent profit responsibility leads to much greater success and profitability than closely-controlled, centrally administered operations. Part of the price of this success and profitability is an occasional situation of suboptimization, due to pettiness, bickering, or just plain managerial cussedness.

SUMMARY

Responsibility accounting centers on the notion that any point within an organization having control over cost or revenue is a responsibility center. The way in which the various responsibility centers discharge their control over cost or revenue is communicated upward in an organization, from lower levels of responsibility to higher levels of responsibility, through a system of integrated performance reports.

Those responsibility centers having control over cost are known as cost centers. Those having control over both cost and revenue are known as profit centers, and those having control over cost, revenue and investment funds are known as investment centers. The rate of return formula is widely regarded as a method of evaluating performance in an investment center because it summarizes into one figure many aspects of an investment center manager's responsibilities. As an alternative to the rate of return formula, some companies use residual income as a measure of investment center performance. These companies argue that the residual income approach encourages profitable investment in many situations where the rate of return approach might discourage investment.

Transfer pricing relates to the price to be charged in a transfer of goods or an exchange of services between two units (such as divisions) within an organization. The predominant feeling is that the best transfer price is some version of the market price, to the extent that a market price exists for the good or service involved. The use of market price in transfers between units facilitates performance evaluation by permitting both the buyer and the seller to be treated as independent, autonomous units.

QUESTIONS

11–1. In what way does the concept of responsibility accounting give emphasis to a firm's organizational structure?

11–2. Describe the general flow of information in a responsibility accounting system.

11–3. What is meant by the term responsibility center? Could a responsibility center be a person as well as a department, etc.? Does the concept apply to nonmanufacturing as well as to manufacturing activities?

11–4. Distinguish between a cost center, a profit center, and an investment center.

11–5. How is performance in a cost center generally measured? Performance in a profit center? Performance in an investment center?

11–6. What is meant by the terms margin and turnover?

11–7. In what way is rate of return a more exacting measure of performance than the ratio of net income to sales?

11–8. When the rate of return formula is being used to measure performance, what three avenues are open to the manager in improving his overall profitability?

11–9. A student once commented to the author, "It simply is not possible for a decrease in operating assets to result in an increase in profitability. The way to increase profits is to *increase* the operating assets." Discuss.

11–10. X Company has high fixed expenses and is presently operating somewhat above the break-even point. From this point on, will percentage increases in net income tend to be greater than, about equal to, or less than percentage increases in total sales? Why? Ignore income taxes.

11–11. What is meant by the term transfer price, and why are transfer pricing systems needed?

11–12. Why are cost-based transfer prices in widespread use? What are the disadvantages of cost-based transfer prices?

11–13. If a market price for a product can be determined, why is it generally considered to be the best transfer price?

11–14. Under what circumstances might a negotiated market price be a better approach to pricing transfers between divisions than actual market price?

11–15. In what ways can suboptimization result if divisional managers are given full autonomy in setting, accepting, and rejecting transfer prices?

EXERCISES

11–1. Selected operating data for two divisions of Arco Company are given below:

	East Division	West Division
Sales	$50,000	$75,000
Operating assets	20,000	25,000
Net operating income	4,000	5,625
Long-term debt	5,000	6,000

Required:

1. Compute the rate of return for each division, using the rate of return formula.
2. So far as you can tell from the data available, which divisional manager seems to be doing the best job? Why?

11–2. *a.* Company A and Company B each reported an 18 percent rate of return for 19X1. The margin in each company was:

	19X1 Margin
Company A	4%
Company B	9%

What was each company's turnover in 19X1?

b. Sales and operating assets for Company X and Company Y are given below. Compute the margin that each company will have to earn in order to generate a rate of return of 20 percent.

	Sales	Operating Assets
Company X	$20,000	$ 8,000
Company Y	50,000	10,000

11–3. Division A produces a product that can be sold either to Division B or to outside customers. During 19X1, the following activity occurred in Division A:

Units produced	500
Units sold to Division B	100
Units sold to outside customers	400
Unit selling price	$10
Unit cost of production	$ 6

The units purchased by Division B were processed further at a cost of $4 per unit, and sold to outside customers for $15 each. All transfers between divisions are made at market price.

Required:

1. Prepare income statements for 19X1 for Division A, Division B, and the company as a whole.
2. Assume that Division A's manufacturing capacity is 500 units. In 19X2, Division B wants to purchase 200 units from Division A, rather than only 100 units as in 19X1. Should Division A sell the extra units to Division B, or continue selling the units to outside customers? Explain.

11–4. Provide the missing data in the following tabulation:

	Division A	Division B	Division C	Division D
Sales	$500,000	$?	$450,000	$?
Net operating income	20,000	?	22,500	10,000
Operating assets	?	100,000	90,000	?
Margin	?	8%	?	4%
Turnover	?	3	?	?
Rate of return	10%	?	?	16%

11–5. The Transistor Division of Consumer Products, Inc., produces transistors which are sold to the Company's Radio Division, as well as to outside customers. Operating data for the Transistor Division for last year are given below:

	To the Radio Division	To Outside Customers
Sales:		
100,000 units @ $3*	$300,000	
200,000 units @ $4		$800,000
Variable expenses @ $2 and $3	200,000	600,000
Contribution margin	100,000	200,000
Fixed expenses	50,000	100,000
Net income	$ 50,000	$100,000

* $4 outside selling price less expenses applicable to outside sales.

The manager of the Radio Division has just received an offer from an outside supplier to supply the transistors at $2.50 each. The manager of the Transistor Division is not willing to meet the $2.50 price. He argues that it costs him $2.50 to produce and sell a transistor to the Radio Division, so he would show no profit on the Radio Division sales. No additional sales can be made to outside customers.

Required:

1. Show how the Transistor Division manager computed the $2.50 unit cost figure.
2. Should the Transistor Division manager be *required* to meet the outside price of $2.50 for Radio Division sales? Explain.
3. If you were the Transistor Division manager, would *you* meet the $2.50 outside price? Explain.

11–6. Cordell Enterprises has just purchased a large amount of high-speed data processing equipment, and has placed it in a newly organized computer division. The computer division is to provide computer services for all other divisions within the Cordell Enterprises organization. Computer usage is very significant in all divisions.

The computer division charges $300 per hour for computer services, which represents depreciation plus annual operating costs, divided by expected annual usage in hours. Some divisional managers have complained that the charge is too high, and that they can do better outside. The executive committee of the company has decided, however, that the $300 figure will stand as it is, and that divisional managers will not be free to go outside for computer services. As one member of the committee explained, "We know the charge is high, but that equipment represents a major investment, and we need to recover the investment as fast as we can."

Required:

1. Does the $300 figure represent a transfer price?
2. Evaluate the executive committee's decision.

11–7. Selected sales and operating data for three companies are given below:

	Company X	Company Y	Company Z
Sales	$90,000	$140,000	$100,000
Net operating income.	3,600	8,400	4,000
Operating assets.	30,000	70,000	80,000
Stockholders' equity	25,000	60,000	65,000
Minimum required rate of return.	10%	12%	8%

Required:

1. Compute the residual income for each company.
2. Assume that each company is presented with an investment opportunity that would yield a rate of return of 11 percent. Which companies will accept? Reject? Why?

PROBLEMS

11-1. *The Appropriate Transfer Price.* Management Consultants, Inc., is organized into three independent groups:

Engineering Group.
Systems Group.
Personnel Planning Group.

Each group performs consulting services for outside clients, as well as for other groups within the company. The normal pricing and cost structure for each group is:

	Per Consulting Hour		Total Fixed Cost
	Fee	Variable Cost	
Engineering Group	$25	$4	$120,000
Systems Group	30	6	140,000
Personnel Planning Group	27	3	100,000

The company desires to evaluate each group as if it were an autonomous company.

Required:

1. Assume that the Systems Group has need for consulting services from the Engineering Group. The Engineering Group has ample opportunity to utilize its consulting time with outside clients. What transfer price should be charged to the Systems Group? Why?
2. Assume that the going rate for engineering consulting services is $25 per hour. Under the conditions posed in Part 1, is there any reason why the Engineering Group should provide services to the Systems Group for less than this figure? Explain.
3. Again assume the conditions posed in Part 1. Also assume that the systems group has found an engineering firm that will provide the desired consulting services for only $20 per hour. Should the Engineering Group meet this figure in order to keep the business within the company? Explain.
4. Assume again that the going rate for engineering consulting time is $25 per hour. However, the Engineering Group of Management Consultants, Inc., has decided to raise its rate to $30 per hour, and wants to do consulting work for the Systems Group. Should the Systems Group be required to pay the higher price in order to keep the business within the firm? Explain.
5. Assume again that the going rate for engineering consulting time is $25 per hour. The Engineering Group has unused time available, which it is willing to supply to the Systems Group at the

going rate. Should the Systems Group accept the Engineering Group's offer? Explain.

6. Assume again that the Engineering Group has unused time available. The Systems Group has found an outside engineering firm that is willing to do the needed consulting for only $15 per hour. Should the Engineering Group meet this price? Explain.

7. Under the conditions posed in Part 6, if the Engineering Group refuses to meet the $15 hourly rate, should the Systems Group be permitted to go outside for its consulting services? Why or why not?

8. Under the conditions posed in part 6, what is the lowest price that the Engineering Group could accept and still be better off profit-wise than if it did no consulting work for the Systems Group?

11–2. Straightforward Rate of Return Computation. The accounting records of Design Services, Inc., reveal the following information for the prior two years:

	Last Year	This Year
Sales	$60,000	$64,000
Net income	4,500	5,120
Net operating income.........	6,000	6,720
Stockholders' equity	15,000	20,000
Average operating assets	20,000	25,000

Required:

1. Compute the ratio of net income to sales for each year.
2. Compute the ratio of net operating income to sales for each year.
3. Compute the rate of return for each year, using the rate of return formula.
4. Using the data computed in parts 1–3 above, explain why the rate of return is the better measure of managerial performance.

11–3. Choosing an Appropriate Transfer Price. Worldwide Enterprises has just acquired a small company which produces condenser units for refrigerators. The company will operate as a division of Worldwide Enterprises, under the name of the Condenser Division. The newly acquired Condenser Division produces and sells condenser units to various refrigerator manufacturers across the country. The price is $50 per condenser. The president of Worldwide Enterprises feels that the company's own Refrigerator Division should begin to purchase its condenser units from the newly acquired Condenser Division.

Worldwide Enterprises' Refrigerator Division is presently purchasing 400,000 condenser units each year from an outside supplier. The price is $48 per condenser, which represents the normal $50 price less a quantity discount due to the large number of units being purchased.

The Condenser Division's cost per condenser unit is presented below:

Direct materials	$18
Direct labor	14
Variable overhead	6
Fixed overhead	4*
Total cost	$42

* Operating at 2,000,000 units capacity.

The president of Worldwide Enterprises is trying to decide what transfer price should control the sales between the two divisions.

Required:

1. Assume that the newly acquired Condenser Division has sufficient excess capacity to supply all of the Refrigerator Division's condenser needs. Explain why each of the following transfer prices would or would not be an appropriate price to charge the Refrigerator Division on the intracompany sales.

   a. $50
   b. $48
   c. $43
   d. $42
   e. $38

2. Assume that the newly acquired Condenser Division is presently selling all it can produce to outside customers. Under these circumstances, explain why each of the transfer prices given in part 1 (*a*) through (*e*) above would or would not be an appropriate price to charge the Refrigerator Division on the intracompany sales.

11-4. *Residual Income and Rate of Return.* Supply the missing data in the tabulation below.

	Division			
	A	*B*	*C*	*D*
Sales	$50,000	$45,000	$90,000	$75,000
Net operating income	5,000	?	4,500	?
Operating assets	20,000	15,000	?	50,000
Rate of return	?	20%	7.5%	?
Minimum required rate of return:				
Percentage	20%	?	?	6%
Dollar amount	$?	$?	$ 6,000	$?
Residual income	?	750	?	–0–

11-5. *Transfer Pricing and Marketing Decisions.* Pulsar Division produces a component part which is transferred to Quasar Division and used by Quasar Division as an integral part of its finished product. The transfer price is full cost (fixed and variable). Pulsar Division's cost structure is:

Variable cost per unit.	$ 40
Allocated fixed cost per unit	60
Total cost per unit	$100

Upon receiving the component parts from Pulsar Division, Quasar Division adds $50 in variable costs of its own, and sells its finished product to outside customers for $200. Quasar Division's revenues and expenses on a per unit basis are:

		Per Finished Unit
Sales revenue		$200
Variable expenses:		
Added by Quasar Division	$ 50	
Transfer price	100	150
Contribution margin		$ 50

Quasar Division has an order for 10 finished units from an overseas source. The price offered per unit is $125.

Required:

1. Is Quasar Division likely to accept the $125 price offered, or to reject it? Explain.
2. If both Pulsar Division and Quasar Division have excess capacity, would Quasar Division's action benefit or be a disadvantage profit-wise to the company as a whole? Explain.
3. What kind of transfer pricing information is needed by Quasar Division to help in making decisions such as these?

11–6. *Performance Evaluation.* Alicia Symthe Cosmetics, Inc., consists of three major divisions. The financial statements of the separate divisions for 19X7 are provided below:

ALICIA SMYTHE COSMETICS, INC.
Divisional Income Statements
For the Year Ended June 30, 19X7
(in thousands)

	Division		
	A	B	C
Sales	$12,000	$9,000	$20,000
Cost of goods sold	8,000	5,000	12,000
Gross margin	4,000	4,000	8,000
Operating expenses	3,000	3,550	6,400
Net operating income	1,000	450	1,600
Income taxes	600	270	960
Net income	$ 400	$ 180	$ 740

ALICIA SMYTHE COSMETICS, INC.
Divisional Balance Sheets
June 30, 19X7
(in thousands)

	Division		
	A	B	C
Current assets	$1,000	$ 500	$1,500
Fixed assets, net.	2,000	1,500	3,500
Total Assets.	$3,000	$2,000	$5,000
Current liabilities	$ 500	$ 200	$ 600
Long-term liabilities	1,000	800	1,200
Corporate equity	1,500	1,000	3,200
Total Equities.	$3,000	$2,000	$5,000

The company gives the divisional managers great autonomy in making financing and operating decisions. No central headquarters expenses are allocated to the divisions. Top management feels that the performance of the divisions should be evaluated according to the total resources each has at its disposal for productive use.

Required:

1. Compute the rate of return and residual income earned by each division during 19X7. For purposes of computing residual income, assume that top management has set a minimum rate of return of 25 percent.
2. Rank the three divisions in terms of (*a*) rate of return, (*b*) residual income, and (*c*) margin earned.

11–7. *Transfer Pricing.* The Detroit Motor Company has just acquired a new Battery Division. The Battery Division produces a standard 12-volt battery which it sells to retail outlets at a competitive price of $15. The retail outlets purchase about 1,200,000 batteries a year. Since the Battery Division has a capacity of 2,000,000 batteries a year, top management is thinking that it might be wise for the company's Automotive Division to start purchasing from the newly acquired Battery Division.

The Automotive Division now purchases 600,000 batteries a year from an outside supplier, at a price of $14 per battery. The discount from the competitive $15 price is a result of the large quantity purchased.

The Battery Division's cost per battery is shown below:

Direct materials	$ 6
Direct labor	2
Variable overhead.	1
Fixed overhead	2*
Total cost	$11

* Based on 1,200,000 batteries.

Required:

1. If both divisions are to be treated as investment centers, and their performance evaluated by rate of return, what transfer price would you recommend? Why?
2. Assume you are the president of the Detroit Motor Company. What transfer price would be most useful to you in deciding whether the Automotive Division should begin purchasing batteries from the Battery Division? Why?
3. Assume that the Battery Division is now selling 2,000,000 batteries a year to retail outlets. Would your answer to either part 1 or part 2 change? Why?

11–8. *Allocated Corporate Expenses, and Rate of Return.* Darby Products, Inc., consists of three independent divisions—Household Products, Jewelry Products, and Pharmaceutical Products. The household products market is very large, but competition is extremely keen. Therefore, the margin earned by the Household Products division tends to be quite small in comparison with the other two divisions. The condensed income statements of the three divisions for 19X5, the most recent year, are given below:

	Household Products	Jewelry Products	Pharma- ceutical Products
Sales	$12,000,000	$8,000,000	$4,000,000
Less variable expenses	9,000,000	5,000,000	1,500,000
Contribution margin	3,000,000	3,000,000	2,500,000
Less fixed expenses:			
Direct to the division	2,400,000	1,800,000	2,000,000
Allocated from corporate headquarters*	480,000	320,000	160,000
Total fixed expenses	2,880,000	2,120,000	2,160,000
Net operating income	$ 120,000	$ 880,000	$ 340,000

* Allocated on a basis of sales dollars.

Top management of Darby Products, Inc., treats the divisions as if they were separate companies, giving the divisional managers great discretion in making investment and operating decisions. In a recent management development course the executive vice president learned that a popular way of evaluating divisional performance under these circumstances is by the rate of return formula. He has asked the accounting department to compute the rate of return generated by each division during 19X5, and has received the following data:

Household Products	3.20%
Jewelry Products	13.75%
Pharmaceutical Products	17.00%

The executive vice president was shocked when he saw that the Household Products division had earned a rate of return of only

3.2 percent during the year. He was all the more perplexed when he learned that the industry average rate of return for household products is about 7 percent. As the executive vice president walked toward the president's office, he muttered to himself, "I'll give 2 to 1 odds that there's a new manager in that division by the end of the week."

Required:

1. Show how the accounting department computed the rate of return figures given to the executive vice president. Assume that average operating assets for 19X5 are:

Household Products	$3,750,000
Jewelry Products	6,400,000
Pharmaceutical Products	2,000,000

2. What possible criticism can you make of the way the accounting department computed the rate of return figures?
3. Recompute the rate of return figures as you think they should appear. Comment on the results of your computations.

11–9. *Transfer Pricing Dispute.* The Timer Division of Household Appliances, Inc., produces an electronic timing device that is used by the company's Range Division in producing ovens and cooktops. The Timer Division is now operating at its capacity of 800,000 timing devices per year, 40 percent of which is purchased by the Range Division. The Timer Division's income statement for the most recent year is given below:

Sales	$13,440,000
Variable expenses @ $9 per device	7,200,000
Contribution margin	6,240,000
Fixed expenses	3,200,000
Net income	$ 3,040,000

Sales to outside customers (60 percent of the 800,000 unit capacity) are at $18 per timing device. Sales to the Range Division are at $15 per device, due to a quantity discount.

The rapid growth of the electronics field has created intense competition for the Timer Division. Advance Timers, Inc., an outside manufacturer of timing devices, has offered to supply all of the Range Division's timer needs for only $12 per unit.

The manager of the Timer Division will not lower his price to the Range Division. He argues that if he does lower his price, it will result in a loss of $1 per unit of 40 percent of his business:

Total variable expenses (above)	$ 7,200,000
Total fixed expenses (above)	3,200,000
Total expenses	$10,400,000
Cost per unit ($10,400,000 ÷ 800,000 units)	$13
Proposed selling price per unit	$12

Required:

1. Assume you are the president of Household Appliances, Inc. From point of view of the company as a whole, would you urge the Timer Division to lower its price to $12, or would you urge the Range Division to begin purchasing outside? (Because of intense competition, the Timer Division cannot increase its outside sales.)

2. The manager of the Timer Division feels that he should switch production to a new type of timing device, and turn entirely to outside sales. He is confident that he could sell all 800,000 units outside at a $16 unit price. The change in type of timing device produced would require additional fixed costs each year of $100,000, but would reduce variable expenses by $.50 per unit. Would you recommend that the switch in production be made?

11–10. *Level of Operations and Rate of Return.* Trail Blazer, Inc., is a producer and distributor of various motorized recreational scooter, bike, and motorcycle products. The Tote Gote Division produces and distributes a motorized scooter that is very popular among sportsmen for climbing and riding in mountainous terrain. The Tote Gote Division would like to earn a long-run rate of return of 20 percent, and will change its unit selling price as necessary to provide this return. The following data are available on the Tote Gote Division and its product:

Variable cost per scooter.	$ 200
Total annual fixed costs	$1,220,000
Long-run average number of scooters sold each year	10,000
Average operating assets invested in the division.	$1,400,000

Required:

1. Compute the per-unit selling price that will provide the desired rate of return.

2. Although the long-run average number of scooters sold each year is 10,000, as stated above, assume that actual sales fluctuate from 8,500 units to 11,500 units. Compute the margin, turnover, and rate of return that would be realized on sales at the 8,500, 10,000, and 11,500-unit levels of activity. (Use the selling price computed in part 1 for your computations.)

3. What do your computations in part 2 above suggest to you so far as applying the rate of return formula to divisions subject to cyclical movements in the economy?

11–11. *Performance Evaluation, and Motivation.* Dorsey Products has three major divisions. The income statements of the divisions appeared as follows at the end of 19X5:

DORSEY PRODUCTS
Divisional Income Statements
For the Year Ended December 31, 19X5
(in thousands)

| | Division | | |
	A	B	C
Sales	$150,000	$240,000	$300,000
Cost of goods sold	90,000	148,800	165,000
Gross margin.	60,000	91,200	135,000
Operating expenses	45,000	72,000	112,500
Net operating income.	15,000	19,200	22,500
Interest expense.	3,000	5,200	7,000
Income before tax	12,000	14,000	15,500
Income tax (60%).	7,200	8,400	9,300
Net income	$ 4,800	$ 5,600	$ 6,200

All expenses shown above were incurred directly in each division. During 19X5, the average operating assets reported by the divisions were $60,000,000, $100,000,000, and $93,750,000 for A, B, and C respectively. Dorsey Products has a minimum desired rate of return of 16% on assets.

Required:

1. Compute the rate of return earned by each division during 19X5. Rank the divisions from highest to lowest in terms of rate of return.
2. Assume that Division A has an opportunity to add a new product line. The new product line would require an investment of $30,000,000. Interest expense on the investment would be $1,500,000, and net income after taxes would be $1,800,000. What will be the effect on Division A's ranking if it adds the new product line? Will the divisional manager be motivated to add the new product line? Explain. Might it be desirable from point of view of the company as a whole to add the new product line? Explain.
3. Compute the residual income earned by each division, and rank the divisions. How does this ranking compare with the ranking determined in part 1 above?
4. Assume again that Division A can add the new product line mentioned in part 2. What will be the effect on Division A's residual income if the new product line is added? Show computations. Will the divisional manager be motivated to add the new product line? Explain.

11–12. *Transfer Pricing.* This problem is more difficult than preceding problems. Division A produces a component part which can be sold either to outside customers or to Division B. Selected operating data on the two divisions are given below:

Division A

Unit selling price to outside customers. . . . . $		80
Variable production cost per unit.		45
Variable selling and administrative		
expense per unit		2
Fixed production cost in total.		300,000*

Division B

Outside purchase price per unit		
(net of quantity discount). . . . . $		76

* Capacity 20,000 units per year.

Division B has always purchased its component parts from outside suppliers, but now consideration is being given to purchasing component parts from Division A. As the company's president stated, "It's just plain smart to buy and sell within the corporate family when you can."

A study has determined that the variable selling and administrative expenses of Division A would be cut in half for any sales to Division B. Top management wants to treat each division as an autonomous unit with independent profit responsibility.

Required:

1. Assume that Division A has ample excess capacity to handle all of Division B's needs.
   a. What is the highest transfer price that can be justified between the two divisions? Explain.
   b. What is the lowest transfer price that can be justified between the two divisions? Explain.
   c. Assume that Division B finds an outside supplier who will sell the needed component parts for only $70 per unit. Should Division A be required to meet this price? Explain.
   d. Refer to the original data. Assume that Division A decides to raise its price to outside customers to $85 per unit. If Division B is forced to pay this price, and to start purchasing from Division A, will it result in greater or less total corporate profits? How much per unit?
   e. Under the circumstances posed in part (d) above, should Division B be forced to purchase from Division A? Explain.
2. Assume that Division A can sell all that it can produce to outside customers. Repeat (a) through (e) above.

chapter 12

Relevant Costs in Nonroutine Decisions

THE MAKING of decisions is one of the basic functions of a manager. He is constantly faced with problems of deciding what products to sell, what production methods to use, whether to make or buy component parts, what prices to charge, what channels of distribution to use, whether to accept special orders at special prices, etc. At best, decision making is a difficult and complex task. This difficulty is usually increased by the existence of not just one or two, but numerous courses of action that might be taken in any given situation facing a firm.

In decision making, *cost* is always a key factor. The costs of one alternative must be compared against the costs of other alternatives as one step in the decision-making process. The problem is that some costs associated with an alternative may not be *relevant* to the decision to be made. To be successful in decision making, a manager must have tools at his disposal to assist him in identifying relevant and irrelevant costs, so that the latter can be eliminated from his decision framework. The purpose of this chapter is to acquire these tools, and to show their application in a wide range of decision-making situations.

COST CONCEPTS FOR DECISION MAKING

Three cost terms discussed in Chapter 2 are particularly applicable to this chapter. These terms are differential costs, opportunity costs, and sunk costs. The reader may find it helpful to turn back to Chapter 2 and refresh his memory of these terms before reading on.

Identifying Relevant Costs

What costs are relevant in a decision? The answer is easy. *All* costs are relevant in a decision, *except:*

1. Sunk costs.
2. Future costs that *do not differ* between the alternatives at hand.

All decisions involve the future. Nothing can change what has happened in the past. The future may be only minutes or hours away, but any decision made now can only have its effect then. It follows, therefore, that the essential framework from which a decision is made must of necessity be based on *expected future data.* Past or historical costs (sunk costs), having already been incurred, are not relevant to future events and decisions.

Not all future costs are relevant in decision making. Those which do not differ between the alternatives under consideration must be ignored. That is, if a cost will be incurred regardless of which of several alternatives is selected, then it cannot possibly be of any help in deciding which alternative is best. Such costs must be eliminated from the manager's decision framework, as irrelevant to the decision to be made.

In sum, a manager's approach to decision making must involve the following steps, so far as quantitative matters are concerned:

1. Assemble *all* costs associated with *all* alternatives under consideration.
2. Eliminate those costs which are sunk.
3. Eliminate those costs which do not differ between the alternatives under consideration.
4. Make a decision based on the remaining cost data. These remaining costs will be the costs that are *relevant* to the decision to be made.

Cost Relevance versus Cost Precision

There is a difference between cost relevance and cost precision. Managers sometimes confuse relevance with precision, thinking that they mean the same thing. Actually, they are very different ideas. A cost can be very precise, but yet totally irrelevant to the decision at hand. To illustrate, assume that the purchasing agent's salary is $30,000 per year. This figure is precise, but it may be totally irrelevant to a decision about whether to purchase a new piece of factory machinery.

A relevant cost is one that is *pertinent to the decision at hand,* and that must be considered if the manager is to make the best possible choice among alternatives available.

SUNK COSTS ARE NOT RELEVANT COSTS

One of the most difficult conceptual lessons that managers have to learn is that sunk costs are never relevant in decisions. The tendency to want to include sunk costs within the decision framework is especially strong in the case of book value of old equipment. We focus on book value of old equipment below, and then consider other kinds of sunk costs in the latter part of the section and in other parts of the chapter. We shall see that regardless of the kind of sunk cost involved, the conclusion is always the same—sunk costs must be eliminated from the manager's decision framework.

Book Value of Old Equipment

Assume the following data:

Old Machine		Proposed New Machine	
Original cost	$10,000	List price new	$12,000
Remaining book value	$ 8,000	Expected life	4 years
Remaining life	4 years	Disposal value in 4 years	–0–
Disposal value now	$ 3,000	Annual variable expenses	
Disposal value in 4 years	–0–	to operate	$16,000
Annual variable expenses		Annual revenue from sales	$50,000
to operate	$20,000		
Annual revenue from sales	$50,000		

Should the old machine be disposed of and the new machine purchased? Many accountants and managers alike would say no, since disposal of the old machine would result in a "loss from disposal" of $5,000:

Remaining book value	$8,000
Disposal value now	3,000
Loss if disposed of now	$5,000

Even though the new machine is more efficient than the old machine, there is a general inclination to reason that "we have already made an investment in the old machine, so now we have no choice but to use the machine until we get our money out of it." Although it may be appealing to think that an error of the past (the old machine is only 1 year old) can be corrected by simply *using* the item involved, this, unfortunately, is not correct. The investment that has already been made in the old machine is a sunk cost. The portion of this investment that remains on the company's books (the book value of $8,000) should not be considered in the decision about whether to buy the new machine. We can prove this assertion by the following analysis:

	All Four Years Together		
	Keep Old Machine	*Difference*	*Purchase New Machine*
Sales	$200,000	$ –0–	$200,000
Variable expenses....................	(80,000)	16,000	(64,000)
Depreciation on the new machine.	–0–	(12,000)	(12,000)
Depreciation on the old machine, or loss write-off	(8,000)	–0–	(8,000)
Disposal value of the old machine.	–0–	3,000	3,000
Total net income over the four years........	$112,000	$ 7,000	$119,000

Looking at all four years together, notice that the firm will be $7,000 better off by purchasing the new machine. Also notice that the $8,000 book value of the old machine had *no effect* on the outcome of the analysis. Since this book value is a sunk cost, it must be absorbed by the firm regardless of whether the old machine is kept and used or whether it is sold. If the old machine is kept and used, then the $8,000 book value is deducted in the form of depreciation. If the old machine is sold, then the $8,000 book value is deducted in the form of a loss write-off. Either way, the company bears the same $8,000 deduction.

Focusing on Relevant Costs. What costs in the example above are relevant in the decision concerning the new machine? Following the steps outlined earlier, we should eliminate (1) the sunk costs, and (2) the future costs that do not differ between the alternatives at hand:

1. The sunk costs:
   a. The original cost of the old machine ($10,000).
   b. The remaining book value of the old machine ($8,000).
2. The future costs that do not differ:
   a. The annual sales revenue ($50,000).
   b. The variable expenses (to the extent of $16,000).

The costs that remain will form the basis for a decision. The analysis is:

	All Four Years Together
Reduction in variable expense promised by the new machine ($4,000 per year × 4 years)	$16,000
Cost (depreciation) of the new machine	(12,000)
Disposal value of the old machine.	3,000
Net advantage of the new machine	$ 7,000

Note that the items above are the same as those in the middle column of the earlier analysis.

Depreciation and Relevant Costs. Since the book value of old equipment is not a relevant cost, there is a tendency to assume that depreciation of *any* kind is irrelevant in the decision-making process. This is not a correct assumption. Note above that depreciation on the new machine has been included in the relevant costs, and is a necessary factor in any attempt to assess the desirability of purchasing the new machine. The difference is that the investment in the new machine has *not yet been made*, and therefore does not represent a sunk cost.

Partially Completed Inventory

There is also a tendency to assume that even though past *fixed* costs are not relevant in decisions, the same rule would not apply to past *variable* costs. Again, this is not a correct assumption. All past costs are irrelevant, regardless of whether they are variable or fixed. Consider the following situation:

A firm has 5,000 units of product now in process of production. The units are 80 percent completed. The firm has just discovered that marketing forecasts of expected demand for the product have been far too optimistic, and that the market for the product is already glutted. The following costs have been incurred in bringing the units to a stage of 80 percent completion:

	Per Unit Cost Expended
Direct materials	$ 6
Direct labor	8
Variable overhead.	8
Total	$22

The company has determined that it has two choices as to how to dispose of the partially completed units:

1. The units can be sold for junk at a net disposal price of $2,000.
2. The units can be modified into a slightly different product at an additional cost of $8 per unit. The units can then be sold for $10 each.

Which alternative should be accepted? The company's analysis could take the following form:

	Sell For "Junk" Value	Difference	Process Further
Total sales revenue	$ 2,000	$48,000	$ 50,000
Variable expense already incurred ($22/unit)	(110,000)	–0–	(110,000)
Additional variable expense ($8/unit)	–0–	(40,000)	(40,000)
Net loss.	($108,000)	$ 8,000	($100,000)

As before, the relevant costs are found in the middle column of the analysis. The other costs are irrelevant, and could have been omitted from the computations. The variable costs of $22 per unit are sunk costs, just as the book value of the old machine was a sunk cost in the prior example.

FUTURE COSTS THAT DO NOT DIFFER ARE NOT RELEVANT COSTS

Any future cost that does not differ between the alternatives under consideration is not a relevant cost. As stated earlier, if a company is going to sustain a cost regardless of what decision it makes, then that cost can in no way tell the company which decision is best. The only way a future cost can help in the decision-making process is by being different under one alternative than under another.

An Illustration

To illustrate the irrelevance of future costs that do not differ, let us assume that a firm is contemplating the purchase of a new labor-saving machine. The present cost structure, and the expected cost structure with the machine, are shown below:

	Present Costs	Expected Costs With The New Machine
Units produced	5,000	5,000
Sales price per unit	$ 10	$ 10
Direct materials cost per unit	4	4
Direct labor cost per unit	3	1
Variable overhead cost per unit	1	1
Fixed costs, other.	4,000	4,000
Fixed costs, new machine	–0–	1,000

The new machine promises a saving of $2 per unit in direct labor costs, but will increase fixed costs by $1,000 per period. All other costs, as well as the total number of units produced, will remain the same. Following the steps outlined earlier, the analysis is:

1. Eliminate the sunk costs. (No sunk costs are identified in this problem.)
2. Eliminate the future costs that do not differ:
   a. The sales price per unit does not differ.
   b. The direct materials cost per unit does not differ.
   c. The variable overhead cost per unit does not differ.
   d. The total fixed costs, other, do not differ.

This leaves just the per-unit labor costs, and the fixed costs associated with the new machine:

Savings in direct labor costs (5,000 units at a cost
   saving of $2 per unit). $10,000
Less increase in fixed costs.   1,000
Net cost savings promised by the new machine . . . . $ 9,000

The accuracy of this solution can be proved by looking at *all* items of cost data (both those that are relevant and those that are not) under the two alternatives for a period, and comparing the net income results.

| | 5,000 Units Produced and Sold | | |
	Present Method	Difference	New Machine
Sales	$50,000	$ -0-	$50,000
Variable expenses:			
Direct materials.	20,000	-0-	20,000
Direct labor	15,000	10,000	5,000
Variable overhead	5,000	-0-	5,000
Total variable.	40,000		30,000
Contribution margin	10,000		20,000
Less fixed expenses:			
Other.	4,000	-0-	4,000
New machine	-0-	(1,000)	1,000
Total fixed	4,000		5,000
Net income	$ 6,000	$ 9,000	$15,000

Why Isolate Relevant Costs?

In the preceding example we used two different methods to show that the purchase of the new machine was desirable. First, we considered only the relevant costs; and second, we considered all costs, both those that were relevant and those that were not. We obtained the same answer under both approaches. When students see that the same answer can be obtained under either approach, they often ask the question, "Why both to isolate relevant costs when total costs will do the job just as well?" The isolation of relevant costs is desirable for at least two reasons.

First, only rarely will enough information be available to prepare a detailed income statement as we have done in the preceding examples. Since only limited data normally are available, the decision maker *must* know how to recognize which costs are relevant and which are not. Assume, for example, that you are called upon to make a decision relating to a matter in a *single operation* of a multidepartmental, multiproduct firm. Under these circumstances it would be virtually impossible to prepare an income statement of any type. You would have to rely on your ability to recognize what costs were relevant and what costs were not in order to assemble the necessary data to make a decision.

Second, the use of irrelevant costs intermingled with relevant costs may confuse the picture, and draw the decision maker's attention away from the matters that are really critical to the problem at hand. Furthermore, the danger always exists that an irrelevant piece of data may be used improperly, resulting in an incorrect decision. The best approach is to isolate the relevant items, and to focus all attention directly on them, and on their impact on the decision to be made.

Relevant cost analysis, combined with the contribution approach to the income statement, provides a powerful tool for making decisions in special, nonroutine situations. We will investigate various uses of this tool in the remaining sections of this chapter.

ADDING AND DROPPING PRODUCT LINES

The decisions relating to when to drop old product lines and when to add new product lines are among the stickiest that a manager has to make. In such decisions, many factors must be considered that are both qualitative and quantitative in nature. Ultimately, however, any final decision to drop an old product line, or to add a new product line, is going to hinge primarily on the impact the decision will have on net income. In order to assess this impact, it is necessary to make a careful analysis of the costs involved.

An Illustration of Cost Analysis

As a basis for discussion, let us consider the product lines of the Discount Drug Company. The company has four product lines—drugs, cosmetics, hand tools, and toys. Data for the past month are given in Exhibit 12–1.

EXHIBIT 12–1
Discount Drug Company Product Lines (in thousands of dollars)

	Total	Drugs	Cos-metics	Hand Tools	Toys
Sales	$130	$40	$40	$30	$20
Variable expenses.	86	21	24	26	15
Contribution margin	44	19	16	4	5
Fixed expenses:					
Direct	19	7	7	2	3
Common (allocated according to space occupied)	12	4	4	1	3
Total fixed	31	11	11	3	6
Net income (loss)	$ 13	$ 8	$ 5	$ 1	$(1)

What can be done to improve the Discount Drug Company's overall performance? One of the company's product lines—toys—shows a net loss for the period. Perhaps dropping this product line will improve the company's overall net income. The decision revolves around what costs can be avoided to offset the loss in contribution margin if the line is dropped. We have two classes of costs to consider—direct fixed costs, and common fixed costs.

Direct Fixed Costs. As defined in Chapter 7, a direct cost is one that is *directly traceable* to a particular segment of a business. Therefore, our first inclination is to say that yes, indeed, the direct fixed costs of the toys line could be avoided by dropping the line, since they would disappear if the line itself disappeared. But it rarely is this simple. The problem is that part of the direct fixed costs of the toys line may be *sunk costs* that will continue even if the product line is dropped. A sunk cost cannot be avoided by simply eliminating the segment that it is associated with. For example, a large portion of the direct fixed costs of the toys line may be depreciation on display cases, which will continue even if no toys are being sold. Or, the manager of the toys line may be a long-time employee who will be kept on the payroll even if the product line he is managing is eliminated.

The point is that one cannot just assume that all direct fixed costs will disappear if a particular product line is eliminated. The manager must scrutinize the costs carefully, and determine which direct fixed costs will disappear and which will remain.

In the case of the Discount Drug Company, let us assume that the company's $3,000 in direct fixed expenses shown on Exhibit 12–1 consists of the following items:

Item	Amount	Not Avoid-able	Avoid-able
Depreciation of store fixtures	$1,400	$1,400	
Salary of a long-term employee, who will not be discharged	600	600	
Salaries of employees who will be discharged	1,000		$1,000
Total direct fixed expenses	$3,000	$2,000	$1,000

Common Fixed Costs. Notice from Exhibit 12–1 that common fixed costs have been allocated to the product lines. Deciding what will happen to these common costs if the toys line is dropped is easy. Since the costs are common costs they cannot be avoided by dropping the toys line. The reason is that they consist of general company expenses, such as general management salaries, store rent, etc., that will continue on even in the absence of the toys line. Therefore, they should be marked as being not avoidable, regardless of what decision is made with respect to toys.

The Impact on Net Income. We can now determine the overall impact on net income of dropping the toys line.

	Toys Line		Difference— Overall Company Net Income Increase or (Decrease)
	If Toys Are Retained	*If Toys Are Dropped*	
Sales	$20,000	$ –0–	$(20,000)
Variable expenses	15,000	–0–	15,000
Contribution margin	5,000	–0–	(5,000)
Direct fixed expenses	3,000	2,000	1,000
Common fixed expenses	3,000	3,000	–0–
Total fixed expenses	6,000	5,000	1,000
Net income (loss)	$ (1,000)	$(5,000)	$(4,000)

In sum, if the Discount Drug Company drops the toys line the company's overall net income will *decrease* by $4,000 each period. This decrease is shown in the extreme right column above. The analysis shows that if the toys line is dropped the company will lose $5,000 in contribution margin each period, which will be offset only in part by the avoidance of $1,000 in direct fixed costs. Since the loss in contribution margin exceeds the fixed costs which can be avoided, the decision should be to keep the toys line.

Beware of Allocated Fixed Costs

The conclusion to keep the toys line seems to conflict with the data shown in Exhibit 12–1. Notice from the exhibit that the toys line shows a *net loss* for the period. The explanation for this apparent inconsistency in deciding to keep the toys line even though it shows a loss lies at least in part with the allocated common fixed costs.

One of the great dangers of allocating common fixed costs is that such allocations can make a product line (or other segment of a business) *look* less profitable than it really is. Consider the following example:

A bakery distributed its products through route salesmen, each of whom loaded a truck with an assortment of products in the morning and spent the day calling on customers in an assigned territory. Believing that some items were more profitable than others, management asked for an analysis of product costs and sales. The accountants to whom the task was assigned allocated all manufacturing and marketing costs to products to obtain a net profit for each product. The resulting figures indicated that some of the products were being sold at a loss, and management discontinued these products. However, when this change was put into effect, the company's overall profit declined. It was then seen that, by dropping some products, sales revenues had been reduced without commensurate reduction in costs because the joint manufacturing costs and route sales costs had to be continued in order to make and sell remaining products.[1]

The same thing has happened in the Discount Drug Company as described in the bakery company example above. That is, by allocating the common fixed costs among all product lines, the Discount Drug Company has made the toys line *look* as if it is unprofitable, whereas, in fact, dropping the line would result in a decrease in overall company net income. This point can be seen clearly if we recast the data in Exhibit 12–1, and eliminate the allocation of the common fixed costs. This recasting of data is shown in Exhibit 12–2.

EXHIBIT 12–2
Discount Drug Company Product Lines (in thousands of dollars)

	Total	Drugs	Cos- metics	Hand Tools	Toys
Sales	$130	$40	$40	$30	$20
Variable expenses.	86	21	24	26	15
Contribution margin	44	19	16	4	5
Direct fixed expenses.	19	7	7	2	3
Segment margin.	25	$12	$ 9	$ 2	$ 2
Common fixed expenses	12				
Net income	$ 13				

Source: Exhibit 12–1.

Exhibit 12–2 gives us a much different perspective of the toys line than does Exhibit 12–1. As shown in Exhibit 12–2, the toys line is covering all of its own direct fixed costs, and is generating a $2,000 segment margin toward covering of the common fixed costs of the company. If the toys line was dropped, then this positive segment margin would be lost. In addition, we stated earlier that $2,000 in direct fixed costs (depreciation, etc.) would continue even if the toys line was discontinued. Therefore, the net result of dropping the toys line would be a $4,000 drop in overall company net income, as we computed earlier:

[1] Walter B. McFarland, *Concepts for Management Accounting*, (New York: National Association of Accountants, 1966), p. 46.

Segment margin which will be lost if the toys line
   is eliminated $2,000
Direct fixed costs (depreciation, etc.) which will
   continue even if the toys line is dropped 2,000
Disadvantage of dropping the toys line $4,000

The above computation is simply a different route to the same conclusion we came to in the preceding section—the toys line should *not* be discontinued.

THE MAKE OR BUY DECISION

Many steps are involved in getting a finished product into the hands of a consumer. First, raw materials must be obtained through mining, drilling, growing of crops, raising of animals, etc. Second, these raw materials must be processed to remove impurities, or to extract the desirable and usable materials from the bulk of materials available. Third, the usable materials must be fabricated into desired form, to serve as basic inputs for manufactured products. Fourth, the actual manufacturing of the finished product must take place, with several products perhaps coming from the same basic raw material input (as, for example, several different items of clothing from the same basic cloth input). And finally, the finished product must be distributed to the ultimate consumer.

When a company is involved in more than one of these steps, it is said to be *vertically integrated*. Vertical integration is very common. Some firms go so far as to control *all* activities relating to their products, from the mining of raw materials or the raising of crops right up to the final distribution of finished goods. Other firms are content to integrate on a less grand scale, and perhaps will do no more than produce the fabricated parts which go into their finished products.

A decision to produce a fabricated part internally, rather than to buy the part externally from a supplier, is often called a "make or buy" decision. Actually, any decision relating to vertical integration is a "make or buy" decision, since the company is deciding whether to meet its own needs internally, rather than to buy externally.

The Advantages of Integration

Certain advantages arise from integration. The integrated firm is less dependent on its suppliers, and may be able to insure a smoother flow of parts and materials for production than the nonintegrated firm. For example, a strike against a major parts supplier might cause the operations of a nonintegrated firm to be interrupted for many months, whereas the integrated firm that is producing its own parts may be able to continue operations. Also, many firms feel that they can control quality better by producing their own parts and materials, rather than by relying on the quality control standards of outside suppliers. In addition, the integrated firm realizes profits from the parts and materials that it is "making," rather than "buying," as well as profits from its regular operations.

The advantages of integration are counterbalanced by a number of hazards. A firm that produces all of its own parts runs the risk of destroying long-run relationships with suppliers, that may prove to be harmful and disruptive to the firm. Once relationships with suppliers are severed, they are often difficult to reestablish. If product demand becomes heavy, a firm may not have sufficient capacity to continue producing all of its own parts internally, but then may experience great difficulty in trying to secure assistance from a severed supplier. In addition, changing technology often makes continued production of one's own parts more costly than purchasing from the outside, but this change in cost may not be obvious to the firm. In sum, these factors suggest that although certain advantages may accrue to the integrated firm, the "make or buy" decision should be weighed very carefully before any move is undertaken that may prove to be costly in the long-run.

An Example of Make or Buy

How does a firm approach the make or buy decision? Basically, the matters that must be considered fall into two broad categories—qualitative and quantitative. Qualitative matters deal with issues such as those raised in the preceding section. Quantitative matters deal with cost—what is the cost of producing as compared to the cost of buying? Several kinds of costs may be involved here, including opportunity costs. As a practical matter, opportunity costs can be the most significant factor of all in a make or buy decision.

To illustrate the quantitative end of a make or buy decision, assume that The Bonner Company is now producing a subassembly that goes into its final product. The Bonner Company reports the following costs of producing the subassembly:

	Per Unit	8,000 Units
Direct materials	$ 3	$ 24,000
Direct labor	4	32,000
Variable overhead	4	32,000
Fixed overhead, direct	5	40,000
Fixed overhead, common, but allocated	8	64,000
Total cost	$24	$192,000

The Bonner Company has received an offer from a supplier who will provide 8,000 subassemblies a year at a firm price of $21 each. Should The Bonner Company stop producing the subassemblies, and start purchasing them from the supplier? From a quantitative point of view, this question can be answered only after isolating the relevant costs involved.

Note first that The Bonner Company is allocating a portion of its common fixed costs to the subassemblies. Since these costs are common to all items produced in the factory, they will *continue unchanged* even if the subassemblies are purchased from the outside. The allocated costs, therefore, are not relevant to the decision at hand (since they will not differ between the make or buy alternatives), and should be eliminated from the analysis.

The variable costs of producing the subassemblies (material, labor, and variable overhead) are relevant costs, since they can be avoided by buying the subassemblies from the outside. If the direct fixed costs can also be avoided by buying from the outside, then they, too, will be relevant in the decision. Assuming that *both* the variable costs and the direct fixed costs can be avoided by buying from the outside, the analysis takes the following form:

	Per Unit		*8,000 Units*	
	Make	*Buy*	*Make*	*Buy*
Cost of purchasing		$21		$168,000
Direct materials	$ 3		$ 24,000	
Direct labor	4		32,000	
Variable overhead	4		32,000	
Fixed overhead, direct (can be avoided by buying)	5		40,000	
Total costs	$16	$21	$128,000	$168,000
Difference in favor of continuing to make		$5		$40,000

According to these data, The Bonner Company should reject the supplier's offer, and should continue to make its own subassemblies. Before coming to any final decision, however, The Bonner Company should consider one more factor—the opportunity cost of the space now being used to produce subassemblies.

The Matter of Opportunity Cost

If the space now being used to produce subassemblies *would otherwise be idle*, then The Bonner Company should continue to produce its own subassemblies, and the supplier's offer should be rejected, as we stated above. Idle space that has no alternative use has an opportunity cost of zero.

But what if the space now being used to produce subassemblies would not sit idle, but rather could be used for some other purpose? In that case, the space would have an opportunity cost that would have to be considered in assessing the desirability of the supplier's offer. What would the opportunity cost of the space be? The opportunity cost would be the segment margin that could be derived from the best alternative use of the space.

To illustrate, assume that the space now being used to produce subassemblies could be used to produce a new product line that would generate a segment margin of $50,000 per year. Under these conditions, The Bonner Company would be better off to accept the supplier's offer and to use the available space to produce the new product line.

	Make	Buy
Cost of purchasing (see prior example).		$168,000
Cost of making (see prior example).	$128,000	
Opportunity cost—segment margin foregone on a potential new product line	50,000	
Total cost	$178,000	$168,000
Difference in favor of purchasing from the outside supplier	$10,000	

Perhaps we should again emphasize that opportunity costs are not recorded in the accounts of an organization. They do not represent actual dollar outlays. Rather, they represent those economic benefits that are *foregone* as a result of pursuing some course of action. The opportunity costs of The Bonner Company are sufficiently large in this case to make continued production of the subassemblies very costly from an economic point of view.

UTILIZATION OF SCARCE RESOURCES

Firms are often faced with the problem of deciding how scarce resources are going to be utilized. A department store, for example, has a limited amount of floor space, and therefore cannot stock every product line that may be available. A manufacturing firm has a limited number of machine hours, and a limited number of direct labor hours at its disposal. When capacity becomes pressed, the firm must decide which orders it will accept and which orders it will reject. In making these decisions, the contribution approach is necessary, since the firm will want to select that course of action that will maximize its *total* contribution margin.

Contribution in Relation to Scarce Resources

To maximize total contribution margin, a firm may not necessarily want to promote those products that have the highest *individual* contribution margins. Rather, total contribution margin will be maximized by promoting those products or accepting those orders that promise the highest contribution margin *in relation to the scarce resources of the firm.* This concept can be demonstrated by assuming that a firm has two product lines, A and B. Cost and revenue characteristics of the two product lines are given below:

	A	B
Sales price per unit	$10	$12
Variable cost per unit	5	8
Contribution margin	$ 5	$ 4
P/V ratio	50%	33%

Product line A appears to be much more profitable than product line B. It has a $5 per unit contribution margin, as compared to only $4 per unit for product line B, and it has a 50 percent P/V ratio as compared to only 33 percent for B.

But now let us add one more piece of information—it takes two machine hours to produce one unit of A, and only one machine hour to produce one unit of B. The firm has only 2,000 machine hours of capacity available in the plant per period. If demand becomes strong, which orders should the firm accept, those for product line A or those for product line B? The firm should accept orders for product line B. Even though product line A has the highest *per unit* contribution margin, product line B provides the highest contribution margin in relation to the scarce resource of the firm, which in this case is machine hours available.

	A	B
Machine hours available	2,000 (a)	2,000 (a)
Machine hours required to produce one unit	2 (b)	1 (b)
Units of product that can be produced in one period (a) ÷ (b)	1,000	2,000
Contribution margin per unit	× $5	× $4
Total contribution margin promised	$5,000	$8,000

This example shows clearly that looking at unit contribution margins alone is not enough; the contribution margin promised by a product line must be viewed in relation to whatever resource constraints a firm may be working under.

One of the most common resource constraints is advertising dollars available. Firms typically concentrate their efforts on those product lines that promise the greatest contribution margin per dollar of advertising expended. Another common resource constraint is floor space. The discount department stores and discount food chains have utilized the concept of maximum contribution margin per square foot by concentrating on those product lines that have a rapid turnover, thereby generating large amounts of contribution in small amounts of space available.

The Problem of Multiple Constraints

What does a firm do if it is operating under *several* scarce resource constraints? For example, a firm may have limited raw materials available, limited direct labor hours available, limited floor space, and limited advertising dollars to spend on product promotion. How would it proceed to find the right combination of products to produce under such a variety of constraints? The proper combination, or "mix" of products, can be found by use of a quantitative method known as *linear programming*. Linear programming is a very powerful analytical tool that we shall be discussing in Chapter 17.

JOINT PRODUCT COSTS AND THE CONTRIBUTION APPROACH

The manufacturing processes of some firms are such that several end products are produced from a single raw material input. The meat packing industry, for example, inputs a pig into the manufacturing process and comes out with a great variety of end products, including bacon, ham, spare ribs, pork roasts, etc. Firms that produce several end products from a common input (e.g., a pig) are faced with the problem of deciding how the cost of that input is going to be divided up among the products (bacon, ham, pork roast, etc.) that result. Before we address ourselves to this problem, it will be helpful to define three terms—joint products, joint product costs, and split-off point.

Two or more products that are produced from a common input are known as *joint products*. The term *joint product costs* is used to describe those manufacturing costs that are incurred in producing joint products up to the *split-off point*. The *split-off point* is that point in the manufacturing process at which the joint products (bacon, ham, spare ribs, etc.) can be recognized as individual units of output. At this point some of the joint products will be in final form, ready to be marketed to the consumer. Others will still need further processing on their own before they are in marketable form. These concepts can be shown graphically as follows:

EXHIBIT 12–3
Joint Products

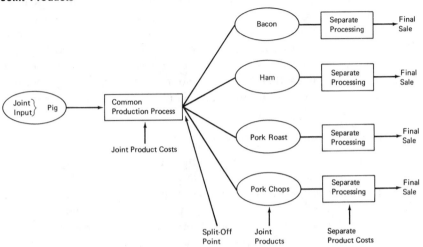

The Pitfalls of Allocation

Joint product costs are really common costs incurred to simultaneously produce a variety of end products. Traditional cost accounting books are full of elaborate approaches to allocating these common costs among the different products at the split-off point. The most usual approach is to allocate the joint product costs according to the relative sales value of the end products.

Although allocation of joint product costs is needed for some purposes, such as balance sheet inventory valuation, such allocations should be used with great caution *internally* in the decision making process. Unless a manager proceeds with care, he may be led into incorrect decisions as a result of relying on allocated common costs. Consider the following situation which occurred in a firm several years ago:

A company located on the Gulf of Mexico is a producer of soap products. It has six main soap product lines which are produced from common inputs. Joint product costs up to the split-off point constitute the bulk of the production costs for all six product lines. These joint product costs are allocated to the six product lines on a basis of the relative market value of each line at the split-off point.

The company has a waste product that results from the production of the six main product lines. Up until a few years ago, the company loaded the waste onto barges, and dumped it into the Gulf of Mexico, since the waste was thought to have no commercial value. The dumping was stopped, however, when the company's research division discovered that with some further processing the waste could be made commercially saleable as a fertilizer ingredient. The further processing was initiated at a cost of $175,000 per year. The waste was then sold to fertilizer manufacturers at a total sales price of $300,000 per year.

The accountants responsible for allocating manufacturing costs included the sales value of the waste product along with the sales value of the six main product lines in their allocation of the joint product costs at the split-off point. This allocation resulted in the waste product being allocated $150,000 in joint product cost. This $150,000 allocation, when added to the further processing costs of $175,000 for the waste, caused the waste product to show a net loss:

Sales value of the waste product after further processing.	$300,000
Less costs assignable to the waste product	325,000
Net loss.	($ 25,000)

When presented with this analysis, the company's management decided that further processing of the waste was not desirable after all. The company went back to dumping the waste in the Gulf.

The Contribution Approach to the Problem

Joint product costs are irrelevant in decisions regarding what to do with a product from the split-off point forward. The reason is that by the time one arrives at the split-off point, the joint product costs have already been incurred, and therefore are sunk costs. In the case of the soap company example above, the $150,000 in allocated joint product cost should not have been permitted to influence what was done with the waste product from the split-off point forward. The analysis should have been:

	Dump in Gulf	Process Further
Sales value	-0-	$300,000
Additional processing costs	-0-	175,000
Contribution margin	-0-	$125,000
Advantage of processing further	$125,000	

By continuing to dump the waste in the Gulf, the company is losing the opportunity to enjoy an additional $125,000 in net income each year.

As a general guide, it will always be profitable to continue processing joint products after the split-off point *so long as the incremental revenue from such processing exceeds the incremental processing costs.* Joint product costs that have *already been incurred* up to the split-off point are sunk costs, and are always irrelevant in decisions concerning what to do from the split-off point forward.

SUMMARY

The accountant is responsible for seeing that relevant, timely data are available for guiding management in its decisions, particularly those decisions relating to special, nonroutine situations. Reliance by management on irrelevant data can lead to incorrect decisions, reduced profitability, and inability to meet stated objectives. *All* costs are relevant in decision making, *except:*

1. Sunk costs.
2. Future costs that will not differ between the alternatives under consideration.

The concept of cost relevance has wide application. In this chapter we have observed its use in equipment replacement decisions, in make or buy decisions, in discontinuance of product line decisions, in joint product decisions, and in decisions relating to the effective use of scarce resources. This list is not inclusive of the possible applications of the relevant cost concept. Indeed, *any* decision involving costs hinges upon the proper identification and use of those costs which are relevant, if the decision is to be made properly. For this reason, we shall continue to focus upon the concept of cost relevance in the next chapter, where we deal with the matter of pricing, and in the two chapters following, where we consider long-run investment decisions.

QUESTIONS

12–1. Define the following terms: incremental cost; opportunity cost; sunk cost.

12–2. Distinguish between cost relevance and cost precision.

12–3. In what way can sunk costs influence future decisions?

12–4. "Sunk costs are easy to spot—they're simply the fixed costs associated with a decision." Discuss.

12–5. "Sometimes depreciation on equipment is a relevant cost in a decision, and sometimes it isn't." Do you agree? Explain.

12–6. "My neighbor offered me $25 for the use of my boat over the weekend, but I decided that renting it out is just too risky." What cost term would you use to describe the $25? Explain.

12–7. "Variable costs and differential costs mean the same thing." Do you agree? Explain.

12–8. Prentice Company is considering dropping one of its product lines. What direct costs of the product line would be relevant to this decision? Irrelevant?

12–9. "If a product line has a negative segment margin, then that's pretty good evidence that the product line should be discontinued." Do you agree? Explain.

12–10. What is meant by the term "make or buy?"

12–11. How does opportunity cost enter into the make or buy decision?

12–12. How will the relating of product line contribution margins to scarce resources help a company insure that profits will be maximized?

12–13. Define the following terms: joint products; joint product costs; split-off point.

12–14. What pitfalls are there in allocating common costs among joint products, from a decision-making point of view?

12–15. What guideline can be used in determining whether a joint product should be sold at split-off point or processed further?

EXERCISES

12–1. Listed below are a number of "costs" for the Wen Corporation:

1. Direct labor
2. Direct materials
3. Variable production overhead
4. Fixed production overhead
5. Variable selling and administrative expense
6. Fixed selling and administrative expense
7. Book value of Machine A
8. Market value of Machine A (current resale)
9. Market value of Machine B (cost)
10. Rate of return available from outside investments

Using the above list, indicate which "costs" are relevant for the following independent cases:

a. The Wen Corporation wants to purchase Machine B to replace Machine A. Both machines have the same capacity, and a remaining life of five years. Machine B will reduce direct labor costs by 30 percent. Other production costs will not change.

b. The Wen Corporation wants to purchase Machine B to increase production and sales. Machine A will continue to be used.

12–2. The Mimoore Printer's Shop prints and distributes daily, weekly, and monthly date books. These date books are printed with various company letterheads, and are used by these companies for advertising purposes. Data for the past quarter are as follows (in thousands of dollars):

	Total	Daily Date Books	Weekly Date Books	Monthly Date Books
Sales	$300	$100	$120	$80
Variable expenses.	180	60	80	40
Contribution margin	120	40	40	40
Fixed expenses:				
Direct	65	30	20	15
Common[1]	30	10	12	8
Total fixed	95	40	32	23
Net income	$ 25	$ -0-	$ 8	$17

[1] Allocation based on sales dollars.

a. Should Mimoore drop the printing of daily date books? Explain. (Assume that all direct fixed expenses associated with the daily date books will be eliminated if the line is dropped.)
b. Recast the above data in a more usable format.

12-3. The Rickson Manufacturing Company manufactures a variety of engines for use in heavy equipment. The company has always produced all of the necessary parts for its engines, including all of the subassemblies. An outside supplier has offered to produce and sell one subassembly to the Rickson Manufacturing Company at a cost of $18 per unit. In order to evaluate this offer, the Rickson Manufacturing Company has gathered the following information relating to its own "cost" of producing the subassemly internally:

	Per Unit	10,000 Units per Year
Direct materials	$ 6	$ 60,000
Direct labor	5	50,000
Variable production overhead	3	30,000
Fixed production overhead, direct	3	30,000*
Fixed production overhead, common, but allocated	5	50,000
Total cost	$22	$220,000

* ⅓ supervisory salaries; ⅔ depreciation of special equipment (no resale value).

a. Assuming there are no alternative uses for the facilities, should the offer be accepted?
b. Assuming that a new product that will generate a segment margin of $50,000 per year could be produced if the subassembly were purchased, should the offer be accepted?

12-4. Bill has just returned from a duck hunting trip. He has brought home 20 ducks. Bill's wife detests cleaning ducks, and to discourage him from further duck hunting has presented him with the following cost estimate per duck:

```
Camper and equipment:
    Cost $4,000. Usable for 8 seasons,
    10 hunting trips per season ...................... $ 50
    Travel expense:
        100 miles @ $.12 per mile (gas, oil, and tires—$.07 per mile;
        depreciation and insurance—$.05 per mile) .............    12
Shotgun shells (2 boxes) ...........................    10
Boat:
    Cost $240. Usable for 8 seasons, 10 hunting trips per season ....     3
    Fine paid for speeding on the way to the river .............    16
Hunting license:
    Cost $30 for the season, 10 hunting trips per season .........     3
Money lost playing poker:
    Loss $18. (Bill plays poker every weekend.) .............    18
1 fifth of "Old Grandad":
    Cost $8. (Used to ward off the cold.) .................     8
Total cost ...................................   $120
Cost per duck ($120 ÷ 20 ducks) ....................   $  6
```

Required:

1. Assuming that the duck hunting trip Bill has just completed is typical, what costs are relevant to a decision as to whether Bill should go duck hunting again this season?
2. Discuss the wife's computation of the cost per duck.

12–5. Kimball Company normally produces and sells 40,000 units of component A each quarter. Each unit of component A has a contribution margin of $5. Fixed overhead costs amount to $160,000 for each quarter.

Employment problems in other companies which purchase component A from Kimball Company have slashed sales to only 5,000 units per month. Kimball Company estimates that the employment problems in the other companies will last for only one quarter, after which time sales of component A will return to normal. However, because of the current low level of sales, Kimball Company is considering closing its plant for three months. If it does, the fixed overhead will drop to $90,000 per quarter. Start-up costs at the end of the shut-down period would total $15,000.

Required:

1. Would you recommend that Kimball Company close its plant, or continue to operate? (You may assume that there are no inventories on hand.)
2. At what level of quarterly sales (in units) would Kimball Company be indifferent as to closing the plant or keeping it open?

12–6. Martin Metal Products is considering replacing Machine A with Machine B. Selected information on the two machines is given below:

	Machine A	Machine B
Original cost new	$40,000	$55,000
Accumulated depreciation to date	24,000	–
Current salvage value	10,000	–
Estimated cost savings each year over		
Machine A.	–	13,000
Remaining years of useful life.	4 years	4 years

Required:

Prepare a computation covering the four-year period which will show the net advantage or disadvantage of purchasing Machine B. Ignore income taxes.

12–7. The Sparks Battery Company produces batteries for sale under its own name to the public. The batteries sell for $18 each; annual sales are 240,000 batteries. The cost per battery is given below:

> Variable production costs $10
> Fixed overhead ($1,200,000 total, divided by
>   240,000 batteries)   5
> Total cost per battery $15

Fixed selling and administrative expenses total $200,000 annually. Variable selling and administrative expenses total $1 per battery.

Faststart Company, which operates a chain of auto supply stores, has offered the Sparks Battery Company $14 per battery on an order of 100,000 batteries. The batteries would be produced carrying the Faststart Company name, and sold through the Faststart stores. The Faststart stores are located in a different part of the country from where the Sparks Battery Company normally sells its batteries.

Because of the bulk order, there would be no variable selling and administrative expenses associated with the sale to the Faststart Company. A machine used to imprint the Faststart Company name on batteries would cost $5,000 and would be usable almost indefinitely.

The Sparks Battery Company has a capacity of 300,000 batteries per year. Faststart Company has made it clear that it will not accept less than 100,000 batteries.

Required:

Would you recommend that the Sparks Battery Company accept the Faststart Company offer? Show all computations.

12–8. Electro Controls, Inc., produces and sells 300,000 units of Product X each year, at a selling price of $20 per unit. The company's cost per unit of Product X is:

> Direct materials . . . . $ 3
> Direct labor   6
> Variable overhead.   2
> Fixed overhead   4
> Total cost per unit $15

The company has received an order from a foreign distributor for 25,000 units of Product X, to be delivered over the next year. The distributor has offered to pay $13 per unit for the 25,000 units ordered. Electro Controls, Inc., would have to purchase a special machine for engraving the name of the foreign distributor on the units he purchased. The machine would cost $35,000, and could be sold for about $20,000 at the end of one year. The sales to the foreign distributor would not disturb regular sales of Product X. The company has sufficient existing capacity to handle the additional units.

Required:

Prepare an analysis showing whether the foreign distributor's offer should be accepted. Ignore income taxes.

12–9. The Moore Equipment Company has been experiencing losses on Product Line 4 for several years. The most recent income statement on Product Line 4 is given below:

Sales		$60,000
Less costs, direct and allocated:		
Manufacturing costs:		
Variable manufacturing costs	$16,000	
Depreciation of equipment (no resale value)	8,000	
Salary of line manager	12,000	
General factory costs–fixed.	6,000	
Total manufacturing costs	42,000	
Selling costs:		
Commissions	4,000	
Freight-out	3,000	
Advertising–direct	10,000	
Total selling costs	17,000	
Other costs:		
General office (allocated on a basis of sales dollars)	5,000	
Purchasing (allocated on a basis of sales dollars)	3,000	
Total other costs.	8,000	
Total costs		67,000
Net loss.		($ 7,000)

The total costs of the General Factory, General Office, and Purchasing will not change if Product Line 4 is discontinued. The discontinuance of Product Line 4 would not affect sales of other product lines.

Required:

Would you recommend that Product Line 4 be discontinued? Show computations.

PROBLEMS

12–1. *Relevant Costs; Purchase of a New Machine.* The Jims Company purchased a machine two years ago at a cost of $48,000. The machine is being depreciated on a straight-line basis. When purchased, the machine was given an estimated life of 12 years, and assigned a zero scrap value.

A computer-controlled machine which performs the same work as the machine purchased by the Jims Company has just come on the market. The new machine sells for $60,000. Although the new machine is more costly to purchase than the old machine, it would slash annual operating costs by $8,000. The new machine would last about 10 years, and have a zero scrap value. The old machine can be sold now for only $16,000, due to the presence of the new machine on the market.

The president of the Jims Company has prepared the following cost analysis:

Savings promised by the new machine		
($8,000 per year × 10 years)		$80,000
Cost of the new machine:		
Purchase price.	$60,000	
Loss on the old machine.	24,000	84,000
Net disadvantage of purchasing the		
new machine		($ 4,000)

The president handed his analysis to the controller and stated, "The loss that we would sustain on the old machine would more than wipe out any savings that the new machine might give us. We can't think about getting rid of that old machine if it means taking a loss on it."

Operating costs of the old machine are $18,000 per year. Sales are expected to remain unchanged at $40,000 per year. Selling and administrative expenses will be $12,000 per year.

Required:

1. Comment on the president's cost analysis.
2. Prepare a summary income statement covering the next 10 years, assuming:
    a. That the new machine is not purchased.
    b. That the new machine is purchased.
3. Analyze the desirability of purchasing the new machine, using only relevant costs in your analysis.

12–2. *Modify or Complete a Product.* The Repeat Electronics Company manufactures a telephone recording device called the Chatterbox. This device sells for $50, and records up to 10 two-minute telephone messages. When first introduced, the Chatterbox met with great success; during the first year 400,000 units were sold. For the current year, production was set at 600,000 units in order to meet an expected increase in demand.

On February 1 of the current year, however, the telephone company announced the availability of a new telephone which has a built-in answering device. This device is equal in quality and performance to the Chatterbox. The new telephone can be installed for only $30.

The Repeat Electronics Company has 40,000 completed Chatterboxes on hand, and an additional 80,000 Chatterboxes which are 60 percent complete as to manufacture. The company is trying to determine what to do with these inventory items. An electronics wholesaler has offered to buy all Chatterboxes available for $25 each.

The partially completed Chatterboxes can be modified into pocket tape recorders at a cost of $14 per unit. The pocket tape recorders can then be sold for $30 each. The normal cost of producing one Chatterbox is given below:

Direct materials	$ 8
Direct labor	12
Variable overhead.	6
Fixed overhead	3
Total cost per unit	$29

Required:

What decision should be made relative to the partially competed Chatterboxes?

12–3. *Discontinuance of a Department.* Sales have never been good in Department C of Stacey's Department Store. For this reason, management is considering eliminating the department. A summarized income statement for the store, by departments, for the most recent quarter is given below:

	A	B	C	Total
Sales	$175,000	$195,000	$102,000	$472,000
Cost of goods sold	70,000	77,600	42,400	190,000
Gross margin.	105,000	117,400	59,600	282,000
Operating expenses:				
Salaries.	18,000	16,000	15,000	49,000
Utilities	2,500	1,900	1,600	6,000
Direct advertising	8,400	6,500	5,000	19,900
General advertising	4,000	4,000	4,000	12,000
Rent on building	15,000	12,000	10,000	37,000
Employment taxes	1,800	1,600	1,500	4,900
Depreciation of fixtures and				
equipment.	12,000	15,000	8,000	35,000
Insurance on inventories, fixtures,				
and equipment	1,800	2,200	1,200	5,200
Property taxes on inventories,				
fixtures, and equipment	600	700	400	1,700
Service department expenses	24,000	31,000	22,000	77,000
Total operating expenses.	88,100	90,900	68,700	247,700
Net income or (loss)	$ 16,900	$ 26,500	$ (9,100)	$ 34,300

The following additional information is available:

1. All departments are housed in the same building. The store leases the entire building at a fixed annual rental rate.

2. If Department C is eliminated, the utilities bill will be reduced by about $500 per quarter.

3. One of the employees in Department C is the president's dim-witted son-in-law. The son-in-law will be transferred to another department if Department C is eliminated. The son-in-law's salary is $2,500 per quarter.

4. The fixtures and equipment in Department C would be transferred to the other departments. One fourth of the insurance and property taxes relate to the fixtures and equipment in Department C.

5. Stacey's Department Store has three service departments—Purchasing, Warehouse, and General Office. One employee in Purchasing and one employee in Warehouse could be discharged if Department C is dropped. The combined salaries and other costs of these two employees is $4,500 per quarter.

Required:

1. Assume that Stacey's Department Store has no alternative use for the space now being occupied by Department C. Should the department be eliminated? You may assume that eliminating Department C would have no effect on sales in the other departments.

2. Assume that Stacey's Department Store has an opportunity to sublease the space now being occupied by Department C, at a monthly rental rate $15,000. Would you advise the store to eliminate Department C, and sublease the space?

12–4. *Make or Buy.* The Calward Corporation, a manufacturer of battery-operated vehicles, has been purchasing brake and accelerator pedals for its vehicles from a local supplier for the past ten years. These pedals are purchased in sets of one brake pedal and one accelerator pedal, at a cost of $8.00 per set. One of Calward's product lines has been discontinued, and as a possible use of the space the firm is considering the alternative of manufacturing pedals internally. The following information has been assembled:

	Per Set		10,000 Sets	
	Make	Buy	Make	Buy
Cost of purchasing		$8.00		$80,000
Direct materials	$1.80		$18,000	
Direct labor	2.40		24,000	
Variable overhead.	.50		5,000	
Fixed overhead, direct (can be avoided by buying)	1.00		10,000	
Total costs.	$5.70	$8.00	$57,000	$80,000

As another alternative, Calward can use the space from the discontinued product line to manufacture an entirely new product. The following data pertain to this new product:

Sales	$55,000
Variable expenses.	20,000
Contribution margin	35,000
Direct fixed expenses (excluding cost for	
the space)	10,000
Segment margin	$25,000

Required:

1. Prepare an analysis to determine whether the firm should make or buy the pedals.
2. If, instead of 10,000 sets of pedals, 20,000 sets were required, should the firm make or buy the pedals? Assume that space is adequate to make the pedals, and that the total direct fixed overhead would not change.

12–5. *Use of Resources.* The Bofin Company has a machine capacity of only 5,000 machine hours per month. In planning next month's production, the following data have been prepared for products A, B, and C.

	A	B	C
Sales price per unit	$14	$15	$12
Variable cost per unit.	7	6	4
Contribution margin	$ 7	$ 9	$ 8
Contribution margin ratio	50%	60%	66⅔%
Machine hours required per unit	6	8	10

Required:

1. Assuming that all units produced can be sold, which product(s) should the firm produce, and how many units should be produced? Show your computations.
2. Assuming that the firm must produce 100 units of Product C because of a long-term contract, what additional products should be produced? Show your computations.

12–6. *Joint Products; Sell or Process Further.* The Brab Corporation produces three main products, A, B, and C, from a single process. Joint product costs up to the split-off point are $250,000. At the split-off point, products A, B, and C have relative sales values of $100,000, $200,000, and $300,000, respectively. In addition to the three main products, the process produces a waste product which can be sold at the split-off point for $25,000, or processed further for $20,000 and then sold for $50,000.

Required:

1. Allocate the joint costs between products A, B, C, and the waste product, based upon the sales value at split-off, assuming that the waste is not processed further.
2. Prepare an analysis to determine whether the waste should be sold at the split-off point, or processed further and sold for $50,000.
3. Assume that Product A can be processed further at a cost of $50,000, and then sold for $130,000. Should Product A be processed further?
4. What general statement can be made with respect to joint costs and the decision to process further?

12–7. *Relevant Costs.* Tacos, Inc., owns a number of highly successful taco houses located at various points throughout a large western metropolitan area. In order to assure itself of a constant supply of tortillas for making tacos, the company operates a small tortilla factory. The torilla factory makes the tortillas and sells them to the company's taco houses for $2.00 per gross (144 tortillas). The factory's income statement for the most recent year is given below:

Sales (16,000 gross of tortillas @ $2.00 per gross).		$32,000
Less variable expenses (16,000 gross of tortillas		
@ $.80 per gross)		12,800
Contribution margin		19,200
Less fixed costs:		
Depreciation of equipment	$6,000	
Salaries and other fixed costs	8,000	14,000
Net income		$ 5,200

Although Tacos, Inc., owns all of the taco house outlets, each taco house has an independent manager who is paid according to the profit he is able to generate from his outlet. The manager of Taco House #4 has just informed the manager of the tortilla factory that he is going to start buying his tortillas from an independent supplier, who is willing to supply all of Taco House #4's tortilla needs for only $1.80 per gross. Taco House #4 purchases 3,000 gross of tortillas each year.

The manager of the tortilla factory (who also is paid according to the profit he is able to generate from his operation), is not happy about the prospect of Taco House #4 going elsewhere for its tortillas, and wants to convince top management that this would be a mistake.

The manager of the tortilla factory would have to discharge one part-time employee if he loses Taco House #4's business. The employee is paid $2,000 per year.

Required:

1. What will be the effect on the tortilla factory's net income if Taco House #4 purchases its tortillas from the independent supplier? Show computations.
2. What will be the effect on Tacos, Inc.'s net income *as a whole company* if Taco House #4 purchases its tortillas from the independent supplier? Show computations.

12–8. *Product Expansion; Make or Buy.* The Jimson Company produces leisure products, including hobby kits. The company has found that the recent energy crisis has caused a significant increase in demand for its products. The hobby kits particularly are selling very well. Sales of the company's most popular hobby kit have now reached capacity, and the company is trying to determine the best way to expand output. Revenue and expense information relating to this hobby kit for the last year are shown below:

	50,000 Hobby Kits Sold
Sales ($12 per kit)	$600,000
Less variable expenses (40 percent of sales)	240,000
Contribution margin	360,000
Less fixed expenses:	
Direct fixed expenses	220,000
Allocated fixed expenses	50,000
Total fixed expenses	270,000
Net income	$ 90,000

The company wants to expand output to 75,000 hobby kits per year. Two alternatives are available for securing the additional output:

1. An outside supplier has offered to produce 25,000 hobby kits per year and sell them to the Jimson Company for $10 each. The kits would then be marketed through the Jimson Company's already established retail outlets.
2. The Jimson Company can expand its own productive capacity. This expansion would result in $145,000 per year in additional direct fixed expenses.

The allocated fixed expenses above are allocated to the product lines on a basis of sales dollars. If sales of hobby kits are expanded to 75,000 kits per year, then this fixed expense allocation will increase from $50,000 to $58,000 per year, to reflect the greater sales. However, the total general expenses being allocated will not change.

Required:

1. Prepare contribution-type income statements based on 75,000 hobby kits sold each year, as they would appear under each of the alternatives above. Which alternative should be selected?

2. Prepare an analysis of the relative desirability of the two alternatives, based only on relevant costs.

3. What nonquantitative matters should be considered in trying to decide between the two alternatives?

12–9. *Relevant Costs.* The costs associated with the acquisition and annual operation of a truck are given below:

Insurance.	$1,600
Licenses and taxes	400
Garage rent for parking.	1,200
Depreciation ($9,000 ÷ 5 yrs).	1,800*
Gasoline, oil, tires, and repairs	.07/mile

* Based on obsolescence, rather than on wear and tear.

Required:

1. Assume that the Dandy Company has purchased one truck, and the truck has been driven 50,000 miles during the first year. Compute the average cost per mile of owning and operating the truck.

2. At the beginning of the second year, the Dandy Company is unsure whether to use the truck, or leave it parked and have all hauling done commercially. What costs above are relevant to this decision?

3. Assume that the company decides to use the truck during the second year. Near year-end an order is received from a customer over 1,000 miles away. What costs above are relevant in a decision between using the truck to make the delivery and having the delivery done commercially?

4. Occasionally the company could use two trucks at the same time. For this reason some thought is being given to purchasing a second truck. The total miles driven would be the same as if only one truck was owned. What costs above are relevant in a decision over whether to purchase the second truck?

12–10. *Discontinuance of a Store.* Superior Markets, Inc., operates three stores in a large metropolitan area. A condensed income statement for the most recent year is presented below:

	Store A	Store B	Store C	Total
Sales	$445,000	$750,000	$675,000	$1,870,000
Cost of goods sold	273,500	401,300	358,600	1,033,400
Gross margin	171,500	348,700	316,400	836,600
Operating expenses:				
Selling	121,000	150,000	142,500	413,500
Administrative	67,310	110,250	100,450	278,010
Total	188,310	260,250	242,950	691,510
Net income (loss)	$ (16,810)	$ 88,450	$ 73,450	$ 145,090

The company is very concerned about Store A's inability to show a profit, and consideration is being given to discontinuing the store. The company has retained you to make a recommendation concerning what to do with Store A. The following additional information is available:

1. The breakdown of the selling expenses and the administrative expenses is:

	Store A	Store B	Store C	Total
Selling expenses:				
Sales salaries.	$ 70,000	$ 90,000	$ 85,000	$245,000
Direct advertising.	12,000	15,000	10,000	37,000
General advertising	3,000	3,000	3,000	9,000
Store rent	25,000	30,000	34,000	89,000
Depreciation of store fixtures	3,500	4,500	3,000	11,000
Delivery salaries.	6,000	6,000	6,000	18,000
Depreciation of delivery equipment.	1,500	1,500	1,500	4,500
Total selling expenses	$121,000	$150,000	$142,500	$413,500
Administrative expenses:				
Store management salaries.	$ 15,000	$ 18,000	$ 16,000	$ 49,000
General office salaries	22,500	45,000	40,500	108,000
Insurance expense on fixtures and inventory	6,000	8,000	8,000	22,000
Utilities	4,500	4,710	4,600	13,810
Employment taxes	6,810	9,540	8,850	25,200
General office.	12,500	25,000	22,500	60,000
Total administrative expenses.	$ 67,310	$110,250	$100,450	$278,010

2. The lease on the building housing Store A can be broken, with no penalty.
3. The fixtures being used in Store A would be transferred to the other two stores.
4. One of the sales personnel in Store A is a long-time employee, who will be retained even if Store A is closed. This employee would be transferred to one of the other stores. His salary is $6,000 per year. All other employees in Store A would be discharged.
5. One delivery crew serves all three stores. Since Store A has relatively few deliveries, there would be no reduction in this crew if the store is discontinued.
6. Employment taxes are 6 percent of salaries.
7. One third of the insurance in Store A is on the store's fixtures.
8. The general office salaries and expenses relate to the general management of Superior Markets, Inc. These expenses are allocated to the stores on a basis of sales dollars.

9. No change in general office salaries and expenses is expected if Store A is dropped.

Required:

1. Prepare a schedule showing the change in revenues and expenses if Store A is discontinued.
2. What recommendation would you make to the management of Superior Markets, Inc?
3. Assume that because of the close location of Store C to Store A, if Store A is closed sales in Store C will increase by at least $150,000 per year. Store C's gross margin rate is 47 percent. Store C has ample capacity to handle the increased sales. What effect would these factors have on your recommendation concerning Store A? Show computations.

12–11. *Relevant Cost Analysis; Book Value.* The Matz Machine Shop purchased a new milling machine one year ago at a cost of $21,000. The machine has been working very satisfactorily, but the shop manager has just received information on an electronically-controlled milling machine that is vastly superior to the machine which has already been purchased. Comparative data on the two machines are given below:

	Present Machine	Proposed New Machine
Purchase cost new.	$21,000	$32,000
Estimated useful life new	7 years	6 years
Cost of installation	–	$ 2,000
Salvage value now.	$10,000	–
Salvage value in 6 years	–0–	4,000
Annual straight-line depreciation	3,000	5,000
Remaining book value	18,000	–
Annual costs to operate	40,000	34,000

The shop manager makes the following quick computation, and exclaims, "There's no way I could buy that new machine. If the boss found out that I took a loss on the old machine, he'd crucify me."

Remaining book value of the old machine.	$18,000
Salvage value now of the old machine	10,000
Net loss from disposal	$ 8,000

Sales from the milling operation are expected to remain unchanged at $90,000 per year indefinitely. Other costs associated with the milling operation total $30,000 annually.

Required:

1. Prepare a summary income statement covering 6 years, assuming:
   a. That the new machine is not purchased.
   b. That the new machine is purchased.
   Would you recommend that the new machine be purchased?

2. Prepare an analysis of the desirability of purchasing the new machine, using only relevant costs.

12–12. *Discussion Questions on Relevant Costs.* The Birch Company normally produces and sells 30,000 units of Product X each month. The company's unit costs at this level of activity are given below:

Direct materials $4
Direct labor 3
Variable overhead 4
Fixed overhead 5
Variable selling 3
Fixed selling 1

Below are a number of questions relating to production and sales of Product X. Unless otherwise stated, *each question is independent of the others.* Assume a normal selling price of $22 per unit, unless a different selling price is given.

Question #1. Assume that the Birch Company has sufficient capacity to produce 40,000 units each month. The company has an opportunity to sell 10,000 units in a foreign market. The only selling costs that would be associated with the foreign order would be $2 per unit in shipping. Legal fees, foreign permits, and other costs of getting the order would be $6,000. What would be the per-unit break-even price on the order?

Question #2. Assume again that the Birch Company has sufficient capacity to produce 40,000 units each month. The company could increase sales by 20 percent above the present 30,000 units each month, if it were willing to increase its fixed advertising by $35,000 monthly. Would the increased advertising expenditure be justified?

Question #3. Five hundred units of Product X produced last month have small blemishes, and it will be impossible to sell these units at regular prices. If the company wishes to sell the blemished units through regular distribution channels, what unit cost figure is relevant for setting a minimum selling price?

Question #4. The United States Army would like to make a one-time-only purchase of 5,000 units of Product X. The contract would call for a fixed fee of $.30 per unit, plus reimbursement for Birch Company's costs of production. Assume that regular sales of Product X have temporarily slumped to only 25,000 units per month. If the Birch Company accepts the Army contract, by how much will profits be increased or decreased from what they would be if only 25,000 units were sold? There would be no variable selling expenses associated with the Army's order.

Question #5. Assume the same situation as described in Question #4, except that the company is presently selling 30,000 units through regular channels. Accepting the Army order would require giving up regular sales of 5,000 units. If the Army contract is accepted, by how much will profits be increased or decreased from what they would be if the 5,000 units were sold through regular channels?

Question #6. Employment problems in the companies that normally purchase Product X from the Birch Company have caused sales to temporarily drop to only 8,000 units per month. The Birch Company estimates that the employment problems will continue for two months, after which time sales will return to normal.

The Birch Company is considering closing its own operations down for the two-month period, rather than operating at a sales level of only 8,000 units per month. The company estimates that if it does close down operations, fixed overhead can be reduced to only $105,000 per month, and that the fixed selling expenses can be reduced by 10 percent per month. Start-up costs after being closed down for two months would total $7,000. Would you advise the Birch Company to cease operations for the two-month period?

Question #7. Assume the same situation as described in Question #6 above. At what level of sales in units for the two months is the Birch Company indifferent as between closing the plant or keeping it open?

Question #8. An outside manufacturer has offered to produce Product X for the Birch Company, and to ship it directly to the Birch Company's customers. This arrangement would permit the Birch Company to reduce its variable selling expenses by one third. The Birch Company's plant would be completely idle but fixed overhead would continue at 60 percent of its present level. What unit cost figure is relevant for comparison against the quotation received from the outside manufacturer?

12–13. *Make or Buy.* The Kemfer Company manufactures a variety of ball point pens. The company has just received an offer from an outside supplier to provide the ink cartridge for the company's Zippo pen line, at a price of $.48 per dozen cartridges. The company is interested in this offer, since its own production of cartridges is nearing capacity.

The Kemfer Company estimates that if the supplier's offer is accepted, the direct labor and variable overhead costs of the Zippo pen line would be reduced by 10 percent, and that the direct materials cost would be reduced by 20 percent.

Under present operations, the Kemfer Company manufactures all of its own pens from start to finish. The Zippo pens are sold through wholesalers at $4.00 per box. Each box contains one dozen pens. Fixed overhead costs charged to the Zippo pen line total $50,000 each period. These fixed overhead costs are common, since the same equipment and facilities are used to produce several pen lines. The present cost of producing one dozen Zippo pens (one box) is given below:

Direct materials	$1.50
Direct labor	1.00
Manufacturing overhead	.80*
Total cost	$3.30

* Includes both variable and fixed overhead, based on production of 100,000 boxes of pens each period.

Required:

1. Should the Kemfer Company accept the outside supplier's offer?
2. What is the maximum price that the Kemfer Company would be willing to pay to the outside supplier per dozen cartridges?
3. Assume that sales of the Zippo pen line increase to 125,000 boxes each period. In order to produce the extra cartridges, the Kemfer Company would incur added fixed expenses of $12,500. Under these conditions, should the supplier's offer be accepted? For how many boxes of Zippo cartridges?

12–14. *Pricing and Joint Products.* (Note to the instructor: Problem 13–9 at the end of Chapter 13 can be assigned very effectively in conjunction with Chapter 12. The problem contains a number of concepts covered in Chapter 12, as well as touching on the problem of pricing.)

Required:

Turn to and solve Problem 13–9 at the end of Chapter 13.

chapter 13

The Pricing Decision

MANY FIRMS have no pricing problems at all. They produce a product that is in competition with other, similar, products for which a market price already exists. Customers will not pay more than this price, and there is no reason for any firm to charge less. Under these circumstances, no price calculations are necessary. Any firm entering the market simply charges the price the market directs it to accept. To a large extent, farm products follow this type of pattern. In these situations, the question isn't what price to charge; the question is simply how much to produce.

In this chapter we are concerned with the more common situation in which a firm is faced with the problem of setting its own prices, as well as deciding how much to produce. The pricing decision is considered by many to be the single most important decision that a manager has to make. The reason is that the pricing of products isn't just a marketing decision or a financial decision; rather, it is a decision touching on *all* aspects of a firm's activities, and as such affects the entire enterprise. Since the prices charged for a firm's products largely determine the quantities customers are willing to purchase, the setting of prices dictates the inflows of revenues into a firm. If these revenues consistently fail to cover all of the costs of the firm, then in the long run the firm cannot survive. This is true regardless of how carefully costs may be controlled, or how innovative the managers of the firm may be in the discharge of their other responsibilities.

Cost is a key factor in the pricing decision. As we have already seen, however, "cost" is a somewhat fluid concept, and sometimes hard to pin down. Our purpose in this chapter is to look at some of the cost concepts developed in earlier chapters and to see how these concepts can be applied in the pricing decision. This chapter is not intended to be a comprehensive guide to pricing; rather, its purpose is to integrate those cost concepts with which we are already familiar into a general pricing framework.

THE ECONOMIC FRAMEWORK FOR PRICING

A large part of microeconomic theory (theory of the firm) is devoted to the matter of pricing. In order to establish a framework for the pricing decision, it will be helpful to review certain of these economic theory concepts. This review will also assist us in showing the relationship between the models involved in microeconomic theory and the concept of incremental analysis discussed in preceding chapters.

Total Revenue and Total Cost Curves

Microeconomic theory states that the best price for a product is that price which maximizes the difference between total revenue and total costs. The economist illustrates this concept by constructing a model such as that shown in Exhibit 13–1.

This model is based on a number of assumptions. The economist assumes, first, that it is not possible to sell an unlimited number of units at the same price. If an unlimited number of units could be sold

EXHIBIT 13–1
Total Revenue and Total Cost Curves
Dollars

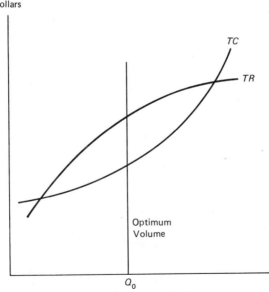

Volume Sold in Units

at the same price, then the total revenue (TR) curve would appear as a straight line, beginning at the origin of the graph. Since the economist assumes that at some point price reductions will be necessary to sell more units, the TR curve is shown increasing at a decreasing rate as quantity sold increases. That is, as price is reduced to stimulate more sales, total revenue will continue to increase for each unit sold, but the *rate* of this increase will begin to decline. As price is reduced more and more, the increase in total revenue will continue to decline, as depicted by the flattening tendency in the TR curve in the exhibit.

The total cost (TC) curve in Exhibit 13–1 assumes that the cost of producing additional units of product is not constant, but rather increases as attempts are made to squeeze more and more production out of a given set of productive facilities. So long as the rate of this increase is less than the rate of increase in total revenue, the company can profit by producing and selling more units of product. At some point, however, the rate of increase in total cost will become equal to the rate of increase in total revenue—that is, at some point the two lines will become parallel to each other. At this point the increase to total cost from producing and selling one more unit of product is exactly equal to the increase to total revenue from that unit of product, and its production and sale yields zero increase in total profits to the firm. This point is shown in the graph in Exhibit 13–1 as quantity Q_0, representing the optimum volume of production and sales for the firm.

At Q_0 volume of units the difference between total revenue and total cost is maximized. If we move to the right of Q_0 volume, total cost is increasing more rapidly than total revenue, and therefore total profits would be decreased. If we move to the left of Q_0 volume, then total revenue is increasing more rapidly than total cost, and the company can profit by further expanding output up to Q_0 level of activity. In sum, Q_0 represents the optimum volume of sales for the firm, and the correct price to charge is the price which will allow the firm to sell this volume of units.

Marginal Revenue and Marginal Cost Curves

These same concepts can be shown in terms of marginal revenue and marginal cost. Marginal revenue can be defined as the addition to total revenue resulting from the sale of one additional unit of product. Marginal cost can be defined as the addition to total cost resulting from the production and sale of one additional unit of product. The economist expresses these concepts in model form as shown in Exhibit 13–2.

The marginal revenue (MR) and marginal cost (MC) curves in Exhibit 13–2 have their basis in the economist's assumption that the total

EXHIBIT 13–2
Marginal Revenue and Marginal Cost Curves

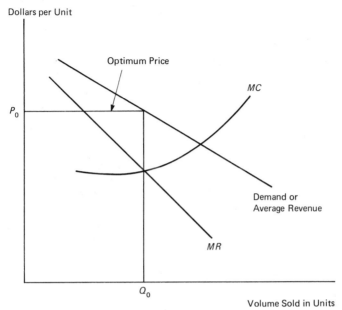

revenue and total cost curves behave in the way depicted earlier in Exhibit 13–1. That is, the marginal revenue and marginal cost curves are derived by measuring the rate of *change* in total revenue and total cost at various levels of activity, and by plotting this change in graph form. Since the total revenue curve in Exhibit 13–1 depicts a declining rate of increase in total revenue, the marginal revenue curve in Exhibit 13–2 slopes downward to the right. And since the total cost curve in Exhibit 13–1 depicts total cost as increasing with volume, the marginal cost curve slopes upward to the right in Exhibit 13–2. As discussed in Chapter 2, the economist's marginal concept is basically the same as the accountant's incremental concept.

Notice that Exhibit 13–2 depicts average revenue, which represents the *average price* obtained for each unit sold, as being greater than marginal revenue. Why is this so? The reason can be shown by means of a simple example. Assume that at a price of $5 per unit 10 units of product X can be sold. If the price is dropped to $4.75, then one additional unit, or 11 units in total, can be sold. The *marginal* revenue from the eleventh unit will therefore be $4.75 (the unit's selling price). But the *average* revenue per unit sold will be $4.98 ($50.00 + $4.75 = $54.75 ÷ 11 units = $4.98 per unit). By this line of reasoning, average revenue will always be greater than marginal revenue, so long as prices must be reduced to sell more units.

The optimum price to charge is determined by the intersection of the marginal revenue and the marginal cost curves. The intersection of these two curves occurs at volume Q_0. This is the same volume as shown earlier in Exhibit 13–1, depicting the point of maximum difference between total revenues and total costs. At volume Q_0 price P_0 should be charged for each unit sold.

Elasticity of Demand

A product's price elasticity is a key concept in any pricing decision. Price elasticity measures the degree to which volume of sales is affected by a change in price per unit. Demand for a product is price inelastic if a change in price has little or no effect on the volume of units sold. Demand is price elastic if a change in price has a substantial effect on the volume of units sold. Salt is a good example of a product that tends to be price inelastic. Raising or lowering the price of salt probably would have little or no effect on the amount of salt sold in a given year.

Whether demand for a product tends to be price elastic or price inelastic can be a crucial factor in a decision relating to a change in price. The problem is that measuring the degree of price elasticity is an extremely difficult thing to do. It's one thing to observe generally that a given product tends to be price elastic, and it's another thing to determine exactly the *degree* of that elasticity—that is, to determine what change in volume of sales will take place as a result of specific changes in price. Yet this is exactly the kind of information that the manager needs in his pricing decision, and the kind of information that he attempts to obtain by carefully planned marketing research programs.

Pricing decisions are further complicated by the fact that cross-elasticity often exists in the demand for certain products. Cross-elasticity measures the degree to which demand for one product is affected by a change in the price of a substitute product. For example, as the price of galvanized pipe goes up, consumers may switch to plastic pipe. One of the problems of measuring cross-elasticity is trying to identify the substitutes for a particular product, and the willingness of consumers to accept those substitutes in place of the product itself. Although problems of this type are often difficult to quantify, the concept of cross-elasticity of demand is an important concept, and cannot be disregarded in the pricing decision.

Limitations to the General Models

Although the models in Exhibits 13–1 and 13–2 do a good job of showing the general outlines of the incremental profit approach to pricing, they must be viewed as being only broad, conceptual guides in pricing decisions. There are several reasons why. First, cost and revenue data available to managers generally are sufficient to provide only rough approximations of the shape of the various cost and revenue curves depicted in the models. As our methods of measurement are improved and refined in years to come this situation may change, but at present managers usually have only a general idea of the shape of the demand curve which they are facing.

Second, the models are directly applicable only in conditions of *monopoly* (no directly competing product in the market) and *monoplistic competition* (many sellers of similar products, with no one seller having a large enough share of the market for other sellers to be able to discern the effect of his pricing decision on their sales). The models are not applicable between these two extremes, where the market is characterized by situations of *oligopoly* (a few large sellers, competing directly with each other). The reason is that the models make no allowance for retaliatory pricing decisions by competing firms, and retaliatory pricing is a prime characteristic of oligopolistic industries.

Where oligopoly exists, the marginal revenue curve of a firm will depend on how the firm's competitors react to price changes. If one firm reduces its prices, then the other firms in the industry probably will retaliate by reducing their prices as well. On the other hand, if one firm increases its prices, its competitors may not follow suit. In such situations, the firm increasing its prices will see its sales drop off sharply, as consumers turn to the firm's competitors. These effects can be seen in a variation of the general pricing model, which is characterized by a *kinked* demand curve, as shown in Exhibit 13–3.

Notice from Exhibit 13–3 that both the demand curve and the marginal revenue curve are kinked at price P_1. Price P_1 is the prevailing price in the industry. Any attempt to expand volume by reducing price below P_1 will result in a severe drop in marginal revenue, since marginal revenue falls off sharply to the right of Q_1, the present volume of sales.

As a practical matter, a kink of this type is likely to appear only if competitor firms are *not* operating at full capacity. If they are operating at full capacity, then they will be unable to absorb extra sales and one firm may be able to raise its prices with little loss of business. If so, then its competitors probably will quickly follow suit and raise their prices as well.

A third limitation to the general models arises from the fact that price is just one element in the marketing of a product. Many other factors must also be considered, which can have a significant impact on the number of units of a product that can be sold at a given price. Among these factors one can find promotional strategy, product design, intensity of selling effort, and the selection of distribution channels.

EXHIBIT 13-3
Kinked Demand Curve Faced by Oligopolistic Firms
Dollars per Unit

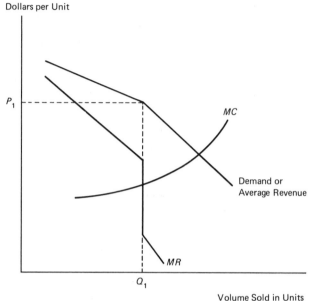

Volume Sold in Units

A final limitation to the general models is that even if business firms had a precise knowledge of the shape of their demand curves, we cannot automatically assume that they would price in such a way as to maximize profits. The reason is that this might bring charges from the public of "profiteering" and "charging all that the traffic will bear." Rather than attempting to maximize profits, many firms seek only to earn a "satisfactory" profit for the company. They think in terms of a reasonable return on the investment which has been made in the company, and strive to set prices in such a way as to earn that return. The concept of a "satisfactory" profit underlies the actions of a great many business firms today.

Although the limitations discussed above preclude the *direct* use of the economic pricing models in pricing decisions, these models nonetheless are highly useful in providing the general framework within which the price setter must work. They state the pricing problem in *conceptual* terms, and as such constitute the starting point in any pricing decision.

PRICING STANDARD PRODUCTS

Not all pricing decisions are approached in the same way. Some pricing decisions relate to the pricing of standard products which are sold to customers in the routine day-to-day conduct of business activities. Other pricing decisions relate to special orders of standard or near-standard products, and still others relate to pricing of special products taken on in an effort to fill out unused productive capacity. In this section we consider the pricing of standard products. The pricing of special orders of various types is reserved to a later section.

Cost-Plus Pricing Formulas

In pricing standard products the key concept is to recognize that selling prices must be sufficient in the long run to cover *all* costs of production, administration, and sales, both fixed and variable, as well as to provide for a reasonable return on the stockholders' investment, if a firm is to survive and grow. This point is often missed by some pricing enthusiasts who seem to imply in their writings that any price above variable or incremental costs is an acceptable price for any product under any circumstances.[1]

In setting normal long-run prices on standard products *all costs* are relevant in the pricing decision, and must be explicitly considered by the price setter if long-run profit goals are to be met. This means that a portion of the fixed costs (even if the fixed costs are sunk) must be considered along with the variable costs, and that the costs of administration and sales must be weighted in along with the costs of production, as prices are set.

The most common approach to the pricing of standard products is to employ some type of *cost-plus* pricing formula. The approach is to compute a "cost" base, and then to add to this base some predetermined markup to arrive at a target selling price. The "cost" in cost-plus is defined according to the method being used to cost units of product. In Chapters 3 and 7 we found that units of product can be costed in two different ways—by the absorption approach or by the contribution approach (with direct costing). We consider both costing methods below, and the approach each takes to cost-plus pricing of standard products.

The Absorption Approach

The absorption approach to cost-plus pricing defines the cost base as the cost to *manufacture* one unit of product. Other costs, such as administration and sales, are provided for through the markup that is added to this base. The mark-up is also structured in such a way as to provide for some desired profit margin above all costs.

---

[1] For a discussion of the circumstances under which variable or incremental costs are useful as a pricing guide, see the section following titled Special Pricing Decisions.

To illustrate, let us assume that the Ritter Company is in the process of setting a selling price on one of its standard products, which has just undergone some slight modifications in design. The accounting department has accumulated the following cost data on the redesigned product:

	Per Unit	Total
Direct materials	$5	
Direct labor	4	
Variable overhead	4	
Fixed overhead (based on 10,000 units)	7	$70,000
Variable selling and administrative expenses	2	
Fixed selling and administrative expenses (based on 10,000 units)	1	10,000

The first step is to compute the full cost to manufacture one unit of product. Once this cost has been determined, it becomes the base in the cost-plus pricing formula, to which the desired markup can be added. For the Ritter Company, the cost to manufacture one unit of product is $20, computed as follows:

Direct materials	$ 5
Direct labor	4
Overhead ($4 variable, plus $7 fixed, or 275% of direct labor cost)	11
Total absorption cost to manufacture one unit	$20

Let us assume that the Ritter Company has a general policy of adding a markup equal to 50 percent of cost to manufacture, in order to obtain its target selling prices. A price quotation sheet for the company prepared under this assumption is presented in Exhibit 13–4.

EXHIBIT 13–4
Price Quotation Sheet—Absorption Basis

Direct materials	$ 5
Direct labor	4
Overhead at 275% of direct labor cost	11
Total cost to manufacture	20
Markup to cover selling and administrative expenses, and desired profit—50% of cost to manufacture	10
Target selling price	$30

As shown in Exhibit 13–4, even though this pricing approach is termed cost-plus, part of the costs involved are buried in the *plus*, or markup part of the formula. The buried costs are those associated with the selling and administrative activities. These costs could be broken out separately and added to the cost base along with the cost to manufacture, but this is rarely done in actual practice. The reason centers on the difficulty that would be involved in making the necessary allocations among the various products of the firm. For example, the salary of the company president would be a common cost among all products. It would be a difficult task to try to allocate his salary in any meaningful way to these products. The great majority of firms feel that selling and administrative costs can be provided for adequately in final, target selling prices by simply expanding the markup over cost to manufacture to include them as well as the desired profit. This means, of course, that the markup must be structured with great care in order to insure that it is sufficient to cover all that it is supposed to cover. More will be said on this point a little later.

Notice from Exhibit 13–4 that the absorption approach to cost-plus pricing makes no attempt to distinguish between costs by behavior (e.g., variable and fixed) in structuring a price quotation sheet. Rather, as is usual with the absorption approach to costing, costs are organized in a *functional* format, according to whether they are associated with production or with some other function of the business.

If the Ritter Company produces and sells 10,000 units of its product at a selling price of $30 each, the income statement will appear as shown in Exhibit 13–5.

EXHIBIT 13–5
The Ritter Company Income Statement—Absorption Basis

Sales (10,000 units @ $30)	$300,000
Cost of goods sold (10,000 units @ $20)	200,000
Gross margin	100,000
Selling and administrative expenses (10,000 units @ $2 variable and $1 fixed)	30,000
Net income	$ 70,000

The Contribution Approach

The contribution approach to preparing price quotation sheets is similar to the absorption approach in that it is structured around the need to cover *all* costs in setting long-run prices. It differs from the absorption approach in that it emphasizes costs by behavior, rather than by function.

In the absorption approach to cost-plus pricing, we found that the cost base consists of the cost to manufacture a unit of product. By contrast, the contribution approach to cost-plus pricing defines the cost base in terms of a product's variable expenses. The cost base includes not just variable manufacturing expenses, but variable selling and administrative expenses as well. A markup is added to this variable expense base designed to cover appropriate fixed costs (production, selling, and administration), and to yield the desired profit on each unit sold.

To illustrate, refer again to the cost data for the Ritter Company. The base to use in cost-plus pricing under the contribution approach would be $15, computed as follows:

Direct materials.	$ 5
Direct labor	4
Variable overhead.	4
Variable selling and administrative expenses.	2
Total variable expenses.	$15

Let us assume that the Ritter Company has found that a markup of 100 percent of variable expenses is adequate to cover allocable fixed expenses and to provide the desired profit per unit. A price quotation sheet prepared under this assumption is shown in Exhibit 13–6.

EXHIBIT 13–6
Price Quotation Sheet—Contribution Basis

Direct materials	$ 5
Direct labor	4
Variable overhead.	4
Variable selling and administrative expense	2
Total variable expenses.	$15
Markup to cover fixed expenses and desired profit—	
100% of variable expenses.	15
Target selling price	$30

Notice again that even though this pricing method is termed *cost*-plus pricing, a portion of the costs are buried in the *plus*, or markup part of the formula. In this case, however, the buried costs are the fixed costs rather than the selling and administrative costs. Again, the reason for not including the fixed costs in the cost base can be traced to the time and difficulty that would be involved in any attempt to allocate. As a practical matter, there is no way to equitably allocate many common fixed costs, as discussed in Chapter 7. Any attempt to do so may result in less usable cost data for pricing, rather than more usable data. In addition, many users of the contribution approach to pricing argue that keeping the cost base free of any element of fixed costs facilitates pricing in special and unusual situations. This point is discussed further in a following section dealing with special pricing problems.

Compare the contribution approach to cost-plus pricing in Exhibit 13–6 to the absorption approach in Exhibit 13–4. Although both approaches are employing the cost-plus concept, notice the difference in the way in which the two approaches handle the cost data, and structure the price quotation sheet. Also notice that the Ritter Company can attain the *same* $30 target selling price by using either costing method.

In order to conclude the Ritter Company example, let us again assume that the company produces and sells 10,000 units of product at a selling price of $30 each. The company's income statement as it would appear under the contribution approach is shown in Exhibit 13–7.

EXHIBIT 13–7
The Ritter Company Income Statement—Contribution Basis

Sales (10,000 units @ $30).		$300,000
Less variable expenses (10,000 units @ $15).		150,000
Contribution margin		150,000
Less fixed expenses:		
Production.	$70,000	
Selling and administrative	10,000	80,000
Net income		$ 70,000

Using Cost-Plus Data

By far the most crucial element in the cost-plus pricing formulas is the percentage markup added to the cost base. We have found that under both the absorption and the contribution approaches to cost-plus pricing some elements of cost are buried in the markup figure. This means that the markup must be sufficient to cover these buried costs, as well as to provide the desired profit per unit. In some situations the percentage markup is more or less standard, and has developed over long years of experience and use. In other situations, however, no standard markups are available, and the markups must be developed by the firm itself. One way of doing this is to set markups according to companywide profit objectives, or according to some desired rate of return on investment.

To illustrate, assume that a firm has found that an investment of $2,000,000 is necessary in order to produce and market 50,000 units of product X each year. It will cost $30 to produce each unit of product X at a 50,000 unit level of activity, and total selling and administrative expenses are estimated to be $700,000. If the firm desires a 25 percent return on investment, then the required markup would be computed as follows:

Desired return on investment (25% × $2,000,000).	$ 500,000
Selling and administrative expenses.	700,000
Total.	$1,200,000 (a)
Cost to manufacture (50,000 units × $30)	$1,500,000 (b)
Required markup—(a) ÷ (b)	80%

The selling price of a unit of product X would be $54:[2]

Cost to manufacture	$30
Markup—80% × $30	24
Target selling price per unit	$54

The problem with a rigid application of an approach such as this is that it tends to ignore the relationship between price and volume. For example, the competitive situation may be such for product X that a selling price of $54 would result in far less than 50,000 units being sold each year. On the other hand, demand may be so great that the company would be swamped with orders.

In order to make cost-plus pricing formulas workable, companies usually do two things. First, they rarely price a product exactly at the target price suggested by the cost-plus pricing formula. The actual selling price will be shaded upward or downward according to the competitive situation prevailing on the market. The mark of the real executive in pricing can be found in his ability to sense the market situation, and in knowing when price adjustments can and should be made. If the executive senses that his competitive position is strong, he will adjust his prices upward; if he senses a strengthening of opposing competitive forces, then he will shade his prices downward. The price setter must recognize that just because a particular margin has been obtainable for the last 20 or 30 years there is no assurance that it will continue to be obtainable. For example, the neighborhood grocery stores suddenly discovered in the 1940s that the margins they had been obtaining for many decades were no longer obtainable because of the development of large chain supermarkets. In turn, the chain supermarkets have discovered in the 1970s that the margins they have enjoyed for nearly three decades are being undercut by the self-serve discount food outlets.

Second, companies will not use the same markup for all product lines, but rather will vary the markup according to custom, need, or general industry practice. For example, one product line may carry a markup of 20 percent whereas another may carry a markup of 60 percent. This is typical of clothing and department stores, where the percentage markup varies by department and occasionally even by item. Jewelry generally has a high markup, whereas stockings carry a relatively low markup.

Why Use Cost Data in Pricing?

If pricing executives end up setting prices according to how they sense the market, then an obvious question at this point is why bother

---

[2] For a detailed discussion of various approaches to computing markups, see A. D. H. Kaplan, Joel B. Dirlan, and Robert F. Lanzillotti, *Pricing in Big Business: A Case Approach* (Washington, D.C.: Brookings Institution, 1958).

using cost data in the pricing decision? Several reasons can be advanced in favor of computing target selling prices by means of the cost-plus approach, even if the resulting prices aren't actually used. First, in making pricing decisions, the manager is faced with a myriad of uncertainties. Cost-plus target prices represent a *starting point,* a way of perhaps removing some of the uncertainties and shedding some light on others. By this means, the manager may be able more easily to feel his way through the thicket, and come up with a price that will be acceptable given the constraints at hand.

Second, cost might be viewed as a floor of protection, guarding the price setter from pricing too low and incurring losses. Although this line of reasoning is appealing and reassuring, the protection offered by the cost floor is more illusionary than real. For one thing, we have already noted that neither the absorption nor the contribution costing approaches include all costs in the cost base. For another thing, unit cost depends on volume. This is because many costs are fixed, and unit cost will therefore depend on the number of units produced and sold. Even though selling prices may be set above total costs, losses may still be incurred if the volume of sales is less than estimated, thereby forcing per-unit costs upward to the point that they exceed the selling price.

Third, formula-based target selling prices may give the price setter some insights into competitors' costs, or help him to predict what a competitive price will be. For example, if a company is operating in an industry where 30 percent markups over cost to manufacture are common, then the company may be able to assume that this same pattern will hold for new products and thereby either predict competitors' prices or price in such a way as to gain quick acceptance of a new product line. On the other hand, by following standard markups over cost, a company may be able to largely *neutralize* the pricing issue, and concentrate on competing in other ways, such as in delivery or in credit terms.

Finally, many firms have such a wide range of products that they simply don't have time to do a detailed cost-volume-profit analysis on every item in every product line. Cost-plus pricing formulas provide a quick and direct way to at least a tentative price that can be further refined as time and circumstances permit.

PRICING NEW PRODUCTS

New products easily present the most challenging pricing problems, for the reason that the uncertainties involved are so great. If a new product is unlike anything presently on the market, then demand will be uncertain. If the new product is similar to existing products already being sold, uncertainty will exist as to the degree of substitution that will develop between the new product and the existing products. Uncertainty will also exist over ultimate marketing costs, etc. In order to reduce the level of these uncertainties, a firm will often resort to some type of experimental or test marketing.

Test Marketing of Products

Many firms have used test marketing with great success in order to gain data relative to the pricing decision. The approach is to introduce the new product in selected areas only, generally at different prices in different areas. By this means the company can gather data on the competition the product will encounter, on the relationship between volume and price, and on the contribution to profits that can be expected at various selling prices and volumes of sales. A price can then be selected that will result in the greatest overall contribution to profits, or that seems best in relation to the company's long-run objectives.

Of course, test marketing is not the same thing as the full-scale production and marketing of a product, but it can provide highly useful information that can help to insure that the full scale effort will be successful. An added benefit can be found in the fact that through test marketing it may be possible to contain any errors in pricing on a small scale, rather than nationwide.

Pricing Strategies

Two basic pricing strategies are available to the price setter in pricing new products. These pricing strategies are known as *skimming pricing* and *penetration pricing*.

Skimming pricing involves setting a high initial price for a new product, with a progressive lowering of the price as time passes and as the market broadens and matures. The purpose of skimming pricing is to maximize short-run profits. In effect, it represents a direct application of the economist's pricing models discussed earlier in the chapter.

Penetration pricing involves setting low initial prices in order to gain quick acceptance in a broad portion of the market. It calls for the sacrifice of some short-run profits in order to achieve a better long-run market position. Whether a firm adopts the skimming or the penetration strategy will depend on what it is trying to accomplish, and on which approach appears to offer the greatest chance for success.

For example, many new products have a certain novelty appeal that causes demand to be quite price inelastic. In these cases, high initial prices are often set and maintained until competitors develop competing products and begin price cutting. As sales volume becomes more sensitive to sales price, prices are slowly reduced until the point is reached where a penetration price is possible that permits access to a mass market. A good example of this type of skimming strategy can be found in the marketing of electronic calculators. Prices of hand-sized calculators started at about $300 in the early 1970s and dropped to less than $25 in about three years' time, finally permitting access to a market so wide that it included the purchasing of calculators for use in weekly grocery shopping. Television sets, stereo sets, automobiles, electronic ovens, and some drug products all went through a similar skimming pricing period before prices were eventually lowered to a mass market penetration level.

One strong argument in favor of skimming pricing is that it offers some protection against unexpected costs in production and marketing of a product. If a new product is priced on a penetration basis and costs are unexpectedly high, then the company may be forced later to raise prices—not an easy thing to do when you are trying to gain wide market acceptance of a new product. On the other hand, if a new product is priced initially on a skimming level, the company has a layer of protection that can be used to absorb any unexpected costs or cost increases. Even if this later causes price reductions to be less than expected, the company will still be in the more favorable position of reducing prices rather than raising them.

Skimming pricing is most effective in those markets where entry is relatively difficult, because of the technology or investment required. The more easy market entry becomes, the less the likelihood that skimming can be carried off very effectively, or at least for a very long period of time. For example, skimming pricing was possible for many years in the computer industry because of technological barriers to entry. By contrast, it is doubtful if skimming pricing was ever much of a factor in the marketing of household cleaning products.

Target Costs and Product Pricing

Our discussion thus far has presumed that a product has already been developed, has been costed, and is ready to be marketed as soon as a price is set. In many cases, the sequence of events is just the reverse. That is, the company will already *know* what price should be charged, and the problem will be to *develop* a product that can be marketed profitably at the desired price. Even in this situation, where the normal sequence of events is reversed, cost is still a crucial factor. The company's approach will be to set *target costs* that can be used as guides in developing a product that can be sold within the desired price range.

This approach is used widely in the household appliance industry, where a company will determine in advance the price range in which it wants a particular product model to sell, and will then set about to develop the model. Component parts will be designed, and then costed item by item to see if the total cost is compatible with the target cost already set. If not, the parts will be redesigned and recosted, and features will be changed or eliminated, until the expected costs fall within the desired targets. Prototypes will then be developed, and again costs will be carefully analyzed to be sure that the desired targets are being met. In these types of situations, the accountant can be of great help to management by continually pointing out the relationships between cost and volume, by segregating relevant costs where needed, and by assisting in the organization and interpretation of cost data.

SPECIAL PRICING DECISIONS

When faced with a pricing decision, which pricing method should the manager use—the absorption approach illustrated in Exhibit 13–4 or the contribution approach illustrated in Exhibit 13–6? If all pricing decisions related to the pricing of *standard* products, the answer would be that it really wouldn't matter which method was used. We have already seen that the same target selling price for a standard product can be obtained using either method. The choice would probably depend on which method was otherwise being used to cost units of product. If the absorption method was otherwise in use, then it would be simpler to go ahead and use it as a basis for pricing decisions as well; the opposite would be the case if contribution costing was otherwise in use.

But all pricing decisions don't relate to standard products, or even to new standard products which fall in the same general category. Many pricing decisions relate to special or unusual situations. For example, a company may get a large order for a standard product but be asked to quote a special, one-time only price. Or a special order may come in from a foreign customer who wants a special price on a standard item on a continuing basis because his order represents business that the company otherwise wouldn't have. A company may have substantial excess capacity and be faced with the problem of pricing special products that are not a part of the regular line, and which are being produced on a limited basis. Finally, a company may be in a competitive bidding situation and forced to bid on many unlike jobs, some of which will be on a more or less continuing basis and others be one-time-only affairs.

All of these situations present *special* pricing problems of one kind or another. Many managers feel that special pricing problems such as those above can be much more easily handled by the contribution approach to pricing than by the absorption approach. The reasons are twofold. First, advocates of the contribution approach argue that it provides the price setter with much more detailed information than the absoption approach, and that this information is structured in a way which parallels the way in which the price setter is used to thinking—in terms of cost-volume-profit relationships. And second, it is argued that the contribution approach provides the price setter with a flexible framework that is immediately adaptable to *any* pricing problem, without the necessity of a lot of supplementary analytical work.

Pricing a Special Order

In order to illustrate the adaptability of the contribution approach to special pricing situations, and to show how the data it presents guide the price setter in his decisions, let us assume the following price quotation sheets for the Helms Company:

Absorption Method		Contribution Method	
Direct materials	$ 6	Direct materials	$ 6
Direct labor	7	Direct labor	7
Overhead at 100% of direct labor	7	Variable overhead.	2
Total cost to manufacture	20	Variable selling and	
Markup—20%	4	administrative.	1
Target selling price	$24	Total variable expenses.	16
		Markup—50%	8
		Target selling price	$24

These price quotation sheets relate to a vacuum pump which the Helms Company manufactures and markets through jobbers. The company has never been able to sell all that it can produce, and for this reason is constantly on the lookout for new business. Let us assume that the Helms Company has just been approached by a foreign distributor who wants to purchase 10,000 pumps at a price of $19 per pump. Should the company accept the offer?

The Absorption Method. The price quotation sheet prepared above by the absorption method is of little help in making the decision. If the Helms Company tries to relate the $20 "cost to manufacture" to the proposed price of $19, then the offer is clearly unattractive:

Sales (10,000 units @ $19)	$190,000
Absorption cost to manufacture (10,000 units @ $20).	200,000
Net loss from the order.	($ 10,000)

On the other hand, since there is excess capacity in the plant, management may be tempted to accept the offer. The dilemma is that no one really *knows* from looking at the price quotation sheet which course of action is best. The pricing system doesn't provide the essential keys that are needed to move in an intelligent way. As a result, whatever decision is made will be made either on a "seat of the pants" basis, or only after much effort has been expended in trying to dig into the cost records for additional information.

The Contribution Method. By contrast, the price quotation sheet prepared by the contribution method provides the company with exactly the framework that it needs in making the decision. Since this price quotation sheet is organized by cost behavior, it dovetails precisely with cost-volume-profit concepts, and guides the decision maker in his decisions without the necessity of doing all kinds of added digging and analytical work in the cost records.

Consider the Helms Company data. Since the company has idle capacity (for which there apparently is no other use), fixed overhead costs are irrelevant in the decision over whether to accept the foreign distributor's offer. Any amount received over unit variable costs (and any *incremental* fixed costs) will increase overall profitability; therefore, rather than relating the proposed purchase price to the $20 "cost to manufacture," the company should relate it to the unit variable costs involved. This is easy to do if the regular price quotation sheet on a product is organized by cost behavior, such as shown above under the contribution method. In the case of the Helms Company, the unit variable costs are $16. Assuming that the unit variable costs associated with the special order will be the same as those associated with regular business, the analysis would be:

Sales (10,000 units @ $19)................................	$190,000
Variable expenses (10,000 units @ $16)....................	160,000
Contribution margin promised by the order (and also increased net income, if fixed costs don't change).................	$ 30,000

In sum, by using the price quotation sheet prepared by the contribution method the Helms Company will be able to see a clearcut short-run advantage to accepting the foreign distributor's offer. Before any final decision can be made, however, the Helms Company will have to weigh long-run considerations very carefully, particularly the impact which accepting this offer might have on future efforts to secure a position in foreign markets. Accepting the $19 price might seriously undermine future negotiations with foreign dealers, and cause disruptions in the long-run profitability of the firm. The Helms Company may feel that it is better to forego the short-run $30,000 increase in contribution margin in order to protect its future long-run market position.

The essential point of our discussion is that the contribution approach to pricing contains a readymade framework within which the price setter can operate in special pricing situations. By organizing costs in a way that is compatible with cost-volume-profit concepts, this approach to structuring price quotation sheets assists the manager in isolating those costs that are relevant in special pricing decisions, and guides him in those decisions from a cost point of view.

The Variable Pricing Model

The contribution approach to pricing can be presented in general model form, as shown in Exhibit 13–8.

EXHIBIT 13–8
The Contribution Approach to Pricing: A General Model

Variable costs (detailed)	XXXX	(Floor)
Fixed costs.	XXXX	Range of
Desired profit	XXXX	Flexibility
Target selling price	XXXX	(Ceiling)

The contribution approach provides a ceiling and a floor between which the price setter operates. The ceiling represents the price that the manager would *like* to obtain, and indeed *must* obtain on the bulk of his sales over the long run. But under certain conditions, the model shows that the manager can move within the *range of flexibility* as far down as the floor of variable costs in quoting a price to a prospective customer. What are the conditions under which a price based on variable costs alone might be appropriate? We can note three:

1. When idle capacity exists, such as in the case of the Helms Company.
2. When operating under distress conditions.
3. When faced with sharp competition on particular orders, under a competitive bidding situation.

When any of these conditions exist, it may be possible to increase overall profitability by pricing *some* jobs, products, or orders at *any amount* above variable costs, even if this amount is substantially less than the normal markup.

We will now examine each of the three special conditions listed above more closely, to see how each relates to the range of flexibility depicted in Exhibit 13–8.

Idle Capacity. There is no need to be concerned about the range of flexibility depicted in Exhibit 13–8 so long as a company can sell all that it can produce at regular prices. That is, no company is going to sell at less than regular prices if regular prices are obtainable.

However, a different situation exists if a company has idle capacity, and that idle capacity can't be used to expand regular sales at regular prices. Under these conditions, any use to which the idle capacity can be put that increases revenues more than variable costs (and any *incremental* fixed costs) will increase overall net income.

The use might come in the form of a special order for a regular product from a customer or source that the company normally does not supply (such as a foreign market). Or the use might come in the form of an order for a special product that the company normally does not produce. Or the use might come in the form of a modification of a regular product to meet a new customer's specifications, or to be sold under the customer's own brand name. In any of these situations, so long as the price received on the extra business exceeds the variable costs (and any *incremental* fixed costs) involved, overall net income will be increased by utilizing the idle capacity.

The Helms Company used earlier is a good example of the sort of situation we are talking about. The company has excess capacity, and there is no prospect of using the excess capacity for regular business. Under these conditions, nothing will be lost by quoting a price to the foreign distributor that is below full cost, or even relaxing the price down very close to the floor of variable costs, if necessary.

Distress Conditions. Occasionally a company is forced to operate under distress conditions, when the market for its product has been adversely affected in some way. For example, demand may virtually dry up overnight, forcing the company to drop its prices sharply downward. Under these conditions, any contribution which can be obtained above variable costs that will be available to help cover fixed costs may be preferable to ceasing operations altogether. If operations cease, then *no* contribution will be available to apply toward fixed costs.

Competitive Bidding. The pricing model illustrated in Exhibit 13–8 is particularly useful in competitive bidding situations. Competition is often hot and fierce in situations where bidding is involved, so companies can't afford to be inflexible in their pricing. Unfortunately, many companies in competitive bidding situations refuse to cut prices in the face of stiff competition, adamantly stating that they price only on a "full cost" basis and don't want the business unless they can get a "decent" price for the work. There are several problems associated with taking this kind of a position on pricing. First, it involves circular reasoning. The so-called decent price is obtained by tacking some markup onto "full cost." But cost is dependent on *volume* of sales, which in turn is dependent on selling price.

Second, as discussed in Chapter 11, there are *two* determinants of profitability—margin and turnover. The "decent" price attitude ignores the turnover factor and focuses entirely on the margin factor. Yet many companies have demonstrated that a more modest margin combined with a faster turnover of assets can be highly effective from a profitability point of view. One way to increase turnover, of course, is to be flexible in bidding, by shading prices in those situations where competition is keen.

Finally, in those situations where fixed costs are high, a company can't *afford* to be inflexible in its pricing policies. Once an investment in plant and other fixed productive facilities has been made, a company's strategy must be to generate every dollar of contribution that it can to assist in the covering of these costs. Even if a company is forced to operate at an accounting loss, this might be preferable to having no contribution at all toward recovery of investment.

CRITICISMS OF THE CONTRIBUTION APPROACH TO PRICING

The major criticism leveled against the contribution approach to pricing is that it leads to suicidal underpricing and to eventual bankruptcy. It is argued that since the aborption approach to pricing includes an element of fixed overhead in the base on which prices are computed, it is superior to the contribution approach, which looks only at variable costs as a base. Including the fixed overhead element in the base under absorption costing is said to make it safer in terms of long-run pricing. Some feel that if variable costs alone are used in the pricing base, the manager may be misled into accepting *any* price over variable costs on a long-run basis for any product.

There are a number of weaknesses to this argument. We should note first that the absorption approach to pricing excludes just as many costs from the pricing base as does the contribution approach. It just excludes *different* costs. For example, the absorption approach doesn't consider selling and administrative costs at all in its base, since the base typically is made up entirely of "costs to manufacture." By contrast, the contribution approach does include variable selling and administrative expenses along with variable production expenses in developing a base for pricing.

Whether or not *any* pricing mechanism results in intelligent pricing decisions will depend in large part on the ability of the price setter to use the data before him. As a practical matter, this means that pricing decisions must be restricted to managers who are qualified to make them. This point has been made very well in an N.A.A. study of actual pricing practices:

> No instance of unprofitable pricing attributable to direct costing was reported, but on the contrary, opinion was frequently expressed to the effect that direct costing had contributed to better pricing decisions. However, companies restrict product cost and margin data to individuals qualified to interpret such data and responsible for pricing policy decisions.[3]

---

[3] Research Report #37, *Current Applications of Direct Costing*, (New York: National Association of Accountants, January 1961), p. 55.

On the other hand, no matter how expert a decision maker may be, his decisions will be faulty if the cost information with which he is working is irrelevant, unclear, or inadequate. Firms that have adopted the contribution approach to pricing have found that the old pricing system often led to incorrect pricing decisions because of faulty data:

> Instances were cited in which management had unknowingly continued selling products below out-of-pocket cost or had decided to withdraw from the market when a substantial portion of the period costs could have been recovered. . . .

> In one interview . . . when direct costing was introduced, analysis demonstrated that contracts which would have contributed to period costs had often been refused at times when the company had a large amount of idle capacity.[4]

THE ROBINSON-PATMAN ACT

In structuring a pricing policy firms must take care to keep their actions within the requirements of the Robinson-Patman Act. The act forbids quoting different prices to competing customers unless the difference in price can be traced directly to ". . . differences in the cost of manufacture, sale, or delivery resulting from the differing methods or quantities in which commodities are to such purchasers sold or delivered." Both the Federal Trade Commission and the courts have consistently held that "cost" is to be interpreted as full cost, and not just incremental or variable costs. This means that in the case of *competing* customers for the *same* goods, price differences cannot be defended on the basis of covering incremental costs alone. Note, though, that we are talking about *competing* customers for the *same* goods. We are not talking about a competitive bidding situation, nor are we talking about a situation in which idle capacity might be used to produce for a noncompeting market, or for some purpose other than production of regular products.

Many states prohibit the sale of goods or services below "cost." Cost is normally either specified as full cost, or so interpreted by the regulating agencies. These regulations all suggest that firms should keep careful records of their costs and of the way their prices are structured in order to be able to answer questions of regulatory bodies.

SUMMARY

The general pricing models of the economist contain the basic framework for pricing decisions. Since these models are conceptual in nature,

---

[4] Ibid.

and since the specific information required for their direct application rarely is available, firms normally rely on pricing formulas to implement the ideas the models contain. Pricing decisions can be divided into three broad groups:

1. Pricing standard products.
2. Pricing new products.
3. Pricing special orders.

Pricing of standard and new products is generally carried out through cost-plus pricing formulas. Such formulas require a cost base, to which a markup is added to derive a target selling price. Cost-plus pricing can be carried out equally well using either the absorption or contribution approaches.

Pricing of special orders is somewhat different, in that in some situations full costs may not be applicable in setting prices. Circumstances may exist in which the price setter may be justified in pricing simply on a basis of variable or incremental costs. In these special pricing situations, price setters often find the contribution approach, with its emphasis on cost behavior, more useful than the absorption approach, which may require considerable reworking of data in order to generate the information needed for a pricing decision.

QUESTIONS

13–1. Why does the economist depict a slowing down of the rate of increase in total revenue as more and more units are sold?

13–2. What is the optimum point of production and what is the optimum price to be charged for a product, as depicted by the total revenue and total cost curves?

13–3. According to the marginal revenue and marginal cost curves, what is the optimum point of production and what is the optimum price to charge for a product?

13–4. What is meant by price elasticity? Contrast a product that is price inelastic to a product that is price elastic.

13–5. Identify four limitations to the economic pricing models.

13–6. What costs are relevant in long-run pricing decisions?

13–7. What is meant by the term "cost-plus" pricing? Distinguish between the absorption and contribution approaches to cost-plus pricing.

13–8. In what sense is the term "cost-plus" pricing a misnomer?

13–9. "Full cost can be viewed as a floor of protection. If a firm always sets its prices above full cost, it will never have to worry about operating at a loss." Discuss.

13–10. Distinguish between skimming pricing and penetration pricing. Which strategy would you probably use if you were introducing a new product that was highly price inelastic? Why?

13–11. What are "target costs," and how do they enter into the pricing decision?

13–12. What problem is sometimes encountered under absorption costing in trying to price special orders?

13–13. Identify those circumstances under which the manager might be justified in pricing at any amount above variable costs.

13–14. Why will net income be maximized (or net loss minimized) when the contribution margin is maximized?

13–15. In what way does the Robinson-Patman Act influence pricing decisions?

EXERCISES

13–1. Cost data relating to a product produced by the Fraser Company are presented below:

	Per Unit	Total
Direct materials	$4	
Direct labor	8	
Variable overhead.	3	
Fixed overhead	5	$25,000
Variable selling and administrative expense	1	
Fixed selling and administrative expense.	2	10,000

The costs above are based on an anticipated volume of 5,000 units produced and sold. The company has a policy of adding a markup of 20 percent of cost to manufacture to obtain target selling prices, or adding a markup of 50 percent of variable costs.

Required:

1. Compute the target selling price under the absorption approach.
2. Compute the target selling price under the contribution approach.

13–2. Barker Company is considering the introduction of a new product. The company has gathered the following information:

Number of units to be produced each year	20,000
Unit cost to manufacture . . . . $	15
Projected annual selling and administrative expenses	50,000
Estimated investment required by the company.	800,000
Desired rate of return on investment	20%

The company uses cost-plus pricing.

Required:

1. Compute the required markup in percentage terms.
2. Compute the target selling price per unit.

13–3. Delsey Company has a capacity of 150,000 motors per year. The company is presently producing and selling 130,000 motors per year at a selling price of $40 per motor. The cost of producing one motor at the 130,000-unit level of activity is given below:

Per Motor

Direct materials	$16
Direct labor	8
Overhead	10
Total cost	$34

The company has a special order for 10,000 motors at a price of $33 each. Selling and administrative costs on the special order would be $2 per motor. The company's fixed overhead costs total $780,000 per year. The company has rejected the order, based on the following computations:

Selling price per motor		$33
Less costs per motor:		
Production cost (above)	$34	
Selling and administrative cost	2	36
Loss per motor		($ 3)

Required:

Should the company have accepted the order? Show computations.

13–4. Advance Technology, Inc., is anxious to enter the electronic calculator market. The company feels that in order to be competitive, the electronic calculator which it produces and sells must not be priced at more than $80. The company wants a 20 percent rate of return on invesment.

In order to produce 10,000 calculators a year, an investment of $800,000 would be required. Selling and administrative expenses would total $140,000 per year.

Required:

Compute the target cost to manufacture one calculator.

13–5. *a.* The way to maximize net income (or minimize a loss) is to maximize the contribution margin. Why is this true?

b. Demonstrate the points you made in part (*a*) above, by using the following information: A company is now selling 10,000 units of product per period at a selling price of $10 per unit. The variable cost per unit is $4, and total fixed costs are $56,000. The company has a special order for 1,000 units at a price of $8 per unit. Prepare income statements with and without the special order.

13–6. To a large extent, the selling price which must be obtained on a product will be dependent on the volume of units that can be sold. Consider the following data on a new product:

Variable production cost per unit	$ 5
Variable selling and administrative expenses per unit	3
Fixed production cost (total)	120,000
Fixed selling and administrative expenses (total)	200,000
Desired markup	80%

The company uses absorption costing for product costing and for pricing.

Required:

1. What would be the target selling price per unit if the company can produce and sell (*a*) 30,000 units each period, (*b*) 60,000 units each period?
2. If the company charges the prices that you computed in part 1 above, will it be assured that no losses will be sustained? Explain.

13-7. The market research division of Ekkof Company has stated that the company's new deluxe product line would be best received on the market at a selling price of $58 per unit. At this price, the market research division projects that 20,000 units could be sold. Costs associated with the new product line are:

Direct materials	$	12
Direct labor		10
Variable overhead.		4
Variable selling and administrative expenses.		3
Fixed overhead (total)		200,000
Fixed selling and administrative expenses (total)		150,000
Desired markup (absorption basis)		75%

Required:

1. Based on the data given above, is $58 per unit an acceptable selling price to Ekkof Company? Show computations.
2. What percentage markup does the $58 per unit selling price represent?

PROBLEMS

13-1. *Target Selling Price and Rate of Return.* The Mickle Company is contemplating entry into a new market in which markups run 80 percent of variable cost. Costs and other information associated with the new product are given below:

Projected annual sales in units.		30,000
Projected variable costs per unit:		
Production	$	12
Selling and administrative		3
Projected fixed costs in total:		
Production		90,000
Selling and administrative		180,000
Projected investment required.		500,000

Required:

1. Compute the target selling price, using the contribution approach.
2. Assume that the Mickel Company will not add a new product line unless it promises a return on invesment of at least 20 percent. On this basis, should the new product line be accepted? Show computations.

13–2. *Percentage Markups and Price Quote Sheets.* Aspen Company produces and markets a number of consumer products, including a toaster. Cost and revenue data on the toaster for 19X5, the most recent year, are given below:

	10,000 Units Sold	
	Total	Per Unit
Sales	$300,000	$30
Cost of goods sold	180,000	18
Gross margin	120,000	12
Selling and administrative expenses.	70,000	7
Net income	$ 50,000	$ 5

Fixed costs comprise $80,000 of cost of goods sold, and $50,000 of the selling and administrative expenses are fixed.

Required:

1. Compute the percentage markup based on the (*a*) absorption approach, and (*b*) the contribution approach.
2. Prepare a model price quotation sheet that could be used by the Aspen Company in judging the acceptability of special orders on toasters at reduced prices. Use the cost data above in your model quotation sheet.

13–3. *Pricing Strategy.* Seals, Sawbuck and Co. is trying to determine the proper pricing strategy to use on its new line of electronic ovens. The company purchases the ovens from a manufacturer according to the following price schedule:

Units Purchased	Unit Cost
Up to 20,000	$200
Over 20,000	180

The ovens are sold to retail consumers through retail outlets located in the western part of the country. Management has been presented with the following two marketing and pricing alternatives:

Alternative #1. Set the regular selling price at $240 per oven. At this price the company estimates that 20,000 ovens can be sold each year. All ovens would be sold at the regular price.

Alternative #2. Set the regular selling price at $240 per oven, but offer periodic "specials" at a price 10 percent off the regular price. The company estimates that 10,000 ovens could be sold at the special price, but that 30 percent of these sales would represent ovens that otherwise would have been sold at the regular price.

Other costs associated with the ovens are:

Sales commission per oven.	$	12
Shipping cost per oven		5
Fixed costs (in total):		
Regular advertising		90,000
Advertising of "specials".		15,000
Allocated general overhead		150,000

Required:

1. Which alternative should the company accept? Show all computations in good form.
2. If the company accepts Alternative #2, what will be the net profit or loss realized from the periodic specials? Show computations.

13–4. *Target Costs and Percentage Markups.* Auto Supply, Inc., is a producer and distributor of auto accessories. The company is anxious to enter the rapidly growing market for long-life batteries. The company feels that to be fully competitive, the battery which it produces and markets cannot be priced at more than $40. At this price, the company is certain that it can capture 5 percent of the present 2,000,000 battery sales made annually in its area.

A study has indicated that the following costs and other data would be associated with the new battery line:

Permanent investment required	$1,200,000
Annual marketing costs:	
Advertising	140,000
Commissions and other ($1.80 per battery).	180,000
Annual administrative costs (salaries).	40,000
Required rate of return on investment	20%

Required:

1. What is the target cost to manufacture one battery?
2. Assume that the target cost to manufacture one battery which you computed above consists of 70 percent variable manufacturing cost and 30 percent fixed manufacturing cost. What percentage markup does the $40 selling price represent under (a) the absorption approach to cost-plus pricing, and (b) the contribution approach?

13–5. *Target Costs and Pricing.* Arborland Vineyards is in the process of developing a new wine. After considerable study, the following target costs have been set for a case of the new wine (based on 10,000 cases):

	Target Costs per Case
Direct materials	$18
Direct labor	5
Variable overhead.	3
Fixed overhead–direct	5
Variable selling	2
Fixed selling	5
Fixed administrative	2
Total target costs.	$40

Arborland Vineyards estimates that adding the new wine will require the following permanent investment of funds:

For working capital. $225,000
For equipment 100,000
Total investment $325,000

The company uses cost-plus pricing. It has been determined that a competitive selling price cannot exceed $45 per case.

Required:

1. *a.* Assume that the company will not produce a new wine unless it provides at least a 40 percent markup, computed by the absorption approach. Under these conditions, are the target costs above acceptable?

   b. How low can the selling price be set and still provide the desired markup?

2. *a.* Redo part 1(*a*) under the assumption that the new wine must provide at least an 80 percent markup, computed by the contribution approach. Under these conditions, are the target costs acceptable?

   b. By how much will the variable costs have to be reduced in order to have a markup of 80 percent, and sell at the competitive $45 price?

3. Refer to the original data. Assume that Arborland Vineyards will not introduce a new wine unless it promises a rate of return on investment of at least 20 percent. If the new wine is produced, the company is certain that 10,000 cases can be sold each year. At what price per case would the new wine have to be sold to provide the desired rate of return on investment?

4. What reductions in target costs would have to be made in order to sell the wine at a competitive $45 per case price, and still realize a 20 percent return on investment?

13–6. *Evaluating a Special Order.* Matheson Motors, a medium-sized producer of electric motors, is located in Pennsylvania. The company distributes its motors in the east coast area. One of the company's most popular motors is the ES2A. A new plant, with an annual capacity of 500,000 motors, has just been constructed to produce the ES2A line. The company is producing and selling 300,000 ES2A motors each year, at the following cost per motor:

	Per ES2A Motor
Direct materials	$20
Direct labor	14
Manufacturing overhead (60% fixed, based on 300,000 motors produced)	10
Shipping expense	2
Sales commission	1
Total.	$47

Other costs associated with the ES2A line are (fixed per year):

Selling $200,000
Administration   100,000
Total fixed costs $300,000

The ES2A motors are sold to east coast distributors for $50 each. The president of Matheson Motors is very anxious to expand sales of the ES2A line. He has just received an offer from a west coast distributor to purchase 100,000 motors per year at a price of $43 per motor. Although there would be no sales commission on this order, the shipping expense per motor would increase by 50 percent. Fixed selling costs would increase by 25 percent.

Required:

1. If the president of Matheson Motors accepts this special price offer, does it appear that he would be in violation of the Robinson-Patman Act?
2. On the basis of the cost data given, would you recommend that the offer be accepted or rejected? Show all computations.
3. What noncost matters should be considered before the offer is accepted or rejected?

13–7. *Distress Pricing.* The Ragged Mountain Mining Company purchased a mine for $1,000,000 in 19X1. The company then expended another $500,000 installing railroad tracks into the mine, setting up supporting beams, and purchasing equipment to process the ore coming out of the mine. The tracks, beams, and equipment were given a ten-year life. It was estimated that the mine contained 1,000,000 tons of ore. Active mining was started in 19X2, and continued through 19X5, with the following average yearly results:

Number of tons of ore mined per year 100,000
Mining costs per ton (exclusive of depletion
and depreciation) $4
Selling price per ton   7

In early 19X6, a competing company discovered massive deposits of the ore just a few miles from the Ragged Mountain Mining Company's mine. The result was that the market became flooded with ore, and the selling price dropped to $5 per ton. The president of the Ragged Mountain Mining Company made a few quick computations, and declared, "We'll have to close the mine. If we keep it open we'll lose $.50 a ton for every ton of ore we mine and sell. At a $5.00 selling price it will be less costly to just close the doors and walk away from the place."

Required:

1. How did the president compute the $.50 per ton loss?
2. Do you agree with the president's decision? Explain.

13–8. *Distress Pricing.* The Marks Toy Company produces and distributes a broad line of games and toys. The company has always used cost-plus pricing, computed by the absorption approach.

In 19X2, hula hoops became very popular with the 8-to-15-year-old set. In order to supply what appeared to be a large and quite permanent demand for a new toy, the company acquired new equipment in 19X2 at a cost of $600,000. The equipment was estimated to be capable of producing 3,000,000 hula hoops before it would have to be replaced. In 19X3, production began. The hula hoops were priced as follows (per unit):

Direct materials	$.10
Direct labor	.05
Overhead (⅓ variable)	.30
Cost to manufacture	.45
Desired markup (60%)	.27
Target selling price	$.72

The selling and administrative expenses were:

Salaries and other fixed expenses (annual)	$15,000
Shipping cost per hula hoop	5¢

In 19X3 and 19X4, the company produced and sold 300,000 hula hoops each year. In 19X5, it suddenly became apparent that hula hoops were more of a fad than a permanent market. Almost overnight, the selling price dropped to $.40 per hula hoop.

The marketing manager has recommended that the company drop the hula hoop line and scrap the special equipment. "It would be insane to continue producing," he reasoned, "At our present level of activity and at a $.40 selling price we would lose $.15 on every unit we sold."

Required:

1. How did the marketing manager compute the $.15 per-unit loss?
2. Do you agree with his recommendation? Explain.
3. Assume that the company has 50,000 hula hoops in the warehouse unsold, and that no more hula hoops will be produced. What is the minimum selling price that the company could accept?

13–9. *Pricing and Joint Product Decisions.* The JES Company has a plant that can either mill wheat into a cracked wheat cereal, or further mill the cracked wheat into flour. The company can sell all the cracked wheat cereal that it can produce at a selling price of $240 per ton. In the past, the company has sold only part of its cracked wheat as cereal, and has retained the rest for further milling into the flour product. The flour has been selling for $295 per ton, but recently the price has become unstable and has dropped to $265 per ton.

Because of this price drop, the sales manager feels that the company should discontinue the milling of flour, and concentrate its entire milling capacity on the milling of cracked wheat to sell as cereal. (The same milling equipment is used for both products.) His feeling is based on the following analysis:

	Cracked Wheat Cost per Ton		Flour Cost per Ton
Raw materials	$200	Cost of cracked wheat used	
Direct labor	12	in milling of flour.	$230
Overhead.	18	Added milling costs:	
Total cost per ton	$230	Added materials.	10
		Added labor.	12
		Overhead.	18
		Total cost per ton	$270

	Cracked Wheat	Flour
Selling price per ton	$240	$265
Cost per ton (above)	230	270
Net profit (loss) per ton	$ 10	($ 5)

The sales manager argues that since the present $265 per ton price for the flour results in a $5 per ton loss, milling of flour should be discontinued, and should not be resumed until the price per ton rises above $270.

The company assigns overhead to the two products on the basis of direct labor hours. Since the same amount of time is required to mill either a ton of cracked wheat or a ton of flour, this overhead charge is the same for either product. Because of the nature of the plant, virtually all overhead costs are fixed. Materials and labor costs are variable.

Required:

1. Do you agree with the sales manager that the company should discontinue milling flour, and use the entire milling capacity to mill cracked wheat if the price of flour remains at $265 per ton? Support your answer with appropriate comments and computations.
2. What is the lowest price that the company should accept for a ton of flour? Again support your answer with appropriate comments and computations.

13–10. *Pricing a Special Order.* The Bestline Furniture Company has been operating at a loss of about $300,000 per year. Last year's income statement is typical:

Sales	$12,500,000
Cost of goods sold	6,000,000
Gross margin	6,500,000
Operating expenses	6,800,000
Net loss	$(300,000)

The company's factory has a capacity of 100,000 machine hours per year, but is being operated at a level of only 60,000 machine hours. The company's fixed overhead costs total $840,000 per year. These costs are allocated to production on a basis of machine hours.

Bestline has received an order from a large TV manufacturer for 10,000 TV cabinets per year. Although Bestline doesn't normally produce TV cabinets, it is considering the offer, since the company is anxious to increase the utilization of its plant. Bestline has determined the following information relating to the order:
1. It will require two machine hours to produce one TV cabinet.
2. Direct materials and direct labor per TV cabinet will total $70 and $20, respectively.
3. Total fixed overhead will not change.
4. Selling expenses will total $9 per cabinet.
5. The TV manufacturer's offer is for a selling price of $125 per cabinet.
6. Administrative expenses will increase by $10,000 per year.

The company has decided to reject the order, based on the following computation:

	Per TV Cabinet	Total
Sales (10,000 cabinets)	$ 125	$1,250,000
Cost of goods sold	115	1,150,000
Gross margin	10	100,000
Operating expenses:		
Selling	9	90,000
Administrative	1	10,000
Total	10	100,000
Net income from the order	$–0–	$ –0–

The company has no alternative uses for its idle capacity.

Required:
1. Show the probable cost breakdown of the $115 cost of goods sold figure.
2. Based on the cost data, do you agree with the decision to reject the order? Show computations.

3. What is the lowest selling price that Bestline can accept per TV cabinet if it wants to eliminate the present net loss in the company as a whole?

13–11. *Pricing a Bid.* Archer instruments produces thermostats for industrial use. The company prices its thermostats at 175 percent of the variable costs required to produce and sell them. This pricing policy has worked very well over the years.

Archer instruments has received an invitation to bid on a government order for 1,000 specially designed thermostats. The company has made the following cost estimates:

Direct materials	$ 70,000
Direct labor	50,000
Variable overhead	10,000
Allocated fixed overhead	20,000
Tools, dies, and other special production costs	30,000
Shipping costs.	5,000
Special administrative costs	5,000
Total costs	$190,000
Cost per thermostat ($190,000 ÷ 1,000)	$190

Archer Instruments is now operating at capacity. If the company takes on the government order, it will have to forego regular sales of $210,000.

Required:

What is the lowest price that Archer Instruments can bid on the government order, without sacrificing current profits?

13–12. *Competitive Bidding.* The Tolby Machine Company designs and produces machine tools to customer specifications. The bulk of the company's business is obtained by competitive bidding. In the latter part of 19X5, the company was invited (along with several other companies) to bid on an order of 50 specially designed jigs needed by a manufacturing firm.

The Tolby Machine Company was very happy to receive the invitation to bid, since business had been very slow for over a year with no prospects for the situation improving. The company estimated the following costs relating to the 50 jigs:

	Total	*Per Jig*
Direct material	$ 50,000	$1,000
Direct labor	40,000	800
Variable overhead	10,000	200
Fixed overhead*	50,000	1,000
Design and cost study	5,000	100
Shipping	7,500	150
Total cost	$162,500	$3,250

* Allocated on a basis of machine hours.

Based on these data, the company has submitted a bid of $3,900 per jig. The price quotation sheet used to compute the bid is shown below:

Direct materials	$1,000
Direct labor	800
Manufacturing overhead	1,200
Total cost to manufacture	3,000
Markup desired—30%	900
Bid price per jig	$3,900

The manufacturer receiving the bid has replied that the bid is too high, and that no bid over $3,300 per jig will be considered. Upon hearing this, the president of the Tolby Machine Company stated, "That lets us out. Our cost is $3,250 per jig. At a bid price of $3,300 the profit we'd make wouldn't be worth the effort."

Required:

What would you advise the Tolby Machine Company to do? Show computations in good form.

chapter 14

Capital Budgeting Decisions

THE TERM capital budgeting is used to describe those actions relating to the planning and financing of capital outlays. Capital budgeting decisions are a key factor in the long-run profitability of a firm. There are at least two reasons why this is true. First, funds available for investment are usually limited, but investment opportunities may be almost limitless. Therefore, the manager must somehow spread his limited investment funds among many competing opportunities, and do so in a way that will provide the greatest possible return to his firm. And second, most investment opportunities are long-term in nature. Once a firm has made a decision to invest in a particular project, it may become locked into that decision for many years into the future even if it later turns out to be less profitable than another would have been.

Because of these factors, capital budgeting decisions are made only after a *thorough evaluation* of the relative merits of every known alternative. We are concerned in this chapter with gaining an understanding of the methods used by managers in making these evaluations.

CAPITAL BUDGETING—AN INVESTMENT CONCEPT

Capital budgeting is an *investment* concept, since it involves a commitment of funds now in order to receive some desired return in the future. When speaking of investments, one is inclined to think of a commitment of funds into corporate stocks and bonds. This is just one type of investment, however. The commitment of funds by a business into inventory, equipment, etc., is *also* an investment in that the commitment is made with the expectation of receiving some return in the future from the funds committed.

Typical Capital Budgeting Decisions

What types of business decisions require capital budgeting analysis? Virtually any decision that involves an outlay now in order to obtain some return (increase in revenue or reduction in costs) in the future. Typical capital budgeting decisions encountered by the businessman are:

1. Cost reduction decisions. Should new equipment be purchased in order to reduce costs?
2. Plant expansion decisions. Should a new plant, warehouse, etc., be acquired in order to increase capacity and sales?
3. Equipment selection decisions. Would machine A, machine B, or machine C do the job best?
4. Lease or buy decisions. Should new plant facilities be leased or purchased?
5. Equipment replacement decisions. Should old equipment be replaced now or later?

Capital budgeting decisions tend to fall into two broad categories— screening decisions and preference decisions. Screening decisions are those relating to whether a proposed project meets some preset standard of acceptance. For example, a firm may have a policy of accepting cost reduction projects only if they promise a return of, say, 20 percent before taxes.

Preference decisions, by contrast, relate to selecting from among several *competing* courses of action. To illustrate, a firm may be considering five different machines to replace an existing machine on the assembly line. The choice as to which of the five machines to purchase is a *preference* decision.

In this chapter, we discuss ways of approaching screening decisions. The matter of preference decisions is reserved until the following chapter.

Characteristics of Business Investments

Some business investments are such that the original sum invested in a project is still existing at the time the project terminates. As an example, if a firm purchases land for $5,000, and rents it out at $750 a year for ten years, at the end of the ten-year term the land will still be intact, and should be salable for at least its purchase price. The computation of the rate of return on such an investment is fairly simple. Since the original investment itself will still be intact at the end of the ten-year period, each year's inflow of $750 is a return on the original $5,000 investment. The rate of return is therefore a straight 15% ($750 ÷ $5,000).

The Problem of Depreciable Assets. A far more common kind of business investment is one that involves *depreciable* assets. An important characteristic of depreciable assets is that they generally have little or no resale value at the end of their useful lives. Thus, any returns provided by such assets must be sufficient to do two things:

1. Provide a return on the original investment.
2. Return the total amount of the *original investment* itself.

To illustrate, assume that the $5,000 investment in the preceding section was made in factory equipment rather than in land. Also assume that the equipment will reduce the firm's operating costs by $750 each year for 10 years. Is the return on the equipment a straight 15 percent, the same as it was on the land? The answer is no. The return being promised by the equipment is much less than the return being promised by the land. The reason is that part of the yearly $750 inflow from the equipment must go to recoup the original $5,000 investment itself, since the equipment will be worthless at the end of its ten-year life. Only what remains after recovery of this investment can be viewed as a return *on* the investment over the ten-year period.

The Time Value of Money. Another characteristic of business investments is that the returns which they promise are likely to extend over fairly long spans of time. Therefore, in approaching capital budgeting decisions it is necessary to employ techniques that recognize the time value of money. Any businessman would prefer to receive a dollar today than a year from now. The same concept applies in choosing between investment projects. Those that promise returns earlier in time are preferable over those that promise returns later in time.

The capital budgeting techniques that recognize these characteristics most fully are those involving *discounted cash flows.* We shall spend the remainder of this chapter illustrating the use of discounted cash flow methods of making capital budgeting decisions. Before discussing these methods, however, it will be helpful to consider the concept of *present value,* and the techniques involved in *discounting.*

THE CONCEPT OF PRESENT VALUE

The point was made above that a businessman would prefer to receive a dollar today than a year from now. There are two reasons why this is true. First, a dollar received today is more valuable than a dollar received a year from now. The dollar received today can be invested immediately, and by the end of a year will have earned some return, making the total amount in hand at the end of the year *greater* than the investment started with. The person receiving his dollar a year from now will simply have a dollar in hand.

Second, the future involves uncertainty. The longer a person has to wait to receive a dollar, the more uncertain it becomes that he will ever get the dollar that he seeks. As time passes, conditions change. The changes may be such as to make future payment of the dollar impossible.

Since money has a time value, the manager needs a method of determining whether a cash outlay made now in an investment project can be justified in terms of expected receipts from the project in future years. That is, he must have a means of expressing future receipts in present dollar terms, so that the future receipts can be compared *on an equivalent basis* with whatever investment is required in the project under consideration. The theory of interest provides the manager with the means of making such a comparison.

The Theory of Interest

If a bank pays $105 one year from now in return for a deposit of $100 now, we would say that the bank is paying interest at an annual rate of 5 percent. The relationships involved in this notion can be expressed in mathematical terms by means of the following equation:

$$F_1 = P(1 + r) \tag{1}$$

where F_1 = the amount to be received in one year, P = the present outlay to be made, and r = the rate of interest involved.

If the present outlay is $100 deposited in a bank savings account that is to earn interest at 5 percent, then $P = \$100$ and $r = .05$. Under these conditions, $F_1 = \$105$, the amount to be received in one year.

The $100 present outlay can be called the *present value* of the $105 amount to be received in one year. It is also known as the *discounted value* of the future $105 receipt. The $100 figure represents the value in present terms of a receipt of $105 to be received a year from now, by an investor who requires a return of 5 percent on his money.

Compounding of Interest. What if the investor wants to leave his money in the bank for a second year? In that case, by the end of the second year the original $100 deposit will have grown to $110.25:

Original deposit	$100.00
Interest for the first year:	
$100.00 × .05	5.00
Amount at the end of the first year	105.00
Interest for the second year:	
$105.00 × .05	5.25
Amount at the end of the second year	$110.25

Notice that the interest for the second year is $5.25, as compared to only $5.00 for the first year. The reason for the greater interest earned during the second year is that, during the second year, interest is being paid *on interest*. That is, the $5.00 interest earned during the first year has been left in the account and has been added to the original $100 deposit in computing interest for the second year. This technique is known as *compounding* of interest. The compounding we have done is annual compounding. Interest can be compounded on a semiannual, quarterly, or even more frequent basis. Many savings institutions are now compounding interest on a daily basis. Of course, the more frequently compounding is done, the more rapidly the invested balance will grow.

How is the concept of compounding of interest expressed in equation form? It is expressed by taking equation (1) and adjusting it to state the number of years, n, that a sum is going to be left deposited in the bank:

$$F_n = P(1 + r)^n \qquad\qquad (2)$$

where n = years.

If $n = 2$ years, then our computation of the value of F in 2 years will be:

$$F_2 = \$100(1 + .05)^2$$
$$F_2 = \$110.25$$

Present Value and Future Value. Exhibit 14–1 shows the relationship between present value and future value, as expressed in the theory of interest equations. As shown in the exhibit, if $100 is deposited in a bank at 5 percent interest, it will grow to $127.63 by the end of five years, if interest is compounded annually.

Computation of Present Value

An investment can be viewed in two ways. It can be viewed either in terms of its future value, or in terms of its present value. If we know the present value of a sum (such as our $100 deposit), we have seen that it is a relatively simple task to compute the sum's future value in n years by using equation (2). But what if the tables are reversed, and we know the *future* value of some amount, but not its present value?

For example, assume that you are to receive $200 two years from now. You know that the future value of this sum is $200, since this is the amount that you will be receiving in two years. But what is the sum's present value—what is it worth *right now*? The present value

EXHIBIT 14–1
The Relationship between Present Value and
Future Value

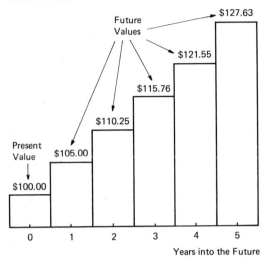

of any sum to be received in the future can be computed by turning equation (2) around, and solving for P:

$$P = \frac{F_n}{(1 + r)^n} \tag{3}$$

In our example, $F = \$200$ (the amount to be received in the future), $r = .05$ (the rate of interest), and $n = 2$ (the number of years in the future the amount is to be received).

$$P = \frac{\$200}{(1 + .05)^2}$$

$$P = \frac{\$200}{1.1025}$$

$$P = \$181.40$$

As shown by the computation above, the present value of $200 to be received two years from now is $181.40, if an interest return of 5 percent is required. In effect, we are saying that $181.40 received *right now* is equivalent to $200 received two years from now, if the investor requires a return of 5 percent on his money. The $181.40 and the $200 are just two ways of looking at the same item.

The process we have just completed is sometimes called *discounting*. We have *discounted* the $200 to its present value of $181.40. Discounting of future sums to their present value is a common practice in business. A knowledge of the present value of a sum to be received in the future can be very useful to the manager, particularly in making capital budgeting decisions. However, we need to find a simpler way of computing present value than using equation (3) every time we need to discount a future sum. The computations involved in using this equation are complex and time-consuming.

Fortunately, tables are available in which most of the mathematical work involved in the discounting process has been done. Table 1 in the Appendix to this chapter shows the discounted present value of *one dollar* to be received at various periods in the future at various interest rates. The table indicates that the present value of one dollar to be received two periods from now at 5 percent is 0.907. Since in our example we want to know the present value of $200, rather than just one dollar, we need to multiply the factor in the table by $200:

$$\$200 \times 0.907 = \$181.40$$

The answer we obtain is the same answer we got earlier using the formula in equation (3).

Present Value of a Series of Cash Flows

Although some business investments are such that they involve a single sum to be received (or paid) at a single point in the future, other investments involve a *series* of cash flows. For example, assume that a firm has just purchased a government bond, in order to temporarily invest funds that are being held for future plant expansion. The bond will yield interest of $500 each year, and will be held for five years. What is the present value of the stream of interest receipts from the bond? As shown in Exhibit 14–2, the present value of this stream is $2,106.00, if we assume a discount rate of 6 percent compounded annually. The discount factors used in this exhibit were taken from Table 1 in the Appendix to this chapter.

EXHIBIT 14–2
Present Value of a Series of Cash Receipts

Year	Factor at 6% (Table 1)	Interest Received	Present Value
1	0.943	$500	$ 471.50
2	0.890	500	445.00
3	0.840	500	420.00
4	0.792	500	396.00
5	0.747	500	373.50
			$2,106.00

Two points are important in connection with this exhibit. First, notice that the farther we go forward in time, the smaller the present value of the $500 interest receipt. The present value of $500 received a year from now is $471.50, as compared to only $373.50 for the $500 interest payment to be received five years from now. This point simply underscores the fact that money has a time value.

The second point is that even though the computations involved in Exhibit 14–2 are accurate, they have involved unnecessary work. The same present value of $2,106.000 could have been obtained more easily by referring to Table 2 in the appendix. Table 2 contains the present value of *one dollar* to be received each year over a *series* of years, at various interest rates. Table 2 has been derived by simply adding the factors from Table 1 together. To illustrate, we used the following factors from Table 1 in the computations in Exhibit 14–2:

	Table 1
Year	*Factors at 6%*
1	0.943
2	0.890
3	0.840
4	0.792
5	0.747
	4.212

The sum of the five factors above is 4.212. Notice from Table 2 that the factor for one dollar to be received each year for five years at 6 percent is also 4.212. If we use this factor, and multiply it by the $500 to be received each year, then we get the same present value of $2,106.00 that we obtained earlier in Exhibit 14–2:

$$\$500 \times 4.212 = \$2,106.00$$

Therefore, when dealing with a *series*, or stream, of cash flows, Table 2 should be used. A series, or stream, of cash flows is known as an *annuity*.

DISCOUNTED CASH FLOWS—THE NET PRESENT VALUE METHOD

Earlier in the chapter the point was made that business investments have two distinguishing characteristics. The first is that they often involve depreciable assets, and the return which the assets provide must be sufficient to recoup the original investment itself as well as to provide a satisfactory yield on the investment. The second is that business investments are generally long-term in nature, often spanning a decade or more. This characteristic lays heavy stress on the necessity to recognize the time value of money in business investment decisions.

If a capital budgeting method is to be fully useful to management, it must be capable of giving full recognition to *both* of the characteristics mentioned above. Although several methods of making capital budgeting decisions are in use, the ones that do the best job are those involving discounted cash flows. The discounted cash flow methods give full recognition to the time value of money, and at the same time provide for full recovery of any investment in depreciable assets. No other capital budgeting method is capable of performing *both* of these functions.

There are two approaches to making capital budgeting decisions by means of discounted cash flow. One is known as the net present value method, and the other is known as the time-adjusted rate of return method. Both methods are discussed in following sections.

The Net Present Value Method Illustrated

The concepts involved in the net present value method of making capital budgeting decisions are best understood by means of a concrete example. Let us assume the following data:

Example A

The Harper Company is contemplating purchasing a machine that is capable of performing certain operations that are now performed manually. The machine will cost $4,941 new, and it will last for five years. At the end of the five-year period the machine will have a zero scrap value. Use of the machine will reduce labor costs by $1,800 per year. The Harper Company requires a 20 percent return before taxes on all investment projects.

Should the machine be purchased? To answer this question it will be necessary first to isolate the cash inflows and cash outflows associated with the proposed project. In order to keep the example free of unnecessary complications, we have assumed only one cash inflow and one cash outflow. The cash inflow is the $1,800 annual reduction in labor costs. The cash outflow is the $4,941 initial investment in the machine.

The investment decision: The Harper Company must determine whether a cash investment now of $4,941 can be justified, if it will result in an $1,800 reduction in cost each year over the next five years, and if the company can get a 20 percent return on its money invested elsewhere.

To determine whether the investment is desirable, it will be necessary to discount the stream of annual $1,800 cost reductions to present value, and to compare this discounted present value to the cost of the new machine. Since The Harper Company requires a return of 20 percent on all investment projects, we will use this rate in the discounting process. Exhibit 14–3 gives a net present value analysis of the desirability of purchasing the machine.

EXHIBIT 14–3
Net Present Value Analysis of a Proposed Project

Initial cost	$4,941
Life of the project (years)	5
Annual cost savings	$1,800
Salvage value	–0–
Desired rate of return	20%

Item	Year(s) Having Cash Flows	Amount of Cash Flow	20% Factor	Present Value of Cash Flows
Annual cost savings	1–5	$ 1,800	2.991*	$ 5,384
Initial investment	Now	(4,941)	1.000	(4,941)
Net present value				$ 443

* From Table 2 in the Appendix.

According to the analysis, The Harper Company should purchase the new machine. The present value of the cost savings is $5,384, as compared to a present value of only $4,941 for the investment required (cost of the machine). Deducting the present value of the investment required from the present value of the cost savings gives a *net present value* of $443. Whenever the *net present value* is positive, as in our example, then an investment project is acceptable. Whenever the *net present value* is negative (i.e., the present value of the cash outflows exceed the present value of the cash inflows), then an investment project is not acceptable.

A full interpretation of the solution would be as follows: The new machine promises slightly more than the desired 20 percent rate of return. This is evident from the positive net present value of $443. The Harper Company could spend up to $5,384 for the new machine and still obtain the 20 percent rate of return it desires. The net present value of $443, therefore, shows the amount of "cushion" or "margin of error" which the company has in estimating the cost of the new machine. Alternatively, it also shows the amount of error that can exist in the present value of the cost savings, with the project remaining acceptable. That is, if the present value of the cost savings were only $4,941, rather than $5,384, the project would still promise the desired 20 percent rate of return.

Emphasis on Cash Flows

In organizing data for making capital budgeting decisions, the reader may have noticed that our emphasis has been on cash flows and not on accounting net income. Although the accounting net income figure is useful for many things, it does not give recognition to the time value of money, i.e., *when* a particular cash flow occurs over time. As we discussed earlier in the chapter, *when* a cash flow takes place is important since a dollar received today is more valuable than a dollar received in the future. Since accounting methods of computing net income do not consider this factor, they will have to be largely ignored in capital budgeting computations. Instead, we will concentrate on identifying *specific cash flows* associated with various investment projects, and on determining *when* these cash flows occur.

In considering an investment project, what kinds of cash flows should the manager look for? Although the specific cash flows will vary from project to project, certain types of cash flows tend to recur, and should be looked for. Usually a cash outflow in the form of an initial investment of some type will be present. In addition, some projects require that a firm expand its working capital in order to service the greater volume of business that will be generated. Any such incremental working capital needs should be treated as part of the initial investment in a project. Also, many projects require periodic outlays for repairs and maintenance, and for additional operating costs.

On the cash inflow side, a project will normally either increase revenues or reduce costs. In regard to this point, notice that *a reduction in costs is equivalent to an increase in revenues*, so far as the ultimate impact on net income is concerned. Cash inflows are also frequently realized from salvage of equipment when a project is terminated. In addition, upon termination of a project, any working capital that is freed for use elsewhere should be treated as a cash inflow.

In summary, the following types of cash flows are common in business investment projects:

Cash Outflows: Initial investment (including installation costs).
                 Increased working capital needs.
                 Repairs and maintenance.
                 Incremental operating costs.

Cash Inflows: Incremental revenues.
                 Reductions in costs.
                 Salvage value.
                 Release of working capital.

Recovery of the Original Investment

When first introduced to present value analysis, students are often mystified by the fact that depreciation is not deducted in computing the profitability of a project. There are two reasons for not deducting depreciation.

First, depreciation is an accounting concept not involving a current cash outflow.[1] As discussed in the preceding section, discounted cash flow methods of making capital budgeting decisions focus on *flows of cash*. Although depreciation is a vital concept in computing accounting net income for financial statement purposes, it is not relevant in an analytical framework that focuses on flows of cash.

A second reason for not deducting depreciation is that discounted cash flow methods *automatically* provide for return of the original investment, thereby making a deduction for depreciation unnecessary. To demonstrate this point, let us assume the following data:

Example B

The Carver Hospital is considering purchasing an attachment for its X-ray machine that will cost $3,170. The attachment will be usable for four years, after which time it will have no salvage value. It is estimated that the attachment will increase revenues from the X-ray department by $1,000 each year. The hospital's board of directors has instructed that no investments are to be made unless they promise an annual return of at least 10 percent.

A present value analysis of the desirability of purchasing the attachment is presented in Exhibit 14–4. Notice that the attachment promises exactly a 10 percent return on the original investment, since the net present value at a 10 percent discount rate is exactly zero.

Each annual $1,000 cash inflow arising from use of the attachment is made up of two parts. One part represents a recovery of a portion of the original $3,170 paid for the attachment, and the other part represents a return *on* this investment. The breakdown of each year's $1,000 cash inflow between recovery *of* investment and return *on* investment is shown in Exhibit 14–5.

The first year's $1,000 cash inflow consists of a $317 interest return (10%) on the $3,170 original investment, plus a $683 return *of* that investment. Since the amount of the unrecovered investment decreases over the four years, the dollar amount of the interest return also de-

---

[1] Although depreciation itself does not involve a cash outflow, it does have an effect on cash outflows for income taxes. We shall take a look at this effect in the following chapter, when we discuss the impact of income taxes on management planning.

EXHIBIT 14–4
Net Present Value Analysis of X-Ray Machine Attachment

Initial cost $3,170
Life of the project (years) 4
Annual incremental revenues $1,000
Salvage value . . . . –0–
Desired rate of return 10%

Item	Year(s) Having Cash Flows	Amount of Cash Flow	10% Factor	Present Value of Cash Flows
Annual incremental revenue	1–4	$ 1,000	3.170	$ 3,170
Initial investment	Now	(3,170)	1.000	(3,170)
Net present value				$ –0–

EXHIBIT 14–5
The Carver Hospital—Breakdown of Annual Cash Inflows

Year	Investment Outstanding During the Year (1)	Cash Inflow (2)	Return on Investment (1) × 10% (3)	Recovery of Investment during the Year (2) – (3) (4)	Unrecovered Investment at the End of the Year (1) – (4) (5)
1	$3,170	$1,000	$317	$ 683	$2,487
2	2,487	1,000	249	751	1,736
3	1,736	1,000	173	827	909
4	909	1,000	91	909	–0–
Total investment recovered				$3,170	

creases. By the end of the fourth year, all $3,170 of the original investment has been recovered.

Limiting Assumptions

In working with discounted cash flows, at least two limiting assumptions are usually made. The first is that all flows of cash occur at the end of a period. This is somewhat unrealistic in that cash flows typically occur somewhat uniformly *throughout* a period. The purpose of this assumption is just to simplify computations.

The second assumption is that all cash flows generated by an investment project are immediately reinvested in another project. It is further assumed that the second project will yield a rate of return at least as large as the first project. Unless these conditions are met, the return computed for the first project will not be accurate. To illustrate, we computed a rate of return for the Carver Hospital in Exhibit 14–4 of 10 percent. Unless the funds released each period are immediately reinvested in another project yielding at least a 10 percent return, then the return computed for the X-ray attachment will be overstated.

Choosing a Discount Rate

In using the net present value method, it is necessary to choose some rate of return for discounting cash flows to present value. In Example A we used a rate of return of 20 percent before taxes, and in Example B we used a rate of return of 10 percent. These rates were chosen somewhat arbitrarily simply for sake of illustration.

As a practical matter, firms put much time and study into the choice of a discount rate. The rate generally viewed as being most appropriate is a firm's *cost of capital.* A firm's cost of capital is not simply the interest rate which it must pay for long term debt. Rather, cost of capital is a broad concept, involving a blending of the costs of *all* sources of capital funds, both debt and equity. The mechanics involved in cost of capital computations are covered in finance texts, and will not be considered here.

Most finance people would agree that a before-tax cost of capital of 18 percent to 20 percent would be typical for an average industrial corporation. The appropriate after-tax figure would depend on the corporation's tax circumstances, but would probably average around 8 to 10 percent.

An Extended Example of the Net Present Value Method

Example C

The Swinyard Company is contemplating adding a new product line. The new product line would be marketable for only five years, after which time it would have to be discontinued. The costs and revenues that would be associated with the new line are:

Cost of equipment required	$80,000
Working capital needed	70,000
Salvage value of the equipment in 5 years	10,000
Annual sales revenues	75,000
Annual out-of-pocket costs for salaries, advertising, etc.	45,000
Overhaul of the equipment required in 4 years	5,000

The Swinyard Company's cost of capital is 12 percent. Would you recommend that the new product line be introduced? Ignore income taxes.

EXHIBIT 14-6
The Net Present Value Method—An Extended Example

				Years 1-5
Sales revenues				$75,000
Out-of-pocket costs.				45,000
Annual net cash inflows				$30,000

Item	Year(s) Having Cash Flows	Amount of Cash Flows	12% Factor	Present Value of Cash Flows
Purchase of equipment	Now	($80,000)	1.000	($80,000)
Working capital needed	Now	(70,000)	1.000	(70,000)
Overhaul of equipment	4	(5,000)	0.636	(3,180)
Annual net cash inflows from sales of the product line	1-5	30,000	3.605	108,150
Salvage value of the equipment	5	10,000	0.567	5,670
Working capital released	5	70,000	0.567	39,690
Net present value				$ 330

This example involves several cash inflows and several cash outflows. The solution is given in Exhibit 14-6.

Notice particularly how the working capital is handled in the exhibit. Also notice how the overhaul of the equipment is handled.

Since the overall net present value is positive, the new product line should be added, assuming that there is no better use for the investment funds involved.

DISCOUNTED CASH FLOWS—THE TIME-ADJUSTED RATE OF RETURN METHOD

The time-adjusted rate of return can be defined as the true interest yield promised by an investment project over its useful life. It can be computed by finding that discount rate which will equate the present value of the investment (cash outflows) required by a project with the present value of the returns (cash inflows) that the project promises. In other words, the time-adjusted rate of return is that discount rate which will cause the net present value of a project to be equal to zero.

The Time-Adjusted Rate of Return Method Illustrated

Finding a project's time-adjusted rate of return can be very helpful to a manager in making capital budgeting decisions. To illustrate, let us assume the following data:

Example D

The Glendale School District is considering the purchase of a large tractor-pulled lawnmower. If the mower is purchased, it will replace hiring men to mow with small, individual gas mowers. The large mower will cost $5,650 and will have a life of 10 years. It will have only a negligable scrap value, which can be ignored. The mower will provide a savings of $1,000 per year in mowing costs because of the labor it will replace.

To compute the time-adjusted rate of return promised by the new mower, it will be necessary to find that discount rate which will cause the net present value of the project to be equal to zero. How do we proceed to do this? The simplest and most direct approach is to divide the investment in the project by the expected annual cash inflow. This computation will give a factor that will be equal to the factor of the time-adjusted rate of return.

$$\frac{\text{Investment in the Project}}{\text{Annual Cash Inflow}} = \text{Factor of the Time-Adjusted Rate of Return}$$

The factor can then be located in the present value tables, to see what rate of return it represents. We will now perform these computations for the Glendale School District's proposed project:

$$\frac{\$5,650}{\$1,000} = 5.650$$

The discount factor that will equate a series of $1,000 cash inflows with a present investment of $5,650 is 5.650. We need now to find this factor in Table 2 in the Appendix to this chapter, to see what rate of return it represents. If we refer to Table 2 and scan along the line for period 10, we find that a factor of 5.650 represents a 12 percent rate of return. Therefore, the time-adjusted rate of return promised by the mower project is 12 percent. We can prove this by computing the project's net present value, using a 12 percent discount rate. This computation is made in Exhibit 14–7.

Notice from Exhibit 14–7 that using a discount rate of 12 percent equates the present value of the annual cash inflows with the present value of the investment required in the project, leaving a zero net present value. The 12 percent rate, therefore, represents the time-adjusted rate of return promised by the project.

The Problem of Uneven Cash Flows

The technique just demonstrated works very well if a projects' cash flows are even. But what if they are not? For example, what if a project

EXHIBIT 14–7
Evaluation of the Mower Purchase Using a 12 Percent Discount Rate

Initial cost				$5,650
Life of the project (years)				10
Annual cost savings				$1,000
Salvage value				–0–

Item	Year(s) Having Cash Flows	Amount of Cash Flow	12% Factor	Present Value of Cash Flows
Annual cost savings	1–10	$ 1,000	5.650	$ 5,650
Initial investment	Now	(5,650)	1.000	(5,650)
Net present value				$ –0–

will have some salvage value at the end of its life, in addition to the annual cash inflows? Under these circumstances, a trial-and-error process is necessary to find that rate of return which will exactly equate the cash inflows with the cash outflows. The trial-and-error process can be carried out by hand, or canned computer programs are available that can perform the necessary computations in seconds. In short, simply because cash flows are erratic or uneven will not in any way prevent a manager from determining a project's time-adjusted rate of return.

The Process of Interpolation

Interpolation is the process of finding odd rates of return that do not appear in published interest tables. It is important, since only rarely will a project have a nice, round rate of return that can be found directly in the present value tables. To illustrate, assume the following data:

Investment required	$6,000
Annual cost savings	1,500
Life of the project	10 years

What is the time-adjusted rate of return promised by this project? We can proceed as before, and find that the relevant factor is 4.000:

$$\frac{\text{Investment Required}}{\text{Annual Cost Savings}} = \frac{\$6,000}{\$1,500} = 4.000$$

Looking in Table 2 in the Appendix to this chapter, and scanning along the line for period 10, we find that a factor of 4.000 falls just between a return of 20 percent and a return of 22 percent. To find the exact rate of return, we will need to interpolate, as follows:

	Present Value Factors	
20% factor.	4.192	4.192
True factor		4.000
22% factor.	3.923	
Difference	.269	.192

$$\text{Time-adjusted rate of return} = 20\% + \left(\frac{.192}{.269} \times 2\%\right)$$

$$\text{Time-adjusted rate of return} = 21.4\%$$

Using the Time-Adjusted Rate of Return

Once the time-adjusted rate of return has been computed, what does the manager do with the information? The time-adjusted rate of return can be compared with the rate of return (usually the cost of capital) that the organization requires on its investment projects. If the time-adjusted rate of return is *greater* than the cost of capital, then the project is acceptable. If it is *less* than the cost of capital, then the project is rejected. A project is not a profitable undertaking if it can't provide a rate of return at least as great as the cost of the funds invested in it.

In the case of the Glendale School District example used earlier, let us assume that the District has set a minimum required rate of return of 10 percent on all projects. Since the mower promises a rate of return of 12 percent, it clears this hurdle, and would therefore be an acceptable investment.

THE COST OF CAPITAL AS A SCREENING TOOL

The cost of capital operates as a *screening* tool, helping the manager to screen out undesirable investment projects. When the time-adjusted rate of return method is being used, this screening takes the form of a *hurdle rate* which a project must clear for acceptance. The hurdle rate is the cost of capital itself. The time-adjusted rate of return promised by a project must be great enough to clear the cost of capital hurdle, or the project is rejected. We saw the application of this idea in the Glendale School District example above, where the hurdle was set at 10 percent.

The cost of capital also serves as a screening tool when the net present value method is used. In this case, the cost of capital becomes the *actual discount rate* used to compute the net present value of any proposed project, as discussed earlier. Any project yielding a negative net present value is rejected.

The operation of the cost of capital as a screening tool is summarized below.

The Cost of Capital As a
Screening Tool

The Net Present Value   The Time-Adjusted Rate of
Method   Return Method

The Cost of Capital is used   The Cost of Capital is used
as the *actual* discount rate in to *compare against* the time-
computing the net present value adjusted rate of return prom-
of a project. Any project with a ised by a project. To be
negative net present value is   acceptable, the project's rate
rejected.   of return cannot be less than
                                 the Cost of Capital

COMPARISON OF THE NET PRESENT VALUE AND THE TIME-ADJUSTED RATE OF RETURN METHODS

The net present value method has a number of advantages over the time-adjusted rate of return method of making capital budgeting decisions.

First, the net present value method is simpler to use. As explained earlier, the time-adjusted rate of return method often requires a trial-and-error process in trying to find the exact rate of return which will equate a project's cash inflows and outflows. No such trial-and-error process is necessary when working with the net present value method.

Second, using the net present value method makes it easier to adjust for risk. The point was made earlier in the chapter that the longer one has to wait for a cash inflow, the greater the risk that the cash inflow will never materialize. To show the greater risk connected with cash flows that are projected to occur many years in the future, firms often discount such amounts at higher discount rates than flows that are projected to occur earlier in time. For example, a firm might anticipate that a project will provide cash inflows of $10,000 per year for 15 years. If the firm's cost of capital was 18 percent before taxes, it might discount the first 10 years' inflows at this rate, and then raise the discount rate to, say, 30 percent or 35 percent for the last five years. The raising of the discount rate would show the greater risk connected with the cash flows that are projected to be received far in the future.

As an alternative, the firm might discount only the first five years' cash inflows at the 18 percent cost of capital rate. The discount rate might then be raised to 25 percent for the next five years, and to 30 or 35 percent for the last five years, to show the increasing risk associated with the passing of time.

No such selective adjustment of discount rates is possible under the time-adjusted rate of return method. About the only way to adjust for risk is to raise the hurdle rate that the rate of return of a project must clear for acceptance. This is a somewhat crude approach to the risk problem, in that it attaches the same degree of increased risk to *all* cash flows associated with a project—those that occur earlier in time as well as those that occur later in time.

Third, the net present value method provides more usable information than the time-adjusted rate of return method. The dollar net present value figure generated by the net present value method is viewed as being particularly useful for decision-making purposes. This point is considered further in the following chapter.

EXPANDING THE NET PRESENT VALUE APPROACH

So far we have confined all of our examples to the consideration of a single investment alternative. We will now expand the net present value approach to include two alternatives. In addition, we will integrate the concept of relevant costs into discounted cash flow analysis.

There are two ways that competing investment projects can be compared using the net present value method. One is the total cost approach, and the other is the incremental cost approach. Each approach is illustrated below.

The Total Cost Approach

The total cost approach is the most flexible and most widely used method of making a net present value analysis of competing projects. To illustrate the mechanics of the approach, let us assume the following data:

Example E

The Harper Ferry Company provides a ferry service across the Mississippi River. One of its ferry boats is in poor condition. The ferry boat can be renovated at an immediate cost of $20,000. Further repairs and an overhaul of the motor will be needed five years from now, at a cost of $8,000. In all, the ferry will be usable for 10 years if this work is done. At the end of ten years, the ferry will have to be scrapped at a salvage value of approximately $5,000. The scrap value of the ferry right now is $7,000. It will cost $16,000 each year to operate the ferry.

As an alternative, The Harper Ferry Company can purchase a new ferry boat at a cost of $40,000. It will have a life of ten years, but will also require some repairs at the end of five years. It is estimated that these repairs will amount to $2,500. At the end of ten years, it is estimated that the ferry will have a scrap value of $5,000. It will cost $12,000 each year to operate the ferry.

The Harper Ferry Company requires a return of at least 18 percent before taxes on all investment projects.

Should the company purchase the new ferry, or renovate the old ferry? The solution is given in Exhibit 14–8.

EXHIBIT 14–8
The Total-Cost Approach to Project Selection

Item	Year(s) Having Cash Flows	Amount of Cash Flows	18% Factor	Present Value of Cash Flows
Buy new ferry:				
Initial investment	Now	($40,000)	1.000	($40,000)
Repairs in 5 years.	5	(2,500)	0.437	(1,093)
Annual cash operating				
cost	1–10	(12,000)	4.494	(53,928)
Salvage of old ferry	Now	7,000	1.000	7,000
Salvage of new ferry	10	5,000	0.191	955
Present value of net				
cash outflows				($87,066)
Keep old ferry:				
Initial repairs	Now	($20,000)	1.000	($20,000)
Repairs in 5 years	5	(8,000)	0.437	(3,496)
Annual cash operating				
cost	1–10	(16,000)	4.494	(71,904)
Salvage of old ferry	10	5,000	0.191	955
Present value of net				
cash outflows				($94,445)
Net present value in favor of				
buying the new ferry				$ 7,379

Three points should be noted from the exhibit. First, observe that *all* cash inflows and *all* cash outflows are included in the solution under each alternative. No effort has been made to isolate those cash flows that are relevant to the decision, and those that are not relevant. The inclusion of all cash flows associated with each alternative gives the approach its name—the *total cost* approach.

Second, notice that the analysis yields a final net present value figure, the same as in our earlier examples of the net present value approach. In Exhibit 14–8, the net present value is positive in favor of buying the new ferry.

And third, notice that the net present value figure *means* the same thing as it did in our earlier examples. It indicates that the new ferry will provide more than the desired 18 percent rate of return.

The Incremental Cost Approach

The incremental cost approach differs from the total cost approach, in that it focuses on relevant costs. The procedure is to pick out those costs and those revenues that are relevant to the decision to be made, and include only them in the discounted cash flow analysis. To illustrate, we will again use the data in Example E relating to the Harper Ferry Company. The solution as to which alternative should be chosen is presented in Exhibit 14–9.

EXHIBIT 14–9
The Incremental Cost Approach to Project Selection

Items	Year(s) Having Cash Flows	Amount of Cash Flows	18% Factor	Present Value of Cash Flows
Incremental investment required to purchase the new ferry	Now	($20,000)	1.000	($20,000)
Repairs in 5 years avoided	5	5,500	0.437	2,403
Savings in annual cash operating costs	1–10	4,000	4.494	17,976
Salvage of old ferry	Now	7,000	1.000	7,000
Difference in salvage in 10 years	10	–0–	–	–0–
Net present value in favor of buying the new ferry				$ 7,379

Three things should be noted from the data in this exhibit. First, notice that the net present value of $7,379 shown in Exhibit 14–9 agrees exactly with the net present value shown under the total cost approach in Exhibit 14–8. This agreement should be expected, since the two approaches are just different roads to the same destination.

Second, notice that the costs used in Exhibit 14–9 are just mathematical differences between the costs shown for the two alternatives in Exhibit 14–8.

Third, notice that in working with the incremental cost approach, it is necessary to proceed from point of view of one of the two alternatives. That is, one must take the position of either buying the new ferry or keeping the old ferry, and then ask himself, "What are the incremental costs and cost savings of this alternative as compared with the other one?" In our computations we have taken the position of buying the new ferry. Therefore, we have listed the incremental costs and cost savings associated with buying the new ferry, as compared with renovating the old ferry.

SUMMARY

Decisions relating to the planning and financing of capital outlays are known as capital budgeting decisions. Such decisions are of key importance to the long-run profitability of a firm, since large amounts of money are usually involved, and since whatever decisions are made may "lock-in" a firm for many years.

A decision to make a particular investment basically hinges on whether the future returns promised by the investment can be justified in terms of the present cost outlay that must be made. A valid comparison between the future returns and the present cost outlay is difficult because of the difference in timing involved. The cost outlay occurs now, and the returns usually come sometime in the future. This problem is overcome through use of the concept of present value, and through employment of the technique of discounting. The future sums are discounted to their present value, in order to be compared on a valid basis with current cost outlays. The discount rate used may be the firm's cost of capital, or it may be some arbitrary rate of return which the firm requires on all investment projects.

There are two ways of using discounted cash flow in making capital budgeting decisions. One is the net present value method, and the other is the time-adjusted rate of return method. The net present value method simply involves the choosing of a discount rate, and then the discounting of all cash flows to present value, as described in the preceding paragraph. If the present value of the cash inflows exceeds the present value of the cash outflows, then the net present value is positive, and the project is acceptable. The opposite is true if the net present value is negative. The time-adjusted rate of return method finds that discount rate which exactly equates the cash inflows and the cash outflows, leaving a zero net present value.

TABLE 1
Present Value of $1.00

$$P = \frac{F_n}{(1+r)^n}$$

Periods	4%	5%	6%	8%	10%	12%	14%	16%	18%	20%	22%	24%	26%	28%	30%	40%
1	0.962	0.952	0.943	0.926	0.909	0.893	0.877	0.862	0.847	0.833	0.820	0.806	0.794	0.781	0.769	0.714
2	0.925	0.907	0.890	0.857	0.826	0.797	0.769	0.743	0.718	0.694	0.672	0.650	0.630	0.610	0.592	0.510
3	0.889	0.864	0.840	0.794	0.751	0.712	0.675	0.641	0.609	0.579	0.551	0.524	0.500	0.477	0.455	0.364
4	0.855	0.823	0.792	0.735	0.683	0.636	0.592	0.552	0.516	0.482	0.451	0.423	0.397	0.373	0.350	0.260
5	0.822	0.784	0.747	0.681	0.621	0.567	0.519	0.476	0.437	0.402	0.370	0.341	0.315	0.291	0.269	0.186
6	0.790	0.746	0.705	0.630	0.564	0.507	0.456	0.410	0.370	0.335	0.303	0.275	0.250	0.227	0.207	0.133
7	0.760	0.711	0.665	0.583	0.513	0.452	0.400	0.354	0.314	0.279	0.249	0.222	0.198	0.178	0.159	0.095
8	0.731	0.677	0.627	0.540	0.467	0.404	0.351	0.305	0.266	0.233	0.204	0.179	0.157	0.139	0.123	0.068
9	0.703	0.645	0.592	0.500	0.424	0.361	0.308	0.263	0.225	0.194	0.167	0.144	0.125	0.108	0.094	0.048
10	0.676	0.614	0.558	0.463	0.386	0.322	0.270	0.227	0.191	0.162	0.137	0.116	0.099	0.085	0.073	0.035
11	0.650	0.585	0.527	0.429	0.350	0.287	0.237	0.195	0.162	0.135	0.112	0.094	0.079	0.066	0.056	0.025
12	0.625	0.557	0.497	0.397	0.319	0.257	0.208	0.168	0.137	0.112	0.092	0.076	0.062	0.052	0.043	0.018
13	0.601	0.530	0.469	0.368	0.290	0.229	0.182	0.145	0.116	0.093	0.075	0.061	0.050	0.040	0.033	0.013
14	0.577	0.505	0.442	0.340	0.263	0.205	0.160	0.125	0.099	0.078	0.062	0.049	0.039	0.032	0.025	0.009
15	0.555	0.481	0.417	0.315	0.239	0.183	0.140	0.108	0.084	0.065	0.051	0.040	0.031	0.025	0.020	0.006
16	0.534	0.458	0.394	0.292	0.218	0.163	0.123	0.093	0.071	0.054	0.042	0.032	0.025	0.019	0.015	0.005
17	0.513	0.436	0.371	0.270	0.198	0.146	0.108	0.080	0.060	0.045	0.034	0.026	0.020	0.015	0.012	0.003
18	0.494	0.416	0.350	0.250	0.180	0.130	0.095	0.069	0.051	0.038	0.028	0.021	0.016	0.012	0.009	0.002
19	0.475	0.396	0.331	0.232	0.164	0.116	0.083	0.060	0.043	0.031	0.023	0.017	0.012	0.009	0.007	0.002
20	0.456	0.377	0.312	0.215	0.149	0.104	0.073	0.051	0.037	0.026	0.019	0.014	0.010	0.007	0.005	0.001
21	0.439	0.359	0.294	0.199	0.135	0.093	0.064	0.044	0.031	0.022	0.015	0.011	0.008	0.006	0.004	0.001
22	0.422	0.342	0.278	0.184	0.123	0.083	0.056	0.038	0.026	0.018	0.013	0.009	0.006	0.004	0.003	0.001
23	0.406	0.326	0.262	0.170	0.112	0.074	0.049	0.033	0.022	0.015	0.010	0.007	0.005	0.003	0.002	
24	0.390	0.310	0.247	0.158	0.102	0.066	0.043	0.028	0.019	0.013	0.008	0.006	0.004	0.003	0.002	
25	0.375	0.295	0.233	0.146	0.092	0.059	0.038	0.024	0.016	0.010	0.007	0.005	0.003	0.002	0.001	
26	0.361	0.281	0.220	0.135	0.084	0.053	0.033	0.021	0.014	0.009	0.006	0.004	0.002	0.002	0.001	
27	0.347	0.268	0.207	0.125	0.076	0.047	0.029	0.018	0.011	0.007	0.005	0.003	0.002	0.001	0.001	
28	0.333	0.255	0.196	0.116	0.069	0.042	0.026	0.016	0.010	0.006	0.004	0.002	0.002	0.001	0.001	
29	0.321	0.243	0.185	0.107	0.063	0.037	0.022	0.014	0.008	0.005	0.003	0.002	0.001	0.001	0.001	
30	0.308	0.231	0.174	0.099	0.057	0.033	0.020	0.012	0.007	0.004	0.003	0.002	0.001	0.001	0.001	
40	0.208	0.142	0.097	0.046	0.022	0.011	0.005	0.003	0.001	0.001						

TABLE 2
Present Value of Annuity of $1.00 in Arrears

$$P_n = \frac{1}{r}\left[1 - \frac{1}{(1+r)^n}\right]$$

Periods	4%	5%	6%	8%	10%	12%	14%	16%	18%	20%	22%	24%	26%	28%	30%	40%
1	0.962	0.952	0.943	0.926	0.909	0.893	0.877	0.862	0.847	0.833	0.820	0.806	0.794	0.781	0.769	0.714
2	1.886	1.859	1.833	1.783	1.736	1.690	1.647	1.605	1.566	1.528	1.492	1.457	1.424	1.392	1.361	1.224
3	2.775	2.723	2.673	2.577	2.487	2.402	2.322	2.246	2.174	2.106	2.042	1.981	1.868	1.816	1.816	1.589
4	3.630	3.546	3.465	3.312	3.170	3.037	2.914	2.798	2.690	2.589	2.494	2.404	2.320	2.241	2.166	1.879
5	4.452	4.330	4.212	3.993	3.791	3.605	3.433	3.274	3.127	2.991	2.864	2.745	2.635	2.532	2.436	2.035
6	5.242	5.076	4.917	4.623	4.355	4.111	3.889	3.685	3.498	3.326	3.167	3.020	2.885	2.759	2.643	2.168
7	6.002	5.786	5.582	5.206	4.868	4.564	4.288	4.039	3.812	3.605	3.416	3.242	3.083	2.937	2.802	2.263
8	6.733	6.463	6.210	5.747	5.335	4.968	4.639	4.344	4.078	3.837	3.619	3.421	3.241	3.076	2.925	2.331
9	7.435	7.108	6.802	6.247	5.759	5.328	4.946	4.607	4.303	4.031	3.786	3.566	3.366	3.184	3.019	2.379
10	8.111	7.722	7.360	6.710	6.145	5.650	5.216	4.833	4.494	4.192	3.923	3.682	3.465	3.269	3.092	2.414
11	8.760	8.306	7.887	7.139	6.495	5.988	5.453	5.029	4.656	4.327	4.035	3.776	3.544	3.335	3.147	2.438
12	9.385	8.863	8.384	7.536	6.814	6.194	5.660	5.197	4.793	4.439	4.127	3.851	3.606	3.387	3.190	2.456
13	9.986	9.394	8.853	7.904	7.103	6.424	5.842	5.342	4.910	4.533	4.203	3.912	3.656	3.427	3.223	2.468
14	10.563	9.899	9.295	8.244	7.367	6.628	6.002	5.468	5.008	4.611	4.265	3.962	3.695	3.459	3.249	2.477
15	11.118	10.380	9.712	8.559	7.606	6.811	6.142	5.575	5.092	4.675	4.315	4.001	3.726	3.483	3.268	2.484
16	11.652	10.838	10.106	8.851	7.824	6.974	6.265	5.669	5.162	4.730	4.357	4.033	3.751	3.503	3.283	2.489
17	12.166	11.274	10.477	9.122	8.022	7.120	6.373	5.749	5.222	4.775	4.391	4.059	3.771	3.518	3.295	2.492
18	12.659	11.690	10.828	9.372	8.201	7.250	6.467	5.818	5.273	4.812	4.419	4.080	3.786	3.529	3.304	2.494
19	13.134	12.085	11.158	9.604	8.365	7.366	6.550	5.877	5.316	4.844	4.442	4.097	3.799	3.539	3.311	2.496
20	13.590	12.462	11.470	9.818	8.514	7.469	6.623	5.929	5.353	4.870	4.460	4.110	3.808	3.546	3.316	2.497
21	14.029	12.821	11.764	10.017	8.649	7.562	6.687	5.973	5.384	4.891	4.476	4.121	3.816	3.551	3.320	2.498
22	14.451	13.163	12.042	10.201	8.772	7.645	6.743	6.011	5.410	4.909	4.488	4.130	3.822	3.556	3.323	2.498
23	14.857	13.489	12.303	10.371	8.883	7.718	6.792	6.044	5.432	4.925	4.499	4.137	3.827	3.559	3.325	2.499
24	15.247	13.799	12.550	10.529	8.985	7.784	6.835	6.073	5.451	4.937	4.507	4.143	3.831	3.562	3.327	2.499
25	15.622	14.094	12.783	10.675	9.077	7.843	6.873	6.097	5.467	4.948	4.514	4.147	3.834	3.564	3.329	2.499
26	15.983	14.375	13.003	10.810	9.161	7.896	6.906	6.118	5.480	4.956	4.520	4.151	3.837	3.566	3.330	2.500
27	16.330	14.643	13.211	10.935	9.237	7.943	6.935	6.936	5.492	4.964	4.525	4.154	3.839	3.567	3.331	2.500
28	16.663	14.898	13.406	11.051	9.307	7.984	6.961	6.152	5.502	4.970	4.528	4.157	3.840	3.568	3.331	2.500
29	16.984	15.141	13.591	11.158	9.370	8.022	6.983	6.166	5.510	4.975	4.531	4.159	3.841	3.569	3.332	2.500
30	17.292	15.373	13.765	11.258	9.427	8.055	7.003	6.177	5.517	4.979	4.534	4.160	3.842	3.569	3.332	2.500
40	19.793	17.159	15.046	11.925	9.779	8.244	7.105	6.234	5.548	4.997	4.544	4.166	3.846	3.571	3.333	2.500

QUESTIONS

14–1. What is meant by the term "capital budgeting"?

14–2. Distinguish between capital budgeting screening decisions, and capital budgeting preference decisions.

14–3. What is meant by the term "time value of money"?

14–4. What is meant by the term "discounting," and why is it important to the business manager?

14–5. Why are discounted cash flow methods of making capital budgeting decisions superior to other methods?

14–6. What is net present value? Can it ever be negative? Explain.

14–7. One real shortcoming of discounted cash flow methods is that they ignore depreciation. Do you agree? Why or why not?

14–8. Identify two limiting assumptions associated with discounted cash flow methods of making capital budgeting decisions.

14–9. If a firm has to pay interest of 8 percent on long-term debt, then its cost of capital is 8 percent. Do you agree? Explain.

14–10. What is meant by an investment project's time-adjusted rate of return? How is the time-adjusted rate of return computed?

14–11. Explain how the cost of capital serves as a screening tool, when dealing with (*a*) the net present value method, and (*b*) the time-adjusted rate of return method.

14–12. Companies that invest in underdeveloped countries usually require a higher rate of return on their investment than they do when their investment is made in countries that are better developed, and that have more stable political and economic conditions. Some people say that the higher rate of return required in the underdeveloped countries is evidence of exploitation. What other explanation can you offer?

14–13. More risky investment proposals should be discounted at lower rates of return. Do you agree? Why or why not?

14–14. If an investment project has a zero net present value, then it should be rejected since it will provide no return on funds invested. Do you agree? Why?

14–15. A machine costs $12,000. It will provide a cost savings of $2,000 per year. If the company requires a 14 percent rate of return, how many years will the machine have to be used to provide the desired 14 percent return?

EXERCISES

(Ignore income taxes on all exercises)

14–1. Which would you prefer to receive, $1,000 at the end of each year for 5 years, or

a. $500 at the end of each year for 11 years, if you can invest money at a 10 percent rate of return?
b. $7,000 at the end of 6 years, if you can invest money at a 12 percent rate of return?
c. $2,000 a year for the 4th through 8th year, if you can invest money at a 20 percent rate of return?
d. $500 at the end of each year for years 1 through 5, plus $800 at the end of each year for years 6 through 10, if you can invest money at an 8 percent rate of return?

14–2. Consider each of the following cases independently:
a. Annual cash inflows that will arise from two competing investment opportunities are given below. Each investment opportunity will require the same initial investment. You desire a rate of return of 20 percent on funds invested. In terms of present values, which investment opportunity is best? Show computations.

Year	Investment X	Investment Y
1	$ 1,000	$ 4,000
2	2,000	3,000
3	3,000	2,000
4	4,000	1,000
	$10,000	$10,000

b. At the end of three years, when you graduate from college, your father has promised to give you a new car that will cost $4,500. How much should he invest now at a 10 percent rate of return in order to have the desired $4,500 in three years?
c. You can purchase an annuity now for $10,000. The annuity will pay you $8,000 per year for the 8th through 10th year in the future, after which it will terminate. If you require a rate of return of 12 percent, is the annuity an acceptable investment?

14–3. Consider each of the cases below independently.
a. Acko Company requires a 14 percent return on all investments. How much will the company be willing to pay for Machine A if the machine will save $8,000 per year for 10 years?
b. Machine B has a projected life of 18 years. It is estimated that the machine will save $4,000 per year in operating costs. What is the machine's time-adjusted rate of return if it costs $29,000 new?
c. Assume that Machine C will yield a 16 percent time-adjusted rate of return. It will last 15 years. If the machine costs $22,300 new, what are the annual cost savings?

14–4. Wriston Company has $15,000 to invest. The company is trying to decide between two alternative uses of the funds. The alternatives are:

	Invest in Project A	Invest in Project B
Investment required	$15,000	$15,000
Annual cash inflows	4,000	–
Single cash inflow at the end of 10 years.	–	60,000
Life of the project	10 years	10 years

Wriston Company's cost of capital is 16 percent.

Required:

Which investment would you recommend the company accept? Show all computations.

14–5. The Doughboy Bakery would like to buy a new bread mixer. The mixer the bakery is considering costs $10,000 new. It would last the bakery ten years, but would require a $4,000 overhaul at the end of the sixth year. After ten years, the mixer could be sold for $1,000.

The Doughboy Bakery estimates that it will cost $800 per year to operate the new mixer. It will replace an old mixer that costs $2,000 per year to operate. In addition, the new mixer will increase output by 18,000 loaves of bread per year. The company realizes a contribution margin of ten cents per loaf.

Required:

1. What are the annual cash inflows that will be provided by the new bread mixer?
2. Assume that the company requires an 18 percent rate of return. What is the mixer's net present value?

14–6. The Barnes Company is contemplating purchasing equipment to exploit a mineral deposit in land to which it has mineral rights. The projected cash flows that would be associated with the investment are given below:

Cost of required equipment	$20,000
Net annual cash receipts	11,000
Working capital needed	10,000
Salvage value of equipment in 4 years	3,000
Overhaul of equipment needed in 3 years	5,000

The company estimates that the mineral deposit would be totally exhausted after four years' operation.

Required:

Assume that the company's cost of capital is 20 percent. Would you recommend the project be undertaken? Use the net present value method.

14–7. Bill paid $12,000 for a bond which he purchased in 19X1. The bond paid interest of $720 each year for five years, after which time Bill sold the bond for $12,400. Bill would like to earn a rate of return of at least 8 percent on all of his investments.

Required:

Did Bill earn an 8 percent return on the bond? Show computations. (Round all dollar amounts to the nearest whole dollar.)

14–8. The Pisa Pizza Parlor is investigating the purchase of a new delivery truck. The truck would cost $5,000 and have a five year useful life. The truck would save $500 per year over the present method of delivering pizzas. In addition, it would result in delivery of about 1,000 more pizzas each year. The company realizes a contribution margin of $1 per pizza.

Required:

1. What would be the annual cash inflows associated with the new truck?
2. Compute the time-adjusted rate of return promised by the new truck. Interpolate to the nearest tenth of a percent.
3. In addition to the data given above, assume that the truck will have a $700 salvage value at the end of five years. Under these conditions, compute the time-adjusted rate of return to the nearest *whole* percent.

PROBLEMS

(Ignore income taxes on all problems)

14–1. *Net Present Value Analysis.* The Darby Pipe Company would like to purchase a new high-speed threading machine that costs $45,000. If purchased, the new machine will replace an old machine that will be sold for its scrap value of $5,000. The company is convinced that the new threading machine can produce the following annual cost savings:

Reduction in materials and supplies used $7,000
Reduction in maintenance required   5,000

The new machine will require about $2,000 more labor cost annually to operate than the old machine, because of its more intricate mechanism. In addition, it will require an overhaul costing $6,000 at the end of six years' use. The new machine will be usable for eight years, after which time it will have a salvage value of $3,000. The Darby Pipe Company requires a rate of return of at least 16 percent on investments of this type.

Required:

Compute the new machine's net present value. Would you recommend purchase?

14-2.   *Replacement Decision.* Alleman Associates has the choice of overhauling its present delivery truck, or purchasing a new one. The company has assembled the following information:

	Present Truck	New Truck
Purchase cost new	$4,000	$5,500
Remaining book value	1,500	–
Overhaul needed now	2,000	–
Annual cash operating costs	3,500	2,500
Salvage value–now	1,000	–
Salvage value–5 years from now	250	1,000

If Alleman Associates keeps the old delivery truck, it will have to be overhauled immediately at the cost shown above. With the overhaul, it can be made to last for five more years. If the new truck is purchased, it will be used for five years, after which it will be traded in on another truck. The company computes depreciation on a straight-line basis. All investment projects are evaluated on a basis of a 20 percent before-tax rate of return.

Required:

1. Should Alleman Associates keep the old truck, or purchase the new one? Use the total cost approach in making your decision. Round to the nearest whole dollar.
2. Redo part 1, this time using the incremental cost approach.

14-3.   *Sensitivity Analysis.* The Big Piney Lumber Company has a saw that has been in use for many years. The saw has a zero disposal value. The company is considering the purchase of a new laser saw that would cost $27,000, but which could save $6,000 per year in cash operating costs and reduced waste. If the new laser saw is not purchased, the company can go on using the old saw almost indefinitely. The manufacturer estimates that the new laser saw will have a service life of 10 years.

Required:

1. Compute the time-adjusted rate of return on the new saw.
2. Since laser saws are very new, the management of the Big Piney Lumber Company is very unsure about the estimated 10-year useful life. Compute what the time-adjusted rate of return would be if the useful life of the laser saw was (*a*) 6 years, and (*b*) 15 years, instead of 10 years.
3. Assume that the life of the saw will be 10 years as originally estimated, but that the annual cost savings would be only $4,000 rather than $6,000. Compute the time-adjusted rate of return.
4. Suppose that the annual cost savings turn out to be $5,000, and that the life of the saw turns out to be 8 years. What would be the time-adjusted rate of return?

14–4. *Lease or Buy Decision.* The Riteway Advertising Agency provides cars for its sales staff. In the past, the company has always purchased its cars outright from a dealer, and then sold the cars after two years' use. The company's present fleet is two years old, and will be sold very shortly. In order to provide a replacement fleet, the company is considering two alternatives:

Alternative #1: Purchase the cars outright, as in the past, and sell the cars after two years' use. If this alternative is accepted, the following costs will be incurred on the fleet as a whole:

Purchase cost	$36,000
Annual cost of servicing, taxes, and licensing	1,200
Repairs, first year of ownership	400
Repairs, second year of ownership	900

At the end of the two-year period, the cars could be sold for $12,000. Another fleet would then be purchased, under the cost conditions indicated above. In all, a four-year time span would be covered by the two purchases.

Alternative #2: Lease the cars from a dealer under a four-year lease contract. The dealer would provide a new fleet of cars immediately, and then take these cars back and provide another new fleet at the end of the second year. The lease cost would be $17,500 per year. As part of this lease cost, the dealer would provide all servicing and repairs, license the cars, and pay all taxes. At the end of the four-year period, the second fleet of cars would then revert back to the dealer, as owner.

If the fleet of cars is purchased, depreciation will be on a straight line basis. Ignore income taxes. The company's cost of capital is 14 percent.

Required:

Would you advise the company to lease or buy its autos?

14–5. *Rental Property Decision.* John Feldman, professor of English at a western university, owns an office building adjacent to the university campus. A realty firm has approached Professor Feldman with an offer to purchase the building and the land on which it stands for $550,000. The realty firm has suggested that the purchase price be paid by a down payment of $250,000 immediately, and yearly payments of $50,000 until the balance is paid in full.

Professor Feldman acquired the rental property 10 years ago at a total cost of $525,000—$50,000 for the land, and $475,000 for the office building itself. He has been depreciating the building by straight-line depreciation, assuming an ultimate salvage value of $75,000. Professor Feldman feels sure that the building can be rented for another 15 years. He also feels sure that in 15 more years the land will be worth twice what he paid for it.

Professor Feldman has kept careful records of the income he has realized from the rental property. These records indicate the following annual income and expenses:

Annual rental revenues.		$75,000
Annual operating expenses:		
Utilities	$14,000	
Depreciation	16,000	
Taxes and insurance	12,000	
Repairs and maintenance	8,000	50,000
Net income		$25,000

In addition to the operating expenses above, Professor Feldman makes a $10,000 mortgage payment each year. The mortgage will be paid off in eight more years. If he sells the property, Professor Feldman will be able to avoid the interest that makes up a part of the annual $10,000 mortgage payment, by paying the mortgage off immediately for $65,000.

Required:

Assume that Professor Feldman can invest money at 6 percent before taxes. Would you recommend that he sell the office building? Show computations, using discounted cash flow.

14–6. *Lease or Buy Decision.* Rightway Stores, Inc., owns a nationwide chain of supermarkets. The company is going to open another store soon, and a suitable building site has been located in an attractive and rapidly growing area. The company has two choices as to how it can acquire the desired building and other facilities needed to open the new store.

Alternative 1: The company can purchase the building site, construct the desired building, and purchase store fixtures. The total cost of these items would come to $1,250,000. This alternative would require the immediate payment of $500,000, and then $250,000 each year for the next three years. The company estimates that the property would be worth about $500,000 in 18 years, the length of time the company would want to occupy the property.

Alternative 2: A large insurance company is willing to purchase the building site, construct a building, and install fixtures to Rightway Stores, Inc.'s specifications, and then lease the completed facility to Rightway Stores, Inc., for 18 years at annual lease cost of $165,000. The insurance company would require a $10,000 security deposit immediately which would be returned at the termination of the lease. The lease would be a "net" lease, in which Rightway Stores, Inc., would be required to pay all costs of insurance, taxes, etc., associated with the property, the same as if Rightway Stores, Inc., were the owner of the property.

Rightway Stores, Inc., estimates that the annual costs of operating the store, exclusive of salaries and depreciation, would be:

Insurance	$ 6,000
Taxes (Property)	18,000
Other	12,000
	$36,000

Rightway Stores, Inc.'s cost of capital is 16 percent.

Required:

Using discounted cash flow, determine whether the company should lease or buy the desired store facilities. Use the total cost approach.

14–7. *Make or Buy Decision.* Cole Company is now purchasing a component part, used in the manufacture of one of its products, from another company. The parts are purchased for $5 each, with a total volume of 20,000 parts being purchased each year. The engineering department of Cole Company has submitted a recommendation that the company begin to produce this part in its own plant. The engineering department has supported its recommendation with the following information:

1. New equipment would have to be purchased to produce the part, at a total cost of $70,000. The equipment would have a ten-year life, and a $5,000 salvage value.
2. A lathe already owned by the company, but not in use, would also be used in production of the parts. The lathe would easily last for 10 years, but would have no salvage value. Its present book value is $24,000.
3. Annual straight-line depreciation on the new equipment would be $6,500; on the presently owned lathe, $2,400.
4. If the parts are produced in Cole Company's own plant, working capital of $20,000 would be needed, to carry raw material and supplies inventories. However, the working capital required to carry finished parts could be reduced by $5,000.
5. Variable production costs per part would be:

Direct labor (0.5 hr @ $4.00 per hour)	$2.00
Direct materials	2.20
Power, supplies, etc.	.20
Total	$4.40

6. No other costs in the Cole Company's plant would be affected by the decision to manufacture the parts. The company applies overhead to production on a basis of $2.00 per direct-labor hour.
7. The company requires a before-tax return of 18 percent on all investments.

Required:

Do you agree with the engineering department's recommendation to produce the parts? Show computations, using the discounted cash flow total cost approach.

14-8. *Investments in Securities.* Mr. Robert Peel had $30,000 available for investment in 19X1. He used the $30,000 to purchase the following three securities during the year:

First Investment: Mr. Peel purchased preferred stock at a cost of $8,000. The stock paid a 6 percent annual dividend. After four years, the stock was sold for $8,300.

Second Investment: Mr. Peel purchased bonds at a cost of $10,000. The interest rate on the bonds was 7 percent, with the interest paid semiannually.* After four years, the bonds were sold for $9,800.

Third Investment: Mr. Peel purchased common stock at a cost of $12,000. The stock paid no dividends, but was sold for $17,800 after four years.

    Mr. Peel's goal is to earn a before-tax rate of return of 8 percent on his investments. Round all amounts to the nearest whole dollar.

Required:

1. On which investment(s) did Mr. Peel earn the desired 8 percent return? Show all computations, using discounted cash flow.
2. Considering all three investments together, did Mr. Peel earn the desired 8 percent return?

14-9. *Equipment Replacement Decision.* The JD Company purchased a new milling machine a year ago at a cost of $35,000. The machine will last the company ten more years, after which it will have a salvage value of $2,000. The JD Company has just been approached by a salesman selling a highly innovative computer-controlled milling machine that costs $50,000. The computer-controlled machine could increase the company's output by about 15 percent, while at the same time reducing per-unit costs. The JD Company's engineering department has prepared the following comparative cost and revenue data:

	Present Machine	Computer-Controlled Machine
Total annual revenues	$100,000	$115,000
Total annual expenses:		
Materials and supplies	30,000	32,000
Maintenance	8,000	15,000
Depreciation	3,000	4,800
Labor	45,000	40,000
Total	86,000	91,800
Net income per year	$ 14,000	$ 23,200

The computer-controlled machine would have a service life of ten years, after which it could be sold for $2,000 salvage. The present milling machine has a book value of $32,000, but it can be sold

---

* In discounting a cash flow that occurs semiannually, the procedure is to halve the discount rate and double the years. Use the same procedure in discounting the proceeds from the sale.

now for $10,000. The president of the JD Company is unenthused about the new computer-controlled machine. He has made the following payback computation:

Cost of the new machine	$50,000
Loss on the old machine ($32,000 – $10,000)	22,000
Total investment in the new machine	$72,000
Net income promised by the new machine	$23,200
Net income provided by the old machine	14,000
Increased net income from the new machine	$ 9,200

$$\frac{\$72,000}{\$9,200} = \underline{\underline{7.8 \text{ years}}}$$

Required:

Use the total cost approach to determine whether the company should purchase the new machine. Since the company views the new machine as being somewhat risky, a discount rate of 24 percent should be used.

14–10. *Accept or Reject a New Product Line.* Environmental Electronics, Inc., has just developed a new electronic device which, when mounted on an automobile, will tell the driver the number of miles the automobile is going per gallon of gasoline. The device can be mounted on any model or make of automobile in a few minutes' time, and with neglible cost. The company is anxious to build facilities to produce the new device in volume, and has made marketing and cost studies to determine probable costs and market potential. These studies have provided the following information.

1. Plant and equipment adequate to produce the new device would cost $5,000,000. This plant and equipment would have a 15-year life, and a $500,000 salvage value.

2. Projected sales in units over the next 15 years would be:

Year	Sales in Units
1	80,000
2	120,000
3	200,000
4	250,000
5–15	300,000

3. Production and sales of the new device would require working capital of $400,000 in order to finance accounts receivable, inventories, etc.

4. Unit variable costs would be:

Direct materials	$ 6
Direct labor	4
Overhead	3
Selling and administrative	2
Total	$15

5. Fixed costs for salaries, maintenance, taxes, insurance, utilities, and straight-line depreciation on the plant and equipment would total $1,800,000 per year.
6. Environmental Electronics, Inc., would sell the devices for $25 each.
7. In order to gain rapid entry into the market, Environmental Electronics, Inc., would have to advertise heavily in the early years of sales. The advertising program would be:

Year	Amount of Advertising
1	$250,000
2	150,000
3–15	50,000

8. Environmental Electronics requires a 12 percent rate of return on investments.

Required:

Suppose the president of Environmental Electronics has asked you to recommend either for or against acquisition of the plant and equipment and production of the new gas-monitoring device. What would be your recommendation? Show computations using discounted cash flow.

14–11. *Discontinuing a Department.* You have just been hired as a management trainee by Marley's Department Store. Your first assignment is to determine whether the store should discontinue its housewares department and expand its appliances department. The store's vice president feels that the housewares space could be better utilized selling appliances, since the appliances have a better markup and move more rapidly. The store's most recent income statement is presented below:

	Appliances	Housewares	Clothing	Total
Sales	$400,000	$50,000	$200,000	$650,000
Cost of goods sold	280,000	40,000	110,000	430,000
Gross margin	120,000	10,000	90,000	220,000
Commissions	40,000	5,000	20,000	65,000
Depreciation	12,000	8,000	10,000	30,000
Other fixed expenses	20,000	8,000	15,000	43,000
Total expenses	72,000	21,000	45,000	138,000
Net income	$ 48,000	($11,000)	$ 45,000	$ 82,000

In the course of your analytical work you have determined the following information:
1. If the housewares department is discontinued, sales of appliances can be expanded by 25 percent. Sales of clothing will be unaffected.

2. The store fixtures being used in the housewares department could not be used in the expanded appliances department. These fixtures would have to be sold for their salvage value of $6,000. The fixtures will last for eight years more, after which they will have zero sale value.

3. Since appliances are much more expensive than housewares items, the store would have to expand its working capital investment in inventories and accounts receivable by $20,000.

4. The added level of appliance sales would carry the same proportionate variable expenses as current appliance sales.

5. Expanding the appliances department would require an expenditure of $60,000 for renovation and new fixtures. These fixtures would have an eight-year life and a $4,000 salvage value.

6. The store uses straight-line depreciation. If the fixtures now being used in the housewares department are sold, then all depreciation now being charged to that department will disappear.

7. The "other fixed expenses" in the housewares department represent the salary of a long-time employee, who will be retained regardless of whether the housewares department is retained or discontinued.

8. The store has a before-tax desired rate of return of 16 percent on all investments.

Required:

Make a recommendation to the vice president as to whether the housewares department should be discontinued and the appliances department expanded. Use discounted cash flow, covering an eight-year period. Use the incremental cost approach.

14–12. *Equipment Acquisition: Uneven Cash Flows.* Ellis Company is using a single Model 400 shaping machine in the manufacture of one of its products. The company is expecting to have a large increase in demand for the product, and is anxious to expand its productive capacity. Two possibilities are under consideration:

Alternative 1: Purchase another Model 400 shaping machine to operate along with the currently-owned Model 400 machine.

Alternative 2: Purchase a Model 800 shaping machine, and use the currently-owned Model 400 machine as standby equipment. The Model 800 machine is a high-speed unit, with double the capacity of the Model 400 machine.

The following additional information is available on the two alternatives:

1. All machines have a ten-year life from the time they are first used in production. Scrap value is nominal, and can be ignored. Straight-line depreciation is used.

2. The cost of a new Model 800 machine is $40,000.

3. The Model 400 machine now in use cost $18,000 three years ago. Its present book value is $12,600, and its present market value is $10,000.

4. A new Model 400 machine costs $22,000 now. If the company decides not to buy the Model 800 machine, then the currently owned Model 400 machine will have to be replaced in seven years at a cost of $25,000. The replacement machine will have a market value of about $18,000 when it is three years old.

5. Production over the next ten years is expected to be:

Year	Production in Units
1	40,000
2	50,000
3	60,000
4-10	65,000

6. The two models of machines are not equally efficient in output. Comparative variable costs per unit are:

	Model 400	Model 800
Materials per unit....................	$0.22	$0.40
Direct labor per unit	0.42	0.15
Supplies, lubricants, etc. per unit	0.06	0.05
Total variable cost per unit	$0.70	$0.60

7. The Model 400 machine is less costly to maintain than the Model 800 machine. Annual repairs and maintenance on a single Model 400 machine are $2,500.

8. Repairs and maintenance on a Model 800 machine, with a Model 400 machine used as standby, would total $3,800 per year.

9. No other factory costs will change as a result of the decision between the two machines.

10. The Ellis Company requires a before-tax rate of return of 20 percent on all investments.

Required:

1. Which alternative should the company choose? Show computations, using discounted cash flow.

2. Suppose that the cost of labor increases by 10 percent. Would this make the Model 800 machine more or less desirable? Explain. No computations are needed.

3. Suppose that the cost of materials doubles. Would this make the Model 800 machine more or less desirable? Explain. No computations are needed.

chapter 15

Further Aspects of Investment Decisions

WE CONTINUE our discussion of capital budgeting in this chapter by focusing on three new topics. First, we focus on income taxes and their impact on the capital budgeting decision. Second, we focus on methods of ranking competing capital investment projects, according to their relative desirability. And third, we focus on methods of making capital budgeting decisions, other than discounted cash flow.

INCOME TAXES AND CAPITAL BUDGETING

In our discussion of capital budgeting in the preceding chapter, the matter of income taxes was omitted for two reasons. First, many organizations have no taxes to pay. These organizations include schools, hospitals, and governmental units on local, state, and national levels. Use of capital budgeting techniques by these organizations will always be on a before-tax basis, as illustrated in the preceding chapter. Second, the topic of capital budgeting is sufficiently complex that it is best absorbed in small doses. Now that we have laid a solid groundwork in the concepts of present value and discounting, we can explore the effects of income taxes on capital budgeting decisions with little difficulty.

The Concept of After-Tax Cost

If someone were to ask you how much the rent is on your apartment, you would probably answer with the dollar amount you pay out each month. If someone were to ask a businessman how much the rent is on his factory building, he might answer by stating a lesser figure than the dollar amount being paid out each month. The reason is that rent is a tax-deductible expense to a business firm, and expenses such as rent are often looked at on an *after-tax* basis, rather than a before-tax basis. The true cost of a tax-deductible item is not the dollars paid out, but the amount of the payment that will remain after taking into consideration *any reduction in income taxes* that the payment will bring about. An expenditure net of its tax effect is known as *after-tax cost*.

After-tax cost is not a difficult concept. To illustrate the ideas behind it, assume that two firms, A and B, normally have sales of $15,000 each month, and cash expenses of $5,000 each month. Firm A is considering an advertising program that will cost $2,000 each month. The tax rate is 60 percent. What will be the after-tax cost to Firm A of the contemplated $2,000 monthly advertising expenditure? The after-tax cost is computed below:

	Firm A	Firm B
Sales	$15,000	$15,000
Expenses:		
Regular	5,000	5,000
New advertising program	2,000	–0–
Total	7,000	5,000
Net income before taxes	8,000	10,000
Income taxes (60 percent)	4,800	6,000
Net income	$ 3,200	$ 4,000
After-tax cost of the new advertising program	$800	

The after-tax cost of the advertising program would be only $800 per month. This figure must be correct, since it measures the difference in net income between the two companies, and since their income statements are identical except for the $2,000 in advertising paid by Firm A. In effect, a $2,000 monthly advertising expenditure would *really* cost Firm A only $800 *after taxes*.

A formula can be developed from these data that will give the after-tax cost of *any* cash expenditure. The formula is:

$$(1 - \text{Tax Rate}) \times \text{Total Amount Paid} = \text{After-Tax Cost} \qquad (1)$$

We can prove the accuracy of this formula by applying it to Firm A's $2,000 advertising expenditure:

$$(1 - .60) \times \$2,000 = \$800 \text{ After-Tax Cost of the Advertising Program}$$

The concept of after-tax cost is very useful to the manager, since it measures the *actual* amount of cash that will be leaving a company as a result of a particular expenditure decision. In integrating income taxes into capital budgeting decisions, it will be necessary to place all revenue and expense items associated with a project on an after-tax basis.

In the case of revenues and other *taxable* cash receipts, the after-tax cash inflow can be obtained by a simple variation of the expenditure formula used above:

$(1 -$ Tax Rate$) \times$ Total Amount Received

$\qquad\qquad\qquad$ = After-Tax Benefit (net cash inflow)   (2)

We emphasize the term *taxable* cash receipts above, since not all cash inflows are taxable. For example, the release of working capital at the termination of an investment project would not be a taxable cash inflow.

The Concept of Depreciation Tax Shield

The point was made in the preceding chapter that depreciation deductions in and of themselves do not involve cash flows. For this reason, depreciation deductions were ignored in Chapter 14 in all discounted cash flow computations.

Even though depreciation deductions do not involve cash flows, they do have an impact on the amount of income taxes that a firm will pay, and income taxes *do* involve cash flows. Therefore, as we now integrate income taxes into capital budgeting decisions, it will be necessary to consider depreciation deductions to the extent that they affect tax payments.

An Illustration. To illustrate the effect of depreciation deductions on tax payments, let us compare two firms, X and Y. Both firms have annual sales of $20,000, and cash operating expenses of $10,000. In addition, Firm X has a depreciable asset, on which the depreciation deduction is $3,000 per year. The tax rate is 60 percent. A cash flow comparison of the two firms is given in Exhibit 15–1.

Notice from the exhibit that Firm X's net cash inflow exceeds Firm Y's net cash inflow by $1,800. Also notice that in order to obtain Firm X's net cash inflow, it is necessary to add the $3,000 depreciation deduction back to the company's net income. This step is necessary since depreciation is a noncash deduction on the income statement.

Exhibit 15–1 presents an interesting paradox. Notice that even though Firm X's net cash inflow is $1,800 *greater* than Firm Y's, its net income is much *lower* than Firm Y's (only $2,800, as compared to Firm Y's $4,000). The explanation for this paradox lies in the concept of the *depreciation tax shield.*

The Depreciation Tax Shield. Firm X's greater net cash inflow comes about as a result of the *shield* against tax payments that is provided by depreciation deductions. Although depreciation deductions involve

EXHIBIT 15–1
The Impact of Depreciation Deductions on Tax Payments—A Comparison of Cash Flows

	Firm X	Firm Y
Sales	$20,000	$20,000
Expenses:		
Cash operating expenses.......................	10,000	10,000
Depreciation expense	3,000	–0–
Total.................................	13,000	10,000
Net income before taxes.......................	7,000	10,000
Income taxes (60 percent)......................	4,200	6,000
Net income	$ 2,800	$ 4,000
Cash inflow from operations:		
Net income, as above	$ 2,800	$ 4,000
Add: The noncash deduction for depreciation	3,000	–0–
Total cash inflow.........................	$ 5,800	$ 4,000
Greater amount of cash available to Firm X............	$1,800	

no outflows of cash, *they are fully deductible* in arriving at taxable income. In effect, depreciation deductions *shield* revenues from taxation, and thereby *lower* the amount of taxes that a company must pay.

In the case of Firm X above, the $3,000 depreciation deduction taken involved no outflow of cash to the firm. But yet this depreciation was fully deductible on the company's income statement, and thereby *shielded* $3,000 in revenues from taxation. Were it not for the depreciation deduction, the company's income taxes would have been $1,800 higher, since the entire $3,000 in shielded revenues would have been taxable at the regular tax rate of 60 percent (60 percent × $3,000 = $1,800). In effect, the depreciation tax shield *has reduced Firm A's taxes by $1,800*, permitting these funds to be retained within the company, rather than going to the tax collector. Viewed another way, we can say that Firm A has realized an $1,800 *cash inflow* (through reduced tax payments) as a result of its $3,000 depreciation deduction.

Because they shield revenues from taxation, depreciation deductions are generally referred to as a "depreciation tax shield." The reduction in tax payments made possible by the depreciation tax shield will always be equal to the amount of the depreciation deduction taken, multiplied by the tax rate. The formula is:

Depreciation Deduction × Tax Rate
         = Tax Savings from the Depreciation Tax Shield   (3)

We can prove this formula by applying it to the $3,000 depreciation deduction taken by Firm X in our example:

$3,000 × 60% = $1,800 reduction in tax payments (shown as "Greater amount of cash available to firm X" in Exhibit 15-1)

As we now integrate income taxes into capital budgeting computations, it will be necessary to consider the impact of depreciation deductions on tax payments, by showing the tax savings provided by the depreciation tax shield.

The Best Depreciation Method

The most widely used depreciation methods are straight-line, sum-of-the-years-digits, and double-declining balance. If a firm is interested in minimizing taxes, which depreciation method should be chosen? Since the cash flow benefits associated with depreciation deductions arise as a result of the tax shield which they provide, that method should be chosen which provides the largest present value of tax savings over the life of an asset. Exhibit 15-2 compares the three depreciation methods, in terms of the present value of the tax savings which they provide on a hypothetical asset costing $100,000.

As shown in Exhibit 15-2, the double-declining balance method provides the largest present value of tax savings resulting from the depreciation tax shield. The sum-of-the-years'-digits method provides the second largest present value, and the straight-line method provides the smallest present value. This example goes far to explain why firms often prefer the accelerated depreciation methods over the straight-line method. Since the accelerated methods provide the bulk of their tax shield early in the life of an asset, the present value of tax savings which they provide will always be greater than the present value of tax savings under the straight-line method.

The point should be emphasized that all three depreciation methods provide the *same total* dollars of tax savings in *absolute* terms. That is, each method provides $60,000 in *absolute* dollars of tax savings over the four-year life of the asset, as shown in the tabulation below:

Year	Straight-Line	Sum-of-the-Years'-Digits	Double-Declining Balance
1	$15,000	$24,000	$30,000
2	15,000	18,000	15,000
3	15,000	12,000	7,500
4	15,000	6,000	7,500
Total dollars of tax savings	$60,000	$60,000	$60,000

EXHIBIT 15–2
Tax Shield Effects of Depreciation, on a Present Value Basis

Cost of the asset	$100,000
Life of the asset	4 years
Salvage value	–0–
Desired rate of return	15% after taxes
Income tax rate	60%

Method of Depreciation	15% Factor	Present Value of Tax Savings
Straight-Line Depreciation:		
Annual depreciation ($100,000 ÷ 4 = $25,000):		
Depreciation deduction $25,000		
Multiply by 60% . . . . X 60%		
Income tax savings, years 1–4 . . . . $15,000	2.855	$42,825

Sum-of-the-Years'-Digits Depreciation:

Year	Multiplier*	Depreciation Deduction	Tax Shield: Income Tax Savings @ 60%		
1 . . . . 4/10		$40,000	$24,000	.870	$20,880
2 . . . . 3/10		$30,000	$18,000	.756	13,608
3 . . . . 2/10		$20,000	$12,000	.658	7,896
4 . . . . 1/10		$10,000	$ 6,000	.572	3,432
					$45,816

Double-Declining Balance Depreciation:

Year	Book Value	Rate†	Depreciation Deduction	Tax Shield: Income Tax Savings @ 60%		
1 . . . . $100,000		50%	$50,000	$30,000	.870	$26,100
2 50,000		50%	25,000	15,000	.756	11,340
3 25,000		50%	12,500	7,500	.658	4,935
4 12,500		50%	12,500	7,500	.572	4,290
						$46,665

* The denominator for the sum-of-the-years'-digits method is: $1 + 2 + 3 + 4 = 10$

$$S = \frac{n(n + 1)}{2}$$

or

$$S = \frac{4(4 + 1)}{2} = 10$$

where S = sum of the years
n = life of the asset
† The percentage rate for the double-declining balance method is: 2 × straight line rate = 2 × 25% = 50%. The asset is depreciated to zero salvage value in the 4th year.

The difference between the three depreciation methods lies in the *present value* of these tax savings. Notice that the accelerated methods provide most of their tax savings *early* in the life of the asset, as compared to the straight-line method. Since money has a time value, this earlier availability of the tax savings increases the present value of the total tax savings stream. In sum, by providing large depreciation tax shields early in the life of an asset, accelerated methods of depreciation defer taxes to the future, thereby making more dollars of cash available for use *now* in a business.

Comprehensive Example of Income Taxes and Capital Budgeting

Armed with an understanding of the concepts of after-tax cost, after-tax revenue, and depreciation tax shield, we are now prepared to examine a comprehensive example of income taxes and capital budgeting. Assume the following data:

The Daily Globe newspaper has an auxiliary press that was purchased three years ago at a cost of $56,000. The press is being depreciated by the straight-line method, with no provision for salvage value. The press will last four more years, but it will need an overhaul in two years at a cost of $8,000. The overhaul will be fully deductible for tax purposes when incurred. The operating costs of the press are $48,000 each year, exclusive of depreciation. Although no salvage value is being recognized for tax purposes, the press will have a salvage value of about $3,000 at the end of four more years.[1]

The Daily Globe is thinking about selling the old press and purchasing a new press. The old press can be sold right now for $25,000. A new press will cost $50,000, and will be used only four years, after which time it will be salable for $5,000. If the new press is purchased, it will be depreciated by the sum-of-the-years'-digits method. No salvage value will be recognized for tax purposes. The new press will cost $40,000 each year to operate.

The tax rate is 60 percent. The Daily Globe requires a return after taxes of 10 percent on all investments in fixed assets.

Should the Daily Globe keep its old press, or buy the new press? As explained in the preceding chapter, there are two ways to approach a capital budgeting decision such as this one—by the total cost approach, or by the incremental cost approach. Exhibit 15–3 contains the solution

---

[1] Section 167(f) of the *Internal Revenue Code* permits a taxpayer to ignore salvage value up to 10 percent of the cost of an asset in computing depreciation deductions. Therefore, if an asset cost $20,000, and had a salvage value of $3,000, only $1,000 of the salvage value would need to be recognized in computing depreciation deductions for tax purposes.

from the total cost approach, and Exhibit 15–4 contains the solution from the incremental cost approach.

Since the total cost approach is more widely used than the incremental cost approach, we will focus our discussion on it. The following points should be noted about the data and computations in Exhibit 15–3:

1. The initial investment of $50,000 in the new press is included in full, with no reductions for taxes. The tax effects of this investment are considered in the depreciation deductions.
2. Annual cash operating costs are kept separate from depreciation deductions. These are unlike items, and should not be mixed together. The annual cash operating costs are included in present value computations on an after-tax cost basis.
3. The tax savings provided by the depreciation deductions are included in present value computations in exactly the way illustrated and discussed earlier in the chapter (see Exhibit 15–2).
4. Since The Daily Globe does not consider salvage value when depreciating assets, book value at the end of four years will be zero for both the old and the new presses. Therefore, the entire salvage value in each case will be fully taxable. The net cash inflow to the company is computed by multiplying the salvage value by (1 — Tax Rate), as discussed earlier in the chapter.
5. The computation of the cash inflow from the disposal of the old press is somewhat more involved than the other items in the exhibit. Note that *two* cash inflows are connected with the disposal of the old press. The first is a $25,000 cash inflow in the form of the sale price. The second is a cash inflow of $4,200 resulting from the tax shield provided by the loss sustained on the sale. This tax shield functions in the same way as the tax shield provided by depreciation deductions. That is, the loss on disposal of the old press (the difference between the sale price of $25,000 and the book value of $32,000) is fully deductible from income in the year the loss is sustained. This loss shields income from taxation, thereby causing a reduction in the income taxes that otherwise would be payable. The tax savings resulting from the loss tax shield are computed by multiplying the loss by the tax rate (the same procedure as for depreciation deductions).
6. The overhaul of the old press is treated the same as any other cash expenditure, and included in the analysis on an after-tax cost basis.
7. Generally, any gains on sales of depreciable assets used in a business are taxed as ordinary income, just as losses are deductible as ordinary losses. Only under very narrow circumstances can such gains ever be taxed as capital gains, even in part. The tax laws in this matter are very complex, and expert tax advice should be sought if doubt exists as to the proper classification of a gain.

EXHIBIT 15–3

Comprehensive Example of Income Taxes and Capital Budgeting: Total Cost Approach

Item and Computations			Year(s) Having Cash Flows	Amount of Cash Flows	10% Factor	Present Value of Cash Flows
Buy the New Press:						
Initial investment			Now	($50,000)	1.000	($50,000)
Annual cash operating costs		$40,000				
Multiply by 1 − 60%		× 40%				
After-tax cost		$16,000	1–4	(16,000)	3.170	(50,720)
Depreciation deductions:						

Year	Multiplier	Depreciation Deduction	Tax Shield: Income Tax Savings @ 60%					
1	4/10	$20,000	$12,000	1	12,000	.909	10,908
2	3/10	15,000	9,000	2	9,000	.826	7,434
3	2/10	10,000	6,000	3	6,000	.751	4,506
4	1/10	5,000	3,000	4	3,000	.683	2,049

Item and Computations			Year(s) Having Cash Flows	Amount of Cash Flows	10% Factor	Present Value of Cash Flows
Salvage value, fully taxable since						
book value will be zero		$5,000				
Multiply by 1 − 60%		× 40%				
Net cash inflow		$2,000	4	2,000	.683	1,366
Cash flow from disposal of the old press:						
Book value now						
($56,000 − $24,000)	$32,000					
Sale price now	25,000	$25,000				
Loss on disposal	$ 7,000					
Income tax savings @ 60%	× 60%	4,200				
Total cash inflow from disposal		$29,200	Now	29,200	1.000	29,200
Present value of costs						($45,257)

Keep the Old Press:

Annual cash operating costs	$48,000			
Multiply by 1 − 60%	× 40%			
After-tax cost	$19,200	1–4	($19,200)	3.170	($60,864)
Depreciation deduction	$ 8,000			
Multiply by 60%	× 60%			
Income tax savings	$ 4,800	1–4	4,800	3.170	15,216
Salvage value, fully taxable since book value will be zero	$ 3,000			
Multiply by 1 − 60%	× 40%			
Net cash inflow	$ 1,200	4	1,200	.683	820
Overhaul at end of year two	$ 8,000			
Multiply by 1 − 60%	× 40%			
After-tax cost	$ 3,200	2	(3,200)	.826	(2,643)
Present value of costs					($47,471)
Net present value in favor of purchasing the new press					$ 2,214

EXHIBIT 15–4
Comprehensive Example of Income Taxes and Capital Budgeting: Incremental Cost Approach

Item and Computations	Year(s) Having Cash Flows	Amount of Cash Flows	10% Factor	Present Value of Cash Flows
Initial investment	Now.....	($50,000)	1.000	($50,000)
Savings in annual cash operating costs $8,000				
Multiply by 1 − 60% ..... × 40%				
Net annual savings $3,200	1–4.....	3,200	3.170	10,144

Difference in Depreciation:

Year	New Press	Old Press	Difference	Tax Savings @ 60%				
1.....	$20,000	$8,000	$12,000	$7,200	1.....	7,200	.909	6,545
2.....	15,000	8,000	7,000	4,200	2.....	4,200	.826	3,469
3.....	10,000	8,000	2,000	1,200	3.....	1,200	.751	901
4.....	5,000	8,000	(3,000)	(1,800)	4.....	(1,800)	.683	(1,229)

Difference in salvage value:				
Salvage of the new press $5,000				
Salvage of the old press 3,000				
$2,000				
Multiply by 1 − 60% ..... × 40%				
Net cash inflow ..... $ 800	4.....	800	.683	546
Disposal value of the old press now (see computations in Exhibit 15–3)	Now.....	29,200	1.000	29,200
Overhaul avoided in two years on the old press $8,000				
Multiply by 1 − 60% ..... × 40%				
Net cash inflow $3,200	2.....	3,200	.826	2,643
Net present value in favor of purchasing the new press.....				$ 2,214

Note: The figures in this exhibit are derived from the *differences* between the two alternatives given in Exhibit 15–3.

Finally, two points should be noted on an *overall* basis in both Exhibits 15–3 and 15–4. First, notice that all cash flows involving tax-deductible costs and taxable revenues have been placed on an after-tax basis, by multiplying the cash flow in each case by one minus the tax rate $(1 - 60$ percent$)$. Second, notice that the depreciation deductions and loss deductions have been multiplied *by the tax rate itself* (60 percent) to determine the tax savings (cash inflow) resulting from the tax shield. *These two points should be studied with great care, until both are thoroughly understood.*

PREFERENCE DECISIONS—THE RANKING OF INVESTMENT PROJECTS

In the preceding chapter we indicated that there are two types of decisions to make relative to investment opportunities. These two types of decisions are screening decisions and preference decisions, respectively. Screening decisions have to do with whether or not some proposed investment is acceptable to a firm. We discussed ways of making screening decisions in the preceding chapter, where we studied the use of the cost of capital as a screening tool. Screening decisions are very important, in that many investment proposals come to the attention of management, and those that are worthwhile must be screened out from those that are not.

Preference decisions come *after* screening decisions, and attempt to answer the following question: "How do the remaining investment proposals, all of which have been screened and provide an acceptable rate of return, rank in terms of preference? That is, which one(s) would be *best* for the firm to accept?" Preference decisions are much more difficult to make than screening decisions. The reason is that investment funds are usually limited, and this often requires that some (perhaps many) otherwise very profitable investment opportunities be foregone.

Preference decisions are sometimes called *ranking* decisions, or *rationing* decisions, because they attempt to ration limited investment funds among many competing investment opportunities. The choice may be simply between two competing alternatives, or many alternatives may be involved, which must be ranked according to their overall desirability. Either the time-adjusted rate of return method or the net present value method can be used in making preference decisions.

Time-Adjusted Rate of Return Method

When using the time-adjusted rate of return method to rank competing investment projects, the preference rule is: *The higher the time-adjusted rate of return, the more desirable the project.* If one investment project promises a time-adjusted rate of return of 18 percent, then it is preferable over another project which promises a time-adjusted rate of return of only 15 percent.

Ranking projects according to time-adjusted rate of return is widely used as a means of making preference decisions. The reasons are probably twofold. First, no additional computations are needed beyond those already performed in making the initial screening decisions. The rates of return themselves are used to rank acceptable projects. And second, the ranking data are easily understood by management. Rates of return are very similar to interest rates, which the manager works with every day.

Net Present Value Method

If the net present value method is being used to rank competing investment projects, the present value of the cash flows of one project cannot be compared directly to the present value of the cash flows of another project, unless the investments in the projects are of equal size. For example, assume that a company is considering two competing investments, as shown below:

	Investment A	Investment B
Investment required	$50,000	$5,000
Present value of cash inflows	51,000	6,000
Net present value	$ 1,000	$1,000

Each project has a net present value of $1,000, but the projects are not equally desirable. A project requiring an investment of only $5,000, that produces cash inflows with a present value of $6,000, is much more desirable than a project requiring an investment of $50,000 that is capable of producing cash inflows with a present value of only $51,000. In order to compare the two projects on a valid basis, it is necessary in each case to divide the present value of the cash inflows by the investment required. The ratio which this computation yields is called the *profitability index*. The profitability index on each of the investments above is computed below:

	Investment A	Investment B
Present value of cash inflows	$51,000 (a)	$6,000 (a)
Investment required	$50,000 (b)	$5,000 (b)
Profitability index (a) ÷ (b)	1.02	1.20

The preference rule to follow when using the profitability index to rank competing investment projects is: *The higher the profitability in-*

dex, the more desirable the project. Applying this rule to the two investments above, Investment B should be chosen over Investment A.

In computing the investment in a project, the cash outlays should be reduced by any salvage recovered from sale of old equipment being replaced. Investment in a project also includes any working capital that the project may require, as explained in the preceding chapter.

Comparing the Preference Rules

The profitability index is conceptually superior to the time-adjusted rate of return as a method of making preference decisions. This is because the profitability index will always give the correct signal as to the relative desirability of alternatives, even if the alternatives have different lives and different patterns of earnings. By contrast, if lives are unequal, the time-adjusted rate of return method can lead the manager to make incorrect decisions.

Assume the following situation:

Parker Company is considering two investment proposals, only one of which can be accepted. Project A requires an investment of $5,000, and will provide a single cash inflow of $6,000 in one year. Therefore, it promises a time-adjusted rate of return of 20 percent. Project B also requires an investment of $5,000. It will provide cash inflows of $1,360 each year for six years. Its time-adjusted rate of return is 16 percent. Which project should be accepted?

Although Project A promises a time-adjusted rate of return of 20 percent as compared to only 16 percent for Project B, Project A is not necessarily preferable over Project B. It is preferable *only* if the funds released at the end of the year under Project A can be reinvested at a high rate of return in some *other* project for the five remaining years. Otherwise, Project B, which promises a return of 16 percent over the *entire* six years, is more desirable.

Let us assume that the company in the example above has a cost of capital of 12 percent. The profitability index approach to ranking competing investment projects would rank the two proposals as follows:

	Project A	Project B
Present value of cash inflows:		
$6,000 received at the end of one year at 12 percent (factor of 0.893)	$5,358 (a)	
$1,360 received at the end of each year for six years at 12 percent (factor of 4.111)		$5,591 (a)
Investment required	$5,000 (b)	$5,000 (b)
Profitability index (a) ÷ (b)	1.07	1.12

The profitability index indicates that Project B is more desirable than Project A. This is in fact the case if the funds released from Project A at the end of one year can be reinvested at only 12 percent (the cost of capital). Although the computations will not be shown here, in order for Project A to be more desirable than Project B, the funds released from Project A would have to be reinvested at a rate of return *greater* than 14 percent for the remaining five years.

OTHER APPROACHES TO CAPITAL BUDGETING DECISIONS

The discounted cash flow methods of making capital budgeting decisions are relatively new. They were first introduced on a widespread basis in the 1950s, although their appearance in business literature predates this period by many years. Discounted cash flow methods have gained widespread acceptance as accurate and dependable decision-making tools. Other methods of making capital budgeting decisions are also available, however, and are preferred by some managers.

The Payback Method

The payback method centers around a span of time known as the *payback period*. The payback period can be defined as the length of time that it takes for an investment project to recoup its own initial cost out of the cash receipts it generates. In business jargon, this period is sometimes spoken of as "the time that it takes for an investment to pay for itself." The basic premise of the payback method is that the more quickly the cost of an investment can be recovered, the more desirable is the investment.

The payback period is expressed in years. The formula used in computing the payback period is:

$$\text{Payback Period} = \frac{\text{Initial Outlay}}{\text{Uniform Annual Cash Receipts}} \qquad (4)$$

Notice from the formula that depreciation is ignored in computing the payback period. To illustrate the mechanics involved in payback computations, assume the following data:

The Concord Company needs a new milling machine. The company is considering two machines, Machine A and Machine B. Machine A costs $15,000 and will reduce annual operating costs by $5,000. Machine B costs only $12,000, but will also reduce annual operating costs by $5,000.

Required:
Which machine should be purchased? Make your calculations by the payback method.

$$\text{Machine A payback period} = \frac{\$15,000}{\$5,000} = 3.0 \text{ years}$$

$$\text{Machine B payback period} = \frac{\$12,000}{\$5,000} = 2.4 \text{ years}$$

According to the payback calculations, The Concord Company should purchase Machine B, since it has a shorter payback period than Machine A.

Evaluation of the Payback Method

The payback method is not a measure of profitability. It is a measure of how quickly investment dollars can be recouped. This is a major defect in the approach, since a shorter payback period is not always an accurate guide as to whether one investment is more desirable than another. To illustrate this point, consider again the two machines used in the example above. Since Machine B has a shorter payback period than Machine A, it *appears* that Machine B is more desirable than Machine A. But if we add one more piece of data, this illusion quickly disappears. Machine A has a projected ten-year life, and Machine B has a projected five-year life. It would take two purchases of Machine B to provide the same length of service as a single purchase of Machine A. Under these circumstances, Machine A would be a much better investment than Machine B, even though Machine B has a shorter payback period. Unfortunately, the payback method has no inherent mechanism for highlighting differences in useful life between investments for the decision maker. Such differences can be very subtle, and relying on payback alone can cause the manager to make incorrect decisions.

A further criticism of the payback method can be found in the fact that it does not consider the time value of money. A cash inflow to be received several years in the future is weighed equally with a cash inflow to be received right now. To illustrate, assume that for an investment of $8,000 you can purchase either of the two following streams of cash inflows:

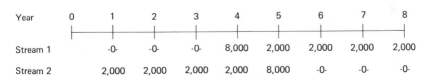

Year	0	1	2	3	4	5	6	7	8
Stream 1		-0-	-0-	-0-	8,000	2,000	2,000	2,000	2,000
Stream 2		2,000	2,000	2,000	2,000	8,000	-0-	-0-	-0-

Which stream of cash inflows would you prefer to receive in return for your $8,000 investment? Each stream has a payback period of 4.0

years. Therefore, if payback alone was relied on in making the decision, you would be forced to say that the streams are equally desirable. However, from point of view of the time value of money, Stream 2 is much more desirable than Stream 1.

On the other hand, under certain conditions, the payback method can be very useful to the manager. For one thing, it can help him to identify the "ballpark" in weeding out investment proposals. That is, it can be used as a screening tool to help answer the question, "Should I consider this proposal further?" If a proposal doesn't provide at least some minimum payback period, then there might be no need to consider it further. In addition, the payback period is often of great importance to new firms that are "cash poor." When a firm is cash poor, a project with a short payback period, but low rate of return, might be preferred over another project with a high rate of return, but a long payback period. The reason is that the company may simply need a faster return of its cash investment.

Payback and Uneven Cash Flows

When the cash inflows associated with an investment project are erratic or uneven, the simple payback formula which we outlined earlier is no longer usable, and the computations involved in deriving the payback period can be fairly complex. Consider the following data:

Year	Investment	Cash Inflow
1	$4,000	$1,000
2		–0–
3		2,000
4	2,000	1,000
5		500
6		3,000
7		2,000
8		2,000

What is the payback period on this investment? The answer is 5.5 years, but to obtain this figure it is necessary to balance off the cash inflows against the investment outflows on a *year-by-year* basis. The steps involved in this process are shown in Exhibit 15–5. By the middle of the sixth year, sufficient cash inflows will have been realized to recover the entire investment of $6,000 ($4,000 + $2,000).

The Simple Rate of Return Method

The simple rate of return method is another capital budgeting technique that does not involve discounted cash flows. The method is also known as the financial statement method, the unadjusted rate of return

EXHIBIT 15–5
Payback and Uneven Cash Flows

Year	(1) Beginning Unrecovered Investment	(2) Additional Investment	(3) Total Unrecovered Investment (1) + (2)	(4) Cash Inflow	(5) Ending Unrecovered Investment (3) − (4)
1	$4,000		$4,000	$1,000	$3,000
2	3,000		3,000	–0–	3,000
3	3,000		3,000	2,000	1,000
4	1,000	$2,000	3,000	1,000	2,000
5	2,000		2,000	500	1,500
6	1,500		1,500	3,000	–0–
7	–0–		–0–	2,000	–0–
8	–0–		–0–	2,000	–0–

method, and the book value method. It derives its popularity primarily from the fact that it is supposed to parallel conventional financial statements very closely in its handling of investment data.

Unlike other capital budgeting methods we have discussed, the simple rate of return method does not focus on cash flows. Rather, it focuses on accounting net income. The approach is to estimate the revenues that will be generated by a proposed investment, and then to deduct from these revenues all projected operating expenses associated with it, *including depreciation*. This net income figure is then related to the required investment in the project, as shown in the following formula:

Simple Rate of Return

$$= \frac{[\text{Incremental Revenue}] - \left[\begin{array}{c}\text{Operating Expenses} \\ \text{(including depreciation)}\end{array}\right]}{\text{Initial Investment}} \quad (5)$$

Or, if the project is a cost reduction project, the formula becomes:

$$\text{Simple Rate of Return} = \frac{\text{Reduction in Costs} - \text{Depreciation}}{\text{Initial Investment}}$$

Example

Brigham Tea, Inc., is a processor of a non-tannic acid tea product. The company is contemplating the purchase of equipment for an additional processing line. The additional processing line would increase revenues by $10,000 per year. Cash operating expenses would be $4,000 per year. The equipment would cost $24,000 and have a 12-year life. No salvage value is projected.

Required:

1. Compute the simple rate of return.
2. Compute the time-adjusted rate of return, and compare it to the simple rate of return.

By applying the formula for the simple rate of return found in equation (5), we can compute the simple rate of return to be 16.7 percent:

Simple Rate of Return =

$$\frac{\left[\begin{array}{c}\$10,000 \text{ Incremental} \\ \text{Revenues}\end{array}\right] - \left[\begin{array}{c}\$4,000 \text{ Cash Operating Expenses} \\ + \$2,000 \text{ Depreciation}\end{array}\right]}{\$24,000 \text{ Initial Investment}}$$

Simple Rate of Return = 16.7 percent

This rate, however, is far below the time-adjusted rate of return of approximately 23 percent:

$$\text{Time-Adjusted Rate of Return} = \frac{\$24,000}{\$6,000^2} = \text{Factor of } 4.000$$

$$\text{Time-Adjusted Rate of Return} = \frac{\text{Approximately 23 Percent from Table 2,}}{\text{Scanning across the 12-year Line.}}$$

Criticisms of the Simple Rate of Return

The most damaging criticism of the simple rate of return method is that it does not consider the time value of money. A dollar received ten years from now is viewed as being just as valuable as a dollar received today. This defect becomes more significant the farther one goes forward in time. Notice from our computations above (involving a 12-year life) that the simple rate of return (16.7 percent) is much less than the time-adjusted rate of return (23 percent). The longer the expected life of a project, the more severely the simple rate of return method will understate the project's true rate of return. This understatement becomes less pronounced as the life of a project becomes shorter.

A further criticism of the simple rate of return method is that it often proves to be misleading in its basic approach. The method is supposed to parallel conventional financial statements closely in its handling of data. Yet studies show that this parallel is rarely present.[3] The problem is that conventional accounting practice tends to write costs off to expense very quickly. As a result, the net income and asset structure actually reflected on financial statements may differ substantially from comparable items in rate of return computations, wherein costs

---

[2] $10,000 increased revenues, minus $4,000 cash expenses.

[3] See *Research Report 35, Return on Capital as a Guide to Managerial Decisions,* National Association of Accountants (December 1959), p. 64.

tend to be expensed less quickly. This disparity in handling of data is especially pronounced in those situations where rate of return computations are carried out by nonaccounting personnel.

The Choice of an Investment Base

In our examples, we have defined the investment base for simple rate of return computations to be the entire initial investment in the project under consideration [see the formula in (5)]. Actual practice varies between using the entire initial investment, as we have done, and using only the *average* investment over the life of a project. As a practical matter, which approach one chooses to follow is unimportant. If the average investment is used, rather than the entire initial investment, then the resulting rate of return will be approximately doubled.

SUMMARY

Unless a company is a tax-exempt organization, such as a school or a governmental unit, income taxes should be considered in making capital budgeting computations. When income taxes are a factor in a company, cash expenditures must be placed on an after-tax basis by multiplying the expenditure by one minus the tax rate. Only the after-tax amount is used in determining the desirability of an investment proposal. Similarly, taxable cash inflows must be placed on an after-tax basis by multiplying the cash inflow by one minus the tax rate.

Although depreciation deductions do not involve a present outflow of cash in a company, they are valid expenses for tax purposes, and as such affect income tax payments. Depreciation deductions shield income from taxation, resulting in decreased taxes being paid. This shielding of income from taxation is commonly called a depreciation tax shield. The savings in income taxes arising from the depreciation tax shield are computed by multiplying the depreciation deduction by the tax rate itself. Since accelerated methods of depreciation provide the bulk of their tax shield early in the life of an asset, they are superior to the straight-line method of depreciation, from a present value of tax savings point of view.

Preference decisions relate to ranking two or more investment proposals according to their relative desirability. This ranking can be performed using either the time-adjusted rate of return or the profitability index. The profitability index, which is the ratio of the present value of a proposal's cash inflows to the investment required, is generally regarded as the best way of making preference decisions when discounted cash flow is being used.

Instead of using discounted cash flow, some companies prefer to use either payback or the simple rate of return in evaluating investment proposals. Payback is determined by dividing a project's cost by the annual cash inflows which it will generate, in order to find how quickly the original investment can be recovered. The simple rate of return is determined by dividing a projects' accounting net income either by the initial investment in the project or by the average investment over the life of the project. Both payback and the simple rate of return can be useful to the manager, so long as they are used with a full understanding of their limitations.

QUESTIONS

15–1. Why is it important to understand capital budgeting on a before-tax basis, as well as on an after-tax basis?

15–2. What is meant by after-tax cost, and how is the concept used in capital budgeting decisions?

15–3. What is a depreciation tax shield, and how does it affect capital budgeting decisions?

15–4. Why are accelerated methods of depreciation superior to the straight-line method of depreciation, from an income tax point of view?

15–5. Assume that an old piece of equipment is sold at a loss. From a capital budgeting point of view, what two cash inflows will be associated with the sale?

15–6. Assume that a new piece of equipment costs $30,000. The tax rate is 60 percent. Should the new piece of equipment be shown in the capital budgeting analysis as a cash outflow of $30,000 or as a cash outflow of $12,000 (i.e., $30,000 times 1 − 60%)? Explain.

15–7. Assume that a company has cash operating expenses of $15,000 and depreciation expense of $10,000. Can these two items be added together and treated as one in a capital budgeting analysis, or should they be kept separate? Explain.

15–8. What is meant by the term "payback period?" How is the payback period determined?

15–9. Under what conditions will the simple rate of return tend to approximate the time-adjusted rate of return?

15–10. Refer to Problem 14–9 in the preceding chapter. Do you agree with the president's payback computation in this problem? Explain. Ignore taxes.

15–11. Distinguish between capital budgeting screening decisions, and capital budgeting preference decisions. Why are preference decisions more difficult to make than screening decisions?

15–12. What is the preference rule for ranking investment projects under time-adjusted rate of return?

15–13. What is the preference rule for ranking investment projects under the net present value method?

15–14. Can an investment with a profitability index of less than 1.00 be an acceptable investment? Explain.

15–15. What is the major criticism of the payback and simple rate of return methods of making capital budgeting decisions?

EXERCISES

15–1. *a.* Carbo Company now spends $50,000 each year on advertising. The company is contemplating increasing its advertising to $70,000 each year. What would be the after-tax cost of the increased advertising, if the company pays taxes of 55 percent on income?

b. Black Company has just purchased a new machine that will increase revenues by $30,000 per year. If the company pays combined income taxes at a 60 percent rate, what will be the annual after-tax cash inflow from revenues provided by the new machine?

c. Irbin Company has just hired a new assistant controller at an annual salary of $24,000. The controller has indicated to the president of Irbin Company that the new assistant controller is costing the company $10,560 "after taxes." What is Irbin Company's tax rate?

d. Pilling Company has just purchased a new computer at a cost of $140,000. If the computer has a five-year life and the tax rate is 60 percent, what are the annual cash flows resulting from the depreciation tax shield? Use straight-line depreciation.

15–2. *a.* Boudine Beverage Company has a machine with a book value of $18,000. If the company sells the machine for $12,000 what will be the effect on cash flows, after taxes? Assume a tax rate of 60 percent.

b. The Colver Chemical Company has just sold a piece of equipment for $8,000. The equipment had a book value of $5,000. What will be the effect of this sale on cash flows, after taxes? Assume a tax rate of 60 percent.

15–3. Andy's Auto Rentals has just purchased a piece of car washing equipment at a cost of $30,000. Although the equipment will have a $2,000 salvage value at the end of its five-year life, salvage value is not considered in computing depreciation for tax purposes. The company uses sum-of-the-year's-digits depreciation, and the tax rate is 60 percent. Assume a discount rate of 8 percent, after taxes.

a. Compute the present value of the cash flows resulting from the depreciation tax shield each year.

b. Assume that the equipment is sold for its salvage value at the end of five years. What is the present value of the cash flows resulting from the sale, after taxes?

15–4. The Riverdale Publishing Company is investigating the purchase of a new collating machine to replace a presently owned hand-operated collating machine. The new machine would cost $18,000, and have a ten-year life. Its scrap value in 10 years would be $1,000.

If the new machine is purchased, the old machine will be kept and used on a standby basis. The operator of the old machine is paid a salary of $6,000 per year. If the new machine is purchased, the operator will be discharged, but given severance pay of $500. The severance pay will be paid and deducted for tax purposes in the first year of operation of the new machine. The company uses straight-line depreciation, and ignores salvage value in computing depreciation deductions.

Required:

Compute the net present value of the new collating machine, assuming the company requires an after-tax return of 10 percent on investments of this type. Use a tax rate of 60 percent.

15–5. A company is considering two investment alternatives. Relevant cost and revenue information on the two alternatives is given below:

	Alternative A	Alternative B
Investment in machinery and equipment.	$20,000	–
Investment in working capital	–	$20,000
Net annual revenues or cost savings.	6,000	6,000
Life of the project	8 years	8 years

At the end of eight years the equipment will have no salvage value. Straight-line depreciation will be used. At the end of eight years the working capital can be released for investment elsewhere. The company requires an after-tax return of 8 percent on all investments. The tax rate is 60 percent.

Required:

1. Compute the net present value of each investment alternative.
2. Compute the profitability index for each investment. Which alternative should be accepted? Rejected?

15–6. The Roper Construction Company plans to purchase a piece of equipment for use in construction of a large dam. The following information is available on the equipment:

Purchase cost new.	$50,000
Annual cost savings that will be realized from use of the equipment	21,500
Repairs required in the second year.	500
Salvage value in 4 years (ignored for purposes of computing depreciation deductions)	1,000

The company requires an after-tax return of 12 percent on all equipment purchases. The tax rate is 60 percent.

Required:

1. Compute the net present value of the equipment investment, assuming that straight-line depreciation is used. Does the equipment provide the desired 12 percent rate of return?

2. Compute the net present value of the equipment investment, assuming that sum-of-the-years'-digits depreciation is used. Does the equipment provide the desired 12 percent rate of return? How do you explain the difference in rate of return between part 1 and part 2?

15-7. The Tyler Transport Company has just purchased a new barge for hauling freight on the Mississippi River. The barge cost $90,000. Other data are given below:

Annual cash inflow (before taxes) expected from use of the new barge	$32,500
Salvage value of the barge in 5 years (ignore in computing depreciation)	8,000
One-time-only inspection and seaworthiness certification cost (expensed in Year 1).	1,000

The company uses sum-of-the-years'-digits depreciation, and desires an after-tax return of 14 percent on all equipment. The tax rate is 60 percent.

Required:

Does the new barge promise at least the minimum desired rate of return? Show computations by the net present value method. Round to the nearest whole dollar.

15-8. Nick's Novelties, Inc., is considering the purchase of a new type of pinball machine to place in amusement houses. The machines would cost $4,000 each, have a six-year useful life, and have an ultimate salvage value of $400 each. The company estimates that average annual revenues and expenses per machine would be:

Revenues from customers		$2,000
Operating expenses:		
Maintenance, taxes, etc.	$400	
Depreciation.	600	
Commission to amusement house.	500	1,500
Net income		$ 500

Required:

1. Assume that Nick's Novelties, Inc., will not purchase new equipment unless it promises a payback period of less than 3.5 years. Would you recommend purchase of the pinball machines? Ignore taxes.

2. Assume that Nick's Novelties, Inc., will not purchase new equipment unless it promises a simple rate of return of at least 12 percent. Would you recommend purchase of the pinball machines? (Compute investment at initial cost.) Ignore taxes.

15–9. Noyes Company is considering two machines, only one of which can be purchased. Cost and other information on the two machines is given below:

	Machine #1	*Machine #2*
Cost of the machine	$10,000	$12,000
Annual savings in cash operating costs	5,600	3,200
Life of the machine	5 years	6 years
Depreciation method to be used	SL	SL

Neither machine will have any salvage value. The tax rate is 60 percent. The cost of capital is 10 percent.

Required:

1. Compute the net present value of each machine. (Round to the nearest whole dollar.)
2. Compute the profitability index for each machine.

15–10. The following data relate to a piece of equipment just purchased by the Darley Company:

Purchase cost	$23,375
Annual cost savings that will be provided by the equipment	5,000
Life of the equipment	15 years
Cost of capital of the company	16%

Required:

Compute the following (round computations to the nearest dollar):
a. The payback period. Ignore taxes.
b. The simple rate of return. Ignore taxes.

15–11. Information on four investment proposals is given below.

Proposal Number	*Investment Required*	*Present Value of Cash Inflows*	*Net Present Value*	*Life*
1	$ 8,000	$ 9,800	$1,800	5 years
2	11,000	10,200	(800)	7
3	7,000	9,100	2,100	6
4	14,000	16,200	2,200	6

Required:

Rank the proposals in terms of preference.

PROBLEMS

15–1. *Net Present Value Analysis.* Chris's Travel Service is located in a large western city. The company specializes in recreational travel, and is considering the purchase of a large bus to provide sightseeing tours of the area. A 40-passenger bus can be purchased for $30,150. After 6 years' use the bus will be traded in on a replacement or sold for $6,000. The costs of operating the bus for a single season are estimated as follows:

Salaries.	$ 6,000
Maintenance.	1,100
Fuel.	9,500
Promotion	3,000
Licenses and taxes	400
Insurance	2,000
Total.	$22,000

The travel service estimates that the tours would average two full bus loads a day, for a 150-day season. The cost for a tour would average $2.50 per person. The management of Chris's Travel Service feels that the investment in the bus would have to yield a return of at least 10 percent, after taxes, to make the venture worthwhile. The company uses sum-of-the-years'-digits depreciation, and recognizes salvage value in computing depreciation deductions. The tax rate is 60 percent.

Required:

By use of the net present value method, determine whether the bus should be purchased.

15–2. *Depreciation Methods and Rate of Return.* John Belmont, manufacturing vice president of Atlantic Industries, has been anxious for some time to purchase a new piece of equipment for use in the plant. The equipment would cost $360,000 and have an eight-year life. It would have a final salvage value of $20,000.

Mr. Belmont has just received an analysis from his staff indicating that the equipment will not provide the 12 percent after-tax rate of return required by the company. In making this analysis, Mr. Belmont's staff estimated that the new equipment would generate net income before taxes of $65,000 per year. Straight-line depreciation of $45,000 per year was deducted in arriving at the $65,000 figure. The company does not consider salvage value in computing depreciation deductions. The tax rate is 60 percent.

The controller of Atlantic Industries has told Mr. Belmont that he should instruct his staff to use sum-of-the-years'-digits depreciation in their analysis. Somewhat irritated by this suggestion, Mr. Belmont replied, "You accountants and your fancy bookkeeping methods! What difference does it make what depreciation method we use—we have

the same investment, the same income, and the same total depreciation either way. That equipment just doesn't measure up to our
rate of return requirements. How you make the bookkeeping entries
for depreciation won't change that fact."

Required:

1. Compute the net present value of the new equipment, using
   straight-line depreciation.
2. Compute the net present value of the new equipment, using
   sum-of-the-years'-digits depreciation.
3. Explain to Mr. Belmont how the depreciation method used can
   affect the rate of return generated by an investment project.

15–3. *Equipment Replacement Decision.* A medium-sized manufacturing
company has been concerned for some time about the cost of its
data-processing operations. The company now has a manual system
in operation, but is considering the purchase of a small computer
in order to reduce data-processing costs. The following information
is available:

1. The company's present manual system involves the following
   direct cash expenses each month:

Salaries.	$6,000
Forms and supplies	500
Payroll taxes and other.	2,000
Total.	$8,500

2. The equipment, etc., associated with the manual system is fully
   depreciated, and has zero salvage value.
3. Several of the employees associated with the manual system
   would have to be discharged. They would be given severance
   pay of $10,000, which would be paid and fully tax deductible
   in the first year of operation of the new computer.
4. The new computer would cost $90,000, and have a 10 percent
   salvage value in three years.
5. The company uses sum-of-the-year's-digits depreciation, and considers salvage value fully in computing depreciation deductions.
6. The annual costs of operating the new computer would be:

Salaries.	$45,000
Forms and supplies	7,100
Payroll taxes and other.	3,700
Total.	$55,800

7. The company's after-tax cost of capital is 10 percent. Assume
   a tax rate of 60 percent.

Required:

1. Compute the annual savings in cash expenses that will be provided by the new computer.

2. Decide whether the computer should be purchased, using discounted cash flow. Round to the nearest whole dollar.

15-4. *Equipment Replacement Decision.* The Coral Lake Resort has recently purchased 30 new motorized golf carts for use on its exclusive golf course. The carts cost the resort considerably more than had been planned, and the manager of the resort is now wondering if they will provide the 14 percent after-tax rate of return that the resort's board of directors requires on all equipment purchases. The manager has asked you to make the necessary computations to determine if the 14 percent rate of return will be realized. You have determined the following information:

1. The total cost of the carts was $40,000. The carts will have a $4,000 salvage value in ten years.
2. Thirty old golf carts were sold that had a total book value of $8,000. The sale price totaled $5,000. Depreciation on the old carts would have totaled $800 per year for the next ten years.
3. The board of directors insists that straight-line depreciation be used on all equipment. Salvage value is not considered in computing depreciation deductions.
4. The 30 new golf carts are expected to generate net income each year of $10,000 (before depreciation and income taxes) above what the old carts would have generated.
5. The Coral Lake Resort's income tax rate is 60 percent.
6. The 30 new carts will require an overhaul at the end of the sixth year, costing a total of $5,000.

Required:

Use discounted cash flow to determine whether the new golf carts will provide the required 14 percent rate of return. Round to the nearest whole dollar. Use the incremental cost approach.

15-5. *Payback; Discounted Cash Flow.* Sal's Soda Shop is investigating the purchase of a new soft ice cream dispensing machine that is capable of dispensing several different flavors at one time. The machine costs $10,000. It will have an eight-year life, and a $2,000 scrap value. The following annual operating results are expected if the machine is purchased:

Increase in annual revenues		$8,000
Increase in expenses:		
Operating expenses.	$5,900	
Depreciation.	1,000	6,900
Net income before taxes		1,100
Income taxes (30%).		330
Net income		$ 770

Sal's Soda Shop expects an after-tax return of 10 percent on all equipment purchases. Straight-line depreciation will be used.

Required:

1. What is the payback period on the new machine?
2. Will the machine provide the minimum 10 percent return required by Sal's Soda Shop? Show computations by discounted cash flow. Round to the nearest dollar.
3. Compute the new machine's profitability index.

15–6. *Comparison of the Total Cost and Incremental Cost Approaches.* Cache Dairies, Inc., is considering the purchase of a new milk separator. The separator would cost $120,000. After five years' use the separator could be sold for $12,000, but this salvage value would not be considered in computing annual depreciation deductions. The new separator would provide considerable savings in annual operating costs, as shown below:

	Old Separator	New Separator
Salaries.	$34,000	$24,000
Supplies	6,000	5,000
Utilities.	8,000	6,000
Cleaning and maintenance	22,000	5,000
Total annual operating costs	$70,000	$40,000

If the new separator is purchased, the old separator will be sold for its present salvage value of $30,000. If the new separator is not purchased, the old separator will be used for five more years, then scrapped for a $2,000 salvage. The old separator's present book value is $50,000. The old separator is being depreciated by the straight-line method, with salvage value ignored for depreciation purposes. The new separator would be depreciated by the sum-of-the-years'-digits method. If kept and used, the old separator would require repairs costing $40,000 in one more year. These repairs would be expensed immediately. Cache Dairies, Inc.'s after-tax cost of capital is 18 percent. The tax rate is 60 percent.

Required:

1. Determine whether the new milk separator should be purchased, using the total cost approach to discounted cash flow. Round to the nearest whole dollar.
2. Repeat part 1, this time using the incremental approach to discounted cash flow.

15–7. *Simple Rate of Return and Payback.* Bostitch Company uses a large stapling machine in the manufacture of one of its products. The machine is well built, and could last the company for at least another eight years. Bostitch Company has learned that a smaller but equally productive stapling machine is now on the market that could provide some savings in annual operating costs over the present machine. Comparative cost data on the two machines are given below:

	Old Machine	New Machine
Original cost.	$18,000	$16,500
Remaining useful life.	8 years	8 years
Salvage value in 8 years.	-0-	500
Annual depreciation	1,500	2,000
Annual operating costs excluding depreciation.	35,000	31,600

The company deducts salvage value in computing depreciation charges. If the new machine is purchased, the old machine will be scrapped at a negligible scrap value.

Required:

1. Compute the simple rate of return promised by the new machine. If the company requires a minimum return of 10 percent on initial investment, would you recommend purchase? Ignore taxes.
2. Assume that a used equipment dealer will give the company $5,000 cash for the old stapling machine. Under these conditions, what would you say the "cost" would be of the new machine? Compute the simple rate of return. Ignore taxes.
3. Refer to the original data. Compute the payback period for the new machine. If the company requires a payback period of no more than five years, would you recommend purchase of the new machine? Ignore taxes.
4. If the company can get $5,000 cash for the old stapling machine, as stated in part 2 above, what would be the payback period for the new machine? Ignore taxes.

15–8. *Make or Buy Decision.* Western Instruments, Inc., uses 50,000 electronic components each year in the manufacture of a sensing device for alarm systems. At present, the company is manufacturing the electronic components in its own factory at the following cost per unit:

Direct materials	$2
Direct labor	4
Variable overhead.	1
Allocated general factory overhead	1
Total cost per unit	$8

The purchasing agent for Western Instruments, Inc., has found a supplier that will provide the electronic components to Western Instruments, Inc., for only $7.90 each. If the electronic components are purchased from the outside supplier, the equipment now being used to produce the components can be sold for $20,000. The equipment has a book value of $30,000. If the company continues to manufacture the components, the equipment will be depreciated at $6,000 per year for five years. After five years it can be sold for a scrap value of $2,000. Western Instruments, Inc.'s after-tax rate of return is 14 percent. The tax rate is 60 percent.

Required:

1. Should the company continue to make the electronic components, or buy them from the outside? Use the total cost approach in making your decision.
2. Assume that the space now being used to produce the components could be used to manufacture another product that would provide a before-tax margin (after all direct costs) of $45,000 per year. Would your answer to part 1 change? Explain.

15–9. *Preference Ranking of Investments Proposals.* Curry Company is investigating five different investment opportunities. The company's cost of capital is 10 percent. Information on the five investment proposals under study is given below:

Proposal Number	Invest- ment Required	Present Value of the Cash Inflows, at a 10% Rate	Net Present Value	Life of the Project	Time- Adjusted Rate of Return
1	$24,000	$28,360	$4,360	6 years	16%
2	18,000	21,669	3,669	12 "	14
3	15,000	18,674	3,674	6 "	18
4	18,000	20,918	2,918	3 "	19
5	17,000	16,013	(987)	6 "	8

Required:

1. Compute the profitability index for each investment proposal.
2. Rank the five proposals according to preference, in terms of:
   a. Time-adjusted rate of return.
   b. Profitability index.
3. Which ranking do your prefer? Why?

15–10. *Comparison of the Total Cost and Incremental Cost Approaches.* The Queensway Touring Lines is considering replacing the boiler system in one of its smaller touring boats. As a new management trainee with the company, you have been given responsibility for making the decision. You have gathered the following information relative to the boiler system now in operation on the boat, and relative to the proposed new boiler system:

	Old Boiler System	New Boiler System
Cost of the system new.	$11,000	$ 9,450
Accumulated depreciation to date	5,000	–
Remaining life.	6 years	6 years
Salvage value now.	4,000	–
Salvage value in six years.	500	900
Annual operating costs, excluding depreciation.	24,000	22,000
Repairs needed in three years	2,000	–
Depreciation method used	SL	SOYD

The Queensway Touring Lines does not consider salvage value in computing depreciation deductions. The change in boiler systems would have no effect on total annual revenues from the touring boat. If the new boiler system is installed, the old system will be sold for its current salvage value. The company requires an after-tax return of 8 percent on all investments. Assume a tax rate of 60 percent.

Required:

1. Using the total cost approach to discounted cash flow, determine whether the new boiler system should be installed on the touring boat. Round to the nearest whole dollar.
2. Repeat part 1, this time using the incremental cost approach to discounted cash flow.

15-11. *Depletion; Uneven Cash Flows.* The Magic Mountain Mining Company has an opportunity to purchase the mineral rights on a piece of land for $100,000. Other information relevant to this investment opportunity is given below:
1. The land contains 50,000 tons of mineral deposits. If the rights to these mineral deposits are purchased, extraction of the deposits will proceed as follows:

Year	Tons Mined and Sold
1	4,000
2	8,000
3	20,000
4	10,000
5	8,000

2. If the mineral rights are purchased, the $100,000 cost would be depleted on a basis of the number of tons mined and sold each year.
3. The selling price of the mineral would be $20 per ton. This price is expected to remain unchanged for quite some time.
4. Equipment costing $50,000 would have to be purchased to mine

the mineral deposits. The equipment would have only nominal residual value when extraction was complete. The company uses straight-line depreciation.

5. Annual out-of-pocket costs for salaries, insurance, utilities, etc., would total $30,000.
6. Variable out-of-pocket costs for supplies, labor, overhead, selling expense, etc., would total $12 per ton.
7. After all mineral extraction was completed, the company would have to spend $60,000 to restore the land to its natural condition.
8. The Magic Mountain Mining Company's after-tax cost of capital is 12 percent. The company's tax rate is 45 percent.

Required:

Determine whether the company should purchase the mineral rights and proceed with mining, as outlined above. Use discounted cash flow in your analysis. Round to the nearest whole dollar.

15–12. *A Comparison of Investment Alternatives.* John Pitts is a professor in a large western university. Professor Pitts has just received an inheritance of $100,000 from his father's estate, and he is wondering how he can best invest the sum between now and the time of his retirement at age 65. Professor Pitts's position with the university pays him a salary of $25,000 per year. This salary is expected to remain unchanged if Professor Pitts stays with the university until his retirement in 12 years. Professor Pitts is considering two alternatives for investing his inheritance.

Alternative #1. The first alternative would be to purchase $100,000 in municipal bonds, which would mature in 12 years. The bonds would bear interest at 8 percent, which would be tax-free and paid semiannually. (In discounting a cash flow that occurs semiannually, the procedure is to halve the interest rate and double the periods.)

Alternative #2. The second alternative would be to purchase a business of his own, which he would operate. Professor Pitts could purchase a well-established retail store for $100,000. The following information relates to this alternative:

1. Of the purchase price, $48,000 would be for fixtures and other depreciable items. The remainder would be for inventory and other working capital items.
2. The store building would be leased. At the end of 12 years, if Professor Pitts could not find someone to buy out the business, it would be necessary to pay $2,000 to the owner of the building in order to break the lease.
3. Straight-line depreciation would be used on the depreciable items. These items would have negligible residual value in 12 years.
4. Sales would average $112,000 per year. Out-of-pocket costs, including rent on the building, would total $76,500 per year (exclusive of income taxes).

5. Since Professor Pitts would operate the store himself, it would be necessary for him to leave the university if this alternative is selected. Professor Pitts's tax rate is 30 percent.

Required:

Advise Professor Pitts as to which alternative he should select. Use discounted cash flow in your analysis. Round to the nearest whole dollar. Use an after-tax rate of return of 8 percent. Use the total cost approach.

part three

Specialized Topics for Further Study

chapter 16

Inventory Planning
and Control

INVENTORY is usually one of the largest categories of assests, representing a major investment of funds. Because of the magnitude of the investment involved, managers are anxious to keep inventory at its *optimal* level.

What is the *optimal* level of inventory? It is that level which will exactly balance off the costs of carrying too little inventory against the costs of carrying too much inventory. If the investment in inventory is too large, then unnecessary costs are incurred. These costs include the costs of obsolescence, spoilage, insurance, etc. If the investment in inventory is too small, production can be disrupted, work flows can become uneven, and sales can be lost.

Our purpose in this chapter is to explore the methods available to managers for finding and maintaining that level of inventory which is neither too large nor too small, but rather optimal in relation to the needs of the firm.

THE NEED FOR INVENTORIES AND FOR INVENTORY CONTROL

With the development of computer technology and other forms of automation, significant advances have been made in inventory planning and control over the last few decades. Despite these advances, the point has not been reached where inventories are unneeded. In order for inventories to be unneeded, production and sales would have to occur at the same moment. Such an innovation is still far into the future for most industries.

It is hard to imagine any firm operating without an adequate stock of inventory. The reason is that inventories perform a vital cushion function in nearly all business firms. They cushion against imbalances in supply and demand, as well as against erratic movements in the production process.

Inventory Records versus Inventory Control

Are inventory records and inventory control the same thing? The answer is no. Inventory records are simply one of the facilitating tools of inventory control. Massive detailed records do not constitute control in and of themselves. Many firms fail to understand this point. Such firms often have rooms full of impressive inventory records, detailed down to the last thumbtack. Despite the existence of such records, or the spartan diligence with which they may be kept, inventory may still not be in control.

"Control" as we view it here does not relate to shuffling of paper, updating of perpetual inventory cards, or counting of paper clips. It relates to the *level of investment* in inventory. Inventory can be said to be in "control" when the level of investment is optimum in relation to the needs of a business.

Inventory records may be helpful in *maintaining* the optimum level of investment in inventory once that level has been determined, but they do not constitute control in and of themselves.

Inventory Ratios versus Inventory Control

Since inventory control relates to the level of investment in inventory, the manager must have tools at his disposal which will help him to determine when the level of investment is "just right" in relation to the needs of his firm. In order to maintain an inventory level that is "just right," the manager needs to know two things: (1) how much inventory to order at a time, and (2) how often to place orders. Several methods of determining this information are discussed later in the chapter.

The question at this point is "How do financial ratios enter into the inventory control picture?" Can ratios such as the inventory turnover ratio tell the manager how much inventory to order at a time, or tell him how often to place orders? The answer is no. Financial ratios are *broad* in scope, and for this reason don't provide the detailed information needed for day-to-day decision making. Ratios such as the inventory turnover are useful to the manager in much the same way that inventory records are useful. They can assist the manager in reviewing and maintaining the proper level of investment in inventory once it has been determined, but they do not constitute inventory control in and of themselves.

In fact, too great a reliance on ratios can lead to costly errors in inventory planning. For example, firms are often admonished to increase their inventory turnover. But consider the following:

> An infinite turnover can be achieved by carrying no inventory whatsoever. But such an inventory policy would not be a good policy because a company with no inventory would be continuously buying, expediting . . . . Turnover is worth improving, yes, but only if there is no substantial increase in ordering cost and only if there is no substantial loss of sales resulting from excessive stockouts.[1]

Divergence of Functional Viewpoints

One of the interesting things about inventories is that they are viewed so much differently in the various functional areas of a firm. These differences in viewpoint are important to recognize early in our discussion, since they can have an impact on the inventory policies ultimately adopted by a firm. We will look at the contrasting viewpoints of four major functional areas—finance, purchasing, production, and sales.

Finance. The finance manager would like to see the investment in inventory pared down as much as possible. The reason is that he is responsible for seeing that adequate investment funds are available when needed in a company. Every dollar that can be sliced out of inventory simply means another dollar available for use elsewhere—and there are times when the needs elsewhere can be very pressing. For this reason, the finance manager is often inclined to look very longingly at the investment funds tied up in inventory, and will press his case for minimum inventory levels.

Sales. The sales manager, by contrast, wants large amounts of inventory on hand at all times. The larger the inventory level, the more sure he is of being able to supply what a customer wants, when the customer wants it. The sales manager lives in more or less constant fear of competitors being in a better position to service customers than he is. For this reason, he will do all in his power to convince others of the need to expand stocks of merchandise, and to expand centers for distribution. Moreover, the sales manager is always anxious to have production respond instantly in filling requests for special production runs, no matter how small they may be.

Production. The production manager, on the other hand, is interested in production runs that are as continuous as possible, thereby building up large stocks of particular items. Frequent production changeovers increase set-up costs, changeover costs, learning time, and generally lower the overall efficiency of the production process. For this reason,

---

[1] *Techniques in Inventory Management* (New York: National Association of Accountants, Research Report No. 40, 1964), p. 96.

the production manager will not be interested in building up small stocks of large numbers of items, or in meeting requests from the sales department for special production runs.

Purchasing. Finally, the purchasing officer likes to buy in large quantities, so that he may take advantage of discounts and more favorable freight rates. Often, special buys will present themselves that offer an opportunity to achieve large savings through advance buying. But the funds required to carry large stocks may deplete bank accounts just at a time when the finance manager is scraping the barrel to provide investment funds needed elsewhere in the firm.

The inventory policy of a firm must be structured in such a way as to recognize this divergence of viewpoints. Profits cannot be maximized by recognizing the needs of one functional area to the exclusion of all others. A firm's inventory control policy must be one that blends the needs and objectives of all functional areas to the common good of the company as a whole.

COSTS ASSOCIATED WITH INVENTORY

There are three groups of costs associated with inventory. The first group represents the costs of ordering inventory. The second group represents the costs of carrying inventory. The third group represents the costs of not carrying *sufficient* inventory. Examples of costs associated with each group are given below:

Costs of ordering inventory:

1. Clerical costs.
2. Transportation costs.

Costs of carrying inventory:

1. Storage space costs.
2. Handling costs.
3. Property taxes.
4. Insurance.
5. Obsolesence losses.
6. Interest on capital invested in inventory.

Costs of not carrying sufficient inventory:

1. Customer ill will.
2. Quantity discounts foregone.
3. Erratic production (expediting of goods, extra set-up, etc.).
4. Inefficiency of production runs.
5. Added transportation charges.
6. Lost sales.

The simplest and most direct method of inventory control is to choose that level of investment in inventory which will minimize the total of these three classes of costs. However, this is not easily done. Notice that the three classes of costs are in direct conflict with each other. For example, as inventory levels increase, the costs of carrying inventory also increase, but the costs of not carrying sufficient inventory will decrease. Attempts at total cost minimization are also complicated by the fact that many of these costs are extremely difficult to identify and to measure.

In computing the costs of carrying inventory, *fixed* space costs should be included *only* if they change with the level of inventory being carried. The reason is that if a cost does not change with the level of inventory being carried, then it cannot be a factor in deciding what level of investment will result in total cost minimization. Examples of fixed space costs which generally do not change with the amount of inventory being carried are rent and depreciation.

We now turn our attention to those specific methods available to the manager for finding that level of investment in inventory which is "just right" in relation to the needs of his firm, and which will bring about the total cost minimization spoken of above.

INFORMAL INVENTORY CONTROL METHODS

The inventory of many firms is large in terms of number of items carried in stock, as well as in terms of dollar investment. It is not unusual for firms to have inventories containing 40,000 to 50,000 separate items. Not all of these inventory items need to be controlled in the same way. Control of some items can be very informal, whereas others may require elaborate quantitative techniques such as discussed later in the chapter. The manager must use his own judgment to determine what control procedures are needed in a particular situation.

Eyeball Review

Perhaps the least formal of all inventory control methods is the "eyeball review." The manager, supervisor, or purchasing officer simply makes a visual review of the adequacy of inventory stocks from time to time, and places orders as needed. Few, if any, records are kept of purchase dates, purchase amounts, or rates of usage. One rather obvious side-effect of the eyeball review method is that stockouts (running out of goods) are frequent. Yet this method of inventory control is more widely used than one would think, even in larger organizations.

A close relative of the eyeball review method is the "stockout method." This approach calls for placing orders for additional merchandise whenever the last item in the prior order has been sold. Nearly everyone has had the experience of going into a store to purchase an item, only to be told something like the following: "Looks like we just sold the last one—guess I'll have to put in an order for another batch." The cost of these approaches to inventory control in terms of lost opportunities is beyond calculation.

The Two-Bin Method

Some variation of the "two-bin" method is often used in situations where large numbers of small items are involved, as with nails, screws, and similar materials. Two bins are filled initially with the materials. One bin is used at a time. When it is emptied and consumption of the second bin is begun, an order is placed to refill the first bin. Although highly informal, this method is used effectively even in large organizations for control of some inventory items.

A variation of the two-bin method is the "red line" method. A red line is placed part way down the side of a container. When items have been withdrawn down to the red line, a refill order is placed. The red line is placed at a point far enough from the bottom to allow receipt of the new order before the container is completely emptied. This acts as an informal safety stock for the company. The author has seen both the red line and the two-bin methods in use in major steel companies across the nation.

MORE FORMAL INVENTORY CONTROL SYSTEMS

Although the informal inventory control methods are useful in some situations, more formal approaches are needed for most items of merchandise and materials. Two widely used approaches are the "tag system" and the "ABC method."

The Tag System

Variations of the tag system can be used with or without perpetual inventory records. The approach entails placing coded tags on all items of stock. As units are sold or placed into production, the tags are removed and controlled.

If perpetual inventory records are in use, the tags form a basis for entries directly in the inventory records of stock on hand. The records may be "keyed'" to designate reorder points, much like the red line on the barrels mentioned earlier. Whenever sufficient merchandise has been sold or goods used to bring the stock level down to a designated point, an order is automatically placed. Frequently, the perpetual inventory records carry a notation as to the quantity to be purchased in order to bring stocks back up to the desired level.

If perpetual inventory records are not in use, the tags are accumulated and used as a basis for reordering at specified points of time. For example, a firm may have a policy of ordering on a weekly basis. In this case, the tags accumulated over the prior week are simply sorted and organized, thereby forming the basis for the order. One weakness of this method is that it requires large safety stocks if sales or usage tend to fluctuate from period to period. Tag systems of this type are in widespread use in clothing and appliance stores.

The ABC Method

To assist in inventory control, many firms find it helpful to classify inventory items into groups. This approach is particularly useful in those situations where a firm has many different items of inventory, and its stocks of these items are very large. A technique known as the *ABC method* is often employed as a means of classifying inventory into various groups, and as an assist in controlling the groups once they have been formed. For example, the major automobile manufacturers use the ABC method of inventory classification to assist in the control of parts and supplies needed for assembly lines.

Using the ABC Method. The approach of the ABC method is to list inventory items according to average annual usage, weighted by the cost per unit. To illustrate, assume that the Detroit Motor Company has 12 inventory items which it uses in the production of a particular manufactured component. All 12 items are purchased from outside suppliers. They are listed according to average annual usage in column 2 of Exhibit 16–1.

EXHIBIT 16–1
Inventory Listing According to Annual Usage—Parts and Supplies

(1) Item	(2) Average Usage	(3) Cost per Unit	(4) Total Cost (2) × (3)	(5) ABC Classification
B6.	3,000	$20.00	$60,000	A
CD56.	2,000	22.00	44,000	A
X22.	15,000	1.00	15,000	C
B7.	11,000	2.00	22,000	B
H32.	10,000	3.00	30,000	B
MNK5	30,000	.50	15,000	C
106.	2,000	8.00	16,000	B
B8.	8,000	12.00	96,000	A
B9.	5,000	9.00	45,000	A
X21.	45,000	.30	13,500	C
X23.	60,000	.10	6,000	C
H44.	18,000	2.00	36,000	B

Each item in Exhibit 16–1 has been placed in either an A, a B, or a C classification, according to the total dollar volume of the item's annual usage. This total dollar volume (column 4) is obtained by multiplying the average annual usage by the cost per unit. Those items with a large dollar volume of usage are placed in an A classification. As the dollar volume of usage diminishes, we move down through the B and C classifications, with those items requiring the smallest dollar volume placed in the C category.

A total cost figure is then obtained for each classification, by adding together the total costs of the separate items in each classification. Each classification is also summarized according to the number of units of inventory it contains. Exhibit 16–2 contains a cost and unit summary for the inventory items appearing in Exhibit 16–1.

EXHIBIT 16–2
ABC Classification of Parts and Supplies (from Exhibit 16–1)

| | *Items* | | *Dollars* | |
Classification	Number of Inventory Units	Percentage of Total Units	Total Cost	Percentage of Total Cost
Group A.	18,000	8.6%	$245,000	61.5%
Group B.	41,000	19.6	104,000	26.1
Group C.	150,000	71.8	49,500	12.4
	209,000	100.0%	$398,500	100.0%

Interpreting the Data. Having now summarized the inventory items into the three groups, we can see that Group A represents only 8.6 percent of the total number of items, but yet represents 61.5 percent of the total dollar volume of inventory. By contrast, Group C represents 71.8 percent of the total number of inventory items, but only 12.4 percent of the total dollar volume. Clearly, most of the Detroit Motor Company's efforts shoud be directed toward the control of Group A items. By controlling the inventory items in this group, the company will be controlling the bulk of the cost of its parts and supplies. The company's strategy will be to maintain a minimum supply of Group A items on hand. The reason is that Group A items are very expensive, and even a small amount of overstocking can be very costly to the company. For this reason, items in the Group A category will be ordered very frequently in small lots, thereby keeping the stock on hand at a minimum. The thinking is that the added costs arising from more frequent ordering will be less than the added costs that would be involved in carrying larger stocks on hand.

Group C, by contrast, involves so little dollar cost that the Detroit Motor Company probably will be better off cost-wise to order less frequently in larger physical volumes. Quite ample stocks of Group C items very likely can be maintained without incurring excessive inventory carrying costs. The less frequent ordering will result in reduced clerical costs, reduced handling costs, and reduced shipping charges.

Group B items fall between the two extremes. The items in this group will be controlled in the way that is best cost-wise, taking into consideration the concepts discussed for groups A and C above.

In summary, all Group A items and many Group B items will be controlled almost on a hand-to-mouth basis, because of the high costs of carrying stocks of goods. Other Group B items and all Group C items will be stocked in more ample amounts, because of the lower carrying costs. One major auto manufacturer uses four inventory classifications, A–D. The company keeps 2 days' supply of Group A items on hand, 5 days' supply of Group B items on hand, 12 days' supply of Group C items on hand, and at least 20 days' supply of Group D items on hand.

COMPUTING THE ECONOMIC ORDER QUANTITY

The point was made earlier in the chapter that the inventory control problem has two dimensions—how much to order, and how often to do it. The "how much to order" is commonly referred to as the *economic order quantity*. It is the order size that will result in the *lowest total annual costs* for the inventory item in question. We will consider three approaches to computing the economic order quantity—the tabulation approach, the graphic approach, and the formula approach.

The Tabulation Approach

In computing the economic order quantity, there are two classes of costs that must be considered. These costs are:

1. The costs of ordering inventory.
2. The costs of carrying inventory.

Both of these classes of costs were discussed earlier in this chapter. In our earlier discussion we stated that the manager tries to maintain that level of investment in inventory which will minimize his total costs. Therefore, in computing the economic order quantity, the task is to find that order level which will minimize the total annual costs of ordering and carrying inventory.

The Trade-Off between Ordering Costs and Carrying Costs. Given a certain annual consumption of an item, a few large orders placed each year will result in far less ordering costs than placing many orders of a small quantity each. For example, if a firm uses 5,000 units of an inventory item each year, it might place only two orders of 2,500 units each. This would result in few ordering costs. On the other hand, the firm could place 2,500 orders of only two units each. This would result in many ordering costs.

Unfortunately, those actions which result in low *ordering* costs will trigger high inventory *carrying* costs. The reason is that the larger the number of units purchased with each order, the higher the *average* inventory level. And, of course, the higher the average inventory level, the higher the costs of carrying inventory.

The manager's problem, therefore, is to find that trade-off between ordering costs and carrying costs which will result in the least total annual cost of ordering and carrying inventory. We will now develop an example to show how this is done, by using the *tabulation approach* to computing the economic order quantity.

An Illustration. To illustrate the tabulation approach to computing the economic order quantity, let us assume that a manufacturer uses 3,000 units of a subassembly each year. The subassemblies cost $20 each. Other cost data are given below:

> Inventory carrying costs, per unit, per year . . . . $.80
> Cost of each purchase order placed (clerical, etc.). $10

What is the economic order quantity for the subassemblies? To answer this question, we will need to assume various order sizes, and make a tabulation of the *total annual costs* that will be associated with each order size. Exhibit 16–3 contains such a tabulation for the subassemblies in our example, assuming order sizes ranging from 25 units to 3,000 units each.

Notice from Exhibit 16–3 that the carrying cost of inventories $[C(0/2)]$ increases as the cost of purchase orders placed $[P(Q/0)]$ decreases. For example, if subassemblies are purchased in order sizes of 25 units each, the annual cost of carrying inventories is only $10, whereas the cost of placing the purchase orders is $1,200. By contrast, if only one order of 3,000 units is placed each year, the costs are just reversed. It will then cost $1,200 to carry inventories through the year, but it will cost only $10 to place purchase orders. As stated earlier, finding the economic order quantity involves a trading off of these opposing costs.

Interpreting the Data. As we scan the computations in Exhibit 16–3, we can see that the *minimum* total costs will be obtained by purchasing in order sizes of 250 to 300 units each. Therefore, the economic order

EXHIBIT 16–3
Tabulation of Costs Associated with Various Order Sizes

Symbol*		Order Size in Units								
		25	50	100	200	250	300	400	1,000	3,000
$O/2$	Average inventory in units.	12.5	25	50	100	125	150	200	500	1,500
Q/O	Number of purchase orders	120	60	30	15	12	10	7.5	3	1
$C(O/2)$	Annual carrying cost @ $.80 per unit.	$ 10	$ 20	$ 40	$ 80	$100	$120	$160	$400	$1,200
$P(Q/O)$	Annual purchase order cost @ $10 per order.	1,200	600	300	150	120	100	75	30	10
T	Total annual cost	$1,210	$620	$340	$230	$220	$220	$235	$430	$1,210

* Symbols: O = Order size in units (see headings above).
Q = Annual quantity used, in units (3,000 in this example).
C = Annual cost of carrying one unit in stock.
P = Cost of placing one order.
T = Total annual cost.

quantity must lie somewhere between these two amounts. If we wanted to add more columns to our exhibit, we would find that the economic order quantity is about 275 subassemblies per order. That is, an order size of 275 subassemblies will *minimize* the total annual costs associated with ordering and carrying inventory.

One drawback to the tabulation approach is that it may require many computations to finally "zero in" on a precise figure. Nevertheless, the method is conceptually sound, and represents a considerable improvement over most of the inventory control methods discussed earlier in the chapter.

The Graphical Approach

The economic order size can also be obtained by a graphical approach. A graphical solution to the subassembly example used in the preceding section is presented in Exhibit 16–4. Notice that the graph in this exhibit contains three cost curves—one for total cost, one for the per-unit inventory carrying costs, and one for the cost of placing a purchase order. The cost data used in Exhibit 16–4 have been taken from Exhibit 16–3.

EXHIBIT 16–4
Graphical Solution to Economic Order Size

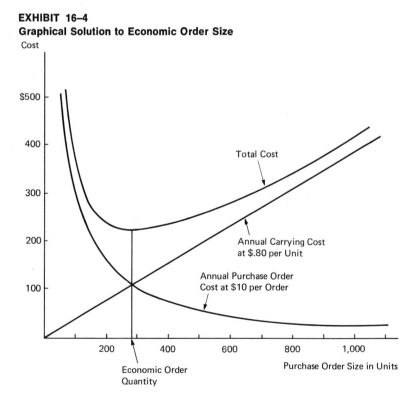

The graphical solution indicates that the economic order quantity is about 275 units, the same quantity we obtained by the tabulation approach. Notice that the *total costs* in the graph are lowest at the point where the annual carrying costs and the annual purchase order costs are equal. The economic order quantity will always be found at this point.

The graphical approach is particularly useful to the decision maker, in that he can see the behavior and relationship of the various costs over wide ranges of activity.

The Formula Approach

In addition to the tabular and the graphical approaches, the economic order quantity can also be found by means of a formula. The derivation of the formula is based on a concept illustrated in the graphical approach. That concept is that the economic order quantity will always be found at the point where carrying costs and order costs are equal. For those of mathematical bent, we can say that at this point the derivative of total annual cost with respect to order size is zero.[2] The formula used to compute the economic order quantity is usually expressed as follows:

$$0 = \sqrt{\frac{2QP}{C}} \qquad (1)$$

where 0 = the order size in units, Q = the annual quantity used in units, P = the cost of placing one order, and C = the annual cost of carrying one unit in stock. Interpreting the symbols in the formula, we can say that the economic order quantity will be equal to the square root of two times the annual quantity used times the cost per order, divided by the annual cost of carrying one unit in stock.

Substituting with the data used in our preceding example, we have:

Q = 3,000 subassemblies used per year
P = \$10 cost to place one order
C = \$.80 cost to carry one subassembly in stock for one year

$$0 = \sqrt{\frac{2(3,000)(\$10)}{\$.80}} = \sqrt{\frac{\$60,000}{\$.80}} = \sqrt{75,000}$$

$$0 = 274 \text{ (the economic order quantity)}$$

---

[2] The derivation of the formula is:

(1) $T = \dfrac{QP}{0} + \dfrac{OC}{2}$ (3) Set $\dfrac{dT}{d0} = 0; \dfrac{C}{2} - \dfrac{QP}{0^2} = 0$ (5) $0^2 = \dfrac{2QP}{C}$

(2) $\dfrac{dT}{d0} = \dfrac{-QP}{0^2} + \dfrac{C}{2}$ (4) $C0^2 = 2QP$ (6) $0 = \sqrt{\dfrac{2QP}{C}}$

Notice that the economic order quantity of 274 obtained by the formula approach differs only slightly from the 275 figure obtained by the graphical and tabular approaches. Although more accurate data can be obtained with less effort from the formula approach, it has the drawback of not providing as great a *range* of data as the other two approaches. So far as decision making is concerned, this drawback can be important. It is always helpful to a decision maker to have as much data available as possible.

Limitations to the Formula Approach

There are two important limitations to use of the formula approach. One is that the per unit carrying cost must be constant. The other is that the per-unit purchase price must be constant.

Any variation in the *per-unit* carrying cost of inventory will make it impossible to use the formula approach. The reason is that the formula *assumes* that per-unit carrying costs will be the same, regardless of the quantity of inventory being carried on hand. In some firms it may cost less *per unit* to carry large amounts of inventory than it does to carry smaller amounts of inventory. If this is true, then the tabulation approach to computing the economic order quantity must be used, rather than the formula approach.

Any variation in the per unit *purchase price* of inventory will also make it impossible to use the formula approach. The purchase price may vary because of quantity discounts which are offered on large purchases. If quantity discounts are available, then again the tabulation approach must be used in computing the economic order quantity. The quantity discounts available would be deducted from the total annual ordering and carrying costs, to arrive at net annual costs:

	Order Level in Units			
	500	*1,000*	*1,500*	*2,000*
Annual carrying cost	$XX	$XX	$XX	$XX
Annual purchase order cost	XX	XX	XX	XX
Total annual cost	XX	XX	XX	XX
Less quantity discounts	XX	XX	XX	XX
Net annual cost	$XX	$XX	$XX	$XX

The Economic Order Range

The graph in Exhibit 16–4 shows a pronounced tendency for total cost to flatten out between 200 and 300 units. This tendency is a common characteristics of EOQ graphs—that is, total cost will always tend to flatten out over some limited range.

Because of this characteristic, most firms in actual practice look for a minimum cost *range*, rather than simply for a minimum cost *point*. In the case of the subassemblies in our example, the manager would scrutinize the graph, notice the flattening out of total costs between the 200 and 300 subassembly order sizes, and choose an order quantity somewhere in this *range*. Although the order quantity chosen by this approach may not be precisely the economic order quantity, the difference in total annual costs will be very small.

As a practical matter, many suppliers require that all purchases be made in certain round lot sizes, rather than in any lot size that the customer may wish to designate. For example, the supplier of subassemblies in our illustration may require that purchases be in round lots of 100. In this case, it would not be possible to order in the precise economic order quantity of 274 units. Rather, the firm would choose an order size somewhere in the *range* of 200 to 300 units, probably using the figure of 300 units since it falls at the lower end of the minimum cost range. The total costs for this figure would be very close to the total costs for the actual economic order quantity of 274 units.

The Use of Estimated Data

Managers occasionally feel that computation of the economic order quantity would not be useful for their firm, since the only cost data available are based on estimates. The fear usually is that use of estimated cost data will result in wide errors when applied to the formula, or when inserted onto the graph. This concern is unfounded. One of the real advantages of the analytical approaches to computing the economic order quantity is that they are highly useful even if the cost data available are only approximations of the actual costs.

To illustrate, let us assume the following *actual* cost data:

$Q = 10,000$ units used each year
$P = \$15$ cost to place one order
$C = \$.75$ cost to carry one unit in stock for one year

Given these *actual* costs, the economic order quantity would be:

$$0 = \sqrt{\frac{2(10,000)(\$15)}{\$.75}} = \sqrt{\frac{\$300,000}{.\$75}} = \sqrt{400,000}$$

$$0 = 633 \text{ (the economic order quantity)}$$

Let us assume, however, that the company *estimates* its inventory carrying costs to be $1.00, due to the lack of availability of the actual cost figure of $.75. In this case, the economic order quantity would be computed to be:

$$0 = \sqrt{\frac{2(10,000)(\$15)}{\$1.00}} = \sqrt{\frac{\$300,000}{\$1.00}} = \sqrt{300,000}$$

$$0 = 548 \text{ (the economic order quantity)}$$

At first glance it may appear that using the estimated cost figure of $1.00 has thrown the company far off of its goal. Notice that the 548 unit order size using estimated data is considerably less than the actual economic order quantity of 633 units. But in comparing the total annual costs associated with each order size, we get a more accurate picture of the effect of using estimated data:

	Total Annual Costs Using the Actual EOQ of 633 Units	Total Annual Costs Using the Incorrect EOQ of 548 Units
Inventory carrying costs:		
(633/2) × $.75	$237	
(548/2) × $.75		$206
Purchase order costs:		
(10,000/633) × $15	237	
(10,000/548) × $15		274
	$474	$480
Difference in total annual cost	$6	

Using an estimated figure of $1.00 for inventory carrying costs has resulted in a difference of only $6 in total additional costs. This $6 compared to the optimal costs of $474 represents an error of only about 1.3 percent—hardly enough to put the company out of business.

The moral is that the use of even roughly approximated data will usually place the manager in touch with the minimum total cost *range*. As discussed in the preceding section, it is the minimum total cost range that the manager usually is interested in finding anyway.

Production Runs

The economic order quantity concept can also be applied to the problem of determining the optimal size of production runs. Deciding when to start and when to stop production runs is a problem that has plagued machine shops for years. The problem can be solved quite easily by inserting the *set-up cost* for a new production run into the economic order quantity formula in place of the purchase order cost. The set-up cost includes the labor costs, etc., involved in getting facilities ready for a run of a different production item.

To illustrate, assume that the Chittenden Company has determined the following costs associated with one of its product lines:

Q = 15,000 units produced each year
P = $150 set-up costs to change a production run
C = $2 to carry one unit in stock for one year

What is the optimal production run size for this product line? It can be determined by using the same formula as used to compute the economic order quantity:

$$0 = \sqrt{\frac{2(15,000)(\$150)}{\$2.00}} = \sqrt{\frac{\$4,500,000}{\$2.00}} = \sqrt{2,250,000}$$

0 = 1,500 (economic production run size in units)

Notice that the relatively high set-up costs require that production runs be relatively large in size. The Chittenden Company will minimize its overall costs by producing in runs of 1,500 units each.

DETERMINING THE REORDER POINT

The point has been made several times in the chapter that the inventory control problem has two dimensions—how much to order, and how often to do it. The analytical approaches to computing the economic order quanity tell us how much to order. We need now to determine how often orders should be placed. In business jargon this is known as determining the *reorder point*.

The reorder point is dependent on three factors. First, on the economic order quantity. Second, on what is termed the *lead time*. The lead time can be defined as the interval between when an order is placed and when the order is finally received from the supplier. Finally, the reorder point is dependent on the rate of usage during the lead time.

Constant Usage during the Lead Time

If the rate of usage during the lead time is known with certainty, determining the reorder point is a relatively simple task. It involves little more than multiplying the daily rate of usage by the number of days lead time required, and reordering when inventory stocks reach that level. The formula is:

Reorder Point = Lead Time × Average Daily or Weekly Usage

The computation of the reorder point is shown both numerically and graphically in Exhibit 16–5.

EXHIBIT 16–5
Determining the Reorder Point—Constant Usage
Economic order quantity ....500 units
Lead time........................3 weeks
Average weekly usage ....50 units
Reorder Point = 3 Weeks × 50 Units per Week = 150 Units.

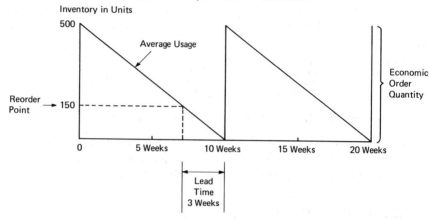

The reorder point for the data presented in Exhibit 16–5 would be 150 units. That is, the company will automatically place a new order for 500 units when inventory stocks drop to a level of 150 units, or three weeks supply, left on hand.

Variable Usage during the Lead Time

The previous example assumed that the 50 units per week usage rate was constant, and known with certainty. Although some firms enjoy the luxury of certainty, the more common situation is to find considerable variation in the rate of usage of inventory items from period to period. If usage varies from period to period, the firm that reorders in the way illustrated in Exhibit 16–5 may soon find itself out of stock. A sudden spurt in demand, a delay in delivery, or a snag in processing an order may cause inventory levels to be depleted before a new shipment arrives.

Companies that experience problems in demand, delivery, or processing of orders have found that they need some type of buffer to guard against stock-outs. Such buffers are usually called *safety stocks*. Safety stocks serve as a kind of insurance against greater than usual demand, and against problems in ordering and delivery of goods. Their size is determined by deducting *average usage* from the *maximum usage* that can be reasonably expected during a period. For example, if the firm in the preceding example was suddenly faced with a situation of variable demand for its product, it would compute a safety stock as follows:

Maximum expected usage per week. . . . . . 65 units
Average usage per week . . . . 50 units

Excess . . . . 15 units
Lead time . . . . X3 weeks

Safety stock . . . . 45 units

How does the necessity to maintain a safety stock affect the computation of the reorder point? The reorder point is determined by *adding the safety stock to the average usage during the lead time.* In formula form, the reorder point would be:

Reorder Point

= (Lead Time X Average Daily or Weekly Usage) + Safety Stock

Computation of the reorder point by this approach is shown both numerically and graphically in Exhibit 16-6.

EXHIBIT 16-6
Determining the Reorder Point—Variable Usage
Economic order quantity . . . . 500 units
Lead time . . . . 3 weeks
Average weekly usage . . . . 50 units
Maximum weekly usage . . . . 65 units
Safety stock . . . . 45 units
Reorder Point = (3 Weeks X 50 Units per Week) + 45 Units = 195 Units

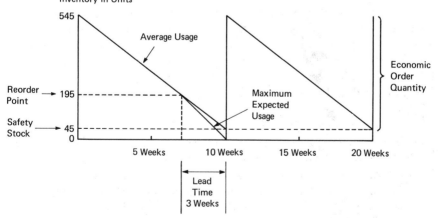

Determining the Optimum Safety Stock

The size of the safety stock will be determined in part by demand forecasts, and in part by the "feel" the decision maker has for the item involved, based on past experience. In deciding on a final figure to carry in stock, consideration must also be given to the *costs* that will be involved.

We noted earlier that there are three groups of costs associated with inventory:

1. The costs of ordering inventory.
2. The costs of carrying inventory.
3. The costs of not carrying sufficient inventory.

We have found that determining the economic order quantity is a matter of minimizing the total costs associated with groups 1 and 2. Determining the optimum safety stock is a matter of minimizing the total costs associated with groups 2 and 3, so far as the safety stock is concerned.

If too large a safety stock is carried, then carrying costs for insurance, taxes, etc., will be excessive. If too small a safety stock is carried, then lost sales, customer ill will, etc., will cut into profits. In short, the optimum safety stock has been attained when the costs of carrying an additional unit of inventory are exactly counterbalanced by the costs of not carrying the additional unit. A number of very promising statistical approaches to determining this point can be found in specialized books on inventory control.[3]

HUMAN JUDGMENT AND THE DIGITAL COMPUTER

With the advent of the high-speed digital computer, more and more inventory control systems are being automated. In fact, one of the important advantages of quantitative inventory control methods is that they can be largely dehumanized. Once economic order quantities, reorder points, and safety stocks have been computed, the entire system can be automated and operated with a minimum of dependence on human judgment.

Even though the digital computer carries out its work with incredible speed and efficiency, the fact that it is on the job does not eliminate entirely the need for an element of human judgment. The writer recalls a situation a number of years ago where the inventory control system was largely computerized. One item in inventory was hemp rope, which was used in production of one of the company's products. The company used 2,500 feet of rope each month. It was intended that this quantity be purchased and on hand at the beginning of each month's operations.

---

[3] See Thomson M. Whitin, *Theory of Inventory Management,* 2d ed. (Princeton, N.J.: Princeton University Press, 1957); and Joseph Buchan and Ernest Koenigsberg, *Scientific Inventory Management* (Englewood Cliffs, N.J.: Prentice-Hall, Inc., 1963).

In error, the computer was programmed to order 25,000 feet of rope each month. Many months went by, and one warehouse was nearly full of hemp rope before anyone questioned why so much was being purchased. When the warehouseman was asked why he didn't question the quantity of rope being accumulated, he replied, "The computer said that we ought to be buying 25,000 feet of rope a month, and I don't question that computer."

SUMMARY

Inventories are needed in nearly all business firms. They provide protection against imbalances in supply and demand, against erratic movements in the production process, and against difficulties in obtaining shipments from suppliers. Although inventories provide protection to a firm, they do so at a cost. Because these costs are often very high, it is important that inventory levels be carefully controlled. The optimum inventory level is that level which will sustain smooth operation at the least total annual cost. In order to maintain inventory at its optimum level, the manager must be able to determine two things—how much inventory to order at a time, and how often to place orders.

The "how much to order" question is resolved by determining the economic order quantity. The economic order quantity is that quantity which will minimize the total annual costs of ordering and carrying inventory. It can be determined by the tabulation approach, by the graphical approach, or by the formula approach.

The "how often to place orders" question is resolved by determining the reorder point. The reorder point is a function of the lead time required to obtain a shipment from a supplier, multiplied by the daily or weekly usage during the lead time. If usage during the lead time varies, then a safety stock may be needed to provide protection against stockouts.

QUESTIONS

16–1.   What is the optimal level of inventory in a firm?

16–2.   "We keep detailed records on every single item that we carry in inventory, and the records are updated on a daily basis. No firm in the industry has better inventory control than we do." Discuss.

16–3.   "The higher the inventory turnover, the better the inventory control." Do you agree? Why or why not?

16–4.   In what ways do the viewpoints of the officer in charge of finance and the officer in charge of sales differ, so far as inventory is concerned?

16–5.   List at least three costs associated with a company's inventory policy that do not appear as an expense on the income statement.

16–6. What three classes of costs are associated with a company's inventory policy? Which of these classes of costs is the most difficult to quantify?

16–7. What is a "two bin" inventory system?

16–8. What is meant by the term "economic order quantity"? Name three ways of determining the economic order quantity.

16–9. What trade-offs in costs are involved in computing the economic order quantity?

16–10. "Managers are more interested in a minimum cost *range* than they are in a minimum cost point." Explain.

16–11. "Computing the EOQ may be useful in some firms, but it would never work in our company. The best we can do is estimate our inventory carrying and order costs. The estimates would never work in an EOQ formula." Discuss.

16–12. How can the EOQ formula be modified to determine the optimal size of production runs?

16–13. Define "lead time" and "safety stock".

16–14. What function do inventories serve in a business firm?

EXERCISES

16–1. Classify the following either as (*a*) costs of carrying inventory, or (*b*) costs of not carrying sufficient inventory:
1. Air freight on a rush order of a critical part needed in production.
2. Interest paid on investment funds.
3. State and local taxes on personal property.
4. Spoilage of perishable goods.
5. Excessive set-up costs.
6. Customers lost through inability of the company to make prompt delivery.
7. Quantity discounts lost as a result of purchasing in small lots.
8. Fire insurance on inventory.
9. Loss sustained when a competitor comes out with a less expensive, more efficient product.
10. A general feeling of ill will among customers, due to broken delivery promises.

16–2. 1. The Hurd Company uses 8,000 units of a certain part each year. The company has determined it costs $40 to place an order for the part from the supplier, and $4 to carry one part in inventory each year. Compute the economic order quantity for the part.
2. Assume that the Hurd Company's ordering costs increase to $50 per order. What will be the effect on the economic order quantity? Show computations.
3. Assume that the Hurd Company's carrying costs increase to $5 per part. (Ordering costs remain unchanged at $40.) What will be the effect on the economic order quantity? Show computations.

16–3. Bedford Motor Company uses 3,125 units of Part S-10 each year. The cost of placing one order for Part S-10 is estimated to be about $10. Other costs associated with Part S-10 are:

	Annual Cost per Part
Insurance.	$.10
Property taxes.	.06
Interest on funds invested	.05
Other	.04
Total cost	$.25

Required:

Compute the economic order quantity for Part S-10.

16–4. Selected information relating to an inventory item carried by the Sikes Company is given below:

Economic order quantity.	700 units
Maximum weekly usage	60 units
Lead time	4 weeks
Average weekly usage.	50 units

Sikes Company is trying to determine the proper safety stock to carry on this inventory item, and the proper reorder point.

Required:

1. Assume that no safety stock is to be carried. What is the reorder point?
2. Assume that a full safety stock is to be carried.
   a. What would be the size of the safety stock in units?
   b. What would be the reorder point?

16–5. Foley Automotive Accessories, Inc., sells a complete line of auto parts and accessories. The company purchases its batteries from the Acid Battery Works at a cost of $10 per battery, and sells them at retail for $15 each. Other selected information relating to the batteries is given below:

Number of batteries sold each year.	?
Economic order quantity	200 batteries
Purchase order cost, per order.	$8.00
Annual cost of carrying one battery in inventory.	.50

Required:

Compute the number of batteries sold each year.

16–6. The Classy Cassette Company distributes cassettes on a retail level. The series R-4 cassette is one of the company's most popular models.

This model is very expensive to carry in inventory, however, so the company is anxious to keep inventories at a minimum level. The following information has been assembled on the R-4 cassette:

Economic order quantity	800 cassettes
Annual carrying cost	$1/cassette
Annual sales.	16,000 cassettes
Lead time	1.5 weeks
Maximum weekly sales.	400 cassettes

Required:
1. Assume that the company does not want to carry a safety stock. What is the reorder point? Round all figures to the nearest whole unit.
2. Assume that the company wants to carry a full safety stock.
   a. Compute the safety stock. Round all figures to the nearest whole unit.
   b. Compute the reorder point.

16–7. The Aspen Machine Shop has a customer that has been purchasing 10,000 special order die castings each year. The customer normally orders 1,000 castings at a time, and this has made it necessary for the Aspen Machine Shop to make 10 separate production runs each year. The Aspen Machine Shop would like to avoid having to make 10 runs each year, if possible.

The shop's cost analyst estimates that it costs $500 to set up for a run of the die castings. Variable production costs per casting total $10. Inventory carrying costs are 10 percent per year. The shop is quite sure that the customer will purchase another 10,000 castings during the coming year.

Required:

Compute the most economic production run size. Round to the nearest whole casting.

PROBLEMS

16–1. *Economic Order Quantity and Safety Stock.* Dexter Manufacturing Company uses 100,000 units of Material A each year. The material is used evenly throughout the year in the company's production process. A recent cost study indicates that it costs $.60 to carry one unit of Material A in stock for a year. The company estimates that the cost of placing an order for Material A is $75.

On the average, it takes six days to receive an order from the supplier. Occasionally, orders do not arrive for nine days, and at rare intervals (about 1 percent of the time) orders do not arrive for eleven days. Each unit of Material A costs the Dexter Manufacturing Company $4. The company works an average of 360 days per year. Round all figures to the nearest whole unit.

Required:

1. Compute the economic order quantity.
2. What size safety stock would you recommend for Material A? Why?
3. What is the reorder point for Material A in units?
4. Compute the *total cost* associated with ordering and carrying Material A for a year.

16–2. *Estimating Carrying Costs.* Bateman Company is trying to determine its inventory carrying costs. The following data have been developed:

Insurance on inventory . . . . 4% of inventory value
Rent of storage facility . . . . $12,000 per year
Interest on investment funds . . . . 10% borrowing rate
Property taxes . . . . 6% of inventory value

Bateman Company sells a single product, which is purchased from a supplier according to the following price schedule:

0– 4,000 units . . . . $12.00 per unit
4,001– 8,000 units . . . . 11.50 per unit
8,001–12,000 units . . . . 11.00 per unit
12,001–24,000 units . . . . 10.25 per unit

The company purchases a total of 24,000 units each year. Assume that the average inventory in units is equal to one half of an average order from the supplier (i.e., if the average order from the supplier was 8,000 units, then the average inventory would be 4,000 units in stock).

Required:

1. Compute the total annual cost of carrying inventory, assuming average orders from the supplier of 4,000 units, 8,000 units, 12,000 units, and 24,000 units.
2. Using the data computed in part 1, compute the per unit carrying cost of inventory at each order level.
3. Are the per unit carrying costs which you have computed in part 2 usable in the EOQ formula? Why or why not?

16–3. *Economic Order Quantity and Safety Stock.* Myron Metal Works, Inc., uses a small casting in one of its finished products. The castings are purchased from a foundry located in another state. In total, Myron Metal Works, Inc., purchases 24,000 castings per year, at a cost of $8 per casting.

The castings are used smoothly and evenly throughout the year in the production process, on a 360-day-per-year basis. The company estimates that it costs $60 to place a single purchase order, and about $2 to carry one casting in inventory for a year. The high carrying costs result from the need to keep the castings in carefully controlled temperature and humidity conditions, and from the high cost of insurance.

Delivery from the foundry generally takes six days, but can take as much as ten days. The days delivery time and the percentage of occurrence are shown in the following tabulation:

Delivery Time	Percentage of Occurrence
6 days	75% of the time
7 days	10 of the time
8 days	5 of the time
9 days	5 of the time
10 days	5 of the time
	100%

Required:

1. Compute the economic order quantity.
2. Assume that the company is willing to assume the risk of being out of stock 15 percent of the time. What would be the safety stock? The reorder point?
3. Assume that the company is willing to assume the risk of being out of stock only 5 percent of the time. What would be the safety stock? The reorder point?
4. Assume a 5 percent stockout risk, as stated in part 3. What would be the total cost of ordering and carrying inventory for one year?

16–4. *EOQ Sensitivity Analysis.* Jensen Brothers, Inc., uses 8,000 pounds of Material X each year. The material cost $50 per pound, and is used evenly in the production process throughout the year. The company estimates that it costs $20 to place an order for Material X.

The company has never attempted to control inventory, in terms of level of investment. In the past, Material X has been purchased twice each year, in orders of 4,000 pounds each. The supplier stipulates that orders must be in multiples of 100 pounds.

Cost analysis has determined that the cost of carrying inventory is about $2 per pound per year. Material X costs the company $80 per pound to purchase.

Required:

1. Compute the economic order quantity and the number of orders that should be placed each year.
2. Assume that the carrying cost can be pared down to only $1.50 per pound per year. What would be the effect on the EOQ?
3. Assume the original data. If increased costs of paper and handling push ordering costs up to $30 per order, what will be the effect on the EOQ?
4. Assume the original data. What annual cost savings will be realized if the company abandons its current purchase policy, and purchases in the economic order quantity?

16–5. *Safety Stocks.* Marcy's, Inc., a large department store, has made a study of the sales of one of its most popular lines. The study covered a period of 100 weeks, and revealed the following sales of the line, in units:

(1) Number of Weeks	(2) Sales in Units	Weighted Sales in Units (1) × (2)
2.	100	200
6.	200	1,200
12.	250	3,000
20.	300	6,000
24.	350	8,400
16.	400	6,400
10.	450	4,500
6.	500	3,000
4.	600	2,400
100		35,100

Weighted average sales = 351 units per week.

The lead time required to receive an order of this line from the supplier is one week. The following additional data are available:

Economic order quantity	684 units
Cost to place one order.	$20.00
Annual carrying cost per unit	3.00

Required:

1. Assume that no safety stock is to be provided. What is the reorder point? What percentage of the weeks will stockouts occur?
2. Assume that the store can tolerate no stockouts. What size safety stock in units would be required?
3. Assume that a 96 percent protection against stockouts is adequate. What size safety stock in units would be required? What would be the cost of maintaining this safety stock?
4. As a manager, how would you use the cost data computed in part 3 in determining whether the safety stock is justified?

16–6. *Changing Carrying Costs and EOQ.* Allison Company sells a single product. This product is purchased from a manufacturer, and sold by Allison Company at the retail level. Allison Company has developed the following data relating to its inventory carrying costs:

Interest cost on invested funds	10% of inventory value
Property taxes.	8% of inventory value
Space cost (rent, etc.).	$15,000 per year
Insurance on inventory.	6% of inventory value
Annual sales	12,000 units of product

Allison Company purchases units of product from the manufacturer according to the following price schedule:

Units	*Price per*
Purchased	*Unit*
0– 1,000	$10.00
1,001– 2,000	9.90
2,001– 6,000	9.80
6,001–12,000	9.70

Allison Company's sales take place smoothly throughout the year, so the company's average inventory is equal to one half of the average purchase order in units.

Required:

1. Compute the *total* annual inventory carrying costs, assuming average purchase orders of 1,000 units, 2,000 units, 6,000 units, and 12,000 units.
2. Assume that it costs $200 to place one purchase order. Which of the four purchase order levels in part 1 should the company use? Treat the savings from quantity discounts as a reduction in total annual ordering and carrying costs. (Hint: Use the tabulation approach to EOQ.)

16–7. *Tabulation Approach to EOQ.* Yales Jewelers, Inc., purchases 30,000 one-quarter carat diamonds each year for various mountings. Pertinent information relating to the diamonds is given below:

Purchase cost per diamond.	$30
Cost to carry one diamond in inventory for one year	5
Cost of placing one order to the company's supplier	40

The maximum order which the insurance company will permit is 1,500 diamonds. The minimum order which the supplier will permit is 300 diamonds, with all orders required to be in multiples of 300 diamonds. The company has been purchasing in the maximum allowable volume of 1,500 diamonds per order.

Required:

1. By use of the tabulation approach to EOQ, determine the volume in which the company should be placing its diamond orders.
2. Compute the annual cost savings that will be realized if the company purchases in the volume you have determined in part 1 above, as compared to its present purchase policy.

16–8. *Tabulation Approach to EOQ.* The Tolby Manufacturing Company uses 15,000 ingots of Klypton each year. The Klypton is purchased from a supplier in another state, according to the following price schedule:

500 ingots	$30.00 per ingot
1,000 ingots	29.90 per ingot
1,500 ingots	29.85 per ingot
2,000 ingots	29.80 per ingot
2,500 ingots	29.75 per ingot

The Tolby Manufacturing Company sends its own truck to the supplier's plant to pick up the ingots. The truck's capacity is 2,500 ingots per trip. The company has been getting a full load of ingots each trip, making 6 trips each year. The cost of making one round trip to the supplier's plant is $500. The paperwork associated with each trip is $30.

The supplier requires that all purchases be in round 500-ingot lots. The company's cost analyst estimates that the cost of storing one ingot for one year is $10.

Required:

1. By use of the tabulation approach to EOQ, compute the volume in which the company should be purchasing its ingots. Treat the savings arising from quantity discounts as a reduction in total annual trucking and storing costs.
2. Compute the annual cost savings that will be realized if the company purchases in the volume which you have determined in part 1 above, as compared to its present purchase policy.

16–9. *ABC Method of Inventory Control.* Smuthers Company has introduced a new product line to be manufactured in its plant. The component parts required by the new line are listed below, along with estimated annual usage and per-part costs.

Parts Stock No.	Estimated Annual Usage in Units	Per-Part Cost
A6.	1,180	$25.00
A7.	19,000	.10
A8.	600	35.00
D2.	3,500	4.00
D3.	3,000	3.80
D4.	8,000	.20
G6.	3,800	3.50
G7.	1,500	22.00
K1.	20,000	.05
K2.	7,000	.50
K3.	2,000	15.00
M3	16,000	.02

The company uses the ABC method of selected control as an assist in deciding on purchase policies for parts. ABC categories are segregated as follows:

A—Approximately the highest 70% of parts cost.
B—Approximately the next highest 25% of parts cost.
C—Approximately the lowest 5% of parts cost.

Required:

1. Assign each part item into either an A, a B, or a C category, according to the company's policy.

2. Prepare a tabulation, such as illustrated in Exhibit 16–2, which will show management the breakdown of items and costs as between the A, B, and C categories.
3. State in broad terms the inventory policy that should be followed for the A, B, and C categories, respectively.

16–10. *Inventory Control Systems.* You have been engaged to install an accounting system for the Kaufman Corporation. Among the inventory control features Kaufman desires in the system are indicators of "how much" to order "when." The following information is furnished for one item, called a "komtronic," which is carried in inventory:

a. Komtronics are sold by the gross (12 dozen) at a list price of $800 per gross f.o.b. shipper. Kaufman receives a 40 percent trade discount off list price on purchases in gross lots.
b. Freight cost is $20 per gross from the shipping point to Kaufman's plant.
c. Kaufman uses about 5,000 komtronics during a 259-day production year but must purchase a total of 36 gross per year to allow for normal breakage. Minimum and maximum usages are 12 and 28 komtronics per day, respectively.
d. Normal delivery time to receive an order is 20 working days from the date a purchase request is initiated. A stockout (complete exhaustion of the inventory) of komtronics would stop production, and Kaufman would purchase komtronics locally at list price rather than shut down.
e. The cost of placing an order is $30.
f. Space storage cost is $24 per year per average gross in storage.
g. Insurance and taxes are approximately 12 percent of the net delivered cost of average inventory, and Kaufman expects a return of at least 8 percent on its average investment (ignore ordering costs and carrying costs in making these computations.)

Required:

1. Prepare a schedule computing the total annual cost of komtronics based on uniform order lot sizes of one, two, three, four, five, and six gross of komtronics. (The schedule should show the total annual cost according to each lot size.) Indicate the economic order quantity.
2. Prepare a schedule computing the minimum stock reorder point for komtronics. This is the point below which reordering is necessary to guard against a stockout. Factors to be considered include average lead period usage and safety stock requirements.

(AICPA, adapted)

chapter 17

Quantitative Decision Techniques

THE DECISION-MAKING role is one of enormous complexity. The variables involved in many decisions are so numerous that managers are being forced more and more to turn to mathematics and statistics for tools to assist in the decision-making process. As a result, the quantitative sciences are developing many new and extremely useful approaches to the solving of business problems.

We are concerned in this chapter with gaining some familiarity with certain of these newer approaches to decision making. The point must be stressed, however, that the material covered in this chapter represents no more than an introduction to the use of quantitative methods in solving business problems. Real expertise can be obtained only by specialized study in the areas of quantitative controls.

OPERATIONS RESEARCH

The use of quantitative approaches to the solving of business problems has become so widespread that it has led to the birth of a completely new discipline. This new discipline is still somewhat in the formative stages, but it is well enough developed to be given the general title of *operations research*. The discipline involves the development of mathematical and statistical models that are designed to assist the manager in complex decision-making situations.

The Thrust of Operations Research

Operations research (OR) is primarily *planning* oriented, rather than *control* oriented. That is, it assists the manager in defining alternatives, and in comparing one alternative against another. It also assists the manager in selecting the alternative that best fills the need at hand. The approach is one of *model building*, where the variables associated with a particular objective are defined and then observed as they interact one with another. The purpose of OR is to assist the manager in making more rational decisions, by providing him with more information than he would otherwise have available in a complex situation.

As we begin our study of OR techniques, the reader should keep clearly in mind that the quantitative methods involved in OR in no way eliminate or reduce the importance of the experience and intuition of the individual manager. Rather, these methods *amplify* the value of experience and intuition by assisting the manager to *utilize* his experience and intuition in an orderly way in the decision-making process.

Model Building

The real heart of OR lies in the developing of mathematical and statistical models. Models attempt through mathematical expressions to portray the real world as clearly as possible in a condensed but highly usable way. They define in mathematical terms the characteristics and variables associated with a real situation, and then illustrate the relationships between the variables which they have defined. Most people have used models at some time in their lives. Accountants and managers use models constantly, although the models are rarely recognized for what they are. Financial statements, for example, are models of the actual financial structure of a business firm.

Models are enormously practical tools. Perhaps their greatest value lies in their ability to assist the manager in seeing the consequences of a particular decision without going to the cost and difficulty involved in having the actual experience. That is, if a model can be constructed of a particular phase of a firm's operations, the manager can observe the effect on the model of various alternatives he is considering. Thereby, he can choose that alternative which will yield the result he desires, without incurring a large amount of cost or losing a great deal of time in fruitless trial-and-error efforts.

In short, models take much of the guesswork out of complex decisions. They become the manager's laboratory, in which he can isolate and evaluate relevant variables, and, through the use of the digital computer provide orderly and practical solutions to problems. We should note here that without the availability of the computer much of the development that has taken place in OR would not have been possible. Many models are so complex that they become impractical to use in the absence of the computer.

LINEAR PROGRAMMING

Linear programming is a mathematical tool designed to assist management in making decisions in those situations where constraining or limiting factors are present. Limiting factors might include, for example, a scarcity of raw materials needed in the production of a company's products, or a plant with inadequate machine time to produce all of the products being demanded by a firm's customers. Linear programming is designed to assist the manager in putting together the "right" mix of products in situations such as these, so that the scarce resources of the firm (e.g., raw materials, machine time) can be utilized in a way that will maximize profits.

Characteristics of Linear Programming Problems

Business problems having the following general characteristics tend to lend themselves most readily to a linear programming solution:

1. There is some *objective function* which management feels must be maximized or minimized. For example, the objective might be to *maximize* the contribution margin of the firm, through the mix of products produced and sold. Alternatively, the objective might be to produce a mix of products that will *minimize* the use of labor time or machine time.

2. There are *constraints* under which the company must operate that limit the extent to which the objective function can be maximized or minimized. For example, if the objective is to maximize contribution margin, the company may be constrained in terms of the availability of raw materials for production, the availability of manpower or machine hours, or the availability of distribution channels.

3. The objective function and constraints cited in 1 and 2 above must lend themselves to algebraic expression. If algebraic expression is possible, the result is a model which describes in mathematical terms the activity or problem under study.

4. The relationships involved in 1 and 2 above must be *linear* in nature, or sufficiently close to being linear that an assumption of complete linearity will not adversely affect a solution.

Fortunately, many business problems lend themselves to a linear programming solution, as we shall see in the following sections.

A Graphical Approach to Linear Programming

The basic idea behind linear programming is to find an optimum solution to a problem in the face of limiting or constraining factors.

To demonstrate a linear programming analysis, let us assume the following data:

> A firm produces two products, X and Y. The contribution margin per unit of X is $8, and the contribution margin per unit of Y is $10. The firm has 36 hours of production time available each period. It takes 6 hours of production time to produce one unit of X and 9 hours of production time to produce one unit of Y.
>
> The firm has only 24 pounds of raw material available for use in production each period. It takes 6 pounds of raw material to produce one unit of X and 3 pounds of raw material to produce one unit of Y.
>
> Management estimates that no more than 3 units of Y can be sold each period. The firm is interested in maximizing contribution margin. What combination of X and Y should be produced and sold?

There are four basic steps in a linear programming analysis:

1. Determine the objective function and express it in algebraic terms.
2. Determine the constraints under which the firm must operate, and express them in algebraic terms.
3. Determine the area of feasible product combinations on a graph. This area will be bounded by the constraint equations derived in "2" above, after the constraint equations have been expressed on the graph in linear form.
4. Determine from the area of feasible product combinations that mix of products which will maximize (or minimize) the objective function.

We shall now examine each of these steps in order, by relating them to the data in the example above.

1. The objective function equation: Determine the objective function and express it in algebraic terms.

In our example, the objective is to maximize contribution margin. For each unit of X that is sold $8 in contribution margin will be realized, and for each unit of Y that is sold $10 in contribution margin will be realized. Therefore, *total* contribution margin for the firm can be expressed by the following equation:

$$Z = 8X + 10Y \tag{1}$$

where Z = the total contribution margin that will be realized with an optimal mix of X and Y; X = the number of units of product X that should be produced and sold to yield the optimal mix; and Y = the number of units of product Y that should be produced and sold to yield the optimal mix.

2. The constraint equations: Determine the constraints under which the firm must operate, and express them in algebraic terms.

From the data in our example we can identify three constraints. First, only 36 hours of production capacity are available. Since it requires 6 hours to produce one unit of X and 9 hours to produce one unit of Y, this constraint can be expressed in the following form:

$$6X + 9Y \leq 36 \qquad (2)$$

Notice the inequality sign $(\leq)$ in the equation. This signifies that the total production of both X and Y taken together cannot *exceed* the 36 hours available, but that this production *could* require *less* than the 36 hours available.

The second constraint deals with raw material usage. Only 24 pounds are available each period. It takes 6 pounds of raw material to produce one unit of X and 3 pounds to produce one unit of Y. This constraint can be expressed in the following algebraic terms:

$$6X + 3Y \leq 24 \qquad (3)$$

The third constraint deals with market acceptance of product Y. The market can absorb only 3 units of Y each period. This constraint can be expressed as follows:

$$Y \leq 3 \qquad (4)$$

3. *The area of feasible product combinations: Determine the area of feasible product combinations on a graph.*

A graph containing the constraint equations [equations (2)–(4) above] is presented in Exhibit 17–1. In placing these three equations on the graph, we have asked the questions, "How much product X could be produced if all resources were allocated to it, and none were allocated to product Y?"; and "How much product Y could be produced if all resources were allocated to it, and none were allocated to product X?" For example, consider equation (2), dealing with production capacity. A total of 36 hours of production capacity is available. If all 36 hours are allocated to product X, 6 units can be produced each period (since it takes 6 hours to produce one unit of X, and 36 hours are available). On the other hand, if all 36 hours of production capacity are allocated to product Y, then 4 units of Y can be produced each period (since it takes 9 hours to produce one unit of Y, and 36 hours are available).

If All Production Capacity Is Allocated to Product X	*If All Production Capacity Is Allocated to Product Y*
$6X + {-0-} \leq 36$	${-0-} + 9Y \leq 36$
$X = 6$	$Y = 4$

EXHIBIT 17–1
A Linear Programming Graphical Solution

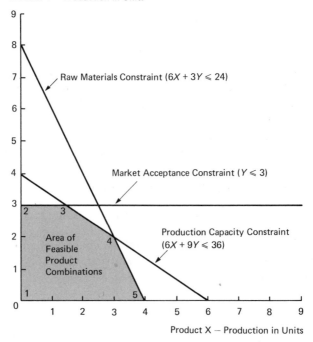

Therefore, the line on the graph in Exhibit 17–1 expressing the production constraint equation [equation (2)] extends from the 6-unit point on the X axis to the 4-unit point on the Y axis. Of course production *could fall anywhere* on this constraint line; the points on the axes (6,4) simply represent the *extremes* that would be possible.

The equation associated with the raw materials constraint [equation (3)] has been placed on the graph through a similar line of reasoning. Since 24 pounds of raw materials are available, the firm could produce either 4 units of X or 8 units of Y, if all of the raw materials were allocated to one or the other (since it takes 6 pounds to produce a unit of X, and 3 pounds to produce a unit of Y). Therefore, the line expressing the equation extends from the 4 unit point on the X axis to the 8 unit point on the Y axis. Again, production *could fall anywhere* on this constraint line; the points on the axes (4,8) simply represent the *extremes* that would be possible.

Since the third constraint equation [equation (4)] concerns only product Y, the line expressing the equation on the graph does not touch the X axis at all. It extends from the 3-unit point on the Y axis and runs horizontal to the X axis, thereby signifying that regardless of the number of units of X that are produced, there can never be more than 3 units of Y produced.

Having now plotted on the graph the lines representing the three constraint equations, we have isolated the *area of feasible product combinations*. This area has been shaded on the graph. Notice that the area of feasible product combinations is formed by the lines of the constraint equations. Each line has served to limit the size of the area to some extent. The reason, of course, is that these lines represent *constraints* under which the firm must operate, and thereby serve to *limit* the range of choices available. The firm could operate *anywhere* within the area of feasible product combinations. One point within this area, however, represents an optimal mix of products X and Y that will result in a maximization of the objective function (contribution margin). Our task now is to find precisely where that point lies.

4. *The optimal product mix: Determine from the area of feasible product combinations that mix of production which will maximize the objective function.*

The optimal product mix will always fall on a *corner* of the area of feasible product combinations. If we scan the graph in Exhibit 17–1 we can see that the area of feasible product combinations has five corners. The five corners will yield the following product mixes between X and Y (starting at the origin, and going clockwise around the area of feasible product combinations):

	Units Produced	
Corner	*X*	*Y*
1........0		0
2........0		3
3........1½		3
4........3		2
5........4		0

Which production mix is optimal? To find the optimal mix we will need to calculate the total contribution margin promised at each corner. We can do this by referring to the unit contribution margin data given in the objective function equation.

$$Z = 8X + 10Y \qquad (1)$$

This equation tells us that each unit of X promises $8 of contribution margin, and that each unit of Y promises $10 of contribution margin. Relating these figures to the production mixes at the five corners, we find that the following total contribution margins are possible:

X		Y		Total Contribution Margin
$8(0)	+	$10(0)	=	$ 0
8(0)	+	10(3)	=	30
8(1½)	+	10(3)	=	42
8(3)	+	10(2)	=	44
8(4)	+	10(0)	=	32

The firm should produce 3 units of X and 2 units of Y. This production mix will yield a maximum contribution margin of $44. Given the constraints under which the firm must operate, it is not possible to obtain a greater total contribution margin than this amount. Any production mix different from 3 units of X and 2 units of Y will result in *less* total contribution margin.

Why Always on a Corner?   It was stated earlier that we will always find the optimal product mix on a *corner* of the area of feasible product combinations. Why does the optimal mix always fall on a corner? Look at the objective function equation again for a moment [equation (1)]. This equation expresses a straight line with a $-\frac{4}{5}$ slope. Place a ruler on the graph in Exhibit 17–1 extending from the 8 point on the Y axis to the 10 point on the X axis (a $-\frac{4}{5}$ slope). Now bring your ruler down toward the origin of the graph, taking care to keep it parallel to the line from which you started. Note that the first point which your ruler touches is the corner of the area of feasible product combinations showing a production mix of 3 units of X and 2 units of Y. Your ruler touches this point first because it is the farthest point from the origin in relation to the objective function line. Therefore, that point must yield the greatest total contribution margin for the firm. Any point closer to the origin would result in less total contribution margin.[1]

Direction of the Constraint

Exhibit 17–1 shows the direction of all of the constraints to be *inward* toward the origin of the graph. The direction of the constraint will always be inward, so long as the constraint equation is stated in terms of less than or equal to ($\leq$).

The direction of the constraint will be *outward* away from the origin of the graph whenever the constraint equation is stated in terms of

---

[1] The objective function line could coincide with one of the lines bounding the area of feasible product combinations. In this case, a number of different product combinations would be possible, each resulting in the same total contribution margin. However, our statement that the solution will always be found on a corner is still true even under these conditions, since the product mix at the corners of the line would yield the same total contribution margin as any point on the line.

greater than or equal to ($\geq$). To illustrate, assume the following constraint:

X weighs 4 oz. and Y weighs 9 ozs. X and Y must be mixed
in such a way that their total weights is at least 72 ozs.

Constraint equation: $4X + 9Y \geq 72$ ozs.

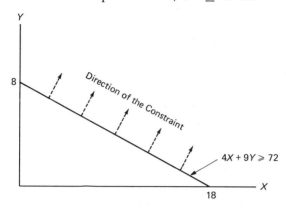

Since the direction of this constraint line is upward rather than downward, the area of feasible product combinations will be found *above* it, rather than below it. Constraints expressed in terms of *greater than or equal to,* as illustrated above, can be found in any linear programming problem, but are most common in *minimization* problems.

The Role of Shadow Prices

The linear programming solution which we completed earlier provided management with a very valuable piece of information—how much of product X and how much of product Y to produce each period. However, the value of linear programming doesn't stop here. The technique is capable of providing answers to many other questions that may arise in the course of operations.

For example, if demand for product X becomes very strong, the firm may consider expanding production capacity beyond the 36 hours now available. If capacity is expanded by, say, five hours, how will profits be affected? If capacity is expanded, it will be necessary to purchase more than 24 pounds of raw materials. If the firm has to pay a substantial premium for the additional pounds of raw materials, how will this affect profits? On the other hand, how will profits be affected if raw materials become more scarce, or if production capacity is reduced through strikes or breakdowns?

These are all questions of great economic significance. Answers to questions such as these can be obtained through sensitivity analysis using linear programming *shadow prices*. A shadow price can be defined as the *value of a marginal unit* of a scarce resource.

The Computation of Shadow Prices

Since a shadow price is the value of a *marginal* unit of a scarce resource, the shadow price associated with any scarce resource can be computed by varying the available amount of the scarce resource by *one unit*, and observing the impact of the change on total contribution margin. The extent to which total contribution margin is changed will equal the shadow price for the scarce resource under examination.

We will demonstrate the computation of shadow prices by returning to the data used in the preceding example. The equations which we used to express the constraints associated with production capacity and with raw materials are given below:

$$\text{Production capacity constraint: } 6X + 9Y \leq 36 \qquad (2)$$
$$\text{Raw materials constraint: } \quad 6X + 3Y \leq 24 \qquad (3)$$

The Shadow Price of Production Capacity. We stated earlier that to find the shadow price associated with any scarce resource it is necessary to vary the available amount of that scarce resource by one unit, and to observe the effect of the change on total contribution margin. Therefore, to find the shadow price associated with production capacity, we will need to increase the available amount of capacity from 36 hours to 37 hours, and then to solve the constraint equations for new values for products X and Y.[2]

$$6X + 9Y \leq 37 \text{ [Increased from 36 hours; see equation (2) above]}$$
$$\underline{6X + 3Y \leq 24 \text{ [Unchanged; see equation (3) above]}}$$
$$6Y = 13$$
$$Y = 2\tfrac{1}{6}$$

Subtracting one equation from the other, we find the new production volume for Y to be $2\tfrac{1}{6}$ units. By substituting this value back into one of the equations, we find the new production volume for X to be $2\tfrac{11}{12}$ units.

$$6X + 9(2\tfrac{1}{6}) = 37$$
$$6X + 19\tfrac{1}{2} \quad = 37$$
$$6X \qquad\quad = 17\tfrac{1}{2}$$
$$X \qquad\quad = 2\tfrac{11}{12}$$

---

[2] In finding new values for products X and Y, we could construct a graph as we did in Exhibit 17–1. However, since we are dealing with only two equations and two unknowns, it is quicker and easier to solve the equations directly for the new values of X and Y.

In other words, if the firm had 37 hours of production time available, rather than 36 hours, it would produce $2^{11}/_{12}$ units of product X and $2\frac{1}{6}$ units of product Y. In our earlier solution using 36 hours of production time, the production mix was 3 units of X and 2 units of Y.

To find the shadow price associated with the extra hour of production time, we need now to insert the new values of X and Y into the objective function equation, and to observe the impact of the changed production mix on total contribution margin.

$$Z = 8X + 10Y$$
$$Z = 8(2^{11}/_{12}) + 10(2\frac{1}{6})$$
$$Z = 23\frac{1}{3} + 21\frac{2}{3}$$
$$Z = 45$$

If 37 hours of production capacity are available, the firm will realize $45 in total contribution margin. In our earlier solution using 36 hours of production capacity, the total contribution margin was only $44. Therefore, since increasing production capacity by one hour increased the total contribution margin from $44 to $45, the shadow price associated with production time is $1. For each hour that production capacity can be increased, the firm can increase total contribution margin by $1. The inverse also holds true. Each hour of production capacity that is *idle* will *reduce* total contribution margin by $1.

The knowledge of the shadow price associated with a scarce resource is an extremely useful piece of information. To cite one widely used application, if the cost of increasing capacity by 1 hour is only $.40, then the company in our example would be well advised to proceed with its expansion plans. The expenditure of the $.40 would return back $1 in additional contribution margin.

The Shadow Price of Raw Materials. We will now use the same procedure to compute the shadow price associated with raw materials. We will increase the raw materials available by 1 pound, and then solve for new production volumes for X and Y.

$$6X + 9Y \leq 36 \text{ [Unchanged; see equation (2) above]}$$
$$\underline{6X + 3Y \leq 25} \text{ [Increased from 24 pounds; see equation (3) above]}$$
$$6Y = 11$$
$$Y = 1\frac{5}{6}$$

Substituting the new production volume of $1\frac{5}{6}$ units of Y back into one of the equations, we find the new production volume for X to be $3\frac{1}{4}$ units:

$$6X + 3(1\frac{5}{6}) = 25$$
$$6X + 5\frac{1}{2} = 25$$
$$6X = 19\frac{1}{2}$$
$$X = 3\frac{1}{4}$$

If 25 pounds of raw materials are available, the firm will produce $3\frac{1}{4}$ units of product X and $1\frac{5}{6}$ units of product Y. To find the shadow price associated with the extra pound of raw materials, we will need to insert these new values for X and Y back into the objective function equation, and to observe the impact of the changed production mix on total contribution margin.

$$Z = 8X + 10Y$$
$$Z = 8(3\frac{1}{4}) + 10(1\frac{5}{6})$$
$$Z = 26 + 18\frac{1}{3}$$
$$Z = 44\frac{1}{3}$$

Since our earlier solution with 24 pounds of raw materials available yielded only $44 in total contribution margin, we can see that the shadow price associated with this scarce resource is $\frac{1}{3}$ of a dollar, or $.33. If raw materials cost less than $.33 a pound, the firm can profit by purchasing additional amounts as they become available. The extent to which the firm will profit by the additional purchases will be the difference between the price paid and the $.33 shadow price.

The Simplex Method

In our examples we have dealt with only two products, X and Y. When more than two products are involved in a linear programming problem, the graphical method no longer is adequate to provide a solution. In these cases, a more powerful version of linear programming is needed. This more powerful version is commonly called the *simplex* method.

The simplex method is considerably more complex in operation than the graphical method, even though the principles underlying its operation are identical to those already discussed in connection with the graphical method. Generally, linear programming simplex solutions are carried out on the digital computer. The mechanics of the method are covered in most advanced managerial accounting texts.

Applications of Linear Programming

Linear programming has been applied to an extremely wide range of problems in many different fields. Decision makers have found that is is by far the best tool available for combining manpower, materials, and facilities together to the best advantage of a firm. Although the use of linear programming has been most extensive in the industrial, agricultural, and military sectors, it has also been applied to problems in economics, engineering, and the sciences. In addition, linear programming has been used widely in solving problems associated with the space program in this country.

In this section, a few of the broader applications of linear programming are given, with the thought in mind of demonstrating the versatility of linear programming in solving a wide range of problems.

Production and Inventory Control. Many business firms are faced with a seasonal demand for their products. These firms have found that producing in uneven spurts to meet fluctuating demand often results in excessive production costs. On the other hand, producing at an even level throughout the year often results in large inventories on hand, causing inventory carrying costs to be excessive. Linear programming has been used very successfully in balancing production schedules so that adequate goods are on hand to satisfy demand but yet inventories are not so large as to generate excessive carrying costs. Linear programming is also used extensively in determining product mix, and in deciding which products should be produced in which plant for most effective utilization of total facilities available.

Blending Problems. Many situations exist where certain basic components are blended together to produce a product with certain required specifications. Examples would include mixing of feed for cattle, mixing of tobacco ingredients for cigars and cigarettes, blending sausage ingredients, and blending gasoline. In the case of gasoline, oil refineries are faced with the problem of taking a number of crude oil products and blending them into different grades of gasoline. By considering the characteristics of the various crude oil products available, and by considering the characteristics desired in the final gasoline product, linear programming can be used to put together those ingredients that will produce the desired product at the least cost. Much the same approach is used in producing cattle feeds. Usually the feeds have some minimum nutritional requirement that must be met. Linear programming is used to meet that requirement at the least possible cost.

Routing and Assignment Problems. A version of linear programming known as the *transportation method* is widely used in routing and assignment problems. The railroads, for example, have found it very helpful in moving empty boxcars from one place to another. Empty boxcars may be needed at certain points, but located at entirely different points. Linear programming is used to determine how to get the empty cars to the desired points with the least time and cost. This same technique is also used to assist in locating warehouse facilities in such a way as to provide the most efficient service to customers at the least cost. Linear programming is now being used extensively to assist in structuring routes for salesmen over sales territories. The objective is to cover a sales territory in the least time and at the least travel cost.

Other Applications. Linear programming has also been used in traffic control problems, in minimizing trim loss in paper mills, in structuring executive compensation programs, in plywood and paneling production in saw mills, and in investment portfolio management.

PROBABILITY ANALYSIS

Much of the discussion throughout this book has assumed that the decision maker was working under conditions of certainty with respect to future events. That is, we have assumed that the decision maker has known with perfect certainty what the results would be of a particular decision. If a new product line was about to be introduced, we have assumed that the decision maker *knew* how many units could be sold. If a new machine was about to be purchased, we have assumed that the decision maker *knew* by how much the machine would reduce annual operating costs. This assumption of certainty has been a useful approach up to this point, since it has permitted us maximum freedom to focus on the *use* of data without becoming bogged down in the uncertainty problem.

It would be nice, of course, to have a world of perfect certainty. The decision maker's only problem would be to determine what future events were relevant to a particular problem, and the solution would then become obvious. The world is not characterized by conditions of certainty, however, so we must now relax our earlier assumptions, and consider what avenues are available to the decision maker in coping with uncertain situations.

One OR technique, *probability analysis,* has been developed in direct response to the need to operate under conditions of uncertainty. This OR technique has proved to be particularly useful in business situations, and is fast becoming an indispensable tool for both the accountant and the manager.

Objective versus Subjective Probabilities

A probability simply means that there is some statistical chance that a particular event will occur. Several events may be possible in a given situation. Each event will carry some probability, or statistical chance, that it will occur rather than the other events in the situation being considered.

Objective Probabilities. In some cases, the probability of an event occuring can be objectively determined. For example, if you toss a coin in the air, there is one chance in two that it will fall heads. The probability of heads is therefore $\frac{1}{2}$, or .5. The probability of tails is also $\frac{1}{2}$ or .5, since there is an equal chance of getting tails on the toss. The sum of the probabilities of the two events is given below:

Event	Percentage Chance of Occurrence	Probability
Heads	50%	.5
Tails	50	.5
	100%	1.0

The sum of the probabilities of the events associated with a particular situation will *always* add to 1.0. This is because the probability assigned to a particular event gives the relative chance of that event happening in comparison to the relative chance of the other events happening, and the events are mutually exclusive. That is, no two can happen at the same time. The probabilities associated with the tossing of a coin are objective in the sense that they can be (and have been) verified by observation.

Many business problems are such that the probability of the events associated with the problem can be objectively determined. These are situations where a large backlog of historical experience is available to which the decision maker can turn. For example, a firm may have detailed records available showing the level of demand for its products at various seasons of the year. Under these conditions, the probability of selling a given number of units of a particular product during a particular season of the year could be objectively determined by simply turning to the records.

Subjective Probabilities. On the other hand, other business problems are such that no past experience is available at all. If no past experience is available, the decision maker must outline the range of events that in his judgment *could* happen, and assign to each event some probability of occurrence. These probabilities will be based entirely on the decision maker's subjective judgment, or feel, for the situation at hand. Probabilities established in this manner are known as *subjective probabilities*. The point should be emphasized that subjective probabilities are not just pulled out of thin air. Rather, they are determined by the decision maker drawing upon all of the insight, intuition, judgment, and personal experience that he can bring to bear upon the problem at hand.

Many business problems are such that subjective probabilities can be assigned, and the problem then solved via mathematical probability theory. This OR tool for decision making is illustrated in the following sections.

Expected Value Tables

Assume that the Titan Company, a manufacturer of washing machines, has just made a sale of 500 machines to a laundromat chain. The machines are under a warranty which states that the Titan Company must provide servicing and parts for the machines for one year. The Titan Company is trying to determine the best way in which to handle this warranty obligation. Three options are available:

1. A servicing and repair firm will make all service calls and provide all parts for the washers for the one-year period for a flat fee of $15,000.
2. A second servicing and repair firm will provide all required parts for the one-year period and make up to 1,500 service calls for a fee of $10,000. Additional service calls will be made at a charge of $5 each.
3. A third servicing and repair firm will provide all required parts for the one-year period and make up to 2,000 service calls for a fee of $12,500. Additional service calls will be made at a charge of $5 each.

Which option should be accepted? The choice depends on the number of service calls that actually will be made during the one-year period. The problem is that the Titan Company doesn't know how many service calls will be made. The Titan Company is therefore faced with the necessity of making a decision under conditions of uncertainty.

Setting the Probabilities. The Titan Company's approach should be to determine as best it can the probabilities that certain volumes of service calls will actually materialize. The way in which these probabilities are determined will depend on the extent and quality of information available. Records may be available for prior sales of similar machines that may give a clear pattern of the range of probable service calls. If such records are available, then *objective* probabilities can be determined.

On the other hand, records of past experience may not be available to use as a basis for setting objective probabilities. The lack of such records, however, will not relieve the Titan Company of the necessity to make a decision. It will just make the decision more difficult, and wrap it more tightly in a cloak of uncertainty. If no prior records are available, the Titan Company will have little choice other than to gather all of the facts, evidence, etc., that can be assembled, and on the basis of judgment, intuition, and feel for the situation assign subjective probabilities to the chance of certain levels of service calls actually materializing over the next year.

We will assume that the Titan Company has determined, either through objective evidence gleaned from extensive records, or from subjective evaluation of the problem, that a maximum of 3,000 service calls can be expected over the next year. The probabilities which the Titan Company has assigned to various levels of calls up to a maximum of 3,000 are given below:

Number of Service Calls	Chance of Occurrence	Probability of Occurrence
1,500 or less.	40%	.4
2,000.	30	.3
2,500.	20	.2
3,000.	10	.1
	100%	1.0

Constructing the Expected Value Table. With data available on the probability of certain levels of service calls materializing, the Titan Company can construct a series of *expected value tables*. These tables are shown in Exhibit 17–2.

EXHIBIT 17–2
Expected Value Tables

	(1) Event (Number of Calls to be Made)	(2) Probability	(3) Conditional Value	Expected Value (2) × (3)
		Table 1		
Option 1:	All calls	1.0	$15,000	$15,000
		Table 2		
Option 2:	1,500 or less.	.4	$10,000	$ 4,000
	2,000.	.3	12,500	3,750
	2,500.	.2	15,000	3,000
	3,000.	.1	17,500	1,750
				$12,500
		Table 3		
Option 3:	2,000 or less.	.7	12,500	$ 8,750
	2,500.	.2	15,000	3,000
	3,000.	.1	17,500	1,750
				$13,500

The construction of the tables in Exhibit 17–2 warrants a word of explanation. Notice in the "Event" column that all events associated with an option are listed. In the case of Option 1, the only event that can occur is for the servicing firm to make all calls. Under the other two options, however, a series of events is possible, depending on the separate servicing terms being offered. (Refer back to the servicing terms under the three options.)

Under the "Probability" column, the probability of the various events materializing is given. Notice in each case that the sum of the probabilities adds to 1.0. These are the probabilities that were derived earlier by the Titan Company, either through objective evidence or through subjective evaluation.

The "Conditional Value" column indicates the total cost that will be incurred if the number of service calls under the "Event" column are actually made. For example, under Option 2, if 2,000 service calls are made, the Titan Company will be required to pay the basic contract price of $10,000 plus $5 for the number of service calls over 1,500. Since there would be 500 calls above this figure, an additional $2,500 would be added onto the basic $10,000, bringing the total cost to $12,500, as shown in the table.

The "Expected Value" column is a product of the conditional value multiplied by the probability of occurrence. This column is then totaled to give the expected value associated with each option. Since the Titan Company is interested in minimizing cost, the option that has the *least* expected value is the most desirable alternative. This would be Option 2, with an expected value of $12,500. Therefore, the Titan Company should accept the offer of the second servicing and repair firm.

Other Applications

An expected value table can be used in solving many business problems dealing with uncertainty. To show another, less complex example of expected value, assume the following data:

Montier Company is trying to forecast sales for 19X4. The company has gathered the following information:

Level of Sales	Probability
$100,000	.3
150,000	.4
200,000	.2
250,000	.1

Required: Compute the sales forecast for 19X4.

(1) Event	(2) Probability	(3) Conditional Value	Expected Value (2) × (3)
A	.3	$100,000	$ 30,000
B	.4	150,000	60,000
C	.2	200,000	40,000
D	.1	250,000	25,000
			$155,000

The sales forecast would be set at $155,000 for 19X4.

Payoff Tables

A variation of the expected value table that is used in some probability analysis is known as a *payoff table*. To illustrate its use, assume the following information:

A street vendor sells several items of fruit, including bananas. He buys his bananas on Monday for sale during the week. Any bananas remaining at the end of the week are discarded, since the market for overripe bananas is somewhat limited. The vendor purchases his bananas for $.05 per pound, and sells them for $.12 per pound.

During some weeks the vendor sells as few as 50 pounds, but during other weeks he is able to sell as many as 500 pounds. He is anxious to maximize his profits from bananas, but he is uncertain as to how many pounds of bananas to purchase each week to accomplish this. If too many bananas are purchased, the spoilage losses cut into his profits. On the other hand, if too few are purchased, then sales are lost.

The vendor needs first to determine the range of demand for bananas. He then needs to determine the probabilities associated with the various levels of demand within this range. Assume that he determines (either by objective evidence or by subjective evaluation) these values to be as follows:

Demand for Bananas in Pounds	Probability Of Occurrence
50.	.05
100.	.10
200.	.30
300.	.30
400.	.15
500.	.10
	1.00

Since the vendor purchases his bananas for $.05 a pound and sells them for $.12 a pound, his profit per pound sold is $.07, and his loss per pound unsold is $.05. These data can now be organized into a payoff table, as shown in Exhibit 17–3.

The construction of this table requires a word of explanation. First, notice that the demand for bananas is given in the extreme left column. In the next column the table shows the probability of the various levels of demand actually materializing. The table then shows what the profit result would be for weekly purchases of bananas ranging from 50 pounds to 500 pounds. Under each purchase alternative there are two columns, one marked "CV" and one marked "EV." These notations stand for "conditional value" and "expected value." The dollar amounts in these col-

EXHIBIT 17–3
Payoff Table

Purchases of Bananas in Pounds

Event (Demand)	Prob- ability	50		100		200		300		400		500	
		CV	EV	CV	EV	CV	EV	CV	EV	CV	EV	CV	EV
50 lbs.	.05	$3.50	$ .18	$1.00	$ .05	$-4.00	$- .20	$-9.00	$- .45	$-14.00	$- .70	$-19.00	$- .95
100 lbs.	.10	3.50	.35	7.00	.70	-2.00	- .20	-3.00	- .30	- 8.00	- .80	-13.00	-1.30
200 lbs.	.30	3.50	1.05	7.00	2.10	14.00	4.20	9.00	2.70	4.00	1.20	- 1.00	- .30
300 lbs.	.30	3.50	1.05	7.00	2.10	14.00	4.20	21.00	6.30	16.00	4.80	11.00	3.30
400 lbs.	.15	3.50	.52	7.00	1.05	14.00	2.10	21.00	3.15	28.00	4.20	23.00	3.45
500 lbs.	.10	3.50	.35	7.00	.70	14.00	1.40	21.00	2.10	28.00	2.80	35.00	3.50
			$3.50		$6.70		$11.50		$13.50		$11.50		$ 7.70

Note: See the explanation of this table in the accompanying text.

umns are computed in exactly the same way as the conditional value and expected value amounts in the expected value table in the preceding exhibit.

To illustrate, assume first that the vendor purchases 100 pounds of bananas each week, and assume second that he purchases 200 pounds of bananas each week. Under these two different assumptions, what would be the CV and EV associated with weekly sales of 50 pounds of bananas? These computations are shown below:

Purchase 100 Pounds, Sell 50 Pounds		*Purchase 200 Pounds, Sell 50 Pounds*	
Conditional value (CV):		Conditional value (CV):	
Profit from pounds sold		Profit from pounds sold	
(50 lbs. × $.07).	$3.50	(50 lbs. × $.07).	$3.50
Loss from pounds unsold		Loss from pounds unsold	
(50 lbs. × $.05).	(2.50)	(150 lbs. × $.05)	(7.50)
	$1.00		($4.00)
Expected value (EV):		Expected value (EV):	
(Conditional value times the		(Conditional value times the	
probability of the event)		probability of the event)	
$1.00 × .05	$ .05	$4.00 × .05	($ .20)

The reader should trace these figures into the table in Exhibit 17–3. All other figures in the table are computed in the same way that we have computed these. For each pound of bananas that the vendor sells, he will make a profit of $.07; for each pound left unsold at the end of the week, he will sustain a loss of $.05.

Since the vendor is interested in maximizing his profits, the alternative with the *highest* expected value will indicate the optimum number of pounds of bananas to purchase each week. This would be 300 pounds, which will result in weekly profits of $13.50 (see Exhibit 17–3). The fact that during some weeks the vendor will lose sales of 200 pounds of bananas (during weeks when he could have sold 500 pounds) is immaterial. Profits will be maximized by purchasing only 300 pounds each week.

The Value of Perfect Information

We have just determined that the best alternative open to the vendor is to purchase 300 pounds of bananas each week, from which profits of $13.50 will be realized. Actually, another alternative is open to our vendor friend. He can wait and try to get additional information before committing himself to a particular course of action. Often executives want to dig into the facts a little deeper before launching off in a certain direction. Additional information, through sampling, is always obtainable if one is willing to pay the price. The question is, what price is additional information worth?

The Impact on Profits. The worth of additional information will depend on the impact it will have on profits. If it is necessary to pay more for information than it can yield in increased profits, then the information obviously isn't worth going after. On the other hand, the increased profits accruing from a small amount of additional information may be so great that almost any cost can be justified.

The payoff table provides the decision maker with a tool for assessing the value of additional information. This value can then be measured against the cost of securing that information, to determine whether the expenditure would be worthwhile.

An Illustration. To illustrate how the value of additional information can be measured, let us return to the data in our street vendor example. Assume for the moment that the vendor has perfect information. That is, assume that he has secured a source of information that tells him at the beginning of each week exactly how many pounds of bananas can be sold during that week. The vendor is able, then, to purchase precisely that many pounds, and he is able to end each week with neither spoilage nor unsold merchandise. Under these conditions, his payoff table would appear as shown in Exhibit 17–4.

EXHIBIT 17–4
Payoff Table with Perfect Information

(1) Event (Demand)	(2) Prob- ability	(3) CV with Perfect Information	EV with Perfect Information (2) × (3)
50 lbs.	.05	$ 3.50	$ .18
100 lbs.	.10	7.00	.70
200 lbs.	.30	14.00	4.20
300 lbs.	.30	21.00	6.30
400 lbs.	.15	28.00	4.20
500 lbs.	.10	35.00	3.50
			$19.08

Since we are assuming that the vendor has perfect information, the amount demanded in Exhibit 17–4 (column 1) is exactly the amount sold each week. Therefore, the conditional value is simply $.07 profit per pound times the number of pounds sold. Under these conditions, the probability (column 2) represents the *actual* percentage of weeks that the various levels of demand will materialize. The expected value column in the table shows that if the vendor had access to this perfect information, his weekly profits would be $19.08.

What would this source of perfect information be worth to the vendor? Since he can expect to earn only $13.50 a week without perfect information, he would be willing to pay up to the *difference* between this figure and the $19.08 that he can earn *with* the perfect information. This difference is $5.58. Therefore, if the vendor could obtain perfect information for any cost less than $5.58 per week, he would be justified in paying the price.

As a practical matter, of course, perfect information does not exist in the real world. Even so, the *broad concept* which we have just developed is an extremely useful guide in attempting to assess the value of additional information. This is true even if that information is less than perfect. By determining what he would be willing to pay for *perfect* information, the decision maker can more objectively determine what he would be willing to pay for *imperfect* information.

SUMMARY

The decision making process is so complex and involves so many variables that the manager often finds it beneficial to employ various quantitative decision techniques found in the mathematical and statistical sciences.

One such technique is linear programming. Although linear programming has many applications, its basic purpose is to assist the manager in arriving at the optimum solution to a problem in the face of limiting or constraining factors.

Probability analysis is another very useful quantitative decision technique. Probability analysis is often employed when a decision must be made under conditions of uncertainty. The technique involves the establishment of a range of possible events, and the assignment of some probability factor to each event. The probabilities can be assigned either on the basis of objective evidence gleaned from past experience, or on the basis of subjective evaluations on the part of the decision maker. These probabilities are used to determine an overall expected value, which serves as a guide to the decision maker in his decision.

Although quantitative decision techniques such as linear programming and probability analysis are somewhat new on the business scene, they have come to be trusted and recognized as powerful and indispensable decision-making tools.

QUESTIONS

17–1. What changes in kinds of information supplied by accounting would you expect to follow a widespread adoption by management of quantitative techniques such as linear programming and probability analysis?

17–2. Is operations research planning oriented, or control oriented? Explain.

17–3. Most mathematical techniques rely heavily on models of some type. What is the value of model building in attempting to solve business problems?

17–4. Can the following equation be described as a model?

$$\text{Assets} = \text{Liabilities} + \text{Owners' Equity}$$

Explain why the equation is or is not a model.

17–5. What does linear programming attempt to achieve for the decision maker?

17–6. Schloss Company has decided to use linear programming as a planning tool. The company can't decide whether to use marginal contribution per unit or gross profit per unit in its linear programming computations. Which would you suggest? Why?

17–7. Define "objective function" and "constraint" as these concepts relate to linear programming.

17–8. Sever Company produces two products. Product A has a contribution margin per unit of $10. Product B has a contribution margin per unit of $8. Explain why a linear programming analysis might suggest that the company produce more of product B than product A. (Ample market exists for either product.)

17–9. What is meant by an "area of feasible product combinations?"

17–10. Sometimes a linear programming solution will show that it is more profitable to have some idle capacity than it is to utilize all capacity available. Prepare a linear programming graph for two products, X and Y, that shows such a solution. Assume three constraints— capacity and raw materials for both products, and market acceptance for product Y. No numbers are needed on the graph—just assumed constraint lines and an assumed objective function line touching the optimal product mix point.

17–11. What is meant by the term "shadow price?" How is a shadow price determined?

17–12. Give five applicatons of linear programming in solving business problems.

17–13. Differentiate between an objective probability and a subjective probability.

17–14. All companies faced the same general economic conditions in the first ten years after World War II. Some companies invested heavily in expansion and growth during this period, whereas other companies kept large portions of their assets in liquid form. What influence did subjective probabilities have on the actions of management in each case?

17–15. What is meant by the term "expected value?"

EXERCISES

17–1. Consider the three following equations:
Maximize:

$$Z = 2X + 5Y$$

Subject to the constraints:

$$2X + 4Y \leq 10$$
$$X + 3Y \leq 6$$

Required:

Solve for X and Y by means of the linear programming graphical method.

17–2. The objective function and constraint equations for Mercer Company are given below:
Maximize:

$$Z = 3A + 4B$$

Subject to:

$$2A + 3B \leq 12$$
$$4A + B \leq 14$$
$$B \leq 2$$

Required:

Solve for A and B by means of the linear programming graphical method.

17–3. Murl Company produces two products, Awls and Pows. Two types of material, A and B, are used in the production of each product. The quantities required by product are:

	Material A	Material B
Awls	3 lbs.	2 lbs.
Pows	1 lb.	2 lbs.
Total available.	10 lbs.	12 lbs.

Market conditions are such that no more than five Pows can be sold. Contribution margin of the Awls and Pows is $3 and $2 per unit, respectively.

Required:

1. Prepare an objective function equation, and constraint equations for the Awls and Pows.
2. Determine how much of each product should be produced, by means of the linear programming graphical method.

17–4. Stoner Products, Inc., uses 2 lbs. of material A in the manufacture of both its large and small mugs. The large mugs also require 3 ozs. of material B. The small mugs do not use material B. Both size mugs use material C. The large mugs use 3 ozs., and the small mugs use 1 oz. The contribution margin of the large and small mugs is $3 and $2, respectively. The amount of materials available each period is:

$$
\begin{array}{ll}
\text{Material A} & \text{8 lbs.} \\
\text{Material B} & \text{9 ozs.} \\
\text{Material C} & \text{6 ozs.}
\end{array}
$$

Required:

1. Assume that the company wishes to maximize contribution margin. Prepare an objective function equation, and constraint equations.
2. Determine how much of each product should be produced each period by means of the linear programming graphical method.

17–5. Miers Company desires to maximize contribution margin. The company has determined by a linear programming analysis that contribution margin is maximized by producing and selling three units of product X and two units of product Y. This mix of production and sales yields a total contribution margin of $34. The company's objective function and constraint equations are:

$$Z = 6X + 8Y$$
$$2X + 3Y \leq 12 \text{ (Constraint equation for material \#1)}$$
$$2X + Y \leq 8 \text{ (Constraint equation for material \#2)}$$

Required:

Determine the shadow price of material #2.

17–6. The Meriweather Company is trying to determine the cost savings that probably will be realized from purchasing a newer, more efficient lathe. The company's industrial engineers have made a study of the problem, and have prepared the following data:

	Annual Savings	*Prob- ability*
Most pessimistic estimate	$30,000	.2
Most likely estimate	40,000	.7
Most optimistic estimate	50,000	.1

Required:

Use an expected value table to show the probable annual cost savings arising from purchase of the new lathe.

17–7. Barney's Brewery has just discovered a tantalizing new wine that is to be priced at $10 per bottle. Barney's variable costs per bottle are $6. The company's marketing division estimates the following range of sales at the $10-per-bottle price:

| | Annual | |
	Sales in Bottles	Probability
	10,000.	.1
	20,000.	.3
	30,000.	.4
	40,000.	.2

Required:

By use of an expected value table, compute the expected value of annual contribution margin from sales of the new wine.

PROBLEMS

17–1. *Straightforward Maximization Problem.* The Haag Company can produce two different products, A and B. The company has four manufacturing operations—Cutting, Sanding, Assembly, and Packing. Product B goes through all four operations. Product A goes through all operations except Assembly. The manufacturing requirements in terms of hours per unit are given below for A and B for each of the company's operations:

	Product A	Product B
Cutting Operation.	2	3
Sanding Operation	3	1
Assembly Operation	–	4
Packing Operation	1	1

Each operation is limited in terms of number of hours available. The available hours by operation are: Cutting—30 hours; Sanding—15 hours; Assembly—24 hours; and Packing—8 hours.

Each unit of product A which is sold yields $3 in contribution margin, and each unit of product B which is sold yields $4 in contribution margin. The company wishes to maximize contribution margin.

Required:

1. Prepare equations to express the objective function, and each of the constraints.
2. Determine the optimum mix of products A and B, using the graphical method of linear programming.

17–2. *Graphical Method, with Shadow Prices; Maximization.* The Farrow Fertilizer Company produces two high-quality fertilizer products— Nitro-X and Nitro-Y. Each fertilizer product is produced in batches. One batch of Nitro-X yields a contribution margin of $6, and one batch of Nitro-Y yields a contribution margin of $10. The company is anxious to maximize contribution margin. Either product can be sold in unlimited quantities. Two raw materials go into the production of both Nitro-X and Nitro-Y, although not in the same proportions, as shown in the table below:

	Material A	*Material B*
Nitro-X usage per batch	4 lbs.	3 lbs.
Nitro-Y usage per batch	3 lbs.	6 lbs.
Total raw material available each day	60 lbs.	90 lbs.

Required:

1. Prepare equations to express the objective function and the constraints.
2. Determine how many batches of Nitro-X and of Nitro-Y should be produced each day. Use the linear programming graphical method, with Nitro-X on the horizontal axis and Nitro-Y on the vertical axis.
3. Assume that material B must be purchased in 15-pound bags, and that a single bag costs $16. What is the shadow price of one bag of material B?
4. By how much would daily profits be increased by purchasing an additional bag of material B each day?

17–3. *Optimum Production Mix to Maximize Profits.* Bill Sagers has just retired, and is anxious to open a small pottery business to occupy his time. Mr. Sagers has decided to produce just two items initially— pots and bowls. The local pottery supply house has indicated that because of shortages in supplies, Mr. Sagers can be allowed only 80 pounds of high quality clay each week, and only 11¼ gallons of glazing material.

Mr. Sagers has purchased a used kiln, which he feels can be operated about 60 hours per week. His wife will package all finished products, and will have a maximum of about 11 hours per week to work for the pottery business. Mr. Sagers has determined the following additional information:

		Per Batch	
Operation	*Item Needed*	*Pots*	*Bowls*
Moulding	Clay	8 lbs.	5 lbs.
Glazing	Glaze	5 qts.	3 qts.
Firing	—	4 hrs.	6 hrs.
Packaging	—	1 hr.	1 hr.

Mr. Sagers feels that no more than nine batches of bowls can be sold each week. The pots yield $50 in profits per batch, and the bowls $40 per batch. Mr. Sagers wishes to maximize his profits.

Required:

1. Prepare equations to express the objective function, and each of the constraints. Identify pots as X and bowls as Y.
2. Determine how many batches of pots and how many batches

of bowls should be produced each week. Identify pots as *X* and bowls as *Y* on your linear programming graph.

17–4. *Minimum Vitamin Requirement at Least Cost.* The Frisky Dog Kennel has found that its animals must receive a minimum daily requirement of 20 units of Vitamin A and 24 units of Vitamin B in order to stay healthy and active. Two different rations are on the market containing Vitamins A and B. One pound of Ration X contains 5 percent of the minimum daily requirement of Vitamin A, and 12 percent of the minimum daily requirement of Vitamin B. One pound of Ration Y contains 10 percent of the minimum daily requirement of Vitamin A, and 8 percent of the minimum daily requirement of Vitamin B.

Ration X costs $.20 per pound whereas Ration Y costs $.50 per pound. The kennel can purchase unlimited quantities of either ration. A mixing machine is used to mix the two rations together to get the desired mix that provides the Vitamin A and Vitamin B requirements mentioned above. The mixer cannot hold more than 300 pounds of ration at a time.

The company wants to provide the minimum daily vitamin requirement at the least possible cost.

Required:

1. Prepare equations to express:
    a. The objective function.
    b. The constraints under which the proper vitamin mix must be obtained.
2. Determine the mix of Ration X and Ration Y which will provide the minimum daily vitamin requirement at the least possible cost.

17–5. *Optimum Candy Mixture; Cost Minimization.* (Based on a situation described by Miller and Starr, *Executive Decisions and Operations Research,* pp. 217–22.) The Happy Valley Candy Company produces and sells a box of candy made up of caramels and creams. The company would like to find the optimal mixture of the two kinds of candy, in order to meet the specifications per box as outlined in the following table:

	Caramels	Creams	Per Box
Weight per piece.	1.2 ozs.	0.6 ozs.	18.0 ozs. or more
Number of pieces	?	?	25 or more
Cost per piece	$.03	$.02	$.66 maximum cost

The company wants at least six caramels in each box of candy. The company can produce either caramels or creams in unlimited numbers, so the objective is to minimize the cost of candy going into each box. The mixture will not affect the selling price per box.

Required:

1. Prepare equations expressing the objective function, and the constraints under which the company must operate.
2. Determine the optimal mix of caramels and creams in order to minimize the total cost per box of candy. Use a linear programming graph, with caramels on the horizontal axis (X), and creams on the vertical axis (Y).

17–6. *Cost Minimization.* (Prepared from a situation described by Naylor and Byrne, *Linear Programming*, Wadsworth Publishing Company, p. 45.) Recycled Metals, Inc., has received an order from a customer who wants to purchase a minimum of 2,500 pounds of scrap metal. The customer requires that the scrap metal contain at least 1,200 pounds of high-quality aluminum that can be melted down and used in fabrication. The customer also requires that the scrap delivered to him contain no more than 480 pounds of unfit metal. By "unfit" the customer means metal that contains so many impurities that it can't be melted down and used at all.

Recycled Metals, Inc., can purchase aluminum scrap metal from either of two suppliers. The scrap being sold by the two suppliers contains the following proportions of high-quality aluminum and unfit scrap:

	Supplier A	Supplier B
High quality aluminum.	80%	30%
Unfit scrap.	20%	15%

Either supplier has unlimited quantities of scrap metal available. Supplier A charges $.25 per pound, and Supplier B charges $.12 per pound. Recycled Metals, Inc., would like to minimize the total cost it will have to pay to acquire the needed scrap metal to fill the customer's order.

Required:

1. Prepare equations to express the objective function and the constraints under which Recycled Metals, Inc., must make its purchase.
2. Determine the amount of scrap metal which should be purchased from each supplier, by using the linear programming graphical method.

17–7. *Expected Value Computations.* (Based on situations suggested by Miller and Starr, *Executive Decisions and Operations Research*, pp. 77–98). Several expected value problems are presented below. Each is independent of the others.

1. An appliance manufacturer sells two different models of toasters. The company has found that 70 percent of its sales are for the less expensive toaster, priced at $20. The remaining sales

are for the more expensive toaster, priced at $30. What is the expected purchase price of the toasters?

2. The Fearless Finance Company has found that 15 percent of its customers default on an average of 30 percent of their loans each year. What is the expected percentage of default each year for the company?

3. The Starr Company has paid dividends of $.80 per share in five of the last ten years, $.60 per share in four of the last ten years, and $.90 per share once in the last ten years. What is the expected dividend payment?

4. A large mail-order house has discovered that 15 percent of the orders for a particular item are returned by the purchaser. A cost analysis has determined that each return costs the company $.80 in handling and transportation. What is the expected extra cost per unit for returns of the item?

5. An investor has $1,000 to invest. He can invest in alternative A, which will yield a 4½ percent return, or alternative B, which will yield a 6 percent return. However, both alternatives are risky. Alternative A has a 90 percent chance of paying off, and alternative B has a 65 percent chance of paying off. Which alternative has the largest expected value?

17–8. *Expected Value Computations.* (Based in part on situations suggested by Miller and Starr, *Executive Decisions and Operations Research*, pp. 77–98.)

1. An auto dealership is conducting a lottery. The prize is a new car valued at $6,000. The dealership expects to sell 50,000 tickets at $.50 each. What is the expected value of the new car?

2. A manufacturing company receives shipments from its supplier in $10,000 orders. The company's records show that 10 percent of the time a complete shipment will be lost or destroyed, 15 percent of the time one fifth of a shipment will be damaged beyond use, and 5 percent of the time 10 percent of a shipment will be damaged beyond use. What is the maximum amount that the company should pay for insurance per shipment?

3. A state lottery sells 1,000,000 tickets each week. The tickets cost $.50 each. Three prizes are awarded weekly:

Prize	Number of Winners
$50,000	2
$25,000	5
$10,000	10

What is the expected value per ticket?

4. The "numbers game" is an illegal, but widely played, game of chance. The player bets whatever amount he likes on a three-digit number from 001 to 999. After all bets are placed, a three digit number is drawn randomly. If it is the player's number, and that number is, say, 423, he wins 500 times what he bet. If the number is, say, 812, he wins 900 times what he bet,

etc. Assume a player bets $2 on number 557. What is the expected value of his bet?

17–9. *Payoff Table; Perfect Information.* About three years out of every ten, State University has a really good basketball team and draws large crowds. The problem is that State University's fieldhouse is too small to hold the crowds that come out in the years the team is good. For this reason, the university is thinking about renting a huge domed arena owned by a professional basketball team and playing its games there in good years. Unfortunately, it is not possible to tell whether the team is going to be good or bad until the year is already under way.

If the university rents the domed arena, and the basketball team turns out to be a good team, then profits for the season from attendance will be $620,000. If the university rents the domed arena, and the team proves to be a poor one, then the university will lose $180,000 because of poor attendance and inability to cover the rent out of gate receipts.

If the university does not rent the domed arena, and the team turns out to be a good team, then profits for the season will be only $190,000 (because of not being able to get many spectators into the university's small fieldhouse). If the university does not rent the arena, and has a poor team, then profits will be $30,000 for the season.

Required:

1. Prepare a payoff table, and determine whether as a long-run policy the university should rent or not rent the domed arena.
2. A local sports commentator hasn't missed in over 30 years in predicting whether State University is going to have a good team or a bad team. He demands $25,000 for telling State University in advance whether the coming year's team is going to be good or bad. Should the university be willing to pay the $25,000 for the "perfect" information each year? Show computations.

17–10. *Payoff Table; the Value of Perfect Information.* Mr. A. Precott owns and operates the Happy Valley Fruit Farm. Mr. Precott's largest crop consists of his sweet cherries. He can market his sweet cherries in one of two ways:

1. A local cannery will purchase the cherries six weeks in advance of harvest at a profit to Mr. Precott of $60,000. If frost ruins the cherries during this six-week period, then the contract price is automatically adjusted so that Mr. Precott's profit is only $10,000.
2. Mr. Precott can wait until after harvest and sell the cherries to the highest bidder. This alternative will yield him a profit of $100,000 each year unless the cherries are ruined by a frost prior to harvest. In the event of frost, he will suffer a loss of $25,000. Mr. Precott notes from the Farmer's Almanac that a

killing frost occurs in his area during the critical six-week period prior to harvest about 40 percent of the time.

Required:

1. Prepare a payoff table, and determine whether Mr. Precott should establish a long-run policy of selling to the cannery.
2. A local weather forecaster has spent his life studying weather patterns of the area, and claims that he can predict without fail years in which frost will occur. How much should Mr. Precott be willing to pay each year for such "perfect" information concerning frost? Show computations.

17–11. *Payoff Table.* Adonis, Inc., operates a number of men's hair-styling shops. The company is contemplating a shop in a new location, and is trying to determine how many hair stylists to hire to staff the shop. Each stylist can style 20 heads a day. The price is $3 per styling. The shop can hold up to five stylists. The company estimates the following volume of business in a normal 20-day month:

Volume	Number of Days	Number of Customers
Heavy.	4	100
Medium	10	60
Light	6	40

Each stylist employed in the shop is paid $40 per day. Stylists can only be hired on a permanent basis, i.e, no part-time work. The company wants to maximize daily profits from the shop.

Required:

Prepare a payoff table to determine how many stylists should be employed in the shop, and determine the daily profits.

chapter 18

"How Well Am I Doing?" –Financial Statement Analysis

No MATTER how carefully prepared, all financial statements are essentially historical documents. They tell what *has happened* during a particular year or series of years. The most valuable information to most users of financial statements, however, concerns what probably *will happen* in the future. The purpose of financial statement analysis is to assist statement users in *predicting the future* by means of comparison, evaluation, and trend analysis.

THE IMPORTANCE OF STATEMENT ANALYSIS

Virtually all users of financial data have concerns that can be resolved to some degree by the predictive ability of statement analysis. The stockholder is concerned, for example, about matters such as whether he should hold or sell his stock, about whether the present management group should remain or be replaced, and about whether the company should have his approval to sell a new offering of senior debt. The creditor is concerned about matters such as whether income will be sufficient to cover the interest due on his bond or note, and about whether prospects are good for his obligation to be paid at maturity. The manager is concerned about matters such as dividend policy, availability of funds to finance future expansion, and the probable future success of operations under his leadership.

The thing about the future that statement users are most interested in predicting is profits. It is profits, of course, that provide the basis for an increase in the value of the stockholder's stock, and that encourage the creditor to risk his money in an organization. And it is largely profits that make future expansion possible. The dilemma is that profits are uncertain. For this reason, one must have certain analytical tools to assist in interpreting the key relationships and trends that serve as a basis for judgments of potential future success. Without financial statement analysis, the story that key relationships and trends have to tell may remain buried in a sea of statement detail.

In this chapter we consider some of the more important ratios and other analytical tools used by analysts in attempting to predict the future course of events in business organizations.

Importance of Comparisons

Not only are financial statements historical documents, but they also are essentially static documents. They speak only of the events of a single period of time. However, statement users are concerned not just with the present, but with what the *trend of events* has been (and will be) over time. For this reason, financial statement analysis directed toward a single period is of limited usefulness. The results of financial statement analysis are of value only when viewed in *comparison* with the results of other periods, and in some cases, with the results of other firms. It is only through comparison that one can gain insight into trends, and make intelligent judgments as to their significance.

Unfortunately, comparisons between firms within an industry are often made difficult by differences in accounting methods in use. If one firm, for example, values its inventories by Lifo and another firm values its inventories by average cost, comparisons between the two firms will be of limited usefulness, and can be downright misleading. One must be on constant guard, therefore, to be sure that a proper basis exists for any comparisons that are made.

The Need to Look beyond Ratios

There is a tendency for the inexperienced analyst to assume that ratios are sufficient in themselves as a basis for judgments about the future. Nothing could be further from the truth. The experienced analyst realizes that the best-prepared ratio analysis must be considered tentative in nature, and never conclusive in itself. Rather than an end, ratios should be viewed as a *starting point,* as indicators of what to pursue in greater depth. They raise many questions, but rarely answer any by themselves.

To solidify his judgments, the analyst must take a careful look at industry trends, technological changes in process or anticipated, changes in consumer tastes, changes in economic factors both regionally and nationally, and at changes taking place within the firm itself. A recent change in a key management position, for example, might rightly serve as a basis for much optimism about the future, even though the past performance of the firm may have been very mediocre.

STATEMENTS IN COMPARATIVE AND COMMON-SIZE FORM

As stated above, few figures appearing on financial statements have much significance standing by themselves. It is the relationship of one figure to another, and the amount and direction of change from one point in time to another, that is important in financial statement analysis. How does the analyst key in on significant relationships? How does he dig out the important trends and changes in a company? Three analytical techniques are in widespread use:

1. Dollar and percentage changes on statements.
2. Common-size statements.
3. Ratios.

All three techniques are discussed in following sections.

Dollar and Percentage Changes on Statements

A good beginning place in financial statement analysis is to put statements in comparative form. This consists of little more than putting two or more years' data side by side. Statements cast in comparative form will underscore movements and trends, and may give the analyst many valuable clues as to what to expect in the way of financial and operating performance in the future. Comparative financial statements for Brickey Electronics Company, a hypothetical firm, are shown in Exhibits 18–1 and 18–2.

Horizontal Analysis. Comparison of two or more years' financial data is known as *horizontal analysis.* Horizontal analysis is greatly facilitated by showing changes between years in both dollar *and* percentage form, as has been done in Exhibits 18–1 and 18–2. Showing changes in dollar form helps the analyst to zero in on key factors which have affected profitability or financial position. For example, observe in Exhibit 18–2 that sales for 19X2 were up $4,000,000 over 19X1, but that this increase in sales was more than negated by a $4,500,000 increase in cost of goods sold.

Showing changes between years in percentage form helps the analyst to gain *perspective,* and to gain a feel for the *significance* of the changes

EXHIBIT 18–1

BRICKEY ELECTRONICS COMPANY
Comparative Balance Sheet
December 31, 19X1, and December 31, 19X2
(in thousands of dollars)

	19X2	19X1	Increase (Decrease) Amount	Per-cent
Assets				
Current Assets:				
Cash	$ 1,000	$ 2,570	$(1,570)	(61.1)
Accounts receivable, net	6,000	4,000	2,000	50.0
Inventory	8,000	10,000	(2,000)	(20.0)
Prepaid expenses	500	200	300	150.0
Total Current Assets	15,500	16,770	(1,270)	(7.6)
Property and Equipment:				
Land	4,000	4,000	-0-	-0-
Buildings and equipment, net	9,500	6,000	3,500	58.3
Total Property and Equipment	13,500	10,000	$ 3,500	35.0
Total Assets	$29,000	$26,770	$ 2,230	8.3
Liabilities and Equity				
Current Liabilities:				
Accounts payable	$ 6,000	$ 4,200	$ 1,800	42.9
Accrued payables	500	300	200	66.7
Current portion of bonds payable	500	500	-0-	-0-
Total Current Liabilities	7,000	5,000	2,000	40.0
Long-term Liabilities:				
Bonds payable, 5%	7,500	8,000	(500)	(6.3)
Total Liabilities	14,500	13,000	1,500	11.5
Stockholders' Equity:				
Preferred stock, $100 par, 6%, $100				
liquidation value	2,000	2,000	-0-	-0-
Common stock, $10 par	6,000	6,000	-0-	-0-
Additional paid-in capital	1,000	1,000	-0-	-0-
Total Paid-in Capital	9,000	9,000	-0-	-0-
Retained earnings	5,500	4,770	730	15.3
Total Stockholders' Equity	14,500	13,770	730	5.3
Total Liabilities and Equity	$29,000	$26,770	$ 2,230	8.3

that are taking place. One would have a different perspective of a $1,000,000 increase in sales if the prior year's sales were $2,000,000 than he would if the prior year's sales were $20,000,000. In the first situation the increase would be 50 percent—undoubtedly a significant increase for any firm. In the second situation the increase would be only 5 percent—perhaps a reflection of just normal growth.

EXHIBIT 18–2

BRICKEY ELECTRONICS COMPANY
Comparative Income Statement and Reconciliation
of Retained Earnings
For the Year Ended December 31, 19X1, and December 31, 19X2
(in thousands of dollars)

	19X2	*19X1*	*Increase (Decrease)* Amount	Percent
Sales	$52,000	$48,000	$4,000	8.3
Cost of goods sold	36,000	31,500	4,500	14.3
Gross margin	16,000	16,500	(500)	(3.0)
Operating expenses:				
Selling expenses.	7,000	6,500	500	7.7
Administrative expenses	5,000	5,200	(200)	(3.8)
Total operating expenses	12,000	11,700	300	2.6
Net operating income.	4,000	4,800	(800)	(16.7)
Interest expense	375	400	(25)	(6.3)
Net income before taxes	3,625	4,400	(775)	(17.6)
Income taxes (60%)	2,175	2,640	(465)	(17.6)
Net income	1,450	1,760	$ (310)	(17.6)
Dividends to preferred stockholders,				
$6 per share (see Exhibit 18-1)	120	120		
Net income remaining for common				
stockholders	1,330	1,640		
Dividends to common stockholders				
($1 per share)	600	600		
Net income added to retained				
earnings	730	1,040		
Retained earnings, beginning of year	4,770	3,730		
Retained earnings, end of year	$ 5,500	$ 4,770		

Trend Percentages. Horizontal analysis of financial statements can also be carried out by computing trend percentages. Trend percentages state several years' financial data in terms of a base year. The base year equals 100 percent with all other years stated as some percentage of this base. To illustrate, assume that Glacor Company has reported the following sales and income data for the past five years:

	19X5	*19X4*	*19X3*	*19X2*	*19X1*
Sales	$725,000	$700,000	$650,000	$575,000	$500,000
Net income	$ 99,000	$ 97,500	$ 93,750	$ 86,250	$ 75,000

By simply looking at these data one can see that both sales and net income have increased over the five-year period reported. But how rapidly have sales been increasing, and have the increases in net income kept pace with the increases in sales? By looking at the raw data alone it is difficult to answer these questions. The increases in sales and the increases in net income can be put into proper perspective by stating them in terms of trend percentages, with 19X1 as the base year. These percentages are given below:

	19X5	19X4	19X3	19X2	19X1
Sales	145%	140%	130%	115%*	100%
Net income	132%	130%	125%	115%	100%

    * $575,000 ÷ $500,000 = 115%

Notice that the growth in sales dropped off somewhat between 19X3 and 19X4, and dropped off even more between 19X4 and 19X5. Also notice that the growth in net income has not kept pace with the growth in sales. In 19X5 sales are 1.45 times greater than in 19X1, the base year; however, in 19X5 net income is only 1.32 times greater than in 19X1.

Common-Size Statements

Key changes and trends can also be highlighted by the use of common-size statements. A common-size statement is one that shows the separate items appearing on it in percentage form, rather than in dollar form. Each item is stated as a percentage of some total of which that item is a part. Preparation of common-size statements is known as *vertical analysis.*

The Balance Sheet.   One application of the vertical analysis idea is to state the separate assets of a company as percentages of total assets. A common-size statement of this type is shown in Exhibit 18–3 for Brickey Electronics Company.

Notice from Exhibit 18–3 that placing all assets in common-size form clearly shows the relative importance of the current assets as compared to the noncurrent assets. It also shows that significant changes have taken place in the *composition* of the current assets over the last year. Notice, for example, that the receivables have increased in relative importance, and that both cash and inventory have declined in relative importance. Judging from the sharp increase in receivables, the deterioration in the cash position may be a result of inability to collect from customers.

The Income Statement.   Another application of the vertical analysis idea is to place all items on the income statement in percentage form in terms of total sales. A common-size statement of this type is shown in Exhibit 18–4.

By placing all items on the income statement in common size in terms of sales, it is possible to see at a glance how each dollar of sales is

EXHIBIT 18–3

BRICK
Commoi
December

			Size es
			Χ1
Current Assets:			
Cash			
Accounts receivable, net			14.9
Inventory		21.6	37.4
Prepaid expenses	∠∪∪	1.7	.7
Total Current Assets.	1.,.∪∪	16,770	53.4	62.6
Property and Equipment:			
Land	4,000	4,000	13.8	14.9
Buildings and equipment, net	9,500	6,000	32.8	22.5
Total Property and Equipment	13,500	10,000	46.6	37.4
Total Assets	$29,000	$26,770	100.0	100.0

Liabilities and Equity

Current Liabilities:				
Accounts payable.	$ 6,000	$ 4,200	20.7	15.7
Accrued payables	500	300	1.7	1.1
Current portion of bonds payable	500	500	1.7	1.9
Total Current Liabilities	7,000	5,000	24.1	18.7
Long-term Liabilities:				
Bonds payable, 5%	7,500	8,000	25.9	29.9
Total Liabilities	14,500	13,000	50.0	48.6
Stockholders' Equity:				
Preferred stock, $100 par, 6%, $100 liquidation value	2,000	2,000	6.9	7.5
Common stock, $10 par	6,000	6,000	20.7	22.4
Additional paid-in capital	1,000	1,000	3.4	3.7
Total Paid-in Capital	9,000	9,000	31.0	33.6
Retained earnings.	5,500	4,770	19.0	17.8
Total Stockholders' Equity	14,500	13,770	50.0	51.4
Total Liabilities and Equity	$29,000	$26,770	100.0	100.0

distributed between the various costs, expenses, and profits. For example, notice from Exhibit 18–4 that in 19X2, 69.2¢ out of every dollar of sales went for cost of goods sold, and that only 2.8¢ out of every dollar of sales went for profits.

Common-size statements are also very helpful in pointing out efficiencies and inefficiencies that otherwise might go unnoticed. To illustrate, in 19X2 Brickey Electronics Company's selling expenses increased by

EXHIBIT 18-4

BRICKEY ELECTRONICS COMPANY
Common-Size Comparative Income Statement
For the Year Ended December 31, 19X1, and December 31, 19X2
(in thousands of dollars)

	19X2	19X1	Common-Size Percentages 19X2	19X1
Sales	$52,000	$48,000	100.0	100.0
Cost of goods sold	36,000	31,500	69.2	65.7
Gross margin	16,000	16,500	30.8	34.3
Operating expenses:				
Selling expenses	7,000	6,500	13.5	13.5
Administrative expenses	5,000	5,200	9.6	10.8
Total operating expenses	12,000	11,700	23.1	24.3
Net operating income	4,000	4,800	7.7	10.0
Interest expense	375	400	.7	.8
Net income before taxes	3,625	4,400	7.0	9.2
Income taxes (60%)	2,175	2,640	4.2	5.5
Net income	$ 1,450	$ 1,760	2.8	3.7

$500 over 19X1. A glance at the common-size income statement shows, however, that on a relative basis selling expenses were no higher in 19X2 than in 19X1. In each year they represented 13.5 percent of sales.

RATIO ANALYSIS—THE COMMON STOCKHOLDER

The common stockholder has only a residual claim on profits and assets of a corporation. It is only after all creditor and preferred stockholder claims have been satisfied that the common stockholder can step forward and receive a distribution of profits, or assets in liquidation. A measure of his well-being, therefore, provides some perspective of the depth of protection available to others associated with a firm.

Earnings per Share

An investor buys and retains a share of stock with the thought in mind of a return coming in the future either in the form of dividends or in the form of capital gains. Since earnings form the basis for dividend payments, as well as the basis for any future increases in the value of shares, investors are always extremely interested in a company's reported earnings per share. Probably no single statistic is more widely quoted or relied upon in investor actions than earnings per share, although it has some inherent dangers, as discussed below.

The computation of earnings per share is made by dividing net income remaining for common shareholders by the number of common shares outstanding. "Net income remaining for common shareholders" is equal to the net income of a company, reduced by the dividends due to the preferred shareholders.

$$\frac{\text{Net Income} - \text{Preferred Dividends}}{\text{Common Shares Outstanding}} = \text{Earnings per Share}$$

Using the data in Exhibits 18–1 and 18–2, the earnings per share for Brickey Electronics Company for 19X2 would be:

$$\frac{\$1,330,000}{600,000 \text{ shares}} = \$2.22 \tag{1}$$

Two problems can arise in connection with the computation of earnings per share. The first arises whenever an extraordinary gain or loss appears as part of net income. The second arises whenever a company has convertible securities on its balance sheet. These problems are discussed in the following two sections.

Extraordinary Items and Earnings per Share

If a company has extraordinary gains or losses appearing as part of net income, *two* earnings-per-share figures must be computed—one showing the earnings per share resulting from *normal* operations, and one showing the earnings-per-share impact of the *extraordinary* items. This approach to computing earnings per share accomplishes three things. First, it helps statement users to recognize extraordinary items for what they are—unusual events that probably will not recur. Second, it eliminates the distorting influence of the extraordinary items from the basic earnings-per-share figure. And third, it helps statement users to properly assess the *trend* of *normal* earnings per share over time. Since one would not expect the extraordinary or unusual items to repeat year after year, they should be given less weight in judging earnings performance than profits resulting from normal operations.

In addition to reporting extraordinary items separately, the accountant also reports them *net of their tax effect*. By "net of their tax effect" we mean that whatever impact the unusual item has on income taxes is *deducted from* the unusual item on the income statement. Only the net, after-tax, gain or loss is used in earnings-per-share computations.

To illustrate these concepts, let us assume a fire loss of $3,000, and the following additional items of revenue and expense:

Incorrect Approach

Sales	$50,000	
Cost of goods sold	30,000	
Gross margin.	20,000	Extraordinary gains and losses should not be included with normal items of revenue and expense. This distorts a firm's normal income producing ability.
Operating expenses:		
Selling expenses. $5,000		
Administrative expenses 8,000		
Fire loss 3,000	16,000	
Net income before taxes	4,000	
Income taxes (60%).	2,400	
Net income	$ 1,600	

Correct Approach

Sales	$50,000	
Cost of goods sold	30,000	
Gross margin.	20,000	Reporting the extraordinary item separately and net of its tax effect leaves the normal items of revenue and expense unaffected.
Operating expenses:		
Selling expenses. $5,000		
Administrative expenses 8,000	13,000	
Net operating income.	7,000	
Income taxes (60%).	4,200	
Net income before extra-		
ordinary item	2,800	Original loss $3,000
Extraordinary item:		Less reduction in taxes
Fire loss, net of tax.	(1,200)	at a 60% rate 1,800
Net income	$ 1,600	Loss, net of tax $1,200

The fire loss is fully deductible for tax purposes. Therefore, this deduction will reduce the firm's taxable income by $3,000. If taxable income is $3,000 lower, then income taxes will be $1,800 *less* (60% × $3,000) than they *otherwise* would have been. In other words, the fire loss of $3,000 *saves* the company $1,800 in taxes that otherwise would have been paid. The $1,800 savings in taxes is deducted from the loss that caused it, leaving a net loss of only $1,200.

Extraordinary *gains* will *increase* taxes. The increased taxes are deducted from the extraordinary item, leaving only the net gain that will remain after the added taxes are paid.

To continue our illustration, assume that the company above has 2,000 shares of common stock outstanding. Earnings per share would be reported as follows:

Earnings per share on common stock:
  On net income before extraordinary item ($2,800 ÷ 2,000 shares)* $1.40
  On extraordinary item, net of tax ($1,200 ÷ 2,000 shares) . . . . (.60)

Net earnings per share . . . . $ .80
    * Sometimes called the *primary* earnings per share.

In sum, computation of earnings per share as we have done above is necessary to avoid misinterpretation and misunderstanding of a company's normal income producing ability. Reporting *only* the flat $.80 per share figure would be misleading and perhaps would cause investors to regard the company less favorably than they should.

Fully Diluted Earnings per Share

A problem sometimes arises in trying to determine the number of common shares to use in computing earnings per share. Until recent years, the distinction between common stock, preferred stock, and debt was quite clear. The distinction between these securities has now become somewhat diffused, however, due to a growing tendency to issue convertible securities of various types. Rather than simply issuing common stock, firms today often issue preferred stock or bonds that carry a *conversion feature* allowing the purchaser to convert his holdings into common stock at some future time.

When convertible securities are present in the financial structure of a firm, the question arises as to whether they should be retained in their unconverted form, or whether they should be treated as common stock, in computing earnings per share. The American Institute of Certified Public Accountants has taken the position that convertible securities should be treated *both* in their present and prospective forms. This requires the presentation of *two* earnings-per-share figures for firms that have convertible securities outstanding, one showing earnings per share assuming no conversion into common stock, and the other showing full conversion into common stock. The latter earnings-per-share figure is said to show earnings on a *fully diluted* basis.

To illustrate, let us assume that the preferred stock of Brickey Electronics Company in Exhibit 18–1 is convertible into common on a basis of five shares of common for each share of preferred. Since 20,000 shares of preferred are outstanding, conversion would require issuing an additional 100,000 shares of common stock. Earnings per share on a fully diluted basis would be:

$$\frac{\text{Net Income before Preferred Dividends}}{(600,000 \text{ Original Shares} + 100,000 \text{ Converted Shares})}$$

$$= \frac{\$1,450,000}{700,000 \text{ Shares}} = \$2.07 \quad (2)$$

In comparing equation (2) with equation (1), we can note that the earnings-per-share figure has dropped by $.15. Although the impact of full dilution is relatively small in this case, it can be very significant in situations where large amounts of conve ;ble securities are present.

Price/Earnings Ratio

The relationship between the market price of a share of stock and the stock's current earnings per share is often quoted in terms of a *price/earnings* ratio. If we assume that the market price of Brickey Electronics Company's stock is $45 per share, the company's price/earnings ratio would be computed as follows:

$$\frac{\text{Market Price}}{\text{Earnings per Share}} = \text{Price/Earnings Ratio}$$

$$\frac{\$45.00}{\$2.22 \text{ See Equation (1)}} = 20.3 \tag{3}$$

The price/earnings ratio is 20.3; that is, the stock is selling for about 20.3 times its current earnings per share.

The price/earnings ratio is widely used by investors as a general guideline in gauging stock values. Investors increase or decrease the price/earnings ratio that they are willing to accept for a share of stock according to how they view its *future prospects*. Companies with ample opportunities for growth generally have high price/earnings ratios, with the opposite being true for companies with limited growth opportunities. If investors decided that Brickey Electronics Company had greater than average growth prospects, they might be willing to let the price/earnings ratio for the company rise to 25. In that case we would expect the company's stock to begin selling for about $55 per share ($2.22 EPS × 25.0 P/E ratio).

Dividend Payout and Yield Ratios

An investor holds shares of one stock in preference to shares of another stock because he anticipates that the first stock will provide him with a more attractive return. The return sought after isn't always dividends. Many investors prefer not to receive dividends. Instead, they prefer to have the company retain all earnings and reinvest them internally in order to support growth. Such stocks, loosely termed "growth stocks," often enjoy rapid upward movement in market price. On sale of the stock, investors can then reap their return in the form of capital gains, which receive very favorable treatment from an income tax point of view. Other investors prefer to have a dependable, current source of income through regular dividend payments, and prefer not to gamble on the fortunes of stock prices to provide a return on their investment. Such investors seek out stocks with consistent dividend records and payout ratios.

The Dividend Payout Ratio. The dividend payout ratio gauges the portion of current earnings being paid out in dividends. Investors seeking capital gains would like this ratio to be small, whereas investors who seek dividends prefer it to be large. The ratio is computed by relating dividends per share to earnings per share for common stock:

$$\frac{\text{Dividends per Share}}{\text{Earnings per Share}} = \text{Dividend Payout Ratio}$$

For Brickey Electronics Company, the dividend payout ratio for 19X2 was:

$$\frac{\$1.00 \text{ (see Exhibit 18–2)}}{\$2.22 \text{ [see Equation (1)]}} = 45\% \tag{4}$$

There is no such thing as a "right" payout ratio, even though it should be noted that the ratio tends to be somewhat the same for the bulk of firms within a particular industry. Industries with ample opportunities for growth at high rates of return on assets tend to have low payout ratios, and the reverse tends to be true for industries with limited reinvestment opportunities.

The Dividend Yield Ratio. The dividend yield ratio is obtained by dividing the current dividends per share by the current market price per share:

$$\frac{\text{Dividends per Share}}{\text{Market Price per Share}} = \text{Dividend Yield Ratio}$$

If we continue the assumption of a market price of $45 per share for Brickey Electronics Company stock, the dividend yield is:

$$\frac{\$1.00}{\$45.00} = 2.2\% \tag{5}$$

In making this computation, note that we used the current market price of the stock, rather than the price the investor paid for the stock initially (which might be above or below the current market). By using current market price, we recognize the opportunity cost of the investment in terms of its yield. That is, the investor can sell the stock now for $45 or he can retain it. By choosing to retain the stock he is foregoing the opportunity to acquire some other investment (and the return it would yield) for $45 in its place.

Return on Total Assets

Managers have two basic responsibilities in managing a firm—*financing* responsibilities and *operating* responsibilities. Financing responsibilities relate to how one *obtains* the funds needed to provide for assets in an organization. Operating responsibilities relate to how one *uses* the assets once they have been obtained. Proper discharge of both re-sponsibilities is vital to a well-managed firm. However, care must be taken not to confuse or mix the two in assessing the performance of a manager. That is, whether funds have been obtained partly from credi-tors and partly from stockholders or entirely from stockholders should not be allowed to influence one's assessment of *how well* the assets have been employed since being received by the firm.

The return on total assets ratio is a measure of how well assets have been employed; that is, it is a measure of operating performance. The formula is:

$$\frac{\text{Net Income} + \text{Interest Expense}}{\text{Average Total Assets}} = \text{Return on Total Assets}$$

By adding interest expense back to net income we derive a figure that shows earnings before any distributions have been made to either creditors or stockholders. Thus we eliminate the matter of how the assets were financed from influencing the measurement of how well the assets have been employed.

The return on total assets for Brickey Electronics Company for 19X2 would be (from Exhibits 18–1 and 18–2):

Net income.	$ 1,450,000	
Add back interest expense	375,000	
Total	$ 1,825,000	(a)
Assets, beginning of year	$26,770,000	
Assets, end of year	29,000,000	
Total	$55,770,000	
Average total assets $55,770,000 ÷ 2	$27,885,000	(b)
Return on total assets (a) ÷ (b)	6.5%	(6)

Brickey Electronics Company has earned a return of 6.5 percent on average assets employed over the last year.

Return on Common Stockholders' Equity

One of the primary reasons for operating a corporation is to generate income for the benefit of the common stockholders. One measure of a company's success in this regard is the rate of return which it is able to generate on the common stockholders' equity:

$$\frac{\text{Net Income Less Preferred Dividends}}{\text{Common Stockholders' Equity (total stockholders' equity less preferred stock)}} = \text{Return on Common Stockholders' Equity}$$

For Brickey Electronics Company, the return on common stockholders' equity is 10.6 percent for 19X2, as shown below:

Net income	$ 1,450,000
Deduct preferred dividends	120,000
Net income remaining for common stockholders	$ 1,330,000 (*a*)
Total stockholders' equity	$14,500,000
Deduct preferred stock	2,000,000
Common stockholders' equity	$12,500,000 (*b*)
Return on common stockholders' equity (*a*) ÷ (*b*)	10.6% (7)

Compare the return on common stockholders' equity above (10.6 percent) to the return on total assets computed in the preceding section (6.5 percent). Why is the return on common stockholders' equity so much higher? The answer lies in the principle of *leverage* (sometimes called "trading on the equity").

The Concept of Leverage. Leverage involves the securing of funds for investment at a *fixed rate of return* to the suppliers of the funds, normally with the thought in mind of enhancing the well-being of the common stockholders. If the assets in which the funds are invested are able to earn at a rate of return *greater* than the fixed rate of return required by the suppliers of the funds, then leverage is *positive* and the common stockholders benefit.

For example, assume that a firm is able to earn a return of 8 percent on its assets. If that firm can borrow from creditors at a 5 percent interest rate in order to expand its assets, then the common stockholders can benefit from positive leverage. The borrowed funds invested in the business will earn at a rate of 8 percent, but the interest cost of the funds will be only 5 percent. The difference will go to the common stockholders.

We can see this concept in operation in the case of Brickey Electronics Company. Notice from Exhibit 18–1 that the company's Bonds Payable bear a fixed interest rate of 5 percent. The company's total assets (which would contain the proceeds from the original sale of these bonds) are generating a rate of return of 6.5 percent, as we computed earlier. Since the return on total assets (6.5 percent) is greater than the fixed interest cost of the bonds (5 percent), leverage is positive, and the difference accrues to the benefit of the common stockholders. This explains in part why the return on common stockholders' equity (10.6 percent) is greater than the return on total assets (6.5 percent).

Sources of Leverage. Leverage can be obtained from several sources. One source is long-term debt, such as bonds payable or notes payable. Two additional sources are current liabilities and preferred stock. Current liabilities are always a source of positive leverage in that funds are provided for use in a company with no interest return required by the short-term creditors involved. For example, when a company acquires inventory from a supplier on account, the inventory is available for use in the business, yet the supplier requires no interest return on the amount owed to him.

Preferred stock can also be a source of positive leverage so long as the preferred dividend payable to the preferred shareholders is less than the rate of return being earned on total assets employed. In the case of Brickey Electronics Company, positive leverage is being realized on the preferred stock. Notice from Exhibit 18–1 that the preferred dividend rate is only 6 percent, whereas the assets in the company are earning at a rate of 6.5 percent, as computed earlier. Again, the difference goes to the common stockholders, thereby helping to bolster their return to the 10.6 percent computed above.

Unfortunately, leverage is a two-edged sword. If assets are unable to earn at a high enough rate to cover the interest costs of debt, or to cover the preferred dividend due to the preferred stockholders, *then the common stockholder suffers.* The reason is that part of the earnings from the assets which he has provided to the company will have to go to make up the deficiency to the long-term creditors or to the preferred stockholders, and he will be left with a smaller return than he otherwise would have had. Under these circumstances, leverage is said to be *negative.*

The Impact of Income Taxes. Long-term debt and preferred stock are not equally efficient in generating positive leverage. The reason is that interest on long-term debt is tax-deductible, whereas preferred dividends are not. This makes long-term debt a much more effective source of positive leverage than preferred stock.

To illustrate this point, assume that a company is considering two ways of financing a $100,000 expansion of its assets:

1. $50,000 from an issue of common stock, and $50,000 from an issue of preferred stock bearing a dividend rate of 8 percent.
2. $50,000 from an issue of common stock, and $50,000 from an issue of bonds bearing an interest rate of 8 percent.

Assuming that the company can earn an additional $15,000 each year before interest and taxes as a result of the expansion, the operating results under each of the two alternatives would be:

	#1	#2
Earnings before interest and taxes	$15,000	$15,000
Deduct interest expense (8% × $50,000)		4,000
Net income before taxes	15,000	11,000
Deduct income taxes (60%)	9,000	6,600
Net income	6,000	4,400
Deduct preferred dividends (8% × $50,000)	4,000	
Net income remaining for common.	$ 2,000	$ 4,400 (a)
Common stockholders' equity	$50,000	$50,000 (b)
Return on common stockholders' equity (a) ÷ (b)	4%	8.8%

Notice that the return to the common stockholders under alternative #2 (where bonds are issued) is much higher than it is under alternative #1 (where preferred stock is issued). The reason is that the interest expense on the bonds is tax-deductible, whereas the dividends on the preferred stock are not.

If the company in our hypothetical example above was earning a return on total assets of 6 percent, would leverage be positive or negative? Leverage would be negative in the case of alternative #1, since the return on common stockholders' equity would be less than the return on total assets. Leverage would be positive in the case of alternative #2, since the return on common stockholders' equity would be greater than the return on total assets.

The Desirability of Leverage. The leverage principle amply illustrates that prudent use of debt in the capital structure can substantially benefit the common shareholder. For this reason, most companies today try to keep a certain level of debt within the organization—at least a level equal to that which is considered to be "normal" within the industry. Occasionally one comes across a company which boasts of having no debt outstanding. Although there may be good reasons for a company having no debt, in view of the benefits that can be gained from positive leverage the possibility always exists that such a company is short-changing its stockholders. As a practical matter, many companies, such as commercial banks and other financial institutions, rely heavily on leverage to provide an attractive return on their common shares.

Book Value per Share

Another statistic frequently used in attempting to assess the well-being of the common shareholder is book value per share:

$$\frac{\text{Stockholders Equity} - \text{Preferred Stock}}{\text{Number of Common Shares Outstanding}} = \text{Book Value per Share}$$

The book value of Brickey Electronics Company common stock is:

$$\frac{\$14,500,000 - \$2,000,000}{600,000 \text{ shares}} = \$20.83 \tag{8}$$

If one compares this book value with the $45 market value which we have assumed in connection with the Brickey Electronics Company stock, one might be led to believe that the stock is badly overpriced. It is not necessarily true, however, that a market value in excess of book value is an indication of overpricing. As we discussed earlier, market prices are geared toward future earnings and dividends. Book value, by contrast, purports to reflect nothing about the future earnings potential of a firm. As a practical matter, it is actually geared to the *past*, in that it reflects the balance-sheet carrying value of already completed transactions.

Of what use, then, is book value? Unfortunately, the answer must be that it is of limited use so far as being a dynamic tool of analysis is concerned. It probably finds its greatest application in situations where large amounts of liquid assets are being held in anticipation of liquidation. Occasionally, some use is also made of book value per share in attempting to set a price on the shares of closely held corporations.

RATIO ANALYSIS—THE SHORT-TERM CREDITOR

Although the short-term creditor is always well advised to keep an eye on the fortunes of the common shareholder, as expressed in the ratios of the preceding section, the focus of his attention is normally channeled in another direction. He is concerned with the near-term prospects of having his bill paid on time. As such, he is much more interested in cash flows and in working capital management than he is in how much accounting net income a company is reporting.

Net Working Capital

The excess of current assets over current liabilities is known as net working capital, or sometimes simply as working capital. "Net working capital" is preferred, since the term "working capital" occasionally is used to describe current assets alone. The net working capital for Brickey Electronics Company is given below:

	19X2	19X1
Current assets	$15,500,000	$16,770,000
Current liabilities	7,000,000	5,000,000
Net working capital	$ 8,500,000	$11,770,000

The amount of net working capital available to a firm is of considerable interest to short-term creditors, *since it represents assets financed from long-term capital sources that do not require near-term repayment.* Therefore, the greater the net working capital, the greater the cushion of protection available to short-term creditors, and the greater the assurance that short-term debts will be paid when due.

Although it is always comforting to a short-term creditor to see a large net working-capital balance, his joy becomes full only after he has satisfied himself that the net working capital is turning over at an acceptable rate of speed, and that his obligation could be paid even under stringent operating conditions. The reason is that a large net working-capital balance standing by itself is no assurance that debts will be paid when due. Rather than being a sign of strength, a large net working-capital balance may simply mean that stagnant or obsolete inventory is building up. Therefore, to put the net working-capital figure into proper perspective, it must be supplemented with other analytical work. The following four ratios (the current ratio, the acid-test ratio, the accounts receivable turnover, and the inventory turnover) should all be used in connection with an analysis of net working capital.

The Current Ratio

The elements involved in the computation of net working capital are frequently expressed in ratio form. This ratio is known as the current ratio:

$$\frac{\text{Current Assets}}{\text{Current Liabilities}} = \text{Current Ratio}$$

For Brickey Electronics Company, the current ratio for 19X1 and 19X2 would be:

19X2	19X1
$\frac{\$15,500,000}{\$\ 7,000,000} = 2.21 \text{ to } 1$	$\frac{\$16,770,000}{\$\ 5,000,000} = 3.35 \text{ to } 1$　　　　(9)

Although widely regarded as a measure of short-term debt-paying ability, the current ratio must be interpreted with a great deal of care. A *declining* ratio, as above, might be a sign of a deteriorating financial condition. On the other hand, it might be the result of a paring out of obsolete inventories or other stagnant assets. An *improving* ratio might be the result of an unwise stockpiling of inventory, or it might point up an improving financial situation. In short, the ratio is useful, but tricky to interpret. To avoid a blunder, the analyst must take a hard look at the individual items of assets and liabilities involved.

The general rule of thumb calls for a current ratio of 2 to 1. This rule, of course, is subject to many exceptions, depending on the industry and the firm involved. Some industries can operate quite successfully on a current ratio of slightly over 1 to 1. The adequacy of a current ratio depends heavily on the *composition* of the assets involved. For example, although Company X and Company Y below both have current ratios of 2 to 1, one could hardly say that they are in comparable financial condition. Company Y most certainly will have difficulty meeting its obligations as they come due.

	Company X	Company Y
Current Assets:		
Cash	$ 50,000	$ 5,000
Accounts receivable	50,000	5,000
Inventory	70,000	160,000
Prepaid expenses	5,000	5,000
Total	$175,000	$175,000
Current Liabilities	$ 87,500	$ 87,500
Current Ratio	2 to 1	2 to 1

Acid-Test Ratio

A much more rigorous test of a company's ability to meet its short-term debts can be found in the acid-test, or quick ratio. Merchandise inventory and prepaid expenses are excluded from the total of current assets, leaving only the more liquid (or "quick") assets to be divided by current liabilities:

$$\frac{\text{Cash} + \text{Marketable Securities} + \text{Accounts Receivable}}{\text{Current Liabilities}} = \text{Acid-Test Ratio}$$

The ratio is designed to measure how well a company can meet its obligations without having to liquidate or depend too heavily on its inventory. Since inventory is not an immediate source of cash, and may not even be salable in times of economic stress, it is generally felt that to be properly protected each dollar of liabilities should be backed by at least one dollar of quick assets. Thus, an acid-test ratio of 1 to 1 is broadly viewed as being adequate in many firms.

The acid-test ratios for Brickey Electronics Company for 19X1 and 19X2 are given below:

	19X2	19X1	
Cash	$1,000,000	$2,570,000	
Accounts receivable	6,000,000	4,000,000	
Total quick assets	$7,000,000	$6,570,000	
Current liabilities	$7,000,000	$5,000,000	
Acid-test ratio	1 to 1	1.3 to 1	(10)

Although Brickey Electronics Company has an acid-test ratio for 19X2 that is within the acceptable range, an analyst might be very concerned about several disquieting trends revealed in the company's balance sheet. Notice that short-term debts are rising while the cash position seems to be deteriorating. Perhaps the weakened cash position is a result of the greatly expanded volume of accounts receivable. One wonders why the accounts receivable have been allowed to increase so rapidly in so brief a time.

In short, as with the current ratio, to be used intelligently the acid-test ratio must be interpreted with one eye on its basic components.

Accounts Receivable Turnover

The accounts receivable turnover ratio is frequently used in conjunction with an analysis of net working capital, since it provides at least a rough gauge as to how well receivables are turning into cash. The accounts receivable turnover is computed by dividing sales by the average accounts receivable balance during a period. The turnover figure can then be divided into 365 to determine the average number of days being taken to collect an account.

The accounts receivable turnover for Brickey Electronics Company for 19X2 is:

Accounts receivable:	
Beginning of year	$ 4,000,000
End of year	6,000,000
	$10,000,000
Average balance for year..........	$ 5,000,000

$$\frac{\text{Sales}}{\text{Average Accounts Receivable Balance}} = \frac{\$52,000,000}{\$5,000,000} = 10.4 \text{ Times Turned Over} \quad (11)$$

The average number of days taken during 19X2 to collect an account would be:

$$\frac{365 \text{ Days}}{\text{Accounts Receivable Turnover}} = \frac{365}{10.4 \text{ Times}}$$

$$= 35 \text{ Days Average Collection Period} \quad (12)$$

Whether the average of 35 days taken to collect an account is good or bad depends on the credit terms Brickey Electronics Company is offering to its customers. If credit terms are 30 days, then a 35-day average collection period would be viewed as being very good. Most customers will tend to withhold payment for as long as credit terms will allow, and may even go over a few days. This factor, added to the ever present few slow accounts, can cause the average collection period to exceed normal credit terms by a week to ten days, and should not be a matter for too much alarm.

On the other hand, if the company's credit terms are 10 days, then a 35-day average collection period may be a cause for some concern. The long collection period may be a result of the presence of many old accounts of doubtful collectibility, or it may be a result of poor day-to-day credit management. The firm may be making sales with inadequate credit checks on the companies to whom the sales are being made, or perhaps no follow-ups are being made on slow accounts.

Inventory Turnover

The inventory turnover ratio measures how many times a company's inventory has been sold during the year. It is computed by dividing the cost of goods sold by the average level of inventory on hand:

$$\frac{\text{Cost of Goods Sold}}{\text{Average Inventory}} = \text{Inventory Turnover}$$

The average inventory figure is usually computed by taking the average of the beginning and ending inventory figures. Since Brickey Electronics Company has a beginning inventory figure of $10,000,000 and an ending inventory figure of $8,000,000, its average inventory for the year would be $9,000,000. The company's inventory turnover for 19X2 would be:

$$\frac{\text{Cost of Goods Sold}}{\text{Average Inventory}} = \frac{\$36,000,000}{\$9,000,000} = 4 \text{ Times} \qquad (13)$$

The number of days that it takes to sell the entire inventory one time can be determined by dividing 365 by the number of times the inventory turns over during the year:

$$\frac{365}{\text{Inventory Turnover}} = \frac{365 \text{ Days}}{4 \text{ Times}} = 91\tfrac{1}{4} \text{ Days} \qquad (14)$$

Grocery stores tend to turn their inventory over very quickly, perhaps as often as every 12 to 15 days. On the other hand, jewelry stores tend to turn their inventory over very slowly, perhaps only a couple of times each year.

If a firm has a turnover that is much slower than the average for its industry, then there may be obsolete goods on hand, or inventory stocks may be needlessly high. Excessive inventories simply tie up funds that could be used elsewhere in operations. Managers often argue that they must buy in very large quantities in order to take advantage of the best discounts being offered. But these discounts must be carefully weighed against the added costs of insurance, taxes, financing, and risks of obsolescence and deterioration that carrying added inventories bring.

An inventory turnover that is substantially faster than the average usually is an indication that inventory levels are inadequate.

RATIO ANALYSIS—THE LONG-TERM CREDITOR

The position of the long-term creditor differs from that of the short-term creditor is that he is concerned with both the near-term *and* the long-term ability of a firm to meet its commitments. The long-term creditor is concerned with the near term since whatever interest he may be entitled to is normally paid on a current basis. He is concerned with the long term from point of view of the eventual retirement of his holdings. Since the long-term creditor is usually faced with somewhat greater risks than the short-term creditor, firms are often required to make various restrictive covenants for his protection. Examples of such restrictive covenants would include the maintenance of minimum working capital levels, and restrictions on payment of dividends to common stockholders. Although these restrictive covenants are in widespread use, they must be viewed as being a poor second to *prospective earnings* from the point of view of assessing protection and safety. No creditor wants to go to court to collect his claim; he would much prefer staking the safety of his claim for interest and eventual repayment of principal on an orderly and consistent flow of funds from operations.

Times Interest Earned

The most common measure of the ability of a firm's operations to provide protection to the long-term creditor is the times interest earned ratio. It is computed by dividing earnings *before* interest expense and income taxes by the yearly interest charges that must be met:

$$\frac{\text{Earnings before Interest Expense and Income Taxes}}{\text{Interest Expense}}$$

$$= \text{Times Interest Earned}$$

For Brickey Electronics Company, the times interest earned ratio for 19X2 would be:

$$\frac{\$4,000,000}{\$375,000} = 10.7 \text{ times} \tag{15}$$

Earnings before income taxes must be used in the computation since interest expense deductions come *before* income taxes are computed. Income taxes are secondary to interest payments in that the latter have first claim on earnings. Only those earnings remaining after all interest charges have been provided for are subject to income taxes.

Various rules of thumb exist to gauge the adequacy of a firm's times interest earned ratio. Generally, earnings are viewed as adequate to protect long-term creditors if the times interest earned ratio is 2 or more. Before making a final judgment, however, it would be necessary to look at a firm's long-run *trend* of earnings, and to decide how vulnerable the firm is to cyclical changes in the economy.

The Debt/Equity Ratio

Although the long-term creditor looks primarily to prospective earnings and budgeted cash flows in attempting to gauge the risk of his position, he cannot ignore the importance of keeping a reasonable balance between the portion of assets being provided by creditors and the portion of assets being provided by the stockholders of a firm. This balance is measured by the debt/equity ratio:

$$\frac{\text{Total Liabilities}}{\text{Stockholders Equity}} = \text{Debt/Equity Ratio}$$

	19X2	*19X1*	
Total liabilities	$14,500,000	$13,000,000	(*a*)
Stockholders equity	$14,500,000	$13,770,000	(*b*)
Debt/Equity Ratio (*a*) ÷ (*b*)	1 to 1	.94 to 1	(16)

The debt/equity ratio indicates the amount of assets being provided by creditors for each dollar of assets being provided by the owners of a company. In 19X1, creditors of Brickey Electronics Company were providing $.94 of assets for each $1.00 of assets being provided by stockholders. By 19X2, however, creditors were providing just as much in assets to the company as were its owners.

It should come as no surprise that creditors would like the debt/equity ratio to be relatively low. The lower the ratio, the larger the amount of assets being provided by the owners of a company, and the greater the buffer of protection to creditors. By contrast, common stockholders would like the ratio to be relatively high, since through leverage common stockholders can benefit from the assets being provided by creditors.

In most industries norms have developed over the years that serve as guides to firms in their decisions as to the "right" amount of debt to include in the capital structure. Different industries face different risks. For this reason, the appropriate level of debt for firms in one industry is no necessary guide to the appropriate level of debt for those in a different industry.

SUMMARY

The data contained in financial statements represent a quantitative summary of a firm's operations and activities. If a manager is skillful at taking these statements apart, he can learn much about a company's strengths, its weaknesses, its developing problems, its operating efficiency, its profitability, etc.

Many analytical techniques are available to assist the manager in taking financial statements apart, and to assist him in assessing the direction and importance of trends and changes. In this chapter we have discussed three such analytical techniques—dollar and percentage changes in statements, common-size statements, and ratio analysis. In the following chapter we continue our discussion of statement analysis by focusing on two new topics, funds flow and cash flow, and on their usefulness to the manager in his attempts to assess how well his firm is doing.

QUESTIONS

18–1. What is the basic objective in looking at trends in financial ratios and other data? Rather than looking at trends, to what other standard of comparison might a statement user turn?

18–2. What is meant by the term "leverage"?

18–3. The president of a medium-sized plastics company was recently quoted in a business journal as stating, "We haven't had a dollar of interest-paying debt in over ten years. Not many companies can say that." As a stockholder in this firm, how would you feel about its policy of not taking on interest-paying debt?

18–4. "Preferred stock always results in negative leverage." Do you agree? Explain.

18–5. Distinguish between horizontal and vertical analysis of financial statement data.

18–6. If you were a long-term creditor of a firm, would you be more interested in the firm's long-term or short-term debt paying ability? Why?

18–7. A young college student once complained to the author, "The reason that corporations are such big spenders is that Uncle Sam always picks up part of the tab." What did he mean by this statement?

18–8. What is meant by the yield on a common stock investment? In computing yield why do you use current market value rather than original purchase price?

18–9. What pitfalls are involved in computing earnings per share? How can these pitfalls be avoided?

18–10. A company seeking a line of credit at a bank was turned down. Among other things, the bank stated that the company's 2 to 1 current ratio was not adequate. Give reasons why a 2 to 1 current ratio might not be adequate.

18–11. What is meant by reporting an extraordinary item on the income statement net of its tax effect? Give an example of an extraordinary gain net of its tax effect, and an extraordinary loss net of its tax effect. Assume a tax rate of 60 percent.

18–12. In financial analysis, rather than computing ratios, why not simply study the underlying financial data? What dangers are there in using ratios?

18–13. Assume that two companies in the same industry have equal earnings. Why might these companies have different price/earnings ratios? If a company has a price/earnings ratio of 20 and reports earnings per share for the current year of $4, at what price would you expect to find the stock selling on the market?

18–14. Weaver Company experiences a great deal of seasonal variation in its business activities. The company's high point in business activity is in June; its low point is in January. During which month would you expect the current ratio to be highest? At what point would you advise the company to end its fiscal year? Why?

18–15. Distinguish between a manager's *financing* and *operating* responsibilities. Which of these responsibilities is the return on total assets ratio designed to measure?

EXERCISES

18–1. Consider the following income statement data for the Green Company:

	This Year	Last Year
Sales	$700,000	$620,000
Cost of goods sold	455,000	372,000
Gross margin	245,000	248,000
Selling expenses	70,000	62,000
Administrative expenses	126,000	124,000
Total expenses	196,000	186,000
Net operating income.	$ 49,000	$ 62,000

Required:

1. Express each year's income statement in common-size percentages.
2. Comment briefly on the changes between the two years.

18–2. The Halver Company has reported the following asset, liability, and sales data for the past five years:

	19X5	19X4	19X3	19X2	19X1
Cash	$ 40,000	$ 45,000	$ 55,000	$ 60,000	$ 50,000
Accounts receivable	380,000	340,000	270,000	230,000	200,000
Inventory	625,000	600,000	575,000	550,000	500,000
Total.	$1,045,000	$ 985,000	$ 900,000	$ 840,000	$ 750,000
Current liabilities.	$ 400,000	$ 362,000	$ 325,000	$ 275,000	$ 250,000
Sales	$1,875,000	$1,800,000	$1,725,000	$1,650,000	$1,500,000

Required:

1. Express the asset, liability, and sales data in trend percentages. Use 19X1 as the base year.
2. Comment on the results of your analysis.

18-3. The financial statements of Arby Sales, Inc., are given below:

ARBY SALES, INC.
Balance Sheet
June 30, 19X5

Assets

Cash	$ 8,000
Accounts receivable, net	32,000
Merchandise inventory	45,000
Prepaid expenses	2,000
Plant and equipment, net	100,000
Total Assets	$187,000

Equities

Current liabilities	$ 36,000
Long-term liabilities	50,000
Common stock, $10 par	40,000
Retained earnings	61,000
Total Equities	$187,000

ARBY SALES, INC.
Income Statement
For the Year Ended June 30, 19X5

Sales	$224,000
Cost of goods sold	180,000
Gross margin	44,000
Operating expenses	24,000
Net operating income	20,000
Interest expense	4,000
Net income before taxes	16,000
Income taxes	8,000
Net income	$ 8,000

Accounts receivable and inventory remained relatively constant during the year.

Compute the following:
a. Current ratio.
b. Acid-test ratio.
c. Debt/equity ratio.
d. Accounts receivable turnover in days.
e. Inventory turnover.
f. Times interest earned.
g. Book value per share.

18-4. Refer to the financial statements for Arby Sales, Inc., in Exercise 18-3. In addition to these statements, assume that Arby Sales, Inc., paid dividends of $1.50 per share during the year ended June 30, 19X5. Also assume that the company's stock had a market price of $32 on June 30. Compute the following:
a. Earnings per share.
b. Dividend payout ratio.
c. Dividend yield ratio.
d. Price/earnings ratio.

18–5. The Hilty Company's condensed income statement is given below:

HILTY COMPANY
Income Statement
For the Year Ended September 30, 19X6

Sales	$400,000
Cost of goods sold	300,000
Gross margin	100,000
Operating expenses	60,000
Net income before taxes	40,000
Income taxes (60%)	24,000
Net income	$ 16,000

Included in the operating expenses above is a $5,000 loss resulting from flood-damaged merchandise.

Required:

1. Redo the company's income statement, showing the loss net of tax.
2. Assume that the company has 5,000 shares of common stock outstanding. Compute the earnings per share.

18–6. Selected financial data for Pead Company are given below:

Interest paid on long-term debt	$ 8,000
Net income after interest and taxes	75,000
Total assets	800,000
Long-term debt (8% interest rate)	100,000
Preferred stock, $100 par, 8%	150,000
Total stockholders' equity	650,000

Answer the following:
a. What is the return on total assets?
b. What is the return on common stockholders' equity?
c. Is leverage positive or negative? Explain.

PROBLEMS

18–1. *Extraordinary Gains and Losses, and Earnings per Share.* Merrick, Inc. has 10,000 shares of no par common stock outstanding. The company's income statement for 19X7 as prepared by the company's accountant is given below:

Sales		$200,000
Cost of goods sold		120,000
Gross margin		80,000
Less operating expenses:		
Selling expenses	$15,000	
Administrative expenses	25,000	
Loss from obsolete inventory	20,000	60,000
Income before taxes		20,000
Income taxes (60 percent)		12,000
Net income		$ 8,000

The earnings per share for Merrick, Inc., common stock over the past three years is given below:

	19X6	19X5	19X4
Earnings per share—common . . .	$1.40	$1.20	$1.00

Required:

1. Consider the income statement as prepared by the company's accountant. Why might an investor have difficulty interpreting this statement so far as determining Merrick, Inc.'s ability to generate normal after-tax earnings?
2. Recast Merrick, Inc.'s income statement in better form, showing the inventory loss net of tax.
3. Assume that rather than having a $20,000 loss from obsolete inventory the company has a $20,000 gain from sale of unused plant. Redo the income statement, showing the gain net of tax.
4. Using the income statements which you prepared in parts 2 and 3 above, compute the earnings per share of common stock.
5. Explain how your computation of earnings per share would be helpful to an investor trying to evaluate the trend of Merrick, Inc.'s earnings over the past few years.

18–2. *Effect of Various Transactions on Working Capital, Current Ratio, and Acid-Test Ratio.* Placer Company's working capital accounts at December 31, 19X6, are given below:

Cash	$ 50,000
Marketable securities	30,000
Accounts receivable (net)	200,000
Inventory	210,000
Prepaid expenses	10,000
Accounts payable	150,000
Notes due within one year	30,000
Accrued liabilities.	20,000

During 19X7, Placer Company completed the following transactions:
x. Paid a cash dividend previously declared, $12,000.
a. Issued additional shares of capital stock for cash, $100,000.
b. Sold inventory costing $50,000 for $80,000, on account.
c. Wrote off uncollectible accounts in the amount of $10,000.
d. Declared a cash dividend, $15,000.
e. Paid accounts payable, $50,000.
f. Borrowed cash on a short-term note with the bank, $35,000.
g. Sold inventory costing $15,000 for $10,000 cash.
h. Purchased inventory on account, $60,000.
i. Paid off all short-term notes due, $65,000.
j. Purchased fixed assets for cash, $15,000.
k. Sold marketable securities costing $18,000 for cash, $15,000.
l. Collected cash on accounts receivable, $80,000.

Required:

1. Compute the following amounts and ratios as of December 31, 19X6:

    a. Net working capital.

    b. Current ratio.

    c. Acid-test ratio.

2. For 19X7, indicate the effect of each of the transactions given above on net working capital, the current ratio, and the acid-test ratio. Give the effect in terms of increase, decrease, or none. Item (x) is given below as an example of the format to use:

Transaction	The Effect on		
	Net Working Capital	Current Ratio	Acid-Test Ratio
(x)	None	Increase	Increase

18–3. *Trend and Common-Size Statements Combined with Selected Ratios.* Financial statements for Harcourt Company follow:

HARCOURT COMPANY
Comparative Income Statements
For the Years Ended December 31, 19X6, 19X7, and 19X8
(in thousands of dollars)

	19X8	19X7	19X6
Sales	$10,000	$9,000	$8,000
Cost of goods sold	6,500	5,580	4,800
Gross margin	3,500	3,420	3,200
Selling expenses	500	450	400
Administrative expenses	1,400	860	720
Total expenses	1,900	1,310	1,120
Net income before taxes	1,600	2,110	2,080
Income taxes	960	1,266	1,248
Net income	$ 640	$ 844	$ 832

HARCOURT COMPANY
Comparative Balance Sheets
As of December 31, 19X6, 19X7, and 19X8
(in thousands of dollars)

	19X8	19X7	19X6
Assets			
Current assets	$ 500	$ 600	$ 750
Long-term investments	100	200	250
Plant and equipment (net)	5,500	3,500	2,500
Total Assets	$6,100	$4,300	$3,500
Liabilities and Capital			
Current liabilities	$ 400	$ 300	$ 250
Long-term liabilities	1,900	1,000	500
Capital stock	2,500	2,000	2,000
Retained earnings	1,300	1,000	750
Total Liabilities and Capital	$6,100	$4,300	$3,500

Required:

1. Compute the net working capital for each of the three years.
2. Compute the current ratio for each of the three years.

3. Compute the debt/equity ratio for each of the three years.
4. Express the income statement data in common-size percentages.
5. Express the balance sheet data in trend percentages.
6. Comment on any significant information revealed by your work in parts (1) through (5) above.

18–4. *Leverage through the Use of Long-Term Debt.* (Note to the instructor: Problems 18–5 and 18–6 delve more deeply into the financial statements presented in this problem. Together, problems 18–4, 18–5 and 18–6 provide a comprehensive coverage of the financial ratios presented in this chapter. All or any of them can be assigned— each is independent of the others.)

PALOMAR, INC.
Income Statement and Reconciliation of Retained Earnings
For the Years Ended December 31, 19X1 and 19X2
(in thousands of dollars)

		19X2		*19X1*
Sales		$23,500		$20,500
Cost of goods sold		16,000		14,000
Gross margin		7,500		6,500
Selling expense	$2,000		$1,900	
Administrative expense	3,000	5,000	2,600	4,500
Net operating income		2,500		2,000
Interest expense		500		300
Net income before taxes		2,000		1,700
Income taxes (60%)		1,200		1,020
Net income		800		680
Dividends paid to common shareholders.		525		280
Net income retained		275		400
Retained earnings, beginning of year		6,090		5,690
Retained earnings, end of year		$ 6,365		$ 6,090

PALOMAR, INC.
Comparative Balance Sheets
December 31, 19X1 and 19X2
(in thousands of dollars)

	19X2	*19X1*
Assets		
Current assets:		
Cash	$ 600	$ 590
Accounts receivable (net)	2,900	1,900
Inventories	5,100	3,200
Prepaid expenses	100	100
Total Current Assets	8,700	5,790
Fixed assets, net	6,315	5,600
Other assets	800	750
Total Assets	$15,815	$12,140

Liabilities and Equity

Current liabilities	$ 3,600	$ 2,400
Bonds payable, 8%, due in 10 yrs.	5,500	3,300
Stockholders' equity:		
Common stock, $.50 par value	350	350
Retained earnings	6,365	6,090
Total Stockholders' Equity	6,715	6,440
Total Liabilities and Equity	$15,815	$12,140

Required:

Compute the following for 19X2:
1. Return on average total assets.
2. Return on common equity. Explain fully why the return on average total assets differs from the return on common equity.

18–5. *Common Stockholder Ratios.* Refer to the financial statements in Problem 18–4.

Required:

Compute the following for 19X2:
1. Earnings per share.
2. Assume that Palomar, Inc., has 150,000 shares of convertible preferred stock outstanding. Each share of preferred is convertible into two shares of common. What is the fully diluted earnings per share?
3. Palomar, Inc.'s common stock is selling at 12½. What is the dividend yield ratio?
4. What is the dividend payout ratio?
5. What is the price/earnings ratio? The average price/earnings ratio for firms in Palomar, Inc.'s industry is 15. How do investors regard Palomar, Inc., as compared to other firms in the industry? Explain.
6. Book value per share of common. Does the difference between the 12½ market price and the book value which you have computed suggest that the stock is overpriced? Explain.

18–6. *Creditor Ratios, and Comparison to Industry Averages.* Refer to the financial statements in Problem 18–4 for Palomar, Inc. Palomar, Inc., is a manufacturer of machine tools. The company is contemplating issuing another $2,000,000 in bonds in order to finance a remodeling of its existing plant. The bonds would bear interest at 10 percent. Some stockholders are reluctant to approve additional long-term debt, due to the fact that the machine tools industry is subject to wide-ranging fluctuations in sales and profits. Typical ratios for firms in the machine tools industry are given below:

Current ratio	2.5
Acid test ratio	1.2
Average age of receivables	30 days
Inventory turnover	5.0 times
Times interest earned	8.0 times
Debt/equity ratio	.70 to 1

Required:

1. Assume that you have been approached by a group of stockholders in Palomar, Inc. They present you with the "typical ratios" given above, and ask that you compute these ratios for Palomar, Inc., for both 19X1 and 19X2. (The inventory balance two years ago was $2,500,000; the accounts receivable balance two years ago was $1,700,000.)

2. Comment on the performance of Palomar, Inc., as compared to industry averages, and make a recommendation to the stockholders as to whether they should approve the proposed additional $2,000,000 in long-term debt.

18–7. *Analysis of Inventory and Receivables by Means of Common-Size and Trend Statements, and by Means of Selected Ratios.* At the end of 19X2, the financial statements of the Meredith Sales Company appeared as shown below:

THE MEREDITH SALES COMPANY
Comparative Balance Sheets
December 31, 19X1 and 19X2
(in thousands of dollars)

	19X2	*19X1*
Assets		
Current Assets:		
Cash	$ 200	$ 1,000
Accounts receivable, net	7,000	3,000
Inventory	12,000	6,000
Prepaid expenses	100	100
Total Current Assets	19,300	10,100
Plant and equipment, net	4,200	4,000
Other assets	500	500
Total Assets	$24,000	$14,600
Liabilities and Capital		
Current liabilities	$ 9,000	$ 4,000
Long-term liabilities	1,500	1,500
Total Liabilities	10,500	5,500
Common stock, no par, 500,000 shares	5,100	5,100
Retained earnings	8,400	4,000
Total Liabilities and Capital	$24,000	$14,600

THE MEREDITH SALES COMPANY
Partial Income Statement Data
For the Years Ended December 31, 19X1 and 19X2
(in thousands of dollars)

	19X2	*19X1*
Sales	$50,000	$35,000
Cost of goods sold	35,000	25,000
Net income	5,000	3,000

Late in 19X1, the presidency of The Meredith Sales Company was assumed by Mr. H. R. Pitch. Mr. Pitch had come through the sales end of the company, having previously served as sales manager of the East Coast District, and then as vice president, sales. During 19X2, Mr. Pitch initiated a highly successful drive to expand sales, with sales increasing from $35 million in 19X1 to $50 million in 19X2.

Mr. Pitch knew that 19X2 had been the best year in the company's history, with a net income of $5 million. For this reason he was staggered when he received the balance sheets above and noticed the sharp drop in cash, and the dramatic increase in current liabilities. He muttered to himself, "With fifty million bucks coming in from sales, how could our cash account show a balance of only two hundred thousand? These statements must be goofy."

Required:

1. Express the 19X1 and 19X2 balance sheets in common-size percentages, in terms of total assets and total liabilities and capital. Also express the 19X1 and 19X2 balance sheets in trend percentages, with 19X1 as the base year.
2. For both 19X1 and 19X2, compute the inventory turnover and compute the number of days required to turn the inventory one time. The inventory balance two years ago was $4 million.
3. For both 19X1 and 19X2, compute the accounts receivable turnover, and compute the number of days it takes to collect an account. The accounts receivable balance two years ago was $2 million.
4. Write a short memorandum to Mr. Pitch, explaining why the cash account is down, even though sales and profits are up.

18–8. *Effect of Leverage on the Return on Common Equity.* Mr. H. P. Barney and several other investors are in the process of organizing a new company to produce and distribute a household cleaning product. Mr. Barney and his associates feel that $500,000 would be adequate to finance the new company's operations, and the group is studying three methods of raising this amount of money. The three methods are:

Method A: All $500,000 obtained through issue of common stock.

Method B: $250,000 obtained through issue of common stock, and the other $250,000 obtained through issue of $100 par value, 6% preferred stock.

Method C: $250,000 obtained through issue of common stock, and the other $250,000 obtained through issue of bonds carrying an interest rate of 6%.

Mr. Barney and his associates are confident that the company can earn $100,000 each year before interest and taxes. The tax rate is 60 percent.

Required:

1. Assuming that Mr. Barney and his associates are correct in their earnings estimate, compute the net income that would go to

the common stockholders under each of the financing methods listed above.

2. Using the income data computed in part 1, compute the return on common equity under each of the three methods.

3. Why do methods B and C provide a greater return on common equity than method A? Why does method C provide a greater return on common equity than method B?

18–9. *Determining the Effect of Transactions on Various Financial Ratios.* In the right-hand column below certain financial ratios are listed. Opposite each ratio to the left is a business transaction or event relating to the operating activities of the Hoople Company.

Business Transaction or Event	*Ratio*
1. Issued a common stock dividend to common stockholders.	Earnings per share.
2. Paid accounts payable.	Debt/equity ratio.
3. Purchased inventory on open account.	Acid-test ratio.
4. Wrote off an uncollectable account against the Allowance for Bad Debts.	Current ratio.
5. The market price of Hoople Company common stock increased from 24½ to 30. Earnings per share remained unchanged.	Price/earnings ratio.
6. The market price of Hoople Company common stock increased from 24½ to 30. The dividend paid per share remained unchanged.	Dividend yield ratio.
7. The company declared a cash dividend.	Current ratio.
8. Sold inventory on account at cost.	Acid-test ratio.
9. The company issued bonds with an interest rate of 8%. The company's return on assets is 10%.	Return on common stockholders' equity.
10. The Hoople Company's net income decreased by 10% between last year and this year. Long-term debt remained unchanged.	Times interest earned.
11. A previously-declared cash dividend was paid.	Current ratio.
12. The market price of the company's common stock dropped from 24½ to 20. The dividend paid per share remained unchanged.	Dividend payout ratio.
13. $100,000 in obsolete inventory was written off as a loss.	Inventory turnover ratio.
14. Sold inventory for cash at a profit.	Debt/equity ratio.

15. Changed customer credit terms from 2/10, n/30 to 2/15, n/30 to comply with a change in industry practice.   Accounts receivable turnover ratio.
16. Issued a dividend on common stock.   Book value per share.
17. The market price of the company's common stock increased from 24½ to 30.   Book value per share.

Required:

Indicate the effect that each business transaction or event would have on the ratio listed opposite to it. State the effect in terms of increase, decrease, or no effect on the ratio involved, and give the reason for your choice of answer. In all cases, assume that the current assets exceed the current liabilities both before and after the event or transaction. Use the following format for your answers:

    Effect on Ratio   *Reason for Increase, Decrease, or No Effect*

1.

18–10. *Interpretation of Already Computed Ratios.* Jim Bodkins is a very cautious investor. Before purchasing shares of a company's stock he always investigates the company very thoroughly. Jim presently is interested in the stock of Plunge Enterprises, and has assembled the following data on the company:

	19X3		19X2		19X1	
Current ratio	2.8:1		2.5:1		2.1:1	
Acid test ratio	.7:1		.9:1		1.4:1	
Accounts receivable turnover	8.7	times	9.5	times	10.4	times
Inventory turnover	5.1	times	5.7	times	6.8	times
Sales trend	125.0		112.0		100.0	
Dividends paid per share	Unchanged over the three years					
Dividend yield	5%		4%		3%	
Dividend payout ratio	40%		50%		60%	
Return on total assets	6.8%		6.1%		5.7%	
Return on common equity	7.9%		5.8%		4.7%	

Jim is interested in getting the answers to a number of questions about the trend of events in Plunge Enterprises over the last three years. However, all Jim has to go on is a copy of the current year's (19X3) financial statements, and the ratios given above. Jim's questions are:

a. Is the market price of the company's stock going up or down?
b. Is the amount of the earnings per share increasing or decreasing?
c. Is the price/earnings ratio going up or down?
d. Is the company employing leverage to the advantage of the common stockholder?
e. Is it becoming easier for the company to pay its bills as they come due?

    f. Are customers paying their accounts at least as fast now as they were in 19X1?

    g. Is the total of the accounts receivable increasing?

    h. Is the level of inventory remaining constant?

Required:

    Answer each of Jim's questions, using the data given above. In each case, explain how you arrived at your answer.

18–11. *Extraordinary Loss Net of Tax, and Earnings per Share.* Charlie Boggs is upset. As president of Boggs Enterprises, he is very concerned that the unusual potential of Boggs Enterprises be properly portrayed to investors, particularly since the company will be making a public offering of its stock in a few months. The chief accountant at Boggs Enterprises has just presented the following income statement to Mr. Boggs for the company's recent fiscal year:

BOGGS ENTERPRISES
Income Statement
For the Year Ended January 31, 19X8
(in thousands of dollars)

		Amount	Percent
Sales		$8,000	100.0
Cost of goods sold		5,000	62.5
Gross margin		3,000	37.5
Operating expenses:			
Selling expenses	$ 500		
Administrative expenses	800		
Other expenses	1,500	$2,800	35.0
Net operating income		200	2.5
Income taxes (60%)		120	1.5
Net income		$ 80	1.0

When Mr. Boggs saw the income statement, he moaned, "Just look at that, a net income of only 1% of sales, and the industry average is 5%! When investors see this statement, they'll die laughing! We might as well forget about that stock offering this year. And all because of a fire in an old building that we were going to dump anyway." The fire that Mr. Boggs was referring to was a fire in an antiquated factory building that the company had moved out of several years ago. The building had had a book value of $1,500,000 and was uninsured. The loss is shown under "other expenses" on the income statement above.

Required:

    1. Redo the income statement for Boggs Enterprises in a format that will provide investors with a better perspective of the company's normal operating ability.

    2. Assume that Boggs Enterprises has 50,000 shares of common stock outstanding. Compute the earnings per share as it should be presented in the company's annual report.

18–12. *Comprehensive Problem on Ratio Analysis, with Comparisons to Industry Averages.* Selected financial data from the financial statements of two companies selling similar products are given below.

Data from the Current Year-End Balance Sheets

	Company A	Company B
Cash	$ 15,000	$ 10,000
Accounts receivable	49,500	89,500
Inventory	55,000	117,000
Plant and equipment, net	150,000	240,000
Total Assets	$269,500	$456,500
Current liabilities	$ 56,900	$101,000
Bonds payable	75,000	100,000
Common stock, $10 par	50,000	70,000
Retained earnings	87,600	185,500
Total Liabilities and Capital	$269,500	$456,500

Data from the Current Year-End Income Statements

	Company A	Company B
Sales	$500,000	$700,000
Cost of goods sold	325,000	455,000
Interest expense	6,000	8,000
Net income before taxes	60,000	87,500
Net income	24,000	35,000
Tax rate	60%	60%

Beginning-of-the-Year Data

	Company A	Company B
Accounts receivable	$ 45,500	$ 85,500
Inventory	51,000	113,000
Total assets	250,000	425,000

Other Selected Data

	Company A	Company B
Dividends paid per share	$ 2.50	$ 2.50
Market price per share	72.00	85.00

Industry Averages

Current ratio	2.1 to 1
Acid test ratio	1.1 to 1
Accounts receivable turnover	10.0 times
Inventory turnover	5.7 times
Times interest earned	9 times
Debt/equity ratio	.9 to 1
Dividend yield	4%
Price/earnings ratio	15
Dividend payout ratio	60%
Return on total assets	9%
Return on common equity	15.5%

Required:

1. Compute the following ratios for each company:
   a. Current ratio.
   b. Acid-test ratio.

      c.   Accounts receivable turnover.

      d.   Average collection period for receivables.

      e.   Inventory turnover.

      By use of these ratios, (*f*) tell which company is the better short-term credit risk and why.

2.   Compute the following ratios for each company:

      a.   Times interest earned.

      b.   Debt/equity ratio.

      By use of these ratios and any ratios from part 1, (*c*) tell which company could better take on *additional* long-term debt and why.

3.   Compute the following ratios for each company:

      a.   Earnings per share.

      b.   Dividend yield ratio.

      c.   Price/earnings ratio.

      d.   Dividend payout ratio.

      e.   Return on total assets.

      f.   Return on common equity.

      By use of these ratios and any data from parts 1 and 2, (*g*) tell which company's stock is the better buy and why.

chapter 19

"How Well Am I Doing?" –Statement of Changes in Financial Position

THREE MAJOR statements are prepared annually by most companies—an income statement, a balance sheet, and a statement of changes in financial position. The statement of changes in financial position is less well-known than the income statement or balance sheet, but many view it as being equal in importance. In this chapter our focus is on the development of the statement and on its use as a tool for assessing the well-being of a company.

THE PURPOSE OF THE STATEMENT

The purpose of the statement of changes in financial position is to show the sources and uses of net working capital during an accounting period. The statement is used by managers, investors, and creditors alike to answer such questions as: Why have current assets decreased? What use was made of net income during the period? How was the company's plant expansion financed? Is the company's dividend policy in balance with its operating policies?

Alternate Titles to the Statement

In published corporate reports the statement of changes in financial position is occasionally labeled as a *statement of sources and uses of net working capital,* as a *statement of sources and application of funds,* or simply as a *funds statement.* The term *statement of changes in financial position* is preferred, and should be used in published reports. For convenience in writing, however, the term "funds statement" has the advantage of brevity, and so will be used to some extent in the remaining pages of this chapter.

Working Capital as a Fund of Liquid Resources

To the average layman the term "funds" means cash. To the business-man, however, the term "funds" has a broader meaning. He uses it to refer to his net working capital. The reason becomes obvious when one considers the flow of the circulating assets, and the uses to which short-term financing is put.

The circulating assets are cash, inventory, and accounts receivable. They are so called because they are constantly circulating from one into another. That is, cash is used to purchase inventory. The inventory is then sold to create an account receivable. The receivable is then collected, and the company has cash again. Short-term credit is often used in lieu of cash, in that accounts payable and accrued liabilities are used to meet the short-term financing needs of a company.

The flow of the circulating assets is so constant that the businessman naturally thinks of them as a fund of liquid resources. The *net amount* of these liquid resources available to a firm at any given time is repre-sented by its net working capital—the difference between its current assets and its current liabilities.

CHANGES IN NET WORKING CAPITAL

If net working capital increases during a period, it means that the company generated more liquid resources than it needed for use else-where in the business. The reverse is true if net working capital decreases during a period. As we stated earlier, the purpose of the statement of changes in financial position is to explain fully any change in net working capital during a period. To explain these changes, one must look to the *noncurrent* accounts.

Increases in Net Working Capital

What kind of changes in noncurrent accounts result in increases in net working capital? Refer to the model in Exhibit 19–1. As depicted in the model, increases in net working capital come from five basic sources:

1. Profitable operations.
2. Sales of capital stock.
3. Issue of long-term debt (liabilities).
4. Sales of fixed assets.
5. Sales of other noncurrent assets.

Operations. By far the most significant continuing source of increases in net working capital is operations. The net income which a firm is

EXHIBIT 19–1
Increases in Net Working Capital

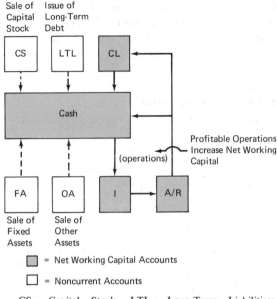

Sale of   Issue of
Capital   Long-Term
Stock   Debt

CS   LTL   CL

Cash

(operations)

Profitable Operations
Increase Net Working
Capital

FA   OA   I   A/R

Sale of   Sale of
Fixed   Other
Assets   Assets

☐ = Net Working Capital Accounts

☐ = Noncurrent Accounts

CS = Capital Stock; LTL = Long-Term Liabilities;
CL = Current Liabilities; FA = Fixed Assets; OA = Other
Assets; I = Inventory; A/R = Accounts Receivable.

able to generate results in a net inflow of circulating assets, which add
to the firm's net working capital balance.

External Sources.   From time to time it becomes necessary to bolster
the net working capital position from external sources. The two external
sources of long-term investment funds are sales of capital stock and
issue of long-term debt.

Sales of Assets.   Although sales of either fixed assets or other assets
(such as patents, copyrights, etc.) also result in increases in net working
capital, these kinds of transactions are fairly infrequent, and cannot
be relied upon as a significant or continuing source of funds.

Decreases in Net Working Capital

As shown in Exhibit 19–2, those actions which will decrease net working capital are basically the reverse of those which will increase it.

Operations.   If operations are unprofitable, then a firm will suffer a
net outflow of resources, resulting in a reduction in circulating assets,
and a decrease in net working capital. Of all the ways for net working
capital to decrease, this is the one that often proves most embarrassing for
management, and the most difficult to explain to investors.

External Drains. If a firm decides to retire capital stock or to retire long-term debt, then net working capital is drained out of the organization. Normally, a decision to retire stock or to retire long-term debt will be made only after much careful advance planning, to be sure that the net working capital position will not be seriously impaired in the process.

EXHIBIT 19–2
Decreases in Net Working Capital

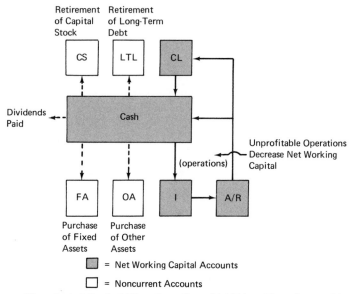

CS = Capital Stock; LTL = Long-Term Liabilities; CL = Current Liabilities; FA = Fixed Assets; OA = Other Assets; I = Inventory; A/R = Accounts Receivable.

Purchase of Assets. A much more common drain on net working capital comes in the form of expansion of productive facilities, and of investment in various other noncurrent assets, such as patents and leaseholds. Investment in these areas is a normal activity for most firms. The danger comes from expanding more rapidly than operations and long-term financing sources will permit, with a resulting drain on the net working capital balance.

Dividends. Finally, net working capital is decreased by payment of dividends to stockholders. Since dividend policy represents an integral part of overall management planning, it is shown as a separate item on the model in Exhibit 19–2. Each firm must decide for itself the level of dividend payments which it feels it can support in light of its needs for expansion of productive facilities and for funds in other areas. A dividend policy that is poorly coordinated with other areas of planning can be disasterous to even a profitable firm.

In summary, decreases in net working capital will result from:

1. Unprofitable operations.
2. Retirement of capital stock.
3. Retirement of long-term debt (liabilities).
4. Purchase of fixed and other noncurrent assets.
5. Payment of dividends.

No Effect on Net Working Capital

There are two groups of transactions that have *no effect* on net working capital. The first group consists of transactions involving *only* current asset and current liability accounts. For example, the collection of an account receivable will have no effect on net working capital. Amounts are simply moved from accounts receivable into cash, with no change occurring in the net working capital balance. Likewise, the payment of a current liability has no effect on net working capital. Both current assets and current liabilities are simply reduced by an equal amount, leaving net working capital unchanged.

The second group consists of transactions involving *only noncurrent* accounts. For example, the issue of a stock dividend has no effect on net working capital. Amounts are simply transferred from Retained Earnings, one noncurrent account, into Capital Stock, another noncurrent account. Net working capital is not affected, because current assets neither leave nor come into an organization as a result of a stock dividend. Another example of a transaction affecting only noncurrent accounts would be the issue of capital stock in exchange for new fixed assets. Since neither current asset nor current liability accounts are disturbed by such a transaction, it will have no effect on a company's net working capital. As a practical matter, however, most analysts would prefer to show the stock-for-fixed assets transaction *as if* two separate transactions had occurred—first, *as if* a sale of capital stock had occurred, and second, *as if* the cash from the sale had been used to acquire fixed assets (even though no cash actually was involved in the fixed asset acquisition). By treating the single transaction as two separate *as if* transactions, it becomes possible to present the elements involved as part of an overall funds flow analysis, whereas treating it simply as an exchange of stock for fixed assets would tend to conceal it from view.[1]

---

[1] For organizations preparing funds statements for inclusion in annual reports the *as if* treatment explained above is a requirement. See APB Opinion 19, *Reporting Changes in Financial Position* (New York: American Institute of Certified Public Accountants, March 1971), p. 373.

THE FUNDS STATEMENT—AN ILLUSTRATION

In order to pull together the ideas considered thus far we will turn to the financial statements of Example Company presented in Exhibits 19–3, 19–4, and 19–5, and prepare a funds statement. Rather than using an elaborate worksheet technique at this point, we will simply reason our way through the analysis, drawing on the concepts which we have developed thus far.

EXHIBIT 19–3

EXAMPLE COMPANY
Balance Sheet
December 31, 19X1 and 19X2

	19X2	*19X1*
Assets		
Current Assets:		
Cash	$ 200	$ 150
Accounts receivable	600	300
Inventory	600	700
Total Current Assets	1,400	1,150
Fixed Assets:		
Plant and equipment	900	700
Less accumulated depreciation	(200)	(150)
Net Fixed Assets	700	550
Long-term investments	300	400
Total Assets	$2,400	$2,100
Equities		
Current Liabilities:		
Accounts payable	$ 800	$ 400
Taxes payable	50	100
Total Current Liabilities	850	500
Bonds payable.	150	500
Stockholders' Equity:		
Capital stock	800	700
Retained earnings	600	400
Total Stockholders' Equity	1,400	1,100
Total Liabilities and Stockholders' Equity	$2,400	$2,100

EXHIBIT 19–4

EXAMPLE COMPANY
Income Statement
For the Year Ended December 31, 19X2

Sales		$900
Cost of goods sold		200
Gross margin		700
Operating expenses:		
Selling expense	$100	
Administrative expense	150	
Depreciation expense	50	
Total expenses		300
Net income		$400

EXHIBIT 19–5

EXAMPLE COMPANY
Statement of Retained Earnings
For the Year Ended December 31, 19X2

Retained earnings, December 31, 19X1	$400
Add: Net income	400
	800
Deduct: Dividends paid	200
Retained earnings, December 31, 19X2	$600

Three Basic Steps to the Funds Statement

There are three basic steps to follow in preparing a funds statement:

1. Find the change in net working capital from the beginning of the period to the end of the period.
2. Analyze the change in each *noncurrent* account, to determine if the change resulted in an increase or a decrease in net working capital.
3. Total the increases and decreases in net working capital obtained in step 2. The difference between the two totals will be the same as the change in net working capital computed in step 1.

Statement of Changes in Net Working Capital

The starting point in a funds statement is to see what change has taken place in the net working capital balance during the period. This change can be computed by preparing a Statement of Changes in Net Working Capital. Such a statement for Example Company is presented below. The statement has been prepared from the balance sheet in Exhibit 19–3.

EXAMPLE COMPANY
Statement of Changes in Net Working Capital
For the Year Ended December 31, 19X2

	19X2	19X1	Net Working Capital Increase (Decrease)
Current Assets:			
Cash.	$ 200	$ 150	
Accounts receivable.	600	300	
Inventory.	600	700	
Total.	$1,400	$1,150	$ 250
Current Liabilities:			
Accounts payable	$ 800	$ 400	
Taxes payable	50	100	
Total.	850	500	(350)
Net working capital.	$ 550	$ 650	$(100)

The Statement of Changes in Net Working Capital indicates that net working capital has decreased by $100 during the past year. What

are the causes of this decrease? From our earlier discussion we know
that the causes can be isolated by analyzing the *noncurrent accounts*
on Example Company's balance sheet.

Changes in Noncurrent Accounts

So far as the end result is concerned, it makes no difference which
noncurrent account we analyze first, nor does it matter in which order
we proceed. This is simply a matter of choice. Since operations usually
represents the most significant source of changes in the funds position,
and one that tends to be watched very closely by investors, most analysts
prefer to start with an analysis of changes in the Retained Earnings
account.

Retained Earnings. From Exhibit 19–3 we can see that Retained
Earnings has increased by $200 during 19X2. What is the cause of this
increase? We can find the answer by looking at the Statement of Retained Earnings in Exhibit 19–5. Notice from Exhibit 19–5 that the $200
increase in Retained Earnings is a *net result* of $400 of net income
earned by the company during 19X2, and $200 of dividends paid to
stockholders during 19X2.

How will these two items affect Example Company's net working
capital position? The model used earlier in Exhibit 19–1 indicates that
net income from operations increases net working capital. On the other
hand, the model used in Exhibit 19–2 indicates that a payment of dividends decreases net working capital. We can begin to organize these
increases and decreases into statement form by labeling the increases
as Sources of Net Working Capital, and the decreases as Uses of Net
Working Capital, as shown below:

>   Sources of Net Working Capital:
>   From operations: net income $400
>
>   Uses of Net Working Capital:
>   To pay dividends $200

Capital Stock. We can now proceed to analyze the other noncurrent
accounts one by one. Since we have already started at the bottom of
the balance sheet, let us continue upward by next looking at the Capital
Stock account. Exhibit 19–3 shows that Capital Stock has increased by
$100 during 19X2. Again, we need to ask ourselves the question, "What
is the cause of this increase?" The most likely answer is that shares
of capital stock were issued for cash during the year. Another answer
could be that shares of capital stock were issued as a stock dividend.
However, in the case of Example Company, the latter alternative seems
unlikely since we see no evidence of a stock dividend charge in the
Retained Earnings account.

A further possibility is that shares of capital stock were issued for new fixed assets. Even if this had happened, most analysts would show it as two separate *as if* transactions, as discussed earlier in the chapter. They would show, first, an issue of capital stock for cash, and then show a use of that cash to purchase fixed assets.

In the case at hand we have no information that the increase in Capital Stock resulted from anything other than a regular sale of shares, so we will treat it in that manner. The model used earlier in Exhibit 19–1 indicates that a sale of capital stock results in an increase in net working capital.

> Sources of Net Working Capital:
> From operations: net income $400
> From sale of capital stock . . . . ¡ . 100←
>
> Uses of Net Working Capital:
> To pay dividends $200

Bonds Payable. The Bonds Payable account in Exhibit 19–3 shows a decrease of $350 during 19X2. About the only action that could account for the decrease would be a retirement of a portion of the bonds, through paying off the bondholders. From the model used earlier in Exhibit 19–2 we have already determined that a retirement of a long-term liability results in a drain on net working capital. Therefore, we can enter this item in our funds statement as a use of funds:

> Sources of Net Working Capital:
> From operations: net income $400
> From sale of capital stock 100
>
> Uses of Net Working Capital:
> To pay dividends $200
> To retire bonds . . . . 350←

Long-Term Investments. As we work our way up the balance sheet in Exhibit 19–3, the next noncurrent account to consider is Long-Term Investments. The decrease of $100 which we note in the account could be the result of either a sale of investments, or a write-off of a portion of the investments as a loss. Since we see no indication on the income statement of any loss write-offs, we will have to assume that a portion of the investments were sold at some time during the year. The model used earlier in Exhibit 19–1 shows that a sale of "other assets" such as long-term investments releases funds to flow back into the working capital pool. Therefore, we can show in our funds analysis that the sale has resulted in an increase in the net working capital position:

> Sources of Net Working Capital:
> From operations: net income $400
> From sale of capital stock 100
> From sale of long-term investments . . . . 100←
>
> Uses of Net Working Capital:
> To pay dividends $200
> To retire bonds 350

Plant and Equipment. The only noncurrent accounts remaining to be considered in Exhibit 19–3 are Plant and Equipment and Accumulated Depreciation. At this point we run into a rather perplexing problem—do we consider the change in Plant and Equipment before or after deducting the related Accumulated Depreciation account? Which we choose will make a difference, since the change before deducting Accumulated Depreciation is an increase of $200, whereas the change after is an increase of only $150. The answer is that we must consider the change in Plant and Equipment *before* deducting Accumulated Depreciation. To do otherwise would open the risk of overlooking important funds transactions.

What would cause the plant and equipment account to increase by $200? The most logical answer is a purchase of new plant and equipment items. From the model used earlier in Exhibit 19–2 we know that a purchase of fixed assets causes a drain on net working capital. The purchase of plant and equipment should, therefore, be entered as a use of funds in our analysis:

> Sources of Net Working Capital:
> From operations: Net income. $400
> From sale of capital stock 100
> From sale of long-term investments 100
> Uses of Net Working Capital:
> To pay dividends $200
> To retire bonds 350
> To purchase pland and equipment . . . . 200←

The Problem of Depreciation

The only noncurrent account remaining to be analyzed is Accumulated Depreciation. The account increased by $50 during the year as a result of a $50 charge for depreciation expense on the income statement (see Exhibit 19–4). Since depreciation is an expense that does not require a present outflow of funds, any depreciation charges on the income statement must be added back to net income, in order to determine the amount of funds generated by current operations. For Example Company, the computation would be:

> Sources of Net Working Capital:
> From operations:
> Net income $400
> Add: Expenses not requiring use of funds—
> depreciation. 50
> Total funds provided by operations . . . . $450←

Depreciation Is Not a Source of Funds. The mechanics of adding depreciation back to net income on the funds statement often leads people to the hasty conclusion that depreciation is a source of funds.

We must state emphatically that depreciation is *not* a source of funds. In fact, the reason for adding it back to net income is because it *does not* involve a flow of funds.

The only funds that can come from operations come from *sales*. If no sales are made, then no funds can be provided by operations, regardless of how large depreciation deductions may be.

Charges Similar to Depreciation. Certain other charges on the income statement also reduce net income without involving an outflow of funds. These charges include depletion, amortization of goodwill, and amortization of patents and leaseholds. Like depreciation, they need to be added back to net income in determining the amount of funds generated by operations during a period.

The Funds Statement

We can organize the results of our analytical work into statement form:

EXAMPLE COMPANY
Statement of Changes in Financial Position
For the Year Ended December 31, 19X2

Sources of Net Working Capital:	
From operations:	
Net income	$400
Add: Expenses not requiring use of funds—	
depreciation.	50
Total.	450
From sale of capital stock	100
From sale of long-term investments.	100
Total Sources	650
Uses of Net Working Capital:	
To pay dividends	200
To retire bonds	350
To purchase plant and equipment	200
Total Uses.	750
Decrease in Net Working Capital	($100)

The net working capital position of Example Company was enhanced during 19X2 by $450 of funds provided by operations, by $100 of funds provided through sale of capital stock, and by an additional $100 of funds provided through sale of long-term investments. These amounts however, were not adequate to cover the drains on net working capital which took place during the year. Dividends of $200 were paid, and $350 of funds were used to retire bonds outstanding. In addition, the company expended $200 for new items of plant and equipment. Altogether, these uses of funds exceeded the sources by $100, causing a reduction in net working capital during the year.

EXHIBIT 19–6

UNIVERSAL COMPANY
Balance Sheet
December 31, 19X1 and 19X2

	19X2	*19X1*
Assets		
Current Assets:		
Cash	$ 200	$ 300
Accounts receivable, net...............	900	500
Inventory	900	1,000
Total Current Assets................	2,000	1,800
Plant and equipment (Note 1)	800	700
Less accumulated depreciation	(300)	(250)
Net plant and equipment	500	450
Intangible assets:		
Patents..........................	300	350
Total Assets	$2,800	$2,600
Liabilities and Equity		
Current Liabilities:		
Accounts payable....................	$ 700	$ 400
Taxes payable......................	400	250
Accrued liabilities	100	150
Total Current Liabilities..............	1,200	800
Mortgage payable	100	200
Stockholders' Equity:		
Common stock	300	200
Preferred stock	150	300
Retained earnings...................	1,050	1,100
Total Stockholders' Equity	1,500	1,600
Total Liabilities and Stockholders' Equity.......	$2,800	$2,600

Note 1: Equipment which had cost $100 new, and on which there was ac-
cumulated depreciation of $75, was sold during the year for its book value of
$25.

Uses of the Funds Statement

The funds statement is highly regarded as a management planning
tool. Although it deals in historical costs, any lack of forward planning,
coordination, or balance in working toward long-run objectives becomes
quickly evident in the story it has to tell. For example, a company
may have as its stated objective to double plant capacity in five years,
using only funds provided through operations. If the company at the
same time is paying dividends equal to earnings and is retiring large
amounts of long-term debt, the discrepancy between long-run plans and
current actions will be highlighted very quickly on the funds statement.

Some of the more significant ways in which managers use the funds
statement include:

1. To coordinate dividend policy with other actions of the company.
2. To plan the financing of additional plant and equipment, the financing of new product lines, and the financing of new marketing outlets.
3. To coordinate total sources of funds and total uses of funds.
4. To find ways of strengthening a weak net working capital position, and thereby strengthening credit lines.
5. To check the implementation of plans and policies.

A WORKING PAPER APPROACH
TO THE FUNDS STATEMENT

The procedure relied on to this point of simply developing a funds statement through logic has allowed us to concentrate our efforts on learning basic concepts, with a minimum of effort expended on mechanics. For many firms, this simple logic procedure is completely adequate as a means of developing a funds statement. The balance sheets of some companies are so complex that a working paper approach is needed to help organize the changes in noncurrent accounts into funds statement form.

A number of working paper approaches to the funds statement are available. The one we have chosen to illustrate relies on the use of T-accounts to assist in analysis and organization of data. In order to illustrate the T-account approach to working paper preparation, we will use the financial statements of Universal Company found in Exhibits 19–6 and 19–7.

EXHIBIT 19–7

UNIVERSAL COMPANY
Statement of Income and Reconciliation of Retained Earnings
For the Year Ended December 31, 19X2

Sales		$2,000
Cost of goods sold.		1,200
Gross margin		800
Operating expenses		500
Net operating income.		300
Interest expense.		25
Net income before taxes		275
Income taxes		125
Net income		150
Retained earnings, beginning.		1,100
Total.		1,250
Less dividends distributed:		
Cash dividends, preferred	$100	
Stock dividends, common	100	200
Retained earnings, ending		$1,050

Note 2: Operating expenses contain $125 of depreciation expense, and $50 of patent amortization expense.

The Statement of Changes in Net Working Capital

The starting point of our analytical work will again be the preparation of a Statement of Changes in Net Working Capital.

UNIVERSAL COMPANY
Statement of Changes in Net Working Capital
For the Year Ended December 31, 19X2

	19X2	*19X1*	*Net Working Capital—Increase or (Decrease)*
Current Assets:			
Cash	$ 200	$ 300	
Accounts receivable	900	500	
Inventory	900	1,000	
Total.	$2,000	$1,800	$ 200
Current Liabilities:			
Accounts payable.	$ 700	$ 400	
Taxes payable	400	250	
Accrued liabilities.	100	150	
Total.	1,200	800	(400)
Net Working Capital	$ 800	$1,000	$(200)

Universal Company has suffered a $200 decrease in its net working capital during 19X2. As before, our objective will be to determine the *causes* of this change in the net working capital balance. Also as before, our basic analytical approach will be to review the changes in noncurrent accounts. The only function the T-accounts will serve will be to assist us in the mechanical process of *organizing* our information as it develops.

The T-Account Approach

In Exhibit 19–8, we have prepared a T-account for each of the noncurrent accounts found on Universal Company's balance sheet. In the T-accounts we have entered the *net change* that has taken place in the various noncurrent accounts during 19X2. Exhibit 19–8 also contains a T-account titled *Net Working Capital*, which we will use to accumulate the sources and uses of net working capital as they develop through our analysis of the noncurrent account changes.

The procedure is to make entries directly in the T-accounts to explain the actions that have caused the changes in the various noncurrent account balances. To the extent that changes in the noncurrent accounts have affected net working capital, appropriate entries are made in the T-account representing net working capital in Exhibit 19–8.

Retained Earnings. As we mentioned earlier in the chapter, the retained earnings account in generally the most useful starting point in

EXHIBIT 19–8

UNIVERSAL COMPANY
T-Accounts Showing Changes in Noncurrent Account Balances
Net Working Capital

Sources	Uses

Plant and Equipment | Accumulated Depreciation | Patents | Mortgage Payable

100 | | 50 | 50 | 100

Common Stock | Preferred Stock | Retained Earnings

| 100 | 150 | | 50 |

developing a funds statement. Exhibit 19–7 presents a detail of the changes in the retained earnings account of Universal Company. We can note from Exhibit 19–7 that net income of $150 was added to retained earnings during 19X2, and that dividends of $200 were charged against retained earnings. The dividends consisted of $100 in cash dividends and $100 in stock dividends. These three items account for the net $50 decrease in retained earnings during 19X2.

We can now enter these three items into the appropriate T-accounts. This is done in Exhibit 19–9.

Entry (1) in the Retained Earnings account shows the increase in retained earnings that resulted from the net income reported for 19X2, and the corresponding increase that would have come about in net working capital. Entry (2) records the payment of cash dividends on preferred stock, and the corresponding drain on net working capital. Entry (3) records the distribution of a stock dividend to common stockholders. Notice that the stock dividend has no effect on net working capital. A stock dividend results in a capitalization of a portion of retained earnings, and involves no outflow of assets.

Notice from Exhibit 19–9 that the three entries fully explain the change during 19X2 of $50 in the retained earnings account. To show that we have fully explained this change, we have drawn a line under

EXHIBIT 19–9

UNIVERSAL COMPANY
T-Accounts After Completion of All Noncurrent Account Analysis
Net Working Capital

	Sources		Uses		
From operations: Net income	(1)	150	(2)	100	To pay cash dividends
From operations:			(4)	150	To retire preferred stock
Patent amortization	(6)	50	(5)	100	To retire mortgage payable
From sale of equipment	(7)	25	(8)	200	To acquire plant and
From operations: Depreciation	(9)	125			equipment

Plant and Equipment		Accumulated Depreciation		Patents		Mortgage Payable	
100			50		50	100	
(8) 200	(7) 100	(7) 75	(9) 125	(6) 50	(5) 100		
100			50		50	100	

Common Stock		Preferred Stock		Retained Earnings		
	100	150			50	
(3)	100	(4) 150		(2) 100	(1) 150	
				(3) 100		
	100	150			50	

Explanation of entries:

(1) To record net income for the period.
(2) To record payment of a cash dividend.
(3) To record a stock dividend.
(4) To record the retirement of preferred stock.
(5) To record the payment of part of the mortgage.
(6) To record the amortization of patent expense.
(7) To record the sale of plant and equipment.
(8) To record the purchase of plant and equipment.
(9) To record depreciation expense for the period.

the three entries, and we have shown that their net effect is a $50 decrease in retained earnings.

Retained Earnings

50				⎰Our analysis of retained earnings must explain why the ⎱account decreased by $50 during 19X2.
(2) 100	(1) 150			⎰We place in the account the entries that explain the $50 ⎱decrease.
(3) 100				
50				⎰To show that we have fully explained the $50 decrease, we ⎱draw a line below the entries, and show their net dollar effect.

Notice from Exhibit 19–9 that debits to the Net Working Capital T-Account represent sources of net working capital, and that credits to the account represent uses of net working capital.

We can now proceed through the remainder of the noncurrent accounts of Universal Company, analyzing the change in each one, and recording the transactions that caused the change directly in the appropriate T-accounts.

Common Stock. Our analysis of retained earnings provided the data needed to explain the $100 increase in common stock during 19X2. As shown in entry (3), the increase is due to the distribution of a stock dividend to common stockholders.

Common Stock

	100
(3) 100	{ Entry (3) fully explains the $100 increase in Common Stock
	100

Preferred Stock. The T-accounts in Exhibit 19–9 show a decrease of $150 in preferred stock during 19X2. Since we have no contrary information, we will have to assume that the decrease has come about through repurchase and retirement of shares. Entry (4) in Exhibit 19–9 shows the repurchase, and its effect on net working capital. Notice from the exhibit that entry (4) fully explains the change in the Preferred Stock account.

Mortgage Payable. Since we again have no contrary information, we will have to assume that the decrease in the mortgage payable account is a result of a retirement of a portion of the liability. Entry (5) in Exhibit 19–9 records the retirement.

Patents. The $50 decrease in the patents account which took place during 19X2 could be the result of a sale of patents. On the other hand, it could also be the result of a writing off of a portion of the patents to expense through amortization. A careful check of Universal Company's income statement in Exhibit 19–7 will reveal that the decrease is a result of amortization. Notice from the footnote to the income statement that during 19X2 Universal Company recorded $50 in patent amortization expense. The effect of the patent amortization on net working capital is shown in entry (6) in Exhibit 19–9.

Amortization of intangibles such as patents has the same effect on net income as does depreciation. It is an expense charge that requires no outflow of funds. Therefore, in computing the funds provided by operations during a period it is necessary to add the amortization back to net income, the same as we add depreciation back to net income.

Plant and Equipment. In order to properly analyze the $100 increase that has taken place in the plant and equipment account during 19X2, it will be necessary to carefully review both Universal Company's balance sheet and its income statement. The increase could simply represent $100 in plant and equipment purchases. On the other hand, there may have been retirements or sales during the year that are concealed in this net change.

From the footnote to the balance sheet we find that certain items of equipment were, indeed, sold during 19X2, at a sale price of $25. The entry at the time of sale would have been as follows:

Cash	25	
Accumulated depreciation.	75	
Plant and equipment.		100

Entry (7) in Exhibit 19–9 records the effects of this transaction on the various T-accounts.

How much did Universal Company expend on plant and equipment *purchases* during 19X2? Overall, we know that plant and equipment increased by $100 during the year (see Exhibit 19–9). Since this $100 increase is what remains *after* the $100 *retirement* of plant items recorded above, purchases of plant and equipment during 19X2 must have totaled $200. Entry (8) in Exhibit 19–9 records these purchases.

Accumulated Depreciation. Universal Company's income statement in Exhibit 19–7 reveals a $125 charge for depreciation expense for 19X2. In accordance with our earlier discussion of depreciation, we will need to record this charge as an *operations related* increase in net working capital, as shown in entry (9) in Exhibit 19–9.

This entry, along with the accumulated depreciation portion of entry (7) above, completes the explanation of the $50 increase in the accumulated depreciation T-account for 19X2, as shown in Exhibit 19–9.

The Completed Funds Statement

The T-accounts in Exhibit 19–9 contain the final results of our funds flow analysis of Universal Company. The net working capital T-account contains the results of those actions which have increased net working capital, and the results of those actions which have reduced net working capital. All that now remains is to organize these data into statement form. This statement is shown in Exhibit 19–10. The reader should review this statement carefully, and as an exercise, state in his own words what has caused net working capital in Universal Company to decrease by $200 during 19X2.

FOCUSING ON CHANGES IN CASH

In preparing a statement of changes in financial position, some firms prefer to focus on cash, rather than to focus on net working capital.

EXHIBIT 19–10

UNIVERSAL COMPANY
Statement of Changes in Financial Position
For the Year Ended December 31, 19X2

Sources of net working capital:
From operations:

Net income	$150
Add: Expenses not requiring use of funds—	
Depreciation	125
Patent amortization	50
Total Funds Provided by Operations	325
From sale of equipment	25
Total Sources.	350

Uses of net working capital:

To pay cash dividends	100
To retire preferred stock.	150
To retire mortgage debt	100
To purchase equipment	200
Total Uses.	550
Decrease in net working capital	($200)

The purpose of the statement then becomes to explain what has caused cash to increase or to decrease during a period.

A statement with its emphasis on changes in cash can be particularly useful to a firm that is experiencing cash problems. The statement can show a firm what its sources of cash were during a period, and show how the cash was used. Such information can be very helpful in planning cash needs, and in maintaining overall control of cash activities.

What Activities Have an Impact on Cash?

In our earlier discussion, when we focused on net working capital, we found that changes in the *noncurrent* accounts contained the key to why net working capital had changed during a period. As we now focus on cash, we will again analyze changes in the noncurrent accounts. But we must also take one additional step. We must also analyze changes in the *current asset* and *current liability* accounts. The reason is that changes in the current asset and current liability accounts have just as much effect on cash as do changes in the noncurrent accounts.

Increases in Cash

Cash can be increased by:

1. Profitable operations.
2. Sales of capital stock.
3. An increase in *any* liability account (current or noncurrent).
4. A decrease in *any* asset account (current or noncurrent).

We discussed earlier how changes in *noncurrent* accounts can affect the funds position. We need now to discuss how changes in *current* asset and *current* liability accounts can affect the funds position when funds are being defined as cash.

Increase in Any Current Liability. In the normal course of events, short-term creditors extend credit to a firm, are paid off, reextend credit, and are paid off again, on a continuing basis period after period. Most firms depend on these short-term creditors as a major source of financing, and for this reason try to keep the turnover going smoothly. If management should make a decision, however, to defer paying short-term creditors, then the volume of accounts due would expand. The result would be that cash that otherwise would have gone to pay creditors would be kept in the organization, and would be available to use internally. By this line of reasoning, one can see that *increases* in amounts due to short-term creditors represent a *source* of cash to a firm.

Decrease in Any Current Asset. Current assets such as inventory and accounts receivable represent an investment of cash. If the level of investment in any current asset is reduced, then cash is freed to flow back into the cash account. Therefore, a decrease in a current asset (such as inventory or accounts receivable) should be entered on the cash flow statement in the "sources of cash" section.

Decreases in Cash

Cash can be decreased by:

1. Unprofitable operations.
2. Retirement of capital stock or payment of dividends.
3. A decrease in *any* liability account (current or noncurrent).
4. An increase in *any* asset account (current or noncurrent).

The only clarification needed is on how changes in current asset and current liability accounts can result in reductions in cash availability.

Decrease in Any Current Liability. We stated in the preceding section that if payments to creditors are deferred the resulting increase in current liabilities represents a source of cash to an organization. By this same line of reasoning, if payments to creditors are accelerated so that overall current liabilities *decrease*, the result will be a net outflow of cash. Therefore, in preparing a cash flow statement, a reduction in a current liability account should be treated as a use of cash.

Increase in Any Current Asset. An increase in a current asset account also represents a use of cash on the cash flow statement. A decision on the part of management, for example, to expand the volume of inventory being carried will cause a drain on the cash account, as cash is tied up in investment in inventory. In like manner, a decision to liberalize credit terms will result in an expanded volume of receivables as customers take longer to pay. The build-up of receivables will result in decreased cash being available internally.

Managers often fail to recognize that an expansion of inventory or receivables represents just as much of an investment decision as a decision to expand the size of the plant and equipment. As a practical matter, an investment in inventories or in receivables can be just as illiquid as an investment in plant and equipment. Once inventories are built up, there always is a reluctance to trim them back down, particularly if customers become used to the greater variety of selection available. And once customers get used to taking longer to pay, it is an extremely difficult task to speed collections up again.

The Cash Flow Statement—An Illustration

A cash flow statement for Universal Company is presented in Exhibit 19–11. This statement is prepared from the financial statements of Universal Company used earlier in the chapter.

EXHIBIT 19–11

UNIVERSAL COMPANY
Statement of Changes in Financial Position
For the Year Ended December 31, 19X2

Sources of cash:
From operations:

Net income	$150
Add: Expenses not requiring use of funds—	
Depreciation	125
Patent amortization	50
Total.	325
From reduction of inventory	100
From expansion of current liabilities.	400
From sale of equipment	25
Total Sources.	850

Uses of cash:	
To expand accounts receivable	400
To pay cash dividends	100
To retire preferred stock.	150
To retire mortgage debt	100
To purchase equipment	200
Total Uses.	950
Decrease in cash.	($100)

The $100 decrease in cash explained by the cash flow statement in Exhibit 19–11 agrees with the decrease in the cash account shown on the balance sheet of Universal Company in Exhibit 19–6. We can summarize the cause of this cash decrease as follows: During 19X2 Universal

Company generated $325 in cash inflow from operations. Additional cash of $100 was obtained from reducing the level of inventories, and cash of $400 was made available through putting off payment of short-term creditors. Cash of $25 was obtained from sale of equipment. The total of these sources of cash was insufficient to cover all of the uses

EXHIBIT 19–12
T-Account Working Papers—Cash Flow Statement

Cash

	Sources		Uses		
From operations: Net Income	(1)	150	(2)	100	To pay cash dividends
From expansion of current			(4)	150	To retire preferred stock
liabilities	(6)	400	(5)	100	To retire mortgage debt
From operations:			(9)	200	To purchase equipment
Patent amortization	(7)	50	(12)	400	To expand accounts
From sale of equipment	(8)	25			receivable
From operations: Depreciation	(10)	125			
From reduction of inventory	(11)	100			

Accounts Receivable

400	
(12) 400	
400	

Inventory

	100
	(11) 100
	100

Plant and Equipment

100	
(9) 200	(8) 100
100	

Accumulated Depreciation

	50
(8) 75	(10) 125
	50

Patents

	50
	(7) 50
	50

Accounts Payable

	300
	(6) 300
	300

Taxes Payable

	150
	(6) 150
	150

Accrued Liabilities

50	
(6) 50	
50	

Mortgage Payable

	100
(5) 100	
	100

Common Stock

	100
	(3) 100
	100

Preferred Stock

150	
(4) 150	
150	

Retained Earnings

50	
(2) 100	(1) 150
(3) 100	
50	

EXHIBIT 19–12 (continued)

Explanation of entries:

(1) To record net income for the period.
(2) To record payment of a cash dividend.
(3) To record a stock dividend.
(4) To record the retirement of preferred stock.
(5) To record the payment of part of the mortgage.
(6) To record financing obtained through net expansion of the current liabilities.
(7) To record amortization of patent expense.
(8) To record the sale of plant and equipment.
(9) To record the purchase of plant and equipment.
(10) To record depreciation expense for the period.
(11) To record cash obtained through reduction of the inventory.
(12) To record cash needed to expand accounts receivable.

of cash during the year. Accounts receivable were allowed to expand by $400, thereby decreasing the amount of cash available for use internally. Cash was used to retire both preferred stock and long-term debt, as well as to purchase equipment and to pay dividends. The result was an overall reduction of $100 in cash available to the firm.

Working papers to support the statement are presented in Exhibit 19–12. The only difference between these working papers and the ones prepared earlier in our analysis of net working capital is that these working papers contain changes in the current asset and current liability accounts, as well as changes in the noncurrent accounts.

SUMMARY

The statement of changes in financial position is one of the three major statements prepared by business firms. Its purpose is analytical, in that it attempts to explain how net working capital has been provided and how it has been used during an accounting period. As such, it is a very useful tool in attempting to assess "how well" a firm is doing, and to assess the quality of its management.

If a firm has been experiencing a cash problem, the statement of changes in financial position can be made to focus on changes in cash, rather than on changes in net working capital. If net working capital is the focus of the statement, then any change in net working capital can be explained by an analysis of the noncurrent accounts. If cash is the focus of the statement, then any change in cash can be explained by an analysis of *all* other accounts, current as well as noncurrent.

QUESTIONS

19–1. What is the purpose of the funds statement?

19–2. How does a funds statement differ from a cash flow statement?

19–3. What are the major sources of net working capital, and what are the major uses of net working capital?

19–4. In determining "funds provided by operations," why is it necessary to add depreciation back to net income? What other income statement items must also be added back to net income in determining "funds provided by operations"?

19–5. What are circulating assets, and why are they called circulating assets?

19–6. What two groups of transactions have no effect on net working capital? Give an example from each group.

19–7. During the current year, a company declared but did not pay a cash dividend of $50,000 and a 5 percent stock dividend. How will these two items be treated on the current year's funds statement?

19–8. 'On December 15 a company borrowed $30,000 from its bank on a 60-day note. Explain how this item will be handled on the company's funds statement and on its cash flow statement for the year ended December 31.

19–9. Under what conditions would the cash flow statement be more useful to a firm than a funds statement? Under what conditions is the funds statement most useful?

19–10. An outside member of the Board of Directors of a small, but rapidly growing manufacturing company is puzzled by the fact that the company is very profitable, but yet never seems to have enough cash to pay its bills on time. Explain to the director how a company can be profitable, yet experience shortages of cash. The company pays no dividends.

19–11. Able Company started the year with $100,000 in accounts receivable. The company ended the year with only $80,000 in accounts receivable. Was this decrease in accounts receivable a source of funds to the company on the funds statement? Explain.

19–12. Appleby Company had a net loss for the year, but yet its funds statement shows a *positive* amount of funds provided by operations. How is this possible?

19–13. A businessman once stated, "Depreciation is one of our biggest sources of funds." Do you agree that depreciation is a source of funds? Explain.

19–14. To the layman, "funds" means cash. Yet when the businessman speaks of funds he generally has net working capital in mind. Why does the businessman think of funds in terms of net working capital?

EXERCISES

19–1. From the following income statement, compute the "funds provided by operations."

ARVID COMPANY
Income Statement
For the Year Ended December 31, 19X7

Sales		$80,000
Cost of goods sold.	$50,000	
Salaries and wages.	12,000	
Depreciation expense.	4,000	
Selling expense	5,000	
Patent amortization.	1,000	72,000
Net income.		$ 8,000

19–2. For each of the following transactions, state whether the items involved would appear on the funds statement for the period. For those items appearing on the funds statement, state whether each item would be a source of net working capital or a use of net working capital, and where appropriate state the dollar amount of the source or use.

1. Sold 500 shares of $100 par value common stock for $110 per share.
2. Retired fully depreciated equipment which had an original cost of $8,000.
3. Purchased $100,000 in inventory on account.
4. Sold fixed assets for $5,000 that had an original cost of $12,000 and accumulated depreciation of $7,000.
5. Declared a cash dividend, $15,000.
6. Purchased $15,000 in fixed assets on a 60-day, 6% note.
7. Amortized goodwill on the income statement, $7,000.
8. Paid the cash dividend in (5).
9. Declared and issued a 5% stock dividend in common on common.
10. $25,000 in long-term debt, due within the next year, was reclassified from a long-term liability status to a current liability status.

19–3. During 19X4, the following events occurred in the Orwell Company:

1. The company issued $25,000 in long-term notes.
2. The company reported net income of $20,000.
3. In order to support an expanded volume of sales, the inventory account increased by $20,000, and accounts receivable increased by $12,000.
4. Depreciation charges for the year totaled $8,000.
5. The company purchased $45,000 in new plant and equipment items.
6. Cash dividends of $3,000 were declared and paid.
7. The company's accounts payable to suppliers increased by $30,000 during the year.
8. No other changes took place in the company.

Required:

Prepare a cash flow statement for the Orwell Company for 19X4, using the data given above.

19–4. Comparative financial statement data for Easy Company are presented below:

	(000 omitted)	
	19X5	*19X4*

Balance Sheet Data

Current assets	$ 25	$20
Fixed assets	100	85
Accumulated depreciation	(30)	(20)
Long-term investments	10	10
Total Assets.	$105	$95
Current liabilities	$ 16	$10
Bonds payable.	5	8
Common stock, no par	65	60
Retained earnings	19	17
Total Equities	$105	$95

Other Selected Data

Net income reported	$ 7
Cash dividends declared and paid	5
Depreciation expense.	10

Required:

1. Prepare a statement of changes in net working capital.
2. Prepare a funds statement for 19X5.

19–5. Comparative financial statement data for the Bonn Company follow:

	(000 omitted)	
	19X7	*19X6*

Balance Sheet Data

Cash	$ 12	$ 9
Accounts receivable, net	40	35
Inventory	90	92
Fixed assets	120	120
Accumulated depreciation	(60)	(50)
Total Assets.	$202	$206
Accounts payable	$ 6	$ 4
Common stock	130	140
Retained earnings	66	62
Total Equities.	$202	$206

Other Selected Data

Net income reported	$ 8
Cash dividends declared and paid	4
Depreciation expense.	10

Required:

Prepare a cash flow statement for 19X7.

19–6. State whether each of the following transactions results in (1) a source of funds, (2) a use of funds, or (3) has no effect on funds. Define funds as net working capital.

  a. A sale of long-term investments.
  b. Retirement of capital stock.

    c. Net income reported for the period.

    d. Purchase of new equipment.

    e. Declaration and issue of a stock dividend.

    f. Sale of capital stock for par.

    g. Retirement of fully depreciated equipment.

    h. Sale of old equipment for its salvage value.

    i. Depreciation charged for the period.

    j. Retirement of long-term debt.

    k. Collection of an account receivable.

    l. Purchase of inventory on account.

   m. Amortization of a patent.

    n. Declaration and payment of a cash dividend.

    o. Reclassification of long-term debt to a current liability status.

    p. Issue of capital stock in exchange for a piece of land.

19-7. Comparative financial statements for GSJ Company follow:

GSJ COMPANY
Balance Sheets
December 31, 19X4 and 19X5

	19X5	*19X4*
Assets		
Current assets	$12	$ 9
Land	9	10
Equipment.	15	10
Accumulated depreciation.	(5)	(3)
Investments	7	7
Total Assets.	$38	$33
Equities		
Current liabilities	7	5
Notes payable	3	6
Common stock	12	9
Retained earnings.	16	13
Total Equities.	$38	$33

GSJ COMPANY
Income Statements
For the Years Ended December 31, 19X4 and 19X5

	19X5	*19X4*
Sales	$27	$20
Cost of goods sold	12	9
Gross margin.	15	11
Operating expenses*	8	6
Net income	7	5
Beginning retained earnings	13	11
Total.	20	16
Deduct cash dividends	4	3
Ending returned earnings.	$16	$13

* Includes $2 depreciation expense each year.

Required:

Prepare a funds statement for 19X5. Working papers are not necessary.

PROBLEMS

19–1. *Funds Provided by Operations.* The following information has been extracted from the annual reports of the Dowd Company:

	This Year	Last Year
Plant and equipment	$50,000	$38,000
Accumulated depreciation—plant and equipment.	22,000	18,000
Net income	9,000	6,000
Depreciation expense.	6,000	4,000
Goodwill amortization	2,000	2,000
Equipment sold during the year for cash at its book value	8,000	
Interest accrued, but not paid during the year	1,500	

You have been able to determine from examining this year's annual report that no retirements of equipment took place other than the sales noted above.

Required:

1. For this year, compute the funds provided by operations. Define funds as net working capital.
2. For this year, assume that Dowd Company had a net loss of $5,000, rather than net income of $9,000. Under this assumption, compute the funds provided by operations.
3. For this year, assume that Dowd Company had a net loss of $10,000, rather than net income of $9,000. Under this assumption, compute the funds provided by operations. Where would you place the "operations" part of the funds statement under this assumption, as a source of funds or as a use of funds? Why?

19–2. *Funds Statement without Working Papers.* The Heber Company's balance sheet accounts at the end of years 1 and 2 are given below:

	Year 2	Year 1
Debits		
Cash	$ 20,000	$ 16,000
Accounts receivable, net	74,000	75,000
Inventory	120,000	104,000
Plant and equipment	300,000	290,000
Long-term investments.	30,000	32,000
Total.	$544,000	$517,000
Credits		
Accumulated depreciation	$ 60,000	$ 44,000
Accounts payable.	100,000	95,000
Mortgage payable	50,000	55,000
Common stock, $10 par	200,000	200,000
Retained earnings.	134,000	123,000
Total.	$544,000	$517,000

The following additional information is available:

1. The change in the retained earnings account between Year 1 and Year 2 can be accounted for as follows:

Retained earnings, Year 1	$123,000
Add net income for Year 2	15,000
	138,000
Deduct cash dividends for Year 2	4,000
Retained earnings, Year 2	$134,000

2. Depreciation expense for Year 2 was $16,000.
3. There were no sales or retirements of equipment during Year 2.

Required:

1. Prepare a statement of changes in net working capital for Year 2.
2. Prepare a funds statement for Year 2, without preparing working papers.

19–3. *Cash Flow Statement without Working Papers.* "Pop" Rafferty has recently purchased a small general store in a rural community. The various account balances changed as follows from the time of purchase to the end of the first six months' of Pop's operation of the store:

	At End of the First Six Months	At Time of Purchase
Cash	$ 1,000	$ 1,500
Receivables	1,500	800
Inventory	6,000	4,100
Fixed assets	8,000	8,000
Accumulated depreciation	(400)	0
Total	$16,100	$14,400
Accounts payable	$ 4,500	$ 4,000
Proprietorship	11,600	10,400
Total	$16,100	$14,400

The local bookkeeper has just presented Pop with the following additional information.

1. Net income for the first six months, $3,000.
2. During the first six months Pop withdrew $1,800 for personal use. Pop can't understand how the cash account could have decreased by $500 if the store really earned $3,000 during the six-month period.

Required:

1. Prepare a cash flow statement for the six-month period. Working papers are not necessary.
2. Explain to Pop what happened to his cash.

19–4. *Cash Flow Model.* Changes in various account balances of the West-over Company over the past year are given below in cash flow model form.

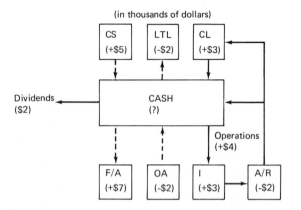

(in thousands of dollars)

The cash inflow from operations has already been adjusted for depreciation and other noncash charges.

Required:

1. Compute the change in the cash account.
2. Did net working capital increase or decrease over the year? Explain.

19–5. *Funds Statement with Working Papers.* The Marcos Company is a small but rapidly growing manufacturer of component parts for the aerospace industry. Competition is very keen, and the company has found that in order to compete effectively it is necessary to be constantly expanding and modernizing its production facilities. The Marcos Company has just approached its banker with a request for a substantially increased line of long-term credit. In support of the loan application, the company's banker has asked for and received the following information:

	(000 omitted)	
	19X6	*19X5*
Current assets (detailed)	$200	$150
Fixed assets	800	700
Accumulated depreciation	(150)	(120)
Long-term investments	30	50
Goodwill	20	25
Total	$900	$805
Current liabilities (detailed)	$140	$100
Long-term notes	230	200
Common stock	300	300
Retained earnings	230	205
Total	$900	$805

From the income statement and from other sources the company's banker has determined that:
1. Net income for 19X6 was $35,000.
2. Cash dividends of $10,000 were declared but not paid during 19X6.
3. $10,000 in fully depreciated equipment was retired during the year. When sold the equipment will have only a negligible scrap value.
4. The goodwill is being amortized against earnings.

Required:

Assume you are a new employee in the loan department of the Marcos Company's bank. The chief loan officer has asked that you prepare the following:
1. A statement of changes in net working capital.
2. T-account working papers for a funds statement.
3. From the information developed in the T-account working papers, prepare a funds statement for 19X6 in good form.

19–6. *Funds Statement with Working Papers.* Adair Enterprises issued $1,000,000 in 8% bonds during 19X6. The bond indenture states that the company must maintain at least a 2.5 to 1 current ratio, or the bonds will be considered to be in default. The management of Adair Enterprises readily agreed to the 2.5 to 1 current ratio stipulation, since the company has always maintained a current ratio of at least 3.0 to 1. For this reason, management was badly shaken at the end of 19X7 to discover that the current ratio had slipped to just 2.5 to 1—the bare minimum required. Relevant financial data are given below for 19X6 and 19X7:

	(000 omitted)	
	19X7	*19X6*
Current assets (detailed)	$ 900	$1,200
Land	300	250
Buildings and equipment.	2,000	1,900
Accumulated depreciation	(400)	(350)
Investments in subsidiaries.	900	625
Patents	65	75
Total.	$3,765	$3,700
Current liabilities (detailed)	$ 360	$ 400
Bonds payable.	1,000	1,000
Preferred stock	400	500
Common stock	1,300	1,250
Retained earnings	705	550
Total.	$3,765	$3,700
Current ratio.	2.5 to 1	3.0 to 1

During the year ended December 31, 19X7:
1. Net income totaled $200,000.
2. Cash dividends declared and paid totaled $45,000.

3. The patents were amortized against net income.
4. Equipment costing $41,000 new was sold for its book value of $17,000.

Required:

To assist the management of Adair Enterprises to understand what happened to the company's net working capital, prepare the following:
1. A statement of changes in net working capital.
2. Working papers for a funds statement.
3. A funds statement in proper form.

19–7. *Cash Flow Statement with Working Papers.* Bill Bergin owns a substantial block of stock in Century Fashions, a clothing manufacturer. Bill has just received a copy of Century Fashions' annual report, in which the following comparative balance sheet data were reported for the year ended January 31, 19X8:

	(000 omitted)	
	19X8	*19X7*
Cash	$ 160	$ 310
Accounts receivable.	500	420
Inventory	875	1,000
Fixed assets	4,600	4,000
Accumulated depreciation.	(1,650)	(1,500)
Investments	300	300
Total.	$4,785	$4,530
Accounts payable.	$ 900	$ 800
Taxes payable	130	75
Mortgage payable	900	1,000
Common stock	2,000	2,000
Retained earnings	855	655
Total.	$4,785	$4,530

After looking over the comparative balance sheet data, Bill commented to a friend, "There's something strange going on here. These balance sheets say that cash decreased by $150,000 during the year, but yet the income statement says that the company earned $250,000. The company only paid $50,000 in dividends, so rather than cash decreasing by $150,000 it seems to me that it should have *increased* by $200,000." The company retired no fixed assets during the year.

Required:

Assume that Bill has asked that you explain the apparent paradox of cash decreasing in the face of a substantial reported net income. Prepare the following:
1. T-account working papers.
2. A cash flow statement for 19X8.

19–8. *Funds Statement.* (This problem and problem 19–9 following are much more rigorous than preceding problems.) Frame Company's 19X9 annual report carried the following items:

	19X9	19X8
Current assets:		
Cash	$ 12,000	$ 13,600
Accounts receivable, net	31,000	29,000
Inventory	80,400	75,200
Prepaid expenses	4,500	4,000
Total.	$127,900	$121,800
Fixed assets:		
Land	50,000	50,000
Equipment	360,500	302,000
Total.	410,500	352,000
Less accumulated depreciation	112,000	90,000
Net fixed assets	298,500	262,000
Investments	52,000	55,000
Patents	135,000	140,000
Total Assets	$613,400	$578,800
Current liabilities:		
Accounts payable	$ 41,200	$ 49,000
Taxes payable	10,300	9,200
Notes payable	10,000	
Total.	61,500	58,200
Notes payable	100,000	160,000
Stockholders' equity:		
Common stock, no par	350,000	250,000
Retained earnings.	101,900	110,600
Total.	451,900	360,600
Total Liabilities and Equity	$613,400	$578,800

The following additional items have also been gleaned from the company's annual report:

1. Net income for 19X9 was $85,300.
2. Depreciation expense during 19X9 totaled $40,000.
3. Cash dividends declared and paid totaled $60,000.
4. $10,000 in fully depreciated equipment was written off the books during the year.
5. Stock dividends of $34,000 were declared and distributed during the year.
6. Equipment with a book value of $32,000 was sold at book value for cash.
7. Six thousand shares of common stock were issued at $11 per share.
8. The patents are being amortized against earnings.

Required:

1. Prepare a statement of changes in net working capital.
2. Prepare T-account working papers for a funds statement for 19X9.
3. Prepare a funds statement for 19X9.

19–9. *Funds Flow and Current Ratios.* The Board of Directors of Tubular Products, Inc., was very impressed by the company's showing in

19X5. Net income more than doubled during the year, although sales increased by only 60 percent. The company's income statement for the year ended November 30, 19X5, is shown below:

TUBULAR PRODUCTS, INC.
Income Statement
For the Years Ended November 30, 19X4 and 19X5
(in thousands of dollars)

	19X5	*19X4*
Sales	$8,000	$5,000
Cost of goods sold	3,700	2,500
Gross margin.	4,300	2,500
Operating expenses	2,900	1,900
Income before taxes	1,400	600
Income taxes	500	200
Net income	$ 900	$ 400

Although the board members were very pleased with the company's operating record, they were disappointed and puzzled over the company's financial condition at the end of 19X5. For the first time in many years Tubular Products, Inc., had a current ratio that was below the industry average of 2.2 to 1. This has concerned the board for two reasons. First, the president of Tubular Products, Inc., is new, 19X5 being his first full year directing the company's affairs. And second, the board is contemplating the issue of a sizable amount

TUBULAR PRODUCTS, INC.
Comparative Balance Sheets
November 30, 19X4 and 19X5
(in thousands of dollars)

Assets	*19X5*	*19X4*
Cash	$ 450	$ 500
Accounts receivable, net	1,150	900
Inventory.	3,100	2,200
Prepaid expenses	50	50
Total Current Assets.	4,750	3,650
Stock of affiliated companies	350	160
Land	500	200
Plant and equipment	5,500	4,890
Accumulated depreciation.	(1,900)	(1,500)
Total Assets	$9,200	$7,400
Equities		
Accounts payable.	$1,775	$1,360
Taxes payable	200	100
Notes payable	500	
Total Current Liabilities.	2,475	1,460
Long-term notes.	1,500	2,000
Common stock, no par	2,500	1,800
Retained earnings.	2,725	2,140
Total Equities	$9,200	$7,400
Current ratio.	1.9 to 1	2.5 to 1

of bonded debt to replace the long-term notes now outstanding, and the board members feel certain that any further erosion of the current position will surely put this move in jeopardy. Comparative balance sheet data are given at the bottom of page 666.

The chairman of the board has asked that you prepare an analysis showing what happened to the company's net working capital during 19X5. In the course of your investigation you have discovered the following items:

1. Cash dividends declared and paid during the year totaled $115,000.
2. The company issued $190,000 of its own stock in exchange for an equal amount of stock in an affiliated company.
3. Fully depreciated equipment costing $100,000 new was retired and removed from the books.
4. A stock dividend of $200,000 was declared and issued during the year.
5. A $300,000 fabricating plant was acquired during 19X5 by giving $200,000 in the company's common stock and $100,000 in cash to cover the purchase price.
6. Depreciation expense for 19X5 totaled $650,000.
7. Unneeded equipment with an original cost of $350,000 was sold for its book value of $200,000.
8. Five thousand shares of common stock were issued at $22 per share.
9. A total of $500,000 in long-term notes were reclassified during the year as current liabilities, since these notes will fall due within the coming year.

Required:

1. Prepare a schedule of changes in net working capital.
2. Prepare T-account working papers for a funds statement.
3. Prepare a funds statement.
4. Based on your work in parts 1–3 above, comment to the board on whether a problem exists in relation to the company's net working capital.

19–10. *Case on Cash Flow Analysis.* Early in 19X7 Mr. Robert Gilmore was made president of the Turnbow Sales Company. Prior to assuming the presidency of the company, Mr. Gilmore had been sales manager and then vice president of sales. Mr. Gilmore was widely regarded as a hard-hitting and extremely capable sales executive, but he had little patience with financial matters. He constantly warned the financial staff to not bother him with what he termed "nit-picky nickle and dime stuff."

During 19X7, under Mr. Gilmore's direction, the Turnbow Sales Company launched a very successful program to expand sales by 25 percent. As a result, 19X7 was the most profitable year in the company's history. Comparative income statements for 19X6 and 19X7 are given below:

(000 omitted)

	19X7	19X6
Sales	$50,000	$40,000
Cost of goods sold	30,000	24,000
Gross margin.	20,000	16,000
Operating expenses:		
Selling	7,500	5,000
Administrative	4,400	4,400
Depreciation.	1,100	1,000
Total.	13,000	10,400
Income before taxes	7,000	5,600
Income taxes	3,000	2,400
Net income	$ 4,000	$ 3,200

Mr. Gilmore was very pleased with the 19X7 operating results. For this reason he was staggered when he received a call from the company's bank indicating that the Turnbow Sales Company's account was overdrawn. The company's year-end comparative balance sheet revealed the following:

(000 omitted)

Assets	19X7	19X6
Current Assets:		
Cash	$ (20)	$ 2,300
Accounts receivable.	9,520	6,000
Inventory	17,500	12,000
Total Current Assets.	27,000	20,300
Investments	1,200	2,000
Plant and equipment	19,600	17,500
Accumulated depreciation.	(4,800)	(4,000)
Goodwill.	2,000	2,200
Total Assets	$45,000	$38,000
Equities		
Current Liabilities:		
Accounts payable.	$13,500	$ 9,850
Taxes payable	500	300
Total Current Liabilities.	14,000	10,150
Long-term debt	6,000	6,500
Common stock	15,000	13,000
Retained earnings.	10,000	8,350
Total Equities	$45,000	$38,000
Net working capital.	$13,000	$10,150

Mr. Gilmore was all the more perplexed when he noted from the statements above that the company's net working capital had increased during 19X7. After mulling over the statements for a while, he exclaimed, "These statements just don't make sense. We've had the most profitable year in our history, our working capital is up, but yet we don't have a dime in the bank. It looks like the more we make, the poorer we get."

Assume that you are the chief financial officer in the Turnbow Sales Company, and that it is your responsibility to explain to Mr. Gilmore what happened to the company's cash during 19X7. To assist in your explanation, you have gathered the following additional data:

1. Plant and equipment was purchased during 19X7 in the amount of $2,500,000.
2. The company sold $800,000 in investments at cost during 19X7 in order to bolster the weak cash position.
3. The goodwill is being amortized against earnings.
4. Some $500,000 in long-term debt fell due and was paid during the year.
5. Equipment costing $400,000 was sold during 19X7 at its book value of $100,000.
6. Cash dividends totaling $1,500,000 were declared and paid during the year.
7. Ten thousand shares of common stock were sold for $115 per share.
8. Stock dividends of $850,000 were declared and distributed during the year.

Required:

1. Prepare T-account working papers for a cash flow statement.
2. Prepare a cash flow statement.
3. Write a brief memo to Mr. Gilmore explaining the *chief* causes of the decrease in cash during 19X7.

Index

Index

This book has been set in 10 and 9 point Caledonia, leaded 2 points. Part numbers are 24 point (large) Helvetica Medium and chapter numbers are 24 point (large) Helvetica Medium and 30 point Helvetica Medium. Part and chapter titles are 24 point (small) Helvetica Medium. The size of the type page is 27 × 45½ picas.